SAMPSON TECHNICAL INSTITUTE

NOR
STATE BO/
DEPT. OF CC
LIBRARIES

Library
Sampson Technical Institute

LA
205
D5
1971

A

HISTORY OF EDUCATION

IN

THE UNITED STATES

BY

EDWIN GRANT DEXTER, Ph.D.

9949
6-25-75

BURT FRANKLIN
NEW YORK

Published by LENOX HILL Pub. & Dist. Co. (Burt Franklin)
235 East 44th St., New York, N.Y. 10017
Originally Published: 1906
Reprinted: 1971
Printed in the U.S.A.

S.B.N.: 8337-40741
Library of Congress Card Catalog No.: 70-161007
Burt Franklin: Research and Source Works Series 758
History of Education 6

Reprinted from the original edition in the New York Public Library.

PREFACE

In presenting this volume under the dignified title of *A History of Education in the United States*, I fully recognize that I may to many seem presumptuous. "Is our educational story," they will say, "so small a matter as to be placed between two covers; or is the author one of those dangerous complacents who 'knows not, and knows not that he knows not'?" Neither of these queries can be answered wholly in the negative, for the complete narrative is a long one, and no man can know it in all its details. Yet the difficulty is not one which can mend itself with time. If it were, there might be less excuse for the present work, which is offered more as a report of progress than as a final word upon the subject. In its preparation I have been governed by the belief that the most crying need of the student of our educational history is a considerable mass of definite fact upon which to base his own generalizations, or with which to interpret those of others, rather than extended philosophical discussions of historical trend. Current educational literature is rich in the latter, though comparatively barren of the former, and when it does appear, is of necessity disconnected. That the work is, then, essentially institutional — perhaps more appropriately termed a Chronicle than a History — is a part of the plan, and if a defect, is one fully reckoned with, for of two evils the lesser has seemed to me to be the omission of the philosophy rather than the fact. When the book is used as a text for classroom work, the former can well be supplied by the instructor; when used by the general reader, the references have been so selected as to supply the lack. These are probably more profuse than would be necessary to meet the needs of most readers, yet are so classified through the use of different kinds of type as to constitute, in a sense, three separate bibliographies. In the reference lists at the ends of the chapters, the authors whose names are printed in bold-faced type are cited in the text of the chapter; those printed in italics are deemed especially important, while those in common type are not without value, and should be read by the student making an exhaustive study of the subject. The selections are largely made from works which are likely to be found in the library of the educator, and would certainly be included in that of any normal school, or college, or in a public library of any pretension. I refer particularly to Barnard's *American Journal of Education*, the Reports of the United States Commissioner of Education, the Proceedings of the National Educational Associations, files of the leading educational journals (*Educational Review, School Review,* and *Education* are most frequently cited), and the Herbert B. Adams Contributions to American Educational History, published as circulars of information by the United States Bureau of Education, together with a limited number of other circulars from the same source. When the book is used as a text, all of these works should be readily accessible to the student.

The book is so arranged as to be studied in either one of two ways: chronologically throughout, by using the marginal references printed in bold-faced type. When this is done, the whole book will be covered in connection with Part I; or chronologically only for the development of elementary and secondary education, higher and special education being considered topically.

To follow this plan, the bold-faced marginal references should be disregarded.

I should be ungracious if I did not acknowledge my indebtedness to educators in every part of the country for their courtesy and kindness in supplying specific information for use in the volume. Rich as we are in historical sources, many facts of importance in a study like this are only in the possession of isolated individuals who must be appealed to or the quest abandoned. Almost without exception my appeals — which in some instances must have seemed inordinate — have been promptly responded to. The state superintendents of public instruction have been especially sinned against by me in this respect, though no class of educators, from our national commissioner to the teacher in the rural school, has been entirely exempted; and I am alike grateful to them all.

Particularly am I under obligations to my colleagues, Mr. J. E. Miller and Professor E. C. Baldwin, the former for work in the preparation of material, several of the chapters in Part I being largely based upon his studies; to the latter for invaluable aid in the revision of manuscript. I am under obligations also to members of the State Library School of the University of Illinois for the revision of references. And to any reader who will call my attention to inaccuracies which must have crept into the work in spite of every precaution, I shall be equally grateful.

EDWIN GRANT DEXTER.

THE UNIVERSITY OF ILLINOIS,
    April 24, 1904.

CONTENTS

PART I

THE GROWTH OF THE PEOPLE'S SCHOOLS

CHAPTER I

CHAPTER II

CHAPTER III

CHAPTER IV

CHAPTER V

CHAPTER VI

CHAPTER VII

CHAPTER VIII

CHAPTER IX

CHAPTER X

CHAPTER XI

CHAPTER XII

CHAPTER XIII

CHAPTER XIV

PART II

HIGHER AND SPECIAL EDUCATION

CHAPTER XV

CHAPTER XVI

CHAPTER XIX

CHAPTER XX

CHAPTER XXI

CHAPTER XXII

PART III

EDUCATIONAL EXTENSION

CHAPTER XXIV

CHAPTER XXV

CHAPTER XXVI

MAPS

History of Education

PART ONE

THE GROWTH OF THE PEOPLE'S SCHOOLS

CHAPTER I

BEGINNINGS IN VIRGINIA

THE history of education in the United States, even in the narrower sense of the history of its schools, has its beginning with the first permanent English settlement. Although the Spanish had for more than one hundred years been making paths in the American wilderness and the French had raised their flag on the Florida shores, that permanency of occupation which is a prerequisite to organized educational effort was nowhere discoverable until the Virginia settlement of 1607, and was lacking there at the beginning.

In the spring of that year one hundred and five men settled at Jamestown. They did not come to build homes, but to seek wealth in a land that was thought to glitter with gold. Among them were twelve common laborers, four carpenters, several masons and blacksmiths, and forty-eight gentlemen. Such were these pioneers. Only a few of them were married, and these had left their families in England. The first few years were full of mismanagement and consequent suffering. The early settlers were in no way fitted for a battle with the wilderness. They came to find gold, not to make homes, and it was not until repeated disappointment in the former quest had thoroughly disheartened them that they were willing to accept the latter alternative. For the first ten years of the settlement we find no evidences of schools, and even then they originated largely as missionary ventures of the English Church. In 1616 the king ordered the Bishop of London to collect money for a college to be founded in Virginia, and during the next three years some £1500 were raised and sent over. In 1618 the following instructions were given to Governor Yardly:—

Neill[1], p. 147.

"Whereas by a special grant and license from his Majesty, a general contribution hath been made for building and planting a college for the training up of the children of those infidels in true religion, moral virtue, and civility, and for other godliness, we do, therefore, according to a former grant and order, hereby ratify, confirm, and ordain that a convenient place be chosen and set out for the planting of a university at the said Henrico in time to come, and that in the meantime, preparation be made for the building of the said college for the children of the infidels according to such instructions as we shall deliver. And we will ordain that ten thousand acres, partly of the lands they impaled and partly of the land within the territory of the said Henrico, be allotted and set out for the endowing of the said university and college with convenient possessions."

Neill[1], p. 137.

Professor Adams, in speaking of this grant, says:—

"The proposed grant, which was duly made, included one thousand acres for an Indian college; the remainder was to be the foundation of a seminary of learning for the English."

Adams, p. 11.

Warren and Clark, p. 22.

The Virginia Company also gave more than £100 for a house, and several books toward a library.

Sir Edwin Sandys, the treasurer of the Company, was back of this educational movement. By this time it had become evident that the Virginia project was more than a mere prospecting venture for gold,—was, in fact, to be a permanent English occupation,—and the city of London sent one hundred children to the colony, together with private donations amounting to £500, to aid in their maintenance until they should be self-supporting, the Virginia Company agreeing

" that all these children should be educated and brought up in some good trade or profession, so that they might gain their livelihood by the time they were twenty-one years old, or by the time they had served their seven years' apprenticeship."

Robinson, I, p. 40.

That these juvenile settlers were very acceptable to the colony is shown by the fact that more were asked for and sent over in 1620, on the same conditions.

Robinson, I, p. 24.

Before the close of the summer of 1620 Sandys, with the help of friends, succeeded in sending 1261 persons to America. It was also through him that " ninety young women of good breeding and modest manners were induced to emigrate to Jamestown " in the same year.

Ridpath, p. 73.

The lands granted to the college were in part settled by the colonists, under the agreement that one-half of the profits should be retained by the tenants, while the other half should be used " getting forward the work and for the maintenance of the tutors and scholars."

Clews, p. 350.

While the records apply indiscriminately the terms " college " and " university " to this projected institution of learning, it is plain that since untutored savages and children were to be its students, the words lacked entirely their modern meaning. Doubtless the work with the former had a distinctly religious aim, though the following instructions given to Governor Wyatt in 1621 indicate that the practical side was not to be neglected. He was " to use means to convert the heathen, viz., to converse with some; each town to teach some children fit for the college intended to be built . . . to put prentices to trades, and not let them forsake their trades for planting, or any such useless commodity."

Hening, I, pp. 114, 115.

But the terrible massacre of 1622, which depopulated the college lands and left the handful of survivors with no thought except for personal safety, put an end to it all, and it is doubtful even if any actual instruction was ever given by this earliest prospective American University.

At least one other definite attempt to found schools had been made previous to the catastrophe of 1622. The records show that in the previous year one Dr. Copeland collected from passengers on one of the ships of the East India Company £70 to be used in building a church or school in Virginia. When this came to the notice of the court, a committee was appointed to take the matter in hand. This committee decided that a school was most needed, and that tö apply the money to that purpose, rather than to the erection of churches,

Neill, p. 328.

would best meet the wishes of the donors. In view of these conditions, they resolved "for the erecting of a free school, which, being for the education of children and grounding of them in the principles of religion, civility of life, and humane learning, seemed to carry with it the greatest weight and highest consequence unto the plantation as that whereof both church and commonwealth take their original foundation and happy estate, this being also like to prove a work most acceptable unto the planters, through want whereof they have been hitherto constrained to their great cost to send their children from thence better to be taught. . . . That in honor of the East Indy benefactors, the same should be called the East Indy School, who shall have precedence before any other to prefer their children thither to be brought up in the rudiments of learning. . . . That this, as a collegiate or free school, should have dependence upon the college in Virginia, which should be made capable to receive scholars from the school into such scholarship and fellowship of said college, shall be endowed withal for the advancement of scholars as they arise by degrees and deserts in learning. That for the better maintenance of the schoolmaster and usher intended there to be placed, it was thought fit that it should be moved at the Next Quarter Court, that one thousand acres of land should be allotted unto the said school, and that five persons, besides an overseer of them, should be forthwith sent upon this charge . . . and that, over and above this allowance of land and tenants unto the schoolmaster, such as send their children to this school should give some benevolence unto the schoolmaster, for the better increase of his maintenance. . . . That the planters there be stirred up to put their helping hands towards the speedy building of the said school, in respect their children are like to receive the greatest benefit thereby in their education; — that those that exceed others in their bounty and assistance hereunto shall be privileged with the preferment of their children to the said school before others that shall be found less worthy."

The Quarter Court referred to above, approved the report of the committee; but because the court found trouble in securing a schoolmaster, his appointment was delegated to the colonial authorities. Workmen were sent over in 1622 to erect a house, and the following year the East India Company collected some money and gave it to the Virginia council to be expended on the school. A teacher, Caroloff, was brought to the colony, but conditions at the time of his arrival were not favorable for educational movements, and nothing more is heard of the East India School in Virginia.

Considering the magnitude of the disaster of 1622, and the suffering which it entailed, it could hardly have been expected that immediate attention should be given to the needs of the young; and it is somewhat surprising to find that in 1624 Sir Edwin Palmer secured the grant of an island — probably for better protection — in the Susquehanna, for the "founding and maintenance of [margin: Neill[2], p. 83.] a university and such schools in Virginia as shall there be erected, and shall be called '*Academia Virginiensis et Oxoniensis*.'"

Like its predecessors, this educational attempt proved, for various causes, abortive; and at Palmer's death was lost sight of.

This year, 1624, is, however, memorable in our educational history as marking the initiation of school legislation. The General Assembly decided that each borough or hundred should by some just means secure a number of Indian children, who were to be educated " in true religion and a civil course in life; of which children the most towardly boys in wit and graces of nature (are) to be brought up by them in the first elements of literature, so as to be fitted for the college intended for them, that from thence they may be sent to that work of conversion."

Fiske, I, p. 246.

The records fail to show what the results of this move were; but there is reason to believe that they were more successful than their predecessors had been, and that some schools were actually established.

In 1634 or 1635, began an era of schools in Virginia founded by private bequest. At that time one Benjamin Symms left by will two hundred acres of land and eight cows for a free school in Elizabeth County. This school was to be for the parish of Elizabeth City and Kiquotan. The justices of the peace of the county, together with the minister and church wardens of the city parish, and their successors, were to be trustees of the funds. The school opened in 1636.

Brown[1], pp. 48, 49, 149.

Fiske, II, p. 246.

In 1643 the General Assembly, presided over by Governor William Berkeley, confirmed the will, encouraging others to make like provisions : —

Hening, I, p. 252.

" Be it enacted and confirmed upon consideration had of the godly disposition and good intent of Benjamin Symms, deceased, in founding by his last will and testament a free school in Elizabeth County, for the encouragement of all others in like pious performances, that the said will and testament with all donations therein contained concerning the free school and the situation thereof in the said county and the land of pertaining to the same, shall be confirmed according to the true meaning and godly intent of the said testator, without any alienation or conversion thereof to any place or county."

In a record dated 1649 (possibly 1647) this school is further alluded to as follows : —

" I may not forget to tell you we have a free school, with two hundred acres of land, a fine house upon it, forty milch kine, and other accommodations to it ; the benefactor deserves perpetual memory ; his name is Mr. Benjamin Symms, worthy to be cherished. Other petty schools we have, too." Mass. Hist. Col.
XIX, p. 119.

Other schools of a similar character were established soon after the middle of the seventeenth century. Fiske mentions four : Captain John Moon's school, founded in 1655 ; Richard Russell's, in 1667 ; Mr. King's, in the same year; and the Eaton School, sometime prior to 1689. He also expresses his belief that several others took their origin at about the same time, though nothing is on record concerning them, unless it be in the parish books of the region. Of the four schools mentioned, Fiske, II, p. 246. the first was founded through the benevolence of John Moon, who left four cows for educational and charitable purposes. A school in Newport parish, Isle of Wight County, seems to have been the result.

The Eaton School, which Fiske places some time before 1689, was in the same region as the Symms School. Professor Brown thinks it was endowed sometime before 1646 by Thomas Eaton with 250 acres of land. The Symms and Eaton funds were finally united, and their income now goes to the Hampton High School. Brown, p. 49.

In addition to these four private schools, at least one other has left a definite record of itself. It was founded in Newport County in 1675, by Henry Peasley, who devoted to its support six hundred acres of land, ten cows, and one breeding mare. Later several slaves were added to its endowment by others. Regarding the subjects taught in these schools and the number of pupils who received their benefits, we know nothing.

If we are to judge by legislation enacted by the Assembly of Virginia previous to 1650, there must either have been many other schools in operation in the colony, or teaching of an elementary nature was common in the home.   It is certain that laws for compulsory education would not have antedated the general prevalence of schools, and we find the following law relative to orphans on the statute books for 1646 : —

"All overseers and guardians of such orphans are enjoined by the authority aforesaid to educate and instruct them according to their best endeavors in Christian religion and in rudiments of learning, and to provide for them necessaries according to the competence of their estates."

Clews, p. 355.   All legislation with reference to orphans after this date prescribed some education.   Of compulsory education Fiske says : —

"There was, after 1646, a considerable amount of compulsory primary education in Virginia, much more than is generally supposed, since the records of it have been buried in the parish vestry books. In the eighteenth century we find evidences that pains were taken to Fiske, II, p. 246, educate colored people."

Industrial education had its advocates in those days. Some parents were not training their children to work as it was thought proper, and though very poor, they were unwilling to bind their children out to others who could teach them some trade.   To remedy this, the Assembly decreed in 1646 — "that the commissioners of the several counties respectively, do, at their discretion, make choice of two children in each county at the age of eight or seven years at the least, either male or female, which are to be sent up to James City between this and June next, to be employed in the public flax houses under such master or mistress as shall be there appointed in carding, knitting, and spinning.

And that the said children be furnished from the said county with six barrels of corn, two coverlets, or one rug and one blanket, one bed, one wooden bowl or tray, two pewter spoons, a sow shote of six months old, two laying hens, with convenient apparel, both linen and woollen, with hose and shoes. . . . And it is further thought fit that the commissioners have caution not to take up any children but from such parents who by reason of their poverty are disabled to maintain and educate them." At the same time provisions were made Hening, I, p. 336. for the erection of two houses, each twenty feet by forty feet, for the accommodation of these children, ten thousand pounds of tobacco being appropriated to meet the expense."

When the colonial Assembly met in 1660, a new effort was made to establish schools. Here, as in New England, the needs of the church called for action. The following decree explains the condition : —

"Whereas the want of able and faithful ministers in this country Hening, II, p. 25. deprives us of those great blessings and mercies that always attend upon the service of God, which want, by reason of our great distance from our native country, cannot in probability be always supplied from thence, Be it enacted, that for the advance of learning, education of youth, supply of the ministry and promotion of piety, there be land taken upon purchases for a college and free school and that there be with as much speed as may be convenient, housing erected thereon for entertainment of students and scholars."

This same Assembly also provided for the raising of money with which to carry on this work : —

"Be it enacted that there be a petition drawn up by this Grand Assembly to the King's most excellent Majesty for his letters patent to collect and gather the charity of well disposed people in England for the erecting of colleges and schools in this country. . . ."

Funds were to be solicited among the colonists, as Hening, II, well as in England. Even Governor Berkeley and the p. 30. members of the Assembly contributed, as the following record shows : —

Hening, II, p. 37. "The Right Honorable his Majesty's Governor, Council of State, and Burgesses of the present Grand Assembly have severally subscribed several considerable sums of money and quantities of tobacco (out of their charity and devotion) to be paid . . . , after a place is provided and built upon for that intent and purpose. . . . That the commissioners of the several counties do at the next following court in their several counties, subscribe such sums of money and tobacco, . . . as they think fit, and that they also take the subscriptions of such other persons at the said courts, who shall be willing to contribute towards the same."

Hening, II, p. 37. And, lest any should escape who were willing to aid in the cause, it was ordered that word should be sent to the different churches that an opportunity might be given to all.

Hening, II, p. 517, Praiseworthy as were their efforts, it is to be feared that the results were not far-reaching. As late as 1671, Governor Berkeley, when questioned concerning instruction in the colony, said : —

"The same course that is taken in England out of towns; every man according to his ability instructing his children. . . . But, I thank God, there are no free schools nor printing, and I hope we shall not have these hundred years; for learning has brought disobedience and heresy and sects into the world, and printing has divulged them and libels against the best government. God keep us from both!"

Adams, p. 14. In 1691 the legislature sent Dr. William Blair to England to secure a charter for the college which had often been under discussion, but which had never been established. He returned the following year with the royal document from which sprang the College of William and Mary.

REFERENCES

Adams, Herbert B. College of William and Mary. Circ. Inf. No. 1, 1887. Am. Ed. Hist. No. 1. (Contains bibliography.) — *Boone*, Richard G. Education in the United States. N.Y. 1889. — **Brown**, Elmer E. The Making of our Middle Schools. N.Y. 1902. (Contains an extensive bibliography.) — **Clews**, Elsie W. Educational Legislation and Administration of the Colonial

Governments. Columbia University Pub. 1899. — Fiske, John. Old Virginia and her Neighbors. — *Jones*, D. R. State Aid to High Schools. Univ. Calif. Pub. 1903. (Includes all states of the Union.) — Hening, William W. The Statutes-at-large. (Collection of Laws of Virginia.) — Neill, Edward D. (1) History of the Virginia Company of London. (2) Virginia Vetusta. — Ridpath, John Clark. History of the United States. — Robinson, Conway. Proceedings of the Virginia Company of London. (In collections of Va. Historical Society.) — Warren, S. R., and Clark, S. N. Public Libraries in the United States.

CHAPTER II

DUTCH SCHOOLS IN THE NEW NETHERLANDS

IN the year 1633 the first school was established by the Dutch at New Amsterdam, with Adam Roelandsen as teacher. For this school two distinctions may with some justice be claimed: First, that of being the earliest in the colonies of which we have any definite record; and second, being the longest in continuous service, since its lineal descendant is still in active operation. As has been shown in the previous chapter, several attempts to found schools had been made in the Virginia colony previous to this time, all of which had come to naught, unless we may suppose that the Assembly action of 1624 was productive of results. Since we cannot be certain of this, the claim of priority maintained by the school of the Dutch Reformed Church at New Amsterdam seems valid.

The settlement in Manhattan Island was at this time twenty years old. The first rude huts had been built there in the winter of 1613–1614 by the stranded crew of a Dutch trading vessel.

The following year a fort was erected, and the name New Amsterdam given to the settlement. Ten years later (1623) thirty families, sent out by the Dutch West India Company, landed on the island, eight of them remaining, while the rest sailed on up the river and made permanent settlement at Fort Orange (Albany). These Dutch settlers, unlike the early adventurers in Virginia, came to found homes. Soon after their arrival a colonial government was established, with Peter Minuit as governor, and in 1626 the Island of Manhattan — twenty

Henrico School, etc., p. 2.

thousand acres — was purchased of the Indians for $24. From this time on the growth of the settlement was rapid. This was due in part to special concessions made to settlers in the New Amsterdam colonies. In 1629 the West India Company issued the so-called "charter of exemptions," under which all colonists were given freedom from taxation for a period of ten years, together with special privileges of landholdings, trade, and self-government. In return for these liberal terms, the settlers were, however, enjoined as follows by the company : —

Clews, p. 19.

"The Patroons and the colonists shall, in particular, endeavor to find out ways and means whereby they may support a minister and schoolmaster, that thus the service of God and zeal for religion may not grow cool and be neglected among them, and they shall, for the first, procure a comforter of the sick there."

O'Callaghan[1],
II, p. 557.

The last-named functionary seems to have been an important officer in the colony. Even previous to this formal demand for his services (1626), Sebastian Jan Crol and Jan Huyck had each acted in the capacity, which was both spiritual and medical. Since their duties were often, in the later days of the colony, performed by the schoolmaster, it has been inferred by some that Crol and Huyck had also kept school.

Of this we find no sufficient corroboration. It is however certain that in 1633 the colony found itself in a position to comply with that part of the company's injunction having to do with the school, and Roelandsen was sent from Holland to be its master.

Dunshee, p. 28.

The work of the school was strictly elementary in its nature. Whereas the colonists in Virginia seem to have been actuated by the missionary spirit in the establishment of schools principally for Indians and orphans, and the Puritans in New England recognized at first only a need for higher education for the maintenance of a learned clergy, the Dutch began at the bottom, with their own children.   In the matter of popular education they were leaders.

Roelandsen's career seems to have been a checkered one.   He was involved in no less than fifteen lawsuits, one of which he brought against a debtor for the payment of a wash bill.   This would lead us to wonder whether the schoolmaster of those days, among his varied duties, was public laundryman.   In another case at law he was defendant in a suit for passage-money from Holland.   This he won, having proved that he worked his way, while his son, who was his fellow-passenger, "said the prayers."

Appendix A.

Pratt, pp. 870–871.

Of the exact character of his school work, which he relinquished in 1638, we know nothing.   In the same year we find the first record of a public tax for school purposes.   Among a series of laws relating to various matters of public importance is the following : —

> " Each householder and inhabitant shall bear such tax and public charge as shall hereafter be considered proper for the maintenance of clergymen, comforters for the sick, schoolmasters, and such like necessary officers."

O'Callaghan[1], I, p. 112.

Pratt, p. 836.

Within the next few years at least one other private school was established and presided over by Jan Stevensen, and it is not improbable that there were more. This might be inferred by the fact that "as early as 1642, it was customary, in marriage contracts, whenever the bride was a widow having children, for the parties to 'promise to bring up the children decently, according to their ability, to provide them with necessary clothing and food, to keep them at school, to let them learn reading, writing, and a good trade;' to which was sometimes added 'as honest parents ought and are bound to do, and as they can answer before God and man.'"

This would certainly have been impossible unless schools had been available.

That they were not, however, very much in evidence is shown by one of the first public utterances of the renowned Peter Stuyvesant upon his arrival as director-general of the colony in 1647. He said : —

Van der Kemp, VII, p. 106.

"Whereas, by want of proper place, no school has been kept in three months, by which the youth is spoiled, such is proposed, where a convenient place may be adapted to keep the youth from the street and under a strict subordination."

It is evident that by this he must have meant official public school, for Stevensen's school was at that time in operation. A marked distinction was made between these two classes of schools. The teacher of the former was a public official, and his appointment rested jointly with the West India Company and the Classis of Amsterdam.

Dunshee, p. 23.

Usually when reference to a school is found in the records, it is to the official public school. From the first organization of schools in New Amsterdam, till 1808, when a special board of trustees was appointed, the management and supervision of this school was in the hands of the deacons. During the period of Dutch rule, no private teacher could follow his calling without a license from civil and ecclesiastical authorities. This fact seems to have given rise to much trouble on the part of some of the early aspirants to schoolroom honors.

Dunshee, p. 33.

Fernow, II, p. 348.

Because Jacob van Corler had disregarded the rule and had "arrogated to himself to keep school," he was warned not to teach until he had solicited and obtained from the director and council "an act *in propria forma*." The people, however, were on his side, and when he was ordered "not to keep any school," they found "themselves greatly interested thereby, as their children had forgot what the above-named Jacob van Corler had to their great satisfaction previously taught them in reading, writing, and cyphering, which was much more than any other person, no one excepted ; therefore they

Certification of Teachers, Appendix H.

20007030

request that the above-named Corler may be allowed
again to keep school; and although the above-named
burgomasters and two schepens have spoken verbally
thereon to your Honors and your Honors were not
pleased to allow it, for reasons thereunto moving your
Honors, they therefore, in consequence of the humble
supplication of the burghers and inhabitants aforesaid, again request that your Honors may be pleased
to permit the above-named Corler again to keep
school."

The director-general and the council were, however,
obdurate, replying that " school-keeping and the appointment of schoolmasters depend absolutely from the
jus patronatus, in virtue of which we interdicted school-
keeping to Jacob van Corler, as having arrogated it to
himself without our orders — in which resolutions we
do as yet persist." Corler was seemingly refused permission merely because he had attempted to teach without consulting the authorities, for, when he was first
warned to desist, it was only until he should receive permission in legal form.

Van der Kemp,
XX, p. 215.
The requirements for certification seem not to have
been very rigid. At least because Johannes van Gelder
(1662) was " tolerably well acquainted with reading and
writing, it has happened that several of the principal inhabitants of this city advised and encouraged him too,
to open a public school," and so he petitioned for and
was granted the privilege of " keeping school."

Broadhead, I,
p. 506.
In 1649 the "Nine Men "[1] drew up a " Remonstrance,"
explaining to the Fatherland their grievances. Their
minister had gone, and conditions were discouraging.
As for education, they said : —

" There should be a public school, provided with at least two
good masters, so that, first of all, in so wild a country, where there

[1] The people elected eighteen men, from whom the governor selected
nine as an advisory board.

are many loose people, the youth be well taught and brought up, not only in reading and writing, but also in the knowledge and fear of the Lord. As it is now, the school is kept very irregularly; one and another keeping it according to his pleasure, and as long as he thinks proper."

This complaint, coming from the representation of the people, and implying neglect on the part of the higher officers, moved the director to make reply through his secretary, Cornelis van Tienhoven. He acknowledged that the new schoolhouse, toward which the "commonalty had contributed something," was not yet built, but that the blame was with the churchwardens who had charge of the funds. That the youth were in want of schools only to the extent of the "circumstances of the country." The communication closed with the somewhat ironical retort: —

"If they (the people of New Netherlands) are such patriots as they appear to be, let them be leaders in generous contributions for such laudable objects, and not complain when the Directors requested a collection toward the erection of a church and a school."

In 1650 the classis, at Amsterdam, took cognizance of conditions in the colony and sent over "a schoolmaster, who shall also act as comforter of the sick. He is considered an honest and pious man. . . . The Lord grant that he may for a long time exemplify the favorable testimony which he carried with him from here to the edification of the youth." O'Callaghan[1], **I,** p. 317.

The path of these Dutch schoolmasters was not strewn with roses. A further account may put the reader into closer sympathy with them. In 1654 William Verstius asked the classis for an increased salary, but in this he was not successful. In his resignation, which promptly followed, he states that "there are now several persons fully competent to acquit themselves in this charge." Van der Kemp, IV, p. 23.

Van der Kemp, X, p. 6.

Harmanus van Hoboocken was appointed to take the place of Verstius. The salary, the work, and appointive power are seen in the minutes of March 23, 1655: —

". . . The Noble Lords of the Supreme Council, with the consent of the respected Consistory of this city, appointed Harmanus van Hoboocken as chorister and schoolmaster of this city at 35 guilders [1] per month, and 100 guilders annual expenditures; who promises to conduct himself industriously and faithfully, persuant to the instructions already given, or hereafter to be given."

The council minutes for August 11 contain the following with reference to Hoboocken : —

"A petition being read of Harmanus van Hoboocken, now chorister in this city, soliciting — as he is burdened with a wife and four small children, without possessing any means for their sustenance — that his salary be paid to him monthly, or at least, quarterly, so is, after deliberation given an apostil as long as the supplicant remains in service, he may depend on the punctual payment of his salary."

Van der Kemp, X, p. 81.

A census of New Amsterdam in 1656 showed 120 houses and 1000 inhabitants. The increase in population and the partial destruction of the schoolhouse by fire again brings the teacher before the council. The accounts of this event do not agree in all points, but the following is given as being fairly satisfactory : —

"To the Honorable Lords, Burgomasters, and Schepens of the city of New Amsterdam : Harmanus van Hoboocken, schoolmaster of this city, respectfully requests that your Honors would be pleased to grant him the Hall and the side room for the use of the school and as a dwelling, inasmuch as he, the petitioner, does not know how to manage for the proper accommodation of the children, during the winter, for they much require a place adapted for fire, and to be warmed, for which their present tenement is wholly unfit. He, the petitioner, burdened with a wife and children, is greatly in need of a dwelling for them; and . . . he anticipates great inconvenience, not knowing how to manage for the accommodation of the school children; and if your Honors cannot find any, he, the petitioner, requests your Honors to be pleased to allow him the rent of the back room where Geurt Coerten at present occupies, which he, the petitioner, would freely accept for the present, as he is unable to pay so heavy a rent as a whole house amounts to."

Pratt, p. 885.

[1] A guilder is equal to about 40 cents.

The court could not grant the petition in full as the rooms were out of repair, but he was allowed 100 guilders yearly with which to secure suitable rooms.

That the development of schools was extremely slow is shown by the following extract from a formal report sent to Holland from New Amsterdam in 1657 : —

". . . It is to be added that (to our knowledge) not one of all these places, whether Dutch or English villages, hath a schoolmaster, except the Manhattans, Beverwyck, and now are also at Fort Casmir, on the South River;· and though some parents would give their children some instruction, yet they experience much difficulty, . . .; 1. Because some villages are only in their first establishment, and whilst people come naked and poor from Holland, they have not means to provide a minister and schoolmaster; 2. Because there are few qualified persons in this country who can or will teach."   Pratt, p. 846.

In 1658 the colonists thought that they had come to the point where they might maintain more than an elementary school. Reverend Driesius was the first to urge a Latin school and its advantages. He even expressed his willingness to be the teacher. A petition was sent to the managers of the company, in which the following paragraph relating to the Latin school also hints at the very elementary instruction that had been given in the schools : —

"Laying before your Honors the great augmentation of the youth of the Province and place, which yearly increases more and more, and finds itself now very numerous, and though many of them can read and write, the burgers and inhabitants are nevertheless inclined to have their children instructed in the most useful languages, the chief of which is the Latin tongue; and as there are no means to do so here, the nearest being at Boston, in N. England, a great distance from here, and many of the burgers and inhabitants of this place and neighborhood having neither the ability nor the means to send their children thither, we shall therefore again trouble your Honors, and humbly request that your Honors would be pleased to send us a suitable person for master of a Latin school, in order that our children may be instructed in, and study such language, not doubting but were such person here, many of the neighboring places would send their children hither to be instructed in that tongue ;

hoping that, increasing from year to year, it may finally attain to an Academy, whereby this place, arriving at great splendor, your Honors shall have the reward and praise next to God the Lord who will grant his blessing to it. On your Honors sending us a school-master, we shall endeavor to have constructed a suitable place or school."

O'Callaghan[2], III, p. 233.

The following year (1659) Dr. Alexander Carolus Curtius, a professor in Lithuania, was engaged and sent over to take charge of the school. He was to have a salary of 500 florins[1] per year, one-fourth of this to be paid him before embarking, so that he might procure some needed books. He was to have 100 guilders with which to provide some necessary articles, and besides was to have a garden and orchard given him in New Amsterdam. He might give private instruction, if it did not interfere with his teaching in the Latin school. On July 4 he appeared in court and was told that the city would allow him 200 florins yearly as a present. The treasurer also gave him an order for 50 florins besides, which he accepted with thanks. Being a physi-cian, he also practised medicine. He did not meet the expectations of the people or of the company. The court complained that he was taking too much pay from his pupils, and the people said that he did not keep order, for the pupils "beat each other and tore the clothes from each other's backs." His reply to the patrons was that his hands were tied, as some of the parents forbade him punishing their children. Besides all this, he was involved in a suit about the price of a hog. Losing the suit did not make him any more popu-lar than he had been. As a result of all his troubles, it was thought best to have a new teacher.

Pratt, pp. 852–857.

In 1660 Hoboocken again petitioned for an allow-ance, since he was "behindhand with the building of the school, and for divers other reasons." The council decided to pay him "his current year's salary . . . at a

[1] A florin is worth about 40 cents.

more convenient season . . . and his allowance is henceforth abolished."

O'Callaghan[2], III, p. 407.

School-teaching was sometimes taken up as a last resort. Jan Juriaense Becker, "through the caprices of the unsteady fortune . . . has been compelled to become a tavern-keeper . . . for which he nearly sacrificed all what he possessed — and whereas the supplicant is apprehensive that many difficulties, and even poverty is threatening him and his family," being an old employee of the company he asked that he might be employed as a writer for the company, and if that was not possible, "that then the supplicant might be permitted to keep school, to instruct the youth in reading, in writing, etc." This touching appeal was favorably heard, and he was granted permission "to keep school."

Van der Kemp, XXIV, p. 374.

In January of 1662 Rev. Ægidius Luyck arrived at New Amsterdam and became the successor to Curtius in the Latin school. His salary seems not to have been fixed at first, so that some anxiety arose on his part. In a petition, after some explanation, he says: —

"I offer, notwithstanding, cheerfully to continue my service, but solicit most earnestly and humbly that the Director General, with his high and faithful Council, that it may please them to provide me with a decent salary, so as I cannot doubt, it shall meet their approbation, as well knowing that I cannot live on the small payment which is received from my disciples — and as a laborer deserves his wages — and if I might obtain a favorable resolution, my ardor and zeal to acquit myself well to my duty must of course increase — by which I am encouraged to remain."

Van der Kemp, XXI, p. 257.

So serious did the matter of salary become, that he even petitioned for permission "to sail — on a short trip — under God's guidance to the Fatherlande; to solicit there in person." The case was finally settled by allowing "the Rev. Aegidius Luyck" wampum to the amount of 1000 guilders annually, one-half of which was to be paid by the company.

Luyck first came to the colony to be private instructor

to Director Stuyvesant's children, and it was because of his success in teaching them, that others requested that he should be appointed to continue the Latin school. In 1663 he reports twenty pupils, among whom were two from Virginia and two from Fort Orange. At the same time he was expecting ten or twelve more from these places. He was also arranging for some of them to board with him. When the English took possession, he took the oath of allegiance. In 1665 he was in Holland, assisting Stuyvesant in justifying the surrender of New Amsterdam without resistance. He returned to New Amsterdam, and at the recapture in 1674 he was burgomaster. When the English again took possession he refused to take the oath and returned to Holland.

Pratt, passim.

Mr. Pratt, in his *Annals of Public Education in the State of New York*, gives a list of thirty teachers who taught in that colony during the Dutch rule; of these teachers, ten conducted private, and twenty public, schools; some for a short period, others for a number of years.

On the whole, we cannot fail to be impressed with the conscientious attempts of the sturdy Dutch burghers to provide schools for their children. Thirty masters in as many years among a population as limited as was that in the New Netherlands even at the time of the British occupancy, is a worthy showing, though those masters — like others before and since — were not all that might be desired.

REFERENCES

Boone, Richard G.   Education in the United States. — **Broadhead**, John R.   History of the State of New York. — Brown, Elmer E.   The Making of our Middle Schools.   N.Y. 1902. — **Clews**, Elsie W.   Educational Legislation and Administration of the Colonial Governments.   Columbia University Pub.   1899. — Draper, Andrew S.   Public School Pioneering in New York and Massachusetts.   Ed. Rev. Vols. III, IV, and V. — Dunshee, Henry.   History of the School of the Reformed Dutch Church in New York.

N.Y. — **Fernow**, Berthold. The Records of New Amsterdam. — *Martin*, George H. Public School Pioneering. Ed. Rev. Vols. IV and V. — **O'Callaghan**, Edward B. (1) New York Colonial Documents. (2) New Amsterdam Records. — **Pratt**, Daniel J. Annals of Public Education in the State of New York. References in this chapter are to the Eighty-second Regent's Report of the State of New York. Contains a bibliography. Many of the references in this chapter are also found in Pratt. — **Van der Kemp**, Francis A. Albany Records.

CHAPTER III

Massachusetts Bay

THE sturdy settlers upon the New England coast played a much more important part in the making of our school system than had their predecessors in Virginia, or those at the mouth of the Hudson. These were of quite different stock. While the Virginia settlements were peopled with adventurers, or at best by those who hoped soon to return to the mother country, and New Amsterdam with the poorest of Dutch peasantry, within the veins of the first New England colonists ran blood as blue as any in old England, and the first step of each upon the rugged shore was with the full consciousness that it would never be retraced. Though willing to undergo hardships and privations for conscience' sake, they set to work energetically to lessen them as much as was in their power. Physical hardships they could put up with without a murmur, but spiritual and intellectual deprivations — never. So they early set up schools, patterned as closely as possible after those which they had attended in the mother country. The early comers, especially to the Boston colony, were singularly well fitted for the task of establishing them. Never since, in the history of our country, has the population as a class been so highly educated as during the first half-century of the Massachusetts settlements. One man in every 250 had been graduated from an English university, and both clergy and laity had brought from home enviable reputations for superior service both in church and college.

It was but natural, then, that the fear so often expressed that education and religion might die with the first generation, should result in the establishment of institutions for their perpetuation. The first was the Latin Grammar School, though antedating Harvard College but two years. The prime mover in the enterprise is generally conceded to have been Rev. John Cotton, one of the most brilliant products of Emanuel College, Cambridge, where he had remained some years after graduation, as tutor. During his subsequent pastorates in England, as well as in his native town, he had been much interested in the grammar schools. No better leader could have been found for such a movement among a cultivated and refined people, of whom Palfrey says : —

"In all its generations of worth and refinement, Boston has never seen an assembly more illustrious for generous qualities . . . than were the magistrates of the young colony who welcomed Cotton and his fellow voyagers at Winthrop's table."

Palfrey, I, p. 367.

It was in 1635 that the town-meeting voted "that our brother Philemon Parmount shall be interested to become schoolmaster for the nourturing of children with us," and the long career of the school was fully started. This was almost exactly five years after the first settlement in Boston, and fifteen after the beginning at Plymouth.

Brown, p. 34.

Unfortunately we know but little about Parmount. His connection with the school did not last for more than a year, and tradition has it that after going into the wilderness of New Hampshire as one of the followers of Anne Hutchinson, he was one of the founders of Exeter in that state. Certain it is that he was a settled pastor there in 1638. In 1636 we find record that "at a general meeting of the richer inhabitants there was given toward the maintenance of a free school with us, Mr. Daniel Maud, being now also chosen thereunto."

Clews, p. 61.

The list of "richer inhabitants," some forty in number, who subscribed to the fund, is headed by the name of Governor Vane, followed by his deputy John Winthrop and William Bellingham, each of whom gave £10, and

Winthrop, p. 295 note.

since the entire sum pledged was but £40 6s., the remainder must have been given in small sums. Besides his regular salary, Maud had assigned to him a "garden plot" upon condition of building thereon if need be. He continued as teacher until 1642, when he took up a pastorate at Dover, New Hampshire, thus following the path of his predecessor, Parmount. Private subscriptions did not long remain the sole support of the school, though the rate bill and tax were not resorted to in the earliest years, the first direct reference to fees being in 1679. To supplement the fees the town granted certain islands, and in some instances, the rents accruing from these possessions were devoted to the support of the school. For example, in 1641 it was voted that Deere Island should be improved and the

Clews, p. 61.

income derived from it devoted to a free school. But that the income from such a source could not have been sufficient to meet the expenses of the school is evident from the fact that in 1644 the island was leased for three years at £7 a year. In 1660 the general court granted Boston one thousand acres of land for the support of its schools.

The fame of the Boston Latin School rests not alone upon the fact that it was the first school to be started in the colony, but perhaps fully as much upon its great good fortune in having at its head for more than a third

Cheever.

of a century the illustrious Ezekiel Cheever. So far as we have record, Cheever had begun his work as a teacher in 1642 in New Haven, going to Ipswich in 1651, to Charlestown in 1661, and removing to Boston in 1670, where he passed the remainder of his long and useful life. Seldom has a teacher been more praised by his contemporaries, nor mourned by his friends. His funeral sermon was preached by Cotton Mather, who also wrote a poem in honor of his former teacher, in both of which he bestows great praise on Cheever and his work. The poem begins : —

> " You that are men, and thoughts of manhood know,
>   Be just now to the man that made you so."

But he finds himself unable to write as he should,

> " Ink is too vile a liquor, liquid gold
>   Should fill the pen, by which such things are told . . .
>   His work he loved : oh, had we done the same :
>   Our play days still to him ungrateful came.
>   And yet so well our work adjusted lay,
>   We came to work as if we came to play."

In speaking of his life, he continued : —

> " He died . . . in the ninety-fourth year of his age : after he had been a skillful, painful, faithful schoolmaster for seventy years."
> " We generally concur in acknowledging that New England has never known a better schoolmaster."

All joined Mather in speaking his praises. Cheever's *Accidence* was the first great text-book in colonial times. It was a beginning Latin book, and so great was its popularity that it commanded considerable respect, even in the nineteenth century. The last edition was printed in 1838. Text-books, p. 217.

Charlestown in 1636 joined in the educational movement inaugurated by Boston, and arranged with William Witherell " to keep a school for twelve month, to begin the eight of August, and to have £40 this year." Since nothing is said as to the source of the money, it would seem that the expenses were to be met by the public. This school was not, however, wholly free in 1647, being supported in part by the rent from some islands and the income from the Mystic Weir. Martin[2], p. 49.

In 1659 the general court granted Charlestown one thousand acres of land, on condition that it be improved and used for the support of the school. If these condi- Clews, p. 62.

tions could not be complied with by Charlestown, the land was to be given to the town that should meet the requirements.

Bush³, p. 1171.

In 1637 Rev. John Fiske, wealthy and well educated, settled at Salem and began to teach school. In this work he continued until early in 1640, when the town-meeting appointed a "young Mr. Norris" in his stead. Norris seems to have been successful, for he taught the children of Salem for upwards of thirty years. Thereafter the school had graduates of Harvard for its masters for more than a century.

Martin², p. 50.

Not all of our town schools of to-day can boast of such a record. The school was supported by subscriptions from the patrons, while the town rate provided for the children of the poor.

The first public school in America to be supported by direct taxation "upon the inhabitants of a town" was established at Dorchester, Massachusetts, in May, 1639.

In 1636 David Thompson had settled upon Thompson's Island, off the coast of the colony town, and in 1638 he gave the island to the town on the payment of twelvepence yearly rental. Having transferred the island to the town, the town council met May 20, 1639, and adopted the following order : —

"It is ordered the twentieth day of May, 1639, that there shall be a rent of £20 a year imposed forever on Thompson's island, to be paid by every person that hath propriety in said island, according to the proportion that any such person shall from time to time enjoy and possess there, and this toward the maintenance of a school in Dorchester. This rent of £20 a year to be paid to such schoolmaster as shall undertake to teach English, Latin, and other tongues, also writing. The said schoolmaster to be chosen from time to time by the freemen, and it is left to the discretion of the elders and the seven men for the time being whether maids shall be taught with the boys or not. For the levying of this £20 yearly from the particular persons who ought to pay it according to this order, it is further ordered that some man shall be appointed by the seven men for the time being to receive this, and on refusal to levy it by distress, and not finding distress, such person as so refuseth payment shall forfeit the land he hath in propriety in said island."

Here, the first teacher was the Rev. Thomas Waterhouse.

Dorchester, as we see, had its first school in 1639. In 1645 the town appointed a committee of three "wardens or overseers of the school." These men, residents of Dorchester, were to hold office for life unless for a "weighty" reason they be removed. This first school committee appointed by any municipality in this country put the schools in touch with the town-meeting, and no doubt laid the foundation of our present local board of directors. Text-books, p. 210.

The town-meeting of Newbury in 1639 granted ten acres of land to Anthony Somerby "for his encouragement to keep school one year." It was decided to raise the teacher's salary — £20 — by town rate. A committee was appointed to have charge of the school, and there was some talk of building a schoolhouse. The following year it was decided "that the town should pay £24 by the year to maintain a free school at the meeting-house." Yet the vote seems not to have been by any means unanimous, since seventeen residents "desired to have their dissents recorded." Bush⁸, p. 1171.

It was in 1636 that the general court took up the question of higher education, and the result was the founding of Harvard College. Ten years later, in 1641, it anticipated its later enactment for the furtherance of elementary education by appealing to the elders of the church to prepare "a catechism for the instruction of youth in the grounds of religion." Harvard Col. p. 225 *et seq.* Clews, p. 58.

The fact that these matters were put into the hands of the elders, and that merely a catechism was asked for, has caused this act to be regarded as a religious rather than as an educational move. But at that time the clergy were the acknowledged educational leaders, and the civil and religious interests were closely united. That the youth should be instructed " in the grounds of religion " meant much to a people who used the Bible in the court room as freely as in the pulpit, who made it the foundation of their civil as well as of their religious laws. That their children should be able to understand and read that book which had so much to do with their laws and lives concerned them greatly, and was a weighty reason for establishing schools.

Except for these two enactments, the first of which was special (Harvard College) and the second of little educational purport, the Massachusetts law of 1642 was the first upon the statutes in any way affecting education in the colony. This was, however, far-reaching in its consequence; and because of its wise provisions, deserves perpetuation.

Appendix B.

In it the court recognized that in many instances the children were not being trained " in learning and labor and other employments which may be profitable to the commonwealth," and emphasized the responsibility of parents and masters in the matter. Recognizing with wonderful foresight the needs of a democratic community, when we consider its lack of experience under such a form of government, the court instructed the selectmen to make investigation from time to time, and place in better guardianship those children that were being neglected. It did not as yet make the instruction of the youth a public responsibility, though it did insist that they should be taught in the home. Should any parents or masters refuse to render proper accounts, they were to be fined, and their children taken from them. Should the difficulties of enforcing the law prove too great for the overseers, they could call upon the civil authorities.

Here was also ample provision for practical industrial education, the tools and the material for the work to be provided by the several towns. Both boys and girls were within the provisions of the law, and their conduct toward each other was to be carefully guarded. These colonists seem to have caught the spirit of the old Jewish saying, " He that does not teach his son a trade does the same as if he taught him to steal."

If the act of 1642 does not free the people of Massachusetts from the charge of being merely religious bigots, that of 1645 may show further what they considered "profitable to the commonwealth." It was then Clews, p. 60. decreed by the court that " whereas it is conceived that the training up of youth to the art and practice of arms will be of great use to this country in divers respects . . . that all youth within the jurisdiction from ten years old to the age of sixteen years, shall be instructed by some one of the officers of the band."

It is not known just when the school at Cambridge began; but in 1643 Elijah Corlett had "very well ap- Corlett. proved himself for his abilities, dexterity, and painfulness in teaching and educating the youth under him."

Brown, p. 40.

This school was never large, only nine students being in attendance in 1680. Corlett continued to teach until his death, which occurred forty-three years after we first hear of him as a teacher. He was known as a good instructor, but a "very poor" man. The Cambridge school had some Indian pupils for whom a special grant had been made; the others paid regular fees. The town, however, felt that the teacher deserved better treatment than he was receiving, and in 1648 "it was Martin[2], p. 49. agreed at a meeting of the whole town, that there should be land sold of the common for the gratifying of Mr. Corlett for his pains in keeping a school in the town, the sum of £10, if it can be attained, provided it shall not prejudice the cow common."

Fortunately for the gratifying of Mr. Corlett the " cow common " proved adequate for the needs; and six months later the records allude to the payment of £10

Bush³, p. 118a.
as a gift.   In 1654 the town again came to his relief by
levying a rate for his benefit.

From the Hopkins charity fund he was granted an
annual appropriation of £7 10s., but he never had more
than the bare necessities of life.   His successors at
Cambridge for a hundred years had the same struggle
for existence.

Clews, p. 62.
In 1659 the town was granted one thousand acres of
land by the general court on " condition that they forever appropriate it " to the grammar school.   Should
they fail to do so, the benefit was to pass to the nearest
town that did support a grammar school.

Bush³, p. 118o.
Cotton Mather places Corlett by the side of Ezekiel
Cheever in the well-known lines : —

> " 'Tis Corlett's pains and Cheever's we must own,
> That thou, New England, are not Scythia grown."

He further speaks of him as, " that memorable old
schoolmaster in Cambridge from whose education our
college and country have received so many of its worthy
men that he is himself to have his name celebrated in
our church history."

Brown, p. 40.
Roxbury opened a school in 1645.   The record runs : —

" The inhabitants of Roxbury, in consideration of their religious
care of posterity, have taken into consideration how necessary the
education of their children in literature will be to fit them for public
service, both in the church and commonwealth, in succeeding ages ;
they therefore unanimously consented and agreed to erect a free
school."

Mass. Col. Rec.
IV, pt. i, p. 438.
The teacher's salary was fixed at £20, appropriated
from the rents of certain lands which were to be forever
devoted to the support of the school.   A committee of
seven was appointed.   Vacancies on this committee
were to be filled by the founders or their heirs.   If,
however, after a reasonable length of time, vacancies
should not be so filled, then the rest of the committee

was to make the appointment. This committee was to select the teacher and have general supervision of the school and its funds. This was a private school with a permanent endowment. In 1660 the general court gave the town five hundred acres of land for the support of a free school.

In 1671 Thomas Bell left by will two hundred acres of land to support the children of the poor of Roxbury. This was turned over to the school. At times citizens complained much because of the private nature of the school. The opposition to it became so great that in 1669 a committee was appointed by the court to study the question and effect an amicable settlement. The investigation proved favorable to the school, and the court supported the trustees. Provisions were also made for the levying of taxes, in case the income of the school fell short of the required amount. But it was expressly stated "that the said donors be absolutely and wholly free from any such levy or imposition. That the levy be equally made on all inhabitants, excepting only those that do, by virtue of their subscription, pay the full proportion of the annual charges." *Mass. Col. Rec. IV, pt. ii, p. 457.* *Clews, p. 62.*

Roxbury was the home of Rev. John Eliot, the apostle to the Indians. As an early advocate of education, he deserves rank by the side of Cotton. Of him and his work Cotton Mather says: — *Eliot.*

"I cannot forget with what ardor I ever heard him pray, in a synod of these churches which met at Boston. . . . 'Lord, for schools everywhere among us, O that our schools may flourish. That every member of this assembly may go home and procure a good school to be encouraged in the town where he lives. That before we die we may see a good school encouraged in every plantation of the country.' God so blessed his endeavors that Roxbury could not be content without a free school in the town; and the issue of it has been one thing which has made me almost put the title of *Schola Illustris* upon that little nursery; that is, Roxbury has afforded more scholars, first for the college and then for the public, than any town of its bigness, or, if I mistake not, of twice its bigness, in all New England." *Mather, Vol. I, Bk. 3, p. 498.* *Bush[3], p. 1169.*

These six schools, established in the first half of the seventeenth century, together with one at Braintree, which seems to have been started as early as 1645, furnished the students for Harvard College, and the work which they were doing may be roughly estimated by its entrance requirements. They were all in a sense secondary schools, since admission to them presupposed at least some slight knowledge of the English language. Since even so much proficiency was not by any means the rule with the children of the colony, in spite of the admonition of the act of 1642, the general court again turned its attention to educational matters, and in 1647 framed the most important school law of our whole history. This law marks a tremendous step forward; so far forward, in fact, that the people had hardly caught up with it in two centuries' time, with the result that its enforcement was practically impossible. Yet it has been the model for a vast amount of subsequent legislation, and may be taken as the mother of all our school laws. It contained all the essentials of the purest democracy. The teacher was to be appointed by the people and paid by the people " to teach all such pupils as shall resort to him, to write and read," without a shadow of class distinction. Nor was the law simply permissive; it was mandatory as well, requiring that schools be established, and that a fine of £5 await those communities that failed to observe its edicts. There was to be an elementary school for towns of fifty families and a grammar school for those of one hundred families. But like so many laws enacted since its day, this one had its weak point, well-nigh ruining its usefulness. The fines were too small. The town disposed to do so could pay its fine much cheaper than it could keep its school, and we are forced to believe that many were so disposed to do. In fact, it has been said that Boston alone, of all the towns within the colony, complied fully with the law of 1647 during each of the years that it was on the statute books.

Appendix C.

Appendix B.

The defects were, however, discovered in time and remedied by increasing the fines to be imposed for non-compliance.

In 1649 Watertown decided to build a schoolhouse, and voted the necessary funds. " John Sherman was appointed to procure the schoolhouse built; and to have it built 22 foot long: and 14 foot wide and 9 foot between joints." In looking about for a teacher, the selectmen "agreed that John Sherman shall wright a letter: in the Townes name: unto David Michell of Stamfourth to Certify to him: the Townes desire of him: to come and keepe schoole in the towne." Evidently they failed to secure Michell, for the next year Richard Norcross was chosen "Schoole master for the chilldren to Read and Write and Soe much of Lattin, according to the order of the Court, as allso if any of the s^d towne have any maidens, y^t have a desire to learne to write y^t the s^d Richard should attend them for the learning off them: at allso y^t he teach such as desire to Cast acompt, and y^t the towne did promise to allowe the s^d Richard for his imployment thirty pounds for the yeare."

Martin[4], p. 577.

In this instance the teacher was elected by a vote of the town, the town fixed the studies except Latin, and of that the court's order — enough to fit for the university — was to be followed. Girls might be taught, but they were not to be admitted to the school, it seems, since the teacher was to "attend them." Norcross was reëlected annually for twenty-five years. At the end of that period the town seems to have adopted measures of economy, since they wished to hire a teacher "as cheap" as they could. In 1679 Norcross was again engaged, and that expenses might be diminished as much as possible, he was to teach English and Latin scholars at the schoolhouse for eight months, and during the four summer months "Latin Scholars and writers" at his own house. His salary was fixed at £20. The people objected to this agreement, and as a result the school was kept at the schoolhouse the entire year and his salary raised to £25.

A contract with Norcross for the year 1651 throws some light on the school.

" An agreement Between the Towne and Mr. Richard Norcross. That Mr. Richard Norcross shall attend the keeping of a schoole within the Bounds of Watertowne where the Towne shall appoynt. That he use his best endeavor to instruct all such psons as shall be sent unto him in Inglish writing or Lattin according to the Capassity of the pesons and that it is in the Liberty of any Inhabitant to send his sonnes or servant for a weeke or two and to take them away agayne at his plesure and therefore the sayd Mr. Norcross is to keepe a strict accounte of the nomber of weekes that every one Dooth Continue, And that every pson that learnesth Inglish shall pay 3*d* a weeke and such as write or Lattin shall pay 4*d* and that Mr. Norcross is to give notice to the pertickler parents of theyre just Due according to this order and If any pson shall neglect to bring unto his house his full Due by the 29th of the 8th month in 52 that then he shall bring a note of the names and the sums of theyr debt unto the 7 men who are hereby required to take some speedy Course to him to his due.   This order consented to By Mr. Richard Norcross."

When the salary was not fully paid by fees the town made up the shortage.

Appendix B.   An act of the Massachusetts general court, passed in 1652, throws an interesting light, not only upon what the schools had accomplished, but upon what they were expected to accomplish in the future.   According to this act the number of students in the college was increasing.

Mass. Col. Rec. VI, pt. i, p. 100.   For the time being, the supply of learned men for " magistrates, associates in courts, physicians, and officers in the Commonwealth, and of teaching elders in the churches " was sufficient, but the young men after completing their education were wont to " seek for and accept employment " elsewhere ; and, as a result, it was becoming " more and more difficult to fill places of most emminence as they are empty or wanting."   " If timely provision be not made it will tend much to the disparagement, if not to the ruin, of the Commonwealth." In this there appears nothing that would narrow the work of education merely to providing a learned ministry.

In 1654 the court passed an act that took into consideration not only the moral standing of the teacher but also insisted upon his orthodoxy. Hinsdale, p. 1232.

" *Ordered*, Forasmuch as it greatly concerns the welfare of this country that the youth thereof be educated not only in good literature, but sound doctrine, this court doth therefore commend it to the serious consideration and special care of the overseers of the college and the selectmen in the several towns not to admit or suffer any such to be continued in the office or place of teaching, educating, or instructing of youth, or child, in the college or schools that have manifested themselves unsound in the faith or scandalous in their lives, and not giving due satisfaction according to the rules of Christ."

In 1671 the court for weighty reasons increased the fine for towns that failed to keep a grammar school from £5, as decreed by the act of 1647, to £10; but the hesitation on the part of the constables to serve the warrants upon the guilty towns seems largely to have negatived the effect of the change. We can interpret this unwillingness to enforce the law only as evidence that the public was not in sympathy with it and that, with the new generation, educational ideals were becoming lower. Yet in spite of this, school laws were enacted from time to time, that of 1683 requiring that towns of five hundred families and more maintain two grammar schools, while the fines imposed by that of 1647, even as amended, were doubled. Appendix B.

But the colony was rapidly growing, in spite of the Indian wars, the frontier pushing westward, and many of the towns in its wake setting up schools. Besides those already mentioned, the following schools seem to have been established previous to 1700 within the Massachusetts Bay Colony, or in regions immediately tributary to it within the state.

Dedham	. . . . . .	1653	Concord	. . . . .	1680
Newbury	. . . . . .	1658	Barnstable	. . . .	1682 (?)
Northampton	. . . .	1667	Taunton	. . . . .	1682
Hingham	. . . . . .	1670	Woburn	. . . . .	1685
Duxbury	. . . . . .	1677	Lynn	. . . . . .	1687
Rehoboth	. . . . . .	1678	Marblehead	. . . .	1698 (?)

Plymouth Colony

Although the colonists at Plymouth were tardy in the setting up of schools, we have evidence that their children were not wholly neglected. This comes in the form of an indignant reply made as early as 1623, to a rumor that seems to have been current in England that "their children were not catechised nor taught to read." "This is not true," it ran, "in neither part thereof : for divers take pains with their own as they can. Indeed, we have no common school for want of a fit person or hitherto means to maintain one, though we desire to begin." There seems, however, to have been at least one school in the colony in 1635, for we find in a contract which the widow of Dr. Fuller made in receiving an apprentice, the agreement "to keep him at school for at least two years." Such would hardly have been made had there been no schools.

Palfrey, II, p. 45.
Plymouth Rec.
I, p. 37.

Yet that the instruction of children, even in the home, was not general, even as late as 1650, or at least that it was not efficient, is indicated by an action of the general court of the colony in that year. It runs : —

Hinsdale, p. 1258.

> 1658. It is proposed by the Court vnto the seuerall Townshipes of this Jurisdiction as a thinge they ought to take into theire serious consideration That some course may be taken that in euery Towne there may be a schoolmaster sett vp to traine vp children to reading and writing.

Since this same act was repeated in 1663, we must believe that "the seuerall Townshipes" did not "take into theire serious consideration" this "thinge they ought."

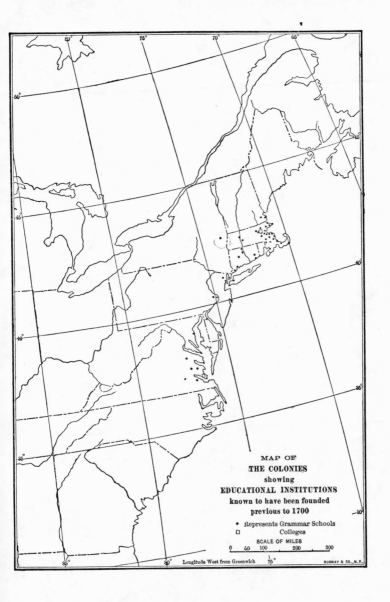

MAP OF
THE COLONIES
showing
EDUCATIONAL INSTITUTIONS
known to have been founded
previous to 1700

• Represents Grammar Schools
□   "   Colleges

SCALE OF MILES
0   50   100   200   300

Longitude West from Greenwich   75°

BURWAY & CO., N.Y.

By this time a dozen towns had been incorporated, but there could not have been such a thing as public schools. A whole generation, then, grew up without the advantages of instruction with which other colonies were providing their children.

An unsuccessful attempt at establishing grammar schools was made in 1667, when the court decided that each town of fifty families shall raise £12 by tax for the support of the same.

In 167c the court opened the way for a school by "granting all such profits as may or shall accrue annually to the colony from fishing with nets or seines at Cape Cod for mackerel, bass, or herring, to be improved for and towards a free school in some town in this jurisdiction, for the training up of youth in literature for the good and benefit of posterity, provided a beginning were made within one year after the said grant." *Plymouth Hist. Soc. Col. XIV, p. 80.*

The town of Plymouth, by opening a school, secured this income from fishery privileges, amounting to £33 a year. The town also voted lands for the school, and private contributions were made. A schoolhouse was built "not only for the better accommodating of the scholars, but also for the schoolmaster to live and reside in." The first public schoolmaster, Mr. John Morton, opened the school in 1671. He was "to teach the children and youth to read the Bible, to write, and to cast accounts." The following year Mr. Corlett of Harvard was chosen teacher, and the school was raised to a grammar grade. He taught Greek and Latin, but the people were not so much interested in these languages, and in 1674 they voted that their "children be taught to write and cypher besides that which the country expects from the said school." In this same year the rents from the fishery were again voted to the school "if a competent Number of scholars shall appear to be devoted thereunto, which this Court judges not to be less than eight or ten.' Certainly public sentiment was *Small, p. 521.* *Appendix B.*

in need of an awakening. The law of 1677 shows that this awakening was at hand.

This law was a marked advance over anything which had preceded it in the colony; and a number of towns availed themselves of the advantages which it offered. But in 1692 the Plymouth Colony was united with that of Massachusetts Bay, and the law of 1647, with its various amendments, became operative throughout the entire country.

The Connecticut Colonies

In speaking of the schools of Connecticut, the late Dr. Hinsdale said: —

Hinsdale, p. 1240.

> "No State has a more honorable educational record, taken altogether, than Connecticut. No other of the old States can show such a connected series of public and private transactions relating to schools and education, extending from the foundation of the Commonwealth down to the opening of the present educational area, some fifty or sixty years ago. Accordingly, the State affords the best possible opportunity to study continuously the history of popular education from the feeblest beginnings."

Steiner, p. 16.

Very little time was lost in getting schools under way after the first settlements were made in Connecticut. Hartford was but four years old when, in 1639, Rev. John Higginson opened the first; and if, as seems probable, one was started in New Haven the same year, schools there were practically coincident with the founding of the town.

The only evidence we have that New Haven had a school at so early a date is the following record: —

Am. Jour. Ed. 4: 662.

> "Thomas Fugill is required by the Court to keep Charles Higginson (?), an indentured apprentice at school one year, or else advantage him as much in his education as one years schooling comes to."

It hardly seems probable that schooling would be mentioned in the formal action of the court, if there had been no schools in the New Haven Colony, where Fugill resided.

Late in the year 1641 the court at New Haven con- Steiner, p. 16. sidered seriously the matter of public education, and voted "that a free school be set up in this towne and our pastor, Mr. Davenport, together with the magistrates, shall consider whatt yearly allowance is meet to be given to it out of the common stock of the towne, and allso whatt rules and orders are meet to be observed in and about the same."

The first teacher of the school resulting from this action was Ezekiel · Cheever, until 1644 at an annual salary of £20; but for the remainder of his service, which terminated in 1650, £30. It was during his connection with the New Haven school that he wrote his renowned *Accidence*.

The serious purpose in the minds of the founders of Text-books, p. 217. these early schools is shown by the following statement regarding the New Haven school, which was to be " . . . for the better training up of youthe in this towne, that through God's blessing they may be fitted for public service hereafter, either in church or commonwealth."

But the Hartford settlers were in no way behind their neighbors at New Haven. Previous to 1642 a schoolhouse had been erected, though that it was not always used for purely educational purposes may be inferred from the record that there were stored within it "two large guns, and carriages and other things belonging to the town." Perhaps, however, these were but the necessary accompaniments of a school situated as was that at Hartford in those days. In the following year (1643) it was voted Steiner, p. 16.

"That Mr. Andrew should teach the children in the school one year next ensuing from the 25th of March, 1643, and that he shall have for his pains £16; and therefore the townsmen shall go and inquire who will engage themselves to send their children; and all that do so shall pay for one quarter at the least, and for more if they do send them, after the proportion of twenty shillings the year, and if they go any weeks more than an even quarter, they shall pay sixpence a week; and if any would send their children who are not able to pay for their teaching, they shall give notice of it to the townsmen, and they shall pay it at the town's charge; and Mr. Andrew shall keep the account between the children's schooling and himself, and send notice of the times of payments and demand it; and if his wages do not come in, the townsmen must collect and pay it; or if the engagements come not to sixteen pounds, then they shall pay what is wanting at the town's charge."

This record shows in what an energetic, whole-hearted manner those old settlers, in a town less than eight years old, attacked the school question. The plan was not to see whether there were enough generously minded people in the community to support the school, but to hire the teacher, complaints or no complaints, assure him of the full salary, and then go out among the people for the children. They drew the mark and jumped to it, and jumped the farther for having drawn it.

By 1648, Hartford had outgrown its school accommodations, and it was decided in a town-meeting that " the necessities of the town and the desires of many, calling for some provision to be made for the keeping of a school with better conveniency than hitherto hath been attained, the want whereof hath been both uncomfortable to those who have been employed in that service and prejudicial to the work under hand, which is looked as conducing much to the good of the present age, and that of the future." At the same time it was also " agreed and consented to by the town that £40 shall be paid in the way of a rate to the townsman for the time being carrying on the said work. . . ." But this, it was felt, would be far from enough to build the kind of home that was needed. Therefore, provisions were made for receiving such private donations as any might be disposed to make; and it was expressly stated "that the building so erected shall not be diverted to any other use or

Hinsdale, p. 1240.

employment, but in the way of schooling without the consent of the parties that shall contribute."

In 1650 the first codification of the Connecticut laws Appendix B. was made, and the famous articles under the titles "Children" and "Schools" remained upon the statute books for more than 150 years, slightly modified from time to time, so as to give them greater efficiency. In both the influence of the Massachusetts legislation is plainly noticeable.

As may be seen from the law, education is insisted upon because "it is of singular behoofe and benefitt to any commonwealth." The rights of the parents are recognized, but in case they neglected their duty and did not teach children at least enough to enable "them to fully read the English tongue," and understand "the capital laws" a fine of 21*s.* was to follow. Religious training was also made obligatory.

For those who could not or would not go farther, an opportunity was given to train children up in some "trade profitable to themselves and the commonwealth." There was every reason in those days for an insistence upon a familiarity with the "capital laws." As the life to come was held to depend upon a knowledge of the "principles of religion," so the present depended to an extent that seems almost incredible in these later days, upon full understanding of them. The following sections from the capital laws of the 1650 codification (and there were many more of a similar nature) will serve to illustrate the importance of this.

"SECTION 14. If any child or children above sixteen years old Hinsdale, p. 1242. and of sufficient understanding, shall curse or smite their natural father or mother, he or they shall be put to death; unless it can be sufficiently testified, that the parents have been very unchristianly negligent in the education of such children, or so provoke them by extreme and cruel correction that they have been forced thereunto to preserve themselves from death or maiming.

"SECTION 15. If any man has a stubborn, or rebellious son of sufficient understanding and years, viz., sixteen years of age, which will not obey the voice of his father, or the voice of his mother, and that where they have chastized him, he will not hearken unto them ; then may his father or mother being his natural parents lay hold on him and bring him to the magistrates assembled in court, and testify unto them that their son is stubborn, and rebellious, and will not obey their voice and chastisement, but lives in sundry notorious crimes, such a son shall be put to death."

It was in the same year (1650) that the Connecticut colony enacted its first law with reference to Indian education. The order was "that one of the teaching elders of the churches in this jurisdiction, with the help of Thomas Stanton, shall be desired, twice at least in every year to go amongst the neighboring Indians and endeavor to make known to them the counsels of the Lord, . . . and Mr. Governor and Mr. Deputy, and other magistrates are desired to take care to see the thing attended, and with their presence so far as may be convenient encourage the same."

Hinsdale, p. 1252.

The work among the Indians was to be evangelical, " wherein the glory of God and the everlasting welfare of the poor, lost, naked sons of Adam is so deeply concerned." In 1654 the court asked that Homas Mynor send his son John to Hartford, that he might prepare himself in school for work among the Indians. The court was ready to "provide for his maintainance and schooling." Schools, however, had preceded legislation, there having been one at Guilford, founded in 1646, and another at Farmington, taught by the parish minister from 1648 to 1697. References to this school are found in the records as late as 1736.

Bush³, p. 1177.
Steiner, p. 16.

The school at New Haven had been started as a Latin school, but by 1652 it had become quite elementary in character. In the early part of this year, " the Governor acquainted the court that he heard the school master is somewhat discouraged, because he hath so many English scholars, which he must learn to spell, which was never the town's mind, and it was now ordered that the school master shall send back such scholars, as he sees doth not answer the first agreement with him, and the parents of such children were desired not to send them."

Yet it seems that the matter was not easily settled. Hinsdale, p. 1243. Later in the year the governor again memorialized the court, and stated what had been done with reference to securing a teacher. He had written to two teachers, but had not yet heard from either. " But now Mr. Janes has come to town, and is willing to come hither again if he may have encouragement." In case one of the teachers to whom the governor had written should come Mr. Janes was "willing to teach boys and girls to read and write if the town saw fit." The town was willing to "allow him at least £10 a year out of the treasury, and the rest he might take of the parents of the children he teacheth by the quarter, as he did before, to make a comfortable maintainance." Many were of the opinion that there should be two teachers, "for if a Latin school master come, it is feared he will be discouraged if many English scholars come to him."

In 1655, when the New Haven Colony contained seven towns, the law made ample provision for the education of children. In each settlement the "officials were from time to time to have a vigilant eye over their brethren and neighbors. . . ." Parents and masters must endeavor "either by their own ability and labor, or by employing such schoolmasters or other helps and means as the plantation doth afford or the family may conveniently provide" to teach children and apprentices "to be able duly to read the scriptures and other good and profitable printed books in the English tongue . . . and in some competent measure to understand the main grounds and principles of the Christian religion necessary to salvation."

Parents and masters who violated the law were to be fined, after due warning, 10s. for the first offence. If in three months after the first fine, any failed to comply with the law, they were to be fined 20*s*. If after a Hinsdale, p. 1245. second fine "the said deputies, officer, or officers, shall still find a continuance of the former negligence, if it be not obstinacy, so that such children or servants may be in danger to grow barbarous, rude, and stubborn through ignorance, they shall give due and seasonable notice that every such parent and master be summoned to the next court of magistrates, who are to proceed as they find cause, either to a greater fine, taking security for due conformity to the scope and intent of this law, or may take such children or apprentices from such parents and masters, and place them for years — boys till they come to the age of one and twenty, and girls till they come to the age of eighteen years, with such others who shall better educate and govern them, both for the public conveniency and for the particular good of the said children or apprentices."

Clews, p. 83.

In this law the education of girls is included with that of boys, as the last lines distinctly state.

In 1657 the court was asked to devise some means "to further the setting up of schools." The answer of the court was "that in every plantation, where a schoole is not already set up and maintayned, forthwith indeavors shall be used that a schoolemaster be procuried that may attend the worke." One-third of the teacher's salary was to be paid by the town, and two-thirds by parents of the pupils.

Clews, p. 84.

Yet the people felt the need of something better in the way of schools than anything which they had yet known. In 1659 "the Court looking upon it as their great duty to establish some course that (through the blessing of God) learning may be promoted in this jurisdiction as a means for fitting instruments for public service in church and commonwealth, did order that £40 shall be paid by the treasurer for the furtherance of a grammar school for the use of the inhabitants of this jurisdiction and that £8 more shall be disbursed by him for procuring books . . . as suitable for this work."

The object was to establish a school for the entire New Haven Colony. A committee, with the governor at the head, was appointed to locate and start the school. Guilford offered a house for the proposed school, and insisted that if the " school should be settled in any other place . . . the like allowance should be made by that plantation where it falls." *Hoadley, p. 301.*

But three years later (1662) the two Connecticut colonies of Hartford and New Haven were united; and we find no record that the proposed school was ever started. In speaking of the schools in New Haven previous to the union, Dr. Barnard says: —

" It is due to historical truth, to ascribe to the early, enlightened, and persevering labors of Theophilus Eaton and John Davenport, the credit of establishing in New Haven, before it ceased to be an independent colony, *a system of education*, at that time without a parallel in any part of the world, and not surpassed in its universal application to all classes, rich and poor, at any period in the subsequent history of the State." *Am. Jour. Ed. 4 : 655.*

Another stanch friend of education was Edward Hopkins, who more than once had been governor of Connecticut, and who left by will the greater part of his estate for the benefit of schools in his colony. He had been eminently successful, both in private and public life. Called to England on business, he had intended to return, but died there in 1657. In writing from London to Davenport in 1656 he says: " That which the Lord hath given me in those parts, I ever designed the greatest part of it for the furtherance of the worke of Christ in those ends of the earth." *Hopkins.*

In his will, he states: —

" The sovereign Lord of all creatures giving in evident and strong intimations of his pleasure to call me out of this transitory life unto himself, it is the desire of me, Edward Hopkins, esq., . . . to thus *Rep. Com. Ed. 1899–1900, 2 : 1282.*

dispose of the estate the Lord in mercy hath given to me. . . . And the residue of my estate in New England I do hereby give and bequeath to my father, Theophilus Eaton, esq., Mr. John Davenport, Mr. John Gulick, and Mr. William Goodwin, in full assurance of their trust and faithfulness in disposing of it according to the true intent and purpose of me the said Edward Hopkins, which is to give some encouragement in their foreign plantations for the breeding up of hopeful youths in a way of learning, both at the grammar school and college, for the public service of the country in future times. . . ."

Brown, p. 46.

Two of these trustees were from the New Haven, and two from the Connecticut Colony. Church troubles at Hartford interfered with a settlement of the funds until 1664, when £400 was given to Hartford, £412 to New Haven, and £308 to Hadley, for the support of schools, and £100 to Harvard College.

Appendix D.

The New Haven school founded upon the Hopkins bequest — the well-known Hopkins Grammar School — was started in 1660, with Jeremiah Peck as master. He was "to teach the scholars Latin, Greek, and Hebrew, and fit them for college." It is evident that the schoolmaster was to be a personage of some dignity, for in addition to £40 a year from the colony, £10 from the town of New Haven, and the tuition of the pupils from without the colony, he was to have "a settled habitation, not at his own charge," and his "property and person" were to be exempt from taxation. When, besides all this, he was given one week's vacation each year "to improve as the case may require," he left the formal record that he was well satisfied. The people, however, were not, and in less than a year's time the general court closed the school, asserting that "the end is not attained for which it was settled, no way proportionable to the charge imposed."

Steiner, p. 22.

According to a report made a few months previous to the closing of the school, the people of New Haven took but little interest in it, and the fault was perhaps not all with the teacher. In the words of Davenport, who presented the report : —

" The Committee for ye schoole made it a great objection against the keeping of it up, that this towne did not send scholars, only five or six ; therefore, if ye would not have ye benefit taken away, you should send your children to it constantly and not take them off soe often : and, further said that he was in the schoole and it grieved him to see how few schollars were there."

After the unsuccessful attempt at a grammar school, George Pardee taught an elementary school at New Haven. Not even £60 could secure a teacher qualified to conduct a Latin school, though Pardee was " willing to do what he was able " ; but he acknowledged " he had lost much of what learning he formerly had obtained." He was ready " to teach English and to carry them in lattine so far as he could ; also to learn them to write. . . . He was also advised to instruct the youths in point of manner, there being a great fault found in that respect, as some exprest." Pardee taught at New Haven for at least thirteen years ; and, in spite of his lack of knowledge, seems to have been successful, for " several persons say they find some fruit of his labors in their children and did desire he might go on yet longer."

In 1666 the united colonies were divided into four Hoadley, p. 176. counties, with Hartford, New London, New Haven, and Fairfield the chief towns in each. Six years later the court granted each county six hundred acres of land " to be improved in the best manner that may be for the benefit of a grammar school . . . and to no other use or end whatsoever."

The act establishing the county grammar school reads : —

" *And it is further ordered,* That in every county there shall be set up and kept a grammar school for the use of the county, the master thereof being able to instruct youths so far as they may be fitted for college."

At this same time the teacher was exempted from military service and from taxes.

Again in 1677 the law was amended. Because some

county towns failed to support the Latin school as the law directed " to move, excite, and stir up the attendance of so wholesome an order."

Hinsdale, p. 1245.

"*It is ordered by this court*, That if any county town shall neglect to keep a Latin school according to order, there shall be paid a fine of ten pounds by the said county towns to the next town in that county that will engage and keep a Latin school in it, and so ten pounds annually till they shall come up to the attendance of this order; the grand jury to make presentment of the breach of this order to the county court of all such breaches as they shall find after September next.

Hoadley, I *i*, p. 307.
Hinsdale, p. 1245.

"*It is also ordered by this court*, Where schools are to be kept in any town, whether it be county town or otherwise, which shall be necessary to the maintaining the charge of such schools, it shall be raised upon the inhabitants by way of rate, except any town shall agree to some other way to raise the maintenance of him they shall employ in the aforesaid works, any order to the contrary notwithstanding."

If a town failed to support a school more than three months in the year, it was ordered to pay a fine of £5 for every defect, to the Latin school in the county. At the same time the fine for failing to keep a county grammar school was fixed at £10.

Steiner, p. 28.

In 1678 the inhabitants of the village of Paquanake, being four miles distant from Fairfield, employed a teacher for their children, since the distance to the town school was great. They asked to be relieved from the taxes levied to support the school at Fairfield, but the town refused their request. When the matter was carried to the general court, the answer was : —

Clews, p. 94.

"To the county court of Fairfield, to grant unto the inhabitants of Paquanake so much out of their county revenue by customs, fines, etc., so much as their rate shall come to, toward the maintenance of a grammar school at Fairfield, and also this court doth recommend it to the said court of Fairfield to improve so much of their county revenues as they can spare besides for the settlement and encouragement of a grammar school there."

Hinsdale, p. 1246.

With reference to elementary schools it was decided —

"That every town, when the Lord shall have increased their families to thirty in number, shall have and maintain a school to teach children to read and write, on the penalty expressed in the former law."

Though the laws were stringent and the courts watchful, many were growing up in ignorance. A new law was enacted in 1690, because there were "many persons unable to read the English tongue." The members of the grand jury were to visit once a year at least "each family they suspect" neglecting the education of "all children under age and servants." Masters and parents found guilty were to be "fined 20s. for child or servant" whose teaching was being neglected. *Am. Jour. Ed. 4:693.*

At the end of the seventeenth century there do not seem to have been, in spite of all the favorable legislation, more than the six schools mentioned in the united colonies of Connecticut. *Yale Col. p. 237 et seq.*

Rhode Island

The freedom of thought, for the enjoyment of which Roger Williams established the Providence Plantations in 1636, extended itself to every phase of social as well as religious development; and since school legislation savored of coercion, none was enacted for nearly two centuries. Yet schools sprang up here and there within the present limits of the state, even in the earlier colonial period. The first was at Newport, when in 1640 it was voted that one hundred acres should be laid forth and appropriated for a school for encouragement of the poorer sort, to train up the youth in learning. *Stockwell, p. 5.*

Providence, too, in 1663, set aside 106 acres of land "for the maintenance of a school in this town." But for the most part the schools were private enterprises. Regarding them there is little record, and opinion as to their number and distribution is extremely contradictory. In one record, dated 1716, we find the statement that *Medical Ed. p. 328.*

Tolman, p. 20.
Libraries, p. 482.

Brown Univ.
p. 259 *et seq.*

"there were schools of all kinds, although no uniform, organized system," while Samuel, writing a half-century later, says: —

> "As respects schools previous to 1770, they were but little thought of; there were in my neighborhood three small schools, perhaps about a dozen scholars in each. Their books were the Bible, spelling book, and primer. Besides this, there were two or three women schools. When one had learned to read, write and do a sum in the rule of three, he was fit for business."

Newspapers,
p. 505.

In 1789 the question of public education was systematically taken up by the citizens of Providence and vigorously championed by Mr. Joseph Howland. Little resulted, until the year 1800, when by legislative enactment each town in the state should maintain at the expense of the town "one or more free schools for the instruction of the white inhabitants between the ages of 6 and 20." Reading, writing, and common arithmetic were the required subjects. Under this law, Providence opened free schools in 1800. The present school system of the state rests upon the school law of 1828.

New Hampshire

Clews, p. 164.

Bush[2], p. 11.

Until 1680 the territory of New Hampshire was a part of Massachusetts Bay Colony and subject to the provisions of the school ordinance of 1647. Although there are few records of schools in the earlier years, the fact that Boston's first two teachers settled there — Parmount at Exeter, and Maud at Dover — leads us to believe that they were not neglected. In those of which we have account, girls seem to have been, for colonial times, particularly favored. When the town of Hampton engaged John Legat as schoolmaster, in 1649, it was for "all the children . . . both male and female (which are capable of learning) to write, read, and cast accounts."

Dartmouth Col.
p. 265 *et seq.*

And when Dover, in 1658, voted to raise £20 a year

for the support of a teacher, it was distinctly stated that it was for " all the children " within the township.

In the first year of New Hampshire's independence (1680) was passed a general school law, requiring the selectmen of each town to raise by assessment money for erecting and repairing houses of worship, parsonages, and schoolhouses, and for securing a teacher for the town. The fine for non-compliance with this law was fixed at £10. During the years following this act other laws, both for elementary and grammar schools, were enacted — only to be shamefully neglected. This neglect led to the passage of a law in 1719 which was practically a copy of the Massachusetts ordinance of 1647, with a fine of £20 instead of £5 for non-compliance. The law, with slight modifications, remained in force for many years.

Maine

Since Maine was, until as late as 1820, a part of Hall. Massachusetts, its school history all through colonial times is bound up with that of the latter state. Being on the frontier, schools were slow in getting a start, if we may judge from the frequent references in the records to " presentiments " served upon towns by the grand jury for failure to comply with the school ordinances. Nathaniel Freeman seems to have been the first teacher within the present boundaries of the state, he having been engaged in 1701 to " ceep scool " for all the inhabitants of York. In 1728 the town of Portland opened a school with the very frank admission inserted in the records that it was " to prevent the town's being 'presented.' " Three years later (1733), whether for a similar reason or not is not stated, it " voted. to have a scool Master for the year Insuing, and left it with the selectmen to provide one at the charge of the Town, and to order whare it should be kept as convenient as can for the advantage of the whole Town." The selectmen employed Mr. Hicks for £2 8s. 10d. for the year. For many years the settlements in Maine were in almost continued struggle with the Indians. But gradually schools worked their way eastward along the coast, and by the time of the Revolution were widely scattered.

Yet, that the advantages had not been ideal, may be learned from conditions at Canaan in 1728, when Samuel Weston taught a class of married men. Samuel Wood was schoolmaster in this same town in 1796. He did not confine himself exclusively to the old paths, but introduced the newspaper into his school, which "proved a very interesting document to the young." Schools were in operation in Buxton in 1761, in New Gloucester in 1764, in Machias in 1774, and in Norridgewock in 1779. With the passage of the Massachusetts school law in 1789 the school district was fully legalized and remained the unit of organization for more than a century. Before the end of the eighteenth century 161 towns had been incorporated within the present limits of the state of Maine, but in only 7 is there any record of a grammar school. Probably not more than this number had the required 100 families.

Bowdoin Col.
p. 272.

Vermont

Bush[1], p. 11.

This state had practically no school history during the colonial period. The first settlement was not made until 1724; and during the next half-century only occasional schools were maintained. So far as we know, the first was at Guilford, in 1761. The Constitution adopted in 1777, however, decreed "that a school or schools shall be established in each town by the legislature for the convenient instruction of the youth."

REFERENCES

Barnard, H. History of Common Schools in Connecticut. Am. Jour. Ed. 5 : 114. — **Brown,** E. E. Making of the Middle Schools. N.Y. 1902. — Burton, W. The District School as it Was. Boston, 1833. — **Bush,** George C. (1) History of Education in Vermont. Circ. Inf. No. 4, 1900. Am. Ed. Hist. No. 29. (2). History of Education in New Hampshire. Circ, Infor. No. 3, 1898. Am. Ed. Hist. No. 22. (3) The First Common Schools of New England. Rep. Com. Ed. 1896–1897, 2 : 1165. — Champlin, Rev. J. T. Educational Institutions in Maine while a District of Massachusetts. In Maine Hist. Col. 1881. — **Cheever,** Ezekiel (biog.). Am. Jour. Ed. 1 : 297. — **Clews,** Elsie M. Educational Legislation and Administration of the Colonial Government. Columbia University Pub. 1899. — **Coffin,** History of Newbury. Constitutional Provision respecting Education. Am. Jour. Ed. Vol. 17. — **Corlett,** Eliza (biog.). Am. Jour. Ed. 30 : 743. — *Dickinson,* J. W. Brief Descriptive Sketch of the Massachusetts School System. Boston, 1893. — *Draper,* Andrew S. Public School Pioneering in New York and Massachusetts. Ed. Rev. 3 : 313. — Edwards, B. B. Education and Literary Institutions. Am. Quart. Reg. 5 : 273. — Eliot, John (biog.). Am. Jour. Ed. 27 : 25. — Emerson, G. B. Education in Massachusetts. Boston, 1869. — English High and Latin Schools (Boston). Am. Jour. Ed. 13 : 34. — *Gove,* Aaron. Education in the Colonies. N. E. A. 1900 : 305. — **Hall,** Edward W. History of Higher Education in Maine. Circ. Inf. No. 3, 1903. Am. Ed. Hist. No. 36. — **Hinsdale,** B. A. Documents illustrative of American Educational History. Rep. Com. Ed. 1892–1893. Vol. 2. — Hoadley, Charles. Records of the Colony and Plantations of New Haven. New Haven. — Hopkins, Edward (biog.). Am. Jour. Ed. 28 : 177. — Hyde, William DeW. Education in Maine. In Davis's New England States. 1897. — Johnson, Clifton. The Country School in New England. N.Y. 1893. — **Martin,** G. H. (1) Brief Historical Sketch of the Massachusetts Public School System. Boston, 1893. (2) The Evolution of the Massachusetts School System. Boston. (3) Massachusetts Schools before the Revolution. N. E. Mag. N. S. Vol. 9. (4) Early Education in a Massachusetts Town. Ed. 15 : 577. — **Massachusetts Colonial Records.** Boston. — **Mather,** Cotton. Magnalia. — *Mayo,* A. D. Early Common Schools of New England. Rep. Com. Ed. 1894–1895, 2 : 1551. History of Education in the North Atlantic States. Rep. Com. Ed. 1897–1898, 1 : 355. — Nelson, A. H. The Little Red Schoolhouse. Ed. Rev. 23 : 304. — *Olmstead,* D. Observations on the School System of Connecticut. Am. Inst. of Instr. Sec. 1838, p. 95. — **Palfrey,** J. G. History of New England. 2 vols. Boston,

1858 and 1860. — Perin, J. W.   History of Compulsory Education in New England.   Meadville, Pennsylvania.   1896. — **Plymouth Historical Society Records.**   Plymouth. — Public Schools of Massachusetts.   Boston, 1900.   (Eight monographs prepared for the Paris Exposition.) — *Simonds,* J. W.   Schools as they were in New Hampshire.   Am. Jour. Ed. Vol. 28. — **Small,** W. H.   The New England Grammar School.   Sch. Rev. 10 : 521. — **Steiner,** Bernard C.   History of Education in Connecticut.   Circ. Inf. No. 2, 1893.   Am. Ed. Hist. No. 14. — **Stockwell,** Thomas B.   History of Public Education in Rhode Island from 1663 to 1876.   Providence, 1877. — Taylor, J. O.   The District School.   Philadelphia, 1835. — **Tolman,** William H.   History of Higher Education in Rhode Island.   Circ. Inf. No. 1, 1894.   Am. Ed. Hist. No. 18. — Winship, H. E.   Great American Educators.   N.Y. 1900. — **Winthrop,** John.   History of New England from 1630 to 1649.   Boston, 1853.

CHAPTER IV

EDUCATIONAL DEVELOPMENTS IN THE OTHER COLONIES

FROM the three centres of colonial crystallization, which have been discussed somewhat fully as regards school history for the seventeenth century, went out in great part the pioneer schoolmasters who made the educational history of the colonies which followed. It is true that even before the close of the period which has been covered, the Swedes had a foothold in Delaware, and William Penn had established his Plantation in the region which now bears his name, neither entering the country through the doorway of already established settlements. But, with these exceptions, and perhaps one or two others in the far South, the country was being occupied by a pushing out of old frontiers, rather than by an establishment of new.

Delaware

When, in 1640, the queen of Sweden sent out her little colony to the American wilderness, it was with the instruction that "the patrons of this colony shall be obliged to support at all times as many ministers and schoolmasters as the number of inhabitants shall require." Powell, p. 12.

Two years later the governor was ordered "to urge instruction and virtuous education of the young." Just to what extent and in what manner the Swedes observed the injunctions is not known; but there is every indication that they did not neglect them. Books were sent over from the mother country, and proved a great help. At the close of the seventeenth century most of the Text-books, p. 210.

Swedes were able to read.   Schools were comparatively abundant.   The minister very commonly was the schoolmaster, and the efficiency of the school was determined by his own fitness for the work.   As the English gradually settled in the colony, their language more and more prevailed, and the distinctively Swedish school and language became things of the past.   The Dutch from New Amsterdam also found their way into Delaware, bringing their schools with them.   The earliest of these teachers was Ernest Pietersen, who taught in New Armstel (now New Castle) in 1657.

The Society for the Propagation of the Gospel was active in promoting the cause of education in many of the colonies, and the ministers and other missionaries sent out under its supervision very commonly engaged in teaching school as a part of their work.   In 1705 this society located Rev. George Ross at New Castle, Delaware.   Twenty years later he gave the following account of the educational conditions : —

Powell, p. 36.

"There are some private schools within my reputed districts which are put very often into the hands of those who are brought into the country and sold for servants.   Some school masters are hired by the year, by a knot of families who, in their turn entertain him monthly, and the poor man lives in their houses like one that begged an alms, more than like a person in credit and authority. When a ship arrives in the river it is a common expression with those who stand in need of an instructor for their children, *let us go and buy a school master*.   The truth is, the office and character of such a person is generally very mean and contemptible here, and it cannot be other ways 'til the public takes the Education of Children into their mature consideration."

Schools in Delaware were under both private and church control.   The Friends opened a school at Wilmington in 1765, which has been in operation since its foundation.   The Presbyterians in 1767 moved one of their schools from Pennsylvania, and established it at Newark, where it became an academy of no mean standing.   Delaware made its first direct land grant for education in 1772 by voting a lot to New Castle for a school. The constitution of 1792 recognized the need of public education, and four years later the legislature began to enact laws for establishing schools. A school fund was started in 1797. In 1817 the first draft was made upon it by appropriating $1000 for each county for instructing the children of poor parents in reading, writing, and arithmetic. Several schools were opened, and the work was continued for a few years, but the "high spirited and brave people" were indignant, and the "pauper school," as it was called, did not prosper.

From time to time laws were enacted intended to raise money "to pay the tuition of poor children" (1829, 1832, 1835), and to devote certain special taxes to school purposes (United States surplus revenue in 1837), but it was not until 1861 that it was made obligatory upon the school committees of the separate districts to levy a tax for school purposes. Even under this latter law schools prospered but poorly. There was no state supervision, nor is there to-day; no provision for the examination of teachers, and no schools whatsoever for the colored race. The better class of citizens soon felt these conditions to be deplorable, and after much agitation, a general school law was passed in 1875, which is the basis of the present system of free public schools. It provides free education for the children of both races, and has placed the schools of the state upon a substantial footing.

Hist. Sketches, p. 55.

Delaware Col. Powell, p. 86.

Coeducation, p. 432.

Text-book legislation, p. 219; Library legislation, p. 485; Sch. organization, App. F; St. Supt. Pub. Ins., App. G; Cert. of teachers, App. H; Teachers' Inst., App. I; Comp. Ed. Laws, App. J; Ed. Statistics, App. K.

Pennsylvania

When William Penn first visited his American grant in 1682, he found it already occupied by some six thousand European colonists, mostly Swedes who had crossed the river from Delaware. At least one school was in operation. This was at Upland, and the record of it is from the courts, for the teacher had, in 1679, sued a Mr. Williams for " 200 guilders for teaching his children to read the Bible."

Penn's first " Frame of Government" made ample provisions for schools; and, in harmony with it, the Assembly arranged for the education of all the youth. In 1682 it was enacted that the laws of the province should from time to time be published, and that this published volume should be one of the books taught in the schools. The Assembly of the following year passed several Hinsdale, p. 1263. school laws, in which the following points are worthy of special mention : (1) all who have charge of children must see that they can read and write by the time they are twelve years old. (2) All children shall be taught a useful trade. (3) All those who neglect these provisions shall be fined £5 for every child neglected. Schools were started the same year, and numerous records show that the law was enforced.

In 1689 the Friends Public School was founded at Philadelphia, and eight years later was formally chartered. This was the beginning of the famous William Penn Charter School which has figured so prominently in the educational history of Philadelphia. It was under the control of the Friends, but open to all classes and to both sexes. To all who were unable to pay for its privileges, it was free.

Libraries, p. 482. For some reason, the Penn Charter of 1701, unlike that of 1681, made no mention of schools ; and, since it was in force until 1776, schools within the Plantation made but slow progress.

Moreover, the conflict between the English and the German settlers was unfavorable to the growth of public education. When, however, the state failed to establish a general system of education, churches and separate commissions founded schools for themselves.

The expenses were, as a rule, defrayed by fees. Wickersham says : —

> "The educational policy for 150 years after the coming of Penn was to make those who were able to do so pay for the education of their children, and to educate the children of others free."

Although the long struggle between the races was a serious drawback to educational progress in Pennsylvania, still, in some instances, national prejudice gave way to present needs, and the two nationalities worked in harmony. This was the case in the Germantown Academy, or Union School, which was founded in 1761. The leader in this movement was Christopher Sower, a prominent printer who took great interest in education.

Other towns soon established schools of a similar character. What was perhaps the earliest book of a pedagogical nature to appear in the country, was from the pen of Christopher Dock, a master of one of the early Pennsylvania schools. Dock must have had a genius for reform in teaching, for as early as 1725 he was using a blackboard in his school, a hitherto unknown thing in teaching, and his "*School-ordnung*" was strangely ahead of the times.

The Moravian schools at Bethlehem and Nazareth, established before the middle of the eighteenth century, were among the best in the country, and received pupils from every one of the colonies. Colonists from Connecticut, who settled in the Wyoming Valley about the middle of the eighteenth century, although politically troublesome, contributed not a little to the educational history of the state. In 1768 it was decided that each township within the settlement should reserve 960 acres of land for the support of "the gospel ministry and the schools." In many, the schools received but a minor share of the apportionment; still, they were not neglected, — some in the valley even now are receiving the benefits of the original grant. Besides the income from

Wickersham, p. 180.

Medical Ed. p. 328.

Wickersham, p. 482.

Boone, p. 36.

Newspapers, pp. 504, 505.

"The Junto," p. 550.

Nazareth Acad. p. 429.

Univ. of Penn. p. 250 *et seq.*

Univ. of Penn. Law Sch. p. 317.

Art Ed. p. 401.

Ed. of Deaf, p. 471.

Lafayette Col. p. 274.

Deckman Col. Haskins, p. 42.

Franklin and Marshal Col. Haskins, p. 66.

Hist. Sketches, p. 331.

Haverford Col. Haskins, p. 90.

High Schs.
p. 171.

Ed. of Feeble-
minded, p. 476.

Penn. St. Col.
Haskins, p. 183.

Teachers' Inst.
p. 393.

Normal Schs.
p. 378.

Lehigh Univ.
p. 276.

Towne Sci. Sch.
p. 353.

Bryn Mawr
Col. p. 439.

Phila. Sch. Org.
p. 194.

Pittsburg Sch.
Org. p. 195.

Wharton Sch.
Finance, p. 420.

Coeducation,
p. 433.

the lands, tuitions were paid, each patron contributing an amount determined by the number of children he had in school. The Wyoming Valley system of schools remained in force until 1834, when a state system was established by law. This was the beginning of free schools for the entire state. The law constituted each county of the state a school division, and each township, ward, or borough, a district. Six school directors were elected by the voters in each district, and two inspectors for each appointed by the county court. The latter were to visit each school every three months and report to the state superintendent. The law, however, contained an optional clause, which made it possible for districts to violate its intent until 1854, when it was made operative upon all school offices to enforce it to the letter. The available funds rapidly increased through favorable legislation. Normal schools, which were established in various parts of the state, were largely academic in their character, and met to a considerable extent the demands for secondary education, while the many colleges upon private foundation have adequately supplied that of a higher grade.

Text-book legislation, p. 219; Library legislation, p. 485; Sch. organization, App. F; St. Supt. Pub. Ins., App. G; Cert. of teachers, App. H; Teachers' Inst., App. I; Comp. Ed. Laws, App. J; Ed. Statistics, App. K.

New Jersey

New Jersey, situated as it was, at about the centre of the early colonies, received an overflow from them all. The Dutch crossed the Hudson from New Amsterdam; the English from the New Haven Colony had but little farther to come, and entered in considerable numbers, while the Swedes from Delaware, and English and German settlers under Penn coming up the coast, made no inconsiderable contribution to its early population. Each of these peoples figured in the school problem, though in some cases only to increase its complications. The Dutch had the first school in the field, Engelbert Steen-huysen having established one in 1661 or 1662, at Bergen. Some years later it was ordered by the council that " all shall be bound to pay their share toward the support of the preceptor and schoolmaster," thus making it a publicly supported school. But public sentiment does not seem to have been ready for such a move, for the sheriff was frequently called upon to " proceed to im-mediate execution against all unwilling debtors." With the Dutch supremacy at New Amsterdam over, the English proved too strong for the Hollander influence in New Jersey; and soon the English language and methods predominated in the schools. They brought with them their school customs, and when Woodbridge was chartered in 1669, one hundred acres of land were set apart for school purposes. But for all that, twenty years elapsed before a school was established.

Newark had its first school in 1676, taught by John Catlin. In the contract they bound him to " do his faith-ful, honest, and true endeavor to teach the children, or servants of those as have subscribed, the reading and writing of English, and also arithmetic, if they desire it ; as much as they are capable to learn and he capable to teach them within the compass of this year." The Scotch-Irish and the Quakers also settled in New Jersey. Here, as elsewhere, schools soon made an appearance among them. In 1682 the Assembly of West Jersey granted the Island of Matinicunk, about three hundred acres in the Delaware River to Burlington, " from hence-forth and forever hereafter for educational purposes." In accordance with this grant, the revenues of the island are regularly used in the support of the Burlington schools. In 1693 and 1695 East Jersey enacted laws authorizing the inhabitants of any town to meet and elect three men, who should have charge of school matters. As for school tax, if any refused to pay their

Murray, p. 11.

assessment, their property was to be sold to an amount sufficient to satisfy all school claims.

In 1702 East and West Jersey, which had hitherto been separate provinces, were united and placed under the governor of the colony of New York. During the seventy-five years of this arrangement, which extended to the time of the Revolution, no school legislation was enacted, what schools there were being purely of a vol-

Log Col.
p. 245.

untary type. Some of these, as the famous Log College of William Tennent at Neshameny, were grammar schools of no mean character; but by far the greater number were of a most elementary nature. About the middle

Princeton Col.
p. 245.
Rutgers Col.
p. 263.

of the century Princeton College was founded, and just previous to the Revolution Rutgers College at New Brunswick. With the close of the War of the Revolution, much of which had been fought upon New Jersey

Theological Ed.
p. 309.

soil, interest in education at once became manifest, and academies at once sprang up in many parts of the state. In 1816 a public school fund was started through the appropriation of $15,000, which during the next two years was increased to more than $100,000, and in 1824 still further augmented by the addition each year of one-tenth of the state tax. Seven years later (1831) educa-

Hist. Sketches,
p. 262.

tional progress received a setback through the abolition of the previously enacted free school law and provision made only for schools for poor children, the rest of the fund being given to private and parochial schools. This was, however, only temporary, and in 1839 the previous law was reëstablished, with many improvements.

Stevens Inst.
p. 347.

In 1845 another advance was made by the appointment of the state superintendent of schools. With this move, and the establishment of a state normal school, educational progress through legislation ceased until after the Civil War. Such general progress had, however, been made throughout the state that in 1867 a

Coeducation,
p. 432.

thoroughly modern school law was passed, which with some modification is in force to-day.

Text-book legislation, p. 219; Library legislation, p. 485; Sch. organization, App. F; St. Supt. Pub. Ins., App. G; Cert. of teachers, App. H; Teachers' Inst. App. I; Comp. Ed. Laws, App. J; Ed. Statistics, App. K.

Maryland

The first schoolmaster to make his way across the Potomac from Virginia seems to have been Ralf Crouch, who lived upon the Maryland side of the river from 1639 to 1659, and "opened schools for the teaching of the humanities." The sentiment there was, as it had been in Virginia, on the whole opposed to free schools for the people; so, except in the case of orphans and dependents, public education was little favored during the colonial period, and far on into that of our national life. Catholic missionary and parochial schools have played an important part in the educational history of the state; the first of the former, for the Indians, having been established as early as 1677. That there must have been something of a market for teachers at about this time, either for service as private tutors or in the schools, is evident from a statement made in 1678 by Jonathan Boucher, rector at Annapolis. It runs : — Steiner, p. 16.

Fiske, p. 249.

". . . not a ship arrives with either redemptioners or convicts, in which schoolmasters are not regularly advertised for sale, as weavers, tailors, or other trade: with little other difference that I can hear of except perhaps that the former do not usually fetch so good a price as the latter."

But when one recalls the slight offences for which men were imprisoned at that time, due allowance will be made for some of these "convicts."

In 1696 a serious attempt seems to have been made to found county schools throughout the colony. It included the creation of a corporation of not to exceed twenty members, including the governor and other high officials, who were to receive bequests and donations for the purpose, and to have general control Steiner, p. 22.

of the schools. To increase the fund, the colony, in 1704, imposed duties on various imports and exports, such as liquor, tobacco, beef, and pork, and even negroes and Irish servants, though we cannot believe that the latter were included within the excise list for any other reason than to check the growth of the Catholics, Maryland having become by this time largely Protestant. Although every encouragement was given to the county schools, up to 1717 but one had been started, and the plan was given up as a failure An occasional private school, however, seemed to flourish. In 1745 an advertisement of the Kent County School in Chestertown stated "that young gentlemen are boarded and taught the Greek and Latin tongues, writing, arithmetic, and merchants' accounts, surveying, navigation, the use of globes, by the largest and most accurate in America, also any other parts of Mathematics, by Charles Peale. N.B. Young gentlemen may be instructed in fencing and dancing by very good masters." Peale was the father of the famous portrait painter of that name.

Another school of considerable reputation was opened by James Hunt in Blandensburg in 1773. He had the name of being an excellent teacher and possessed a fine library and some philosophical apparatus with which to illustrate his work. He was, we are told, in the habit of taking his pupils to the court-house, that they might have practical demonstrations in rhetoric and oratory.

At about the beginning of the nineteenth century various benevolent societies for the education of the poor began to be incorporated. They were largely in control of elementary education until 1812, when a state fund was started through the levying of a tax on banks. In 1826 the first direct school tax was imposed. This, however, failed of any important results, since it had to be submitted to each county for popular approval, and even then was dependent upon district taxation for sup-

Newspapers, p. 505.

Steiner, p. 37.

Medical Ed. p. 330.

Theological Ed. p. 310.

Art Ed. p. 403.

U. S. N. A. p. 357.

Hist. Sketches, p. 165.

port. For nearly forty years the state suffered under the provisions of this law, each county being subject to the caprice of its voters, in many instances a majority being wedded to the idea of privately supported schools, with consequently disastrous results to free education.

But in 1865, when the country was in the throes of the Civil War, a new law was passed, remedying the defects of its predecessor, and with later advances made in 1868 and 1872 working legislation was had under which the schools have prospered.

Text-book legislation, p. 219; Library legislation, p. 485; Sch. organization, App. F; St. Supt. Pub. Ins. App. G; Cert. of teachers, App. H; Teachers' Inst. App. I; Comp. Ed. Laws, App. J; Ed. Statistics, App. K.

Agricult. Ed. p. 361.

Normal Schs. p. 378.

Negro Ed. Chapter XXII.

Johns Hopkins Univ. p. 278.

Fort Wood Sum. Sch. p. 519.

Woman's Col. of Balt. p. 440.

Coeducation, p. 432.

North Carolina

Southward from Virginia there were no schools until after the beginning of the eighteenth century. Charles Griffin seems to have been the first professional teacher in North Carolina, he having come from the West Indies about the year 1705 and settled in Pasquotank County. He held the combined position of churchwarden and schoolmaster, making such a success in the latter calling that, according to the record of the time, "even the Quakers send their children to his school."

Weeks, p. 138 I.

Later, Griffin was elected reader and clerk at Chowan, with a salary of £20 a year, and accepted the call, "notwithstanding the large offer" made him to remain at Pasquotank.

Several schools of a semi-religious nature were established throughout the Carolinas during the first half of the eighteenth century, usually in connection with the churches. In 1745, North Carolina attempted to found a system of free schools, a law to that end being enacted; but since it was only permissive, little resulted. Somewhat later German settlers from Pennsylvania came to the colony in considerable numbers, in some instances establishing schools, while at about the same time the Presbyterian denomination in the state of New York sent a number of missionaries into the South, with the result that several churches and schools in North Carolina were established. The first academy in the state was founded at Wilmington, about 1760.

Smith, p. 26.

Many others followed in 1829, 186 having been chartered. One of the most successful of them was founded in 1764, at Newbern. The legislature authorized the building of the house, and granted a charter, the first in the colony. The master was to be of the Church of England, and to have a license from the governor. To educate the poor, a tax of a penny a gallon was levied on all spirituous liquor imported into the Neuse River for seven years. The following year two lots were granted to the school; and the trustees were given the right to collect by law the unpaid subscriptions.

State Univ.
p. 284.

North Carolina and Pennsylvania were the first states to provide for schools in their constitution. As early as 1817 an attempt was made to establish a very complete system of schools; but the measure failed to pass the legislature, and public schools received little encouragement. Another futile attempt to better school conditions was made by the legislature in 1825, but it was not until 1839 that anything definite was accomplished. It provided for the division of the state into 1250 school districts, each with its schoolhouse and a proportionate part of the state literary fund (then about $100,000 annually) devoted to its support. The bill provided for county adoption, but this was not very generally made. The plan was slightly modified in 1844, but remained practically the basis of school organization until after the Civil War. With the new problems which its completion entailed, fresh legislation was enacted, and the constitution of 1868 contained a free school clause providing education for every child for at least four months of each year. Although under many diffi-

Hist. Sketches,
p. 297.

Ed. of Deaf,
p. 471.
St. Bd. of Ed.
p. 199.

Teachers' Inst.
p. 393.

Negro Ed.
Chapter XXII.

Agricult. Col.
p. 362.

Normal Schs.
p. 378.

Coeducation,
p. 432.

culties, substantial progress has been made since that time.

Text-book legislation, p. 219; Library legislation, p. 485; Sch. organization, App. F; St. Supt. Pub. Ins. App. G; Cert. of teachers, App. H; Teachers' Inst. App. I; Comp. Ed. Laws, App. J; Ed. Statistics, App. K.

South Carolina

In South Carolina school legislation dates from 1701, though five years earlier we hear of some slaves being taught to read that they might embrace the Christian religion. This suggests a mission school. All the early legislation was special, having to do only with the establishment of a free school at Charleston. This was made possible through a gift of money made by "several well disposed christians," and sixteen commissioners were appointed for founding, erecting, governing, and visiting the school." According to the charter the master must be a "member of the church of England, in sympathy and full fellowship of the same," and be able to teach Latin, Greek, and mathematics. He was to receive £100 per annum out of the public treasury. The commissioners might appoint twelve students to be taught free. Each person that subscribed £20 toward the school might nominate a student who would be entitled to free tuition for five years. The fee for all other students was fixed at £4 a year. John Douglas was the first master. Provisions were also made (should the attendance at once demand it) for an usher and an assistant to teach writing, arithmetic, merchants' accounts, surveying, navigation, and practical arithmetic. He, like the head master, was to be paid partly from the public funds and partly from the fees. It was also provided that each parish might appoint a suitable place for a school, and receive from the public treasury £12 toward the building of a house. While the legislature was making its plans, the society for the Propagation of the Gospel opened a school at Charleston in 1711.

Newspapers, p. 505.

In 1722 a new law was enacted, which aimed at nothing less than schools for all. "By this act the justices of these courts were authorized to purchase lands, erect a free school, in each county and precinct, and to assess the expense upon the lands and slaves within their respective jurisdictions." There were other schools of the same class, some founded by individual enterprise, some by societies. The oldest of these was the *South Carolina Society*, which was founded about 1737. One that did very much in education was the *Winyaw Indigo Society* at Georgetown. Its work dates from 1756. Its school was much more than a charity school. McCrady says, "this school for more than a hundred years was the chief school for all the eastern part of the country, between Charleston and the North Carolina line, and was resorted to by all classes." The income from the endowment founded by this society now goes to the support of the Georgetown high school.

Merriwether, p. 217.

A colony from Dorchester, Massachusetts, located at Dorchester, South Carolina, where it remained until 1752. In 1724 and 1734 acts were passed to establish a school for them. Several individuals had already bequeathed considerable sums for educational purposes. Among these was Richard Beresford, who in 1722 left £6500 for the advancement of "liberal learning." The school founded upon the bequest was situated in the parish of St. Thomas and St. Dennis, near Charleston, and was one of the prominent schools of the state down to the time of the Civil War. At the close of the Revolution, South Carolina had eleven public and three charitable grammar schools, beside eight of a private nature. In 1826 thirty-two academies had been established, and there were at about the same time nine thousand pupils in the elementary schools; but these were entirely inadequate, and as late as 1847 a legislative com-

State Univ. p. 284.

Hist. Sketches, p. 362.

Ed. of Deaf, p. 471.

mittee reported that "nothing was done worthy so sacred a cause as education." Yet this was more largely because of a lack of knowledge of how to proceed with the work than a lack of interest in it, as considerable sums of money had from time to time been appropriated to school purposes. It was not until after the Civil War that anything like a system of public schools was organized. This was in 1870, and the bill provided for a state superintendent of public instruction, county boards of school examiners with power to certificate teachers, and as generous a financial support for the schools as a depleted state treasury would allow. Schools have rapidly multiplied, and on the whole education has since prospered within the state.

Agricult. Col. p. 362.

Negro Ed. Chapter XXII.

Normal Schs. p. 378.

Coeducation, p. 432.

Text-book legislation, p. 219; Sch. organization, App. F; St. Supt. Pub. Ins. App. G; Cert. of teachers, App. H ; Teachers' Inst. App. I ; Comp. Ed. Laws, App. J; Ed. Statistics, App. K.

Georgia

The first educational attempts made within the present state of Georgia were in the nature of mission schools for the Indians, conducted by the Moravians. These came to an end when the settlement removed to Pennsylvania in 1738. The next, by George Whitfield and James Habersham, who as early as 1740 had founded a charitable school for orphans and dependents. This school developed into one of the most prominent educational institutions in the South during the colonial period. When the state constitution was framed in 1777, it contained an educational clause stating that "schools shall be erected in every county of the state and supported at the general expense of the state as the Legislature shall hereafter point out." Six years later a law was enacted which was the beginning of the "poor school" system of the state. According to it, the governor might grant one thousand acres of vacant land for the establishment of a school in each county. By

Jones, pp. 22 *et seq*.

State Univ. p. 284.

1800 six academies had been founded; by 1829, sixty-four; and by 1840, one hundred eighty-six. This very rapid growth was largely fostered by legislative action taken in 1823, providing for the distribution of $500,000 equally among the free schools and academies of the state.

Georgia kept pace with the other Southern states by establishing in 1868 a system of schools "to be forever free to all children of the state." A board of education and a state school commissioner were established for its control, and its immediate supervision given to trustees in each district. Revenues were derived from a poll tax, taxes upon exhibitions, etc., and from the earnings of the Western and Atlantic Railway. The constitution made it obligatory to support separate schools for the two races — as was common in the South. In 1875 there were 114,648 white children and 55,268 black — a little less than one-half the school population for the former and one-third for the latter.

Ed. of Deaf, p. 471.

Hist. Sketches, p. 68.

Negro Ed. Chapter XXII.

Agricult. Col. p. 362.

Atlanta Sch. Org. p. 195.

Normal Schs. p. 378.

Coeducation, p. 432.

Text-book legislation, p. 219 ; Library legislation, p. 485; Sch. organization, App. F; St. Supt. Pub. Ins. App. G; Cert. of teachers, App. H; Teachers' Inst. App. I; Comp. Ed. Laws, App. J; Ed. Statistics, App. K.

REFERENCES

Haskins, C. H., and Hull, W. I. History of Higher Education in Pennsylvania. Circ. Inf. No. 4, 1902. — Historical Sketches of State School Systems (each state). Rep. Com. Ed. 1876. — Jones, Charles E. Education in Georgia. Am. Ed. Hist. No. 5. Circ. Inf. No. 4, 1888. — Merriwether, Colyer. History of Higher Education in South Carolina. Circ. Inf. No. 3, 1888. Am. Ed. Hist. No. 4. — Murray, David. History of Education in New Jersey. Circ. Inf. No. 1, 1899. Am. Ed. Hist. No. 23. — Powell, Lyman P. History of Education in Delaware. Circ. Inf. No. 3, 1893. Am. Ed. Hist. No. 15. — Smith, Charles Lee. History of Education in North Carolina. Circ. Inf. No. 2, 1888. Am. Ed. Hist. No. 3. — Steiner, Bernard C. History of Education in Maryland. Adams Series, No. 19. Circ. Inf. No. 2, 1894. Am. Ed. Hist. No. 19. — Wickenham, James P. History of Education in Pennsylvania. Lancaster, 1886.

CHAPTER V

LATER EDUCATIONAL DEVELOPMENT IN THE EARLY COLONIES

Virginia

THE College of William and Mary, established in 1689, fostered the educational interests of the Old Dominion. Private schools other than those which had preceded it were established from time to time; and in 1724, out of twenty-nine parishes, seventeen supported schools of some sort. More largely, too, than in the Northern colonies, it was the custom of the Virginia planters to procure private tutors for their children, or to send them abroad to be educated, so the colony was but little worse off educationally than were the better parts of New England. In 1779 Thomas Jefferson drew up a bill providing for free schools and the training of all free children, both male and female, in reading, writing, and arithmetic. His whole plan included elementary, secondary, and higher education; but his ideas were in advance of the time, and the plan was not favorably received. In 1796 he secured the passage of his bill, but the act was only permissive, and consequently was without effect.

Virginia made its first general provision for elementary education in 1818. By this act $45,000 was appropriated each year from the income of the literary fund. This money was given to the counties. The county authorities used the money for the support of charity schools, which were maintained in various towns. The better class of people would not patronize these "poor

Col. Wm. and Mary, p. 234 et seq.

Symms Sch. et al. p. 6.

Univ. of V. Law Sch. p. 319.

schools," but provided for their children in private inst.
tutions or by family tutors. As a result, popular educa
tion suffered.

Ed. of Deaf,
p. 471.
Hist. Sketches,
p. 399.
Ed. of Blind,
p. 474.
An. Message,
1843.

Minor changes were made in the law from time to
time; but even as late as 1843 provision had been
made, according to Governor McDowell, to give only
sixty days' schooling annually to one-half the indigent
children of the state, as the grand result, "and that
it [the law] was little more than a costly and delusive
nullity which ought to be abolished and another and
better established in its place." This was attempted in

Hampton Inst.
p. 457.
Agricult. Ed.
p. 362.
Normal Schs.
p. 378.

1846, through the passage of a law establishing school
districts, county commissions, and district trustees. But
like so much other school legislation, the adoption of
the law was made optional with the counties, and nothing
like a state system of schools resulted. But after the
Civil War, when in 1870 Virginia adopted a new con-

Coeducation,
p. 432.

stitution, a full state system of free schools was established, with state and county superintendents, and all the
machinery for complete organization. And it is working well.

Text-book legislation, p. 219; Sch. organization, App. F; St. Supt. Pub.
Ins. App. G; Cert. of teachers, App. H; Teachers' Inst. App. I; Comp.
Ed. Laws, App. J; Ed. Statistics, App. K.

District of Columbia

When the District of Columbia was organized in 1804,
an elaborate plan was formulated for a system of educational institutions to comprise "schools for teaching
the rudiments of knowledge; a college in which the
higher branches should be taught; and a university for
the acquisition of the highest range of studies." The
first of these three classes of schools has been in operation these many years, but the favorable opportunity
which has been awaited for the other two has never
come. From the first the schools have been entirely

under governmental control. Thomas Jefferson, when President, was chairman of the earliest committee having the matter in charge, and schools were opened in 1806. In order that the tuition might be free to the " poor children," certain taxes (on slaves, dogs, liquors, and public exhibitions) were in part devoted to their support. Children from well-to-do families paid $5 each quarter. All schools were, however, made free in 1848. In 1869 a superintendent of schools was appointed, and in 1874 the schools of the entire district placed under the control of a board of nineteen trustees, all to be residents of the district.

Columbian Univ. p. 273.

Normal Schs. p. 378.

Colored schools were organized by act of Congress passed in 1862.

The schools of the district are lavishly provided for, and are of a high degree of excellence. The many advantages which may be derived from the government libraries and museums, as well as from the diplomatic life of the capitol, has given rise to many private and endowed institutions of higher instruction, both of an academic and professional character.

Text-book legislation, p. 219; Sch. organization, App. F; St. Supt. Pub. Ins. App. G; Cert. of teachers, App. H; Teachers' Inst. App. I; Comp. Ed. Laws, App. J; Ed. Statistics, App. K.

West Virginia

Until 1861 this state was a part of Virginia; but in that year the western counties of the old state refused to secede from the Union, and formed a separate state organization. It immediately provided for the formation of a fund to aid in the support of free schools, and instructed the legislature to set up, as soon as practicable, a complete system of public schools throughout the state. This was brought about a few years later, and has steadily developed to the present time.

State Univ. p. 284.

Normal Sch. p. 378.

Coeducation, p. 432.

Text-book legislation, p. 219; Sch. organization, App. F; St. Supt. Pub. Ins. App. G; Cert. of teachers, App. H; Teachers' Inst. App. I; Comp. Ed. Laws, App. J; Ed. Statistics, App. K.

New York

83d Regents
Rep. p. 632.

When the Dutch were forced to haul down the flag in the New Netherlands, the greater number of the schoolmasters either returned to Holland or removed to other colonies, and the Dutch schools ceased to be an important factor in education. But the English were slow in setting up theirs, no definite public action having been taken relative to education until 1702, when "one able, skillful and orthodox person to be schoolmaster" was appointed in New York City, his salary of £50 being raised by public tax. That there had been schools during the previous years of British occupancy, and that their teachers had been "orthodox" we may gather from a specific requirement in force that all teachers from abroad be licensed by the Archbishop of Canterbury, and those from within the colony, by the governor. Since the latter was as good a churchman as the former, we may not doubt as to the religious character of the work, though we may wonder what the academic prerequisites to certification may have been.

The school founded in 1702 was continued only for seven years.

Somewhat more pretentious, and also more successful, was a project set on foot in 1732 to establish a school in New York City in which Latin, Greek, and mathematics should be taught. Public provisions were made for the practical support of the school and for the free instruction of twenty young men from the various counties of the state, who should be recommended by the county officials. The justices of the Supreme Court, the rector of Trinity Church, and the mayor, recorder, and aldermen of the city of New York, were constituted a committee to visit and manage the school. They were given power to secure and remove the teacher. In this committee we see the beginning of a long struggle carried on in New York to remove the schools from the domination of the church and put them under state control. In 1754 Columbia College was founded. Up to the time of the Revolution, the elementary schools in New York City were largely fostered and supported by the Society for the Propagation of the Gospel.

Medical Ed. p. 329.
Columbia Col. p. 253 *et seq.*

The first state legislation regarding schools seems to have been made in 1786, when it was ordered that unappropriated lands within the state should be laid out in townships ten miles square, and that in each of them one section should be reserved for the "gospel and schools" and one "for promoting literature." Special appropriations were also made to help academies.

In 1795 a general school law was enacted "for the purpose of encouraging and maintaining schools in the several cities and towns of this state, in which the children of the inhabitants residing in this state shall be instructed in the English language, or be taught English grammar, arithmetic, mathematics, and such other branches of knowledge as are most useful and necessary to complete a good education."

Sherwood, p. 520.
Union Col. p. 272.

One hundred thousand dollars was appropriated from the state treasury each year for five years toward the partial support of the schools. Three years later (1800) there were 1350 public schools, with an attendance of 60,000 pupils. At the end of the five years, for which this law was enacted, repeated efforts were made to renew it, but all failed. The people felt that some "religious society" should provide the opportunities for an education. Because many were without the means for securing even elementary training, the "Public School Society of the City of New York" was chartered in 1805. This society was composed of the leading men of the city, and aimed to establish a free school "for the education of such poor children as do not be-

Theological Ed. p. 310.
Regents, p. 78.
Agricult. Ed. pp. 361, 363.
U. S. M. A. p. 355.
Columbia Law Sch. p. 380.
Hamilton Col. p. 273.
P. I.
Ed. of Deaf, p. 471.
Learned Soc. p. 553.
Hist. Sketches, p. 237.

long to, or are not provided for, by any religious society." This society had control of the schools of New York City for forty-eight years. As early as 1784 the state board of regents had been appointed primarily to aid in the reconstruction of Columbia College, but later it was given further powers, and it has for more than a century now been in charge of all forms of private education within the state. When, in 1812, a state superintendent of schools was appointed, the public school system was put into his hands.

The state was particularly fortunate in securing as the first incumbent of this office Mr. Gideon Hawley, a man of unusual ability, and to him much of the success of subsequent school development may be ascribed. The school law adopted at the time of his appointment provided for the districting of the state for school purposes, and that the school fund be distributed on a per capita basis of school population. Inspection and the examination of teachers were made the duties of the township commissioners. These duties, however, so seriously interfered with the other functions of these officers, that in 1841 county superintendents were provided for, and two years later the township officials were relieved of their school duties. But in 1847 the county superintendents were in turn deposed (reinstated in 1856), and thus a sad blow struck to the efficiency of the school system.

In 1849 a free system of schools was provided for the entire state which, in spite of much opposition during the earlier years of its existence, even bringing about its abolition for a time, has stood the test and has become one of the strongest and most efficient in the country. Since 1867, when the final important step in its completion was taken, every move has been a progressive one.

The latest action, taken in February, 1904, was the creation of a school commissioner, to be elected (after six years, the first appointment to be by the legislature) by the board of regents, and intended to combine the functions of that board with those of the state super-intendent of public instruction. A. S. Draper was appointed as the first incumbent of the new office. It is too early as yet to say what the results of the plan may be, but seemingly it does away with certain defects inherent in the old dual system of administration.

Coeducation, p. 432.

Text-book legislation, p. 219; Library legislation, pp. 485, 495; Sch. organization, App. F; St. Supt. Pub. Ins. App. G; Cert. of teachers, App. H; Teachers' Inst. App. I; Comp. Ed. Laws, App. J; Ed. Statistics, App. K.

Massachusetts

The early colonial grammar school did thorough work in the classics, as the Harvard entrance requirements show. These schools were modelled after the English grammar schools, with which the first colonists were familiar, and in which many of them had been trained. They differed, however, from the English school, in that they did not have the large endowment which made the English school an independent institution. We have seen how lands and funds were set aside for the support of education in the colonies; but the income from these sources were not sufficient to provide a healthy support. We have also seen provisions for levying and collecting tax for schools, but the people were not always zealous in complying with these laws. The eighteenth century saw many new settlements made; and with these, new schools were opened. But in efficiency the schools were on the decline. The schools as they existed were not always those that the law pre-scribed. The many wars, together with the poverty and the increasing trouble with the mother country, were not favorable to education.

Appendix C.

Am. Jour. Ed. 27 : 62.

The Puritans had feared that the education they had brought with them was in great danger of perishing with them, and from some accounts it would seem that their fears were justified. In 1701 the Massachusetts court complained that the law was "*shamefully neglected* by divers towns, and the penalty thereof not required." This was a condition not peculiar to Massachusetts alone. To remedy this growing evil, the fine for failing to support a grammar school, which in 1692 had been fixed at £10, was increased to £20. Not only were schools neglected, but teachers were poorly prepared for the work of competent instruction. As a means toward insuring better teachers, a law was enacted which required every grammar school teacher to be approved by the minister of the town, and of the two nearest towns, or by any two of them. Providing against any abuse of this privilege, the law stipulated "that no minister of any town shall be deemed, held, or accepted to be schoolmaster of such town within the intent of the law."

Recognizing the lack of teachers, and with a view of drawing men into this profession, several laws conferring special favors were enacted. In 1692 they were exempted from tax; in 1692, from military service; and in 1699, from guard duty. It was, perhaps, the scarcity of teachers and the unwillingness of the people to carry the financial burden which the schools necessarily imposed, that developed, during this period, the moving school. Towns that felt too poor to support a school alone, would often combine and hire a teacher in common. How long the school should be taught in each town so combining was determined by the amount it had subscribed toward the teacher's salary.

Perhaps nothing illustrates the general trend of educational affairs in Massachusetts during the eighteenth century better than the school law of 1789. This was a step backward when compared with previous laws; but as the others could not be enforced, and this was intended as something which could be, it comes nearer

Margin notes:

Training of teachers, p. 371 *et seq.*

Newspapers, p. 504.

Evening Sch. p. 542.
Am. Acad. Arts and Sci. p. 552.

giving the true state of affairs. Among the features of this law were the following : —

1. The district system was legalized. The district school became a necessity because of the rural population that was too far removed from town to share in the benefits of a town school.

2. Towns of 50 families were to support an English school at least six months during the year. This might be in one or any number of sessions. The old law had required the school to be in session throughout the year. These schools were to instruct in reading, writing, the English language, arithmetic, orthography, and decent behavior. This was an enlargement of the curriculum.

3. Towns of 100 families were to continue schools for a length of time equal to twelve months of the year.

4. Towns of 150 families were to support a grammar school for six months; and, in addition, a school to instruct children in the English language for twelve months in the year. These schools might be in any number of terms and places.

5. Towns of 200 families were to support a grammar school and an English school each for a length of time equal in the aggregate to twelve months of the year. The old law had required a grammar school in each town of 100 families, but the law was continually violated. In speaking of this, Charles Hammond says : —

"Indeed it is not certain that any locality, save Boston, has constantly complied with this provision of the ancient statutes."

6. All teachers were to be college graduates, and "shall produce satisfactory evidence thereof." Instead of this qualification, however, it was sufficient to present a certificate from "a learned minister, well skilled in the Greek and Latin language, settled in the town or place where the school is proposed to be kept," or from two equally well qualified ministers near by. This certifi-

Williams Col. p. 272.
Amherst Col. p. 273.
Am. Lyceum, p. 569.
Harvard Med Sch. p. 329.

Hist. Sketches,
p. 179.

Harvard Law
Sch. p. 318.

High. Schs.
p. 171.

Ed. of Deaf,
p. 471.

Theological Ed.
pp. 310–11.

Ed. of Blind,
p. 474.

Mt. Holyoke
Col. p. 435.

Perkins Inst.
p. 476.

St. Bd. of Ed.
p. 200.

Agricult. Ed.
p. 361.

Normal Schs.
p. 374 *et seq.*

Teachers' Inst.
p. 393.

Lawrence Sci.
Sch. p. 352.

Tufts Col.
p. 276.

Worcester Inst.
Tech. p. 346.

Trans. of pupils,
p. 189.

Kindergarten,
p. 166.

Art Ed.
p. 403.

Martha's Vin.
Sum. Inst.
p. 527.

Boston Sch. Org.
p. 194.

Smith Col.
p. 439.

Wellesley Col.
p. 438.

cate must bear witness, not only to the scholastic attainments, but also the moral qualifications of the teacher. A settled minister could not be considered a schoolmaster within the intent of this act.

7. The penalty for neglecting to support a school according to law was fixed at £10 for the towns of 50 families, towns that failed to support the grammar school were fined £30, and for other towns the fine was £20 and £30.

8. As for truant officers, the minister, the selectmen, or other persons appointed for this purpose, should " use their best endeavors " that all should attend the schools. They were also to visit the schools, at least once in six months, and to "inquire into the regulation and discipline thereof, and the proficiency of the scholars therein, giving reasonable notice of the time of their visitation."

9. Recognizing the fact that there would be need of schools, even more elementary than those provided for in this act, it was provided that the teachers of such schools must also secure a certificate. The penalty for violating this provision was fixed at 20*s.*

10. Only citizens of the United States were eligible as teachers. The fine for violating this provision was fixed at the rate of 20*s.* a month. This was certainly meant to be prohibitive. In this is shown the hostile feelings that had culminated in the Revolution.

This law, with its unfortunate emphasis upon the district unit of organization, was in force with but slight modification until 1826, with but little real progress on the part of the schools. In that year a more business-like administration of its provisions was arranged for, through the election of school committees of not less than five persons, chosen at the annual town-meeting, empowered to visit schools, report upon them to the governor, and to examine and certificate teachers. Again, eight years later (1834), a great advance was made in the establishment of a permanent school fund. But the most important move in the school history of the state came in 1837. This was the creation of a state board of education, with Horace Mann as its first secretary; an act which inaugurated the great educational revival, which, in some respects, made our national educational system. Developments since that time, too rapid even to summarize in a brief outline, have made the schools of Massachusetts models which nearly every other state in the Union has followed as a copy.

Radcliffe Col. p. 442.
Harvard Sum. Sch. pp. 515, 535.
Marine Bi. Lab. p. 520.
Concord Sum. Sch. p. 521.
Northfield Sum. Conf. p. 523.
Coeducation, p. 432.
Ed. Revival, Chapter VII.

Text-book legislation, p. 219; Library legislation, pp. 484, 485; Sch. organization, App. F; St. Supt. Pub. Ins. App. G; Cert. of teachers, App. H; Teachers' Inst. App. I; Comp. Ed. Laws, App. J; Ed. Statistics, App. K.

Connecticut

In 1750 Connecticut enacted a school law which contained all the essential features of a previous law of 1700, with some additions. The chief points were: —

1. Towns of 70 families, having but one ecclesiastical society, and ecclesiastical societies that have 70 families shall maintain, at least, one good school for eleven months of the year. Towns and societies of less than 70 families need continue their school only one-half the year. Hinsdale, p. 1251.

2. Every head county town shall maintain a grammar school throughout the year.

3. Toward the support of these schools, the colonial treasurer shall pay annually to those towns that keep their schools according to law, the sum of 40s. on every £1000 in the lists of towns.

4. Local school funds that had been begun by the sale of lands in 1733, shall be a perpetual fund for the support of schools.

5. In case the general tax and local funds are insufficient to support schools according to law, the required amount shall be raised, one-half by the tax, the

other by rate fee, unless some other method shall be agreed upon by the community.

6. The civil authorities and selectmen shall inspect the schools at least quarterly. They shall note the character of the instruction, suggest improvements, and report to the general assembly all disorder and misapplication of funds. The tax of 40s. on the £1000 proved more than the colonists could pay during the stress of the French and Indian War, and in 1754 was fixed at 10s. In 1766 it was made 20s.; and was in 1767 again raised, this time to 40s.

Steiner, p. 31.

Later, Connecticut encouraged public schools and discouraged those of a private character. About the middle of the eighteenth century the "Separatists" had a large following and set up a school, "The Shepherd's Tent," in the house of one of their adherents. The object of this school was to train "exhorters, teachers, and ministers." Of this the assembly did not approve, and passed a law forbidding any one to maintain a school of any sort, except such as had already been provided by law, except by "special lycence" from the assembly.

This law was the result of heated religious discussion, but it did not prevent private academies from springing up near the end of the colonial period.

Theological Ed. p. 312.

The first school on the order of an academy was established by Governor Trumbell at Lebanon in 1743. The school was limited to thirty pupils, and was supported by tuition fees. For more than thirty years it was kept by Matthew Tisdale, a Harvard graduate, and its fame drew pupils even from the West Indies and the Southern colonies. The "Union School of New London" was incorporated in 1774. This school was to prepare for the college, and also to furnish a thorough English education. It had a long and useful career.

Legal Ed. pp. 316, 319.

Finally, the control of the schools passed into the hands of local districts or "school societies." The societies were distinct from the old "ecclesiastical society" which once had control. The laws bringing about this change were enacted in 1795 and 1798. The support of the schools was to come from the income of the permanent funds. Each district or society was to appoint a committee of not more than nine competent persons, who were to have complete control of the school. The county grammar school was no longer required, but societies might, upon a two-thirds vote, establish a school of higher grade than elementary. It is not to be expected that the people were anxious for such schools at a time when they approved of the re-pealing of the old law. In 1799 the school law was again changed. A tax of $2 was levied on each $1000, but nothing was said as to the length of the school session. As a consequence, there was no uni-formity in this respect, and the schools were closed when the funds ran out. The new system did not prove successful. *(Conn. Acad. Arts and Sci. p. 553.)*

As a result of the lack of school supervision the schools ran down, and Connecticut, like the other states, found that her children were being neglected. There were, however, signs of an awakening. In 1825 the governor called attention to the insufficiency of the schools, and on his recommendation several towns adopted the Lancasterian system. In 1826 there was an attempt to secure state supervision of the common schools, and in 1827, at Hartford, a society was organized to that end. Ten years later, Henry Brainard was ap-pointed secretary of the state board of education, and the period of real, though interrupted, progress in state education was begun in Connecticut. *(Ed. of Deaf, p. 470. Shef. Sci. Sch. p. 352. Teachers' Inst. p. 392.)*

At the same time was passed an act "for the better supervision of the common schools," and providing for a complete system of organization. In 1856 the "school societies" were abolished, and their powers and duties transferred to the towns which appointed school visitors with duties similar to those of the school committees in *(Hist. Sketches, p. 43. Normal Schs. p. 377. Agricult. Col. p. 362.)*

Coeducation,
p. 432.

Massachusetts.   Connecticut has a large school fund, and its educational institutions of every class are generously supported.

Text-book legislation, p. 219; Library legislation, p. 485; Sch. organization, App. F; St. Supt. Pub. Ins. App. G; Cert. of teachers, App. H; Teachers' Inst. App. I; Comp. Ed. Laws, App. J; Ed. Statistics, App. K.

Rhode Island

Hist. Sketches,
p. 352.

According to the Rhode Island school law of 1828, which is the parent of all subsequent educational legislation within the state, $10,000 was appropriated annually from the treasury for the support of free schools. This was to be supplemented by an annual tax within each town, the amount to be determined at the town-meeting.   The town also appointed school committees of from five to twenty-one persons, with power to examine and appoint teachers and to visit the schools. The state appropriation has been gradually increased;

Teachers' Inst.
p. 393.
Normal Schs.
p. 378.
Barnard.

in 1839 to $25,000; in 1854 to $50,000, and in 1870 to $90,000.   In 1845 provisions were made for "advanced" (secondary) instruction, when desired, and for school libraries accessible to all the inhabitants of the town. The real efficiency of the schools of the state may be

Agricult. Col.
p. 362.
Brown Woman's
Col. p. 442.

attributed to the work of Henry Barnard, who in 1843 was invited to serve as the first state superintendent of public instruction, and devoted two years of incessant labor to the solution of its then most unfortunate school tangles.

Text-book legislation, p. 219; Library legislation, p. 485; Sch. organization, App. F; St. Supt. Pub. Ins. App. G; Cert. of teachers, App. H. Teachers' Inst. App. I; Comp. Ed. Laws, App. J; Ed. Statistics, App. K.

Maine

Hist. Sketches,
p. 153.
Colby Col.
p. 273.

One year after its separation from Massachusetts and admission to the Union as a separate state, Maine passed a school law.   Under it not less than 40 cents for each inhabitant was to be devoted to the maintenance of its free schools. In each town and plantation too, a school committee of from four to seven persons was provided for, with duties similar to those of corresponding committees in Massachusetts. A school agent was also to be appointed by the town, for each district, with general supervisory duties.

Theological Ed. p. 310.

High Schools, p. 171.

In 1827 authority was given to form districts out of two or more towns — a provision arising out of necessity of the thinly settled regions.

But nothing like a standardization of the schools of the state was brought about until 1846, when a state board of education was organized. This was later abolished, but much progress had been made under it, and with the appointment in 1854 of a state superintendent, the schools were systematized and placed upon a substantial footing. County supervisors of schools were authorized in 1869, and a compulsory law requiring three months' schooling for all between the age of nine and fifteen years passed in 1875. Since that time the general requirements have been much stiffened.

Teachers' Inst. p. 393.

Normal Schs. p. 378.

State Univ. p. 284.

Trans. of pupils, p. 189.

Coeducation, p. 432.

Text-book legislation, p. 219; Library legislation, p. 484; Sch. organization, App. F; St. Supt. Pub. Ins. App. G; Cert. of teachers, App. H; Teachers' Inst. App. I; Comp. Ed. Laws, App. J; Ed. Statistics, App. K.

New Hampshire

Little independent school action was taken by New Hampshire after its separation from Massachusetts (1680) until 1789, when it was decreed that there should be English grammar schools maintained in all "ordinary towns," and grammar schools, in which Greek and Latin should be taught in all shire and half shire towns. In 1808 an advance was made in general organization, through the establishment of school committees for towns and parishes, and twenty years later a supervisor for each district.

Hist. Sketches, p. 253.

Dartmouth Med. Sch. p. 329.

Libraries, p. 484.

At about the time of this latter action (1828) a "literary fund" was made available for the schools.

The next move was the appointment of a state commissioner (1846), who was later deposed (1850), and his place taken by county commissioners. In 1867 a reconstruction was again made, and a state board of education constituted, together with a state superintendent of education. The latter has persisted, though the former was abolished in 1874. Since 1848 graded schools have been provided for.

Text-book legislation, p. 219; Library legislation, pp. 484, 485; Sch. organization, App. F; St. Supt. Pub. Ins., App. G; Cert. of teachers, App. H; Teachers' Inst. App. I; Comp. Ed. Laws. App. J; Ed. Statistics, App. K.

Vermont

Vermont was settled by families from the older New England states, who followed the latter closely in the organization of schools. The first school law appeared on the statute books in 1782, and established the district

system with the regular officers for its administration. Not until 1825 was any legislation of importance enacted, but in that year legal provision was made for the creation of a school fund. Two years later (1827) a state commissioner of public schools was established,

empowered to recommend text-books, to superintend the district school committees, and to collect school statistics.

In 1856 a state board of education was organized, and continued until 1874, when it was replaced by a state superintendency. All the machinery for normal and higher instruction is in operation.

Text-book legislation, p. 219; Library legislation, p. 484; Sch. organization, App. F; St. Supt. Pub. Ins. App. G; Cert. of teachers, App. H; Teachers' Inst. App. I; Comp. Ed. Laws, App. J; Ed. Statistics, App. K.

REFERENCES

Adams, Herbert B. Thomas Jefferson and the University of Virginia. Circ. Inf. No. 1, 1888. Am. Ed. Hist. No. 2. — Barnard,

Henry. Am. Jour. Ed. Vol. 27 ; 17 : 32 ; 4 (biog.). Am. Jour. Ed. 1 : 659, 15 : 605. — *Bush*, George C. (1) History of Higher Education in Massachusetts. Circ. Inf. No. 6, 1891. (2) History of Education in New Hampshire. Circ. Inf. No. 3, 1898. (3) History of Education in Vermont. Circ. Inf. No. 4, 1900. — Earle, Alice Morse. Customs and Fashions in Old New England. — Fiske, John. Old Virginia and her Neighbors. Vol. II. — Hinsdale, B. F. Documents Illustrative of American Educational History. Rep. Com. Ed. 92–93 : 1225–1414. — **Historical Sketch of State School Systems** (each state). Rep. Com. Ed. 1876. — *Hough*, B. F. Constitutional Provisions in Regard to Education in the Several States. Circ. Inf. No. 7, 1875. — *Johnson*, Clifton. The Old-time District School. Outl. 76 : 568. — **Martin**, George H. Evolution of the Massachusetts Public School System. N.Y. 1894. — *Mayo*, A. D. The American Common School in New England from 1790 to 1840. Rep. Com. Ed. 94–95, p. 1551. Education in Southwestern Virginia. Rep. Com. Ed. 1890–1891 : 881. — *Morgan*, B. S., and Coch, J. F. History of Education in West Virginia. Charleston, 1891. — *Randall*, S. S. Common School System of the State of New York. Troy, 1851. History of the Common School System in the State of New York. N.Y. 1871. — **Regents' Report**, 83d. Albany, N.Y. — Rice, J. M. The Public School System of the United States. N.Y. 1893. — Schools as they were in the United States, Sixty and Seventy Years Ago. Am. Jour. Ed. Vol. 13. — Sherwood, Sidney. History of Higher Education in the State of New York. Circ. Inf. No. 3, 1900. Am. Ed. Hist. No. 28. — Steiner, Bernard C. History of Education in Connecticut. Circ. Inf. No. 2, 1893. — *Tolman*, William H., History of Education in Rhode Island. Circ. Inf. No. 1, 1894. — *Whitehill*, A. R. History of Education in West Virginia. Circ. Inf. No. 1, 1902.

CHAPTER VI

THE GROWTH OF THE ACADEMIES

As the grammar schools throughout the early colonies declined in efficiency toward the latter part of the eighteenth century, a new institution was coming to the front, and providing a means of education that was far-reaching. This was the academy, the successor of the old grammar school, and the forerunner of the modern high school. From about the time of the Revolution, until the middle of the nineteenth century, it was the undisputed leader in secondary education; and although now in a sense deposed by the public high school, the academy has not by any means outlived its usefulness. In their inception, academies were of two general classes : (1) The local academy, which aimed to do little more than to supply the educational needs of its immediate neighborhood; and (2) the academy of a more pretentious type, with a course of considerable breadth, drawing its students from a wide field. The former were frequently but ephemeral, while the latter possessed often considerable endowment, and were established upon a permanent basis. The academy was essentially a private institution, but as will be shown later, in many instances received such substantial recognition from the state as to warrant its inclusion under the public school system. So closely did the early academies resemble their predecessors, the grammar schools, that it is not easy to determine the first, either as to time or place. The first, however, to become incorporated was one in Philadelphia, founded in 1753, through the efforts of Benjamin Franklin. In Massa-

Germantown
Acad. p. 61.

chusetts the first to incorporate was the Phillips Academy at Andover, started in 1778, though not chartered until two years later. Phillips Academy at Exeter, New Hampshire, was founded at about the same time. Dummer Academy was the third to be chartered in New England, being incorporated in 1782; though its history begins in 1761, when Lieutenant-governor Dummer bequeathed his mansion and 330 acres of land for the establishment and support of a school. Two years later the school was opened at Byfield, Massachusetts. Because of the celebrity of its first master, Samuel Moody, it may rightly be called the mother of the New England Academy. For nineteen years Master Moody managed this school, and made it, says Charles Hammond, "the best type of an English grammar school that had existed on American soil since the days of Ezekiel Cheever." And again he says, "There is no doubt that the long and successful career of Master Moody at Byfield led to the establishment of the Phillips Academies and of Leicester."

Master Moody was indeed an exceptionally successful teacher. In 1746 he graduated from Harvard and began teaching the York Grammar School in the province of Maine. This was the only public school in the region. Under his instruction were educated a number of boys who later became famous. Governor Dummer had provided in his will that the town or parish committee should have control of the funds of his school, and should appoint the teacher. In looking for a master, they determined upon Master Moody. He was appointed for life, and could be removed only in case the overseers of Harvard considered him "immoral and incompetent." Master Moody was no less successful in training men at Byfield than he had been at York. One of his pupils was Samuel Phillips, Jr., who was the chief factor in securing the founding of the Phillips Academy at Andover. Another of his pupils was Eliphalet Pearson. Phillips

Newark Acad.
p. 63.

Wm. Penn. Sch.
p. 60.
Wilmington
(N.C.) Acad.
p. 68.
Nazareth Acad.
p. 61.

Moody.

Rep. Mass. Bd.
Ed. (40th)
p. 188.

Warren Acad.
p. 260.

Phillips.

and Pearson were intimate friends in college; and when Andover was being planned, it was with the understanding that Pearson, because of his special fitness, should become its first master.

Rep. Mass. Bd.
Ed. (40th)
p. 220.

The constitution of Andover limited the number of students to thirty, and gave preference to those who sought instruction "in the learned languages." Others were not to be admitted unless the number was incomplete for one month. Thirteen pupils enrolled on the opening day, and before the end of the month the full number — thirty — was in attendance, and the rule limiting the enrolment to that number was discarded.

P. 428.

Leicester Academy, in Worcester County, was the third to be incorporated in Massachusetts. This was in 1784. At that time there was not a single school in the county higher than the district school. Indeed the whole central and western parts of the state were without schools of high grade. When the legislature was petitioned for a charter, it conditioned the granting of it upon the securing of £1000 as an endowment, in addition to the building, which had been already secured. The endowment was to insure some permanency to the institution, and shows the caution as well as the wisdom of the legislators in the matter. The £1000 was secured and the charter granted within a month after the legislature had made that a condition.

Westford Acad.
p. 428.

Bradford Acad.
p. 428.

When the law of 1789 was enacted, the academies were ready to coöperate with the state. As early as 1797 they had risen to sufficient importance to call for the attention of the legislature. Because others were seeking charters, the general assembly of Massachusetts appointed a committee from its own number to study the question of academies, their relation to the state, and what the state's attitude should be in the future toward them. The committee found that already fifteen academies had been chartered. Of this number, six had received a grant of one township each of state

Acads. in Ga.
p. 72.

land; and one, a grant of fifteen thousand acres. Of the remaining eight, some had been endowed by towns and individuals, while others had no endowment. Upon the recommendation of the committee, a law was enacted in behalf of academies, favorable to the policy of granting state aid, and considering all parts of the state entitled to equal grants. But before lands were granted to any academy in the future, there must be a permanent fund of at least $3000, provided either by individuals or communities. The amount of land to be granted to a single academy was fixed at a half township. This amount was then voted to each of several academies, on condition that they should within three years secure an endowment of $3000. The same amount was promised to five counties on like conditions.

Am. Jour. Ed. 17:74.

This law recognized the academy as a part of the public school system, though the school itself was only a semi-public institution. The land that was granted at this time was within the province of Maine. Under the protection of the state the academies multiplied rapidly. While their spread was not conducive to the growth of the public school sentiment, still we must not forget that they came in at a time when there was a vast educational field unoccupied, and one that would have remained unoccupied but for them. Barring the fact that they fostered a sentiment for private, rather than for public schools, their influence was good. They became educational centres in their respective communities, and broadened the life of that great class that could never hope to go to college; while, on the other hand, they were the college fitting schools. So well did they do their work, that the colleges were able to raise their entrance requirements materially. As a rule they were manned by young men full of zeal, who inspired the pupils with a desire for the best in life, and who sent them out to occupy positions of trust in the state and the church. These same teachers often brought out

new and improved text-books, and thus became the
means of raising the standard of teaching.

Acads. in N.Y.
p. 375.
To trace the development of academies in the different
colonies would be a long task.   A general idea of their
growth and decline may be gathered from the following
table, which gives the incorporation of academies for a
century, in several states.   The table is necessarily incomplete : —

	—— to 1800	1801–1820	1821–1840	1841–1860	1861–1880
Maine	5	20	31	34	8
New Hampshire . .	10	18	59	23	25
Vermont	10	24	22	10	9
Massachusetts . .	17	19	78	40	15*a*
New York	19	33	176	183	123*b*
Maryland	5	24	40	23	—
North Carolina . .	30	113	43*c*	—	—
Georgia	6	14	—	—	—
Totals . . .	102	265	449	313	180

a closes with 1877.   *b* closes with 1873.   *c* closes with 1825.

But the tremendous proportions to which the academy
system had grown at the zenith of its influence is
shown by the table on page 96, which gives its status
in 1850.

Academies of the more pretentious sort were primarily
fitting schools for the colleges, and their courses were,
consequently, largely classical.   The others devoted
more time to the common studies.   Pupils sometimes
entered at seven years, though nine was more commonly
considered the proper age.   Discipline was strict and
punishment severe.   The following, written in 1860 by
Am. Jour Ed.
32 : 873.
one of the first pupils at Phillips, Andover, will give some
idea of the work.

"Monitors kept an account of all a student's failures, idleness,
inattention, whispering, and like deviation from order, and at the
end of the week were bestowed substantial rewards for such self-
indulgences, distributed upon the head and hand with no lack of
strength or fidelity."

After mentioning Cheever's *Accidence*, Corderius, Nepos, and Virgil, with possibly some other author as the texts in Latin, the same writer continues : —

" Our grammar was ' Ward's,' in which all the rules and explanations were in Latin, and we were drilled sedulously in writing this language far enough to get into the university. Our studies in Greek were very superficial. Gloucester's Greek Grammar was our guide in that language, and a thorough ability to construe the four Gospels was all required of us to enter college.

" In that day arithmetic was begun at the university. The degree of preparation for college and the amount of studies within it, are not worthy of remembrance, when compared with the means of acquirement now presented to the aspiring student."

If this last statement was true for 1860, how much more applicable is it to-day.

REFERENCES

Academies, Mass., policy of. 40th Rep. Mass. Bd. Ed. 1875–1876. — *Academies*, Statistics of. Am. Jour. Ed. Vol. 30. — *Bartlett*, S. C. The New England Academy. Rep. Com. Ed. 1896–1897, 2 : 1183. — Bradford Academy. Am. Jour. Ed. 30 : 595. — Cheney, M. L. High School Legislation in California since 1876. Pacific Ed. Jour. 11 : 122. — Dummer Academy. Am. Jour. Ed. 30 : 763. — Hopkins Grammar School. Bacon, L. W. New Haven, 1860. Am. Jour. Ed. 28 : 275. — Lawrence Academy. Am. Jour. Ed. 2 : 49. — Leicester Academy. Am. Jour. Ed. 28 : 798 and 30 : 777. — **Moody**, Samuel. Am. Jour. Ed. 28 : 785. — Norwich Free Academy. Am. Jour. Ed. 3 : 191. — Phillips Academy, Andover. Am. Jour. Ed. 30 : 669. — Phillips Academy, Exeter. Bell, Charles H. Exeter, 1883. — **Phillips**, Samuel (biog.). Am. Jour. Ed. 6 : 75. — Steele, G. M. Has the New England Academy outlived its usefulness? Ed. 15 : 513. — Tomlinson, E. T. The Field and Work of the Academy. Ed. 5 : 127. — *Tucker*, G. Educational Statistics of the Census of 1840. Am. Jour. Ed. 24 : 171. — Virginia Military Institute. Am. Jour. Ed. 23 : 825. — William Penn Charter School. Philadelphia, 1880. — Winterbotham, Rev. W. View of the United States of America. Am. Jour. Ed. 24 : 137.

THE FOLLOWING TABLE SHOWS THE STATUS OF THE
AMERICAN ACADEMY IN 1850: —

	Number	Teachers	Pupils	Annual Income [1]
Alabama	166	380	8,290	$224,279
Arkansas	90	126	2,407	34,308
California	6	5	170	20,392
Columbia, District of . .	47	126	2,333	84,040
Connecticut	202	329	6,996	152,120
Delaware	65	94	2,011	53,498
Florida	34	49	1,251	22,742
Georgia	219	318	9,059	184,849
Illinois	83	160	4,244	47,678
Indiana	131	233	6,185	73,219
Iowa	33	46	1,111	11,180
Kentucky	330	600	12,712	306,507
Louisiana	143	354	5,328	283,003
Maine	131	232	6,648	64,966
Maryland	223	503	10,787	239,083
Massachusetts	403	521	13,436	354,521
Michigan	37	71	1,619	31,953
Minnesota	1	1	12	—
Mississippi	171	297	6,628	144,732
Missouri	204	368	8,829	183,403
New Hampshire	107	183	5,321	52,591
New Jersey	225	453	9,844	300,242
New Mexico	1	1	40	—
New York	887	3,136	49,328	1,015,249
North Carolina	272	403	7,822	222,695
Ohio	206	474	15,052	201,077
Oregon	29	44	842	24,495
Pennsylvania	524	914	23,751	570,501
Rhode Island	46	75	1,601	37,423
South Carolina	202	333	7,467	205,489
Tennessee	264	404	9,928	175,926
Texas	97	137	3,389	77,732
Utah	13	—	—	2,221
Vermont	118	257	6,864	56,159
Virginia	317	547	9,068	351,007
Wisconsin	58	86	2,723	19,899
Total	6,085	12,260	263,096	5,831,179

[1] Estimated in part. Am. Jour. Ed. 1 : 308.

CHAPTER VII

THE EDUCATIONAL REVIVAL

ALTHOUGH public elementary education had been, after a fashion, established in the older states of the North by the end of the first third of the nineteenth century, its conditions were anything but ideal. The previous fifty years had been a period of intense struggle, economic, social, religious, and educational. The War of the Revolution had left the three millions of people composing the population, impoverished; and the difficulties with Great Britain, which continued up to the close of the War of 1812, made them uncertain, even of the future. The states west of the Alleghanies were being opened up, and, although full of promise for the future, were drawing off many of the brightest and most energetic young men from the Eastern states, leaving that region impoverished. During all the time, the schools, which are, after all, the barometer of social and economic success, were running down. It is true that colleges were springing up, and that academies were in their most prosperous condition, but neither of these institutions was for the people. The most deplorable features of the district system of school organization were dominant in the common schools. Although it was a time which produced great leaders, this seems to have been in spite of the schools, rather than because of them. Great teachers there were here and there, and good schools; but most of the latter were within the private rather than the public system, and touched but a comparatively small proportion of the people. Schools of the early colonial type. which had been essentially seventeenth-century transplantations from Europe, were outgrowing their general usefulness, and as yet the right thing had not been found with which to replace them. In 1837 the state of Massachusetts was paying but $2.73 per pupil for the education of its children, a sum only about one-tenth that of the present cost, and less than even the poorest communities of the South are now devoting to it. There was absolutely no such thing known as the pedagogical supervision of the schools, and not a public institution for the training of teachers in the country. Such were the educational conditions in the East when, in 1837, Massachusetts first organized its state board of education. The far-reaching influence of this move was due to two things : first, the fact that general conditions were ripe for a period of educational progress; and, second, that the right man was at hand to become its leader. Neither one could have accomplished much without the other, but the combination was a most happy one. To it we may ascribe the tremendous growth in common school education which the country has since seen.

Horace Mann, the first secretary of the Massachusetts board, was born in Franklin, Massachusetts, in 1796. Left fatherless at the age of thirteen years, his boyhood days were full of hardships. Able to attend school but a few weeks in each year, he was, even in those earlier years, impressed with the weakness of the instruction which was open to him, a fact that did much to spur him on in the unremitting warfare he waged during the later years of his life against just such schools as he had known in his youth. He was, however, an insatiate reader, having read the town library, a present from Benjamin Franklin in recognition of the name, through ; and even at fifteen he had acquired such a veneration for a book that, in his own words, "I would as soon stick a pin into my own flesh as into the pages of a book." At about the age of nineteen years he met his first real teacher, fitted for college in six months, entered Brown University, and was graduated with the class of 1819. Both previous to his entrance to college and during the years of his course, Mann had taught a country school. When, after having studied law, practised successfully for several years, and after election to the Massachusetts legislature from Dedham, the town of his residence, he was appointed to the responsible position of secretary of the state board of education, he was not without deep conviction on the subject of popular education, nor without determination to make the office, which was created for him, count for much.

During the twelve years of his secretaryship Mr. Mann's accomplishments were little short of stupendous. Never strong of constitution, they were broken into by occasional periods of ill health, which necessitated leisure for recuperation ; but with these few exceptions, he labored constantly for the upbuilding of the schools of the state. No task was too hard nor distasteful for him to undertake, if it counted toward that end. Everywhere that teachers could be brought together, he was present to address them even at the sacrifice of energy on his part that reduced his fragile health almost to the breaking point. Every important phase of the public school question was not only touched upon by him, either in his public lectures or printed reports, but when he felt that the occasion demanded, fought out to the bitter end, against all opposition. Volumes have been written upon his educational campaigns, which Bibliography, p. 102. comprise some of our most important contributions to the literature of the schools. So it is necessary here only to point out some of the more important ones.

First and foremost: Mann was opposed to the district P. 81. system of organization, characterizing the ordinance of 1789 which authorized it as "the most unfortunate law on the subject of common schools ever enacted in the state." He urged the town unit of administration and adequate supervision, for, as he sometimes said, he was superintendent of schools in every district of the state.

Second: He urged the apportionment of an adequate public school fund. When he took up the work, such a fund existed in Massachusetts, but largely on paper. Now the state provides for a fund of $5,000,000, besides which — and it comes largely through appeals to public generosity made by Mann — more than $10,000,000 are raised annually within the state by taxation for public school purposes.

P. 374 *et seq.*

Third: He was one of the prime movers in the campaign for normal schools and better trained teachers.

Appendix J.

Fourth: He fought strenuously for a longer school year.

In 1837 one-third of the children within the state were without any school advantages whatsoever, while a large proportion of the remainder attended school but two or three of the winter months, or a few weeks in the summer. In 1839 the minimum school year for all districts was fixed at six months, and it has been steadily lengthened, until now every child in the state is forced to take seven full years' schooling of forty weeks each, with the privilege of extending those years to twelve or thirteen.

Fifth: He was indefatigable in his labors for good, clean, sanitary schoolhouses: fit "temples of science" as he denominated them. The accounts which he gives of the school buildings, as he found them during his first official journeys about the state, seem incredible. Almost universally in the country districts and in the smaller towns they were dilapidated and ill kept, if not even filthy, and it is to be feared that many of the larger cities were not without offence. During the twelve years of Mann's secretaryship, $1,000,000 were put into public school buildings.

P. 219.

Sixth: Mann urgently strove to bring about some uniformity in text-books. At the beginning of his work, he found three hundred different sets in use in the state. Yet before its close he was able, not only to bring about some approximation to uniformity, but even to raise the general quality not a little. To-day in Massachusetts, as in many other states, all text-books are provided the pupils at public expense.

Seventh: He was able to look beyond the schools as factors in education, and to recognize the public library as an important feature. The public library revival dates from the period of Mann's secretaryship. Chapter xxiv.

The merest glance over these, a few of Horace Mann's accomplished results, is enough to convince one of the efficiency of his service, as well as of the fact that they are in the exact lines along which our public school systems, not only in Massachusetts, but in every state of the Union, have made their progress.

In 1849 Mann was succeeded in the Massachusetts secretaryship by Barnas Sears, subsequently representing his state in Congress for a brief period, and died, in 1859, as president of Antioch College in Ohio. His great work had, however, been accomplished in Massachusetts, and has been continued practically along the lines he laid out, ever since.

In 1846 special agents of the board of education were appointed, who have added much to its efficiency. In 1854 city and town superintendents of schools were authorized. In 1869 towns were empowered to expend public funds for the conveyance of children to schools, and the whole question of the consolidation of rural schools inaugurated. P. 200.

P. 189.

In 1882 the school district system, after fifty years of controversy, was finally abolished: one year later evening schools were authorized; and the next (1884), a free text-book law enacted. P. 183 *et seq.*
Chapter xxvii.
P. 219.

Free high school instruction was required of every town in 1891, the school year extended to eight months, three years later; and in 1902 a law went into effect requiring every town and city to employ a superintendent of schools, either singly or in combination with other towns.   In all these moves we can see Horace Mann and his influence.

In other states in the East the educational developments of the last half-century have been largely attempts to accomplish these same results.   It is true that within each state, school growth has shown a certain individuality (certain steps in the Massachusetts plan have never been taken by some states and probably never will be), while others have taken their places.   Yet these differences do not seem to be sufficiently great to warrant a detailed discussion in a volume of this character, of the more recent growth of school systems in the older states. Particular facts regarding that growth are brought out in the topical discussions which comprise the other chapters, while the present conditions are shown in the brief statistical statements to follow, largely made up from the various tables in the latest report of the United States Commissioner of Education.

Appendix K.

REFERENCES

Harris, W. T. Horace Mann. Ed. Rev. 2: 105–119. — *Horace Mann*. Rep. Com. Ed. 1895–1896, 1 : 887 (includes bibliography). — Mann, Horace. Lectures on Education. Boston, 1840. — Mann, Mary. Life and Works of Horace Mann. Boston, 1865. Horace Mann. Ed. 3: 255–265. — *Martin*, G. H. Horace Mann and the Revival of Education in Massachusetts. Ed. Rev. 5: 434. — *Massachusetts*. Board of Education Annual Reports for the years 1838–1849. Boston (very valuable). — *Mayo*, A. D. Horace Mann and the Great Revival of the American Common School, 1830–1850. Rep. Com. Ed. 1896–1897, 1 : 715.

CHAPTER VIII

EDUCATIONAL DEVELOPMENT IN THE MIDDLE WEST

ALTHOUGH the older colonies, and especially those of New England, furnished the battlefields upon which most of the great educational conflicts have been fought out, the conditions west of the Alleghanies were sufficiently different from those of the far East to leave plenty of problems for the pioneer schoolmen of the westward moving frontier. In the early days of the Middle West the settlers came from the Eastern states across the mountains, rather than from the Eastern countries across the ocean, and they had learned their lessons of popular education well. They already believed firmly, that the public school should not follow the frontier afar off, but that it should keep pace with it; and not infrequently the schoolhouse was the first public building erected in the settlements, preceding even the meeting-house. The migrations into the West were from one portion of a republic to another portion of that same republic, and those institutions which had taken long years to evolve in the older states were adopted, ready made, in the newer. The federal government encouraged this adoption, including in the official act which incorporated the Northwest Territory (from which the older states west of the Alleghanies were formed) the following clause : —

"Religion, morality, and knowledge being necessary to good government and the happiness of mankind, schools and the means of education shall forever be encouraged."

These were no idle words. Although not intended to be mandatory in any narrow sense, they were, nevertheless, prophetic. No other newly occupied country in the whole world's history has ever seen schools established so nearly coincident to the first settlements, nor schools of so high an order in so short a time.

In some respects the West has caught up with, and passed the earlier settled region to the East. Its schools contain a larger proportion of the children of school-going age, both in the elementary and secondary grades. It has, too, a larger total number of pupils in the schools, and makes a greater annual expenditure for school purposes than does any of the other geographical divisions studied by the commissioner of education. But these latter facts may be ascribed to a larger total of population. Secondary and higher education is particularly developed in the Central states, nearly one-half the institutions in each of these classes being found there. It has been preëminently the home of coeducation, the first college in the country admitting both sexes, (Oberlin) being within its borders, while the lower schools have been

Appendix K. coeducational from the start, almost without exception.

Ohio

When the " Ohio Company " first made settlement at Marietta, on the north bank of the Ohio River, a " second New England " was planned, and schools were an indispensable part of the enterprise. Seemingly, the schoolmaster was among the first comers to the settlements; and, that he began operations immediately, may be judged from the fact, that in 1788, but one year after the town was established, $200 was sent out by Manasseh Cutler, to pay him and the minister. Possibly, one man received it all. Within a few years four schools

Mayo[1], 1526. were in operation in Marietta.

Beginning with 1802, academies were incorporated, and, as settlements increased, private schools multiplied. Legislation aiming to encourage schools of these classes dates from 1817, when it was made possible for any six or more persons to incorporate and establish a school. As may be supposed, none of these schools was of a very high grade.   Of them, Barnard says : —

"Schools worthy of remembrance between 1802 and 1820 were known only in the most enterprising towns.   The mass of the people had privileges in such 'common' institutions of learning as might be expected among communities in which school teachers were tolerated, but neither examined for qualifications nor encouraged for merit."

Am. Jour. Ed. 6 : 82.

The first public school law was enacted in 1821. This was based on a New York ordinance, and was merely permissive.   It provided for the districting of the township, school committees, and the levying of rate bills.   Because of the failure of this law, a new and mandatory one was enacted in 1825, which may be regarded as the real beginning of the public school system in Ohio.   In it provisions were made for the organization of districts, a county school tax (which continued until 1851), and the certification of teachers by examiners appointed by the county court of common pleas.   Since the examiners were also to visit the schools at intervals, we have here the anticipation of a general plan of supervision.   By a clause inserted in the school law in 1829, it was made possible for cities to organize separate districts apart from the township, and a few years later Cincinnati availed itself of the privilege, taking out a special charter.   Almost coincident with the Eastern educational revival under Horace Mann in 1837, a popular wave of public school enthusiasm struck Ohio.   As a result, a state superintendent of public instruction was appointed (Samuel Lewis), and Calvin E. Stowe was sent to Europe to study and report upon elementary education.   The school law of 1838, which followed these moves, plainly favored the township, rather than the district unit of organization.

Western Res. Univ. p. 274.

Ed. of Deaf, p. 471.

Oberlin Col. p. 274.

Marietta Col. p. 275.

Ed. of Blind, p. 474.

Ed. of Feeble-minded, p. 476.

Teachers' Inst.
p. 393.
The township clerk was made virtually the superintend-ent of schools, with considerable authority, while further provisions were made for the separate incorporation of cities.   The first real encouragement was given to graded schools through the passage of the "Akron Law" in 1847.

This provided for a number of primary schools as soon as the city funds should warrant them, and also High Schs.
p. 171. for a grammar school.   Two years later it was enacted that any village, town, or city, with two hundred or more inhabitants, might organize on a similar basis, if the people so voted.   The school law of 1853 abolished Reading Circle,
p. 396. the "rate," and made schools free.   It also took the first step toward the consolidation of rural districts Case Sch.
p. 347. under the township system; though it was not until 1885 that a law was enacted enabling township, village, and special school districts to unite and maintain a high school.   What will perhaps prove to be a final blow to the district school within the state was dealt by the law of 1900, which provided for a vote on the cen-Trans. of pupils,
p. 190. tralization of the schools of any township.   By this act the township board of education must submit the ques-Cin. Univ.
p. 277. tion to popular vote upon petition signed by one-fourth of the citizens.   As a result of this law, Ohio is one of the leaders in the movement for the consolidation of the rural schools.

Cleveland,
p. 192.
The public schools of Ohio, especially in the cities, are of a high order, Cleveland having a unique and Cincinnati,
p. 195. seemingly very successful form of organization.   Small colleges have multiplied almost beyond all precedent; Ohio Colleges,
Appendix K. and, together with the State University, bring the facilities for higher education almost to the very doors State Univ.
p. 284. of all the inhabitants.   State normal schools have never been maintained, though departments of education in Coeducation,
p. 432. several of the colleges are endeavoring to supply the lack.

Text-book legislation, p. 219; Library legislation, p. 484; Sch. organization, App. F; St. Supt. Pub. Ins. App. G ; Cert. of teachers, App. H; Teachers' Inst. App. I; Comp. Ed. Laws, App. J; Ed. Statistics, App. K.

Indiana

The first school of which we have any record within the present state of Indiana was taught by a French missionary, M. Revet, at Vincennes, in 1793. Ten years later there was a school at Charleston, and in 1806, when the first territorial legislature convened, the Vincennes University was established, primarily with special reference to the needs of the Indians, though only one ever entered. State Univ. p. 284.

In 1824 a general school law was enacted, providing for township trustees who had power to locate districts, appoint sub-trustees, examine teachers, and erect schoolhouses. The method of erecting these houses was unique ; all able-bodied male persons, except minors, being required to work one day each week until the building was completed. All such who failed to perform the required labor, or to pay the equivalent in building material, were subject to a fine of thirty-seven and one-half cents for each day's default. But the law left matters wholly in the hands of the voters, with the result that enterprising communities pushed schools, while others neglected them.

It was at this time that attention was turned to the county seminary, which had a wide influence for a quarter of a century. The first such institution was Union Seminary, incorporated in 1825. By 1843 twenty-four similar schools had been incorporated. Some of them developed into higher institutions, as, for instance, the State University and Wabash College. Beside the county seminaries, were private and denominational schools. The first of these was Corydon Seminary, incorporated in 1816. Their number increased, till by 1850 thirty-seven had been granted charters. Follow-

ing the general law of 1824, changes had been made
from time to time; but in 1852 an ordinance was enacted,
which contains the substance of the present school law.
This provided for a school tax, township libraries, graded
schools in urban centres, and the township unit of organization.   The school tax was opposed by many, and the
supreme court declared it unconstitutional.   A new law

Woodburn,
p. 46.

met the same fate, but in 1867 one was enacted that
stood the test.

In 1873 the state board of education began to commission high schools.   These schools are entitled to send
their pupils on certificate to the leading colleges, to
which they are admitted without an examination.   In
1898 the board adopted a course of study for these
schools, which in 1902 was fully revised.

Ed. of Deaf,
p. 471.

Teachers' Inst.
p. 398.

Ed. of Blind,
p. 474.

Boone, p. 65.

Rose Polytech.
p. 348.

The first convention of Indiana teachers of which we
have record was held as early as 1836.   There was a
Northern Indiana Teachers' Institute in 1849.   The
present organization, known as the State Teachers'
Association, was organized in Indianapolis in 1854.   In
1856 the *Indiana School Journal* commenced publication, and until 1865 was an organ of the State Association.

The common school system comprises the following
officers : —

Superintendent of public instruction.

State board of education (Superintendent being president).

County superintendent.

City and town trustees.

Township trustees.

Indianap. Sch.
Org. p. 195.

Normal Schs.
p. 378.

Purdue, p. 351.

Coeducation,
p. 432.

The university system consists of the State University
(at Bloomington), founded as the Indiana College in
1829, changed to Indiana University in 1838; the State
Normal School (at Terre Haute), founded in 1865 for
the express purpose of training teachers for the common
schools; and the Purdue Industrial University (at La-

fayette); its foundation was laid in 1862, but it was not opened until 1874.

Text-book legislation, p. 219; Library legislation, p. 485; Sch. organization, App. F; St. Supt. Pub. Ins. App. G; Cert. of teachers, App. H; Teachers' Inst. App. I; Comp. Ed. Laws, App. J; Ed. Statistics, App. K.

Illinois

There is a tradition that in the early years of the eighteenth century the French established a college at Kaskaskia, which existed as late as 1754, but of this we have no certain record. The zeal of the Jesuits along educational lines makes it seem probable, however, that they would have founded schools of some sort, though that they had an institution worthy in any sense of the title College, is extremely doubtful. But it is certain that as early as 1783 John Seeley kept a school in an abandoned cabin in Monroe County, and that the school was continued the next year by Francis Clark. Other schools soon followed in the neighboring counties. As early as 1804 an evening school was kept by John Messenger, a surveyor and one of the makers of Peck and Messenger's map of early Illinois. In the northern part of the state settlements were made later, the first school in Cook County having been started in 1816.

The legislature of 1819 incorporated three academies, Willard, Madison at Edwardsville, Washington at Carlyle, and p. xcix. one at Bellville. The charters of the first two mentioned provided for the free instruction of poor children, and also that as soon as the financial conditions should permit, provisions should be made for the teaching of girls.

The first general school law was enacted in 1825, and it provided for a system of free schools. This law was in advance of public sentiment, as was plainly shown by its speedy repeal. In fact no state outside of New England had at the time a school ordinance which even approximated the Illinois law of 1825 in its educational bearing. It provided for free schools in each county, the examination of teachers by district trustees, and the levying of local school taxes. Two years later it was made ineffective by a legislative provision that no person should be taxed for schools "without his consent," and Illinois lost its opportunity for educational leadership in the West. Additions were, however, frequently made to the school laws; and in 1840 they were fully revised, but with little general improvement.

In 1840 and in 1843 there was special legislation with reference to academies, which were springing up in considerable numbers. Some few were chartered with the special privilege of receiving public moneys on the same basis as the public schools, but this practice never became general. At about the same time a law was passed exempting from taxation land to the extent of 10 acres, owned by any educational institution, while for colleges and seminaries the amount exempted was 160 acres, if actually used for school purposes, together with all buildings and equipment.

The appointment of the first state superintendent, Ninian Edwards, in 1854, was followed by a law in 1855 which abolished the "rate" and made instruction free. Up to this time the private and denominational schools had occupied the field, but now a change set in, and many of the academies became the free graded schools of their communities. Rural districts multiplied, libraries were established, and schools were in session nearly seven months of the year. In 1889 the school law was thoroughly revised and, with amendments since made, the union of districts for one common high school has been made possible. Such legislation has not, however, as yet made possible such a union of the common schools.

Illinois extending as it does from Lake Michigan to the mouth of the Ohio River, the schools have been

Ed. of Deaf, p. 471.

Ed. of Blind, p. 474.

Rockford Col. p. 435.
Ed. of Feeble-minded, p. 476.
Teachers' Inst. p. 393.
Normal Schs. p. 378.
St. Bd. of Ed. p. 200.
Northwestern Univ. p. 275.
State Univ. p. 284.
Univ. of Chicago, p. 278.
Township H. S. p. 190.

Chicago Sch. Org. p. 194.

affected to a marked degree both by Northern and Southern influences. Although as a class they are of a high degree of excellence, the greatest diversity and variation is shown, and probably Illinois shows greater local differences in schools than any other state in the Union.

Coeducation, p. 432.

Text-book legislation, p. 219; Library legislation, p. 484; Sch. organization, App. F; St. Supt. Pub. Ins. App. G; Cert. of teachers, App. H; Teachers' Inst. App. I; Comp. Ed. Laws, App. J; Ed. Statistics, App. K.

Michigan

There is a record that Cadillac, in the days when he was commander at Detroit, offered to provide funds for the establishment of a school at the fort for the French and Indians; but whether in the stirring times such was actually done, we do not know. If not, a mission school, started in 1755, seems to have been the first within the present state. Twenty years later (1775) Detroit had a schoolhouse. And beginning with about that time, schools were maintained in nearly all the permanent settlements. They were, however, of the most primitive sort, usually kept in log cabins, and the instruction went no farther than the three R's.

McLaughlin, p. 15.

In Michigan school legislation began from the top, since the first enactment was to provide for a college or university, with a system of preparatory schools as feeders. The former did not immediately materialize; but several of the latter were established, and during their continuance occupied the place of the academy. No action was taken in support of the common schools until 1827, when a law was enacted which was almost an exact counterpart of the Massachusetts school ordinance of 1647. It, however, provided for the licensing of teachers, and imposed a penalty of $200 — certainly intended to be prohibitory — upon any teacher who failed to comply. Yet the law proved non-effective so far as any increase in the number of schools was concerned, since no town was required to support a teacher, if two-thirds of the votes decided " that they would not comply with the law." Two years after its passage the law was modified in such a way as to make it more effective, and at the same time more nearly to meet existing conditions.

But interest in education was not wanting. In 1830 a ladies' seminary was incorporated. At the same time Detroit had an elementary school which possessed many of the essential characteristics of the modern kindergarten. A covered wagon was provided to take the children to and from the school, where a bed was in readiness for the sleepy little tots, if the session proved too long.

Mich. Pioneer
Col. 1 : 369.

With the appointment in 1836 of John Pierce as state superintendent of public instruction (and he was the first to hold such an office west of Pennsylvania), together with the provisions made for education in the constitution then adopted, an era of school activity was entered upon. The next year a school law was passed providing for a system of schools to be maintained, in part

Ag. Ed. p. 361.

by local taxes and state appropriations, and in part by " rate." This was a long step in advance ; but it did not make free schools, nor, in fact, were such generally established in the state until 1869. Under the law of

State Univ.
p. 284.

Teachers' Inst.
p. 393.

Normal Schs.
p. 378.

Detroit Sch.
Org. p. 195.

Sch. Mines,
p. 351.

1837 schools in the poorer localities fared but indifferently, since many parents removed their children when the public funds were exhausted, to avoid paying the fee ; and, as a result, schools were often closed after a very brief term. In 1842 Detroit organized its schools upon a graded basis. And one year later, a law was enacted providing for a similar course in other cities. The union of school districts was also authorized. Under this law, city and town supervision of schools was stimulated and education in the larger centres of population prospered. That the work in the rural communities might also be better organized, county superintendents were provided for in 1867; but eight years later this Coeducation, p. 432. action was reversed. Since that time Michigan has been without school officers under that name, though the chairman of the board of county commissioners performs the duties of the office.

Text-book legislation, p. 219; Library legislation, p. 485; Sch. organization, App. F; St. Supt. Pub. Ins. App. G; Cert. of teachers, App. H; Teachers' Inst. App. I; Comp. Ed. Laws, App. J; Ed. Statistics, App. K.

Wisconsin

In 1791 James Portier opened a school at Green Bay. Even though his pupils were all from a single family, we must give him credit for being the first teacher within the present state of Wisconsin. He was, moreover, a quarter of a century ahead of his time, for it was not, so far as is known, until 1817 that a second school was established. This was at Prairie du Chien. Settlements were by this time springing up with some Whitford. rapidity, and other schools soon followed.

In 1820 Rev. Eleazer Williams, who later won some fame as the pretended Dauphin of France, conceived the idea of locating the "Six Nations" of New York at Green Bay. He was in the employ of the Episcopal Missionary Society; and, in 1823, started a school with an attendance of fifty white and half-breed children, on the Fox River, opposite Shanty Town. A few years later, the society erected buildings at a cost of $9000, in which the children lived and were instructed. The school was intended especially for Indians and half-breeds, who were admitted between the ages of four and fourteen. Branch schools were established; but after a period of sixteen years, the work was discontinued, not however, until it had exerted a strong influence upon educational development in the region.

Until 1836 the schools were all of a private nature, and supported entirely by tuition; but in that year, Ed. of Blind, p. 474. under the laws of Michigan Territory, a public school

Teachers' Inst.
p. 393.
State Univ.
p. 284.
Normal Schs.
p. 378.

was organized in Milwaukee. In the same year Wisconsin was organized as a separate territory, and adopted the Michigan school laws almost bodily. Then, for a series of years, school development was somewhat retarded by a continual tinkering with educational legislation; but in 1849 the school code was modernized, and a rapid growth followed. By a legislative act in 1858, adjoining school districts were permitted to unite for the support of a common school, and, in 1875, high schools, supported in part by the state, were established. These schools are under a more or less direct supervision of the state department of public instruction. Recently (1899) Wisconsin has provided for a system of county training schools for teachers, and six such schools have already been established. In 1901 similar county institutions for instruction in agriculture and domestic science have been made a part of the school system, the state being the first to make this move. Four such schools are in operation, each receiving $4000 from the state.

Coeducation,
p. 432.

Milwaukee Sch.
Org. p. 195.

Text-book legislation, p. 219; Library legislation, p. 484; Sch. organization, App. F; St. Supt. Pub. Ins. App. G; Cert. of teachers, App. H; Teachers' Inst. App. I; Comp. Ed. Laws, App. J; Ed. Statistics, App. K.

Minnesota

Although mission schools for the Indians had been in operation in Minnesota as early as 1834, there seems to have been no school for white children until 1847, when the first was established at St. Paul. This was the result of a philanthropic movement started by a Dr. Williamson, and furthered by the National Educational Society, which sent out the first teacher, Harriet Bishop. A log hut 10 ft. × 12 ft., which had been used as a blacksmith shop, was pressed into service as a schoolhouse. Two years later, in the same cabin, the first public meeting within the territory for the purpose of establishing a school system was held.

The first territorial legislature, convened in 1849, enacted a school law, providing for a two and one-half mill tax for school purposes, as well as arranging for special levies for the erection of buildings. It also recognized the township as the unit of organization, and provided for the election of trustees, who had power to examine and hire teachers. Each township containing five families was constituted a district for school purposes. This might be increased to two districts, when twice that number were resident within the township. This law remained in force until 1861. In 1851 there were thirteen school districts and but five schoolhouses within the state, with a total enrolment of 250 pupils. Three years later (1854) the township unit of organization was replaced by the district, and the county commissioners empowered to subdivide the township. The question of graded schools arose early in the '60's, the town of St. Anthony (now Minneapolis) first being empowered, by special legislation, to establish a graded system. In 1864 the act was made general in the schools of the state. We cannot, however, suppose that the teaching was of a very high order, since the average monthly pay of males was but $21, while for the females it was but $13.

Hamlin Univ. Greer, p. 171.
Teachers' Inst. p. 393.

Greer, p. 94.
Normal Schs. p. 378.
Carlton Col. Greer, p. 153.
State Univ. p. 284.
Greer, p. 147.

The first legislation with reference to high schools was passed in 1878. Under it, the sum of $400 was granted to each such school upon the condition that pupils be admitted from any part of the state, and that the work be of such a character as to prepare the graduates to enter the sub-freshman class at the university. Provisions were also made for state inspection of the schools. With the exception of the period from 1879 to 1881, this plan of state aid to the high schools has been continued with the best of results, in 1900 no less than 140 receiving $1000 each.

Macallister Col. Greer, p. 17.

St. Paul and Minnap. Sch. Org. p. 195.
Greer, p. 86.

Secondary schools which cannot fully comply with the educational requirements of the law, are given $200 each.

Coeducation, p. 432.

Text-book legislation, p. 219 ; Library legislation, p. 485 ; Sch. organization, App. F ; St. Supt. Pub. Ins. App. G ; Cert. of teachers, App. H ; Teachers' Inst. App. I ; Comp. Ed. Laws, App. J ; Ed. Statistics, App. K.

Iowa

Primitive school conditions in the Middle West are graphically pictured in a description of one of the first schoolhouses erected within the state of Iowa.

Parker, p.15.

" It was built of round logs, the spaces between them chinked and then daubed with mud. About five feet from the west wall on the inside and five feet high another log was placed, and running clear across the building. Puncheons were then fixed on this log and in the west wall, on which the chimney was built. Fuel could then be used of any length not greater than the width of the building, and when it was burned through in the middle, the ends were crowded together. In this manner was avoided the necessity of so much wood chopping. There was no danger of burning the floor, as there was none. The seats were made of stools or benches constructed by splitting a log, hewing off the splinters from the flat side and then putting four pegs into it from the round side for legs. The door was made of clapboards. On either side a piece of one log was cut out and over the aperture was pasted greased paper, which answered for a window. Wooden pins were driven into the log running lengthwise immediately beneath the windows, upon which was laid a board, and this constituted the writing desks."

In the early days of the territorial régime, and even well into the period of its state organization, such structures were the homes of the public schools. They answered their purposes well, though that they were inexpensive is shown by the fact that in 1846, when Iowa was admitted to the Union as a state, the one hundred log schoolhouses then in use were valued at $125 each. The first one was used for school purposes in 1830, when Benjamin Jennings opened a school near the present site of Keokuk. Within a decade forty more were doing service. During territorial days little was done for the schools of the state by legislative enactment, though each of the three governors urged such action strongly. But the state constitution, adopted in

1846, was pronounced in its educational demands. It provided for a state superintendent, the creation of a public school fund, and a system of public schools based upon the district system of organization. An elaborate school law was enacted in 1858 : it had been prepared by Horace Mann and Amos Dean, the latter, Chancellor of the State University, who had previously been appointed a committee to provide a system of education suitable for the state. This law abolished the " rate " and made the schools free to all white children from five to twenty-one; established the office of county superintendent; gave aid to county institutes; authorized county high schools; and made the township the unit of organization with provision for sub-districts. State Univ. p. 284. Teachers' Inst. p. 393.

The county high school idea was borrowed from Jefferson. Several counties attempted to establish such schools, but without success. In 1870 a second county high school law was enacted; but the town and city high schools had already become so numerous that the law was without much influence. Guthrie County only seems to have made a success of it. Agricult. Col. p. 362. Parker, 13–14. Normal Schs. p. 378.

In 1870 there were within the state about 7000 ungraded and 212 graded schools, with an average length of session of six months. In 1890 the ungraded schools alone, had doubled in number, while the graded schools had increased to nearly 3500. More than a month, too, had been added to the school year. Coeducation, p. 432.

Text-book legislation, p. 219; Library legislation, p. 485; Sch. organization, App. F; St. Supt. Pub. Ins. App. G; Cert. of teachers, App. H; Teachers' Inst. App. I; Comp. Ed. Laws, App. J; Ed. Statistics, App. K.

Missouri

The first school within the present state of Missouri was taught by J. B. Trabeau in St. Louis, in 1774. His service in the schoolroom was an unusual one, for, more than forty years later, he was still conducting one Snow, p. 44.

of the two schools then in operation in the town. In 1817 a movement was made to establish a system of schools in St. Louis; but the people were not ready for such action, and it came to naught. It was not until 1838 that the first public school was opened there. The territorial constitution, framed in 1820, provided for a university, and schools within each township, where the children of the poor should be taught free. But this was not followed by direct legislation until 1839, and little activity in school matters was meantime evident. In that year, however, a school law was passed embodying many of the educational ideas of Jefferson, and calling for an elaborate system of state schools, with a university at its head. The plan was, however, impracticable, and was soon modified.

From this time elementary public schools increased. But the private and church academy had no rival until 1853, when St. Louis opened its first high school. During the Civil War schools were seriously interrupted; but in 1866 a new law put them on a better foundation.

In 1860 W. T. Harris began his work as principal of the St. Louis schools. His influence was far-reaching. Through his efforts and those of Miss Susan Blow the kindergarten became a part of the city school system in 1873.

Text-book legislation, p. 219; Library legislation, p. 485; Sch. organization, App. F; St. Supt. Pub. Ins. App. G; Cert. of teachers, App. H; Teachers' Inst. App. I; Comp. Ed. Laws, App. J; Ed. Statistics, App. K.

Oklahoma

When Oklahoma was organized as a territory in 1890 it had already a school population of upwards of thirteen thousand, and no delay was made in establishing a public school system. From the start the schools have, almost without exception, been under public control, there being at present but two private educational institutions within

Margin notes:

Wm. Jewell Col. Snow, p. 67.

Univ. of Mo. p. 284.

Snow, p. 9.

Central Col. Snow, p. 49.

Westminster Col. Snow, p. 93.

Washington Univ. Snow, p. 129.

Drury Col. Snow, p. 103.

Normal Schs. p. 378.

Kindergarten, p. 167.

St. Louis Sch. Org. p. 194.

Coeducation, p. 432.

Agricult. Col. p. 362.

the territory. The first high school was established at Kingfisher in 1889, and has been followed by fifteen others, two of which are for colored pupils. Within the state are also a university, an agricultural college, and three normal schools, one of which is for the colored race.

Ter. Univ. p. 285.

Normal Schs. p. 378.

Coeducation, p. 432.

Text-book legislation, p. 219; Library legislation, p. 485; Sch. organization, App. F; St. Supt. Pub. Ins. App. G; Cert. of teachers, App. H; Teachers' Inst. App. I; Comp. Ed. Laws, App. J; Ed. Statistics, App. K.

Kansas

With the promptness in school matters which has always characterized the West, a school was established at Wyandotte, now Kansas City, Kansas, in 1844, almost as early, that is, as the first settlers reached the state. This was seemingly the first school for white children, though at least six years previous to its establishment a mission school had been in operation among the Shawnee tribe of Indians; and it is quite possible that others also had been started. But the real beginnings of educational growth date from 1855, when the great army of emigrants reached the state in their white-topped wagons, and began the making of their prairie homes. The vicinity of Lawrence was the earliest to be settled, and led in school matters during the first few years. Previous to 1859 the schools were nearly all of a private character, though even two years earlier a territorial superintendent of public instruction had been appointed, and some attempts made to encourage public schools through legislative enactment. Some idea of the rapidity with which the country was filling up at about this time may be gained from the fact that Douglas County, the one in which the capital of the state is situated, had, on January 1, 1859, but 5 school districts, while six months later the number had increased to 30. This is characteristic of school growth in the Eastern counties.

Blackmar.

Baker, Univ. Blackmar, p. 119. Washburn Col. Blackmar, p. 130.

Ottawa Univ. Blackmar, p. 139.

Teachers' Inst. p. 393.

Univ. of Kan.
p. 284.
Blackmar, p. 23.

By 1866, 222 school districts had been organized; in 138 of them schools were being taught at a cost of about $12,000. Approximately one-half of this was raised by taxation, while the other half came from private contribution. Since the admission of Kansas to the Union as

Agricult. Col.
p. 362.

a state in 1861, a complete system of public schools, "including common schools and schools of a higher grade, comprising normal, preparatory, college, and

Normal Schs.
p. 378.

university departments," has been a requirement of the constitution — all free to both sexes. The immense extent of public school lands has made it possible to fulfil this requirement very perfectly, providing a public school for every 185 of the inhabitants. Besides others,

Blackmar, p. 19.

a considerable number of private schools and colleges have been chartered. There was little demand for high

Coeducation,
p. 432.

schools until about 1870; but since that time they have developed rapidly, those in the larger cities being most excellently sustained.

Text-book legislation, p. 219; Library legislation, p. 485; Sch. organization, App. F; St. Supt. Pub. Ins. App. G; Cert. of teachers, App. H; Teachers' Inst. App. I; Comp. Ed. Laws, App. J; Ed. Statistics, App. K.

Nebraska

Caldwell.

In matter of time, school development in Nebraska paralleled very closely that in its sister state Kansas. Within it, the first mission school was at Belvue in 1836, and the first public school at Brownville in 1855.

In this latter year, the first territorial legislature enacted laws establishing a school system with the state librarian as superintendent of instruction. Provisions were made for school districts, for the certification of teachers, and for levying taxes. Schools of a higher grade were allowed, but their support was to come from fees and not from public funds. In 1858 the Iowa law, which carried with it the township unit of organization, was adopted almost bodily, and remained in force until

1867, when it was set aside, and laws based on the Ohio system enacted. By this move the district system was established and has been in practice ever since, although frequent attempts have been made to change. Township high schools were authorized by law in 1858, but few, if any, have been established. Beginning in 1867, town and city high schools were established by special legislative acts; and in 1873 a general law was passed providing for them, and also for the organization of all incorporated towns as separate districts. The former may tax themselves to the extent of 2 per cent for school purposes, while the rural districts may add ½ per cent to that amount. High schools have had a very rapid growth in the state. In 1888 there were 119 such schools, with an enrolment of 5404 pupils. Ten years later the numbers were 415, and 14,123 respectively. Since 1895 these schools have been open without tuition to the pupils of the district schools from any part of the state.

Univ. of Neb. p. 284.

Caldwell, p. 17.

Teachers' Inst. p. 393.

Doane Col. Caldwell, p. 183.

Univ. of Omaha, Caldwell, p. 158.

Normal Schs. p. 378.

Coeducation, p. 432.

Text-book legislation, p. 219; Library legislation, p. 485; Sch. organization, App. F; St. Supt. Pub. Ins. App. G; Cert. of teachers, App. H; Teachers' Inst. App. I; Comp. Ed. Laws, App. J; Ed. Statistics, App. K.

The Dakotas

The territory now comprising the states of North and South Dakota was detached from Minnesota and separately organized in 1861. It was first colonized in 1859, and in spite of the several Indian wars which occurred within the next few years, a school was in session in Bon Homme County (South Dakota) as early as 1861, and the educational organization of the territory was perfected two years later. At that time there were no public schools, and but a few private schools. By 1867, however, 29 school districts had been organized, attended by 421 pupils, while two private schools accommodated 160 more. In 1878 the number of districts had increased to 401 with an enrolment of 7150. The territorial school organization included a state superintendent of public instruction, a county superintendent, and three directors for each district.   In 1888 the territory was divided, and the two separate states admitted to the Union.   At that time there were within the borders of North Dakota 35 graded and 1366 common schools.   Two years later the state opened an agricultural college and two normal schools.   A general school law for a uniform and complete school system was among the first enactments of the legislature.   In 1895 the governor, the president of the State University, and the state superintendent were appointed a state high school board with power to appoint an assistant.   This board is to visit once a year and report on the condition of such high schools as maintain at least a two-years' course and admit without tuition students from any part of the state.   For the help of these schools the state set aside annually $10,000 to be distributed as follows : To each school that maintains a four-years' course, $400; a three-years' course, $300; and a two-years' course, $200.   This money is to be used for securing better equipment for the schools. The constitution provides for a large fund, fixing the minimum price of school lands at $10 per acre.   The educational progress has kept pace with other industries, and the enrolment in the public schools of 1902 was almost 84,000.

The educational development within the southern of the sister states has been similar.   During its territorial days (1883) a university had been established at Vermilion, which was continued under state control.   Its public schools are in a flourishing condition, and, owing to the generosity of the state in the granting of public lands, well supplied.

Marginal notes:

State Univ. p. 284.

Agricult. Col. p. 362.

Sch. of Mines, p. 351.

Normal Schs. p. 378.

State Univ. p. 284.

Agricult. Col. p. 362.

Normal Schs. p. 378.

Coeducation, p. 432.

Text-book legislation, p. 219; Library legislation, p. 485; Sch. organization, App. F; St. Supt. Pub. Ins. App. G; Cert. of teachers, App. H; Teachers' Inst. App. I; Comp. Ed. Laws, App. J; Ed. Statistics, App. K.

REFERENCES

Allen, W. F., and Spencer, D. E. Higher Education in Wisconsin. Circ. Inf. No. 1, 1889. — Blackmar, Frank W. Higher Education in Kansas. Circ. Inf. No. 2, 1900. Am. Ed. Hist. No. 27. — Boone, R. G. History of Education in Indiana. N. Y. 1893. — Caldwell, H. W. History of Education in Nebraska. Circ. Inf. No. 3, 1902. Am. Ed. Hist. No. 32. — Columbian History of Education in Kansas. Topeka, 1893. — Educational Influence of the Ordinance of 1787. N. E. A. 1887 : 118. — Greer, John N. History of Education in Minnesota. Circ. Inf. No. 2, 1902. Am. Ed. Hist. No. 31. — Hinsdale, B. A. History of Education in the Western Reserve. Ohio Archeol. and Hist. Soc. Pub. 1898. — *Historical sketch of state school systems* (each state). Rep. Com. Ed. 1876. — Knight, George W. and Commons, J. R. History of Higher Education in Ohio. Circ. Inf. No. 5, 1791. — *Mayo*, A. D. Education in the Northwest during the First Half-century of the Republic, 1790–1840. Rep. Com. Ed. 1894–1895, p. 1513. Development of the Common Schools in the Western States. Rep. Com. Ed. 1898–1899, 1 : 357. — McCarthy, E. F. M. Western State Education (in Education for the People). 1895, p. 82. — McLaughlin, Andrew C. History of Higher Education in Michigan. Circ. Inf. No. 4, 1891. Am. Ed. Hist. No. 11. — Michigan Pioneer Collection, Vol. I. — Parker, Leonard F. Higher Education in Iowa. Circ. Inf. No. 6, 1893. Am. Ed. Hist. No. 17. — Salmon, Lucy. M. Education in Michigan during the Territorial Period. Ed. 8 : 12. — Smart, J. H. Indiana Schools and the Men who made Them. Cincinnati, 1876. — Smith, W. L. Historical Sketch of Education in Michigan. Lansing, 1881. — Snow, Marshall S. Higher Education in Missouri. Circ. Inf. No. 2, 1898. Am. Ed. Hist. No. 21. — Venable, W. H. First Schools in the Ohio Valley. N. E. A. 1889 : 231. — Whitford, W. C. Annual Report of Superintendent of Public Instruction of Wisconsin, 1876. Historical Sketch of Education in Wisconsin. — *Willard*, Samuel. Illinois School Report, 1883–1884. Brief History of Early Education in Illinois. — Woodburn, J. A. Higher Education in Indiana. Circ. Inf. No. 1, 1891. Am. Ed. Hist. No. 10.

CHAPTER IX

THE SOUTHERN STATES

THE South, although in some parts settled early, has been slow in establishing an organized system of public schools. In the earlier years this was due largely to a prevailing sentiment against such school organization, and in favor of private schools, or education within the family by means of tutors. As a consequence, the poorer classes were not educated, or were forced to attend the so-called " pauper school." There were, however, many private schools and academies of a high order throughout the South, and those who were able to pay for educational opportunities found them in abundance. Especially was this true of the girls, for the South was a leader in the founding of seminaries for them. But it was not until the close of the Civil War that the states took up the problem of the education of the masses, and most manfully have they struggled with it since that time, in the face of odds not equalled in any other part of the country. Many conditions have made the problem difficult. First, the region, never a wealthy one, had been impoverished by the tremendous expense of a war fought within its own confines, with all the devastation which that means. Second, six million of totally uneducated colored people had been freed and left upon their hands for assimilation and some form of education. This involved the setting up of a double system, with all the extra expense which such a plan involves. Third, the population was largely rural, necessitating a greater outlay of money to bring the school to every child than though it had been more fully urban;

and fourth, no part of the country had so large a proportion of its population within the limits of school age as it; a most encouraging fact from some points of view, but perplexing to the financiers of public school problems.

Yet, previous to 1870, every Southern state had made constitutional and legislative provisions for free schools and a general system of education. Twelve had some form of state control, eight had provided for county supervision, normal schools had been started in six, agricultural and industrial colleges in a still larger number, and progress had been made in grading the schools in the large cities. It is true that the North had helped in this work through the Peabody and other funds, and the federal government had extended its aid; but the great bulk of the labor and funds came from the South P. 455. itself. Considering that but thirty years have elapsed since its educational machinery was really started, magnificent progress has been made. In that time the percentage of total population enrolled in the schools, as well as of children of school age, has doubled; the actual number of pupils attending school more than quadrupled; ten days have been added to the school year, and the per capita expenditure for school purposes nearly doubled. The South to-day taxes itself more heavily for its schools in proportion to its wealth than does the great Western portion of our country, though not as yet quite so heavily as the North and East.

Yet, in spite of the fact that the South has for a generation made such rapid progress in school matters, its start was from such a plane as to leave much to be done before they are upon the same footing of general excellence as the other portions of the country. Appendix K.

Kentucky

Mrs. Jane Comes, the wife of one of the earliest settlers at Harrodsburg, taught the first school in Kentucky. This was probably in the spring of 1776, when the colony was not more than a year old. The following year there was a school at McAgee's Station. Others soon followed. These earliest schools were private, and must have been very primitive in character. They were the first representatives of the " Old-field," or " Hedgerow" schools.

The Virginia legislature made its first grant for education in Kentucky in 1780, by setting aside 8000 acres of land for an academy, as soon as it should be convenient to establish one. Three years later, 20,000 acres were granted for founding Transylvania University, and trustees were named. This was to be a state institution, though it was never without denominational flavor. Though called a university, the institution was little more than an academy. The first instruction in connection with it was in the home of Rev. David Rice, at Danville, in 1785. During the next ten years a number of schools, both of elementary and secondary grades, were opened within the various settlements and had a fair attendance. In the closing years of the century, educational interest centred about the academies, more than 30 being established in different parts of the state. Each was given 6000 acres of land by the legislature and was also granted permission to raise $1000 by lottery. These privileges were soon extended to each county for school purposes, and previous to 1820, 47 of them had county academies in operation, some of which, by special enactment, had received double the usual grant of land. But they led but a precarious existence. Educational sentiment had not yet been properly aroused, the people were not willing to tax themselves for school purposes, the lands were poorly managed, and the academies soon languished. But their failure served to turn popular attention to educational questions, and in 1821 a committee was appointed by the legislature to make a study of the school systems

Lewis, p. 30.

Transylvania Univ.
Lewis, p. 35.

Center Col.
Lewis, p. 110.

Ed. of Deaf,
p. 471.

of the East and to suggest remedies for the difficulties in Kentucky. Barnard calls the report of this committee "one of the most valuable documents upon common school education that had at that time appeared." This report favored the New York system, with its local taxes supplemented by state appropriations. Unfortunately, the legislature took no action, except to print the report.

Am. Jour. Ed. 27 : 335.

The schools of Louisville led those of the state. Here, in 1829, was a free school, conducted on the Lancasterian system. The city appropriated $2050 for its support for a year, but at the end of that time the system of fees was again adopted, and the free school was a thing of the past. But in 1840 tuition fees were abolished and the schools of Louisville made free. Night schools were established especially for apprentices in 1834. In this same year there was appointed a school agent, whose duty it was to visit all the schools each quarter and report upon their condition. His duties were soon enlarged, and by 1838 corresponded in general to those of the present city superintendent.

Georgetown Col Lewis, p. 141.

Evening Schs p. 541.
Louisville, p. 193.

A system of public schools for the state was made possible by a law of 1838, which included the following provision : a school fund, a state board of education, a superintendent of schools, school districts with trustees for each, county commissioners, and a local school tax. At this time there were 175,000 children of school age, of whom perhaps not more than half had enjoyed any school advantages. But because of opposition and indifference it was not until 1853 that the law was in operation in every county of the state. During the Civil War but little educational progress was made, and at its close the question of negro education was added to the already unsolved school problems. The Peabody and other funds contributed throughout the North for this purpose aided materially in its solution, but the burden of the work has been undertaken by the state. In 1866 all taxes paid by the negroes, except such as were

Univ. of Louisville, Lewis, p. 261.

Ed. of Blind, p. 474.

Ed. of Feeble-minded, p. 476.

Kentucky Uni7 p. 284.
Lewis, p. 83.

needed for the support of the charitable institutions of the race, were devoted to these schools. A little later a negro poll tax was established and devoted to the same purpose, and since that time the state has made generous appropriations. In 1884 an act was passed calling for the election of county superintendents of schools by popular vote, and under the direction of these officials the schools have prospered.

Better attendance, too, has been secured by the compulsory school law of 1896, which requires at least eight weeks of continuous attendance per year on the part of children between the ages of seven and fourteen.

Text-book legislation, p. 219; Sch. organization, App. F; St. Supt. Pub. Ins. App. G; Cert. of teachers, App. H; Teachers' Inst. App. I; Comp. Ed. Laws, App. J; Ed. Statistics, App. K.

Tennessee

"It is the indispensable duty of every legislature to consult the happiness of a rising generation, and fit them for an honorable discharge of the social duties of life," is a part of the preamble to the act which chartered Davidson Academy at Haysboro in 1785. And when the North Carolina legislature passed the act, it also endowed the academy with 240 acres of land, and declared all the school's property exempt from taxes for ninety-nine years. The school opened the following year in a stone church, where it continued for at least twenty years, with Rev. Thomas Craighead as teacher. This was the beginning of Nashville University. In 1806 Congress granted to Tennessee 100,000 acres for each of two colleges; 100,000 acres for academies, one in each county, and 640 acres for every district six miles square for school purposes. By a single act the legislature incorporated twenty-seven boards of trustees who should have charge of the academies and lands of their several counties. Unfortunately the public lands and

gricult. Col.
362.

ormal Schs.
378.

egro Ed.
hapter XXII.

ewis, p. 329
* seq.

oeducation,
. 432.

State Univ.
p. 284.

funds of Tennessee were not well handled, and have never brought to the support of schools what they were expected to contribute. The early legislation did not provide for special elementary schools, as is clearly shown in a declaration of 1817 that colleges and academies "should form a complete system of education." In 1830, however, there was formed a definite plan for public instruction, beginning with the elementary work. At that time provisions were made for organizing school districts, with five trustees to each, who were to select county commissioners, hire teachers, and report annually to the commissioners, who in turn were to report to the legislature. If legislative enactments could have brought it to pass, Tennessee would have had one of the best school systems in the country. The amount of money appropriated by the state was not, however, sufficient to support the schools, and the people were not ready to tax themselves for the education of the children of others. As a result, the school term was short, and education was largely a private concern. At the close of the war each county was given supreme control of its own schools, with the result that in 1872 only twenty-nine out of ninety-three counties levied any tax. Some of the counties had "not a single school, either public or private, in operation." The following year (1866) the state superintendent's office was revived, and county superintendents and district directors were appointed. These changes met with serious opposition, but on the whole schools began to improve. In 1891 a law was passed providing for graded schools, five years being devoted to primary work and three to higher instruction.

Ed. of Deaf, p. 471.

Ed. of Blind, p. 474.

Normal Schs. p. 378.

Negro Ed. Chapter XXII.

Coeducation, p. 432.

Text-book legislation, p. 219; Library legislation, p. 485; Sch. organization, App. F; St. Supt. Pub. Ins. App. G; Cert. of teachers, App. H; Teachers' Inst. App. I; Comp. Ed. Laws, App. J; Ed. Statistics, App. K.

Arkansas

Shinn.

The first settlement in Arkansas was at Arkansas Post in 1686. At an early date the Jesuits had schools for teaching the Indians, but for the beginning of effective education we must come down to the nineteenth century. In his *History of Education in Arkansas*, J. H. Shinn says that in 1820 there were private schools of some repute in their respective localities. The first school law with reference to public education was passed in 1829, seven years later. Batesville Academy — the first of many similar institutions that followed — was incorporated. Provisions were made for admitting the poor of the county without tuition, and for free instruction for all, as soon as the funds would warrant. In selecting teachers and officers, and in admitting students, all religious tests were forbidden. This same tolerance was not shown, however, in the Napoleon Public School, chartered two years later, when it was distinctly stated that " prosylites of abolition or Mormon doctrines " should be excluded.

In 1843 a general school law was passed fixing the subjects to be taught, and providing for a county board of education, whose duty it should be to distribute funds, examine teachers, and visit the schools at least once a year. Temperance legislation began in 1856, by prohibiting the sale of liquor in quantities less than forty gallons within three miles of Talcon Academy. This seems to have met with favor, and the next legislature

Shinn, p. 22.
State Univ.
p. 284.
Shinn, p. 64.

extended the same provisions to six other schools. But conditions were not favorable for free schools. It was not until 1867 that an act was passed basing the support of education upon the assessed wealth of the state. A general school law followed, but during the

Normal Schs.
p. 378.
Negro Ed.
Chapter xxii.

reconstruction period, its workings were not always satisfactory. However, there was some progress, and in 1870 more than $500,000 was expended for education, three-fifths of which came from direct taxation. At that time there were 70,000 children in school; but such had been the neglect of previous years, that the census showed 112,000 inhabitants who could not read, and 133,000 who could not write. With the opening of the State University at Fayetteville in 1872, and a branch normal at Pine Bluff three years later, was laid the foundation for the substantial progress that has since been made.

Ark. Col.
Shinn, p. 102.

Hendrix Col.
Shinn, p. 108.

Coeducation,
p. 432.

Text-book legislation, p. 219; Sch. organization, App. F; St. Supt. Pub. Ins. App. G; Cert. of teachers, App. H; Teachers' Inst. App. I; Comp. Ed. Laws, App. J; Ed. Statistics, App. K.

Louisiana

Although Louisiana was settled in the earlier years of the eighteenth century, it was by French adventurers rather than by homeseekers. It is not surprising, therefore, that during their entire occupancy of the region, we find only occasional, and not very successful, attempts to establish schools. The first was by a company of Ursuline nuns who, together with some Capuchin monks, came to New Orleans in 1727. The former conducted a hospital as well as a school for girls, more than twenty pupils being in the latter in the year 1728. The monks seem not to have taken very extensively to educational work, though one of them, Father Cecil, is said to have been "engaged in the instruction of boys."

Fay.

Fay, p. 10.

Seemingly these schools were maintained but for a few years; and so far as we know, no others were provided to take their place until after the Spanish possession of the territory, which took place in 1761. Eleven years later, several Spanish teachers were sent over in an attempt to change the prevailing language; but so firmly was the French tongue established that the schools which they set up were but poorly attended. At no time had they more than thirty pupils, while in eight French schools which were in operation there were upward of four hundred. Educational conditions at about the beginning of the eighteenth century are set forth in the following quotation from a volume published in 1803.

Fay, p. 20.

" There is in this country no other public institution appropriated to the education of youth, except a mere school established by the government and comprised of say fifty children almost all from poor families where instruction is given in French and Spanish, in reading, writing and cyphering, and the convent of nuns who have a few boarding pupils and keep a class for day pupils."

A school for boys had, however, been kept for a few years, but failed for lack of support. But in 1805 the University of New Orleans was founded. This was a comprehensive educational institution, on the plan of the University of France, and included schools of all grades in various parts of the territory, as well as libraries, and the college to be situated in New Orleans. Funds to the extent of $50,000 annually were to be raised by lottery. After a few years, however, the whole scheme was set aside as impracticable. The year following that of the establishment of the university saw the passage of a free school law which, however, remained upon the statute books for but a single year, and was productive of no results.

At about that time legislative appropriations for school purposes became common, the county being made the custodian of such funds.

Academies, too, were springing up, and in 1821 $800 was appropriated for each, with the understanding that eight pupils should be instructed free, and be furnished with books, quills, and paper.

Fay, p. 3.
Tulane Univ.
p. 275.
High Sch.
p. 171.
Negro Ed.
Chapter xxii.
State Univ.
p. 284.

At the same time a county tax of $1000 was authorized, and $800 was allowed to each county that had not yet supported a school. In 1847 a free school act was adopted, fixing the school age at six to sixteen, granting at least three years of schooling to all under twenty-one, providing a property and poll tax, a state superintendent, and county superintendents, with an allowance of $300 for the work of the latter. In 1851 the county superintendent's office was abolished and the schools were put in charge of directors, who served without pay. The county superintendents were reinstated in 1879, when other provisions for schools were also made by the new constitution.

New Orleans Sch. Org. p. 195. Normal Schs. p. 378. Coeducation, p. 432.

Text-book legislation, p. 219; Sch. organization, App. F; St. Supt. Pub. Ins. App. G; Cert. of teachers, App. H ; Teachers' Inst. App. I ; Comp. Ed. Laws, App. J; Ed. Statistics, App. K.

Texas

At an early date French and Spanish missionaries settled in Texas. In 1714 some of these located at San Antonio, building stone chapels which were so constructed " as to make them serve at once for churches, schools, and dwellings, as well as forts." These seem to have been the first schoolhouses. From 1620 to 1820 the Spaniards occupied the territory and made strong efforts to convert and educate the Indians. There were schools at different places, as at El Paso about 1806, but it was not until 1829 that the Mexican government organized what may be termed a public school system. And even then free tuition was limited to five poor pupils in each school. The schools were conducted on the Lancasterian plan. In them were taught " reading, writing, arithmetic, the dogmas of the Catholic religion, and all of Akerman's catechisms of arts and sciences." But the English speaking inhabitants were not satisfied with this provision, and petitioned for an endowment with which to establish primary schools. The government acceded to their wishes by granting 17,713 acres of land to be used for this purpose. However, little resulted from this action, and in 1834 only four schools were in operation. In 1836 Texas declared its

Lane, p. 1.

independence from Mexico, and among the first acts of the new republic were the chartering of an academy, a college, and a university. Its Congress, too, was liberal in the granting of lands for school purposes, as it might well have been, giving to each county four leagues (17,712 acres).

Though the constitution of 1845, which was enacted when Texas was admitted to the Union as a state, made it the duty of the legislature to establish a system of public schools, nine years passed before this was done. The first school under the new provisions was opened at San Antonio. During the reconstruction period Texas fared better than some of the states, because she was silent on the question of separate schools for the two races, and so was free to have schools for both, while in some states the presence of the negroes meant separate systems of schools.

As at present organized, the state school system consists of independent school districts for grammar and primary schools, subject to the subdivision of counties for community schools ; municipal control of schools in cities, towns, and villages organized for the purpose and local taxation to supplement the school fund apportioned by the state. This latter is very large, since each county is in control of four leagues of land for school purposes, and, as new counties are organized, a like amount is appropriated to them from the public domain. These lands are usually sold to good advantage, and the public school fund of Texas is by far the largest of any state in the Union.

Text-book legislation, p. 219; Library legislation, p. 485 ; Sch. organization, App. F ; St. Supt. Pub. Ins. App. G ; Cert. of teachers, App. H ; Teachers' Inst. App. I ; Comp. Ed. Laws, App. J ; Ed. Statistics, App. K.

Mississippi

During the greater part of the period of French and Spanish influence in Mississippi, there seem to have

---

Margin notes:

Baylor Univ.
Lane, p. 65.

State Univ.
p. 284.
Lane, p. 123.
Agricult. Col.
p. 362.
Normal Schs.
p. 378.
Negro Ed.
Chapter XXII.
Coeducation,
p. 433.

Mayes.

been neither private nor public schools in the territory, though private tutors were to some extent employed by the more wealthy of the planters. But, in the closing years of the eighteenth century, a colony of New Englanders made a settlement and established a number of schools, all of a private nature. Doubtless more would have arisen in other parts of the territory had it not been for the scarcity of properly qualified teachers. Mayes, p. 22. According to the records, many persons who aspired to the position had acquired such vicious habits that parents could not intrust their children to them.

Mississippi early shared with the other Southern states the honor of providing schools for the girls. As early as 1801 Rev. David Kerr, assisted by his wife and daughters, conducted a ladies' seminary, "the first public female school" in that part of the South. One year later, the legislature granted a charter to Jefferson College, this being the first public authorization of an institution of learning. Because of lack of funds, instruction was not begun until 1811. In the meantime, however, Washington Academy had been established. The buildings of this institution were transferred to the college, and a preparatory school serving the needs of the community was continued. The general support of the school was from tuition fees, though it had the benefits of some public land, as well as some special assistance from the legislature. Up to 1820 the state had done nothing toward education, beyond the establishing of a dozen academies, and during the next twenty years the same policy was continued, though the number of colleges and academies at the end of that period was more than a hundred. Most of these had a brief and uneventful history.

Through the persistent efforts of Governor Brown, the first law looking toward a general school system State Univ. was enacted in 1846. But even this was non-effective, p. 284. since it was possible for any township to reject its pro- Mayes, p. 118.

visions if the majority of the heads of families filed a written protest each year. There was much opposition to the law, and frequent changes were made. The tendency was, however, toward particular laws for special communities, while all outside of these communities were neglected. No general system was established before the Civil War.

The legislature of 1870 provided for an elaborate school system, making each county and each city with more than five thousand inhabitants a school district. County superintendents were to be appointed by the state board of education; but several years lapsed before any provisions were made for paying these officers, and, as a result, their supervision was inefficient. The people at first opposed the school tax, but the records show a marked improvement in school conditions within a few years. The provisions for special districts were extended, and in 1878 were made to include all towns of more than one thousand inhabitants. The schools in these districts are moreover less graded, and are, in many localities, gradually crowding out the private schools.

Ag. Col. p. 363.

Negro Ed. Chapter XXII.
Agricult. Col. p. 362.
Normal Schs. p. 378.
Coeducation, p. 432.

Text-book legislation, p. 219; Library legislation, p. 485; Sch. organization, App. F; St. Supt. Pub. Ins. App. G; Cert. of teachers, App. H; Teachers' Inst. App. I; Comp. Ed. Laws, App. J; Ed. Statistics, App. K.

Alabama

Clark.

It is doubtful if during the French or Spanish occupancy of the present state of Alabama, schools of any kind were maintained, though as early as 1742 the governor of the province made a formal application to the French government for a college. About 1810, however, John Pierce, a native of New England, set up a school at Boat House, on the Tenas River. This seems to have been the first. One year later an academy was incorporated at Saint Stephens, in Washington County, and in 1812, another at Huntsville, in Tombigbee County.

To these the territorial legislation gave $1000. No other schools seem to have been founded previous to the admission of Alabama to the Union as a state in 1819.

The city of Mobile was the first in the state to attempt to establish a system of public schools (1826). This was done under a special law enacted for the county. The law gave considerable liberty to the county board of school commissioners, authorizing them "to establish and regulate schools, and to devise, put in force, and execute such plans and devices for the increase of knowledge, educating youth, and promoting the cause of learning in said county, as to them may appear expedient."

In 1837 the legislature gave permission to the trustees of Boston Academy, which was in process of erection, to raise $50,000 by means of a lottery.

It also authorized a school tax, and required schools to be maintained outside of the city of Mobile.

With the establishment of La Grange College by the Methodists in 1830, there sprang up a number of denominational schools that wielded a powerful influence in the state up to the Civil War. Along with these schools were other private academies that followed the same course as in other states.

It was not until 1852 that Mobile had a system of graded schools, the first in the state. The old academy was sold, and the city established public schools. It was at this time that teachers were first required to hold a certificate. The lack of properly qualified teachers continued to be a hindrance to progress until 1879, when a new law required all teachers to pass an examination and to furnish a certificate of moral fitness. The effect of this law was very beneficial. In 1850 there were 166 academies and 1152 public schools in the state, with an enrolment of about 36,000 pupils. Twenty-five years later, the number of pupils had increased to nearly 150,000.

Clark, p. 220.

State Univ. p. 284.

Negro Ed. Chapter XXII.

Normal Schs. p. 377.

Tuskegee, p. 458.

Coeducation, p. 432.

Text-book legislation, p. 219; Sch. organization, App. F; St. Supt. Pub. Ins. App. G; Cert. of teachers, App. H; Teachers' Inst. App. I; Comp. Ed. Laws, App. J; Ed. Statistics, App. K.

Florida

Bush.

Unless it were in connection with some of the early Spanish settlements, there seems to have been no popular interest in education in Florida until 1831, and then the interest seems to have been but short-lived. In that year some public-spirited citizens of Tallahassee, deploring the lack of schools, formed what was known as the Florida Educational Society. This was an institution not unlike the American Lyceum in its organization, though established primarily to arouse interest in public education. Branches of the society were formed in several towns of the territory, and schools were established; but in a few years interest in the project subsided, and we hear nothing more of it. But school legislation soon followed. In 1835 the register of the land office was charged with the duty of selecting and collecting the various lands, granted by Congress "for schools, seminaries, and other purposes," and four years later, three school trustees were ordered to be chosen in each township. The township lands were not merged into a common fund for school purposes, but each township committee leased its own lands (the 16th section), and applied the proceeds as it deemed wise. In some instances the money was turned over to a private school, and probably in no case was the school receiving it entirely free. In 1849 and 1850 new school ordinances were enacted, authorizing public schools for white children to be supported by county taxes not to exceed $4 annually for each child of school age. This limit would seem to have been unnecessary, since but two counties levied any school tax whatever. No further school legislation of any importance was enacted until 1869, when the present public school

Am. Lyceum, p. 569.

Bush, p. 12.

system was established. Fairly generous financial provisions were made for schools, state and county superintendents appointed, and "boards of instruction" for each county established. The effect of this law was immediately felt, and under it the schools steadily improved. Whereas, in 1850, there were but 10 academies and 69 common schools in the state, with but 3129 pupils in all, and ten years later, only about double that number, in 1873 the number of public schools had increased to 400, and in 1880 to 1131, with an enrolment of more than 40,000 pupils. The Agricultural College has now become the State University (1903).

Bush, p. 20.

Negro Ed.
Chapter XXII.

Agricult. Col.
p. 362.

Normal Schs.
p. 378.

Teachers' Inst.
p. 393.

Coeducation,
p. 432.

Text-book legislation, p. 219; Sch. organization, App. F; St. Supt. Pub. Ins. App. G; Cert. of teachers, App. H; Teachers' Inst. App. I; Comp. Ed. Laws, App. J; Ed. Statistics, App. K.

REFERENCES

Bush, George Cary. History of Education in Florida. Circ. Inf. No. 7, 1888. — *Candler*, W. A. Education Progress in the South since 1865. N. E. A. 1889 : 339. — Clark, Willis G. History of Education in Alabama. Circ. Inf. No. 3, 1889. — Curry, O. H. Education at the South. Am. Inst. of Instr. Lectures, 1881. — Fay, Edwin W. History of Education in Louisiana. Circ. Inf. No. 1, 1898. — Frost, W. G. Educational Pioneering in the Southern Mountains. N. E. A. 1901 : 555. — *Historical Sketch of State School Systems* (each state). Rep. Com. Ed. 1876. — Johnston, R. M. Early Educational Life in Middle Georgia. Rep. Com. Ed. 1894–1895, 2 : 1699. — *Gilman*, D. C. Thirty Years of the Peabody Educational Fund. At. Month. 79 : 161. — Lane, J. J. History of Education in Texas. Circ. Inf. No. 2, 1903. — Lewis, Alvin F. History of Higher Education in Kentucky. Circ. Inf. No. 3, 1899. Am. Ed. Hist. No. 26. — Mayes, Edward. History of Education in Mississippi. Circ. Inf. No. 2, 1899. — *Mayo*, A. D. Development of the American Common Schools in the Atlantic and Central States of the South, 1830 to 1860. Rep. Com. Ed. 1899–1900, 1 : 427. The American Common School in the Southern States during the First Half Century of the Republic. Rep. Com.-Ed. 1895–1896, 1 : 267. The South at School. Am. Inst. of Instr. Lectures, 1881. — Merriam, Lucius S. Higher Education in Tennessee. Circ. Inf. No. 5, 1893. Am. Ed. Hist. No. 16. — Perry, William F. Genesis of Public Education in Alabama. Atl. Hist. Soc. Trans. 1898. — Ruffner, Henry. Some Historical Documents bearing upon Common School Education in Virginia and South Carolina previous to the Civil War. Rep. Com. Ed. 1899–1900, 1 : 381. — Russel, A. J. History of the Common Schools of Florida. Tallahassee, 1884. — Shinn, Josiah H. History of Education in Arkansas. Circ. Inf. No. 1, 1900. — Smith, E. B. Education in the South. (Address delivered before Congregational Club. Chicago, 1888.) — *Weeks*, Stephen B. The Beginnings of the Common School System in the South. Rep. Com. Ed. 1896–1897, 2 : 1379. — White, Greenough. The South, Past and Present. Sch. Rev. 7 : 148.

CHAPTER X

THE WESTERN STATES

UNLIKE the great central portion of our country, the territory farther west was not occupied, though a regularly moving frontier, which took up the land for agricultural purposes and promised permanent homes from the very beginning. It was, rather, taken possession of by civilization, through a series of unrelated migrations to particular localities far removed from other settled territory, from which centres of population little frontiers were sent out, until the at first isolated settlements have left little wholly unoccupied land between their borders. This peculiarity of occupation, and especially, in some instances, the reasons underlying the special migrations, have influenced educational development to some extent; but in the end, the result has been the same as in the Eastern portions of our country, and to-day we find the public school a flourishing institution, even in the remotest corners of this vast Western domain. Although, as a whole, the latter figures as the newest portion of the United States, it had within it, in the present territory of New Mexico, a permanent European settlement before the Pilgrim had set foot on Plymouth Rock, or the English flag was raised at Jamestown. But the old Spanish civilization of Coronado and his band, though permanent, was not militant, and cannot be said to have influenced, in any important way, subsequent educational development of any portion of the country. Of the migrations of English-speaking people into the Western territory, the first of any magnitude was that of the Mormons to the region of the Great Salt Lake.

This was a religious pilgrimage made by home-seekers, and the resulting institutional and educational life was that of a community realizing its permanency from the start. In this respect it differed from the next two *crusades*, that to California in 1849, and to Colorado ten years later, which were for gold. The resulting settlements showed, in the most glaring way, all the peculiarities of the mining-camp. In the earlier years, when the population lacked women and children, and when what few families there were, were ready to set out at a moment's notice for more promising fields, schools were few, and in many instances those that existed were hardly worthy of the name. Yet such conditions have been typical of almost the whole mountain region of the West, for the gold fevers of '49 and '59 have broken out in nearly every one of its states and territories. At first, only those who failed in the quest for gold turned to agriculture and allied pursuits. These proved the richness of the fields, and others were not slow to follow their example. Now, in spite of its vast mineral wealth, the whole region, with the exception of some few restricted portions, figures primarily for its agricultural resources.

Its schools rank high. Although but thinly settled, the region enrolls a greater percentage of its school population (five to eighteen years) in its schools than does any other part of the country. In its expenditure, too, for school purposes it is generous, exceeding any other portion of the country in per capita outlay, and nearly doubling that for the country as a whole. No group of states has a better reason to be proud of its educational accomplishments than those of the Rocky Mountain region.

Appendix K.

New Mexico

The Spanish settlements in New Mexico date from the latter part of the sixteenth century, and without doubt, mission and parochial schools were maintained from nearly the beginning. In the year 1806 we have the record of 480 children in such schools at Santa Fé alone. A quarter of a century later, parochial schools were being maintained in several other towns within the territory. These schools had many of the characteristics of those of southern Europe. In the summer months the session began at 6 A.M., and in the winter but an hour later. The instruction was largely in Spanish. No attempts seem to have been made to supplement the private schools with those upon a public foundation until 1854–1855. Then the legislature passed a permissive public school law, which, however, required the action of the counties to become operative. There, the popular vote was so overwhelmingly against the schools (5016 against, 37 for), as to leave no doubt as to the feeling of the people on the question of public schools. About ten years later, a new law was enacted, providing for a school in each settlement, and levying a tax of 50 cents for each pupil. The probate judge was to perform the duties of the county superintendent, and the justice of the peace was authorized to employ the teachers, and require the boys and girls to attend school from November to April. It seems, however, that the law was not always enforced, for during the school year of 1870–1871 only 1.4 per cent of the total population was enrolled in the schools ; within the next decade the enrolment had increased to 3.98 per cent, while at the same time 19.67 per cent of the total population of the entire country was attending school. Since that time both the laws and the school conditions have improved. The population of New Mexico is largely a Spanish-speaking people, a fact which introduces conditions into the public school problem which have been hard to meet, and which have retarded the progress of public education within the territory.

Ter. Univ. p. 285.

Sch. of Mines, p. 351.

Agricult. Col. p. 362.

Normal Schs. p. 378.

Coeducation, p. 432.

Text-book legislation, p. 219; Library legislation, p. 485; Sch. organization, App. F; St. Supt. Pub. Ins. App. G; Cert. of teachers, App. H; Teachers' Inst. App. I ; Comp. Ed. Laws, App. J; Ed. Statistics, App. K.

Colorado

Previous to the year 1859, but little was known of the territory included within the present state of Colorado. The "forty-niners," en route to the gold fields in California, had crossed it in large numbers, and an occasional fur trader or explorer had visited it; but to the great mass of the people it was known only as an undefined portion of "The Great American Desert."

But in 1858 a band of miners, known in history as Green Russell's party, spent some months in the mountains of the region just west of the present city of Denver; and their reports of gold brought great crowds of prospectors to the new country during the following year, almost paralleling the stampede of a decade before to the regions of the Golden Gate. Although at first but few of the settlements contained any women and children, still a few schools were established, the first being at Boulder, in 1860.

By 1861 the increase in population had been such as to justify Congress in establishing the territory of Colorado, the region having previously been a part of Kansas. At the time, the number of school children within the boundaries of the entire territory were hardly sufficient, had they been gathered into one district, to have formed a first-class district school. Nevertheless, there was an excellent beginning. The schools of Colorado remained in a somewhat chaotic condition until 1870. The school funds were frequently misappropriated. The legislature of 1870 made provisions for a State School of Mines. The act also provided that the governor, by and with the consent of the legislative assembly, "should appoint a suitable person to the office of State Superintendent, who shall hold the office for two years at a salary of $1000 per year." Since that time educational development has been rapid, and the schools

Sch. of Mines,
p. 351.

Colo. Col.
p. 277.

Le Rossignol,
p. 7.

State Univ.
p. 284.

Teachers' Inst.
p. 393.

Le Rossignol,
p. 19.

Agricult. Col.
p. 362.

Denver Univ.
p. 276.

Le Rossignol,
p. 31.

Normal Schs.
p. 378.

Colo. Sum. Sch.
p. 531.

compare favorably with those in any portion of the country.

Coeducation, p. 432.

Text-book legislation, p. 219; Library legislation, p. 484; Sch. organization, App. F; St. Supt. Pub. Ins. App. G; Cert. of teachers, App. H; Teachers' Inst. App. I; Comp. Ed. Laws, App. J; Ed. Statistics, App. K.

Utah

In Utah schools are practically coincident with the coming of the Mormons, the vanguard of whom arrived in the summer of 1847. The main body, however, did not reach the valley of the Great Salt Lake until the following year. At first, education among these settlers was almost entirely of an elementary nature, since there were many, even among the adults, who were unable to read or write. The necessity of educating the adults in the rudimentary subjects was so great that a parents' school was soon established at Salt Lake City, for the heads of families and for the training of teachers. Brigham Young was one of the pupils in this school. Primary and other schools were immediately opened in all the principal settlements, and for those who were sufficiently advanced, classes were organized as early as the winter of 1848–1849 for the study of ancient and modern languages. The *Frontier Guardian* reports (May 30, 1849) that "there have been a large number of schools, the past winter, in which the Hebrew, Greek, Latin, French, German and English languages have been taught successfully."

State Univ. p. 284.

During the '60's the various denominations were busy establishing mission schools, and were making much progress educationally. This was the means of arousing the Mormons, and some attempts were even made at higher education.

In 1870 schools were private, and the support came from "fees"; 20,772 pupils were enrolled in the 262 private schools. There was, however, at this time, a

growing feeling that education should be free.   Ten
years later the legislature arranged for school districts,
and a tax for building and repairing schoolhouses.   It
had been the custom, in Mormon settlements, to keep
the school in the meeting-house.   When this new law
came into operation, many of these became the schoolhouses of their respective districts.   Interest in public
education continued to grow, and in 1885 the schools
were being largely supported by public funds.   By 1890

Agricult. Col.
p. 362.
it was strong enough to occupy largely the field that
once had been held by the denominational schools.

Normal Schs.
p. 378.
The constitution of 1895 prohibits both the legislature
and the state board of education from prescribing the
text-books to be used in the common schools, and requires the metric system to be taught throughout the

Coeducation,
p. 432.
state.   In 1902 Utah ranked twelve in the enrolment
of school population.

Text-book legislation, p. 219; Library legislation, p. 485; Sch. organization, App. F; St. Supt. Pub. Ins. App. G; Cert. of teachers, App. H;
Teachers' Inst. App. I; Comp. Ed. Laws, App. J; Ed. Statistics, App. K.

California

As early as 1767 the Spanish had made settlements
within the boundaries of the present state of California,
and before the close of the century had established
eighteen missions, mostly in the central and southern
parts.   These were in charge of a considerable number

Rep. Com. Ed.
98–99: 446.
of priests.   Although it is known that in connection
with these missions, schools were kept, they have left no
permanent record of themselves.   Of their exact character we are consequently ignorant.   For the beginning
of anything even suggestive of an educational system,
we must come down almost to the middle of the nineteenth century.

In the fall of 1847 the town council of San Francisco
built a small schoolhouse.   Soon after, the citizens met

and elected a school committee — the first in California. Thomas Douglas, a Yale graduate, was employed as teacher. The principal support of the school was the tuitions, though the sum of $400 was appropriated by the town, in order that the poor might receive free instruction. The gold excitement of 1849 left little thought for education in the minds of the people; so this school was short-lived. But the rush to the gold fields brought hundreds and thousands to the state; and it was not long before private and denominational schools were established in the more populous districts. In the winter of 1850–1851 the legislature took action favorable to public education by appointing a state superintendent of schools, and providing for school districts, together with committees whose duties it was to build schoolhouses and to secure proper teachers. At this time, so rapid had been the immigration, the school population was estimated at six thousand, though the public schools were confined almost wholly to San Francisco and a few of the larger mining-camps. The next legislature levied a school tax, and provided that its income should be shared by the parochial schools which had been established in considerable numbers.

The question of public support of private schools was literally fought out, and in 1855 it was decided that only those schools which were conducted by teachers examined and approved by legal officers, and in which no sectarian doctrines were taught, should share in the public funds. San Francisco had its first high school in 1856. Because some of the city officers found that a high school might not be legally considered a common school, they named it " The Union Grammar School." However, at the end of the year, their fears were removed, and it was allowed to take the name of high school. The first state normal school dates from 1862. Following this, in 1865–1866, came a revision and advance in legislation that marked the beginning of free common schools for every rural district in the state.

State Univ.
p. 284.
Normal Schs.
p. 378.
Leland Stanford
Univ. p. 278.
St. Bd. of Ed.
p. 200.
San Fran. Sch.
Org. p. 194.
Mills Col.
p. 438.
Coeducation,
p. 432.

California, in 1863–1864, adopted the policy of authorizing the state board of education to select a uniform series of text-books for rural districts.   The scope of this law was broadened until (1885) the board was authorized to edit, or cause to be edited, a series of text-books, and to have them printed by the state.   These books were then to be sold to pupils at cost.   The plan has not proved entirely satisfactory.   There seems to be a general feeling that the books are not equal to those put out by private enterprise.   Furthermore, though the state is printing the books at a loss, the price is greater than that asked for the ordinary school texts in open market.

Text-book legislation, p. 219; Library legislation, p. 485; Sch. organization, App. F; St. Supt. Pub. Ins. App. G; Cert. of teachers, App. H; Teachers' Inst. App. I; Comp. Ed. Laws, App. J; Ed. Statistics, App. K.

Arizona

As was the case with so many of the Western states, parochial schools were in the field in Arizona before any public provision was made for education.   The latter was first attempted in 1864, when at its first session the territorial legislature passed a bill providing schools in the larger settlements, and also for a system of rural schools as soon as they should be needed.   An appropriation was made at this time for a mission school. Seemingly, the cities felt little need for school legislation, since Prescott alone availed itself of its privileges. Four years later (1868) another school ordinance was passed, establishing both territorial and county superintendents of schools, but since no mandatory tax was levied, the officers had for several years no schools to supervise.   In fact, the governor's report for the year 1871 shows that there was not a public school in the territory. This, however, does not mean that there were no educational privileges, since parochial schools existed in some numbers. But, within a few years of the passage of the law, considerable interest was manifested in public schools. Districts were organized in the thinly settled regions, the towns established graded systems, and in 1880 about 10 per cent of the population was enrolled in the schools. This was, roughly speaking, one-half of the school population. Since that time the improvement has been gradual, educational conditions in Arizona being now well up to those of similar portions of the country.

Ter. Univ. p. 285.

Normal Schs. p. 378.

Coeducation, p. 432.

Text-book legislation, p. 219; Library legislation, p. 485; Sch. organization, App. F; St. Supt. Pub. Ins. App. G; Cert. of teachers, App. H; Teachers' Inst. App. I; Comp. Ed. Laws, App. J; Ed. Statistics, App. K.

Nevada

The constitution of 1864 made provisions for a school system, beginning with the primary school and extending through all grades to the State University. In addition to those provisions which were commonly made in state constitutions at that time, a paragraph was included, requiring all teachers to take an oath to support and protect the Constitution and government of the United States, " bearing true faith, allegiance and loyalty to the same," etc., and also the following : —

"And I do further solemnly swear or affirm, that I have not fought a duel, nor sent or accepted a challenge to fight a duel, nor been a second to either party, nor in any manner aided or assisted in such duel, nor been knowingly the bearer of such challenge or acceptance, since the adoption of the constitution of the State of Nevada, and that I will not be so engaged or concerned, directly or indirectly, in or about any such duel during my continuance in office. And further, that I will well and faithfully perform all the duties of the office of ——, on which I am about to enter, (if an oath) so help me God; (if under affirmation), under the pains and penalties of perjury."

Whether or not it was difficult to find teachers who fulfilled all the requirements I cannot say; but there was in 1870–1871 only a trifle over 7 per cent of the population in school. At the end of the next decade the percentage had doubled. The State University first opened at Elko in 1874. The work at first was that of an ordinary academy. Two years later it was moved to Reno, and was organized with six departments. There being no normal school in the state, the university offers courses for teachers. Because of local conditions, Congress allowed the land granted for an agricultural college to be used in establishing the College of Mines. With a population of about 43,000, the schools of Nevada are necessarily few. Of a total enrolment of 7295 for the year 1901–1902, all but 4.7 per cent were in the public schools.

State Univ.
p. 284.

Coeducation
p. 432.

Text-book legislation, p. 219; Sch. organization, App. F; St. Supt. Pub. Ins. App. G; Cert. of teachers, App. H; Teachers' Inst. App. I; Comp. Ed. Laws, App. J; Ed. Statistics, App. K.

Oregon

In Oregon the earliest settlements were along the Columbia and Willamette rivers. Hardly had they been made when missionaries• arrived, and schools were put in operation. As early as 1835, a Mr. Edwards started a school near the village of Chamfrog, and the next year twenty-five children were brought in from Fort Prairie and placed in his school; but sickness broke out among them, and the enterprise was abandoned. Still other schools soon sprang up throughout the settlements. The people were interested, not only in the education of their own children, but in that of the Indians, and several mission schools were established. Among others, was the so-called Indian Manual Labor School, established in 1842 by the Methodists, which was later merged into the Oregon Institute. From

1840 to 1850 a number of small schools were opened; some were under the control of the Catholics, others, of the Protestants. Through the pioneer work of these denominational schools, here, as in the other states, the public system was evolved. The first move in that direction on the part of the legislature was made in 1849, when it was voted that the interest arising from the money received from the sale of school lands should be used for public school purposes. This was only a small step, but it made possible the first public school at Oregon City in the year following. The legislature of 1853–1854 made further provisions for schools by devoting certain fines to their support, and providing for a local tax. While these laws were being enacted, and the work of establishing the school system was being pushed, the different denominations continued the building of academies and colleges. Both the Agricultural College (chartered in 1868) and the State University (opened in 1876) were private institutions before they came under state control.

State Univ. p. 284.

Agricult. Col. p. 362.

Normal Schs. p. 378.

Coeducation, p. 432.

Text-book legislation, p. 219; Sch. organization, App. F; St. Supt. Pub. Ins. App. G; Cert. of teachers, App. H; Teachers' Inst. App. I; Comp. Ed. Laws, App. J; Ed. Statistics, App. K.

Washington

The early history of this state parallels very closely that of Oregon. Previous to its organization as a separate territory in 1863, private and denominational schools were to be found here and there in the various settlements, and there is every evidence that the colonists were deeply interested in educational matters. A school law had been passed as early as 1854; and from that time schools had been supported, at least in part, by taxation. In 1870, 4760 pupils were in attendance at 154 public schools, while 358 were served by private schools. Ten years later (1880) the figures for public

State Univ. p. 284.

schools were 9827 and 415. Since that time the growth has been rapid, especially during the decade of the '90's, when the mining interest in Alaska brought many thousands of people to the state. The first high school was established at Seattle in 1883, and although there were but four others in the state previous to 1890, they have since multiplied rapidly, 76 being reported for the year 1902. Many of these, however, have but a two years' course. The State University at Seattle is in a flourishing condition, maintaining departments of law and science, as well as arts. Six other institutions of college grade, as well as three normal schools, are situated in various parts of the state.

Normal Schs. p. 378.

Agricult. Col. p. 362.

Coeducation, p. 432.

Text-book legislation, p. 219; Library legislation, p. 485; Sch. organization, App. F; St. Supt. Pub. Ins. App. G; Cert. of teachers, App. H; Teachers' Inst. App. I; Comp. Ed. Laws, App. J; Ed. Statistics, App. K.

Idaho

Soon after the organization of Idaho as a separate territory in 1863, the general supervision of the public schools was delegated to the comptroller, who for many years performed the duties without special compensation. County superintendents and the rural district officers were a part of the general organization. The early growth of schools was, however, slow. In 1866 there were but 14 within the territory, with an enrolment of 436 pupils, while as late as 1874 the comptroller states that at Boise City, the capital and largest city, "during the whole of 1873 there was no school, and but four months taught during 1874." But in 1880 the whole number of schools within the territory had increased to 155, attended by 6758 pupils. From this time the growth has been steady. The State University at Moscow was established in 1892. Normal schools are maintained at Albion and Lewiston.

State Univ. p. 284.

Normal Schs. p. 378.

Coeducation, p. 432.

Text-book legislation, p. 219; Library legislation, p. 485; Sch. organization, App. F; St. Supt. Pub. Ins. App. G; Cert. of teachers, App. H; Teachers' Inst. App. I; Comp. Ed. Laws, App. J; Ed. Statistics, App. K.

Montana

A territorial school law passed in 1864 provided for schools only as they could be maintained from an income from certain fines and by rates. It was not until 1874 that a definite school tax was levied. As early, however, as 1868, 25 districts had been organized, with about 700 pupils in attendance. A decade later the numbers had increased to 103 and 2384. The offices of state superintendent and county superintendent have been maintained from the beginning, as well as the usual district officers.

The rapid growth of schools during the last two decades is shown by the fact that in 1890 there was an enrolment of 16,980. It is at present upwards of 45,000.

The first high school within the state was established in 1883 at Butte. But one other, at Anaconda, had its origin in the same decade, the remaining 20 dating their birth since 1890. The higher institutions are a State University, a College of Agriculture and the Mechanics' Arts, and a normal school.

State Univ. p. 284.
Normal Schs. p. 378.
Coeducation, p. 432.

Text-book legislation, p. 219; Sch. organization, App. F; St. Supt. Pub. Ins. App. G; Cert. of Teachers, App. H; Teachers' Inst. App. I; Comp. Ed. Laws, App. J; Ed. Statistics, App. K.

Wyoming

Educational development within this state is a thing of the present generation. With but the meagrest population up to the time of its organization as a territory, and for years afterward, and even this of an extremely unstable character, schools were slow to take root, in 1870 the total number being nine (4 public, 5 private), with an enrolment of 305.

Ten years later but 20 teachers were employed in the territory, and it was not until 1880 that the number of 50 was reached, doing service in 36 different schools and instructing 2000 pupils. At various times in its early history, the auditor, the governor, and the librarian served as territorial superintendent of schools, though in 1880

State Univ.
p. 284.

a separate office was created. In 1886, what is now the State University was established, and this is the only higher institution of learning in the state, its normal department serving as the training school for teachers. The state constitution of 1890 made generous provision for public education, and the schools, though few in number, are well conducted, those in the larger towns com-

Coeducation,
p. 432.

paring favorably with similar systems in the more thickly populated portions of our country.

Text-book legislation, p. 219; Library legislation, p. 485; Sch. organization, App. F; St. Supt. Pub. Ins. App. G; Cert. of teachers, App. H; Teachers' Inst. App. I; Comp. Ed. Laws, App. J; Ed. Statistics, App. K.

REFERENCES

Jones, Mrs. Casey. Historical Sketch of Higher Education on the Pacific Coast, N. E. A. 1888 : 444. — *Hale, Gove,* and *Shattuck.* Education in Colorado. Denver, 1885. — *Historical Sketches of State School Systems* (each state). Rep. Com. Ed. 1876. — Le Rossignol, J. E. History of Higher Education in Colorado. Circ. Inf. No. 1, 1903. — *Stevenson*, J. D. The First Schools in California. N. E. A. 1888 : 676. — *Swett*, John. American Public Schools : History and Pedagogics. New York, 1890.

CHAPTER XI

DEVELOPMENTS IN ELEMENTARY EDUCATION

THE changes in the organization and administration of our common schools, from the time when nearly all the population was rural, and each school consequently had few pupils, to the conditions of to-day, when nearly one-half the people of the country live in towns of considerable size, and approximately eighteen million children are going through the machinery of elementary education, are very great. The curriculum has undergone many modifications, and received additions, until it has lost all resemblance to its former self. But the most important changes have come in the direction of school organization.

A simple machine will do its work even though clumsily constructed; but increase its complexity, and only the most careful adjustment of all its parts will prevent lost motion, or even a total breakdown. The early elementary schools were extremely simple and unorganized. A teacher was provided, who, so far as he was able, gave each pupil from the ABC class to that in the sixth reader, the instruction that fitted his needs. The classes were small, since very few pupils were in the same stage of advancement, and progress was as rapid as the capabilities of the pupil allowed. There was no graded system, so each school was a rule unto itself.

It is impossible to state in any precise way just what the curriculum in these early schools was. There is plenty of record of legislation, but the detail of its administration was left unrecorded. There are no official documents respecting the conditions of the schools themselves; but from the testimony of men who were educated in the common schools prior to 1800, it appears that the course of instruction was limited to spelling, reading, writing, and the elements of arithmetic. It is impossible, however, to suppose that the curriculum remained the same for all the years of our educational history prior to that date, and we have evidence that certain schools made considerable advances during the colonial period.

During the seventeenth century the only subjects taught by legislative requirement in the colonies of Massachusetts Bay, Plymouth, Connecticut, New Amsterdam, and New Sweden, were reading, writing, religion, and capital laws. No reference is made to spelling, which was undoubtedly taught in connection with the reading, nor to arithmetic, although the latter was taught in many of the schools. With the eighteenth century the curriculum underwent considerable modification. Religion and laws were taught together. Arithmetic was generally added, although this was done earliest in the schools of the Middle states, and in the South, rather than in New England, and seems to have had more time devoted to it there. The earliest mention we find of the subject was for Pennsylvania in 1683, when a contract was made with one, Enoch Flower, providing that the children under his tutelage should "learn to read, write and cast accounts."

Clews, p. 281.

It seems probable that ciphering was not generally introduced in the schools of New England until sometime after 1750, though beginnings had been made earlier. Nearly all the records dating after that time mention it in some form, along with reading and writing.

Just when spelling differentiated itself from reading cannot be said with definiteness; but in the records it is not often mentioned as a separate subject until after the Revolution. *Dilworth's Speller*, a very popular text-book, came into favor at about this time, or a little earlier, and may have had something to do with the move. This book contained a little English grammar, and we may infer that this subject received some attention from this time on.

For many years, in fact until well into the nineteenth Chapter xiv. century, even slighter changes were made in the organization of the elementary schools than in their course of study. They were everywhere, even in the larger towns, ungraded, the system consisting of little more than a collection of isolated district schools, each with its own separate building. But as time went on, it became cheaper in thickly populated parts to erect school buildings with several rooms; and even the not over-pedagogical school committees soon recognized an advantage in the plan of roughly classifying the pupils, and of placing the younger ones under a certain teacher, while the older were assigned to others. Here is an anticipation of the present graded system. Yet not for many years, not, in fact, until after the middle of the century, when the city superintendent of schools became a factor, was the division more minute than into the primary and the grammar schools.

Speaking of the primary schools of Boston in 1856, 1903, p. 35. Superintendent Seaver in his report says : —

"The furniture was scanty, only little movable armchairs for the pupils to sit in. There was of course no study in the modern sense of the term. The principle of gradation had not been recognized, and promotions from one teacher's room to another was unknown. It is true that each teacher had six classes, but this meant that her children began with their A B C's with her, and stayed in her room until they were ready for admission to the grammar school, because their teachers were unwilling to impoverish their first classes by parting with their most brilliant pupils."

In many places conditions were not, however, so serious as this. Boston was unusually late in providing for primary schools, and always, until comparatively lately, provided for them but poorly in comparison with what was done for the grammar and secondary grades.

The next stage, although it was omitted in many places, was that of the insertion of the so-called intermediate school between the primary and the grammar, by cutting off one or two years from each, and devoting separate rooms to their work. The step from this plan to that of full yearly grading, with separate rooms and teachers for the work of each year, was not a long one; and, after the appointment of the city superintendent of schools, was rapidly taken. In most of the older cities of the East it came in the decades from 1840 to 1860, though rather in the later than in the earlier years of that period. Now the plan is universal, no city nor town, in the country, large enough to make it profitable, being without its full system of graded schools. In the vast majority the number of annual steps — or grades — is eight, though there are exceptions to the rule. In some few but seven rooms precede the high school, while in a considerably larger number (and most of them are in the New England states) there are nine. This may be due, at least in part, to the earlier legal school age, which generally prevails in that part of the country.

Appendix J.

This graded system of city schools has been the necessary result of the growth of urban population. On the whole, it has worked well, though through it the student who varies materially from the normal type is made to suffer. In the freer organization of the ungraded school, it was possible for the bright student to go a little faster, and the dull ones a little slower than his fellows, without giving rise to any serious administrative problems. In the grades this is not so easy, promotion being usually an annual event, and the stages rigidly differentiated, making it necessary that the same pace be kept by all. Some schools — though altogether too few — are already trying the plan of semi-annual promotion, with the greatest success, except for its strain upon the administrative machinery. No doubt the number of schools doing so will greatly increase within the next few years. The experiment of individual instruction has also been tried; and, although the plan has many strong points, it has not been successfully put into practice in any large city.

Search.

The course of study in the elementary school has undergone so many changes in its evolution from its ungraded state to its present complexity as to make it seem unwise to trace it in detail.

The following suggested programmes, the first taken from the report of the National Educational Association Committee on Rural Schools, and the second, from that of the Committee on Elementary Education, show the best thought of the present day. The first is for an elementary school, admitting of a threefold division of students.

THREE–GRADE PROGRAMME *

Closing Time	Minutes	Primary (C)	Secondary (B)	Advanced (A)
9.10	10	OPENING EXERCISES		
9.35	25	Seat Work †	Arithmetic	Arithmetic
10.00	25	Number On slate or with objects	Arithmetic	Geography
10.25	25	Number	Geography	Geography
10.45	20	Form Work Paper folding, stick laying, etc.	Geography	Geography
10.55	10		RECESS	
11.15	20	Silent Reading	Geography	Grammar
11.35	20	Reading and Spelling	Form Work Map drawing, sand moulding, etc.	Grammar
12.00	25	Excused from School	Reading	Grammar

THREE-GRADE PROGRAMME—*Continued*

CLOSING TIME	MINUTES	PRIMARY (C)	SECONDARY (B)	ADVANCED (A)
1.10	10	†	NOON INTERMISSION	†
1.20	20	Form Work Clay modelling, paper cutting, etc.	Reading	Reading
1.50	20	Silent Reading	Seat Work †	Reading
2.10	20	Reading and Spelling	Animal or Plant Study	U. S. History or Physiology
2.40	30	Writing ^{2} or Language ^{3}	Writing ^{2} or Language ^{3}	Writing ^{2} or Language ^{3}
2.50	10		RECESS	
3.10	20	Number On slate or with objects	Spelling	U. S. History or Physiology
3.35	25	Drawing,^{2} Singing,^{2} or Moral Instruction ^{1}	Drawing,^{2} Singing,^{2} or Moral Instruction ^{1}	Drawing,^{2} Singing,^{2} or Moral Instruction ^{1}
3.50	15	Excused from School	Spelling	Spelling
4.00	10		Arithmetic	Spelling

* From White's School Management. Copyright, 1893, by American Book Co.   † As may be provided for by the teacher.

NOTES: The small figures at right indicate the number of lessons a week.

United States history may be taught the first half of the session, and physiology the second half; or each branch may have two lessons a week.

On Friday the last twenty-five minutes may be devoted to instruction in hygiene, temperance, physics, natural history, etc.

PROGRAMME FOR FULLY GRADED SYSTEM

Branches	1st year	2d year	3d year	4th year	5th year	6th year	7th year	8th year
Reading..........	10 lessons a week		5 lessons a week					
Writing..........	10 lessons a week		5 lessons a week		3 lessons a week			
Spelling Lists.....				4 lessons a week				
English Grammar..	Oral, with composition lessons						5 lessons a week with text-book	
Latin.............								5 lessons
Arithmetic........	Oral, 60 minutes a week		5 lessons a week with text-book					
Algebra...........							5 lessons a week	
Geography........	Oral, 60 minutes a week		5 lessons a week with text-book *				3 lessons a week	
Natural Science + Hygiene	Sixty minutes a week							
U.S. History......							5 lessons a week	
U.S. Constitution..								5 * les.
General History...	Oral, sixty minutes a week							
Physical Culture...	Sixty minutes a week							
Vocal Music.......	Sixty minutes a week divided into 4 lessons							
Drawing..........	Sixty minutes a week							
Manual Training or Sewing + Cookery							One-half day each	
No. of Lessons....	20 + 7 daily exer.	20 + 7 daily exer.	20 + 5 daily exer.	24 + 5 daily exer.	27 + 5 daily exer.	27 + 5 daily exer.	23 + 6 daily exer.	23 + 6 daily exer.
Total Hours of Recitations	12	12	11⅔	13	16¼	16¼	17½	17½
Length of Recitations	15 min.	15 min.	· 20 min.	20 min.	25 min.	25 min.	30 min.	30 mi.

* Begins in second half year.

Of the subjects upon these programmes, nearly all are the common branches, and need no detailed discussion. Upon the latter, appear manual training, sewing, or cookery, and natural science. This last subject, though emphasized by Pestalozzi, Froebel, and other European writers upon pedagogical subjects, gained no hearing in this country until after the middle of the nineteenth century. In 1855 Agassiz invited all the public school teachers who so desired to attend his lectures given at Boston to the undergraduates of Harvard College. Among the teachers who availed themselves of this invitation was Lucretia Crocker, who in 1878 became supervisor of natural history work in the schools of Massachusetts. About 1870 Professor Alpheus Hyatt opened his laboratory to all who wished to come. Saturday morning classes were formed, with him as instructor, and the valuable collection of the Natural History Museum placed entirely at their disposal for demonstrative work. Chapter XIX.

As a result of these lectures, an organization known as the " Teachers' School of Science in New England," was formed in 1871. At first this school was entirely under the direction of Mr. John Cummings, but in 1878–1879 the pecuniary responsibility and control was assumed by Mrs. Pauline Agassiz Shaw and Mrs. Hemenway. Through its instrumentality nearly ten thousand specimens were carried into the public schools of the Eastern states, and the publication of a series of science guides — much used even in the schools of to-day — was begun. Gradually the nature-study movement made its way to every part of the country, no system of schools of any pretension failing to be influenced by it.

Its latest turn is in the direction of agricultural instruction. In point of size, our elementary school system has grown almost beyond the possibility of full comprehension, as is shown by the following table taken from the report of the commissioner of education : — P. 368. 1902, p. xii.

COMMON SCHOOL STATISTICS OF THE UNITED STATES

	1869–1870	1879–1880	1889–1890	1896–1897	1897–1898
I. — General statistics					
Total population	a 38,558,371	a 50,155,783	a 62,622,250	b 71,445,273	b 72,792,617
Persons 5 to 18 years of age	12,055,443	a 15,065,767	a 18,543,201	b 20,484,160	b 20,782,210
Pupils enrolled (duplicates excluded)	6,871,522	9,867,505	12,722,581	14,823,059	15,103,874
Per cent of total population enrolled	17.82	19.67	20.32	20.75	20.75
Per cent of persons 5 to 18 years of age enrolled	57.00	65.50	68.61	72.36	72.68
Average daily attendance	4,077,347	6,144,143	8,153,635	10,052,554	10,356,458
Relation of same to enrolment (per cent)	59.3	62.3	64.1	67.8	68.6
Average length of school term (days)	132.2	130.3	134.7	142.0	143.0
Total number of days attended by all pupils	539,053,423	800,719,970	1,098,232,725	1,427,402,478	1,480,466,644
Average number of days attended by each person 5 to 18	44.7	53.1	59.2	69.7	71.2
Average number attended by each pupil enrolled	78.4	81.1	86.3	96.3	98.0
Male teachers	77,529	122,795	125,525	131,221	132,257
Female teachers	122,986	163,798	238,397	273,737	278,556
Whole number of teachers	200,515	286,593	363,922	404,958	410,813
Per cent of male teachers	38.7	42.8	34.5	32.4	32.2
Average monthly wages of male teachers				$44.62	$45.16
Average monthly wages of female teachers				$38.38	$38.74
Number of schoolhouses	116,312	178,222	224,526	243,753	242,391
Value of all school property	$130,383,008	$209,571,718	$342,531,791	$477,321,190	$495,912,048
II. — Financial statistics					
Receipts:					
From income of permanent funds and rents	—	—	$7,744,765	$9,047,097	$9,333,554
From state taxes	—	—	$26,345,323	$33,941,657	$35,122,035
From local taxes	—	—	$97,222,426	$130,317,708	$135,515,785
From all other sources	—	—	$11,882,292	$18,652,908	$19,862,008
Total received	—	—	$143,194,806	$191,959,370	$199,833,382

COMMON SCHOOL STATISTICS OF THE UNITED STATES—*Continued*

	1898-1899	1899-1900	1900-1901	1901-1902
I. — General statistics				
Total population	b74,178,966	a75,602,515	b77,262,743	b78,544,816
Persons 5 to 18 years of age	b21,090,070	a21,404,322	b21,897,678	22,261,863
Pupils enrolled (duplicates excluded)	15,176,219	15,503,110	15,603,451	15,925,887
Per cent of total population enrolled	20.46	20.51	20.20	20.28
Per cent of persons 5 to 18 years of age enrolled	71.96	72.43	71.26	71.54
Average daily attendance	10,328,396	10,632,772	10,692,091	10,999,273
Relation of same to enrolment (per cent)	68.1	68.6	68.5	69.1
Average length of school term (days)	143.0	144.3	144.2	145.0
Total number of days attended by all pupils	1,477,016,244	1,534,822,633	1,542,074,801	1,594,738,835
Average number of days attended by each person 5 to 18	70.0	71.8	70.4	71.6
Average number attended by each pupil enrolled	97.3	99.0	98.8	100.1
Male teachers	131,207	126,588	123,941	122,392
Female teachers	283,065	296,474	306,063	317,204
Whole number of teachers	414,272	423,062	430,004	439,596
Per cent of male teachers	31.7	29.9	28.8	27.8
Average monthly wages of male teachers	$45.25	$46.53	$47.55	$49.05
Average monthly wages of female teachers	$38.14	$38.93	$39.17	$39.77
Number of schoolhouses	244,833	248,279	249,969	254,076
Value of all school property	$523,679,996	$550,069,217	$576,963,089	$661,571,307
II. — Financial statistics				
Receipts:				
From income of permanent funds and rents	$9,007,887	$9,152,274	$9,823,482	$10,522,343
From state taxes	$35,341,064	$37,886,740	$38,476,250	$38,330,589
From local taxes	$144,897,878	$149,486,845	$161,245,764	$170,779,586
From all other sources	$14,090,384	$23,240,130	$25,422,423	$29,742,141
Total received	$203,337,213	$219,765,989	$234,967,919	$249,374,659

a United States Comm.   b Estimated.

From this table it will be seen that more than one-fifth of our total population is enrolled in the public schools; and that nearly three-fourths of all those of school age are so enrolled; that the number of days attended by those enrolled has increased nearly one-fourth in thirty years; that the total number of school-houses has more than doubled in that time; and that the value of all school property has more than quadrupled. Nothing that I can say can emphasize so strongly as do these figures our national educational development.

Perhaps the most important move of the last quarter-century in elementary education is that which has given us the kindergarten as a part of our public school system. Except with the Dutch in the New Netherlands, the beginning schools had always been less fully provided for in the older states than had those of higher grades, and the kindergarten movement has been slow in gaining headway. But it has now reached every part of the country, and is of almost incalculable benefit. The introduction of the kindergarten into the United States was due to the efforts of Mrs. Elizabeth Peabody of Boston, Massachusetts, who in 1867 visited Germany for the purpose of studying the Froebelian methods, and returned the next year to devote her life to their introduction in this country. Within the next two years several private kindergartens were established in Boston, and in 1870 the first one of a public nature, in one of the city school buildings, though not supported by the school appropriations. Two years later a private kindergarten was opened in New York City, under the direction of Mrs. Boelte — now Mrs. Kraus-Boelte, one of the leaders ever since in the kindergarten movement — who had studied in Germany with the widow of Froebel, the founder of the system. Other private kindergartens, most of them of a charitable nature, were at about this time started in different parts of the country. But the action which more than any other paved the way for the kindergarten as a part of our public school system was taken by the school board of St. Louis at the solicitation of Dr. W. T. Harris, then the superintendent of the St. Louis schools. It was the establishment in 1873 of a public kindergarten under full control of public authorities, and bearing the same relation to the public schools of the city as did any other of the grades. The experiment was a success, and others were rapidly added, demonstrating beyond a doubt the efficiency of the kindergarten as a part of a city school system. In 1874 the number in St. Louis was 4; in 1875, 12; in 1876, 30; in 1877, 40; and in 1878, 53. It is now 125. Regarding the experiment at St. Louis, Miss Blow, who was the gratuitous teacher of the first kindergarten there, says, it " was a crucial one, and had it failed, it would have been difficult to prevail upon other cities to introduce the kindergarten into their schools. There were many ready arguments against such an innovation : the argument from expense : the argument based upon the tender age of the kindergarten children : the argument that kindergartens would spoil the children and fill the primary grades with untractable pupils : the argument that only rarely endowed and therefore rarely to be found persons could successfully conduct a kindergarten. These arguments would have acquired immeasurable force when confirmed by an abortive experiment. Dr. Harris steered the kindergarten course through stormy waters to a safe harbor." With the public kindergarten a success in St. Louis, other cities were not slow to take it up, though in most places it passed through a period of private support before being made a part of the public school system.

In Boston, from 1878 till 1889, Mrs. Quincy A. Shaw supported the entire free kindergarten movement of the city, maintaining as many as 30 at one time. When the city adopted them in 1889, there were 36 teachers and 1074 pupils. Now (1903) the numbers are 167, and 4862.

In 1873 there were in the country 42 kindergartens with 73 teachers and 1252 pupils. The numbers at intervals since are as follows : —

STATISTICS FOR KINDERGARTENS

	Number	Private	Public	Teachers	Pupils
1901	5107	2111	2996	9926	243,447
1898	2884	1519	1365	5764	143,720
1892	1311	852	459	2535	65,296
1885	415	——	——	905	18,832
1880	232	——	——	524	8,871
1875	95	——	——	216	2,809

Of the private kindergartens (which may be seen from the table to nearly equal the public ones in number, though they have but about one-third the total number of pupils) many are maintained as charitable institutions by the various kindergarten associations of the country, of which there are more than four hundred ; many by other benevolent institutions ; while by far the greater number are private enterprises conducted for gain. They vary in every particular, but are generally efficient, and are doing a most valuable work.

From the beginning, it has been recognized that the kindergarten teacher needed special preparation of a character quite different from that of the teacher in the grades, and special training schools were early established. The first was a private institution started in Boston in 1869 under the direction of Miss King. In 1872 Mrs. Kraus-Boelte set up one of a similar nature in New York City, which has ever since been one of the leading training schools for kindergartens. From that time on, their increase has been comparatively rapid, no large city being without one or more. Both the public and the private normal schools, too, have added kindergarten departments in many instances, though the custom has not been by any means universal. At present forty-two of the public normal schools as well as all the institutions classed as teachers' colleges are conducting such departments. In the early days the course was of but a single year. But thoroughly to master the Froebelian philosophy, as well as the technique of kindergarten practice, was found to demand a longer period of study; and now, in all the better institutions, at least two years are devoted to the special kindergarten training course.

REFERENCES

Blow, Susan E. Kindergarten Education. In Butler, Education in United States, Vol. I, Ch. II. — Carter, Joseph. Agriculture as a Science for the Elementary Schools. N. E. A. 1901 : 785. — Cooper, S. B. A Brief Résumé of Kindergarten Growth. N. E. A. 1888 : 330. — *Dewey*, John. The Situation as regards the Course of Study. Ed. Rev. 22 : 26. — Draper, A. S. Duty of the State in relation to the Kindergarten. N. E. A. 1892 : 174. — *Eliot*, Charles W. Shortening and Enriching the Grammar School Curriculum. N. E. A. 1891 : 617. — Harris, W. T. Classification and Instruction in the Rural Schools. N. E. A. 1897 : 121. Elementary Education. N. A. Rev. 160 : 538. — *Hodge*, C. F. Foundations of Nature Study. Ped. Sem. 6 : 536, 7 : 95, 7 : 208. — Jackman, W. F. Natural Science. for the Common School. N. E. A. 1891 : 581. — Lange, D. Nature Study in the Public Schools. N. E. A. 1900 : 404. *Maxwell*, W. H. The Grammar School Curriculum. Ed. Rev. 3 : 472. — Peabody, E. P. Origin and Growth of the Kindergarten. Ed. 2 : 507. — Rice, J. M. The Essentials in Elementary Education. Forum, 22 : 538. — Sabin, Henry. Grading the Country Schools. N. E. A. 1894 : 349. — Search, P. W. The Ideal School, N.Y. 1896. — U. S. Education, Bureau of. Classification in Graded Schools. Rep. 1891–1892, 1 : 601. Early History of the Kindergarten in St. Louis. Rep. 1896–1897, 1 : 899. History of the Kindergarten. Rep. Com. Ed 1874–1875, p. lxiii. — *What Shall the Schools Teach?* W. T. Harris. Forum, 4 : 460. — H. H. Boyten. Forum, 4 : 575. — C. H. Parkhurst. Forum, 5 : 47. — Austin Flint. Forum, 5 : 146. — R. C. Pitman. Forum, 5 : 289. — R. Gilmore. Forum, 5 : 454. — L. F. Ward. Forum, 5 : 574. — S. E. Warren. Forum, 5 : 682. — H. H. Boyesen. Forum, 6 : 92. — A. S. Isaacs. Forum, 6 : 204. — White, E. E. Country School Problems. N. E. A. 1894 : 669. — Young, Mrs. Ella F. Grading and Classification. N. E. A. 1893 : 83.

CHAPTER XII

DEVELOPMENT IN PUBLIC SECONDARY EDUCATION

By the middle of the nineteenth century, public elementary education, supported by taxation, had been established in all parts of the country. There were perhaps restricted localities for which this was not true, but public feeling had been fully aroused to the belief that the hope of the republic rested upon the common school education of all the people. Beyond this point there was the greatest difference of opinion. Only the leaders of thought dared assert that the state should go farther, the great mass of the people believing that beyond this stage, all education should be by private enterprise. Many argued that the common school funds could not be applied legally to the support of higher education. In some states the controversy was spirited. But social and economic conditions were rapidly changing. The head of the family was receiving higher wages; and, as a consequence, the boys and girls were not forced into the ranks of producers at so early an age as formerly. This meant a longer school period, and the educational machinery was quick to adapt itself to the new conditions. The result was the public high school. Public grammar schools had been established in the New England colonies as early as 1635, and in 1639 the school in Dorchester seems to have been supported entirely, or nearly so, by taxation; but with few exceptions, free schools of a secondary grade were almost unknown until well into the nineteenth century.

According to returns secured by the commissioner of education, from 143 out of the 160 cities of over 25,000

P. 170.

P. 28.

inhabitants, the first to establish a public high school with a two to four years' course of study was Boston, Massachusetts, in 1821.   There had been, of course, the colonial grammar schools in considerable numbers, as well as the private academies; but this is the first instance of the class of schools which we now know as the public high school with a fairly well organized course, of a definite length.   Previous to 1840 six other cities, all but one in New England, had established similar schools: Portland, Maine, in 1821; Worcester, Massachusetts, in 1824; New Bedford, Massachusetts, in 1827; Cambridge and Taunton in the same state in 1838; and Philadelphia, in 1839.   Within the next decade seven more high schools had been added to the list in the North Atlantic states, one (New Orleans, 1843) in the South, and three (Cleveland, 1846, Cincinnati, 1847, and Toledo, 1849) in the North Central.   The following table shows the decade of establishment of public high schools as already defined, with from two to four years' courses in the 143 largest cities.   Many of these cities date the foundation of their high schools from some earlier period; but the years used in the preparation of the table are those upon which the courses of study were made, at least sufficiently near the grade of those in the public high schools of to-day as to warrant the use of the term.

Rep. Com. Ed. 1901, 2: 1912.

Brown, ch. xiv.

DECADES OF ESTABLISHMENT OF PUBLIC HIGH SCHOOLS
(WITH TWO TO FOUR YEARS' COURSE) IN CITIES OF
25,000 POPULATION AND OVER

	N. ATLANTIC	S. ATLANTIC	S. CENTRAL	N. CENTRAL	WESTERN	TOTAL
1890–1899	3	1	0	2	1	7
1880–1889	5	0	6	2	4	17
1870–1879	12	6	6	7	3	34
1860–1869	12	1	1	14	1	29
1850–1859	19	—	2	14	1	36
1840–1849	7	—	1	3	—	11
1830–1839	3	—	—	—	—	3
1820–1829	3	—	—	—	—	3
Total	64	8	16	42	10	142

In studying this table, it must be borne in mind that it covers only the large cities of the country, yet they were, with few exceptions, the first to establish public high schools; and, except for the last three decades, the table covers nearly all instances, and is approximately valid for the beginnings of public secondary education in all parts of the country.

Still another table, compiled from tables in the commissioner's report for 1902, shows some interesting facts, since it includes a much larger number of schools. It covers, as will be seen, 3179 in all; all, we may suppose, which could give dates of establishment, comprising roughly one-half those now in existence. A careful inspection, however, of the records upon which the table is based, leads me to believe that in some instances the date given is that of the beginning of the school from which the high school developed, rather than of the public high school itself. Yet this seemed true in but few cases, probably not enough to invalidate the table. It is certain, however, that the earlier schools put down for the Southern and Western states were, at the time indicated, private academies.

DECADES OF ORIGIN OF HIGH SCHOOLS IN THE VARIOUS DIVISIONS OF THE COUNTRY

	N. ATLANTIC	S. ATLANTIC	S. CENTRAL	N. CENTRAL	WESTERN	TOTAL
1900–1902	31	17	30	93	31	202
1890–1899	318	91	161	595	155	1320
1880–1889	142	47	103	508	29	829
1870–1879	121	25	27	298	8	479
1860–1869	60	7	3	103	4	177
1850–1859	67	1	5	34	1	108
1840–1849	27	4	3	9	—	43
1830–1839	10	1	1	2	—	14
1820–1829	6	—	1	—	—	7
Total	782	193	334	1642	228	3179

Exact conclusions drawn from this table would be useless, since, as has been said, it covers but one-half the existing schools. Even then the numbers exceed those given elsewhere by the commissioner, which are that there were in the United States in 1870 about 160 public high schools and in 1880 nearly 800. At the end of each decade since, the numbers for the divisions of the country were as follows : —

Harris, N. E. A. 1901.

	N. ATLANTIC	S. ATLANTIC	S. CENTRAL	N. CENTRAL	WESTERN	TOTAL
1890	786	115	158	1376	91	2526
1900	1448	449	675	3163	270	6005

In 1902 the total number of schools in all these divisions was 6318, with a total enrolment of 541,130 pupils; 485,422 of whom were males and 317,146 females, under a teaching force of 21,778.

The Course of Study

Our first secondary schools were established solely for the preparation of boys for college, and in its inception, at least in the East, the high school was little more than a publicly supported Latin school of the old colonial type. The aim was largely the same, and the course of study differed but little. The latter was rigidly prescribed, and consisted of those subjects which were demanded by the college entrance examinations. Of the Boston Latin School, the classical high school of the city, Superintendent Seaver says in his last report (1903): —

"As in the beginning, so ever since down to the present time, this school has aimed to give the boys of Boston who wished to take it, the best possible preparation for the university. Of course the 'University at Cambridge' was the only one thought of in the earlier years; but, as other universities and colleges have arisen, this school has opened the way to them all. It has always been a classical school."

But in this respect it differs from the vast majority of high schools of the country. The great wave of public secondary school development kept pace with the feeling — in fact, was the measure of the feeling — that the common school education did not meet the demands of everyday life with its necessary complications, and that the high school course should be added, even for those who had no thought of college — that, in fact, the high school should be what it has often been called, the "people's college." This being the case, new questions regarding the course of study arose. The demands of the college entrance board and those of life were soon seen to differ materially. A prescribed classical course which had answered all purposes when supplemented by the broader and more extended study of the four years at college, was found to fit the student but poorly for the active duties of life when not so supplemented, and the schools began trying experiments with the course of study, to see what came the nearest to remedying the defects. This process of experimentation has been going on for many years now, and has even yet not ceased; nor will it, in all probability, until we can have much fuller assurance than we have to-day, that a solution has been reached. The first move in the direction of making the high school more nearly meet the demands of everyday life was through the addition to the still prescribed course, of a number of subjects — each to be taken for a brief period — which, it was thought, would be useful to the student who was not to take the college step. In the decade from 1850 to 1860, when this plan was being exploited, it was not unusual for high schools to require more than twenty separate subjects of all students, and in one instance the number was twenty-nine, and this in a three years' course. The programme of the Boston English High School, with a three years' course, contained, previous to 1860, the following studies: arithmetic, algebra, geometry, geography, general history, history of the United States, reading, grammar, declamation, rhetoric, composition, bookkeeping, natural philosophy, moral philosophy, natural theology, evidences of Christianity, navigation, surveying, mensuration, astronomical calculations, Constitution of the United States, drawing, logic, and French. As might well be supposed, this structure of almost unlimited additions of prescribed subjects soon broke down of its own weight, and the next plan undertaken was that of a subdivision of these subjects into separate courses, each in itself rigidly prescribed, but with election of *course*, possible to the student. These courses were usually designated by names indicating in a general way the character of the subjects included, such as "classical," "Latin scientific," "modern language," etc. This plan had many good features, and is followed in large numbers of schools to the present day. In fact, in a study of the courses of study of 176 high schools made by Professor Phillips, 86 were found to be conducted upon this general plan. Among them are the high schools of St. Louis with 9 such separate courses; Cleveland with 6; Salt Lake City, Milwaukee, and Seattle with 5 each, and Kansas City with 4. The average number of courses for the 86 was 4.5. The fact that the course to be pursued must, in most instances, be selected at the beginning of the first year, when the student can neither be supposed to know his own permanent interests, nor can have advice of much value from the principal, has given rise to the plan of making it possible for the student to take a limited number of electives from subjects not included within the course. In many schools such a plan is in practice, eliminating largely the pedagogical shortcomings of the course system.

The scheme, under which a large number of our best high schools are now being conducted, is not that of separate courses, but one based upon a "core" of subjects prescribed for all, in addition to which a large number of free electives are offered, from which the required number of subjects may be selected, without prescription.

English, three or four years, and mathematics, usually two years, are the most frequent prescriptions under this plan, though history, science, and modern languages are sometimes included. Of 110 schools studied, Professor Phillips found that 17 had 70 per cent or more of the students' time devoted to the free electives; 24 between 50 and 70 per cent; 45 between 40 and 50 per cent, while the remainder had less than 40 per cent. One school at least, that at Galesburg, Illinois, makes no prescription whatever, any subject being taken or rejected at the will of the student. The plan has been in operation there seemingly with good results. Of the class of 1900, consisting of 32 boys and 62 girls, English was taken by all, general history by 97 per cent, botany

Phillips,
Ped. Sem. VII.

Thomson.

by 88 per cent, civil government by 89 per cent, algebra by 75 per cent, physics by 66 per cent, Latin by 56 per cent, and geometry by 46 per cent.

Where sufficient influence, either on the part of the principal or the parents, can be brought to bear upon the pupil to lead him to choose of his own accord a course with no dangerously weak spots, this plan has many strong points; ·but without the certainty of such, it seems almost anarchistic.

The percentages of the total number of students enrolled, who were taking certain studies in the high schools of the country for the years 1890–1901 inclusive, together with certain other facts having to do with the high school enrolment, is shown in the table on the following page.

Rep. Com. Ed. 1902 : 1945.

Some rather striking facts regarding the course of study are shown by this table: First, that the percentage of students who are taking Latin seems to be rapidly increasing, having grown nearly one-fourth in the eleven years covered by the table. In the light of modern educational development it is not easy to account for this. In the higher institutions of learning, the tendency has been in the other direction; but 33 per cent of the students in colleges for men and for both sexes taking the subject in 1901, and when less than 12 per cent of the high school students are preparing for college, it is difficult to see what has given the subject its value in the secondary school. Another, perhaps unexpected, showing is that for the sciences, every one of which, unless we include mathematics in the category, has seemingly decreased in popularity; physics having fallen from 24 per cent to a little more than 18 per cent, chemistry from 10.20 to 7.56 per cent, with most of the others in like proportion. The most plausible explanation of this, it seems to me, is in the more intensive way in which these subjects are studied. Formerly it was the custom for the students to take a little, per-

PER CENT OF TOTAL NUMBER OF SECONDARY STUDENTS IN PUBLIC HIGH SCHOOLS IN CERTAIN COURSES AND STUDIES, ETC.

Students and Studies.	1890–1891	1891–1892	1892–1893	1893–1894	1894–1895	1895–1896	1896–1897	1897–1898	1898–1899	1899–1900	1900–1901
Males	40.27	40.59	40.10	40.45	41.15	41.51	42.36	42.08	41.39	41.64	41.46
Females	59.73	59.41	59.90	59.55	58.85	58.49	57.64	57.92	58.61	58.36	58.54
Preparing for college, classical course	6.04	6.33	7.50	7.87	7.53	7.68	6.62	6.21	6.10	6.02	6.12
Preparing for college, scientific courses	5.80	6.90	7.10	6.43	6.22	6.14	5.55	5.15	5.41	4.80	5.03
Total preparing for college	11.84	13.23	14.60	14.30	13.75	13.82	12.17	11.36	11.51	10.82	11.15
Graduates	12.00	11.48	12.60	12.90	12.11	12.05	12.22	11.79	11.86	11.89	12.13
Graduates prepared for college[a]	28.58	32.44	29.97	26.70	28.08	29.28	29.26	27.45	28.85	30.28	31.27
Studying—											
Latin	41.20	38.88	43.06	44.78	43.97	46.18	48.36	49.67	50.39	50.61	50.45
Greek	3.00	3.08	3.40	3.33	3.10	3.11	3.13	3.12	3.12	2.85	2.63
French	5.70	5.18	6.42	6.81	6.52	6.99	6.86	7.54	7.94	7.78	8.29
German	15.92	10.43	11.92	11.77	11.40	12.00	12.42	13.25	14.01	14.33	15.45
Algebra	52.20	48.93	52.88	56.14	54.27	54.64	55.46	56.13	57.09	56.29	56.96
Geometry	24.60	23.71	26.00	27.20	25.34	26.23	26.71	27.09	27.94	27.39	27.83
Trigonometry		2.37	2.73	2.93	2.53	2.48	2.45	2.27	2.05	1.91	2.04
Astronomy					4.79	4.40	4.21	3.82	3.33	2.78	2.34
Physics	24.00	22.82	23.27	25.29	22.77	22.08	21.09	20.69	20.20	19.04	18.40
Chemistry	10.20	10.17	10.00	10.31	9.15	8.95	8.83	8.30	8.39	7.72	7.56
Physical geography					23.89	25.54	25.38	24.94	24.29	23.37	22.83
Geology					5.00	4.80	4.62	4.37	4.04	3.61	3.44
Physiology					29.95	31.94	30.84	29.98	29.21	27.42	26.60
Psychology					2.74	3.00	2.90	2.74	2.39	2.38	2.19
Rhetoric							34.24	35.97	37.55	38.48	40.71
English literature					32.05	32.34	35.76	40.97	41.75	42.10	45.08
History (other than U.S.)	28.20	30.97	33.88	36.48	34.33	35.28	35.28	37.70	38.32	38.16	38.91
Civics								22.74	21.97	21.66	20.97

a Per cent of total number of graduates.

haps a term, of one science, and then to go on to another, thus figuring in the enrolment of a considerable number. Now a science, once taken, must in many cases be pursued for at least an entire year, thus reducing the number taken, and consequently the total enrolment on the scientific side. We certainly are unwilling to believe that with all the increase in scientific equipment made by our high schools during the decade, that the departments are being less fully utilized, and must conclude that the results may be expressed by the phrase, *non multa, sed multum.*

In length, the high school course has become practically fixed at four years. This following, as it does, the eight, or in some instances, nine years of work in the grades, meets the entrance requirements of any college, and is probably the academic equivalent of at least two years' work in those institutions a half-century ago. Only in the smaller towns, where the common school preparation is deficient, or where a full four years' high school course has not yet been established, would this not be the case. Under the conditions usually existing, the pupils reach the high school at about the age of fourteen years, completing it at eighteen.

The following table shows the ages of those in the high schools of Boston for the years 1902–1903 : —

	12	13	14	15	16	17	18	19 AND OVER	TOTAL
4th year boys	—	—	—	2	9	25	41	40	117
girls	—	—	—	1	33	68	85	68	255
3d year boys	—	—	9	26	104	159	106	47	451
girls	—	—	2	39	180	218	99	33	571
2d year boys	—	3	37	131	213	148	69	26	627
girls	—	5	59	211	283	191	82	26	857
1st year boys	8	79	239	358	272	128	35	11	1130
girls	4	52	259	425	414	201	62	21	1438
Total . .	12	139	605	1193	1508	1138	579	272	5446

Rep. Boston Supt. Schools, 1903, p. 147.

At present there is agitation in educational circles in the direction of adding one or even two years to the course, making it possible for the student to gain that much advanced college standing; but as yet no schools are offering a definitely stated course of that length, leading up to graduation. In a few instances, as at Joliet, Illinois, advanced courses are offered, which may profitably be taken as graduate work; but beyond this the high schools have not yet gone. In breadth the curriculum is rapidly widening, through the introduction of drawing and the fine arts, as well as manual training and the commercial subjects.

Chapter XIX.

Chapter XX.

REFERENCES

For a comprehensive bibliography of secondary education in the United States (several hundred titles), see Brown's *Making of the Middle Schools*, Appendix C.

Addis, Wellford. Federal and State Aid to establish Higher Education. Rep. Com. Ed. 1896–1897, 2 : 1137. — *Aiton*, George B. Principles underlying the making of Courses of Study for Secondary Schools. Sch. Rev. 6 : 369. — Hinsdale, B. A. Sch. Rev. 6 : 606. — Baxter, C. J. The Township High School. N. E. A. 1898 : 308. — Boynton, F. D. A Six-Year High School Course. Ed. Rev. 20 : 515. — *Brooks*, Stratton D. Electives in the Small High School. Sch. Rev. 9 : 593. The Scope and Limitations of the Small High School. Ed. 22 : 434. — *Brown*, Elmer E. Secondary Education in the United States. Sch. Rev. 5 : 84, 139, 193; 6 : 225, 269, 357, 527; 7 : 36, 103, 281; 8 : 485, 540; 9 : 32. — *Butler*, N. M. The Reform of Secondary Education in the United States. At. Month. 73 : 384. Scope and Function of Secondary Education. Ed. Rev. 15 : 15. — Cooley, E. G. Limited Election High School Work. Sch. Rev. 9 : 75. — Corbett, H. R. Free High Schools for Rural Pupils. Sch. Rev. 8 : 213. — *Eliot*, Charles W. Elective Studies in the Secondary School. Ed. Rev. 15 : 442. (See also other papers under same title in this volume.) Recent Changes in Secondary Education. At. Month. 84 : 433. Tendencies of Secondary Education. Ed. Rev. 14 : 417. — Greenwood, James M. High School Statistical Information, N. E. A. 1901 : 490. — Hall, G. Stanley. The High School as the People's College. Ped. Sem. 9 : 63. — *Hanus*, P. H. A Recent Tendency in Secondary Education

Examined. Sch. Rev. 3 : 193. Secondary Education. Ed. Rev. 17 : 346. — Huling, Ray G. The American High School. Ed. Rev. 2 : 23, 40. — *Jones*, R. H. State Aid to Secondary Schools. Univ. of Calif. Pub. 1903. — Laurie, S. S. Public High Schools. Ed. 1 : 247. — Mackenzie, J. C. What constitutes a Secondary School. Sch. Rev. 4 : 532. — Mayo, A. D. The Support of Secondary and Higher Education by the States. Ed. 12 : 262, 335. — Nightingale, A. F. Election in High Schools. Sch. Rev. 9 : 65. The High School. N. E. A. 1889 : 501. — Pickard, J. L. Secondary Schools. Ed. 15 : 21. — *Ramsay*, C. C. The Elective System in High Schools. Ed. 20 : 557. — *Thomson*, F. D. Some Results of the Galesburg Plan. Ed. Rev. 9 : 13.

CHAPTER XIII

THE DEVELOPMENT OF SCHOOL ORGANIZATION AND ADMINISTRATION

THE history of American school administration is a story of unifaction and standardization : of progress from the chaotic conditions under which each little hamlet was doing about what it pleased with its schools, in any way it pleased, without let or hindrance from any outside the community, or adequate supervision by any within it, to those under which it is fully recognized that if the people as a whole are to be educated, definite standards of excellence must be demanded of all schools, and that such can only be maintained through the appointment of responsible officials vested with authority to make demands, and competent to direct the schools in the process of meeting them. The evolution has been from a state of decentralization bordering on anarchy, to one in which there is at least a sufficient degree of centralized power in constituted school authority to make it certain that there can be no absolute school vacua in any part of the land. The whole move has been one of experiment : of feeling about for the best form of organization under which the most perfect schools could be provided for all the people. Some backward steps have been taken, but they have, in every case, been due to mistakes in judgment rather than in purpose ; and although the process is not by any means completed, we have every right to be proud of its results. The various units of organization, and therefore of supervision, which have been set up in this movement toward uniformity are as follows : —

a. The district.
b. The city or town.
c. The county.
d. The state.

Beyond this we have not gone, and perhaps never shall go. There is not with us a federal system of education, as there is in the European countries, our National Bureau of Education having no administrative or executive powers. Not all the units of administration mentioned above are to be found in all the states, some having created their school systems without taking each of the successive steps. The state is, however, in every instance, the supreme power, doing what it pleases through legislation with the schools within its jurisdiction. P. 202

a. THE SCHOOL DISTRICT

This is the smallest unit in school administration and the most democratic feature in our whole political organization. Under the earlier colonial conditions it arose most naturally. As each little settlement extended its boundaries, it became convenient for families so far removed from the centre of population as to make it difficult for them to send their children to the town school, to form a separate nucleus of educational interests and establish a separate school. The region contributing to the separate school formed the school district. In Massachusetts it arose without legal recognition, for the General Court Act of 1647 established the schools upon a town basis; but as the district plan worked well under colonial conditions, it was fully legalized by the act of 1789, and continued to be the dominant school power within the state until well into the nineteenth century, and was not legally abolished until 1882. The functions of administration and supervision were at first performed within them in several ways. The clergyman and "selectmen" of the town within Appendix B.

which the district was situated usually selected the teacher, and performed other necessary duties in connection with the maintenance of the schools; but in an age when quantity of work done by the teacher rather than quality was the important desideratum, supervision, in the modern sense of the word, was entirely lacking. The religious phases of the work were carefully guarded, since the clergymen formed such an important part of the committee; but aside from the regular catechism and an occasional examination upon the sermon of the preceding Sunday, no intellectual tests were made use of. Until the act of 1789, the district, although performing an important function in school matters, was without legal rights. That act, however, gave it privileges which were dangerously extensive, and was declared by Horace Mann in his tenth annual report to be "the most unfortunate law on the subject of common schools ever enacted in the state." Besides the authorization of the school district, it sanctioned the appointment of special committees to look after the schools, the first recognition of any function on the part of a school officer beyond that of the employment and examination of teachers. The really disastrous legislation came, however, in 1801, granting the district the power to raise moneys by taxation, a right which had heretofore been vested in the larger social unit, the town. In actual practice, the district proved too small to be intrusted with final legislation in money matters, in many cases the sentiment among the limited number of voters within a single district being the opposite of generous toward the schools or the district too poor to do much; and although the acts of 1789 and 1801, and similar laws passed in the neighboring states a little later, gave to New England the "little red schoolhouse" in great numbers, they were frequently not very red for want of paint, nor was the teaching within their walls of a very high order. Yet it cannot be denied that much good came from them.

The early district had no such thing within it as school supervision of a pedagogical nature. The school committee was still supreme in matters of general direction, and its activities were little more than clerical. But soon after the passage of the law of 1827, Horace Mann began his campaign for better schools, and with the awakening which came with his secretaryship of the Massachusetts board of education — practically his state superintendency of schools — conditions began to change for the better. School committees in many towns, recognizing that one man could accomplish more by giving his whole time to the work than could several whose interests and time were divided, delegated to a single member, supervisory duties, and had him designated as superintendent of schools. A little later men from without the board, who were skilled in school matters, were selected for these positions, and we have the origin of the modern city superintendent.

In Connecticut the early history of school administration ran parallel to that of Massachusetts, except that there the school district took on an ecclesiastical coloring. The church parish became the school district. When a town had but one parish, the selectmen were in full charge of the school; when it contained more than one, a committee from each was given that authority. This move of giving religious organizations power over the schools was contrary to the general sentiment of religious freedom which pervaded American institutions; and as soon as the intensely religious period of colonial days was passed, the plan was given up, though not without having been taken as a warning in the newer states, many of which have provided by constitution that no religious sect or body shall in any way control the school fund or any part of it. The district school system of New England was copied by nearly all the states in the West, as the population moved in that direction: or it may be that similar conditions gave rise to

Chapter VII.

the same results in school organization without any process of imitation. In any event, except in the South, it was and is the common unit of school organization in the rural districts. In the Southern portions of our country it is prevalent to some extent; but the county there is more generally the unit of civil government, and consequently of school administration. In area and extent the school district is fixed at the convenience of the voters and may, in some instances, be coterminous with the township. When this is so fixed by state legislation, as is the case in Alabama, Indiana, and New Hampshire, the system is, properly speaking, one of township control rather than of district. On the other hand, the district may be extremely limited in area, as is shown by the fact that a number of states have upwards of twelve thousand each. The business of the school district is transacted at the annual school meeting, usually held in the spring, and is practically absolute in its legislative power. In general the duties of the meeting are to elect officers, pass upon financial questions, fix the sites of schoolhouses, and vote upon questions of boundaries. In some instances minor questions of school administration are brought before the school meeting. The number and the character of the officers are usually determined by state law, and vary with different states. Each board of local officers has, however, at least four duties to perform: (1) the reception of moneys from the county or state, or both, (2) its disbursement, (3) the levying, and (4) disbursement of local taxes.

Appendix F.

In some form or other, the district school system exists to-day in a great majority of the states. In Maine, New Hampshire, Vermont, Massachusetts, New Jersey, and Indiana, it has been entirely superseded by the township system, though formerly in vogue. In many others, as, for instance, Rhode Island, Connecticut, Wisconsin, Minnesota, Illinois, the Dakotas, and the upper peninsula of Michigan, it is permissive, and exists alongside of the township system. In some states the district is primarily a subdivision of the town or township; in others, of the county. In nearly all, the voters within the district elect the school officers and levy taxes, though in some those functions are performed by the county. City school systems are usually districts which have obtained, through legislative enactment, special privileges.

No one can deny that the district system has been a necessary step in the evolution of school organization. It was the only available means of bringing the school within the reach of all, and when the population of the country was largely rural, it worked comparatively well.

"Certainly," says President Draper, "the American District School System is to be spoken of with respect, for it has exerted a marked influence upon our citizenship, and has given strong and wholesome impulses to the affairs of the nation." Butler Ed. in U.S. Vol. I, p. 9.

Yet with all its imperfections at its best, conditions have so changed as to limit its usefulness, and even in many parts of our country to make it a menace to educational progress. With the drift of population toward the urban centres, many districts have become so impoverished as to leave but scanty and insufficient revenue for school purposes, and at the same time so depopulated as to leave most of the desks vacant. Since a certain amount of money is necessary to the support of a teacher, no matter how few the pupils, in many cases the cost of education per pupil has become excessively high, while in others this has been guarded against by the employment of the cheapest and most incompetent teachers, to the detriment of the schools. Many schools have been kept in operation with only two or three pupils registered, and in some entire states a considerable proportion have less than five. Gerrymanderings, too, have not infrequently taken place within townships, in such a way as to bring the wealthy portions within a single district, leaving the poorer ones to struggle for the maintenance of an impoverished school. Many other difficulties have arisen; and although the plan had its advantages in the early period of the public school effort, especially while public funds were largely supplemented by tuition fees, it has no advantages to offset its evils, and the future will see it replaced by some system based upon a larger unit of organization, under which the schools may be better supported through a more equable distribution of wealth.

b. TOWNSHIP AND CITY ORGANIZATION

The township and the incorporated city are the units in school organization which are fast superseding the district. Consolidation in school matters is as crying a question as it is in manufacture and finance, and will, perhaps, prove a greater blessing. The township organization is but a merger of districts with practically the same rights and privileges as were invested in each of the original districts. The officers are chosen at the annual town-meetings by all the electors, or, as is sometimes the case, the township is the unit of school government, and the schools are made uniform throughout its extent. It is a less formally democratic and more fully centralized system than the one which it is superseding, and has the advantage of forcing the wealthier portions of the township to contribute to the support of the schools in the poorer communities, thus bringing about a more uniform standard of excellence.

But a comparatively few states, and those for the most part among the older ones, — Maine, New Hampshire, Vermont, Massachusetts, New Jersey, and Indiana, — have a compulsory township organization by legislative enactment. Of these, Massachusetts was the first to abolish the district system, which it did in 1882;

New Hampshire followed in 1886, Vermont in 1892, and Maine in 1893.

In at least twenty-one other states — Connecticut, Florida, Georgia, Illinois, Iowa, Kansas, Louisiana, Michigan, Minnesota, Missouri, Nebraska, Ohio, New York, North Carolina, North Dakota, Nebraska, Pennsylvania, Rhode Island, South Dakota, Tennessee, and Wisconsin — there is permissive legislation looking toward some form of school centralization, though in most of them it is as yet being slightly carried out. Where the township system is being introduced, it has tended to give rise to two distinct classes of schools : first, centralized rural schools in convenient locations throughout the township, usually graded, and with two or more teachers ; second, township high schools. In some instances schools of both these classes exist within the same township, and even in connection with isolated or unattached districts. Such a centralization of schools has given rise to the problem of free transportation of pupils. With many district schools within the township area, no home could be very far from school privileges of some sort ; with three or four schools within the same area, considerable distances must of necessity be travelled by some of the pupils, and some legal provision be made for transportation, if the plan is to be a success. Massachusetts, in 1869, was the first state to expend public funds for the transportation of pupils from the rural district to the town schools, and in 1901 was expending $151,773, or 1.07 per cent of the total school fund, for this purpose. Vermont instituted the plan in 1894, and its expenditure in 1900 was $26,492, or 2.47 per cent of the school fund Maine began it one year later, and in 1901 devoted 3.13 per cent of the fund to the transportation of pupils. The average cost per pupil for transportation within these states is about 8 cents a day, and it has been almost uniformly proven that the plan is a saving in expense, over that of maintaining the larger number of rural schools, as well as one insuring better teachers and equipment, better supervision, greater regularity of pupils' attendance, and a better school spirit.

In a considerable number of the Western states, notably Ohio, which first passed a special law in 1894 authorizing the transportation of pupils in Kingsville and Ashtabula counties, and then made it general in 1898, the plan is in practice.

The township high school, mentioned as another important result of township organization, is being established in those states where the township unit of school organization is permissible, in townships which do not contain an incorporated city or village. In some instances, too, even where such incorporation does exist, the township is made the unit of organization for the high school, in order both to extend its benefits to all within the township limits, and also to make the basis of taxation larger. Indiana, in which the township unit of school organization is compulsory by law, had, in 1902, 502 such schools, with 10,253 pupils. Illinois has 27 township high schools, the first established at Princeton, in 1867.

On the whole, the move in the direction of the township high school is a very encouraging one. It is the only plan by which we can hope to bring the privileges of a secondary school education within the reach of all, and any legislation leading in its direction should be encouraged.

The city unit in school organization is but a district, or collection of districts, or a township in which the schools are usually administered under some law relating to centres of population above a stated minimum, or between definite limits. Such laws exist in every state, and have to do with such matters as those of local taxation and the size of school board. The vast majority of the cities in our country are established under such laws, though a considerable number of the largest ones have appealed to the state legislature for special privileges better adapted to meet local conditions, and have school systems based upon their special charters. Because of this fact, there is no semblance of uniformity in school organization in our largest cities.

Nearly all, however, meet upon the common ground of the school board, and the superintendent of schools. The former is but the cosmopolitan representative of the old school committee of the towns, with its functions modified and enlarged, and its composition much varied. As to size of school boards, we find variations among the fifty largest cities in the country from 84 to 3 in number of members, with an average membership of 12. Throughout the West the numbers run considerably smaller than in the East; the average for the former region being but $10\frac{2}{3}$ to 24 for the latter, with a general tendency in all parts, toward a reduction in size. It seems probable that when the stages of experimentation are over, 9 will be the common number.

In length of term, also, there is great variation among the boards of education in the fifty largest cities. Among them : —

15 cities select members for a term of 2 years
22 cities select members for a term of 3 years
7 cities select members for a term of 4 years
5 cities select members for a term of 6 years
1 city selects members for a term of 7 years.

The method of selection of these officials is either through election by the people, or by appointment. The former method is practised in 32 of the larger cities, appointment in 17, and a combination of the two plans in 2. Of those that elect, 18 do so by wards, and 12 at large. Where the latter method of appointment is in vogue, it is made in two cities on the ward basis, and in 12, at large.

The growing tendency is, however, in the direction of selection at large, rather than as representative of any particular ward or precinct of the city. In those cities where the method of appointment is in vogue, the power is vested in various persons or boards, usually the mayor, who is given the requisite authority, either with, or without the approval of the city council. The table on pages 194 and 195 gives a summary of conditions in several of our great centres of population.

Of our larger cities, Cleveland, Ohio, is the only one which departs in any important way from the general type of school organization. There the school council of seven members is elected at large by the city, each member receiving a salary of $260 per annum. A so-called school director is also elected in the same manner, with a salary of $5000. In business matters his power is practically supreme, even to the extent of vetoing the action of the city council in matters having to do with the schools. He also has the power of appointing the superintendent of schools for an indefinite term, with an annual salary equal to his own. The latter is solely responsible for the educational work of the schools, having full power to appoint, promote, and dismiss all teachers. No other such centralized form of school administration exists anywhere in the country; but the plan has worked well for ten years, and is well worth the careful study of any student of educational organization.

Buffalo might be said to have a plan all of its own, since it is without a school board of any sort, intrusting the management of all school matters to the city council. This would be a dangerous plan to follow, but it has, nevertheless, worked well in that city.

The establishment of the office of superintendent of schools was an early move in city school organization. Its growth was a natural one, and has already been touched upon. Starting almost simultaneously in cities

P. 185.

and towns in various parts of the country, it has become the almost universal custom, nearly ten thousand such officers being now in service. The dates of establishment of the office in some of the principal cities are as follows : —

Buffalo, N.Y.	1837	Newark, N.Y.	1853
Louisville, Ky.	1837	Cleveland, Ohio	1853
St. Louis, Mo.	1839	Chicago, Ill.	1854
Providence, R.I.	1839	Indianapolis, Ind.	1855
Springfield, Mass.	1840	Worcester, Mass.	1855
New Orleans, La.	1841	Milwaukee, Wis.	1856
Rochester, N.Y.	1843	St. Joseph, Wis.	1864
Columbus, Ohio	1847	Albany, N.Y.	1866
Syracuse, N.Y.	1848	Kansas City, Mo.	1867
Baltimore, Md.	1849	Washington, D.C.	1869
Boston, Mass.	1851	Denver, Colo.	1872
New York City	1852	Scranton, Pa.	1877
Jersey City	1853	Philadelphia, Pa.	1883
Brooklyn, N.Y.	1853		

As shown by the table, the cities of Louisville, Kentucky, and Buffalo, New York, may lay claim to having the first city superintendents of schools, priority depending upon the exact day of appointment. This I have not been able to determine, though the appointment at Louisville was previous to September 16 of that year. His title at first was agent of the board of school visitors, but his duties were in every respect those of the later city superintendents. The last of the great cities to create the office was Philadelphia, Pennsylvania, following the lead, not only of those in the list, but of several hundred others of smaller size.

The city superintendents of schools are almost universally elected by the board of education, too frequently for a term of but one year. Their duties and powers are extremely varied, but suggested by the table on page 196, which covers the conditions in 233 cities and towns in Massachusetts.

Rep. Com. Ed. 1902, 1 : 553.

SUMMARY OF LAWS RELATING TO SCHOOL BOARDS OF CERTAIN CITIES[a]

City	Name of School Board	Number of Members	How Chosen	Selected from the City at Large, Wards, or Districts	Term of Office	Vacancies in the Board are filled for the Unexpired Term by—
New York, N.Y.	Board of education of the city of New York.	19	4 chairmen of borough school boards ex officio; to elected by school board of Manhattan and the Bronx; 5 elected by school board of Brooklyn.	Boroughs.	1 year.	Borough school boards.
	School board of the boroughs of Manhattan and the Bronx.	21	Appointed by the mayor.	At large.	3 years; one-third appointed each year.	Mayor.
	School board of the borough of Brooklyn.	45	do.	do.	do.	do.
	School board of the borough of Queens.	9	do.	do.	do.	do.
	School board of the borough of Richmond.	9	do.	do.	do.	do.
Chicago, Ill.	Board of education.	21	Appointed by the mayor, with the approval of the city council.	At large.	3 years; one-third appointed annually.	Mayor with approval of council.
	Board of public education.	37	Appointed by the judges of the court of common pleas.	Wards.	do.	Judges of court of common pleas.
Philadelphia, Pa.	37 boards of directors of sections, or wards.	13 each.	12 elected by the people; member of board of education for the ward is ex officio member of the sectional board.	Sections, or wards.	3 years; one-third chosen annually.	Board of directors in which vacancies exist.
St. Louis, M.	Board of education.	12	Elected by the people.	do.	6 years; 4 elected each alternate year.	Mayor, till next election.
Boston, Mass.	School committee.	24	do.	At large.	3 years; one-third elected each year.	Election by board of aldermen and school committee in joint convention.
Baltimore, Md.	Board of school commissioners.	9	Appointed by mayor and confirmed by second branch of the city council.	do.	6 years; 3 chosen each alternate year.	Mayor with confirmation as described.
San Francisco, Cal.	Board of school directors	4	Appointed by mayor.	City at large.	4 years; 1 appointed each year.	Mayor.

City	Name of board	Number	How chosen	Constituency	Term	Vacancies filled by
Cincinnati, Ohio.	Board of Education.	30	Appointed by mayor.	Wards.	3 years; all elected at the same time.	Board of education.
Cleveland, Ohio.	do.	1 director; 7 members of school council.	do.	At large.	2 years; 3 councillors elected one year and 4 the next.	School council till next municipal election.
Buffalo, N.Y.	No school board; the schools are controlled by city council directly.					
New Orleans, La.	Board of directors.	20	8 appointed by the governor of the state; 12 elected by the city council.	At large.	4 years; one-fourth chosen annually.	Governor or city council; *i.e.* authority which made appointment vacated.
Pittsburg, Pa.	Central board of education.	37	Elected by the several boards of directors of subdistricts, or wards.	Subdistricts, or wards.	3 years; one-third elected annually.	Board of directors of subdistrict in which vacancy occurs.
	37 boards of directors of sub-school districts.	6 each.	Elected by the people of the several subdistricts.	do.	do.	Board in which vacancy occurs.
Washington, D.C.	Board of education.	7	Appointed by commissioners (or general executive officers) of District of Columbia.	City at large.	7 years; 1 appointed each year.	District commissioners.
Detroit, Mich.	Board of education.	16	Elected by the people.	Wards.	4 years; one-half elected at each biennial election.	Mayor, with the confirmation of city council.
Milwaukee, Wis.	Board of school directors.	21	Appointed by commission of 4, which is appointed by mayor.	do.	3 years; one-third appointed each year.	Board of commissioners.
Minneapolis, Minn.	Board of education.	7	Elected by the people.	At large.	6 years; 2 elected at each of two successive biennial elections, and 3 at the next.	Election by the people.
St. Paul, Minn.	Board of school inspectors.	7	Appointed by the mayor.	do.	3 years; 2 appointed each year, except every third year, when 3 are appointed.	Mayor.
Atlanta, Ga.	Board of education.	9	1 from each of 7 wards; elected by mayor and council; mayor and chairman of committee of council on public schools are members *ex officio*.	Wards, except as to *ex officio* members.	5 years; a portion elected each year.	Mayor and council.
Indianapolis, Ind.	Board of school commissioners.	5	Elected by the people.	At large.	4 years; elections biennial; 3 chosen at one election, 2 at the next, etc.	Board of school commissioners till next election.

a Recent reports of the commissioner of education.

DUTIES	NUMBER OF TOWNS IN WHICH CERTAIN DEGREES OF AUTHORITY ARE EXERCISED BY SUPERINTENDENTS				
	None	Advisory	Joint	Full	Unanswered or uncertain
1. Selection of text-books . . .	8	85	44	92	4
2. Selection of reference books . .	9	88	38	93	5
3. Selection of apparatus	6	81	35	103	8
4. Making of course of studies . .	3	41	21	164	4
5. Nomination or certification of teachers	19	67	40	95	12
6. Appointment of teachers . . .	45	89	60	21	18
7. Suspension of teachers . . .	41	104	56	16	16
8. Dismissal of teachers	48	102	61	15	7
9. Inspection and direction of teachers' work	——	3	8	218	4
10. Calling and conducting teachers' meetings	——	2	2	224	5
11. Promotion of pupils	4	16	19	187	7

Not all the officers covered by the table are, strictly speaking, city superintendents, — since in Massachusetts the plan was inaugurated in 1888 by permissive legislation, of consolidating several towns into a single district for purposes of superintendency, one officer being given the direction of all the schools within the district. By an amendment, made in 1891, the minimum salary of such an official was fixed at $1500, enough to insure good service, of which the state pays one-half. Later legislation made it obligatory upon every town to have its schools under the direction of such a superintendent after July 1, 1902, so every school in Massachusetts to-day is under the direction of competent pedagogical experts, and thus is accomplished a move for which Horace Mann practically gave his life.

c. THE COUNTY

Throughout the South, the county has been the general unit in all forms of government, and consequently the basis of school administration. As a result, those functions which were in the earlier times in New England performed by the district school board, such as the examination and appointment of teachers, providing school buildings and raising school funds, etc., are the duties of the county officials. The different states, however, have different methods for the administration of this county school business. In Georgia and Maryland there are no subdivisions of the county for rural school purposes, and it is in all essentials a single district. In several others, the county authorities subdivide the territory, appointing district officials, practically as their agents. This is the case in Alabama, where the congressional township is used for administrative convenience. Florida provides for the formation of districts with limited power within the county; Louisiana recognizes the congressional township much as is the case in Alabama. Mississippi, North Carolina, Tennessee, and Utah make provisions for subdivision, but in each instance subject to county authority.

In all these states where the county is the unit of school organization, as well as in practically all the others, save those in New England, county superintendents of schools are maintained, whose duty it is to have general supervision of the rural schools. Those states, too, at one time or another have had such offices, but have abolished them. New York was the first state to appoint county superintendents of schools (1841), though the office has not been continuous in the state since that time. Previous to 1851 four other states had followed the plan, while all the newer ones have had the office since the beginning of their school legislation. Its function is in most states to examine and certificate

P. 78.

teachers, to keep general records of the school and give them to the state superintendent, and to make one or more visits annually to each school within the county for purposes of general supervision. In some states there is an educational prerequisite to eligibility to the office, though this is by no means the rule, and too frequently the office is made political spoil, and turned over to persons wholly unfitted for the position.

In by far the greater number of the states the office is elective, but in some, variations from the plan exist. In Indiana it is filled by appointment of the township trustees; in Pennsylvania by the school directors within the county; in New Jersey, Mississippi, and Virginia by the state board of education; in Alabama by the state superintendent of public instruction; in Delaware and Florida by the governor; while in North Carolina the appointive power is in the hands of the county board of education, the clerk of the supreme court, and the registrar of deeds. The common term of office is two years, though in Pennsylvania, New York, and New Jersey it is three, and in Illinois, Oregon, and Wisconsin it is four.

Since pedagogical prerequisites to the office of county superintendent of schools are entirely wanting in some states, and only of the meagrest sort in any, variations in efficiency have been more marked within it than any other supervisory school office. In many instances, perhaps it would be safe to say in most, careful and conscientious work is being done; but it is nevertheless true that the political affiliations of the office are such as to introduce more frequent exceptions to this rule than is the case with city superintendents, much to the cost of rural schools in some parts of the country. It must be recognized, however, that the county is too large a unit to make efficient pedagogical supervision of all the schools possible for a single officer, and we cannot doubt that the tendency will be in the direction of its subdivision, either as it has been done in Massachusetts, P. 102. or through a deputation of the duties of the county superintendent to a number of subordinate officials.

d. THE STATE SYSTEM

The state is the unit for general school legislation, and in this it is supreme. Beyond this point it hardly goes, though where a state board of education, or its equivalent, under any title is maintained, some administrative powers are given it. In no sense, however, does the state exercise supervisory powers over the actual work of instruction, since in many states it would be manifestly impossible for the state superintendent of instruction even to visit, for the briefest possible time, all the schools within his jurisdiction in the course of his term of office, and such visitation does not come within the function of the state board.

The state board of education does not exist in all Appendix G. states, and in those in which it does, its functions vary materially. The first state to establish such a general board was New York, through the appointment of its so- P. 78. called board of regents in 1784. This was originally little more than an advisory board for Columbia College at the time of its reorganization at the close of the Revolution; but its powers were gradually increased, until it has the general supervision of all matters having to do with private educational institutions in the state, public schools being under the control of the state superintendent of public instruction. The regents are nineteen in number, and constitute the University of the State of New York.

North Carolina was the next state to establish a state educational board, which it did in 1825, under the title " President and Directors of the Literary Fund." This consisted of the chief justice of the supreme court, the speakers of both houses of the legislature, and the state treasurer. The name state board of education was first used in Missouri in 1835 for a similar body.

P. 98. Massachusetts established its state board of education in 1837. It consists of eight members, one appointed annually by the governor for a term of eight years, together with the governor and lieutenant-governor, *ex officio*. The board is responsible for the management of the state normal schools, the holding of teachers' institutes, the gathering and publishing of statistics, and for the examination and certification of teachers. It employs agents, who visit the teachers' institutes, and in many ways come into direct contact with the school officers of the state. The state board in Connecticut (established 1838) is organized upon much the same plan. The other states present the greatest variation in duties and powers.

In Illinois, where the board was established in 1857, the members are appointed by the governor for a term of six years, and the duties are solely in connection with the management of the State Normal University at Normal.

In California the duties are almost entirely confined to the examination and certification of teachers. The same is true for Kansas, and a large number of other states.

Appendix G. In those states where the members of the board are state officials it is little more than an organization for the transaction of school business and the collection of data. In those in which it is made up of educators chosen for their efficiency in school organization, its influence for good is very great, and it is encouraging to note that the tendency is in the direction of the latter form of organization.

Appendix G. Each state in the Union has an officer, designated in twenty-nine of them as the state superintendent of public instruction, in three as secretary of the state board of education (Massachusetts, Connecticut, and Delaware), and in others superintendent "of common schools," or "of public schools," or "commissioner of public schools," — who is at the head of the public school system of the state.

The first to establish the office was New York, Gideon P. 78. Hawley being appointed to the position in 1813. After eight years the office was abolished and its duties were turned over to the secretary of state, by whom they were usually perfunctorily performed until 1854, in which year the office was reëstablished, and has since been continued. In Maryland, which first had a state superintendent in 1825, and Vermont in 1827, the office has not been continuous, and it remained for Pennsylvania (1833) to set the first unbroken pace. Michigan followed in 1836, and Massachusetts in 1837 with Horace Mann, under the title of Secretary of the State Board of Education. Kentucky was next (also in 1837), and then Connecticut with Henry Barnard, under the same title as Mann's in Massachusetts. His office was, however, abolished in 1842, though resumed by himself seven years later.

Since that time, the general establishment of the office has been rapid, with the newer states dating from the beginning of state organization.

The powers and duties of the superintendents vary greatly in the different states. In New York State he is given sufficient authority to make the office one of dignity and of influence, which are lamentably wanting in many others. There he is a final arbiter in all matters having to do with the schools, and his decisions cannot be reversed by the courts. He may overrule the action of any district or city school board, even closing a school arbitrarily if he deems it wise, or may remove any member of such board. No such power is vested in any other school officer in the country.

In all states it is the duty of the superintendent to collect statistics, and at stated intervals to publish them. He also has control of the state school fund, making the proper apportionments.   In many he directs the examination of teachers for state certificates; in some he is at the head of the institute system.

In the great majority of states he is elected by popular vote, and this fact has in many instances given a political flavor to the office which has worked great harm.   Coming at the end of the ticket, as it usually does in nominating conventions, it is not infrequently apportioned to some geographical locality which has not been represented near its head, irrespective of merit, and so it has sometimes happened that the best man has not been chosen.   But on the whole our state superintendents of public instruction have been men of the highest character and efficiency, and have accomplished all that their legal powers would permit.

e. THE NATIONAL BUREAU OF EDUCATION

The federal government at Washington has never attempted any control over public instruction in the several states, and in this respect offers a marked contrast to the continental countries of Europe.   The need of some national agency which should act in an advisory relation to the schools of the country, collect statistics, and serve as an educational clearing house, was however early felt; and in 1867, upon motion by James A. Garfield, who delivered at the time an address which was a masterly review of American education and its needs, Congress passed a bill establishing a department of education, placing Henry Barnard at its head as commissioner.   He was given a salary of $4000, and was allowed three assistants.   Two years later the department was made a bureau of the interior department, which it still remains.   In 1870 Dr. Barnard was succeeded as commissioner by John Eaton, who served for sixteen years.   Nathaniel H. R. Dawson followed with a term of three years.   In 1889 William T. Harris, the present commissioner, was appointed, and has made the office an increasingly valuable one. Since the establishment of the bureau, annual reports have been issued of from eight hundred to more than twenty-five hundred pages, besides nearly three hundred separate volumes and pamphlets of the greatest value upon a great variety of educational topics. The annual reports contain, besides detailed statistics covering all the educational institutions of the country, special chapters upon the history and philosophy of education in our own and foreign countries, and other subjects invaluable to the student of educational problems. It is safe to say that no other country makes such monumental contributions to the literature of education as we, through these reports.

School Support

In the early days the financial support of the schools was wholly local, either through fees, town taxes, or private bequest. In some instances, as in North Carolina P. 68. with the excise fees, and in Boston and Burlington, New Jersey, where lands were set apart as a source of rev- Pp. 26, 63. enue, and in Plymouth, where fishing rights were disposed of for the same purpose, the school had some particular franchise to depend upon, but such cases are comparatively rare. Public lotteries were also some- P. 256. times made use of as sources of school support, though usually for purposes of higher education. But it was the general rule for the parents of the pupils to pay for the schools outright. As time went on, the custom became general for states to set apart public lands for school purposes. As early as 1733 Connecticut set apart a considerable area to "the perpetual use of the schools." In 1795 the same state turned over to the school fund $1,000,000, the proceeds of the sale of lands in the "Western Reserve." In 1786 New York set apart two lots in each township of unoccupied lands for the uses of the schools, and in 1801 established a permanent school fund by the sale of 500,000 acres of vacant land. Twenty years later Maine disposed of twenty townships for school purposes, while New Hampshire, at about the same time, instituted a tax upon all banks in the state to the same end.

Boone, p. 86.

In most of the older states school funds were established from one source or another; in Virginia — (1810), South Carolina (1811), and North Carolina (1825) by direct state appropriation; in Alabama, Florida, Kentucky, Louisiana, and Tennessee by apportionment of lands. By various acts of Congress, all states admitted to the Union previous to 1848 received the sixteenth section in each township for school purposes, and in those admitted subsequent to that time, the thirty-sixth as well (Utah receiving four sections), making in all 67,893,919 acres, which, at the traditional price of $1.25 per acre, makes a perpetual endowment of nearly $85,000,000. The states have all made material additions to the fund, so that in the year 1901–1902 the total income from the general funds amounted to $10,522,343.

In 1836 the twenty-seven states then organized received from Congress the sum of $42,000,000. Sixteen of them devoted their quotas, in part or in whole, to the public schools, eight turning over the whole sum (Alabama, Delaware, Kentucky, Missouri, New York, Ohio, Rhode Island, and Vermont).

Apart from the national bequests, the entire support of the public schools has come from within the states, either from state taxes, local taxes, or tuition, etc. The exact sums coming from each of these sources for certain years are as follows: —

	1875	1880	1885	1890	1897	1902
Permanent funds . .	—	—	—	$ 7,744,764	$ 9,047,097	$ 10,522,343
State taxes .	—	—	—	26,345,323	33,941,657	38,330,589
Local taxes	—	—	—	97,222,426	130,317,708	170,779,586
All other sources .	—	—	—	11,882,292	18,652,908	29,742,141
Total . .	$88,648,950	$83,940,239	$113,521,895	$143,194,803	$191,959,370	$249,374,659

From 1880 to 1902 the cost per capita for school purposes has increased from $1.56 to $2.99.

REFERENCES

Bardeen, C. W. The Present Status of the Township System (in School Issues of the Day). 1890. No. 8, 184. — Blake, C. G. The Centralization of Schools. Forum, 33 : 103. — Boone, R. G. Education in the United States. N.Y. 1889. — Bonebrake, L. D. The Centralization of the Rural School. N. E. A. 1901 : 804. — *Boykin*, J. C. Organization of City Schools. Ed. Rev. 13 : 232. — Cushing, Grafton D. School Boards. N. E. A. 1903 : 905. — Draper, A. S. Plans of Organization for School Purposes in Large Cities. Ed. Rev. 6 : 1. The Legal Status of the Public Schools. N. E. A. 1889 : 180. Organization and Administration Educational, In Butler's Education in the United States, Vol. I, Ch. 1. The Limits of State Control in Education. Ed. Rev. 1 : 26–32. — Eaton, John. Education by the Government : What has been Done. Ed. 4 : 276. — *Edwards*, Calvin W. School Boards (number of members, terms of service, etc.). N. E. A. 1903 : 898. — Evans, L. B. County Unit in Educational Organization. Ed. Rev. 11 : 369–373. — *Fowler*, William K. Consolidation of the Rural Schools. N. E. A. 1903 : 919 (contains bibliography). — Gilbert, C. B. Large School Boards or Small. Ed. Rev. 4 : 179. — Gove, Aaron. The Rise of the Superintendent. Ed. Rev. 19 : 519. — Greenwood, J. M. Efficient School Supervision. N. E. A. 1888 : 519. — Harris, W. T. The General Government and Public Education throughout the Country. N. E. A. 1890 : 481. — *Hinsdale*, B. A. The Business Side of City School Systems. N. E. A. 1888 : 310. — Holcomb, J. W. The County Superintendent. N. E. A. 1885 : 162. — Holden, Charles. New Departures in School Administration. N. E. A. 1903 : 914. — Hunsicker, B. F. School Boards : Their Functions. N. E. A. 1903 : 910. — *Ingalls*, J. J.   National Aid to the Common Schools. N. A. Rev. 142 : 381. — Jones, L. H.   The Province of the Supervisor. N. E. A. 1897 : 217. — Logan, John A.   National Aid to Public Schools. N. A. Rev. 136 : 337. — M'Donald, J. A.   District System, the Independent. N. E. A. 1897 : 211. — McElroy, E. B.   County Superintendents : Their Relations and Duties to Teachers. N. E. A. 1886 : 336. — Maxwell, W. H.   City School Systems. N. E. A. 1890 : 447. — *Mayo*, A. D.   Original Establishment of Public School Funds. Rep. Com. Ed. 1894–1895, 2 : 1513. — *Patterson*, J. W.   State Supervision. N. E. A. 1890 : 432–439. — Prince, J. T.   Duties of School Superintendents. Ed. 4 : 407.   Consolidation of the Rural Schools. N. E. A. 1903 : 929. — *Prince*, John T.   Evolution of School Supervision, Ed. Rev. 22 : 148–161. — *Rice*, J. M.   Our Public Schools : Baltimore. Forum, 14 : 145.   Buffalo and Cincinnati. Forum, 14 : 293.   St. Louis and Indianapolis. Forum, 14 : 429.   New York City. Forum, 14 : 616.   Boston. Forum, 14 : 753.   Philadelphia. Forum, 15 : 31.   Chicago and St. Paul. Forum, 15 : 200.   Minneapolis. Forum, 15 : 362. — Schaeffer, N. C.   Powers and Duties of State Superintendents. N. E. A. 95 : 350–357. — Swart, J. H.   State Supervision of Schools. N. E. A. 1885 : 439–443. — Upham, A. A.   Transportation of Rural School Children at Public Expense. Ed. Rev. 20 : 241–251. — *United States Education*, Bureau of, Summary of Laws Relating to Compulsory Education. Rep. 1899–1900, 2 : 2596.   City School Systems of the United States. Circ. Inf. No. 1, 1885.   Township School System. Rep. 1877, xxxix.   Development of Educational Systems. Rep. 1876–1877, xl.   Social Unit in the Public School Systems of the United States. Rep. 1894–1895, 2 : 1457–1467.   Conveyance of Children to School.   1894–1895, 2 : 1469–1482 ; 1895–1896, 2 : 1353–1358 ; 1899–1900, 2 : 2258–2284.   Transportation of Pupils to Schools. Rep. 1901, 2 : 2397. — *Watkins*, T. H.   Selection of School Boards : A comparison of Methods in Operation. N. E. A. 1897 : 988. — White, E. E.   Authority of the School Superintendent. N. E. A. 1899 : 314.

CHAPTER XIV

TEXT-BOOKS

WHEN our forefathers crossed the Atlantic to make homes for themselves in America, they brought with them beside the tools for the tillage of the soil, other things they deemed essential to the new civilization which they were to establish. Among their other worldly goods they placed the Psalter, Testament, and Bible, and the little books of their childhood, from which they had learned their letters and their prayers: the *Horn Book*, *A B C*, *Primer*, *Book of Civilitie*, and *Spelling Book*. Together these formed the basis of religion and education in the colonies. But since the education of the young was such an important matter, and since this same education was so largely a process of learning by heart something already in print, the problem of text-books became a very vital one to the schools. In those early days America was very much isolated from Europe. Commerce had not yet bound the two shores of the Atlantic closely together, and, as was natural, books for instruction were scarce. The few which had been brought over were entirely inadequate to meet the school demands, and the problem of text-books bade fair to be a serious one. Not as to-day, the problem of *which one* to select from a multiplicity, but how to get any at all.

The problem solved itself eventually by three gradual steps: First, by the importation of English text-books; second, by reprinting these same books in American printing houses; third, by compiling and printing our own texts.

Although a printing press had been set up in Cambridge as early as 1639, it did not in any way help to solve the text-book problem for more than one hundred years, since it was wholly engaged in turning out controversial pamphlets of a religious nature. It is not strange, therefore, that the needs of the elementary schools were overlooked.

This dearth of books of a secular nature, suitable for school use, had a very marked influence upon the kind of text-books in use in the colonies during the next two centuries. The colonists were a class of people who soon became used to meeting problems with such resources as they had at their command. A scarcity of such books as they themselves had studied was a sore distress, but not one that they could not mitigate, at least temporarily. This they did by what was to them the most logical method. When the colonists lacked *Primer, Spelling Book*, and *A B C* as tools of instruction, they brought into use the Catechism, Psalter, Testament, and Bible. Being a devout people, every family was supplied with these; and they, added to the small stock of special books of instruction, in a way supplied the want.

The religious nature of education in the seventeenth century, particularly in New England, was such as to make the use of church books for school books an easy step. It did not appear a radical departure for the American colonists to press Testament and Bible into the service of elementary education, when primers and other school books were wanting. So thoroughly established did such books become, that they gave their names to the various divisions of pupils, and we find in use such terms as " psalter class," " testament class," and " Bible class." While it was the lack of school books that had brought the church books into use, the substitution was a perfectly satisfactory one to the Puritan of New England. If the Word was the means as well as

Boone, p. 53.

the end of education, so much the better; and this fact perhaps accounts for the long rule of the Testament and Psalter in public and private education in this country.

While the primarily religious works were the most important books of instruction during the earlier decades, it must not be supposed that other kinds of books went out of use entirely. The *Horn Book* was certainly widely used for teaching the letters and other very elementary matter.

The *Horn Book* was a European device, seemingly first used about 1450. It early consisted of a bit of parchment, with the letters and other material for instruction painted or printed upon it, the parchment being fastened to a slab of wood, usually oak, and covered with a thin piece of translucent horn for protection. The whole was made in a form convenient to be carried in the hand, usually of battledore shape. While the *Horn Book*, as above described, existed very early, it did not come into general use until about the beginning of the seventeenth century, and continued to be used until about the end of the eighteenth, though during that period its evolution was through many forms and materials. Tuer, 1:5. Tuer, 2:53, 101, 274.

At first the alphabet was all the reading matter it contained, but later we find other material of an elementary nature. In the later years of the eighteenth century the *Horn Book* became so fully elaborated as to lose all resemblance to its former self. The various folding pasteboard books, and even the samplers of the colonial maidens, were undoubtedly its descendants.

Between the *Horn Book* and Catechism or Psalter, a heterogeneous mass of semi-religious school books of the primer type, imported or brought over by the colonists, afforded the means of progress from the alphabet to higher learning. Among these were the *A B C* and the primer of the old type, which were superseded by the combination *A B C-Primer*, or new primer, which in-cluded the contents of both. Practically all the books used for elementary education during the first century of colonial life were religious in their general nature, but they were religious in varying degree. The Cate-chism, the Psalter, the Testament, and the Bible formed a class of purely theological books, while the *Horn Book*, the *A B C*, the *Primer*, and the *Book of Manners* formed another class, partly devotional and partly secular. These were, however, until well along in the seventeenth century, practically all importations, for the American printing press was slow in getting into active operation.

The first book, or tract, printed in Boston was in 1675; but this was not for use in the schools. Con-necticut Colony did not print its first book until about 1710, while for Rhode Island the date was 1729. In 1694 New York had printed its first book in the shop of William Bradford, and the first brought out in Phila-delphia seems to have been issued by Jansen, the suc-cessor of Bradford, some years later.

In the importations from Europe during the seven-teenth century, we have the fullest evidence that foreign books were the main media of instruction. Be-tween 1650 and 1655 catechisms were especially printed in London for the Dorchester (Mass.) schools. In 1661 the Dutch East India Company provided the public schoolmaster of New Amsterdam with an in-voice of books for the elementary school. In 1696 the King of Sweden sent four hundred primers and five hundred catechisms to the Swedes in Pennsylvania. Of the elementary books, excluding catechisms, published previously to 1700 and listed by Barnard, eighteen were published in England and only two in America. Of these latter the dates are 1685 and 1692.

Throughout the seventeenth century, then, the colo-nies were dependent upon importation from the mother country for the supply of text-books. These were all

Earle, pp. 264–265.

Am. Jour. Ed. 14:601.

Clews, p. 208.

Wickersham, p. 17.

more or less religious in their nature, with biblical texts most widely prevalent. They were, with few exceptions, the work both of English compilers and printers. While this is true for the seventeenth century, the next was one of marked progress toward text-book independence, and the American printer was the largest contributor to the movement. It is difficult to say just when they began to print English books, but it is certain that as early as 1685 a work entitled *The Protestant Teacher for Children* was printed in Boston, but as to the exact character of the book we are in ignorance. It was no doubt a reprint of some English combination A B C primer. Sometime between 1687–1690, there appeared an elementary text destined to be one of the first and most important of the long line of American elementary text-books. It was the *New England Primer*, published by Benjamin Harris at the London Coffee House, Boston, and was itself a reprint of the *Protestant Tutor*, published in London a short time previously by the same Benjamin Harris. This *Primer* seems to have won popular favor at once, for a second edition was announced as early as 1691, and throughout the eighteenth century its success was most startling. Almost innumerable editions were issued by various printers. That some of these were large is shown from the accounts of Benjamin Franklin and David Hall in Philadelphia, who, in the seventeen years between 1749 and 1766, sold 37,100 copies. The *New England Primer* became the most important book of elementary instruction of the times. "There is not and there never was a text-book so richly deserving a history as the primer." It continued to be the most widely used book in America until some time later than 1783, when Webster's *American Spelling Book* appeared. The *New England Primer* was by no means such a text-book as we know to-day. It was a book of deep religious tone, secular matter having at first but little place on its leaves. It contained practically all that the

Am. Jour. Ed. 14 : 606.

Ford, p. 17.

Ford, p. 19.

McMaster, II, p. 570.

Horn Book, the *A B C*, and the primers of the earlier seventeenth century included, and a great deal besides. After a few opening pages, upon which were a frontispiece, Bible quotations, and rhymes, appeared the alphabet in small, capital, and italic letters, followed by vowels, consonants, and double letters. Next came the syllabarium, with its "easy syllables for children," and words from one to six or more syllables. The Lord's Prayer and Creed usually follow. Various alphabetical rhymes came next, including "An Alphabet of Lessons for Youth," full of moral precepts and good advice. The famous poem of John Rogers' Martyrdom filled the succeeding pages, and a catechism, either that of the Westminster Assembly or John Cotton's "Spiritual Milk for American Babes" usually closed the little volume. In certain editions, however, "A Dialogue Between Christ, Youth, and The Devil" were the last words. The editions varied greatly, but the undoubted Puritanical nature of the book can readily be gathered from what has been indicated. The success of the *New England Primer* not only stimulated the printers and booksellers to issue it in numerous editions, but also to import and print similar texts, in the hope of equal success. This latter tendency placed upon the market a number of other primers, no one of which ever approximated the popularity of their prototype and model. Between the years 1730 and 1770 we find advertised a considerable number of *Church of England Primers*, several *Royal Primers*, and quite a crop of elementary books, under such titles as "Instructor," "Plaything," "Token," and "Easy Guide." Most of the latter contained more secular matter than the *New England Primer*. In fact, a growing tendency toward secularization is apparent all through the later years of the century. The *New England Primer* itself very well shows this. At first it was full of religious elements of a distinctly Puritanical kind. Some changes began to creep in, which indicated the presence of a movement toward making school books more useful and more interesting to children — an idea which would not have suggested itself to the old Puritans. With the coming of the great religious awakening in which Whitfield played so important a part, the *Primer* immediately reflected the sentiment of the time, and more religious matter was at once introduced, including, in an addition of 1737, the familiar verses beginning, "Though I am but a little one," and "Now I lay me down to sleep." This period of the evangelization of the *Primer* came between the years 1740 and 1760. It was, however, closely followed by a reaction, which during the Revolutionary period was characterized by an intensely loyal spirit. This passed, attention was directed to devices for attracting and pleasing the children. What was, perhaps, the worst degradation of the *Primer*, in the eyes of the good old Puritans, came when a block of playing cards of the time was inserted as a representation of the Queen. Says Ford : —

"This secularization was an attack by its friends from which the book never quite recovered for the printers having once found how much more saleable such primers were, and parents having found out how much more readily their children learned, both united in encouraging more popular school books, and very quickly illustrated primers, which aimed to please rather than to torture, multiplied.   Ford, p. 51.

While the primer was the most important book up to the time of the Revolutionary War, the popularity of another work, the spelling book, had begun to grow long before that time. About the middle of the eighteenth century there was a gradual differentiation of spelling from reading, giving rise to the new book, which at first was little more than an expansion of the syllabarium of the primer. As was usually the case with new books in colonial times, those earliest used were importations from England. Indeed, there is no evidence that a single speller was published in America during the first century of the colonies. In 1736 Dixon's *English Instructor: the Art of Spelling Improved*, was printed in Boston, as the pioneer, followed by a number of others, the most successful of the earlier ones being Dillworth's *New Guide to the English Tongue*, which achieved considerable popularity. This book had passed through twenty-six English editions; and, after its first American reprint in Philadelphia, in 1757, is said to have run off ninety-eight editions previous to 1778. The book was more than a speller in the modern sense. Besides long lists of words, ranging from the simplest to those of six and seven syllables, it contained reading matter, similarly graded, and consisting of short sentences for beginners, and illustrated fables for the more advanced. While this speller was far less religious than the first *New England Primer*, its tone was still moral and religious. In fact, all the short sentences for beginners in reading were taken from the Psalter, and some of the editions contained the shorter Catechism, showing that the publishers were afraid that a speller alone might be considered too worldly a book. Yet, even with the Catechism, this speller indicates quite a lowering of religious standards.

Wickersham, p. 197.

The Revolution limited the home and foreign supply of text-books; but this was only a pause before an advance. " Scarcely had the war closed when text-books were published in such numbers and quality as to revolutionize the method of teaching." The press fairly teemed with spellers, readers, arithmetics, grammars, geographies, and histories, in quantity and quality such as had never before been known. American authors and American printers had proceeded to win our text-book independence as the American statesman and soldier had won our political independence.[1] In the matter

Boone, p. 66.

Bolles, p. 255.

[1] Together with the constant improvement in the quality of books up to the time of the Revolution, had come a similar increase in the home supply. In 1773 Philadelphia, alone, had thirty-eight book-shops, while Germantown and Lancaster each had two, and the other larger cities were well supplied.

of spelling books, the climax was reached with the famous "blue-backed speller" of Noah Webster, the "beginning of that splendid series of school books which now stands unrivalled." It is interesting to note McMaster, I, how both political and pedagogical conceptions pre- p. 23. sented themselves to the mind of Noah Webster. In the preface to one of his books, he says : —

"In the choice of pieces, I have been attentive to the political interests of America. I consider it as a capital fault in all our schools, that the books generally used contain subjects wholly uninteresting to our youth."

It was precisely that attention which gave us the Webster's *American Spelling Book*, which, next to, if not, indeed, surpassing, the *New England Primer*, has been the greatest inanimate force in American education. This spelling book formed one part of what Webster, perhaps as a tribute to dignified, old-fashioned scholarship, called "A Grammatical Institute of the English Language, comprising an Easy, Concise and Systematic Method of Education, designed for the use of English Scudder, p. 34. Schools in America." The other two parts were a grammar and a reader, though neither attained to any great prominence.

With the *Spelling Book*, the case was, however, quite different, and it is doubtful if, even in modern days of big things, any book has had such a phenomenal sale. It first appeared in 1785, and although it gained a foothold comparatively slowly, by 1815 the sales were estimated at 286,000 copies a year, which number in 1828 had reached 350,000. In 1847 the statement was made that about 24,000,000 copies of the book had been published up to that time, and that the sale was then averaging 1,000,000 copies a year. The popularity of the book continued to the time even of the present generation, the sales for the years 1866–1873 aggregating 8,196,028 copies. By this time, however, competition had become a very different factor from what it had been earlier in the history of the book, and sales rapidly declined. The *American Spelling Book* was clearly modelled after Dillworth's, which it succeeded in popularity; but was fully Americanized and much less religious. It cannot be doubted that Webster felt that he had a real mission in its production, and a genuine pedagogic interest in the American people. In its preface, he says : —

"To diffuse an uniformity and purity of language in America, to destroy the provincial prejudices that originate in trifling differences of dialect, and produce reciprocal ridicule, to promote the interests of literature and harmony in the United States is the most earnest work of the author, and it is his highest ambition to deserve the approbation and encouragement of his countrymen."

His attitude toward a modernized form of spelling, as expressed in the same preface, would seem to place him in the very first rank of spelling reformers.

"The spelling," he says, "of such words as *publick, favour, neighbour, head, prove, phlegm, his, give, debt, rough*, and *well* instead of the more natural and easy method, *public, favor, nabor, hed, proov, flem, hiz, giv, det, ruf, wel* has the plea of antiquity in its favor, and yet I am convinced that common sense and convenience will sooner or later get the better of the present absurd practice."

It may be said that Webster never had the courage to make his book conform to his own principles. With such tools as these were the wits of our eighteenth-century forefathers sharpened, for the great masses of the people never went farther with their schooling than these books could take them. Some few other elementary books made their appearance, such as Bingham's *Columbian Orator*, and *American Preceptor*, Goldsmith's *Roman History*, and Stanford's *The Art of Reading*, but their hold was not strong upon the people.

In the field of numbers, Hodder's *Arithmetic* or *That*

Necessary Art made most easy: being explained in a Familiar Way to the capacity of any that desire to learn it in a little Time, was practically the sole contestant for honors until nearly the end of the century. The first American edition, which was a reprint, appeared in Boston in 1719, succeeded by more than twenty-four others.

The first American to produce an arithmetic of any prominence was Nicolas Pike. His book, *A New and Complete Arithmetic composed for the Citizens of the United States*, was a pretentious volume of 512 pages, the first edition appearing in 1788 from a Newburyport, Massachusetts, press. The edition was followed by many others, printed in various parts of the country, for Pike's *Arithmetic* was the mathematical mentor for more than a generation. Of the 500 and more pages of text, 412 were devoted to arithmetic proper, 60 to plane geometry, trigonometry, and mensuration, 33 to algebra, and 10 to an introduction to conic sections. The arrangement of topics was not materially different from that in our best text-books to-day, and on the whole, the book was a credit to its author and its time. An interesting feature of the earlier edition is the insertion, as an advertisement, of letters of recommendation and approval from various men of note. President Washington, himself, was represented by a lengthy and very commendatory epistle, while the presidents of Harvard, Yale, Brown, Dartmouth, were included in the list.

Rep. Com. Ed. 1897–1898, 1 : 808.

Of text-books strictly for schools of a secondary and higher grade there were comparatively few, the demand being small, and most of these were in the classics. Of them all, Cheever's *Accidence* was by far the most famous, gaining a popularity which carried it far down into the nineteenth century (the last edition was published in 1838). For more than forty years it was practically the only beginner's Latin book in use in the colonies. It has been said : —

Am. Jour. Ed. 1:310.

" His *Accidence* was the wonder of the age, and though, as his biographer and his pupil, Dr. Cotton Mather observed, it had not excluded the original grammar, it passed through eighteen editions before the Revolution and had been used as generally as any elementary work ever known."

The book was small, but 79, 12mo pages, and served as a Latin primer. This completed, the pupil was promoted usually to Lilly's *Latin Grammar*. This book was an English importation, first printed in London in 1755. It was in three parts, containing roughly 300 pages, and was intended to serve the student until he should have acquired a good reading knowledge of the language, and be put to the classic texts themselves.

It would be impossible, within the space available, to discuss with any detail the growth of American text-books during the nineteenth century. Their titles alone would fill a volume. The text-book problems of colonial days have solved themselves; but new conditions have given rise to those no less serious. These are both pedagogic and economic: the first has to do, so far as the administration of the school goes, with the selection of the best, from the mass of the good, bad, and indifferent material in the hands of the pupil, at the least expense to all concerned. Upon both of these questions much legislation has been passed. I shall attempt to do no more than state in a general way what it is. Much has had to do with the unit of area or administration, for which there shall be a uniformity of text-books.

No state in the Union lacks some sort of prescribed uniformity, except Alabama which allows a county option in the matter, which but eleven counties have availed themselves of. In every other state in the Union we have some sort of a prescription, either

1st, district — town or township
2d, county
3d, state

Local uniformity, as covered by class one, is in force (1900) under compulsory statutes in : —

Arkansas	New Hampshire
Colorado	New Jersey
Connecticut	New York
Illinois	North Dakota
Iowa	Ohio
Maine	Pennsylvania
Massachusetts	Rhode Island
Michigan	Vermont
Minnesota	Wisconsin
Nebraska	Wyoming

Compulsory county uniformity is in force in : —

Florida	Mississippi
Georgia	North Carolina
Kentucky	South Dakota
Maryland	West Virginia

In Arkansas this is practically true, and in at least one-half the counties of Iowa is established by popular vote. Indiana maintains county selection in its high school text-books only.

State uniformity prevails in (1900): —

California	Louisiana
Delaware (except city of Wilmington)	Missouri
	Montana
Idaho	Nevada
Indiana (in elementary and grammar schools)	Oregon
	South Carolina
Kansas	Utah
Virginia	

Selection and Adoption

As to selection and adoption, the methods prevailing in the several states are in many respects peculiar to themselves. Under district, town, or township uniformity the local boards are themselves generally the selecting bodies; but in the common districts of New York, the voters in annual meeting exercise this function. Pennsylvania school boards are supposed to select books in consultation with their teachers, and in cities, as in New England, the whole matter is intrusted to the superintendents. The "district boards" of Ohio are limited to an open list of such books as the state text-book commissioners may have previously approved. In Wyoming the state superintendent secures samples and quotations of prices which he places at the disposal of local boards.

Of the eight states having county uniformity, four have special text-book boards, composed usually of both teachers and lay citizens; other states make this a part of the duties of the regular county board of education. To the latter class belongs Florida, which provides that the county superintendent and at least three teachers must be consulted.

Similarly divided also, are those states which have complete centralization : Idaho, Kansas, Missouri, Montana, Oregon, Tennessee, Texas, and Utah have special text-book boards, while the other eight of the list make use of the state board of education.

Nearly all states having county or state uniformity, employ the "bid and contract" system for the purchase of books. That is, sample copies and sealed proposals or bids from publishers are received by the several boards, and both quality and price are considered. California alone publishes its own books, by securing the manuscripts; and a similar publication under contract is authorized by law in Kansas, Indiana, South Dakota, Texas, and Tennessee, and has been tried in Connecticut in the cases of texts in physiology and hygiene.

P. 148.

Supply to Students

The purchasing of books by pupils in the open market is now largely superseded. To indigent children they are provided free in nearly all states. Books are furnished free to all in Maine, Delaware, Maryland, Massachusetts, Nebraska, New Hampshire, New Jersey, Pennsylvania, Rhode Island, Vermont, and Wyoming. By the vote of local school boards, or upon authorization by a local popular vote, they may be so furnished in Colorado, Connecticut, Idaho, Iowa, Kansas, Michigan, Minnesota, Montana, New York (in union districts), North Dakota, Ohio, South Dakota, Washington, and Wisconsin.

REFERENCES

*Ackerman, W. A. Text-book Administration in the United States (Thesis for Higher Diploma, Teachers' College, 1900). — Barnard, Henry. School Books and School Apparatus. Am. Jour. Ed. 32 : 961–969. — Bolles, Albert S. Pennsylvania : Province and State. — Boone, Richard G. Education in the United States. 1889, 66–68. *Clews*, Elsie W. Educational Legislation and Administration of the Colonial Governments. Columbia Univ. Pub. 1899. — Earle, Alice Morse. Description of Horn Book. Chaut. 30 : 452. — Ford, Paul Leicester. The New England Primer. Bookman, 4 : 122–131. — *Greenwood*, James M. American Text-books on Arithmetic. Rep. Com. Ed. 1897–1898, 1 : 789–868 ; 1898–1899, 1 : 781–837. — Hewins, C. M. History of Children's Books. At. Month. 61 : 112–126. McMaster, John Bach. History of the People of the United States. 6 vols. 1884–1900, 2 : 570–571. — *Murray*, David. History of Education in New Jersey. Circ. Inf. No. 1, 1899. Am. Ed. Hist. No. 23. New England Primer. Am. Jour. Ed. 30 : 369–400. — Scudder, Horace E. Noah Webster. Am. Men of Letters Series. — *Suzzalo, Anthony Henry. The Development of the Text-book Problem in Colonial Elementary Schools (Master's thesis, Columbia, May, 1902). — Swett, John (and others). The Relation of the State to Books and Appliances. N. E. A. 1888 : 198. — *Swett*, John. American Public Schools, 1900. — Tuer, Andrew W. History of the Horn

---

* I have quoted these two papers extensively in the preparation of this hapter, and acknowledgments are here made.

Book. 1896, 1 : 132–136. — *U. S. Education*, Bureau of. State Text-book Laws and Systems. Rep. 1888–1889, 1 : 553. Confederate Text-books (1861–1865). Rep. 1898–1899, 1 : 1139–1155. Digest of Laws relating to Text-books, their Selection and Supply. Rep. 1897–1898, 1 : 893. Notes on the History of American Text-books on Arithmetic. Rep. 1897–1898, 1 : 789. — Vest, E. J. Text-books and Public Schools. Ed. 21 : 27. — *Welsh*, Charles. A Forgotten Primer and its Author. Ath. 20 : 94–95. — *Wickersham*, James Pyle. History of Education in Pennsylvania, Lancaster. — Williams, Samuel G. History of Modern Education, 1899 (see Text-books in Index).

PART TWO

HIGHER AND SPECIAL EDUCATION

CHAPTER XV

COLLEGES AND UNIVERSITIES

a. COLONIAL COLLEGES

WHEN the Puritan emigrated from England to America, it was a religious conviction that had brought about his exile from the mother country. He was still in all other respects an Englishman of the times, in whom was deeply ingrafted a love for English institutions. Consequently, when he landed upon the shores of New England, he carried there the English tradition and education. The schools he had known at home, he transplanted to America; and it is not strange that the university, his alma mater, the latest to touch him educationally, and the one which touched him deepest, should have been among the first to take root.

The early settlers of the Massachusetts Bay Colony were largely educated men. In 1638 there were in the four or five settlements of Massachusetts and Connecticut, forty or fifty graduates of Cambridge and not a few Oxonians; roughly, one in every two hundred and fifty of the inhabitants was university bred; a proportion three times as large as at the present day.

The great strength, however, of these men lay, not so much in numbers as in the influence which they exerted over the whole intellectual life of New England. Cotton, Eliot, Hooker, Williams, Ward, Shepard, and Harvard were from Cambridge; Mathew, Dunster, and Davenport from Oxford, though of the Cambridge, rather than of the Oxford type. In general, both universities had much the same aim, method, and curriculum, but each its distinctive type of thought. As Oxford had generally inclined toward conservatism, so Cambridge had shown decided tendencies toward liberalism. Here the doctrines of the Reformation were received much more favorably than at Oxford; and, as a consequence, Mary banished the more ardent reformers, among whom were the more eminent divines of the university. When, under Elizabeth, Cambridge had once more met with royal fàvor, these returned. Many of them had, however, spent the term of their banishment at such Protestant centres as Zürich, Geneva, Frankfort, and Strassburg and come back full of the spirit of Calvin and Zwingli.

Well indeed might Bishop White of Winchester sound the note of alarm in Queen Mary's funeral sermon in the words: —

"The wolves be coming out of Geneva and other places of Germany and have sent their books before, full of pestilent doctrine, blasphemy, and heresy to infect the people."

The return of those exiles meant practically the beginning of Calvinism in England, which, modified to puritanism, was destined to bring about such a momentous change in the history of the nation in 1649.

Gradually the Calvinistic party at Cambridge grew stronger and began to show positive signs of insubordination. Immanuel College, founded in 1583 by Sir Walter Mildmay, was Puritan from the start, although in reply to a query from Elizabeth as to its sentiment, he denied that it was so, adding that he had only "set an acorn," and that God alone knew what the fruit thereof would be when it became an oak.

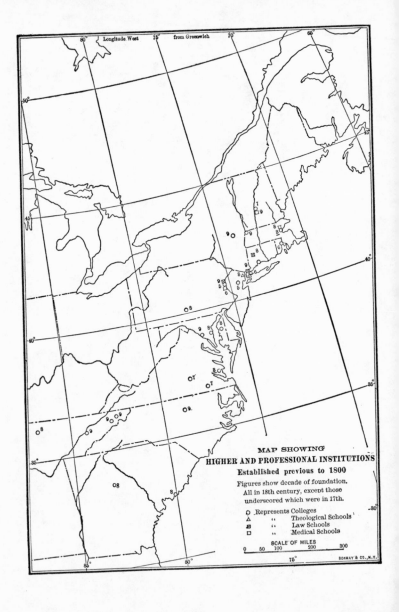

MAP SHOWING
HIGHER AND PROFESSIONAL INSTITUTIONS
Established previous to 1800

Figures show decade of foundation.
All in 18th century, except those
underscored which were in 17th.

○ .Represents Colleges
△ " Theological Schools
⬡ " Law Schools
□ " Medical Schools

SCALE OF MILES
0   50   100   200   300

BORMAY & CO.,N.Y.

No human being could foresee what the "fruit thereof" would be, carried not only over all England, but across the seas, for Cotton Mather says of the college:—

> "If New England hath been in some respects Immanuel's band, it is well; but this I am sure of, Immanuel College contributed more than a little to make it so."

Cotton Mather's *Magnalia.*

Harvard College

It is undoubtedly largely to the intense admiration for, and loyalty to, Immanuel College on the part of these old worthies that we are indebted for the exact type of educational institution known as the American College. Other English colleges, to be sure, sent their sons across the water, and university loyalty was not wanting; but those who were most active in colonial affairs dated not only their intellectual, but their religious freedom of thought to their days at Immanuel, and were hardly settled in their new homes before they set to work to build its New World representative. The move originated not through individual subscription, but through an action of the general court of Massachusetts, which resulted in the foundation of Harvard College. The record is as follows, dated the 8th day of September, 1630:—

> "The Court agree to give Four Hundred Pounds toward a School or College, whereof Two Hundred Pounds shall be paid the next year and Two Hundred Pounds when the work is finished, and the next Court to appoint where and what building."

Quincy, (I) Vol. I, p. 8.

The next general court appointed twelve of the most eminent men of the colony, among them Winthrop, Shepard, Cotton, Wilson, Stoughton, and Dudley, "to take order for a college at Newtown." Not very long after their appointment, the court changed the name of Newtown to Cambridge, "a grateful tribute to the trans-Atlantic literary parents of many of the first emigrants, and indication of the high standing to which they intended the institution they were establishing should aspire.

But none of the money appropriated by the general court had been paid in, nor, indeed, have we any reason to believe it ever was paid over, and the appointed overseers were only beginning to give serious attention to the establishments of the new college when a dissenting clergyman, John Harvard by name, died in Charleston (1638) bequeathing one-half his property and his entire library to the institution.   Although the general court had taken action nearly two years before, and popular interest in the new college had been aroused, nothing visible and tangible had as yet been accomplished ; and we probably may, with justice, ascribe the real beginning of the college to John Harvard's bequest.

Of the man but little is known, though it is certain that he must have been among the most wealthy of the settlers, since his bequest amounted to as much, and possibly considerably more, than the entire amount which the colony was able to pledge.   Just how much the uncertain records of the times make it impossible to say.

It is known that Harvard was a graduate of Immanuel College ; that he had been in the colonies but one year at the time of his death, which was from consumption, and that during that year he had taken a prominent place among the settlers, having served upon several prominent committees.   The testimonies of the times apply to him the epithets of "reverend," "godly," and a "lover of learning."

The catalogue of his library, which document is still treasured among the archives of Harvard College, gives the titles of 260 volumes, which indicate a breadth of scholarship unusual for the period in which he lived.

Valuable as was this contribution of money and books to the course of education in the colonies, the contagion

(margin notes)

Pierce, (I) Vol. I, App. VII.

Harvard.

of Harvard's example seemed almost irresistible, and gave rise to an epidemic of benevolence which assured, at least, the successful launching of the enterprise. The magistrates themselves led the way with a subscription of £200 in books for the library. The more wealthy followed with gifts of £20 and £30. In speaking of donations to the college at these times, and in the years immediately following, Pierce says : —

Pierce, (I) Vol. I, p. 17.

"We read of a number of sheep bequeathed by one man, a quantity of cotton cloth with 9*s.* presented by another ; a pewter flagon worth 10*s.* by a third ; a fine dish, a sugar spoon, a silver-tipt jug, one great salt, one small trencher salt by others ; and of presents or legacies amounting severally to 5*s.*, 9*s.*, £1, £2, etc. What in fact were these humble benefactions ? They were contributions from the *res angusta domi*, from pious, virtuous, enlightened penury to the noblest of all causes, the advancement of education."

And like the widow's mite, they indicate a respect and zeal for the object which would have done greater things, had the means been more abundant. The infant institution was first under the superintendency of Nathaniel Eaton, of unsavory memory. The man seems to have been unfitted in every way for the work which he had undertaken ; and in 1640 was fined and dismissed from service for brutally flogging one of the ushers.

Woodbury, (I) Vol. I, pp. 308–313.

In that year Henry Dunster arrived in the colony, and soon after accepted the presidency of the college, now dignified by that title, and called after Harvard since 1638. Under his administration the first code of laws was formed; rules for admission and principles on which degrees should be granted established.

Dunster was an indefatigable worker; and during the fourteen years of his presidency carried the institution from what were scarcely more than pre-natal squirmings, to at least a healthy infancy. He acted not only as executive head but principal member of the teaching force, with eminent success. His salary seems never to

Appendix C.

have been more than £60 per annum, and judging from the frequent interchanges of letters between him and the officers of the general court concerning its payment, he never received the full amount for any one year, and finally laid down his office with the college considerably his debtor. Early in his administration (1642) was held the first commencement, at which the earliest degrees granted in the colonies were bestowed upon nine men of the first *classis*. In the same year the control of the college was vested in a board of overseers by act of the general court. It consisted of the " Governor, Deputy Governor, Magistrates of the Jurisdiction, and the Teaching Elders of the six adjoining towns." This body was, however, found to be too large for practical purposes, and in 1650 an act was passed by which the college was made a corporation, consisting of the president, five fellows, and a treasurer or bursar, to have perpetual succession by the election of members to supply vacancies, and to be called by the name of " The President and Fellows of Harvard College." Their acts were, however, subject to the approval of the board of overseers, which was continued. In 1654 President Dunster, having publicly expressed himself as opposed to the baptism of infants, was sentenced to public admonition on lecture day, and forced to resign the presidency of the college. His remaining years were spent in Scituate as a preacher of the gospel; and upon his death, in 1659, his remains were carried back to Cambridge at his own request, and interred near the college which he had served so well. President Chauncey, who succeeded Dunster at the college, was a man of much training, sometime Professor of Greek at Trinity College, Cambridge, but since 1838 preacher at Plymouth and at Scituate. About to return to England in 1654, he was earnestly entreated by the general court to undertake the presidency of the college; and, having been promised an adequate salary, accepted.

Appendix C.

Pierce, (I) App. II.

The position he held until 1672, and his term of office Quincy, (I) Vol. I, p. 39. seems to have been a period of severe struggle for sufficient funds to keep the institution on its feet.

Of the general court, and the nature and degree of the patronage which the college received from it during the early years, justice and truth require us to speak in terms of respect and honor, although, in fact, the bounty and favor were only an intelligent self-interest in an institution with whose prosperity its own and that of the country were inseparably identified.

With respect to grants of money, the patronage of the general court during the first period certainly never exceeded, and there is no documentary evidence to show that it equalled, the annual payment of £100 until the year 1673. These payments, with the income of the ferry, were the only revenues of a permanent character which the institution possessed for the purposes of the president and officers.

In the sore straits in which the college found itself during President Chauncey's administration, the town of Portsmouth, New Hampshire, came to its aid in a manner which should bring gratitude to the heart of every Harvard alumnus, and indeed to that of every one who has an interest in higher education. In a letter addressed to the general court, and dated at Portsmouth, in May, 1667, the citizens of that town, after expressing their gratitude for the protection extended them by Massachusetts, say, that "although they had articled with them for the exemption of taxes, yet they had never articled with God and their own consciences for exemption from gratitude, which, while they were studying how to demonstrate, the loud groans of the college came to their ears, and hoping that their example might provoke the rest of the country to an holy emulation in so good a work, and the General Court itself, vigorously to act, for the diverting of the omen of calamity, which its destruction would be to New England," declare that a

Library
Sampson Technical Institute

voluntary collection had been taken among their inhabitants, which authorized the town to pledge the payment of "sixty pounds sterling a year for seven years ensuing to be improved by the Overseers of the college for the advancement of good literature there."

This generous example was followed by many, and measures were immediately adopted for systematically raising funds throughout the colony for a new building to take the place of the old wooden one, it being small and decayed. In consequence, however, of the Indian wars, then raging, the new "Harvard Hall" was not finished until 1677. This building stood till 1764, when it was destroyed by fire. With Chauncey ended the régime of foreign presidents, the institution having furnished its own since his day. His successor, Dr. Samuel Hoar, having taken his bachelor's degree in 1650, later going to England, where Cambridge granted him the Doctorate of Medicine, he returned to this country as an applicant for the presidency of his alma mater, bringing with him letters of recommendation from thirteen clergymen, and was successful in his candidacy. For some reason or other he seems to have lacked the good will of the student body from the very first, and his administration was not a particularly happy one.

In 1685 Rev. Cotton Mather was asked "to take special care of the government of the college, and for that end, to act as President of it." This he did for sixteen years, though a resident minister of Boston throughout practically the entire period.

The early presidents of the college must be regarded as men of unusual attainment for their time. Although the number of students for the first half-century was small, seldom, if ever, during that period exceeding twenty, to be the sole instructor for even so many was no light task, and there was no professor or tutor appointed until 1699.

In that year Henry Flint was appointed first tutor,

and held the position for fifty-four years. No professorship was established until 1721, when Edward Wiggles-
worth was made Hollis Professor of Divinity. During **P. 311.**
the greater part of the eighteenth century the college
was closely identified with the liberal movements, both
in politics and religion, and bore an important part in
the events which led up to the Revolution. In 1775 the
library and classes were removed to Concord, the college
halls given up to the use of the provincial army, and the
president's home occupied for a short while as Washington's headquarters. President Langdon, himself an
ardent patriot, served as chaplain to the troops on
numerous occasions, notably on the eve of the battle of
Bunker Hill. After the evacuation of Boston by the
British, the college resumed its sessions at Cambridge,
and maintained for the ensuing thirty years a high, but
hardly growing reputation, as a seat of learning. For
the latter part of the period the graduating classes aver-
aged about forty. Living salaries were provided for the
president and three professors; those of divinity, mathematics, and Oriental languages. Albert Gallatin, afterward Secretary of the United States Treasury, taught
French as an elective, receiving the fees as his pay. At
this time the first three years of the course were given
largely to Latin, Greek, and Hebrew, the freshmen adding arithmetic, the sophomores algebra and higher mathematics, and the juniors some natural science. The
senior year was given mainly to philosophy. All three
years had more or less oratory and history. In 1782
a medical department was founded with meagre endow- **P. 329.**
ments and scanty equipment, though not until 1831 was
the medical faculty regarded as distinct from the college.

The era of active and incessant growth may be said
to have begun with President Kirkland in 1810. Of
the large endowments, which now sustain numerous
professors and supply a means of support for many
students through scholarships and fellowships, and also

of the funds invested in buildings and grounds, almost the entire amount has accrued from private liberality.

The gifts of the colonial and provincial governments were scanty, and for temporary purposes, if we except the erection of a few buildings. The principal gift of the state of Massachusetts was $10,000 a year for ten years, voted in 1814. From a part of this fund the present University Hall was erected, which remains the chief enduring monument of state generosity.

Harvard and its Surroundings, Moses King.

Until 1865, Harvard was nominally under state control; but in that year a complete divorce took place through legislative action. Under it, bachelors of arts of five years' standing, elect each commencement day five members of the board, who hold office for six years. These need not even be residents of the state.

Thus, after many changes, the government of the University is no longer connected with either church or state, except that this general court of Massachusetts retains the power to allow it — a power, however, which the court does not seek to exercise without the consent of the University itself.

Official guide to Harvard, 1899.

At present, six degrees are awarded on recommendation of the Faculty of Arts and Sciences, the body to which is committed the administration of academic functions. The courses offered in the college — and there are more than five hundred — ordinarily lead to the degree of Bachelor of Arts after a four years' study, though a considerable percentage of the students attain it in less time. The courses in the Lawrence Scientific School lead to the degree of Bachelor of Science, while to properly qualified students in the Graduate School those of Master and Doctor of Arts and of Science are offered.

Six professional schools are administered by separate faculties.

Pp. 311-312.

The Divinity School, with a three years' course leading to the degree of Bachelor of Divinity.

The Law School, also offering a three years' course, P. 318. consisting of more than thirty subjects, with the degree of Bachelor of Laws.

The Medical School, with its building in Boston, offering about the same number of subjects, but requiring P. 329. four years for its completion and the attainment of the degree, Doctor of Medicine.

The Dental School, also in Boston, with a three years' course, leading to the Doctorate of Dental Medicine.

The School of Veterinary Medicine, leading to the appropriate degree in three years, also in Boston, to be discontinued.

The Bussey Institution, situated in Jamaica Plain, a school of Boston, at which a properly qualified student P. 363. may, after passing the required examination, obtain the degree of Bachelor of Agricultural Science. The courses cover scientific agriculture, landscape gardening, and chemistry and natural history as applied to those arts.

The growth of Harvard University, under the long administration of President Eliot, has been rapid and healthy, and it must probably be placed at the head of the higher institutions of learning in our country, not only in point of age but of general influence.

It had, in 1904, 5966 students registered in all departments, with a teaching force of 534. The library contained 607,100 volumes, by far the largest of any of our educational institutions, and ranking third in the country among libraries of all classes. It has graduated, since its foundation, 25,180 students, 14,662 of whom are still living, a veritable army of educated men. Its productive funds amount to $13,119,538. Radcliffe College, P. 442. the affiliated department for women, was incorporated with power to grant degrees in 1894.

Harvard offers 205 scholarships to undergraduates, the annual income from which is $47,755. There are also 41 fellowships in the graduate school, varying in value from $300 to $1000.

Besides these, about $2800 annually — the income of various gifts which the college has received from time to time — is turned over to deserving students, usually in sums not to exceed $50, and a loan fund makes available for student needs an equal sum in addition. In all, Harvard contributes annually nearly $80,000 to the support of its students.

William and Mary

Although the college of William and Mary, the second to be established in the colonies, has not been able to hold its own in point of student body, with most of its other early contemporaries, its intimate connection with colonial matters in Virginia, and its almost unequalled contribution of patriots to the cause of independence, places it in the very front rank of institutions of the anti-revolutionary times. The events leading up to the establishment of the college have already been given, extending back, at least in definite anticipation, to a time antedating by some years the establishment of Harvard. After all previous attempts to found a college in Virginia had come to nought, the colonial assembly conceived the fortunate idea of sending James Blair, a clergyman of high standing, to England to see what could be done there, both in the direction of securing a charter, and moneys for carrying out its privileges. Blair, who was a man of unusual ability, as shown both by the success of this mission and by his subsequent administration of the college, succeeded beyond all hope; he returned in 1693 with a charter signed by their Majesties, William and Mary, together with the snug little sum of £2000 "out of the rents," for the erection of buildings.

Seymore, the attorney-general for the Crown, vexed at what seemed to him the extravagance of their Majesties at a time when an expensive war was being waged and

Chapter I.

every cent needed, flew into a rage upon the presentation of the order for the money by Mr. Blair, telling
him that the funds were needed for "other and better
purposes" than the founding of a colonial college. Upon
the reply by Blair that "the people of Virginia had souls
to be saved," the irate custodian of the Crown's purse
is said to have given vent to the now historical exclama-
tion, "Souls! Damn your souls! Make *tobacco!*" In
spite, however, of the attorney-general, Blair came home
with both the charter and the money. This latter, with
£2500, and perhaps more, which had already been
subscribed by wealthy planters in Virginia, gave the
college, at its start, more wealth than Harvard had
seen during decades of struggle for existence, and freed
it from many of the problems which had been most
perplexing to the New England college. The charter
stated as objects of the college, "that the church of
Virginia may be furnished with a seminary of Ministers
of the Gospel, and that the youth may be properly educated in good manners, and that the Christian faith may
be propagated among the Western Indians to the glory
of Almighty God: to make, found and establish a certain place of universal study or perpetual college of
divinity, philosophy, languages and other good arts and
sciences." The officers were to consist of chancellor,
eighteen visitors or governors, a president or rector, and
six professors, who were to teach one hundred students.
The Bishop of London was appointed as first chancellor, for seven years, and Blair was "created and established first president of the college during his natural
life." Financially, the institution was well provided for
by the terms of the charter, for besides valuable lands,
it was to receive all fees from the surveyor-general's
office, and one penny per pound for all tobaccos exported
from Virginia and Maryland. In return for this munificence — for so it must have seemed when tidings of it
reached its elder brother in the Massachusetts colony —

was demanded one slight and fantastic service which serves to throw light on the ceremonialism of the times; it was that there should be delivered "to us and our successors *two copies of Latin verses yearly,* on every fifth day of November at the house of our Governor or Lieutenant-Governor for the time being." We are not aware that any important contribution to the literature of the period resulted from this demand; but that it was complied with for at least half a century is shown by an item which appeared in the *Virginia Gazette* as late as 1746. It runs: —

> "On this day Se'n night, being the 6th of November, the president, masters, and scholars of William and Mary College, went according to their annual custom in a body to the Governor's, to present his Honor with two copies of Latin verses in obedience to their charter. The President delivered the verses to his Honor, and two of the young gentlemen spoke them."

The site chosen for the college was Williamsburg, the colonial capitol, and the plans for the buildings which were eventually "to be an entire square" were drawn by Sir Christopher Wren. In 1705 the first building was destroyed by fire, together with its entire contents of books and apparatus. Of the course of study at William and Mary during its colonial history, we have but little record, but if "the proof of the pudding is in the eating," it must have been of the sort that makes men, for the story of its graduates is the story of leaders in the movement for independence.

Of eleven members of the Committee of Correspondence appointed by Virginia in 1773, six, including the chairman, Peyton Randolph, were from William and Mary; of the Committee of Safety appointed two years later, six out of eleven; of the thirty-one members of the committee reporting the Declaration of Rights, the chairman and ten others; out of the seven signers of the Declaration of Independence from Virginia, the draftsman of the paper, and four others. Of the thirty-three members of the Continental Congress from the state, the first president of that body and fifteen others were alumni.

Of seven Presidents of the United States born in Virginia, three, Jefferson, Monroe, and Tyler, — as well as John Marshall, the jurist, — were from the same classic halls; altogether a galaxy of men of national reputation not to be equalled in any alumni list of the size in the country; a fact due in part to the location of the college at the focus of patriotic enthusiasm.

In 1776 the first Greek letter fraternity, Phi Beta Kappa, now having chapters in fifty American colleges, and to which only the men (and women) of highest scholastic attainments are admitted, was founded at the college.

The influence of William and Mary remained prominent in Virginia until the time of the Civil War, although the University of Virginia had become a strong competitor for honors. During that conflict, the buildings were again burned and the work suspended, to be revived again after a cessation of hostilities. From that time it has held an honorable, though comparatively unimportant place in the rapidly increasing circle of higher institutions of learning in our country. In 1904 it had an enrolment of 165 students, a faculty of 13, and productive funds amounting to $133,500.

Yale College

Although a number of attempts had been made in the Connecticut Colony in the middle of the seventeenth century to found a college there, in connection with one of which a plot of ground was set apart for the purpose and with another, a fund raised which eventually went to Harvard, nothing was accomplished until 1701. Early in the summer of that year the Rev. James Pierpont, pastor of the New Haven church, a Harvard graduate of 1681, and Abraham Pierson (Harvard, 1668), becoming convinced that the time had come for the establishment of a second college in New England, entered into communication with other interested persons in southern Connecticut and brought about a meeting at Branford, the next town east of New Haven, in September, to consider the project. Tradition says that each appeared at the conference with one or more books which were given as a foundation for the new institution. At a subsequent meeting the details were considered; and on October 16 a charter was granted for a Collegiate School, by the legislature in session at New Haven.

Dexter, (I) p. 9.

A month later, seven of the trustees, established under the charter, met at Saybrook and voted to fix the school there, under the Rev. Mr. Pierson as rector. No student appeared until March, when Jacob Heminway offered himself. On the 16th of the following September commencement exercises were held in Saybrook, at which time the Master of Arts degree was conferred upon four young Harvard bachelors, and also upon Nathaniel Chauncy, who had been privately educated, and whose name leads the list of Yale graduates.

During the same month more students entered, and a tutor was appointed to assist in instruction.

With the exception of £120 in "country pay" from the colonial legislature, as promised by the charter, financial support was entirely from the tuition of the students, which was 30*s.* for undergraduates and 10*s.* for graduates. These did not warrant the rector's resigning his pastoral charge; so, until the date of his death in 1707, he resided in Killingworth.

For the next ten years it would be difficult to name the real seat of the college. The twenty-five or thirty students were scattered over a number of towns in the vicinity of New Haven. As President Hadley has facetiously put it: —

Eliot, (I) p. 47.

"Yale college was founded after a fashion, at the beginning of the last (eighteenth) century, along the north shore of Long Island Sound. For many years it was difficult to say what it was and where it belonged."

After the death of the first rector, — for so the highest officer was called, for fear that an institution of learning dignified with a president would attract notice in England, which would prejudice its charter, — Rev. Samuel Andrew was appointed to the position. He was pastor at Milford. The senior class went to him there, while the two lower classes remained at Saybrook, at first with but one, but later with two, tutors. Of the course of study at this period of Yale's history, we have some account from a letter written to President Stiles in the year 1779 by a graduate of the class of 1714.

"Books of the languages recited in my Day were Tully and Virgil, but without any notes: Burgersdicius and Ramur's *Logick*, also Hereford's *Set Logic*, etc., Pierson's *Manuscript of Physicks*. We recited the Greek Testament; knew not Homer; recited the Psalms in Hebrew; the greatest proficient in the Hebrew and in other languages was Dr. Johnson. We recited Ames's *Medulla* on Saturdays and also his *Cases of Conscience*; sometimes the two upper classes used to dispute syllogistically twice or thrice a week." Steiner, (1) p. 75.

During all these years, the college was without buildings of its own, and in 1716, when the question of erecting a permanent home came up, the colony itself was almost rent in twain by the fight which was waged. Three towns, Hartford, New Haven, and Saybrook, were openly in the field, while Wethersfield and Middletown entertained hopes, and the general assembly had great difficulty in settling the question, which they finally did in 1717, in favor of New Haven.

At about this time Elihu Yale began his bequests to the college, and eventually fixed it in history with his name. He was born in Boston in 1649, moved to England with his parents a few years later, entered the employ of the East India Company as a youth, *Yale.*

and returned to England in later life enormously wealthy, at least for the times. He seems not to have been a man of education nor refinement, as was the first great benefactor of the Massachusetts college; nevertheless, kindly disposed toward education in the colonies, he was induced, largely through the instrumentality of Cotton Mather, to come to the aid of the college in New Haven, which was especially impoverished through the building which was in process of construction. Just before the commencement season of 1718, Yale sent to Boston from England three bales of valuable goods to be sold for the college. There were besides, a portrait of George I, which the university still has, the royal coat of arms which was destroyed during the Revolution, and a case of books. The goods brought £562, which was immediately used in the college building. Of the gift, Steiner says: —

Steiner, (I) p. 81.

"It seems to us small in comparison with endowments to-day, but we must remember that the college received no greater gift from an individual for over a century and that the gift came at a critical time. Without this gift, the trustees could not have finished the building at once, and every moment of delay would have strengthened the Wethersfield faction. This gift crushed it forever."

Gov. E. Yale, p. 242.

Later in the same year more goods were sent over, from which £100 were realized, and at his death Yale bequeathed £500 to the college, but through some difficulty in probating the will, this was never received. With these benefactions, and £618 which had been received from a grant of land made by the general assembly in 1613, the college was in better condition financially than even the most sanguine of its early promoters could have hoped. The building, a wooden structure of three stories containing a chapel, dining room, a library, and twenty-two studies with adjoining bedrooms, was completed and occupied in 1719. It stood until the time of the Revolution, and is said to have had "an air of grandeur."

The remaining years of the Collegiate Institute, for so the college continued to be known until the granting of its charter as Yale College in 1745, comprise a period of slow progress and many internal dissensions of a religious nature. Of the inner life of the college at this time we have some record. Board in the commons cost about 5s. per week, tuition 50s. annually, and the fees at graduation about 40s. more. To gain admission students must "be found expert in both ye Greek and lattin Grammers, as also grammatically resolving both lattin and Greek authors and in making good and true lattin. Every student shall exercise himself in reading Holy Scriptures by himself day by day yt ye word of Christ may Dwell in Him ritchly."

Yale Annals, 346; Steiner, p. 91.

Students are to "avoid profane swearing, lying, needless asserveration, foolish garrulings, Chidings, strifes, railings, jestings, uncomly noise, spreading ill rumors, Divulging secrets, and all manner of troublesome and offensive behavior." "No undergraduate shall, upon pretense of Recreation or any excuse whatever" without permission "be absent from his study or appointed exercise in ye school, except Half an Hour att breakfast, and Half an Hour at Noon after dinner and after ye Evening Prayer till nine of ye clock."

Prayers were at 6 A.M. in summer and at sunrise in winter, and between 4 and 5 P.M. No student could be out of his room after 9 P.M., nor have "a light in his chamber after eleven nor before four in ye morning."

"All undergraduates except freshmen who shall read English into Greek, shall read some part of ye old testament out of Hebrew into Greek in ye morning and shall turn some part of ye new testament out of ye English or lattin into Greek att evening att ye time of Rescitation." In the freshman year on the "five first days of the week" were recitations in Greek and Hebrew, "onely beginning logick at ye latter end of ye year." Sophomores were occupied with "ye logick and with the

exercises of themselves with ye tongues." The juniors
studied principally " Phisicks " while the seniors labored
over "metaphysicks and mathematics, still carrying ye
former studies." The last days of the week were used
by all for " Rhetorick, oratory and divinity."

Berkeley.

In 1738 the trustees ruled that no student should be
admitted without the signature of some responsible person upon his bond for the payments of his dues, a provision still in force.

In 1731 Bishop Berkeley, then a resident of Rhode
Island, having despaired of his Bermuda project, became
interested in the college at New Haven; and upon returning to Europe, made a bequest of a number of
books. In a letter to Dr. Johnson, he said: —

"I have left a box of books to be given away by you. The Greek
and Latin books I would have given to such lads as you think will
make the best use of them, or to the school at New Haven."

Yale Annals,
p. 421.

Besides this, he made out a deed conveying his Rhode
Island farm of ninety-six acres to the college, the income
from the sale of which was to be devoted to "these scholars for their maintenance between first and second degree," the fund still being used for that purpose.

In 1745, nearly twenty-four years after the death of
its first great benefactor, a new charter was granted the
college, which formally changed its name to Yale College
in New Haven. By it, Rector Clap and the ten other
trustees then in office were constituted "an incorporate
society or body corporate and politic : and shall hereafter be known by the name of President and Fellows
of Yale College of New Haven," and were given the
power to appoint " a scribe or register, a treasurer, tutors,
professors, steward, and all other such officers and servants as are usually appointed in colleges and Universities " to " make, ordain and establish all such rules and
ordinances as they shall think proper for the instruction
and education of the students and the ordering, govern-

ing, ruling and arranging of the said college act, which shall be laid before this assembly as often as required and may also be repealed or disallowed by the assembly when they shall think proper." The charter also repealed all former grants of money from the state and appropriated £100 revenue annually. Three years later a second building was erected (1748), at first known as Connecticut Hall, later by the familiar title of South Middle. In 1763 a chapel was erected.

All during this period, and in fact until 1804, the so-called "Freshman Laws" were in force. These were a set of rules enforced by the student body itself, and resembling in many respects those of the fagging system in the great English public schools.

Among them we find : —

"A Freshman shall not play with any member of an upper class without being asked, nor is he permitted to use any acts of familiarity with them, even in study time." "Freshmen are obliged to perform all reasonable errands for any superior, always returning an account of the same to the person who sent them." "When a Freshman is near a gate or door belonging to College or College-Yard he shall look around and observe whether any of his superiors are coming to the same, and, if any are coming within three rods, he shall not enter without a signal to proceed." "Freshmen shall not run in college yard nor up and down stairs or call to any through a window." "It being the duty of Seniors to teach the Freshmen the laws and usages and customs of the college, to this end they are empowered to order the whole Freshman class or any member of it in order to be instructed or reproved at such time and place as they shall appoint, when and where every Freshman shall attend, answer all proper questions and behave decently."

All this sounds very queer to the modern freshman, yet some such system intelligently administered in many of our higher institutions of to-day might not be out of place. The value of a college education is due fully as much to college life as to classroom instruction, and the subtle something which makes the graduate of our older institutions, where ancient customs still persist, look back upon his college days with an almost increasing affection, comes largely from the former.

During the Revolutionary period the work of the college was again scattered. "Tutor Dwight" took some of the students to Wethersfield; Professor Story was asked to go to Glastonbury, and President Daggett was "to visit the different classes as often as he could with convenience."

With the inauguration of Timothy Dwight as president in 1795, Yale began a new era of prosperity. At that time the whole student body numbered only about one hundred, and the faculty consisted of the president, one professor, and three tutors. Dwight was, however, a man of unusual insight, which he manifested first and foremost through a building up and a strengthening of the faculty. Up to this time there had been little permanency in the teaching force. He conceived the idea of securing good men for the teaching positions and making them feel that their life-work was to be the building up of the hitherto struggling institution. In that he succeeded beyond all precedent, as the names of Benjamin Silliman, Jeremiah Day, and James Kingsley, each devoting more than fifty years to the service of the college, amply testify. With such a group of workers, it is no wonder that the succeeding generation of Yale graduates number many of the most famous men of the time.

Steiner, (I) pp. 145–146.

Travels, I, p. 175. President Dwight gives in his travels an outline of the course of study which shows marked improvement over that of a century before.

From this time the development of Yale was steadily in the direction of the great university which it is to-day. The name was changed to Yale University in 1886. In 1846 regular graduate courses of instruction were established, the first degrees being awarded in 1852. The

P. 352. Sheffield Scientific School, always what its name implies rather than a technical school, was founded in 1847 on a coördinate basis with the college.

Four professional schools are maintained: the Medical, the Theological, and the Legal, all established during President Timothy Dwight's administration, and the Art School in 1865.

P. 330.
P. 312.
P. 319.

In 1904, 2975 students were registered at Yale, doing work under an instructional force of 325. The library contained 365,000 volumes. It had graduated in its history 20,900 students, of whom 11,900 were still alive. Its productive funds amounted to $5,000,000.

Princeton College

The educational influences which led to the establishment of the College of New Jersey, later Princeton, may be traced to the famous Log College of William Tennent, pastor of Neshaminy; the religious influences, to the Presbyterian church, which throughout the middle colonies served as a more potent unifying factor among great classes of the people than did even loyalty to kings.

The Log College was unique in the history of American education. Tennent was an Irishman, born in 1673, graduated from Edinburgh in 1695, who came to America in 1716, and in 1727 was settled as pastor of a Presbyterian church, at what was known as the Forks of the Neshaminy. His high views of a liberal education, together with a desire to give its benefits to his sons, led him soon after his settlement to open a school of higher learning and of divinity. He built a log structure which, with Tennent himself, composed the entire plant and teaching force during the twenty years of the school's existence. George Whitfield, who visited Tennent, as he said in his journal, "at the place where young men study now," describes the school as follows:

P. 64.

"It is a log house about twenty feet long, and near as broad; and to me it resembled the school of the Hebrew prophets. From this despised place seven or eight ministers of Jesus have lately been sent forth, more are almost ready to be sent and a foundation is now being laid for the instruction of many others."

With the death of Tennent, some time in the '40's, the school went out of existence; and so completely has the Log College been effaced, that the exact site of the structure is not known.

It had, however, done two things: proved beyond a doubt that the church need not depend upon the old country for its ministers, and demonstrated that the machinery of a successful college need not be elaborate nor beyond the reach of the people. Neither one of these things was lost upon the stanch Presbyterians of East and West Jersey, and the college at Princeton was the result. Its birth was not an easy one, and the story of dissensions regarding charter and location is long. But in 1748 a charter was secured — the one under which, with but slight alteration, Princeton to-day is administered — and its work inaugurated, at Elizabethtown. Of the twenty-three first trustees, six were graduates of Yale, three of Harvard, and three received their training under Tennent at the Log College.

Murray, (I)
p. 212 *et seq.*

The first statement of entrance requirements shows that they did not differ materially from those of Harvard and Yale. The candidate must be able to render Virgil and Cicero's orations into English; translate English into true and grammatical Latin; translate the gospels into Latin or English, and give the grammatical construction of the words. The curriculum was in harmony with the standard of admission; Latin and Greek, and mathematics were studied throughout the entire course. Physical science was represented by natural philosophy and astronomy; logic was studied with a text-book, and its practice secured by discussions. Rhetoric was taught in the same way, and essays and declamations were required; mental and moral philosophy were prominent studies of the higher classes.

From a letter, written in 1750, by a member of the freshman class, we get some idea of the daily programme of studies: —

"But I must give you an account of my studies at the present time. At seven in the morning we recite to the president, lessons in the works of Xenophon in Greek, and in Watts' *Ontology*. The rest of the morning, until dinner time, we study Cicero's *De Oratore* and the Hebrew grammar, and recite our lessons to Mr. Sherman, the college tutor. The remaining part of the day we spend in the study of Xenophon and ontology to recite the next morning. And, besides these things, we dispute once every week after the syllogistic method; — and now and then learn geography."

As was the case with so many of the colonial colleges, the place of permanent location remained a matter of controversy until the time came to erect a building. With the college of New Jersey, this was in 1751.

In May of that year the trustees selected New Brunswick, "Provided the citizens of the place secure to the college £1000 in proclamation money, ten acres for a college campus, and two hundred acres of good land not more than three miles from the town."

The town of Princeton, however, bestirred itself, agreed to exceed the demands, and in 1752 was finally chosen. Two years later the present Nassau Hall was begun, and finished in 1757, being at the time the finest edifice of any character in the colonies, and remaining to-day one of the most venerable and imposing of all our myriad of college buildings. Twice since its erection, in 1802 and in 1855, its interior has been destroyed by fire, but the honest workmanship of its first builders has preserved it in external appearance as it came from the masons. The money required for its construction was raised largely by subscription; about £2000 in England and Ireland, and £400 in the provinces.

The building was first occupied in 1756, opening with seventy students, while at the first commencement at

Princeton, twenty-two were graduated. During the following year Rev. Jonathan Edwards was chosen president, but died within two months of his installation. Although this was by far the shortest presidential term, frequent changes in the executive office had been the rule, and when, in 1768, John Witherspoon was installed president, he was the sixth in a little more than twenty years. His administration was notable both for its length (closed in 1794) and for the important chapters in American history which it helped to write, for no other of our colleges has ever in its history been so intimately associated with national events of the first importance as was Princeton during Witherspoon's presidency. Situated as it was in the geographical centre of the colonies, near the seat of the Continental Congress, it was closely in touch with every move toward colonial freedom, and early became an intellectual breeding-place for patriots. This was undoubtedly due, in part, to two societies, the Well Meaning and the Plain Dealing Clubs, out of which later grew the present Cliosophic and American Whig societies, which as early as 1764 had fought out in mimic on their respective platforms the political problems which were now to be settled on the battlefield. Witherspoon himself was an ardent patriot, besides being a man of great reputation as a teacher and philosopher; and his reputation soon Eliot, (I) p. 200. helped the college into a position of prominence which it had not before occupied. The teaching force increased, endowments were secured, and a larger body of students was attracted and were drawn from a wider territory. Of the relation of Princeton and its venerable Nassau Hall to the political events of the time, Professor Sloan has written: —

"When first completed it (Nassau) was visited by travellers as the largest building then in the colonies. Within the walls of this now venerable and stately pile were quartered the troops of contending British and Americans in the Revolutionary War. The

Continental Congress used it for their sittings when driven from Philadelphia, and adjourned in 1783 to attend the college commencement
in a body. Its walls still bear the imprints of cannon balls used in
the battle of Princeton, and on them hangs a portrait of Washington,
painted by Peale. It was paid for by the money given as a personal
gift by the former for the use of the building by his troops, and fills
a frame which once contained an effigy of George II. Nine signers
of the Declaration of Independence frequented its halls — two were
graduates and three were officers of the corporation which controlled
it — and its windows blazed with light in a grand illumination when
the news of the signing reached the town. Aaron Burr studied in
its classroom ; and his body was borne from its walls to a neighboring
churchyard."

The funds of the college, as well as its buildings,
suffered greatly during the Revolutionary period. Its
library was scattered, its apparatus destroyed, and the
state of New Jersey appropriated the sum of £600
annually for three years for their restoration, an act
which must be considered more in the light of the payment for debt than as a donation. The student body
was gradually increasing, and in 1806 had reached the
number of 200, with a graduating class of 54. The
faculty consisted of a president, four professors, three
tutors, and an instructor in French.

Somewhat later, the college passed through a period
of depression, when less than 75 students were in attendance; but from the year 1830 or thereabouts, there has
been a steady, though at no time a very rapid, increase.
During its later history Princeton has had many noted
men at its head, among whom Dr. McCosh (1868–1888)
perhaps stands at the head. Of his administration we
find the following minutes of faculty action taken at his
death in 1894 : —

Murray, (I)
p. 271.

"The results of his presidency have made a new epoch in our
history. The college has virtually become a university. Its faculty
has been trebled in numbers. Its alumni and friends have rallied
around it with new loyalty. Munificent gifts have poured into its
treasury. Schools of science, of philosophy, of art, of civil and electrical engineering have been founded with endowed professorships;

fellowships, and prizes, and an ample equipment of libraries, numerous laboratories, chapels, dormitories, academic halls, and athletic grounds and buildings. We live among architectural monuments of his energy which other college generations after us will continue to admire."

310.

Princeton has no professional schools, though the Theological Seminary, a separate corporation, is closely affiliated with it. It has always stood for conservatism in matters of instruction, and its courses are less elastic than are those of most of the great universities.

In 1904, 1565 students were enrolled. The faculty numbered 108. It has an alumni list of 8733, of whom 5023 are living. The number of scholarships yielding free tuition is about 80, while 12 graduate-fellowships are maintained. In addition to these, about $3500 is annually distributed through prizes and medals as an inspiration to earnest, scholarly endeavor.

The University of Pennsylvania

Franklin.

In 1749 Benjamin Franklin issued from his press in Philadelphia a little pamphlet entitled "Proposals Relating to the Education of Youth in Pennsylvania." This proved the centre of crystallization about which interest in such matters took form. There had already been maintained in Philadelphia for nine years a charity school for the education of poor children in the elementary branches; but as yet no dignified attempt at higher instruction.

Franklin's pamphlet aroused considerable interest, especially voicing the opinions of large numbers of the thrifty Quakers, since what it proposed was an academy where the study of English should be a prominent feature, asserting that "the time spent in that study [Latin and Greek] might be much better employed in the education for such a country as ours." As a result, a board of twenty-four interested persons was selected, with

Franklin at their head, to organize a school. A considerable sum of money was raised by means of lotteries, private subscriptions, and appropriations from the common council, and instruction began on January 7, 1751. The academy, as organized, was composed of three schools: the Latin, the English, and the mathematical; but in spite of Franklin's sentiments, educational conservatism ruled the board of control, and all, save the former, were allowed to languish. In 1754 a charter was granted the school, and another in 1755, designating the institution as "the College, Academy, and Charitable School of Philadelphia," and carrying with it the customary privileges of granting degrees. The first commencement was held in 1757, with a graduating class of seven. In 1756 a course of study was arranged by the president, covering three years, and comprised readings in Juvenal, Livy, Cicero, Horace, Quintilian, and the Tusculan Questions; the Iliad, Thucydides, Epictetus, and Plato's *De Legibus* formed the work in Greek. Mathematics occupied a prominent place in the course of study, and during the last two years considerable work was done in natural philosophy, chemistry, hydrostatics, prismatics, optics, and astronomy. Ethics and politics, natural and civil law, formed a group of subjects to which more than the usual attention was given. It is perhaps safe to say that no American college was, up to the time of the Revolution, offering courses more liberalizing in their influence than the College of Philadelphia. In 1765 it established a medical department, the first in the country. The Revolutionary P. 328. period was one of sore trial to the institution. Work had to be suspended, its property depreciated, its funds were reduced, but more than all, the general assembly began to interfere with its affairs, and in 1779 took away its charter for various alleged infractions and created a new corporation to be known as "The Trustees of the University of the State of Pennsylvania."

The move was not a success. Public sentiment was with the old college, and in 1789 it was again reëstablished under its former president. There was, however, no field for two rival institutions and in 1791 the college and the university were united, creating the present corporation known as "The Trustees of the University of Pennsylvania." There can be no doubt that the legislative act of 1779 was a severe blow to the cause of higher education in Philadelphia; and it is doubtful whether the university has ever attained as high a relative rank among the higher institutions of our country as the "college" held previous to it.

P. 317.

In the new university there were, besides the Charitable School which was still maintained, three departments, viz.: Arts, Law, and Medicine; the second, as well as the third, being the first of its kind in America. The department of Arts comprised five schools: Philosophy, Grammar, Mathematics, English, and German. In 1810 this plan of organization was abolished. For nearly three-quarters of the nineteenth century the university hardly kept pace with the times. In the college, the course of study was narrowly prescribed, differing but little, in fact, from that laid down in 1756 by President Smith. In all that time, too, it had received only one comparatively small financial bequest. In 1866, however, the curriculum was broadened, elective courses introduced, and the whole course of study materially strengthened. Four years later the present site of the university was secured from the city, buildings erected, and an era of unprecedented prosperity begun. The Towne Scientific School was organized in 1874.

P. 353.

The University of Pennsylvania is in no sense a state university, as are those established under the land grant of 1862. Although in the terms of the final charter the governor of the state must be *ex officio* a member of the board of trustees, and an annual statement of accounts should be laid before the legislature, Pennsylvania has not been more generous in its support than many other states to private institutions within their borders.

The entire state contributions, other than those equally shared by other colleges, consist of an appropriation in 1872 of $100,000 contingent upon the raising of $250,000 by private means, the whole to be used in the erection of a hospital, containing not less than 200 free beds; another $100,000 the next year on a similar basis ($100,000 to be raised), and one in 1889 of $12,500 for a veterinary hospital with the provision that twelve scholarships to be filled by the governor be maintained.

As at present organized, the university includes the following departments: (1) The college, offering courses in the School of Arts and Science, in (*a*) arts and science, (*b*) finance and economy, (*c*) biology, (*d*) music; and, in the Towne Scientific School in (*a*) architecture, (*b*) science and technology, (*c*) mechanical and electrical engineering, (*d*) civil engineering, (*e*) chemistry, and (*f*) chemical engineering; (2) The Graduate School; (3) The Department of Law; (4) of Medicine; (5) of Veterinary Medicine; (6) of Archæology; (7) of Physical Education; (8) of Dentistry; (9) The University Hospital; (10) The Wistar Institute of Anatomy and Biology; (11) The Laboratory of Hygiene; (12) The Veterinary Hospital; (13) The University Library; (14) The Flower Astronomical Observatory.

In 1904 there were about 2500 students enrolled under a faculty of 290. The library contained 225,000 volumes, Nearly 100 scholarships in the college are available, though many of them only to residents of Philadelphia, besides upward of 25 fellowships in the various graduate schools.

Columbia College

In the *New York Mercury* for May 31, 1754, appeared the following: —

" To such Parents as have now (or expect to have) children prepared to be educated in the College of New York.

" I. The Gentlemen who are appointed by the Assembly, to the
Trustees of the intended Seminary or College of *New York* have
thought fit to appoint me to take Charge of it, and have concluded to
set up a Course of Tuition in the learned languages and in the liberal
Arts and Sciences ; they have judged it advisable that I should publish this *Advertisement*, to inform such as have Children ready for a
College Education, that it is proposed to begin Tuition upon the
first Day of *July* next, at the *Vestry Room* in the new School-House
adjoining to Trinity Church in *New York*, which the Gentlemen
of the Vestry are so good as to favor them with the Use of in the
Interim, till a convenient Place may be built.

" II. The lowest Qualifications they have judged requisite in order
to Admission to said College are as follows, viz. That they be able
to read well and write a good legible Hand and that they be well
versed in the five first rules in *Arithmetic*, *i.e.* as far as *Division* and
Reduction : And as to *Latin* and *Greek* that they have a good
knowledge of the *Grammars*, and be able to make grammatical
Latin : and both in construing and parsing to give a good legible
. . . [one line illegible] of *Tully* and of the first books of *Virgil's
Anead*, and some of the first Chapters of the Gospel of St. John in
Greek. . . . In these books then, they may expect to be examined ;
but higher Qualifications must hereafter be expected. . . . And if
there be any of the higher classes in any college, or under private
instruction that incline to come hither, they may expect Admission
to proportionally higher Classes here.

" III. And that people may be better satisfied in sending their
Children for Education to this College, it is to be understood, That
as to Religion, there is no Intention to impose upon the Scholars,
the peculiar Tenets of any particular Sect of Christians, but to incul-
cate upon their tender Minds, the Great Principles of Christianity
and Morality in which true Christians of each Denomination are
generally agreed. And as to the daily Worship in the College,
Morning and Evening, it is proposed that it ordinarily consist of
such a Collection of Lessons, Prayers and Praises of the Liturgy
of the Church as are for the most Part, taken out of the Holy Scriptures, and such as are agreed on by the Trustees to be in the best
manner expressions of our Common Christianity. . . .

" And as to any peculiar Tenets every one is left to judge freely
for himself and to be required only to attend such Places of Worship
on the Lord's Day, as their Parents or Guardians shall think fit to
order or permit.

" IV. The chief Thing that is aimed at in this College, is, to
teach and engage the Children *to know God in Jesus Christ*, and to

love and serve him in all *Sobriety, Godliness,* and *Richness* of Life, with a perfect Heart and a willing Mind: and to train them up in all Virtuous Habits, an all such useful Knowledge as may render them creditable to their Families and Friends, Ornaments to their Country, and useful to the Public Weal in their generation. . . . To which good Purposes it is earnestly desired that their Parents, Guardians and Masters would train them up from their Cradles, under Strict Government, and in all Seriousness, Virtue, and Industry, that they be qualified to make orderly and tractable Members of this Society. And above all, that in order hereunto, they be very careful themselves to set them good Examples of true Piety and Virtue in their own conduct. . . . For as examples have a very powerful Influence over young Minds, and especially, those of their Parents, in vain are they Solicitous for a good Education for their Children if they themselves set before them Examples of Impiety or Profaneness, or of any sort of Vice whatsoever.

Vth and lastly, A *serious, virtuous* and *industrious* Course of Life being first provided for, it is further the Design of this College to instruct and perfect the youth in the learned languages, and in the Arts of *Reasoning* exactly, of *Writing* correctly and *Speaking* eloquently, and in the Arts of *Numbering* and *Measuring,* of *Surveying* and *Navigation,* of *Geography* and *History,* of *Husbandry Commerce* and *Government* : And in the Knowledge of *all Nature* in the *Heavens* above us and in the *Air, Water* and *Earth* around us, and the various kinds of *Meteors, Stones, Mines* and *Minerals, Plants* and Animals, and of everything *useful* for the comfort, the Convenience and elegance of Life in the chief Manufactures, finally to lead them from the study of Nature to the Knowledge of Themselves, and of the God of Nature, and their Duty to him, themselves and one another. And every Thing that can contribute to their true Happiness, both here and hereafter.

This much, *Gentlemen* it is thought proper to advertise you of, concerning the Nature and Design of this college. And I pray God, that it may be attended with all the Success you can wish, for the best good of the rising Generation, to which, while I continue here, I shall willingly contribute my Endeavors to the utmost of my powers, Who am,

> " *Your real friend*
> *and most humble servant*

> " Samuel Johnson.

" N.B. The Charge of the Tuition is established by the Trustees to be only *Twenty-five Shillings* for each Quarter."

Such was the antenatal statement of our Columbia University, setting forth so well, not only the undefined hopes, but the formulated plans, that I have printed it in full. In the same issue of the *Mercury* is still another advertisement bearing upon the new educational project. It is headed " Public Lottery," and states that such will be held as "a further provision toward founding a college for the advancement of learning within the colony, to consist of 5000 tickets at 30 shillings each, 832 of which are to be fortunate." Later in the same year a charter incorporating "the governors of the College of the Province of New York in the city of New York in America," and providing for the establishment of King's College, was granted by George II, and the actual work of instruction begun in the vestry room of Trinity Church. During the following year a tract of land "in the skirts of the city," though taxing the imagination of a modern New Yorker when he learns that it was bounded by Church, Barclay, and Murray streets, was granted the college. A little later a building 30 feet wide and 180 feet long was erected, and occupied for more than a century. Of it Professor Matthews says : —

Eliot, (I) *Four Great Universities.*

" Here Alexander Hamilton and John Jay and Gouverneur Morris laid the foundation of their knowledge. Here the college was revived after the Revolution — King's College no longer, but Columbia — the first use of the name of Columbus in connection with any of the institutions of the continent which he had discovered. Here was worthily continued the tradition of Hamilton and Jay. Here the new college graduated De Witt Clinton and Hamilton Fish, who saw the city — which had had only ten thousand inhabitants when the first class of freshmen met — grow steadily until its population had increased fifty-fold in the space of a century."

For the first year of the college's existence the president was the sole member of the teaching force. With the entrance of the second class his son was appointed tutor ; but for a number of years the faculty did not exceed three. The first commencement was held in 1758, at which time eight bachelor's degrees were conferred and twelve master's, upon graduates of other institutions. In 1767 a medical department was established.

During the Revolutionary period the college building P. 329. was converted into a hospital, the apparatus and books stored, the faculty dispersed, and work practically suspended, though it would seem that some instruction continued to be offered, as we find the record of two students who matriculated in 1777.

Six months, however, after the British evacuated New York "an act for granting certain privileges to the college hitherto known as King's College for altering the name and charter thereof, and erecting a University within the state" was passed by the legislature, and in 1787 a new charter was granted, similar to the old one, but changing the name to Columbia College. The first trustees were all chosen from the board of regents of the State University; and though the institution was an independent corporation, the state made frequent appropriations for its support. In 1809 the requirements for admission to the college were materially stiffened, and the course of study made to include in the freshman year, Cicero's *Letters to Atticus*, Sallust entire, Horace's *Satires*, Dalzel's *Collectanea Majora*, Xenophon's *Memorabilia*, Kent's *Lucian*, double translation Latin verse, Roman antiquities, Euclid's *Elements*, geography, English grammar and reading, English composition and declamation.

The sophomore class read Virgil's *Georgics*, Livy, the *Odes* and *Epistles* of Horace, Demosthenes, Homer, and Herodotus. They continued double translation and Latin composition in prose and verse, also Roman antiquities. In mathematics they took up plane trigonometry and its application, and algebra. They studied geography, elements of rhetoric, English composition, and declamation in English and Latin.

In the junior class were read Cicero on Oratory, Terence, Quintilian, Longinus, and Sophocles. The class also reviewed Horace, Greek and Latin antiquities, and took up Greek composition. English composition was continued with criticism, and the student was required to declaim pieces of his own composition. History and chronology were added to geography and mathematics. Spherical trigonometry and conic sections were taken up. The important studies of this year were natural philosophy and elements of ethics.

In the senior year, to a continuation and review of the subjects formerly pursued, were added astronomy, fluctuation, analysis of intellectual powers, principles of reasoning, and the law of realms and nations. This course remained in practice until 1836, when it was much broadened, and a scientific and literary course added.

In 1857 the college had outgrown its site and moved to the corner of Madison Avenue and 49th Street — a location which at the time was as truly " in the skirts of the city " as the old one had been a century and more before. There it remained for forty years, until it removed to its present magnificent and probably permanent home on Morningside Heights, between 114th and 120th streets. In addition to the medical school, organized in 1767, made independent in 1814 as the College of Physicians and Surgeons, reannexed in 1860, and fully reincorporated as a department of medicine in 1891, are several other professional departments, some of which outnumber in point of students the college itself.

P. 318.

In 1858 the Law School was fully organized, though as far back as 1798 a professorship of law had been established, with James Kent as its incumbent; and it was to Columbia students that his commentaries on American law were first delivered as lectures.

In 1864 the School of Mines was established, and in 1880 that of Political Science.

The latest addition along professional lines was the P. 389.
final incorporation of the Teachers' College, independently organized in 1888, though under a loose affiliation with Columbia, as a professional school for teachers till 1898. The School of Journalism, already announced, though not yet organized, will probably be the next.

In 1889 Barnard College, for women, was affiliated P. 441.
with Columbia very much as Radcliffe College is with Harvard. In 1900 it was, however, incorporated as an undergraduate department for women, instruction being in separate classes, for the most part for undergraduates, though both sexes work together in the graduate school. P. 442.
The latter, which is, strictly speaking, the university, is a very important feature of the Columbia organization, having, in 1902, 609 students registered as candidates for higher degrees. In 1904 the total registration in all the schools and colleges of Columbia was 4512, under a teaching force of 576. The library contained 346,354 volumes. The institution had graduated 16,490 students in the course of its history, and possessed productive funds amounting to $15,026,756.

More than seventy scholarships, for the most part equal to the tuition, are open under various restrictions to the undergraduates of Columbia, and five to those of Barnard College. A considerable amount of money, too, is available for various prizes. In addition to these are upwards of twenty-five fellowships open to graduate students, each of a net value of $500.

Brown University

Brown University, at Providence, Rhode Island, was the sixth higher institution of learning to be founded during colonial times. It was established by the Baptists. In 1762 the Philadelphia Baptist Association, taking cognizance of the difficulties of students of their faith in most of the American colleges, entertained the proposal of Rev. Morgan Edwards, a Philadelphia clergyman, to found, in the colony of Rhode Island, the land of religious freedom, a college to be under the control of their own denomination. James Manning, a graduate of Princeton of the same year, was appointed by the association as its agent to establish "a seminary of polite literature, subject to the government of the Baptists."

In 1764 the friends of the movement obtained from the general assembly a charter for the "College or University in the English colony of Rhode Island in Providence Plantation in New England in America. The trustees and fellows at any time hereafter, giving such more particular name to the college in honor of the greatest and most distinguished benefactor, or otherwise as they see fit."

The charter stated that the corporation should consist of two branches, viz. trustees and fellows, of whom there should be thirty-six in the former and twelve in the latter body. Denominational qualifications were also prescribed; and though the president must always be a Baptist, the three important positions of chancellor, secretary, and treasurer are without religious limitations. The corporation is self-perpetuating, but since 1874 has been filled from nominations made by the alumni. The religious attitude of the university is clearly shown by the following clause in the charter : —

"Furthermore it is hereby enacted and declared: That into the liberal and Catholic institution shall never be admitted any religious tests. But on the contrary all members hereof shall forever enjoy full, free, absolute, and uninterrupted liberty of conscience."

The college at its start, being without funds and unable to support the president, Dr. Manning accepted the pastorate of the Baptist Church at Warren, meanwhile opening a Latin school, which was later moved to Providence, and flourished for more than a century and a quarter. In 1765 instruction of a higher grade was begun, and four years later the first class of seven members was graduated. A tutor was appointed at the beginning of the collegiate work, and no other addition to the faculty until 1774.

Warren had not been looked upon as a permanent seat of the college, and the necessity which had arisen of erecting a college building gave rise to a controversy between various towns of the state for its possession. Final settlement was made in 1770 through its removal to Providence and the erection of University Hall, modelled after Nassau at Princeton, which still remains one of the principal centres of student activity.

In 1776 the work of the college was interrupted by the Revolutionary War, and was not resumed until 1782, University Hall meanwhile being used as a barrack and hospital for the colonial American and French troops.

In 1791, after twenty-nine years of service, President Manning died. At this time the faculty consisted of the president, four professors, and two tutors. The first college funds, amounting to $4500, were collected in England and Ireland by Rev. Morgan Edwards in 1767–1768. During the next two years subscriptions to the amount of $2500 were raised in the South. The former contribution was made a permanent fund; the latter devoted to the construction of buildings. Further gifts were received from the Philadelphia, the Charleston, and the Warren Baptist associations, but they appear to have ceased with the outburst of the Revolutionary War.

President Manning was succeeded in office by Rev. Jonathan Maxey, who resigned in 1802 to accept the presidency of Union College, and was followed by Rev. Asa Messer, Professor of Mathematics and Natural Philosophy in the college, who served for twenty-four years. During his administration a medical school was established and maintained for seventeen years (1811–

1828), but was then discontinued. In 1804 the corporation availed themselves of their chartered rights to give
the college some more definite name, by formally calling
it " Brown University " after Nicholas Brown, an alum-
Brown.   nus, and the first of a distinguished line of benefactors.

Francis Wayland, the fourth president, entered upon
his official duties in 1827. He at once raised the standard of scholarship, and gradually increased the scope of
the instruction. He finally accomplished an entire reorganization of the university on the basis of the elective
principle. In accordance with this " New system " the
bachelor's degree was given for a three years' course,
and the master's degree was given for a four years'
course. Graduate study and special study were both
encouraged ; and the sciences, in accordance with the
spirit of the charter, were made prominent in the curriculum. This system was not put into operation until
1850, and was not fully in force until President Wayland's
retirement, five years later. At the close of his administration in 1855, the university had twenty departments of instruction which, with the years of their
establishment, were as follows : —

Professor of languages and other branches of learning, 1765 ; natural philosophy, 1769 ; law, 1790 (never
taught); natural history, 1784 ; mathematics and astronomy, 1786 ; materia medica and botany, 1811 ; anatomy
and surgery, 1811 ; chemistry, 1811 ; theory and practice of medicine, 1815 (last four discontinued); moral
philosophy and metaphysics, 1811 ; oratory and belles-
lettres, 1815 ; Latin, Greek, 1825. Progress during President Wayland's administration is clearly shown by the
following list of subjects, to which professors or instructors were assigned at the dates annexed : chemistry,
physiology, and geology, 1834 ; moral and intellectual
philosophy, 1834 ; belles-lettres, 1835 ; rhetoric, 1837 ;
Hebrew literature, 1838 ; modern languages and literature, 1843 ; Greek, 1843 ; Latin, 1844 ; French, 1844 ;

history and political economy, 1850; natural philosophy and civil engineering, 1850; chemistry applied to the arts, 1850; rhetoric and English literature, 1851; didactics (*i.e.* pedagogy), 1851; analytical chemistry, 1854.

Since 1855, five men, Revs. Barnas Sears (1855–1867), Alexis Casswell (1867–1871), Ezekiel Gilman Robinson (1871–1889), Elisha Benjamin Andrews (1889–1899), and William Herbert Perry Faunce (1899–   ) (present occupant), have successively occupied the president's chair, and under their direction the university has shown a steady, and in some cases, a rapid growth. More than twenty buildings have been erected upon the campus, or are in process of construction, some of which are among the finest types of American college architecture.

In 1904 the student enrolment was 854, the teaching force 79; volumes in the library 130,000. Six thousand students have been graduated, of whom 2940 are living. About 100 scholarships are open to undergraduates, varying in value from $60 to three or four times that amount, and two fellowships in the graduate departments, each of the income from $10,000.

There are also special aid and loan funds available for students needing temporary financial support.

Rutgers College

The charter under which Queen's College, now Rutgers, at New Brunswick, New Jersey, was founded and is still maintained, was granted in 1766, to the Dutch Reformed Church. A previous charter had been granted, but not used, owing, it is said, to a stated requirement within it that the Dutch language be exclusively used in the college. Whether this was so or not is not certain, but in the second charter is the article : —

"Provided also, that all minutes of the meetings . . . and all regulations relating to the government of the said college, and all accounts relating to the receipts and payments of money shall be made in the English language and no other."

The first meeting of the trustees under the amended charter was held in Hackensack, in 1771, and a spirited contest between that town and New Brunswick carried on for the location of the college, which was finally won by the latter. There seems to have been no president appointed until 1786, though Frederick Frelinghuysen, son of General Frelinghuysen of Revolutionary fame, had been for some years acting as tutor.

During the troublous times from 1776 to 1783 the college made frequent moves from scenes of active hostility, and for a while carried on its work on the Raritan, as is shown by this item, appearing in the *New Jersey Gazette* for January 4, 1779.

"The faculty of Queen's college take this method to inform the public that the business of said college is still carried on at the north Branch of Raritan in the county of Somerset, where good accomodations for young gentlemen may be had in respectable families at as moderate prices as in any part of the state. This neighborhood is so far distant from headquarters that not any of the troops are stationed here, neither does the army in an way interfere with the business of the college. The faculty also take the liberty to remind the public that the representatives of the state have enacted a law by which students at college are exempted from military duty."

The faculty, so far as we are able to discover, consisted of John Taylor, who succeeded Frelinghuysen and continued to hold the important office until 1795, when he became a professor at Union College. In that year the college was closed, and remained so until 1807. Since that time it has had a continued existence of usefulness, though it has never figured among the larger institutions of learning, so far as number of students is concerned. Although originally intended as a fitting school for the ministry of the Dutch Reformed Church, an independent divinity school was established by the

P. 309.

denomination, and the courses have always been those usually found at the smaller academic institutions. By its charter its president and two-thirds of its trustees must be members of that church, though no religious test is required of the students.

In 1904, 226 students were enrolled under a faculty of 28. It had graduated 2126 students, of whom 1236 were still living.

Dartmouth College

Dartmouth College, the latest of the colonial institutions of higher learning to be established, was the outgrowth of an educational attempt to Christianize the Indians, made by Rev. Eleazer Wheelock at his home in Lebanon, Connecticut, in the year 1754. Beginning with two Indian boys, in ten years the number of pupils had increased to thirty, a considerable number of whom were sons of the white colonists. The school attracted considerable attention, and received financial aid both from the assemblies of Massachusetts and New Hampshire, while that of Connecticut recommended contributions from the congregations throughout the colony. In honor of Joshua Moor, a farmer of Mansfield, who made a donation of a house and two acres of land, the institution was called Moor's Indian Charity School, which it in fact still remains on paper, the president and trustees of Dartmouth College holding similar titles in the school, though no actual instruction has been given by the latter since 1849.

In 1763 Wheelock, believing that his school, in order to fulfil best its primary function of educating the Indian, should follow the frontier, cast about for a favorable location in closer touch with Indian settlements. He wrote first to Governor Amherst of Virginia, but receiving no reply, made it known that he was willing to receive offers of land and money from any favorably situated community. These came from all along the New England frontier: Hebron, Connecticut; Pittsfield and Stockbridge, Massachusetts; Chester, Vermont; Harrisburg, New York; and several New Hampshire towns; each offered inducements of land and money. Finally the town of Hanover, New Hampshire, was fixed upon by Wheelock for reasons as follows:—

"It is most central on the river [Connecticut], and most convenient for transportation up and down the river: has convenient communication with Crown Point and Lake Champlain, being less than 60 miles to the former and 140 to the latter, and water-carriage to each, excepting about 30 miles (as they say) and will be upon the road which must soon be opened from Portsmouth and Crown Point and within a mile of the only convenient place for a bridge across said river. The situation is on a beautiful plain: the soil fertile and easy of cultivation. The tract on which the college is fixed, lying mostly in one body and convenient for improvement in the towns of Hanover and Lebanon (N.H.)."

He also adds:—

"There are in this vicinity, in this part of the country which is now settling, more than 200 towns already chartered, settled, or settling, which do, or soon will want goodly ministers."

Dr. Wheelock, just previous to the selection of a site, had procured from George III a charter, a masterpiece of its kind, allowing him to dignify his institution with the title "College," and as a recognition of the aid which Lord Dartmouth had given in the raising of funds in England, it was named after him. In 1770 work was begun upon the new site, an area of six acres cleared of timber and log structures erected.

The hardships and disappointment connected with these first years in the wilderness were so great that nothing but the indomitable perseverance of Wheelock would have brought success; yet before his death in 1779 he had the gratification of seeing seventy-two students graduate and take prominent part in colonial affairs. The War of the Revolution had dispersed his

Bush, p. 142.

Annals, Dartmouth catalogues.

Indian students, and such have only been represented since by an occasional straggler.

We have no exact statement of the course of study for the earliest years of the college, but it seemingly differed but slightly from those of Harvard and Yale, since there were occasional interchanges of students. During Dr. Wheelock's administration there were, upon the faculty, besides himself, two tutors. At his death his son, Dr. John Wheelock, was appointed to the presidency, which he held for thirty-six years. In 1796 candidates for the freshman class "must be versed in Virgil, Cicero's *Select Orations*, the Greek Testament, be able accurately to translate English into Latin, and also understand the fundamental rules of Arithmetic." The course of study for the same year was also stated as follows: —

"The freshman class study the Latin and Greek classics, arithmetic, English grammar and rhetoric. The sophomore class study the Latin and Greek classics, logic, geography, arithmetic, geometry, trigonometry, algebra, conic sections, surveying, belles-lettres and criticism. The junior class studies the Greek and Latin classics, geometry, natural and moral philosophy, and astronomy. The senior class reads metaphysics, theology, and natural and political law. The study of the Hebrew and other oriental languages as also the French language is recommended to the student." Bush, p. 148.

Declamations, orations, and other compositions were regularly required, and it was further stated "that the President attends morning and evening prayers with the students in the chapel, and often delivers lectures to them on ecclesiastical history, or the doctrines of the Christian religion and other important subjects." The college had a hard struggle for existence. Soon after the death of its founder, the treasurer's report showed that if all the property of the corporation were sold at auction, not enough money would be raised to pay its debts. Moneys were, however, raised by subscription, both in this country and abroad, and the lands granted the college becoming more productive, it managed to survive. The great crisis came in 1815, when the legislature of New Hampshire practically discontinued the college, establishing in its place a university with a different president and board of trustees. This action was bitterly fought in the courts, by friends of the college, led by Daniel Webster, a graduate; and, after an adverse decision by the supreme court of the state, was taken to the United States Supreme Court, where the decision was reversed, and the college given all its original rights. It was in connection with this litigation that Webster first came into prominence.

Since that time the development of the college has been similar to that of other New England institutions of its class. For the long period from 1828 to 1863 it was presided over by Rev. Nathan Lord, a man of great administrative force, and under his leadership made substantial progress.

P. 329.

As far back as 1798, a medical school was established which always held a high place. In 1851 the Chandler

P. 353.

School of Science and Arts was founded for the establishment and support of a permanent department or school of instruction in the college, in the practical and useful arts. A school of civil engineering has been

P. 421.

maintained since 1867 and one in administration and finance since 1900.

In 1904 there were 867 students in the entire college, and an instructional force of 72. The library contained 100,000 volumes. Its productive funds amount to $2,500,000.

More than 250 scholarships, varying in value from $50 to $150 are open to undergraduates, and six scholarships ($300), and one fellowship ($500), to graduate students.

b. LATER COLLEGES

In light of the problems which confronted the new republic during and immediately following the struggle for independence, a surprising interest is manifested in higher education at that time, no less than thirteen colleges having been established in the quarter of a century between 1776 and 1800. Although we have no exact records, it is probable that at the end of this period not more than one hundred professors and instructors were connected with the whole group of colleges then established, while but from one thousand to two thousand students were in attendance, and it is doubtful if the total property was worth $1,000,000. No one of these institutions admitted women in any way to its privileges.

At the beginning of the twentieth century (1902) there are no less than 464 colleges and universities for men or for both sexes, 134 of which admit men only to their undergraduate work, while 330 admit both men and women on equal terms. These institutions have 13,952 men and 1994 women on their faculties, 62,430 men and 21,051 women as undergraduates, and 3089 men and 1306 women as resident graduate students. The total property in buildings, grounds, apparatus, etc., amounts to $171,798,822, with productive funds, in addition amounting to $164,298,786. In addition to these institutions for men and both sexes are 131 higher institutions of learning for women alone, with a teaching force of 662 men and 1741 women, 16,964 students, property to the amount of $17,965,152, and productive funds of $7,191,099. These figures mean that in a single century, while the population of the country has increased about 6 times, the number of higher institutions of learning has increased 20 times, the number of instructors 170 times, the number of students at a conservative estimate of 47 times, and the property and productive funds 200 times. Certainly a growth for any country to be proud of, and one never before approximated at any period of the world's history.

It is true that educational advancement cannot be measured solely in numbers of institutions; but except for some few limited regions, the growth in numbers of higher institutions of learning seems not to have exceeded the legitimate demands, and on the whole has been a healthy one, and has extended pretty fully to all parts of our country. The establishment of colleges for men and for both sexes, within the several geographical divisions, made use of by the United States Commissioner of Education in the statistical tables given in his annual reports, is as follows, for each decade of the nineteenth century: —

	N. ATLANTIC	S. ATLANTIC	S. CENTRAL	N. CENTRAL	WESTERN	TOTAL
1890–1899	2	8	13	20	11	54
1880–1889	6	14	11	37	6	74
1870–1879	9	6	16	24	6	61
1860–1869	13	9	13	31	7	73
1850–1859	15	12	8	40	7	82
1840–1849	7	2	8	18	1	36
1830–1839	9	10	4	13	—	36
1820–1829	3	3	5	9	—	20
1810–1819	4	—	1	—	—	5
1800–1809	5	3	—	—	—	8
Total	73	67	79	192	38	449

This table shows that the decade from 1850–1859 was the period of most rapid increase in higher institutions of learning, the decrease in numbers per decade being somewhat gradual since that time.

The map on the opposite page shows graphically the distribution of colleges and universities of our country in the year 1902.

It is impossible to trace, decade by decade, the growth

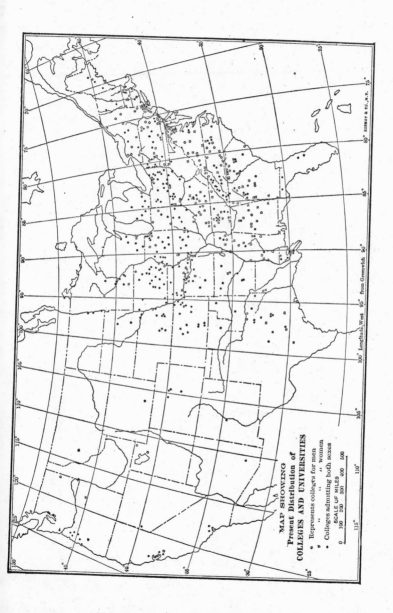

MAP SHOWING
Present Distribution of
COLLEGES AND UNIVERSITIES

• Represents colleges for men
□ " " " women
● Colleges admitting both sexes

SCALE OF MILES
0   100   200   300   400   500

in faculty, student body, and financial status of this group
of institutions for the entire century, for want of records
of these conditions; though, for the latter part of that
period, information is at hand, and is expressed in the
following table: —

	Students : Male and Female	Faculty	Grounds, etc.	Prod. Fund
1875	26,353	3386	41,076,105	33,252,585
1880	32,553	3466	39,623,424	43,431,520
1885	41,848	3890	43,565,413	49,687,378
1890	61,244	7815	64,259,344	74,070,415
1895	63,402	11,582	129,000,000	102,574,808
1904	85,581	15,945	154,529,288	164,298,786

This table is for colleges and universities for men
and those for both sexes, not including higher institutions for women only.

Of the five hundred and more institutions of higher
learning which have sprung up in our country since
the beginning of its independence, but comparatively
few have gained more than a local importance in our
educational history; possibly thirty or forty, besides the
colleges for women, which are treated in another chapter,
and the land grant colleges in a later paragraph in this.

This statement does not mean that the others are not
doing valuable work, nor that the small colleges are not
an important factor in our educational mechanism, but
that their influence is not sufficiently national to warrant individual notice, in a brief survey of American
education.

Some few do, however, seem to demand such notice,
and I make it, fully recognizing the fact that errors in
evaluation are likely to occur. Statistics are not given,
but may be secured from the annual catalogues, which
are easily procurable, or from the *World's Almanac*.

Among those dating their establishment from the

latter part of the eighteenth century, after the Revolution, may well be mentioned Williams, Bowdoin, Union, and Middlebury colleges.

The first of these originated as a free school in Williamstown, Massachusetts, in 1785, though not chartered as Williams College until 1793. When this was done, Harvard entered a formal protest, urging that there was no demand for a second college in the state, and that the cause of education would be injured by the establishment of one. Williams has a beautiful campus, many venerable buildings, and does work of a high standard. Women are not admitted. No professional schools are maintained. The income from nearly $260,000 is devoted to students' aid through scholarships, fellowships, and prizes.

Bowdoin College was founded in 1794, at Brunswick, Maine. It has not only had upon its faculty some of the foremost scientific and literary men of the century and more of its history, but has graduated an unusual number of men of the very highest rank, among them both Longfellow and Hawthorne. A medical school was established in 1820 (?) and is still maintained. Women are not admitted to any of the departments of the college. The income of more than $125,000 is devoted to scholarships and prizes.

Union College, at Schenectady, New York, was founded in 1795. It was to have been called Clinton College, in honor of New York's great governor. Union was one of the first colleges, if not the first, to break away from the old classical course, and place scientific instruction on a plane of equal dignity with it. Certain electives were offered as early as 1797. It maintains, under the regular college course, a school of civil engineering. Women are not admitted to the institution. A large number of scholarships are open under various conditions.

Middlebury College, at Middlebury, Vermont, was

founded in 1800, through the personal influence of President Dwight of Yale. It has always held an honorable place among the smaller New England colleges, and has graduated many eminent men. No professional schools are maintained. Women are admitted. Some forty scholarships are offered.

Hamilton College, at Clinton, New York, is the outgrowth of Hamilton-Oneida Academy, established as an Indian school early in the last decade of the eighteenth century. Its charter as a college was granted in 1812. It has a campus of forty-two acres, many admirable buildings, and has always maintained a high standing. Hamilton offers fifty-five permanent scholarships.

Colby College, at Waterville, Maine, was founded as the Maine Literary and Theological Institution in 1815, and has been successively rechristened Waterville College in 1821, Colby University in 1867, and Colby College in 1900. It is a Baptist institution, offering only academic courses of instruction. Women are admitted P. 443. upon a coördinate, though not strictly a coeducational, basis. Upwards of seventy undergraduate scholarships are maintained.

Amherst College, at Amherst, Massachusetts, was founded in 1821. For nearly fifty years a portion of the board of trustees was filled by the Massachusetts legislature. It offers no professional courses, and is open only to men. The income from more than $285,000 is devoted to student aid in one form or another. The Kellogg fellowship is perhaps the most valuable open to any American college graduate.

Columbian University was founded at Washington, District of Columbia, in 1821. Its buildings are in the heart of the city, in close proximity to many of the national bureaus and departmental libraries. Under the university organization are the college, the Corcoran Scientific School, the School of Graduate Studies, the Law School, the School of Jurisprudence and Diplomacy, the Medical and the Dental School. About fifteen scholarships are available.

P. 441. Western Reserve University, at Cleveland, Ohio, was established as Western Reserve College, at Hudson, in the same state, in 1826, where it remained until 1880. The academic undergraduate department is known as Adelbert College. Besides this college, which is for men, are the Women's College, the Medical and Law colleges and a dental school. Many scholarships and other financial helps to the students are available.

Lafayette College, at Easton, Pennsylvania, was founded in 1826, shortly after the last visit of the illustrious Frenchman of that name to this country, and named in honor of him. Besides its literary courses, it maintains a scientific department of much strength, but no professional schools. It does not admit women. A considerable number of prizes are offered annually.

New York University, which must not be confounded with the University of the State of New York, was organized in 1851. Until recent years it was known as the University of the City of New York, and occupied buildings in Washington Square. In 1894 all save its professional departments was removed to a magnificent site upon University Heights, Fordham, facing the Harlem River. It has many imposing buildings, in connection with one of which, the library, is the so-called Hall of Fame. Besides the college, are schools of Applied Science, Law, Medicine, and Pedagogy. Women are admitted to some of the courses. About thirty scholarships and three fellowships are open.

P. 445. Oberlin College, Oberlin, Ohio, was established in 1833, through Methodist influence, though formally known as Oberlin Collegiate Institute until 1850. A theological seminary and a conservatory of music are maintained. Oberlin has from the start been fully co-educational, being the pioneer in this respect. Fifty or more scholarships are offered.

Tulane University, of Louisiana, is the name under P. 441. which the old University of Louisiana at New Orleans has been known since 1834, when the first of the Tulane bequests, amounting to more than $1,000,000 was received. It has a fine equipment, and is one of the leading institutions of the South. Its departments include the college, the Graduate School, the Women's College, and the colleges of Law and Medicine. More than 150 scholarships are available.

Marietta College, chartered in 1835, was the outgrowth of educational beginnings at Marietta, Ohio, as early as 1797. It was one of the pioneer institutions west of the Alleghanies. No professional courses are offered, and both sexes are admitted. About forty scholarships are open under various conditions.

Rochester University, at Rochester, New York, was founded in 1851, as a result of schism in the faculty and student body of the Hamilton Literary and Theological Institution. It is under the control of the Baptist denomination. More than one hundred scholarships are offered.

The College of the City of New York is, as might be inferred, a part of the school system of New York City, and is entirely supported by municipal taxation. It dates as a college from 1854, though the Free Academy, of which it is the outgrowth, was established seven years earlier. It is intended only for residents of the city. Its entrance requirements are not so rigid as are those of most American colleges, and its students less mature, though the same academic degrees are given. Women are not admitted. The college will occupy, probably about 1905, a magnificent site upon Washington Heights. Since tuition is free, there are no scholarships, though a considerable number of prizes are offered.

Northwestern University, at Evanston, Illinois, was established by the Methodists, in 1855, and has become one of the strong institutions of the Middle West. It maintains, besides the regular college courses, schools of Medicine, Law, Pharmacy, Dentistry, and Music, a number of the schools being in Chicago. The Garrett Biblical Institute is also in close affiliation with the college at Evanston. A free scholarship for the freshman year is granted each high school of Illinois upon the university accredited lists. Six fellowships are open to graduate students.

Tufts College, in the town of Medford, Massachusetts, was founded in 1852, through Universalist interests. P. T. Barnum was a benefactor of the college, having given a building for a museum, and much of its contents. Beside the literary and scientific courses, there are schools of Medicine, Dentistry, and Divinity. The latter are open to women. About seventy scholarships and one fellowship are available.

The University of Denver, at Denver, Colorado, is the outgrowth of Colorado Seminary, a Methodist institution founded in 1864, taking its present name in 1880. It has an extensive campus in the suburbs of Denver, with many fine buildings, including an observatory with a telescope of twenty-inch aperture. Besides the College of Liberal Arts, are maintained schools of Medicine, Law, Theology, Fine Arts, and Dentistry. It is coeducational throughout. Several prizes are open to student competition.

Lehigh University, at South Bethlehem, Pennsylvania, founded in 1865, is especially strong in its scientific equipment. It maintains a school of technology. Women are not admitted to the university. Several prizes of money value are open to student competition.

Cornell University, at Ithaca, New York, one of our country's greatest and most progressive higher institutions of learning, was founded under the land grant of 1862. One-tenth of the entire grant, equal to fifteen hundred square miles, fell to New York State, — the most magnificent educational endowment ever bestowed by a nation to a single institution. After an unsuccessful attempt to found with it, what was to be known as the People's College, all the conflicting interests were united under Ezra Cornell's influence, and the present institution was founded in 1868. Mr. Cornell gave the campus of two hundred acres, than which there is no other in the country of more natural beauty, made many other bequests to the institution, and proved a most efficient guardian of its financial interests. Its entire history is typical of American thrift and foresight. Besides the academic departments, both graduate and undergraduate, there are colleges of Civil Engineering, Mechanical Engineering, Agriculture, and Medicine, the latter in New York City. The State College of Forestry and veterinary colleges are also organically connected with Cornell. One undergraduate scholarship is maintained for each assembly district in the state, in addition to which are some forty or more valuable prizes. Twenty-four fellowships and sixteen graduate scholarships are also offered.

Pp. 349, 363.

Syracuse University, founded at Syracuse, New York, in 1871, is the successor of Genesee College, which had for twenty years been in operation at Lima, New York. It is a Methodist institution. It maintains colleges of Liberal Arts, Fine Arts, Applied Science, Law, and Medicine. Women are admitted.

The University of Cincinnati, at Cincinnati, Ohio, was founded in 1873. It is, in a sense, a municipal institution, since the city appoints a part of its board of trustees; but it is largely maintained by private benefactions. Academic, engineering, medical, law, dental, and technical departments are maintained by the university, or are closely affiliated. Twenty-two scholarships and a limited number of fellowships are open.

Colorado College was established at Colorado Springs, Colorado, in 1874, and is nominally under Congregational supervision. It occupies an enviable position among

Western colleges, and is growing very rapidly, both in equipment and number of students. It is coeducational. No professional schools are maintained. Some twenty scholarships are available.

Pp. 298, 300. Johns Hopkins University, established in Baltimore, Maryland, in 1876, is one of the very first institutions in our country to-day, in which work for advanced degrees is a more prominent feature than are the undergraduate courses. Such, however, have been the conditions there since its inception. A college is maintained, but it is the graduate school that has given Johns Hopkins a reputation for scholarly work unsurpassed by any other institution in the country. Besides the literary and scientific schools of the university there is a medical department. The latter is coeducational, though the others are not. Fifteen graduate scholarships and twenty fellowships are offered by the university.

Leland Stanford Junior University at Palo Alto, California, was founded, and has since been maintained, through benefactions from the Stanford wealth, largely coming as direct gifts from Mrs. Stanford.

In all, several millions has been so turned over. From the start it has been coeducational, though not more than five hundred women may be registered as students at any one time. The university has a beautiful campus, an extensive equipment, and has, for so young an institution, come rapidly to the front rank of American universities. A department of law is maintained as the only professional school. But one scholarship is offered.

The University of Chicago, established by John D. Rockefeller in 1892, is perhaps the most striking example the world has seen of what almost unlimited funds, intelligently expended, can do in a brief time for a higher institution of learning. During the twelve years of its history, it has lived through or jumped over the stages which it took our old Eastern colleges centuries to pass through; and is, so far as material development and elaborateness of organization is concerned, hardly surpassed by any. The university was coeducational for P. 443. the first ten years; but in 1902 instituted the plan of segregation of the sexes. Its sessions are practically continuous throughout the year, the summer work constituting one "quarter." Besides the undergraduate courses, and the Graduate School with a very large enrolment, are schools of Divinity, Medicine, Law, and Education; university extension, too, is conducted on a P. 391. broad scale, and a large number of colleges in all parts of the country are in "affiliated relation" with the university, making possible an interchange of students and certain other privileges. A large number of scholarships are offered to secondary schools in accredited relations to the university, and above seventy fellowships in the Graduate School, ranging in value from $120 to $520.

The State Universities

Although the colleges of colonial days were all private corporations, in nearly every instance they had received moneys or lands by public bequest from the colonies in which they were situated. Harvard was established by an act of the general court of Massachusetts. At William and Mary the charter conferred a land endowment and a portion of the public revenues. The colonial legislature of Connecticut not only made grants of land to Yale College, but for many years in the early eighteenth century made annual appropriations of money. Princeton was first known as the College of New Jersey, and was at least indirectly aided by the legislature through its authorization of a lottery in 1762. The present University of Pennsylvania during its infancy received public money from the city of Philadelphia, the king, and the proprietors of the colony. Columbia, when the College of the Province of New York, was

the recipient of excise moneys.   Brown University was
granted certain exemptions from taxation.   At Rutgers,
the governor was *ex officio* president of the board of
trustees, and Dartmouth was most generously accorded
by the legislature of New Hampshire, large tracts of
land, and on one occasion £500 for the erection of a
new building.   This investment of public funds in colleges was understood by many to carry with it some
sort of state control, but since the institutions were all
more or less under denominational supervision, such was
impossible, and a widespread distrust of them as they were
conducted arose.   This took many forms, and was shared
by men of the most diverse religious and political
opinions.   But it all came virtually to this : That no one
of the colleges fully answered the public needs as regards
higher education.   Every one of them was the college
of a faction or a sect within the commonwealth, and failed
therefore to be the college of the commonwealth in its
entirety.   The democratic spirit which had been rising,
very slowly, since the beginning of the eighteenth century, and the interest in civic affairs, which increased
very rapidly as the Revolution drew on, both tended to
accentuate this feeling of distrust.   It was much more
pronounced in the case of some colleges than of others
but none of them seems to have escaped it entirely.

Brown, (V) p. 17.

As a result, the legislatures in most of the colonies
tried to gain fuller control of the colleges, and make
them more nearly conform to the popular will ; in a
sense, to make state universities of them.   With at
least three — Columbia, University of Pennsylvania,
and Dartmouth — this was actually done, and each had
its brief term of service as a real state institution.
With most of the others the controversy was hard
fought, but they were too firmly established on other
lines to be moved, and retained their original individuality.   But the controversy was not without its effect,
for the Southern states, and those across the Alleghany

Mountains, which were at the point of framing state constitutions, were warned by the difficulties which their older sisters had experienced, and almost without exception made provision for one or more higher institutions of learning under direct state control. In this movement North Carolina took the lead, inserting in the constitution which was framed in 1776 the clause " All useful learning shall be encouraged and promoted in one or more universities; " and although an institution founded upon this clause was opened in 1795, it did not come under full state control until 1821.

In South Carolina a university was under such control in 1801.

As the vast territory of the Middle West was opened up, and constitution after constitution framed, the same wise provision for carrying the public education of the youth to the highest step was made. And it is here that the State University has reached its fullest development. The original interest of all is expressed in the passage from the Indiana constitution written in 1819 : —

" It shall be the duty of the General Assembly, as soon as circumstances will permit, to provide by law for a general system of education ascending in regular gradation from township schools to State University, wherein tuition shall be gratis, and equally open to all."

This is the charter of the American State University — the crown of the public school system.

" Circumstances " permitted in Indiana in 1820, when the Indiana Seminary was established, which later became the State University at Bloomington. In 1817 the territory of Michigan established a college which, in spite of its name, — Catholepistemiad, or University of Michigana, — eventually grew into the great university of that state.

East of the Alleghanies the leaven of state control had not ceased to be active ; and in 1819 Virginia, after an unsuccessful attempt to gain control of the College of William and Mary, established its State University at Charlottesburg. In this enterprise Jefferson was the prime mover; and the wisdom of his plans has been fully demonstrated, not only by the subsequent history of this institution, but of others which have taken it as a model. With the exception of Maine, which founded its university in 1867, no state north and east of the Old Dominion has found place for a state university, for the universities in Pennsylvania, Maryland, and Vermont, though bearing the name of the state, are, in all essentials, private institutions, and the University of the State of New York is but an examining body, without teaching functions. But the establishment of state universities in the West and South came as a matter of course, and has kept pace with the stars upon the flag. Those states which were formed out of public lands — twenty-seven in all — received the donation known to-day as "university lands," and displayed wisdom in varying degrees, in its investment. Nearly all, however, used what was not lost through political jobbery, in one or more higher institutions of learning. These were usually broadly academic in their nature, though not always, as in the case of Illinois which used her grant for the foundation of a normal school. Up to 1862, roughly, a dozen states were maintaining institutions of a higher grade, no one of which was more than a struggling college, with a limited number of students, trying to do what it could upon the meagre revenues of what had been saved from the earlier land grants. Hardly one of these institutions could to-day be considered more than of secondary grade.

Rep. Com. Ed.
1880, p. xxxii.
By the passage in 1862 of the Morrill Act by Congress all this was changed. The act provided for a grant of 30,000 acres of land for each representative and senator in Congress. This land was to be "in place" where the state contained a sufficient quantity of public land subject to sale, at $1.25 per acre; and of scrip, represent-

ing an equal number of acres, where the state did not contain such land. The grant conveyed in all 9,600,000 acres, 1,770,000 of which was land in place, 7,830,000 in the form of scrip. The amount raised by the sale of these, varying in different states from $50,000 to $750,000, was to be devoted to the support in each state of a higher institution of learning, at which technical and agricultural branches should be taught.

Of the purpose of the Morrill Land Grant Act, President Draper says:—

"It had a distinguishing purpose in view. That was to carry the advantages of education to those engaged in manual industries. The older colleges had all pointed toward the time-honored learned professions. Congress recognized the industrial changes consequent upon the introduction of machinery, the advent of steam and electricity as elements in industrial progress, and the material development incident to the civil war. . . . By taking the grants and complying with the fortunate conditions on which they are made, and at the same time giving enthusiastically of their own store to combine therewith the disciplinary and culture studies and supplementing the whole with provision for the old and many new professional courses, the newer states had the most comprehensive university foundation the world has ever seen." Draper, (V), (I)

As a result of this grant, within twenty years practically every state in the Union has established such a school, either in connection with some already existing college or as a new institution. Many of the latter were P. 362. agricultural colleges pure and simple, while in a number of states the money was used in the foundation of a State University which should comply with the requirements as regards courses of instruction. Among the state universities owing their origin to the Morrill Act are those of California, Illinois, Maine, Minnesota, Nebraska, Nevada, Ohio, West Virginia, and Wyoming. At these institutions military training is required of all male students. Coeducation is universal. A part, though not all of the state universities in existence in 1862, were the recipients of their state's allotments of land through the Morrill Act.

The following table shows the states and territories maintaining universities in 1903, together with the year of establishment, and the number of students in each for the years 1875, 1885, and 1903 : —

STATE UNIVERSITIES

	Date of Foundation	1875 Students	1885 Faculty	1885 Students	1903 Faculty	1903 Students
Alabama . .	1831	71	19	207	45	396
Arkansas . .	1872	62	8	67	70	1080
California . .	1868	134	34	197	491	3057
Colorado . .	1877	——	7	71	105	925
Georgia . .	1785	202	10	184	138	2689
Idaho . . .	1889	——	——	——	30	347
Illinois . . .	1868	332	25	247	312	3300
Indiana . . .	1820	134	22	151	70	1285
Iowa . . .	1847	145	16	234	160	1512
Kansas . . .	1864	78	16	180	81	1350
Louisiana . .	1860	8	4	91	27	400
Maine . . .	1867	110	9	84	54	450
Michigan . .	1837	324	44	524	247	2900
Minnesota . .	1868	83	30	54	290	3700
Mississippi . .	1848	55	9	148	18	260
Missouri . .	1840	132	33	573	100	1681
Montana . .	1895	——	——	——	14	300
Nebraska . .	1869	35	16	142	220	2256
Nevada . . .	1886	——	——	——	24	292
N. Carolina .	1789	67	16	207	69	651
N. Dakota .	1883	——	5	——	37	500
Ohio . . .	1870	40	17	64	136	1516
Oregon . . .	1876	——	8	46	71	470
S. Carolina .	1801	86	13	158	16	215
S. Dakota . .	1882	——	——	——	30	450
Tennessee . .	1794	——	11	180	80	618
Texas . . .	1883	——	13	151	109	1300
Utah . . .	1850	——	——	——	28	643
Virginia . .	1825	326	28	306	57	600
Washington .	1861	——	13	6	35	601
W. Virginia .	1867	——	——	——	50	900
Wisconsin . .	1848	216	44	313	187	2810
Wyoming . .	1886	——	——	——	71	200

TERRITORIES

Arizona	1891	——	——	——	23	215
N. Mexico	1891	——	——	——	12	100
Oklahoma	1892	——	——	——	28	410
Total	——	2340	470	4599	3471	41,369

The table shows that in a little more than twenty-five years the number of students in attendance at the state universities has increased nearly twenty times (fourteen institutions added during the period), and that the number upon their faculties to-day exceeds by about one-half, the number of students in 1875. It shows that since 1885 the student body has increased eight times and the faculty seven times. Six out of the ten largest universities in the country (1903) are upon the list, and more than that number which are doing work of as high a character as any.

Financially these institutions are in a prosperous condition. The income from the land grant makes it certain that no one of them can be reduced to absolute penury, and for the most part the states have been generous, and either by means of a "mill tax," or by general appropriations made at each session of the legislature, have provided for their wants. Many of them, too, have been the recipients of private benefaction. In all, tuition is free, or practically so, except in the professional departments. Not all maintain such departments, though of the whole number, thirteen have medical and fifteen legal departments. No one of them supports a theological school.

c. THE DEVELOPMENT OF MODERN UNIVERSITY CONDITIONS

The American college of early colonial days was an institution of learning which took boys at an age, usually varying from twelve to twenty years, who had had, at most, a few years' schooling, put all through the same course of study for a period of four years, and gave them the bachelor's degree. The American university of to-day, in its most elaborated form, is an institution which takes young men and women of an average age of eighteen years and a little more, who have had twelve years' instruction in our primary and secondary school systems, keeps them for periods varying from three years (in special instances) to seven, allowing them to take practically what they want, and giving them one, two, or three degrees according to the length of time spent in study, with the possibility even of adding two or three others, if more than one professional course is taken. The history of Harvard University shows practically every stage in the development from the one to the other of these extremes, and, taking the country as a whole, institutions could be selected which to-day are illustrations of each successive step. The differences between these two extremes in higher education are at least six : viz. those of —

    a. Organization
    b. Requirements for admission.
    c. Elasticity of course.
    d. Length of course.
    e. Graduate work.
    f. Literary and scientific productivity.
    g. General results.

a. In discussing the organization of American colleges and universities, we must at the outset be reminded that the name signifies little. The title "university" is used indiscriminately by institutions of the simplest and of the most elaborate organization, and its original mediæval content, of the four "faculties," is entirely lost. What the typical American college is, has been shown in the earlier pages of this chapter, and need not be further discussed. The American university is modelled after neither the English nor the German types, for the former is but a loose confederation of separate colleges, each on its own foundation; and the latter is essentially a graduate institution, having no distinct college organization whatsoever. Ours, though taking its origin more directly from the English than from the German type, is a combination of both, in that the colleges or faculties within the university are distinctive features, though at the same time integral parts of it, and that graduate work has an important — and increasingly important — place. At Columbia, which illustrates the most elaborate type of organization, the colleges — Columbia and Barnard — give degrees as such (A.B.), while the faculties of Philosophy, Political Science, Pure Science, Applied Science, Architecture, Law, and Medicine as departments of the university grant only (except law) the master's and doctor's degrees. University work is according to this scheme, or will be, when the Law School is put upon a graduate basis, strictly graduate work, and the university degree an advanced degree. This interpretation of university work is being more and more widely accepted, and it may be that in time the term "American university" will be applied only to institutions adequately prepared to offer graduate courses, though in all probability the college, or undergraduate department, will generally be continued as an essential part of the organization.

b. Requirements for Admission

For admission to the early colleges, a definite, though limited amount of study must have been devoted to certain prescribed text-books, mostly classical authors. To-day the other extreme reached by some universities is simply an assurance of that degree of intellectual

Pp. 241, 246, 254, 257, 267.

development possessed by the graduate of a secondary school of recognized standing, without specifying the particular studies the individual student has pursued in reaching that degree of intellectual development. A few institutions exemplify each of these extremes in their entrance requirements, though the great mass is at present pursuing a mediate course. The tendency is, however, in the direction of a lessening of exact subject prescription for entrance. Yet this does not mean a "letting down of the bars," for the general requirements are constantly stiffening — though at the same time broadening — as is shown by the fact that the average age of the college freshman is slowly increasing. At present the entrance requirements of the better class of colleges and universities can be met only by the student who has the equivalent of a full four years' course in the secondary school, in addition to the eight years' elementary course. On the basis of "credits," one credit representing a subject pursued daily (in some instances four times per week) for one year in the secondary schools, forty-five credits is the usual requirement. Although in a few higher institutions none of these credits is definitely prescribed, so far as subject is concerned, usually a varying number — averaging perhaps one-half — must be in certain subjects, as, for instance, mathematics, English, natural science, history, or modern language. The rest may be made up from a large number of subjects approved by the institution to which entrance is sought.

In practice, two methods are made use of for ascertaining the fitness of students for college entrance. The first is through the examination of each individual student in all subjects which he offers for entrance. The second is the acceptance by the colleges of the diploma of the secondary school from which the applicant has come, as fulfilling all requirements. The former is the older method, and is generally in practice with the Eastern institutions. The latter is a later development, and is in vogue with most Western colleges, where special officers are appointed for the examination of each school having a so-called "accredited relation." Each plan has its advantages and its strong advocates. In the Eastern states, where individual examinations are general, many of the higher institutions maintain uniform examinations, which are given in various cities, doing away with the necessity of a journey to the particular institution selected, in order to take the test.

c. ELASTICITY OF COURSE

The course of study in the early American college was wholly prescribed. Each student at a given institution took all that was offered and, consequently, the same as each of his classmates. Gradually, when it seemed necessary to offer a greater number of subjects than time would allow a single student to take, the problem of selection, which is now the basis of our elective system, arose, and the various colleges began to experiment in an attempt to solve it. This was not until late in the eighteenth century, and the college of William and Mary seems to have been the first seriously to grapple with it. At first the college had three schools, and the student passed from one to the other in a fixed order. The lowest was the grammar school, teaching the classics, and, though not pedagogically prerequisite to the others, had been a universal requirement. But in 1770 a rule was passed, allowing "all such youths resident in or out of the college who have acquired a competent knowledge of common or vulgar arithmetic and whose parents or guardians may desire it, to be received into the Mathematical [the next higher] school." A few years later Thomas Jefferson became one of the trustees at William and Mary, and under his influence the course was so broadened that in 1821 he states, in a letter: "at

William and Mary students are allowed to attend the school of their choice, and those branches of science which will be useful to them in the line of life they propose." The same policy was followed from the start at the University of Virginia, which has generally been accredited with its origination. Because of its more conspicuous position among the colleges, it became a model for many and had a great influence in introducing the modern elective system.

The general principle of selection of courses has worked itself into practice in two ways: first, through the arrangement of the subjects of the curriculum into groups which must be elected *in toto*, pedagogical principles governing the selection of subjects for each given group; and, secondly, election, practically unrestricted, of individual subjects. The former is the earlier in general practice, being recognized in the establishment of professional departments in the colleges. Its result was a multiplication of bachelor's degrees, each separate course, leading to separate recognition at commencement. So it was that a quarter of a century ago it was the custom for a college to give from two to six separate bachelor's degrees, indicating the special course, arts, philosophy, science, literature, language, etc., which has been followed. At the present time this modified group system is going out of practice, and with it the degrees; so that A.B. is the only first degree that is given at any of the more prominent institutions (137 in all, among them Harvard, Princeton, Columbia, Johns Hopkins, Pennsylvania, Cornell, Leland Stanford, Vassar, Bryn Mawr, and the state universities of Michigan, Indiana, Virginia, Illinois, and Nebraska).

This second system, that of free elective, is in practice more or less fully in all our higher academic institutions with the exception, perhaps, of a few whose curriculum is so restricted as to make it impossible. In no one is it absolutely unrestricted, since if no other safeguards were put about it, the fact that some subjects are pedagogically prerequisite to others prevents utter license. In some few institutions this is the only restriction; but in by far the larger number, either some few subjects are definitely prescribed, or the breadth of selection is restricted within certain limits, or a combination of both of these plans is in vogue. It is probable, in fact, that no two institutions are administering the elective system in exactly the same manner, though each observes the same general principle. According to Professor Phillips, there were, in 1899, out of ninety- Phillips (III). seven colleges and universities of high rank which he studied, seven, viz.: Cornell, University of Cincinnati, Leland Stanford, William and Mary, and the state universities of Missouri, Virginia, and West Virginia, in which the breadth of elective was unrestricted by rule, while it was practically so in Harvard, Columbia, Yale (1903), and the University of Washington. Johns Hopkins and the University of Kansas, too, varied but slightly from these in their plan. He showed also that thirty-four of the whole number studied (ninety-seven) had 70 per cent or more of their courses elective; twelve had from 50 to 70 per cent elective, and fifty-one, less than 50 per cent. In this latter group are included the larger number of the smaller colleges, only Princeton and Brown of the larger ones being within it.

The whole question of freedom of electives, both in the college and in the secondary school, is one upon which there is a wide difference of opinion among educators. All are agreed that the principle should be recognized, but the exact extent of its administration is the mooted question. Under the early system of prescribed course, it is probably true that efficiency along special lines was sacrificed to general culture: under a system of unrestricted election the reverse might, in individual cases be true. Whether, in the long run, the latter danger is as serious as the former in its results, remains to be seen.

d. Length of Course

P. 251.

Four years has been the length of the American college course, and very few institutions have varied from it. The University of Pennsylvania, in its early years, offered but three years' work, but in general the length of course has been the one feature upon which there has been a practical unanimity of opinion. Four years was, in fact, for a good part of our educational history, the essential requirement for graduation and the measure of accomplishment, rather than the completion of a definite amount of work judged by courses taken. With the introduction of the latter criterion of proficiency — and it is now universal — and the addition of professional departments, the question of shortening the college course has come up, and is to-day one of the important questions in higher education. It is as yet prominent only in a few of the larger universities, where the professional schools are mostly graduate, and is raised by the fact that if the full four years of academic college work is required, students cannot attain the professional degrees until about twenty-six years of age, and cannot hope to be self-supporting in their professions until nearly thirty. This is believed by many to be too long a period to devote to educational preparation for life. The solution of the problem of shortening this period has been attempted in different ways. At Harvard it has been through the arrangement of the courses in such a way that the bright student, especially if he be given university credit for some work done in the secondary school, which is not unusual, may complete the required work for graduation in three years. Large numbers of students at Harvard are now doing so, although the requirements for graduation, measured in courses, are higher than ever before. The so-called "Columbia Plan," which is also in practice in some other institutions, maintains the four years' work for the bachelor's degree, but makes it possible for a student who is planning to enter one of the professional schools of the university to devote a considerable part of his senior college year to work in that school, graduating from it one year earlier than would otherwise be the case. That is, although the college course and the medical course is each four years, the student may complete both courses in seven years. President Butler has also urged the establishment of a distinct two years' college course. Of this plan he says: — Ed. Rev. Sept. 1903, p. 145.

"Whether the completion of such a two years' course should be crowned with a degree is to me a matter of indifference. Degrees are the tinsel of higher education and not its reality. Such a two years' course as I have in mind would imply a standard of attainment at least as high as that required for the degree of A.B. in 1860, which had many characteristics which we of to-day persistently undervalue. . . . The compromise plan as to degrees now becoming so popular, whereby the baccalaureate degree is given either for two years of work in a professional school, or for three years of college study and one year of work in the professional school is disastrous to the integrity of the college course. It deliberately shortens the college course by one year or two, while proclaiming a four-year college course. It is a policy which only university colleges can adopt and independent colleges must suffer if it becomes a fixed and permanent policy."

The plan for a two years' college course here advocated has been in operation for a number of years in the University of Chicago, in connection with the full four years' course. With the completion of the two years' course, a certificate is given granting the title of Associate in the University. The provision meets the need of many who cannot take a longer term of residence, and of those who ought not to take a longer course. Just what the outcome of the whole question of shortening the college course may be, cannot now be said, but as our professions became more and more specialized, it would seem that some concessions of time must be made, or we shall be in danger of seeing the elimination of the baccalaureate degree, as is the case in Germany.

e. Graduate Work

The most important development of our higher institutions of learning during the last fifty years — for it
hardly reaches back farther than that — has been in this
graduate work; that is, in university work, properly
speaking. As that of a professional nature is treated
in the next chapter, those courses of an academic
character only are considered here.

As far back as 1800 there are mentioned in the Harvard catalogues certain "resident graduates," though just
what the character of their work was is not plain; certainly they were not matriculants for advanced degrees.
During the earlier part of the nineteenth century Americans who wished to carry their academic studies farther
than what was demanded in the colleges for the bachelor's degree were forced to go to Europe for proper
instruction. Edward Everett was the first to take a
foreign degree, except in professional subjects, receiving
the Ph.D. from the University of Göttingen in 1819.
During the next quarter of a century a considerable
number of Americans pursued advanced studies abroad,
among them J. G. Cogswell, George Bancroft, and
R. B. Patton. The influence of such men, upon their
return, was sufficient to arouse the somewhat general
interest in advanced instruction to a point of university
action, and about the middle of the century several of
the larger institutions made direct provision for graduate
students. Yale was the first to do so, announcing in its
catalogue of 1847 the establishment of a department of
philosophy and arts for scientific and graduate study.
As early as 1843 Professor Thacher had advocated "the
establishment of a system of advanced instruction for
graduates, which should furnish the opportunities for
continuing their studies beyond what was possible
within the four years' course of the college," and for
some years Professor Silliman had unofficially done this,

P. 244.

but formal action was not taken until 1847. In 1861 the first degrees of Doctor of Philosophy were given to three men. A distinct graduate school was not organized until 1872. In 1874 the old practice of conferring the Master of Arts degree "in course" was changed for the system of granting it only after at least one year of graduate study. The former plan was practised by nearly all the colleges, up to a comparatively recent date, and is with the smaller ones even to-day. It practically allowed every graduate of three years' standing, who made application for it and paid the fees, to receive his master's diploma. The custom did much to lessen respect for the degree. It was, however, so bestowed at Harvard until 1874, at Michigan and Princeton until 1877, at Columbia until 1880, and at Brown until 1891.

In 1856 Columbia formulated an elaborate plan for P. 259. graduate work in three separate schools, viz.: letters, science, and jurisprudence. All led to the degree A.M. The plan was not fully carried out, but in 1881 graduate instruction was emphasized through the introduction of advanced courses in nearly all the college branches of study "open to all bachelors of arts, of science and philosophy, of this or of any other college of equal standing." The degree A.M. was conferred upon the completion of one year's work. The scheme was capable of almost indefinite expansion, and has developed into one of the strongest graduate schools in the country. The Doctorate of Philosophy was first given in 1884.

The Harvard catalogue of 1860 is the first to an- P. 232. nounce any definite plans for graduate instruction there, through the statement:—

"Graduates of the university or of any other collegiate institutions desirous of pursuing studies at Cambridge without joining any professional school may do so as resident graduates."

Until 1872 the degree A.M. only was conferred, but since that date the Ph.D. has been conferred annually to students fulfilling the requirements of at least three years graduate work and an acceptable thesis. This is now the usual requirement for the degree in the larger institutions.

At Princeton, graduate instruction was first offered in 1877–1878. At Cornell and Johns Hopkins, graduate work has been prominent since their organization; and at the latter especially, it has been so emphasized as to give the institution a most enviable reputation for scholarship. The development of graduate instruction during the last twenty years, not only within those institutions in which it was for that time offered, but throughout our whole body of universities, has been very rapid. Many have perhaps attempted it without adequate equipment, and would better have confined their efforts to work of a less advanced character, for which they were fitted, yet the progress as a whole is healthy and most encouraging.

GRADUATE STUDENTS

1871–1872 198	1886–1887 1237
1872–1873 219	1887–1888 1290
1873–1874 283	1888–1889 1343
1874–1875 369	1889–1890 1717
1875–1876 399	1890–1891 2131
1876–1877 289	1891–1892 2499
1877–1878 414	1892–1893 2851
1878–1879 465	1893–1894 3493
1879–1880 411	1894–1895 3999
1880–1881 460	1895–1896 4363
1881–1882 . . . . —	1896–1897 4919
1882–1883 522	1897–1898 4726
1883–1884 778	1898–1899 . . . . —
1884–1885 869	1899–1900 5056
1885–1886 935	1900–1901 6328

Roughly, one-fourth of the students have, during the later years, been registered *in absentia*.

A report made by the Federation of Graduate Clubs shows that in 1897, of the 3204 graduate students in 24 of the leading universities of the country, 35.4 per cent were pursuing literary and language studies; 20.6 per cent, historical and social science studies; 14.2 per cent, natural science; 18 per cent, philosophical studies; 11.1 per cent, mathematical subjects.

The principal advanced degrees conferred for work, other than that of the professional schools, are those of A.M. (Master of Arts), M.S. (Master of Science), Ph.D. (Doctor of Philosophy), and Sc.D. (Doctor of Science). The first is the oldest, having been, as has been shown, conferred by many institutions "in course" for many years. The others are the direct product of graduate schools. The M.S. has commonly been given as a second degree in institutions where the B.S. is conferred, but with the gradual elimination of that degree, is becoming less frequent.

The following table shows the number of Ph.D. and Sc.D. degrees awarded in the United States for 1898 to 1903 inclusive, by the universities offering courses leading to these degrees. The degree Sc.D. was conferred but comparatively few times during these years, (but twice in 1903), and seems to be gradually going out : —

DOCTORATES CONFERRED[a]

	1898	1899	1900	1901	1902	1903	Total
Yale	34	30	26	39	29	36	194
Chicago . . .	36	24	37	36	27	32	192
Harvard . . .	26	24	36	29	31	28	174
Johns Hopkins .	33	38	33	30	17	23	174
Columbia . . .	22	33	21	25	32	39	172
Pennsylvania . .	24	20	15	25	14	29	127
Cornell	19	7	19	21	23	20	109
Michigan . . .	7	4	5	3	10	10	39
Clark	12	5	9	7	1	4	38
New York . . .	5	9	7	6	4	4	35
Wisconsin . . .	5	7	5	5	6	2	30
Virginia . . .	0	2	2	8	6	3	21
Brown	1	3	3	2	2	5	16
Columbian . . .	1	0	5	3	2	4	15
Minnesota . . .	1	2	3	2	3	3	14
California . . .	1	3	2	2	1	3	12
Bryn Mawr . .	3	3	1	2	2	0	11
Princeton . . .	0	3	3	3	1	1	11
Stanford . . .	2	0	2	2	2	1	9
Nebraska . . .	2	1	1	1	0	0	5
Boston	0	0	0	0	0	4	4
Vanderbilt . . .	0	0	3	1	0	0	4
Washington . .	0	2	0	1	0	1	4
Georgetown . .	0	0	0	0	0	3	3
Kansas	0	1	0	0	0	2	3
Lafayette . . .	0	0	0	0	0	3	3
North Carolina .	0	0	0	0	2	1	3
Iowa	0	0	0	0	0	2	2
Lehigh	0	0	0	0	0	2	2
Syracuse . . .	0	1	0	0	1	0	2
Cincinnati . . .	0	0	0	0	0	1	1
Colorado . . .	0	1	0	0	0	0	1
Tulane	0	0	1	0	0	0	1
Missouri . . .	0	1	0	0	0	0	1
	234	224	239	253	216	266	1432

It will be noticed that five universities are distinctly in advance, and that a large majority of the degrees —

[a] From *Science.*

four-fifths — are conferred by seven universities. There has been no considerable change in the position of the universities during the years covered by the records, though there is apparently an increase at Columbia and Michigan, and a decrease at Clark and Johns Hopkins.

Besides the degrees conferred by reputable institutions, fraudulent degrees of all sorts are upon the market, though decreasingly so, owing to stringent legislative action.

Although the degrees A.M. and Ph.D. have been for years, and still are occasionally, given *causa honoris*, sentiment seems to be in favor of doing away with the custom, and of preserving those degrees, as well as some others, from academic prostitution. The Association of Graduate Clubs has taken action in the matter, urging "that the degrees of Ph.D., Sc.D., M.D., and Pd.D. [and A.M.] should never be given *honoris causa* or *in absentia*." L.H.D., S.T.D., D.D., LL.D., D.C.L., and Mus.D. are recognized as honorary degrees.

f. LITERARY AND SCIENTIFIC PRODUCTIVITY

Although in most other respects the American university differs materially from those of the German empire, in the matter of publications it is fast approaching them. In its early days it was what the American college now is, solely an institution for giving instruction. With the introduction of graduate work and better facilities for investigation, together with a more learned faculty, came a change in the attitude toward original work, until now a contribution to the sum total of knowledge is considered a no less important function of the university than is its perpetuation in the classroom. The larger universities make considerable provisions both in matter of instructor's time and in the financial budget, for original research; and large numbers of monographs and special articles appear each year, over the

signatures of the advanced students and of the instructional force. The theses of the candidates for the Ph.D.
degrees alone form no unimportant contribution to human
knowledge. Many of these productions appear in the
literary and scientific magazines, or are privately published; but a number of the larger universities maintain
special publications as a medium for the presentation of
the researches, both of their faculty and students.

At Harvard, ten such serial publications are issued;
at Johns Hopkins, twelve; at Columbia, seven; at the
University of Pennsylvania, eight; and at the University
of Chicago, eight; besides, in most instances, other
magazines of a more general nature edited by members
of the faculty.

Occasional series, moreover, of volumes of a more extended nature, such as the Yale Bicentennial and the
Chicago Decennial publications have been issued, each
comprising studies of much more than an ephemeral
nature. Such a constant contribution to knowledge as
our universities are now making is an educational force
not to be underestimated, and one which bids fair to be
of increasing value as time goes on.

g. THE GENERAL RESULTS

It is difficult to evaluate a force in education, for it
is impossible to say what the conditions would be with
any particular force left out. It is, however, safe to say
that our higher educational institutions are much more
than fulfilling the most sanguine hope of their founders,
in the sturdy men and women which they are turning
out. Of them Professor Thurston says: —

Thurston (VI).

"The great financiers of the country are now usually college
men; the heads of railways are often of that class though they may
have begun at the foot of the ladder; all distinctively learned men
are of that class; our greatest men in literature, science, and art are
practically all educated and cultivated men; the inventors of the

telephone and the telegraph were both educated, and, in fact, learned men; all the great men in medicine and in surgery are college men; all the great lawyers and every great jurist on the bench is of the same rating. We make our Presidents of learned men and usually of college men. The same is true of the members of the cabinet, of the judges on the supreme court bench, of the chiefs of bureaus and practically all men in highly responsible positions. Our foreign ministers and ambassadors, where reflecting special credit upon their country, like Lowell, and White, and Hay, and Chester, have been, not only college men, but distinguished for their attainments in the highest fields of academic learning."

The contribution which the college course makes to a man's success is even in a way capable of statistical demonstration. In a biographical dictionary of living Americans which appeared in 1900 are the names of 8602 who had achieved more than the ordinary success in some calling. A mention of this number of names in the volume in question means, if we assume that every inhabitant of the United States above the age of twenty-one was eligible to such mention, that one in each 600 was so honored. This then, would be our ratio of " success " for all degrees of education — good, bad, and indifferent. We find, however, that of the whole number mentioned, 3237 had received the bachelor's degree in arts, litera-ture, science, or philosophy at some college or university. But a study of the alumni lists of such institutions shows us that after the commencement season of 1899 there were 334,000 living graduates. A comparison of the number mentioned in the book (3237) with this whole number alive shows us that one college graduate in each 106 found a place. Here, then, we have the ratio of success for college graduates. But to carry our process of comparison one step farther: taking 1:600 as the ratio of success for the adult American and 1:106 as that for the college graduate, we find that the proba-bility of success is increased more than 5.6 times by a college education. This tremendous advantage can probably not be attributed entirely to the direct educational effect of such a training, but, to a considerable extent, to the selective influence of the course. Of the whole number of pupils who enter the elementary schools, but a very small percentage continues to the completion of the college course. This comparatively small number of persisters does not fairly represent what our educational machinery could have done with the entire number who started at the bottom, but what that machinery can do with the kind nature had endowed with sufficient energy, determination, and persistence to enable them to withstand the temptations to drop out one by one by the way, and take a seemingly short cut to some *ignis fatuus* of success, but who continue to the end. There is here shown undoubtedly with considerable force the potency of the law of the survival of the fittest, if we take as our criterion of fitness mention in the book in question. This, however, does not invalidate the fact that the college course, either because of its educational or selective influence, increases largely, perhaps to the extent we have shown, the probability that the graduate will gain a favorable place in the public eye.

P. 237.

It is, moreover, possible to show, by means of a still further study of the names in this book, that of the college men, those of high rank in their studies have achieved the greatest success of all. In fifty colleges and universities are chapters of Phi Beta Kappa, the honorary fraternity to which are elected roughly the first one-sixth of the senior class each year. For twenty-two of the colleges studied the names of 2.1 per cent of their living alumni were mentioned in the biographical dictionary, while 5.9 per cent of their Phi Beta Kappa graduates found place there. This would seem to mean that the latter's chances of eminence in his chosen calling are about three times those of his classmates as a whole. It means also, that the college ideal is a true one. The high grade man in college has realized most

nearly the ideal of his *alma mater*. He is its best product, according to its criterion of success, and is given its
highest stamp of approval. If he fails in life, it means
that, judged by another criterion — that of society in its
broadest sense — he is not a success; that the two
criteria are different, based upon different ideals, and, as
a corollary, since life is the final test, that the college
ideal is not a practical one, and that the aim of higher
education is false. If, however, he holds first place in
life, as he did in the preparation for it, we must conclude
that the two ideals, that of the college and that of the
civilization of which it forms a part, are coincident;
that, in terms of the ultimate test, the college ideal is a
good one, and that our American higher institutions of
learning are meeting the demands of modern social and
economic conditions.

REFERENCES

(Roman numerals in connection with marginal references in this chapter indicate division of the Bibliography.)

(I) SPECIAL COLLEGES AND UNIVERSITIES

Bibliography. See Higher Education in the United States.
Columbia Library Bulletin No. 2 (several hundred titles). For historical statements of colleges and universities in the several states,
see numbers of the Adams's series of Histories of Education
(Circ. Inf.) in the bibliographies at the ends of the various chapters
as follows: —

ALABAMA, *Clark* (9); ARKANSAS, *Shinn* (9); COLORADO, *Le
Roisgnol* (10); CONNECTICUT, **Steiner** (5); DELAWARE, *Powell* (4);
FLORIDA, *Bush* (9); GEORGIA, *Jones* (4); INDIANA, *Woodburn* (8);
IOWA, *Parker* (8); KANSAS, *Blackmer* (8); KENTUCKY, *Lewis* (9);
LOUISIANA, *Fay* (9); MARYLAND, *Steiner* (4); MASSACHUSETTS,
Bush (5); MICHIGAN, *MacLaughlin* (8); MINNESOTA, *Greer* (8);
MISSISSIPPI, *Mayes* (9); MISSOURI, *Snow* (8); NEBRASKA, *Cald-
well* (8); NEW HAMPSHIRE, **Bush** (5); NEW JERSEY, **Murray** (4);
NORTH CAROLINA, *Smith* (4); OHIO, *Knight* and *Commons* (8);
PENNSYLVANIA, *Haskins* and *Hull* (4); RHODE ISLAND, *Toll-
man* (5); SOUTH CAROLINA, *Merriweather* (4); TENNESSEE, *Merri-*

man (9); TEXAS, *Lane* (9); VERMONT, *Bush* (5); WEST VIRGINIA, *Whitehall* (5); WISCONSIN, *Allen* and *Spencer* (8). — Amherst College, History of, from 1821 to 1891. New York, 1895. Rev. Seymour Taylor. — Boone, R. G. Recent Colleges. In his Education in the United States. Pp. 158–209 (with bibliography). — Bowdoin College, Historical Sketch of, during the First Century. General Catalogue, 1894. George Thomas Little. — Bowdoin College, History of. Boston, 1882. Nehemiah Cleaveland. — Brown University, History of, with Illustrative Documents. Reuben H. Guild. Providence, 1867. — Columbia College. Harper, 69 : 813–831. — Cornell University. Scrib. 6 : 199–206. — Dartmouth College, History of. Cambridge, 1867. G. T. Chapman. — Dexter, F. B. Sketch of the History of Yale University. — Eliot, C. W. Four Great Universities. — Harvard University, Official Guide. Published by University, 1899. — Harvard, the First American College. Boston, 1886. George Cary Bush. — Harvard University. Scrib. 12 : 337–359. — Kimball, A. R. Yale as a University. Outl. 62 : 771–782. — Pennsylvania University, History of. T. H. Montgomery. Philadelphia, 1900. — Pennsylvania, University of, and Benjamin Franklin. Francis N. Thorp. Circ. Inf. No. 2, 1892. — Pierce. History of Harvard University. — Princeton University, a Brief Account of. A. F. West. Princeton, 1893. — Quincy, J. History of Harvard University. 2 vols. — Rutgers College. Addresses at the Centennial Celebration. J. P. Bradley and others. Albany, 1870. — Union College, Historical Sketch of. T. B. Hough. Rep. Com. Ed. 75–76. — *University of Virginia*, Thomas Jefferson and the. Herbert B. Adams. Circ. Inf. No. 1, 1888. — Vincent, George E. The University of Chicago. Outl. 71 : 839–851. — *William and Mary*, the College of. Herbert B. Adams. Circ. Inf. No. 1, 1887. — William and Mary. History (including the general catalogue from its foundation). Richmond, 1874. — Woodbury. History of New England.

(II) REQUIREMENTS FOR ADMISSION

Admission to College by Certificate. Ed. Rev. 5 : 187, 189, 291, 292, 384, 388 ; 6 : 69, 70. — *Broome*, E. C. A Historical and Critical Discussion of College Admission Requirements. Columbia University, April, 1903. — *Butler*, N. M. Uniform College Admission Requirements, with a Joint Board of Examiners. Ed. Rev. 19 : 68. — *Chase* and *Thurber*, C. H. Tabular Statement of Entrance Requirements to Representative Colleges and Universities of the United States. Sch. Rev. 4 : 341–405. — *Hadley*, A. H. Conflicting Views regarding Entrance Examinations. Sch. Rev. 8 : 583. — *Harris*, W. T. Should Colleges have their Standards of Admission. Ed. 17 : 579. — Keyes, C. H. College Admission Requirements. Ed.

Rev. 19:59. — Lowell, R. Laurence. College Admission Requirements. Ed. Rev. 11:468. — Nightingale, A. F. College Entrance Requirements. N. E. A. 1897:647. — Ramsey, C. C. Report on Admission to College on Certificate and by Examination. Sch. Rev. 8:593–611. — *United States Education*, Bureau of. College Admission Requirements. Rep. 1896–1897:456.

(III) Elasticity of Course

Andrews, E. B. Time and Age in Relation to the College Curriculum. Ed. Rev. 1:133. — Bartlett, S. C. Shortening the College Course. Ed. 11:585. — *Cohn*, A. The Group System of College Studies. N. E. A. 1894:807. — Coulter, J. M. Should the College Course be Shortened? N. E. A. 1891:696. — *Gilman*, D. C. The Shortening of the College Curriculum. Ed. Rev. 1:1. — Mory, William A. The College Curriculum. N. E. A. 1886:358. — Phillips, D. R. The Elective System in American Education. Ped. Sem. Vol. VIII. — United States Education, Bureau of. Courses of Study in Colleges and Universities. Rep. 1888–1889, 2:1224. — *West*, Andrew F. Is there a Democracy of Studies? At. Month. 84:821.

(IV) State Universities

Addis, Wellford, Colleges endowed by Congress for the Benefit of Agriculture and the Mechanic Arts. Rep. Com. Ed. 1895–1896, 2:1243. — *Angell*, J. B. State Universities in the United States. Rep. Com. Ed. 1898–1899, 1:647–655. — Beardshear, W. M. The Function of the Land Grant Colleges in American Education. N. E. A. 1900:463. — Brown, Elmer E. The Origin of American State Universities. Univ. of Cal. Pub. April 10, 1903. — Draper, A. S. (1) State Universities. Outl. 68:768. (2) State Universities of the Middle West. Ed. Rev. 13:313. — Graves, F. P. Ideal of State Universities. Ed. 18:241. — Howard, G. E. The State University in America. At. Month. 67:332. — *Jesse*, R. H. The Influence of the State University on the Public Schools. Sch. Rev. 8:466. The Function of the State University. Science (N. S.), 14:138–143. — Northrup, Cyrus. State Universities. Outl. 59:877. — Pickard, J. L. State Universities of the West. Ed. 20:472. — Swain, Joseph. The State University. N. E. A. 1900:106.

(V) Graduate Work

Hall, G. S. Scholarships, Fellowships, and the Training of Professors. Forum, 17:443.

(VI) Organization and Results

Adams, H. B. American Pioneers of University Extension. Ed. Rev. 2:220. — University Extension in America. Forum,

11 : 510. — *Angell*, J. B.   The Relation of the University to Public Education.   N. E. A. 1887 : 146. — *Brown*, Elmer E.   The University in its Relation to the People.   N. E. A. 1892 : 398. — *Butler*, Nicholas Murray.   The Meaning of Education.   Pp. 125–147. — Cattell, J. McK.   Concerning the American University.   Pop. Sci. Mo. 61 : 170. — Corey, A. M.   Growth of Colleges in the United States.   Ed. Rev. 3 : 120. — Coulter, J. M.   Cost of Undergraduate Instruction. . Ed. Rev. 7 : 417. — *Draper*, A. S.   American Universities and the National Life.   N. E. A. 1898 : 103. — *Eliot*, C. W.   The Older and the Newer Colleges.   Ed. Rev. 16 : 162. — *Gilman*, D. C.   Present Aspects of a College Training.   N. A. Rev. 136 : 526.   University Problems in the United States.   1898. — *Harper*, W. R.   The Small College : its Prospects.   N. E. A. 1900 : 67. — Harris, George.   The Future of the Detached College.   Outl. 71 : 889–891. — Harris, W. T.   The Rise of Higher Education.   Ed. Rev. 16 : 147. — Henderson, C. R.   Plans and Budget for a Small College.   Am. Jour. Sociol. 7 : 721–748. — *Hyde*, W. D.   Adjustment of the Small College to our Educational System.   Outl. 71 : 886–889.   The Future of the Country College.   At. Month. 62 : 721. — Jesse, R. H.   University Education.   N. E. A. 1892 : 120. — Jordan, David Starr.   An Apology for the American University.   N. E. A. 1899 : 213. — Ladd, G. T.   Development of the American University.   Scrib. 2 : 346–360. — *Low*, Seth.   Higher Education in the United States.   Ed. 5 : 1. — *Munsterberg*, Hugo.   Productive Scholarship in America.   At. Month. 87 : 615. — *Perry*, E. D.   The American University.   In Butler's Education in the United States 1900, I : 253–318 (with bibliography). — Powell, L. P.   Ten Years of University Extension.   At. Month. 88 : 393. — Royce, Josiah.   Present Ideals of American University Life.   Scrib. 10 : 376–392. — *Stetson*, H. F.   Shorter College Courses to meet a Popular Demand.   N. E. A. 1890 : 668. — **Thurston**, R. H.   The College as a Leader in the World's Work.   Pop. Sci. Mo. 60 : 346. — *Thwing*, C. F.   College Administration, 1900.   Collegiate Conditions in the United States.   Forum, 33 : 372.   The Endowment of Colleges.   Int. R. 11 : 258–268.   Influence of the College in American Life.   N. A. Rev. 162 : 517.   Three Oldest Colleges.   Ed. 18 : 1.   True Functions of a University.   Nation, 46 : 111–112. — United States Education, Bureau of.   University Extension.   Rep. 1893–1894, I : 951.   University Types and Ideals.   Rep. 1897–1898, 2 : 1435–1452. — *Von Holst*, Hermann E.   Need of Universities in the United States.   Ed. Rev. 5 : 105. — *West*, A. F.   The American College.   In Butler's Education in the United States 1900, I : 209–249.   The Evolution of a Liberal Education.   N. E. A. 1893 : 150.

CHAPTER XVI

PROFESSIONAL EDUCATION

For nearly two centuries after the establishment of the first college at Cambridge, Massachusetts, but occasional and sporadic attempts at specialization in higher education had been made in America. It is true that, during the later years of that period, some few special schools for each of the so-called learned professions had been established, but the students in attendance were so few, and the successes so moderate, as to argue that the people, as a whole, had not felt the need, as yet, of special preparation on the part of their ministers, doctors, and lawyers, beyond what could be had in the academic institutions, and for the two latter professions, apprentice work under some competent practitioner. The earlier colleges had courses especially arranged to meet the needs of the pulpit, and were established in many cases, primarily, as theological schools. The application of their courses to the demands of medical or legal practice was not so direct, though furnishing a broad foundation. It is estimated that among the thirty-five hundred physicians in the country at the close of the Revolution, not more than four hundred had received medical degrees, and it is doubtful, if among the lawyers, the number having received legal instruction in any institution of learning was even so great as that. But as time went on, and the subject-matter to be covered in any adequate professional preparation was increased, the educational machinery adapted itself to the new demands, and special departments, or schools, sprang up wherever the need seemed to be the greatest, some in connection with colleges already founded, and some as separate institutions. Theology was first to enter the field, with medicine second, and law the last among the three great professions. Pharmacy, dentistry, and veterinary practice, as specialties in medicine, followed in order, until we have to-day upwards of five hundred institutions preparing specialists in these various callings.

a. THEOLOGICAL EDUCATION

Although, as has already been said, the earlier colonial colleges were founded, primarily, as feeders for the ministry, they had, by the close of the eighteenth century, to such an extent lost their distinctively religious tone as to make it seem wise, to those especially interested in the perpetuation of denominational creed, to set up separate schools or departments for the protection of its purity. As a consequence, the theological schools arose. Previous to their origin it had not been uncommon for prominent clergymen to take under their special care, one or more candidates for the ministry, and somewhat after the manner of the physician's or lawyer's apprentice, to direct their education. In some few cases, where a considerable number of students were gathered around a single instructor, something approximating a school of theology was organized. Dr. Joseph Bellamy conducted such a private school in Connecticut, near the middle of the eighteenth century, and some of his pupils established similar schools a little later. They had, however, no bearing upon the general development of schools of theology, since such schools were given rise to by the need of the students, while the modern theological seminary is, in almost every case, the embodiment of a desire on the part of a religious denomination to fill its pulpits with men schooled in its own tenets, and practically in every case, though nominally not so in a few, instruction is denominational. They are, as a consequence, all separate institutions, or connected with colleges which at one time were, or still are, under the control of some religious denomination. But 3 of the 148 theological schools in operation in 1902 were avowedly non-sectarian. The others were controlled by more than 20 separate denominations, as follows: —

Roman Catholic .	28
Lutheran (all sects) .	23
Presbyterian (all sects)	21
Methodist (all sects) .	17
Episcopal .	13
Baptist (all sects)	12
Congregational .	10
Dutch Reformed .	6
Christian .	6
Universalists .	3

Several other denominations support one each.

The first religious denomination to establish a theological school in this country was the Dutch Reformed Church in America. In 1784 Dr. John H. Livingston, pastor of the Collegiate Church of New York City, was elected by the synod to be professor of divinity in the church at large. Until 1810 Dr. Livingston, in connection with his pastorate, taught students gratuitously. Other ministers of the denomination, in various localities, were also appointed professors, but all students were required to be examined by Dr. Livingston, and receive a testimonial of proficiency from him before being licensed to preach. About ninety men were thus graduated between the years 1784 and 1810. In the latter year Dr. Livingston gave up his pastoral work, accepted the presidency of Rutgers College at New P. 263 *et seq.* Brunswick, New Jersey, and the professorship of theology therein. Since that time, theological instruction has been conducted there, with the exception of a few years in the early nineteenth century, when work was suspended. Until 1864 the courses in theology constituted a department of Rutgers College; but since that time has been under separate maintenance.

The Roman Catholic denomination was the next to establish a theological school in America, through the foundation of St. Mary's Seminary in Baltimore, in 1791. Its curriculum is, and always has been, broader than that in most theological schools, including courses in philosophy and science. Its start was not encouraging, so far as attendance is concerned, there being but five students during the first three years, and none at all from 1795 to 1797. It is, however, at present in a prosperous condition.

The only other theological institution dating back into the eighteenth century is that of the United Presbyterian denomination, now at Xenia, Ohio, which was founded in 1794, at Service, Pennsylvania. In 1821 it was removed to Chambersburg in the same state, and in 1855, to its present location.

The Congregationalists were first to enter the field in New England, through the establishment of Andover Theological Seminary at Andover, Massachusetts. It was a pioneer in theological instruction, and has been a great force in its denomination, as well as in broader religious movements throughout its entire history. A second school was founded by the Congregationalists at Bangor, Maine, in 1816, and is still in active operation.

The Princeton Theological Seminary, the first, as well as the most influential in the Presbyterian denomination, dates from 1812. At the start it had one professor, three students, and no building of its own. Ten years later it had a faculty of three.

In 1816 the oldest school supported by the Lutheran denomination, Hartwick Seminary, was opened in Otsego County, New York.

The General Seminary of the Protestant Episcopal Church at New York City was the earliest of that denomination, first giving instruction in 1819. For the next two years the work of the seminary was conducted at New Haven, Connecticut, but since 1822 has remained in New York City. It is to-day one of the wealthiest theological schools in the country, with a faculty of nine professors and five instructors.

In 1820 Hamilton Theological Seminary, the first ministerial school of the Baptist denomination, was opened at Hamilton, New York, and has ever since been conducted there. In 1893 the seminary was absorbed by Colgate University, also at Hamilton, and is now the theological department of that institution. In 1825 the Baptists established their second theological school at Newton, Massachusetts.

With these institutions, each of the principal religious denominations, with the exception of the Methodist, had one or more theological schools in operation by the end of the second decade of the nineteenth century. That denomination alone failed to see the importance of special preparation on the part of its ministers; and it was not until 1847 that the first of its seminaries — at Newbury, Vermont — opened its doors. The denomination has, however, during subsequent years, amply made up for its early tardiness in establishing schools, as is shown by the table on page 309.

Boston Univ.

Theology at the Universities

Antedating any of the special schools for theological instruction, divinity had been an academic subject in the curricula of several of the colleges. At the college of William and Mary, the organization almost from the start included a professorship of the subject, and at Harvard the Hollis professorship of divinity dates from 1721, and at Yale a similar chair was established in 1781. Nothing like a definite organization of courses to meet the needs of the prospective minister was, however, attempted at any of the higher institutions of learning already founded, until 1819, when Harvard established a separate faculty of divinity. Yale followed three years later with the founding of its theological department. Since that time nearly fifty colleges and universities have established theological faculties, while more than a dozen independent theological seminaries have entered into such relations with neighboring institutions as to enable their students to enjoy many university privileges. This is illustrated by the relations between the Episcopal Theological School at Cambridge and Harvard University, and the seminaries of the same denomination at New York City and Philadelphia with Columbia, and the University of Pennsylvania, respectively.

With the beginning of the third decade of the nineteenth century, the increase in theological schools was so rapid as to make it unwise, in a work of this character, to consider each separately. The following table shows this growth by decades for each of the geographical divisions of our country made use of by the United States Commissioner of Education in his annual reports:—

THEOLOGICAL SCHOOLS

Year	N. Atlantic	S. Atlantic	S. Central	N. Central	Western	Total
1890–1902	3	3	6	9	2	23
1880–1889	2	4	2	7	—	15
1870–1879	1	1	4	7	2	15
1860–1869	11	4	2	9	1	27
1850–1859	9	—	4	7	—	20
1840–1849	4	—	—	4	—	8
1830–1839	4	2	1	4	—	11
1820–1829	7	2	—	1	—	10
Total	41	16	19	48	5	129

The 129 whose foundation is covered by the period, together with those established at an earlier date, and

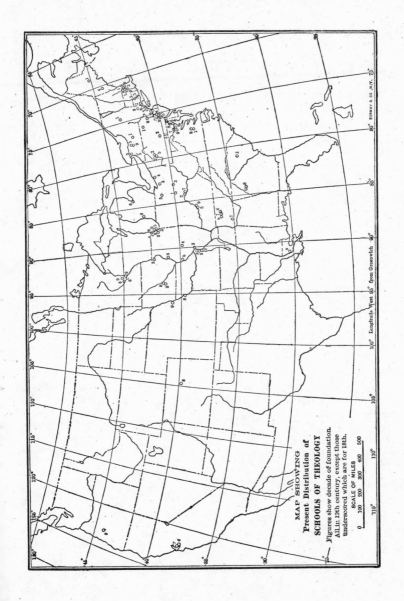

MAP SHOWING
Present Distribution of
SCHOOLS OF THEOLOGY

Figures show decade of foundation.
All in 19th century, except those
underscored which are for 18th.

SCALE OF MILES
0   100   200   300   400   500

several for which the year of establishment could not be ascertained, make 150, the number in active operation in 1902. As will be seen from the table, the decade most prolific of theological institutions was that from 1860 to 1869, with the twelve years since 1890 showing the next largest number. Geographically considered, the Northern states — Atlantic and Central — have two-thirds of the whole number, while the Western states are but meagrely represented, containing roughly but 4 per cent. It is impossible to determine for the earlier part of the nineteenth century the growth in faculty, student body, and annual output of these institutions; but records are available for the latter portion of it, and the figures are given in the following table: —

THEOLOGICAL SCHOOLS

Year	Faculty	Students	Graduates
1902	1034	7343	1656
1900	994	8009	1773
1895	906	8050	1598
1890	744	7013	1372
1885	793	5775	791
1880	633	5242	719
1875	615	5234	782
1870	339	3254	——

Figures (not shown) disclose the fact that there has been a decrease in the total number of theological students for each of the last three years, including 1901, and that the number is now less than it was in 1902. This decrease for the last three years is not for any one denomination alone, for the records show it to be true of each of the seven largest denominations considered separately. The decrease in the number of theological students has shown itself only since 1899, and for the number of graduates, only with the classes of 1901 and 1902. What it may be in the future cannot be told, but in the past the in-

Rep. Com. Ed. 1901, 2: 1735.

crease in theological graduates has much more than kept pace with the increase in the population. The average of the five annual classes in theology from 1880 to 1884, inclusive, was 758, while the average of those from 1897 to 1901 was 1683, an increase of 120 per cent; while the increase in population, as shown by the censuses of 1880 and 1900, was but 52 per cent. Another interesting and encouraging fact to any who may fear for the future of the ministry, is the marked increase in recent years in the number of students in our theological institutions who have already taken their academic college course. The percentage of those who had taken the academic degree for the five theological classes from 1881 to 1885 inclusive, was 23.6, while for the classes from 1896 to 1900 it was 32.6, an increase of no small consequence. With the educated ministry much more than holding its own, we need have no fear for the pulpit. In fact, under those conditions, a decrease in the sum total of clergymen would have some hopeful features about it. The most reliable figures available seem to show that about one minister in four, the country over, is a theological graduate.

The Author, Ed. Rev., Jan., 1903.   A study of the educational preparation of 655 clergymen who are to-day filling prominent pulpits shows the following : —

		PER CENT
a.	No preparation beyond the secondary school	24.4
b.	College training alone	11.9
c.	Professional training alone	12.
d.	Training entirely abroad	7.7
e.	College and professional alone	10.5
f.	College and training abroad	1.4
g.	College and graduate	16.
h.	College, professional, graduate, and abroad	.3
i.	Professional and training abroad	.7
j.	College, graduate, and abroad	1.5

A summary of the important points of this table gives us a percentage of 53.3 for college alone, or in combination; 35.5 for the professional course in all combinations and 29.8 as the total have taken graduate work.

The study of the tabulation of these various kinds of preparation, for decades of graduation, as far back as 1830, throws some light on the gradual changes which have taken place during the last fifty years in the character of education seemingly most conducive to eminence in the pulpit. It shows, first, that the number who stopped with the secondary stage (*a*) has remained practically constant. In the light of recent developments in higher education, this fact is of no great credit to the profession. Second, that the number taking either the college or the divinity course *alone* (*b* or *c*) has decreased to a very marked extent, the percentage in each of these classes being only about one-third that of fifty years before. This fact taken by itself would also seem discouraging, were it not more than compensated for by the more elaborate combinations. For instance, the numbers who had taken both these courses had trebled, while those who had gone still farther and combined graduate work with them, had considerably more than doubled in the same time. In other combinations there were shown to be but slight changes. These fluctuations seem to show that training for leadership in the pulpit is becoming more and more extensive and general rather than intensive and particular; that a mere knowledge of homiletics is not enough; that a liberal *Weltanschauung* is a desideratum. All this is most hopeful from the standpoint of the pew.

The average number of years spent by these eminent clergymen in educational preparation beyond the secondary school was 3.19.

Admission to Theological Schools

Of the 165 theological schools in operation in 1899, 71 required a college degree for admission: 3, the com- Parsons[1], pletion of the junior year; 18, of the freshman year; 19, a three-year high-school course; 6, a two-year; 1, a one-year; 19, a common school education; 4 have no requirements, and 24 are not given.

Length of Course

Of the 150 in 1901, 1 offers a two-year course; 103, a three-year course; 15, a four-year course; 2, a five-year; 1, an eight-year; 4, a varying course, while for the remainder the length is not stated.

For these schools the length of the course in weeks is as follows: 40 weeks, one; 70 to 79, six; 80 to 89, two; 90 to 99, forty-one; 100 to 109, thirty-four; 110 to 119, thirteen; 120 to 129, nineteen; 130 to 139, four; 140 to 149, three; 150 to 159, two; 160, eight; 176, one; 200, one; and 256, one. The others had courses of varying lengths or were not stated. As will be seen, by far the greater number have courses of from 90 to 120 weeks. These include the three-year schools, the year varying from 30 to 40 weeks. A comparison of the figures with those for 1875 shows that but a slight change in the length of the theological course has taken place in the last twenty-four years. Of the 101 institutions for which figures are available for that year, none offered a one-year course; 5, a two-year; 71, a three-year; 1, a three-and-one-half year; 7, a four-year; 1, a four-and-one-half year; 4, a four-year, and 11 a still longer course. The number of months in the school year was about the same for each date, indicating, if anything, a slight decrease in the average length of the theological course for the institutions taken as a class.

b. Legal Education

The first law school in the United States was established at Litchfield, Connecticut, in 1784, by Judge Tappan Reeve, and was conducted there until 1833, in which year it was discontinued. For the first fourteen years of its history Judge Reeves conducted it alone, besides carrying on a large practice. It was customary in those days for lawyers of prominence to have a number of young men in their offices studying law, and in its inception the Litchfield Law School was little more than an elaboration of office method properly organized and supplemented with lectures. As the reputation of the school grew, Judge Gould became associated with Reeve in the work, and instruction took on a more definite form. Both men were brilliant lawyers and had made important contributions to the literature of their profession. But one other instructor was connected with the school; and he, only after the retirement of the former in 1820. Students came to it from every state in the Union, as then constituted, in all 1024 for the entire period of its history, an unusual number of whom rose to positions of great dignity and importance. Ten governors of states, five cabinet officers, two Justices of the United States Supreme Court, eight chief justices of states, forty judges of supreme courts of states, fifteen United States Senators, and fifty Representatives in Congress were among the number: certainly a record of which any school might be proud. The course covered a period of fifteen months, and the tuition for the whole course was $160 — a large sum for those days. No students were taken for less than three months.

Only two other definite attempts to establish schools of law were made in the eighteenth century. Both of these were in connection with colleges already established, and both were failures, if we may judge from the immediate discontinuance of the work. The first was at the University of Pennsylvania in 1791, when Justice Wilson of the United States Supreme Court was elected Professor of Law. His first lecture was delivered under most auspicious circumstances, before an audience in-

Univ. of Pa. p. 250 *et seq.*

cluding President Washington and Cabinet, both houses
of Congress, the Executive and Legislative departments,
the governor of Pennsylvania, Mrs. Washington, Mrs.
Hamilton, and a most distinguished assemblage of representatives of the bar. The course was not, however, continued beyond the first year, and no further attempts at
legal instruction were made at the university until 1817.

Columbia Col.
p. 257.

The second abortive attempt during the century, at
Columbia, in 1797, seems to have given fully as much
promise at the start, for it was made by no less a
legal light than James Kent, author of the famous *Commentaries.* For some reason but a single course of lectures was delivered by Professor Kent, and sixty years
elapsed before a department of law, authorized to grant
degrees, was established at Columbia.

Harvard Col.
p. 233.

It remained for Harvard to establish the first law
school of permanency, with degree-granting privileges;
and this she did in 1817. Until 1870 the degree of
LL.B. was conferred upon all students in attendance
for three terms, but in that year a full two-year requirement was established. The present three-year course
dates from 1877, in which year entrance examinations
were for the first time given. Special students were
admitted without examination as late as 1893. Under
a rule first administered in 1896, only graduates of
approved colleges and those qualified to enter the senior
class at Harvard were to be admitted, and in 1899 the
requirements for entrance were still further stiffened by
demanding a college degree for all. This places the
law school at Harvard upon a full graduate basis, the
first in the country. The school had in 1902 a faculty
of fifteen.

Previous to the establishment of a faculty of law
at Harvard, the University of Maryland, in 1812, had
formally established such a faculty comprising seven
instructors. Only one of them, however, Daniel Hoffman, Esq., seems ever to have given actual instruction

in the subject, and this was not until 1822. Professor Hoffman continued his instruction for "several years" when the work was discontinued, not to be taken up again until 1869, when a final reorganization took place.

Steiner, p. 120.

Yale Col. p. 245.

A law department was first established at Yale College in 1824, though the LL.B. degree was not conferred until 1843. For the first two years after its establishment, the department was practically a distinct institution, though the names of its students were included in the Yale catalogue. It was, however, in 1826, formally adopted. Judge Daggett was the professor in charge, and the school was named after Chancellor Kent. In that year ten students were enrolled; five years later the number had increased to forty-four.

The University of Virginia established a department of law in 1826, and it has been in continuous operation, even during the four years of Civil War, ever since. It was in Jefferson's original plan for the university that law, "Municipal and Foreign, embracing the general Principles, Theory and Practice of Jurisprudence, together with the theory and principles of Constitutional Government," should form a prominent part of the curriculum, and it is to his insistence that the law department was established so early. A two years' course is now maintained.

Univ. of Va. p. 284.

The first law school established west of the Alleghany Mountains was founded in Cincinnati, Ohio, in 1833, in connection with Cincinnati College — an academic institution already in operation. In 1897 the school was absorbed by the University of Cincinnati, and is now the law department of that institution. A three years' course is maintained.

Univ. of Cin. p. 277.

One year after the foundation of legal instruction in Cincinnati, in 1834, a professor of law was added to the faculty in Dickinson College at Carlisle, Pennsylvania. The department was supported by the students enrolled in the courses.

Univ. of N.Y.
p. 274.

As early as 1835 New York University, then the University of the City of New York, took steps in the direction of founding a law department, and requested Benjamin F. Butler to submit plans to that end. Actual instruction was not given, however, until 1838, when three professors were inaugurated. The course was continued only one year, when the work was suspended. It was taken up again in 1859, since which time it has been continuous.

In all there had been up to 1840 ten law schools established in the country, of which at least four had ceased to be active. The entire output of these schools can hardly have exceeded two or three thousand, which, for a population of seventeen million people would mean that professionally educated lawyers were very thinly distributed. The method of studying in law offices as a preparation for practice was almost universal. With the fifth decade of the century a more rapid increase in the establishment of law schools began, though not gathering any very great momentum until considerably later. The following table shows the present distribution (1902) of such law schools, together with the dates of their establishment. The geographical divisions are those made use of by the United States Commissioner of Education in his reports: —

LAW SCHOOLS IN THE UNITED STATES

Year	N. Atlantic	S. Atlantic	S. Central	N. Central	Western	Total
1890–1901	8	4	13	19	4	47
1880–1899	2	1	1	5	2	11
1870–1879	1	5	3	2	1	12
1860–1869	—	3	1	3	—	7
1850–1859	1	2	1	3	—	7
1840–1849	—	1	3	1	—	5
Total	12	16	22	33	7	89

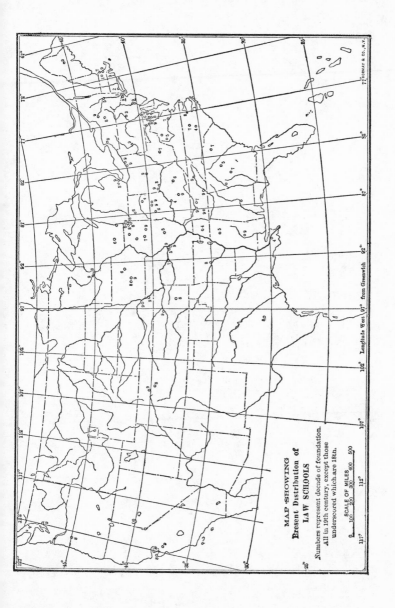

MAP SHOWING
Present Distribution of
LAW SCHOOLS

Numbers represent decade of foundation.
All in 19th century, except those
underscored which are 18th.

SCALE OF MILES
0   100   200   300   400   500

Longitude West 97° from Greenwich

T. SORMAY & CO., N.Y.

As will be seen, the total number established during this period is 89, which, together with those already in operation at its beginning, and two or three, the dates of whose foundation could not be ascertained, give us 102 law schools in operation in the United States in 1902. The fact that considerably more than one-half of these are less than twenty years old, and nearly one-half but ten, shows that we are just now passing through a period of excessive activity in matters pertaining to legal education.

It is not possible to determine with any degree of exactness for the earlier portion of the nineteenth century the increase in teaching force, student body, and size of graduating classes for this group of professional schools, but such facts are available for the last thirty years, and are given in the following table : —

LAW SCHOOLS

Year	Faculty	Students	Graduates
1902	1155	13912	3524
1900	1004	12516	3246
1895	621	8950	2717
1890	346	4518	1366
1885	285	2744	744
1880	229	3134	1089
1875	224	2677	823
1870	99	1653	—

During the period covered by the table, the number of persons engaged in teaching law in the schools of the United States had increased some ten times, the number of students nearly nine, and the average size of the graduating class nearly five times. This has varied materially from year to year, the smallest class for the period being that of 1885, with but 744 members, while the largest, that of 1902, contained 3524. During the thirty years there was in general a marked increase, the average number graduating annually for the first five years of the period being 1128, while for the last five years the average was 3166. A comparison of these figures gives us an increase of nearly 200 per cent for the quarter of a century, in professionally educated lawyers. The figures do not hold true, however, for the legal profession as a whole, since they take no account of those who entered it without the law school diploma. We have to turn to the figures of the tenth and twelfth census for light on that point, and we find from the first that there were in our country in 1880, 64,137 who made a living, or tried to, through the practice of law, while twenty years later the number had swelled to 114,723, an increase of 78 per cent.

From these two sets of figures, we see that the *professionally educated* lawyers have increased 200 per cent in, roughly, twenty-five years, as based upon the annual output, while the number of lawyers of all degrees of education has increased only 79 per cent in but a little less time. The necessary inference is that there is a considerably larger percentage of bachelors of law among those practising before the bar to-day than there was a generation ago. This is not at all to be wondered at, considering the rapid increase in the number of law schools, and the greater stress that is put upon preparation along all professional lines.

It is possible, by a comparison of the number of graduates in law during the last twenty-five years, with the total number of lawyers practising to-day, to determine roughly the percentage of the whole who are professionally educated. The sum total of all the graduating classes for the last twenty-five years is approximately 45,000, and it is safe to say that the whole number of professionally trained lawyers in the country to-day does not exceed that many. But, as has been stated, there were, in 1900, 114,723 in all, so it seems probable that roughly one in two and one-half or 40 per cent have graduated from the law schools. Of the graduates of the law schools for the last twenty years, about 20 per cent, or one in five, had already taken his bachelor's degree in arts or science at some college or university; the number so doing, however, is decreasing from year to year, the percentage being 33.8 for the years 1881–1885, and but 17 for the years 1895–1899.

A study of the educational preparation of 857 lawyers of eminence throughout the country throws some light on the kind of training which seems most conducive to the greatest success, as follows : —

		PER CENT
a.	No preparation beyond the secondary school	39.8
b.	College only	20.3
c.	Law school only	11.5
d.	Training entirely abroad	1.3
e.	College and professional	10.5
f.	College and graduate	9.7
g.	College, professional, and graduate	4.8

The striking thing in this table is the large number who continued their schooling no farther than the secondary stage (*a*). The study by decades gives us little encouragement on this score, since the decrease in this class in the last fifty years has been but 11 per cent (46.2 per cent in 1840, 35.4 in 1890). With so large a number of men able to achieve distinction before the bar without much use of the educational machinery, it would seem as if this were not so essential to success in this profession as in the others. It shows, also, that the schools are not our only educational factors. The study by decades further indicates that the number taking the academic degree alone (*b*) is decreasing (23.1 per cent to 14.6 per cent in fifty years), and that at the same time those depending for success solely upon the professional school (*c*) has considerably more than doubled (11.5 per cent to 27.1 per cent). The large increase in the number taking the professional course alone would seem to imply that intensive study is most conducive to success in law. Of the 857 lawyers covered by the special study, we find that 45.9 per cent had taken the academic degree, either alone or in some combination, which, compared with the 27.2 per cent of the rank and file, gives us a probability of achieving eminence just about doubled through its attainment. As regards the professional course, we have the unexpected showing of a somewhat larger number of bachelors of law among the rank and file of the profession than among the eminent men. This is undoubtedly due in large part to the fact that for earlier decades covered by our study the law school was practically unknown, and also that the large classes of legal graduates of later years have hardly had time to achieve distinction. On the whole, the legal profession is, from the standpoint of the schools, less broadly educated than are the others, and will undoubtedly remain so as long as entrance to it is guarded only by a bar examination which demands but a technical knowledge of the law, and is, the country over, such a variable quantity.

Admission to Law Schools

In the matter of entrance requirements, the law schools of the country differ materially. In many cases, only a knowledge of the rudimentary branches of common school instruction is expected, while in others, though they are very few, a college diploma is demanded. On the whole, the prerequisites to admission are rapidly stiffening, the lead being taken in this respect by the departments of law connected with the colleges and universities. Seventy-six of the total one hundred have such connections. In the greater number, these requirements for entrance to the law departments are the same as to other courses, though they are often interpreted with greater lenience. Of the eighty-six law schools in 1899, the stated requirements for admission were as follows : two required some college work ; three, a four-year high school course ; twelve, a three-year high school course ; eleven, a two-year course ; eight, a one-year course ; twenty-six, a common school education ; sixteen state no requirements ; and eight are not given.

Parsons, *Legal Education,* p. 163.

Length of Course

Appendix E.

For the first half-century of legal education in this country, the courses in the law schools were for the most part loosely organized ; there was no prescribed order for the subjects, and in many cases no definitely prescribed amount of work for graduation. Students frequently attend for a brief period, in order to supplement the work of the office ; but a comparatively small proportion taking all the work offered, or remaining to graduate. In many of the schools but one year's work was offered, and in the remainder, two years'. In 1875 there was but a single school offering more. At about this time, however, the courses began to lengthen, and of the fifty-eight law departments and schools in 1892, no less than fifteen were maintaining a three-year course.

Of the 100 in 1901, 7 offered but one year's work ; 38, two years' ; 53, three years' ; and 2 are giving a four-year course. The total length of the course in weeks for these schools, varying from 34 weeks to 154 weeks, is as follows : —

30–39 weeks, five ; 40–49, four ; 50–59, one ; 60–69, eight ; 70–79, twenty ; 80–89, ten ; 90–99, eleven ; 100–109, twenty-seven ; 110–119, nine ; 120–129, three ; 140–149, one.

The usual school year is 36 weeks, and we find the multiples of this number, 72 and 108 for the two and three year courses, the most common.

Method of Instruction

The method of instruction in vogue in most of our law schools at the present day, as it was in all until a comparatively recent date, is that of the lecture. In some instances this is supplemented by recitation from the text-book. In a comparatively few schools the so-called "case" method is in practice, which consists mainly of a discussion and explanation of a limited number of selected cases intended to cover each point. It is essentially the inductive method applied to legal instruction, and the schools which are making use of it — among them some of the leading schools of the country — argue strongly its superiority. The Moot Court is a feature in nearly all schools.

Admission to the Bar

Even in the earlier colonial days, some formal licensing of practitioners before the bar seems to have been very generally demanded in this country. In Massachusetts, Rhode Island, New Hampshire, and Delaware, the ceremony was simply that of taking an oath, without examination of any sort.

In Virginia and New York the licensing of attorneys was placed in the hands of the governor. In Connecticut the county courts, and in Pennsylvania and South Carolina the justices, were given this power. The tendency has been, however, to place the bar examination in the hands of examiners appointed by the state. The American Bar Association has recommended that the state court of last resort be given this power, and in several states this has been done. The prerequisites to the examination vary with the different states, though in most, from two to three years' legal study is demanded, together with a moderate amount of academic training. The exact conditions for admission to the bar,

Rep. Com. Ed.
1902, 2 : 1503.

as determined by the American Bar Association in 1901, are as follows: —

"Requirements for Admission to the Bar

"A law-school diploma still admits to the practice of law in Alabama, Georgia, Kansas, Louisiana, Michigan, Mississippi, Missouri, Pennsylvania (not in Philadelphia County, except to graduates of the University of Pennsylvania), South Carolina, Tennessee, Texas, Wisconsin.

"No particular period of law study is prescribed in Alabama, Arkansas, California, Georgia, Idaho, Indiana, Kentucky, Massachusetts, Mississippi, Missouri, Nevada, Oklahoma, South Carolina, South Dakota, Tennessee, Texas, Utah, Virginia.

"A period of two years' study is required in Colorado, Kansas, Louisiana, Maryland, Montana, Nebraska, New Mexico, North Carolina, North Dakota, Washington, West Virginia, and Wisconsin.

"A period of three years' study is required in Connecticut, Delaware, District of Columbia, Illinois, Iowa, Maine, Michigan, Minnesota, New Hampshire, New Jersey, New York, Ohio, Oregon, Pennsylvania, Rhode Island, Vermont, Wyoming.

"An examination before a State board of law examiners is now provided for in Colorado, Connecticut, Georgia, Illinois, Iowa, Maine, Maryland, Michigan, Minnesota, Nebraska, New Jersey, New York, Ohio, Rhode Island, Vermont, West Virginia, Wisconsin, and Wyoming.

"In West Virginia the members of the law faculty of the State University constitute the board of examiners."

c. MEDICAL EDUCATION

The medical schools of colonial days in America were the offices of the practising physicians. The ranks of the profession were recruited through the apprentice system, and of the 3000 physicians in practice at the close of the Revolution, it has been estimated that not more than 400 had received the medical degree; and these, with the exception of the 51 graduates from the two schools which had already been founded, had taken them abroad. As, however, was the case in the other learned professions, particularly successful practitioners gathered around them in some instances small circles of

followers, supplemented the work of their regular practice with talks and lectures, for which they sometimes
charged a set fee; and so, with a minimum of organizations, started what might be called medical schools.
Such centres of instruction existed in Philadelphia as
early as 1745, and in New York City in 1750 the human
body was dissected for purposes of medical instruction
before a body of students under the direction of Drs.
John Bond and William Middleton. This was perhaps
the first anatomical laboratory in the country. In
1752 Dr. William Hunter of Newport, Rhode Island, was
conducting such a school, and ten years later Dr. William
Shippen of Philadelphia began annual courses of medical lectures, illustrated by dissections of the human body,
which were continued until the Medical College of
Philadelphia, now the Department of Medicine of the
University of Pennsylvania, was founded in 1765. This

Univ. of Pa.
p. 251.

was the first medical school in the country. Dr. Shippen was appointed Professor of Anatomy and Surgery,
and two other professorships were established in the
school. The first commencement was held in 1769, ten
men receiving the degree of Bachelor of Medicine. This
degree was bestowed somewhat commonly as late as
1813, preliminary to the doctorate, which was given for
a year or more of additional work. At the Philadelphia
school the price of a ticket for a single course of lectures
was fixed at an amount not to exceed "six pistoles"
($20), with an additional matriculation fee of 20s.
Upon graduation, each student was also required to pay
a fee of not less than one guinea to each professor, and
"likewise the usual fees for the seal of his diploma and
for the increase of the library." With the exception of
a brief period during the Revolution, the sessions of the
first medical school have been continuous, though since
1791 it has been an integral part of the University of
Pennsylvania. After that date, the doctorate was the
only degree given by it in medicine. The school now

has a large faculty, and is one of the leading medical schools in the country.

In 1767 a second medical school was established. This was not in its origin a separate school, as its predecessor had been, but a medical department in connection with King's College, now Columbia, at New York City. It began with a faculty of six, one of whom, Dr. Middleton, has already been mentioned as having been active in medical instruction in New York City at a still earlier date. The first degree of Doctor of Medicine to be conferred in the country was bestowed at the commencement of the school in 1770 upon two students who had taken the bachelor's degree a year earlier. Columbia Col. p. 258.

In 1813 the faculty of medicine at Columbia was allowed to resign, in order to accept similar positions in the College of Physicians and Surgeons, established in 1807. Until 1860 the latter was maintained upon an entirely separate basis, and the university had no medical department. In that year, however, the college was again annexed, though in part preserving a separate organization until 1891, when, by an act of the legislature, it became again an integral part of its parent institution. It has to-day one of the first medical equipments in the country.

Harvard was the second of the academic institutions to provide medical instruction, which it did in 1782 by the establishment of a medical department. The first degrees were conferred in 1788, though the doctor's degree not until 1811. In 1810 the work of the school was removed to Boston, where it has since been carried on. It is conducted on a strictly graduate basis. Recent gifts of several millions of dollars lately made the school will, when invested, give it an equipment ahead of any in the country, if not in the world. Harvard Col. p. 233.

For fifteen years after the establishment of the medical department at Harvard, no other school entered the field. The next to do so was Dartmouth College, also a Dartmouth Col. p. 268.

New England institution, founding a medical school in 1798, with Dr. Nathan Smith as Professor of Medicine. Although the faculty of the school has always been particularly strong, it lacked clinical advantages until 1893, when the Mary Hitchcock Hospital was established.

The fifth school of medicine to be established was at Baltimore, Maryland, in 1807, as the Medical Department of the University of Maryland. It began work with a faculty of six and a student body of hardly more than that number. Lectures were at first delivered at the homes of the professors, and occasional clinics were held at the almshouse and at the Maryland Hospital. Work has been continuous since the foundation of this school, which is now in a prosperous condition.

During the decade from 1810 to 1819 two other medical schools were founded in the country: one in connection with Yale College in 1813, the other the Medical College of Ohio, at Cincinnati, Ohio, now the Medical Department of the University of Cincinnati. At the former institution several previous attempts had been made to organize a medical faculty, but without result. The school opened with a faculty of four, and an enrolment of thirty-one students. Latin and natural philosophy were prerequisites to entrance. The student, if a college graduate, must study with a physician three years, and if not a college graduate, four years; and in any case take one full course of lectures, to receive a license to practice. Two courses were required for the degree Doctor of Medicine. In 1814 a class of three was graduated. Since that time the work of the school has been continuous.

Yale Col. p. 245.

These nine schools of medicine had been established in the country and were in operation at the end of the second decade of the nineteenth century. There were, in 1902, 154, of which 123 are of the old school, 10 are eclectic, and 21 homeopathic. Without classification as to kind, the following table shows the geographical

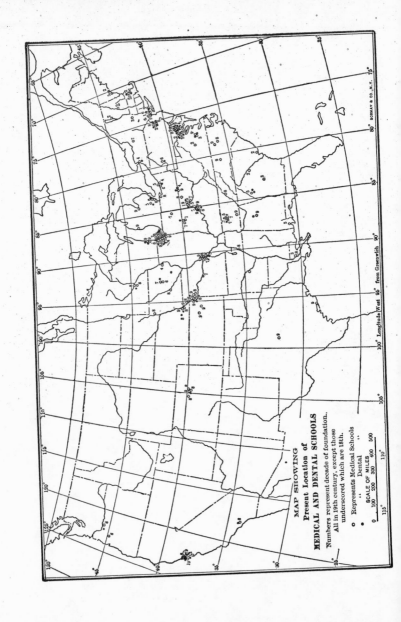

MAP SHOWING
Present Location of
MEDICAL AND DENTAL SCHOOLS

Numbers represent decade of foundation.
All in 19th century, except those
underscored which are 18th.

o   Represents Medical Schools
•   "   Dental   "

SCALE OF MILES
0 100 200 300 400 500

distribution as well as the date of establishment of the 147 which have arisen since 1820.

MEDICAL SCHOOLS

Year	N. Atlantic	S. Atlantic	S. Central	N. Central	Western	Total
1890–1901	3	6	15	17	2	43
1880–1889	4	6	7	11	8	36
1870–1879	2	1	9	9	1	22
1860–1869	4	1	2	5	1	13
1850–1859	3	2	3	4	1	13
1840–1849	2	—	1	5	—	8
1830–1839	1	1	2	1	—	5
1820–1829	3	4	—	—	—	7
Total	22	21	39	52	13	147

As will be seen, the Central states, both South and North, have a large proportion of the whole number. It is a noticeable fact, too, that the last two decades have seen the foundation of nearly one-half of the schools the country over.

In an admirable article Dr. Frank Billings, president of the American Medical Association, says of the medical schools of the country : —

Science, May 15, 1903.

"In the earlier days of our country, the need of physicians was met by the organization of medical schools which were, as a rule, proprietary in character. These schools attempted the education of physicians on the then existing conditions of medicine by teaching in a didactic way the principles and theories of medicine and surgery. The branches usually taught at that time consisted of anatomy, physiology, chemistry, materia medica, obstetrics, the practice of medicine and of surgery. But little opportunity was offered in the great majority of the schools for extensive practical teaching in anatomy or chemistry, and but a moderate amount of clinical work in the so-called practical chairs. The course of medicine in the college consisted of two annual sessions of four or five months. The course was not graded. The student attended all the lectures and clinics taught during his first year, and the second year was a repetition of his first. This class of schools was rapidly increased in the course of time. The chief reasons therefor were the fact that it was recognized that a connection with a medical school was profitable, directly or indirectly. The prestige which the teacher enjoyed among the graduates and the laity brought him a remunerative consultation and private practice. In most of the states it was easy to incorporate and obtain a charter for a medical college. It cost comparatively little to conduct and maintain the institution. Lecture rooms were obtained at trifling cost. The dissecting room was not worthy of the name of laboratory, and the chief expense in maintaining it was the cost of dissecting material, which was usually deficient in quantity and poor in quality. Medical schools were organized all over the country, without reference to the needs of the people. Medical education was prostituted. To obtain a sufficient number of students many institutions showed a most degraded disregard of the moral and mental qualifications of the matriculates. The income of the school was wholly derived from the tuition of students, and no applicant was turned away who had the cash with which to pay his way. To add to the facility of obtaining a medical college course, there were organized in some cities evening schools, the hours of college attendance occurring from 7 to 9 or 10 o'clock at night. These sundown institutions enabled the clerk, the street car conductor, the janitor, and others employed during the day to obtain a medical degree.

" In spite of the general tendency to increase the facility by which a medical degree could be obtained, there was a force at work to improve the methods of medical education. A few older medical colleges and an occasional new one set the standard high in relation to the existing status of medicine. There were earnest, forceful medical men in some of the schools who fought for a higher standard for matriculation and graduation."

That the rapid increase in schools of medicine shown by the previous table, and commented upon by Dr. Billings, was equalled by a growth in faculty, student body, and size of graduating classes, is shown by the following table : —

MEDICAL SCHOOLS

Year	Faculty	Students	Graduates
1902	5029	26,821	5069
1900	4483	25,212	5219
1895	3874	22,887	4827
1890	3987	25,262	4128
1885	2514	13,921	3622
1880	1660	14,006	3230
1875	1172	9,971	2350
1870	588	6,943	—

The sum total of graduates during the twenty-five years' period (112,000) compared with the total number of physicians in the country in 1900 (132,225), makes it seem probable that about three-fourths of the whole number have had the special preparation of the professional school, a much larger proportion than for either law or theology. Of the graduates in medicine, only 7.5 per cent had already taken their academic degree, a much smaller number than of other professions. I have no figures upon which to base a calculation of change in this respect. Of physicians of note, I have the *vitæ* of 540, on which to base a special study of the educational preparation most conducive to success in this profession. The facts disclosed by this study show one of two things : either the medical profession as a whole contains a very small number of uneducated persons, or education is a more necessary stepping-stone to eminence within it than in most other professions, for all but 38 (7 per cent) of our 540 had continued their schooling beyond the secondary stage, and the larger number of these had entered the profession more than forty years ago. A comparison of the professional and academic education of the rank and file in medicine with that of the leaders gives us some striking results. The census figures and those of the commissioner of education for graduates

The Author, Ed. Rev. Jan., 1903.

of the medical school, taken together, show that 74.4
per cent of the whole fraternity are professionally educated, while of our picked men, the percentage is 75.3;
a difference so slight as to indicate that the professional
course alone is at no great premium in the struggle for
recognition. But if we take 7.5 per cent as representing the college-trained physicians, good, bad, and indifferent, we find that the academic degree seems to increase
their chances for success nearly six times, 41.9 per cent
of our eminent men having had that training. It is hard
to see how the college course should be of such vast advantage to the physician, and it is safe to assume that
it is not to him as a simple practitioner that it counts for
so much. Most physicians of note are scientists and
investigators, contributors to their art, as well as expo-
nents of it, and it is along the line of productiveness that
the broader academic training would be most helpful.
For the physicians covered by the special study the
preparation was as follows : —

		PER CENT
a.	No preparation beyond the secondary school	7.
b.	College only	6.7
c.	Medical school alone	43.1
d.	Training entirely abroad	2.9
e.	College and professional	16.3
f.	College and abroad	.7
g.	College and graduate	5.5
h.	College, professional, and abroad	2.8
i.	College, professional, and graduate	8.2
j.	College, professional, graduate, and abroad	1.1
k.	Professional and abroad	3.1
l.	College, graduate, and abroad	1.7

Three particularly interesting things are shown by a
study of these figures from the standpoint of the period
at which practice was begun : —

1. *A decrease in the number of physicians who have
carried their education no farther than the secondary
school.* (*a*) Of those who have been forty years in the

harness, 9.5 per cent were of this class, the number gradually decreasing to 3.6 per cent for those entering it during the last decade. Of course, the rigid restrictions placed upon the practitioner have much to do with this, but even examinations have not been able to do much for some other professions.

2. *A gradual increase in the numbers combining the college course with the professional,* the growth being from 3.4 per cent for the decade 1840–1850 to 22.9 per cent for that from 1890–1900. Although many of the moves in the direction of making medicine strictly a graduate study are too recent to show in our figures, the pioneering of Johns Hopkins is perhaps responsible in part for this increase. Certain it is that the next decade will see much more marked advances in this direction.

3. *A swelling of the numbers who avail themselves of the graduate advantages of our home universities* (*b*), they having increased sixfold in the last fifty years.

As regards training abroad, two things are shown: the number of those who had received their entire education abroad is decreasing (3.4 to 1.8 per cent in fifty years), and, second, those who combine some European study with the college or medical course is on the increase (1.7 to 7.2 per cent in the same period).

The medical profession has a right to be proud of its educational status. It is safe to say that it has distanced all others in the rapid strides with which it has covered the formerly unexplored confines of its field, and recovered it from the mere fetichist and necromancer. Is it too much to ascribe this rapid advance, at least in part, to our educational machinery?

The average time in years devoted by these physicians of eminence to preparation beyond the secondary school was 4.09. This is considerably more time than is invested by members of either of the other learned professions in their educational preparation.

Admission to Medical Schools

Bulletin 8, Jan. 1900, Univ. State of New York.

According to James Russell Parsons, the entrance requirements maintained by the medical schools in the United States in 1899 were as follows:—

"One required a college degree (in 1903, three): 12, a four-year high school course: 3, a three-year course: 12, a two-year course: 97, a one-year course: 29, a common school education, and 2 not stated."

The tendency is in the direction of a stiffening of entrance requirements, especially in the schools which are connected with colleges and universities. Of the whole number, 74 have such connection.

Length of Course

Appendix E.

Of the 154 schools in operation in 1902, but 4 schools had less than a four-year, 2 of this number were offering two years, and 2, three years. In 1903, 3 were put upon a four-year basis. The number of weeks in the school year varies from 22 to 42 weeks, as follows: 1, twenty-two; 6, twenty-four; 44, twenty-six; 4, twenty-seven; 11, twenty-eight; 3, twenty-nine; 26, thirty; 4, thirty-one; 24, thirty-two; 10, thirty-four; 13, thirty-six; 3, forty; 2, forty-two.

In 1875 the courses in the 80 medical colleges of the United States were very much shorter, there being at that time not one offering a four-year course, 32 with a three-year course, 1 with a two-and-one-half year course, 36 with a two-year, 5 with a one-year, and the rest unstated. The number of weeks in the school year was also at that time considerably less, there being 20 schools in which it was 20 weeks or less. On the whole, the length of the medical course has nearly doubled in twenty-five years.

Legal Requirements for the Practice of Medicine

Previous to the Revolution but two colonies had passed any legislation bearing upon the licensing of physicians. New York in 1760 decided that no person should practice medicine in the city of New York without being examined and properly licensed. New Jersey passed a similar law in 1772. Soon after the Revolution, most of the states took action in the matter; and by 1840 nearly all had passed laws intending to protect the people from the imposition of the quacks. To-day such legislation is universal, though differing materially in different states, as is shown by the following table compiled by the commissioner of education.

Rep. 1902, 2 : 1501.

Synopsis of the Requirements for the Practice of Medicine in the United States

Classification. — The states may be classed in four groups, according to the requirements for securing a license to practice.

I. In the first group may be named the states which require an examination, diploma of a recognized medical college, and certain preliminary educational attainments ; viz., Delaware, Louisiana, Maryland, Michigan, New Hampshire, New Jersey, New York, Ohio, Pennsylvania, Wisconsin.

II. In the second group are those requiring an examination and a recognized diploma ; viz., Arizona, California, Connecticut, District of Columbia, Florida, Georgia, Hawaii, Idaho, Illinois, Indiana, Iowa, Maine, Minnesota, Montana, Nebraska, North Carolina, Oklahoma, Porto Rico, South Dakota, Utah, Vermont, Virginia, Washington.

III. In the third group are those requiring an examination only ; viz., Alabama, Arkansas, Kansas, Massachusetts, Mississippi, Missouri, North Dakota, Oregon, Rhode Island, Tennessee, Texas, West Virginia.

IV. In the fourth group are those requiring a diploma of a recognized school or an examination ; viz., Colorado, Kentucky, Nevada, New Mexico, South Carolina, Wyoming.

Mention has not been made of the usual requirements that the applicant shall be twenty-one years of age, of good moral character, and pay a fee varying from $5 to $25. It should be remembered, too, that these regulations are frequently changed by legislative amendments or board provisions.

The Philippines. — The requirements are an approved diploma and an annual tax of $50 to $150, according to income.

Methods in Medical Instruction

In the early days of medical schools, instruction was almost entirely through lectures, in some instances illustrated by means of models and dissections. Gradually text-books were more and more made use of as the supply warranted, and later the laboratory, the clinic, and actual practice in the hospital or at large have been considered very necessary elements. Very recently the "case" method has been followed by a few instructors, and bids fair to become as popular as the same method has in legal instruction. The plan is to secure printed histories of actual cases, which are fully discussed by instructor and students in connection with the actual treatment of similar cases in the clinic or hospital.

At a recent meeting of the National Confederation of State Medical Examining Boards it was voted that before a student should receive the degree of Doctor of Medicine he *should* have attended in a well-equipped medical school, four courses of lectures of at least six months each. These courses to embrace at least 3300 hours actual work in school, including, besides didactic lectures and recitations,

    a. 500 hours laboratory work,
    b. 150 hours practical work,
    c. One or more obstetric cases personally attended,
    d. 750 hours clinical teaching.

All in a school which can command at least 300 hospital or dispensary cases for presentation to its classes. When this shall be the preparation of every young medical practitioner, we need have little fear for the standing of the profession.

d. SCHOOLS OF DENTISTRY

Although the surgical care of the teeth is a matter of record since the time of Herodotus, it is only within a century that such care has formed a specialty in surgery; and it was not until 1839 that the first school for the preparation of such specialists was founded. This was the Baltimore College of Dental Surgery. In 1845 a similar school, now a department of the University of Cincinnati, was established; in 1856 and 1865 schools in Philadelphia; in 1865 one in New York City. These were all separate schools. But in 1867 Harvard founded a dental department, and other universities quickly followed its example, until in 1901 thirty-seven of the fifty-six schools of dentistry are departments of academic institutions, and are to be found in every part of the country.

Univ. of Cin. p. 277.

Harvard Col. p. 223.

The growth in numbers of the student body has been very rapid in the last twenty-five years, there being but 701 students in 1878, to 8420 in 1902, 166 of whom are women. The course is almost uniformly of three years, and the requirements for admission about the same as for the medical schools. The degree, Doctor of Dental Surgery (D.D.S.), is conferred by all the schools upon graduation.

e. SCHOOLS OF PHARMACY

The Philadelphia College of Pharmacy, the first of its kind in this country, was opened in 1822. This was followed in 1823 by the Massachusetts College of Pharmacy; in 1829 by the New York College of Pharmacy; in 1838 by the department of pharmacy of Tulane University in New Orleans; and in 1841 by the Maryland College of Pharmacy. Of late years the growth, both in the number of schools and of students, has been very rapid. In 1878 there were 13 schools, with 1187 students; in 1902 there were 59 schools, with 4427 students, 206 of whom are women. The length of course is usually two years, though 3 schools offer a three-year course, 3 a four-year course and a combination course varying in length. In many, though not all the schools, actual experience in a drug store is a prerequisite to graduation.

f. TRAINING SCHOOLS FOR NURSES

In 1873 there were established in connection with general hospitals in Boston, Salem, New Haven, New York City, and Buffalo, special schools for the training of nurses. These were the first such schools in the country. Six others were opened previous to 1880; 90 between 1880 and 1890; and 350 since that time, — one in nearly all the hospitals of any importance, either for the sick or the insane, in the country. The whole number of pupils in these schools was, in 1901, 11,590, of whom but 1307 are men. In most of the schools the course is two years. The pupils are given a monthly allowance in nearly all schools of from $12 to $24, in return for actual service in the ward. No degree is given.

REFERENCES

GENERAL

Butler, N. M. Professional and Technical Instruction in the University. N. E. A. 1894 : 619. Professional Schools and the American College. Ed. Rev. 24 : 503–517. Colleges and the Professions. Outl. 68 : 242–243. — **Dexter**, E. G. Training for the Learned Professions. Ed. Rev. Jan. 1903. — *Parsons*, J. R. Professional Education. In Butler's Education in the United States, 1900, 2 : 3–21. The Universities and the Professions. Nation, 4 : 425–426. — *White*, A. D. Scientific Education and Industrial Education. Pop. Sci. Mo. 5 : 172. — *Wilson*, Woodrow. Should an Antecedent Liberal Education be required of Students in Law, Medicine, and Theology ? N. E. A. 1893 : 112.

THEOLOGICAL

Boone, Richard G. Theological Education. In his Education in the United States, 1889, pp. 210–212. — Bushnell, Parks. Status of the Theological Seminary. Pub. Opin. 30 : 817–818. — *Dexter*, E. G. Training for the Ministry. Harper's Weekly, June 7, 1903. The Criticisms on Theological Seminaries. Outl. 63 : 732–735. The Education of the Ministers. Nation, 12 : 272–273. — *Eliot*, Charles W. On the Education of Ministers. In his Educational Reform, 1898, pp. 61–86. Evening Theological School, An. Outl. 63 : 620–621. — Hall, Charles. C. Ideal Theology Seminary. Pub. Opin. 24 : 754–755. — *Harper*, William R. Theological Seminaries. Outl. 61 : 89. Innovation in the Theology Curriculum. Pub. Opin. 26 : 114–115. — *McDonnell*, Rev. S. D. Education of Preachers. World's Work, 2 : 837–840. — Munger, Theodore T. The Divinity School and the University. Outl. 70 : 728–733. — **Parsons**, J. R. (1) New York (State) University — College Department Theology. In its Professional Education in the United States, Ser. 1900, v. 6. (2) Theology. In Butler's Education in the United States, 1900, 2 : 22–30. — Taylor, Graham. The Demand upon Theological Seminaries. Pub. Opin. 25 : 818. Theological Education. Ind. 51 : 977–978; 51 : 2709–2713. The Theological Seminaries. Outl. 63 : 436–439. — Vincent, John H. A Non-resident School of Theology. Pub. Opin. 22 : 592–593.

LEGAL

Ashley, Clarence D. The Training of the Lawyer and its Relation to General Education, 1899. — *Batchelder*, Samuel F. Old Times at the Law School (Harvard). At. Month. 90 : 642–655. — Boone, Richard, G. Legal Education. In his Education in the United States, 1900, pp. 212–217. — *Dexter*, E. G. Educational Status of the Legal Profession. Green Bag, May, 1903. — Dicey, A. V. Teaching of the English Law at Harvard. Contemp. 76 : 742–758. — *Meekings*, L. R. Legal Education in the United States. R. of R.'s 10 : 502–507. — New York (State) University — College Department Law. In its Professional Education in the United States. Ser. 1900, v. 7. — *Parsons*, J. R. Law. In Butler's Education in the United States, 1900, 2 : 31–41.

MEDICAL

Boone, Richard G. Medical Education. In his Education in the United States, 1889, pp. 217–221. — Dodson, John M. The Modern University School. — Its Purposes and Methods, 1902. —

Jordan, David Starr. Training of a Physician. Pop. Sci. Mo. 63 : 304–311. Medical Education in New York. Harper, 65 : 668–679. — *Minot*, Charles S. Knowledge and Practice. Science, (N. S.) 10 : 1–11. (Medical Commencement Address at Yale.) New York (State) University — College Department Medicine. In its Professional Education in the United States, Ser. 1900, v. 8. — *Parsons*, J. R. Medicine. In Butler's Education in the United States, 1900, 2 : 42–61. Progress of Medical Education in the United States, Sci. Amer. Sup. 45 : 18499. The raising of Standards in Medical Education. Outl. 70 : 946. — Rusk, E. L. H. Preparation for the Study of Medicine. Science, 19 : 282-284. — *Thwing*, C. F. Best College Education for the Physician. Ed. 13 : 195. — *United States Education*, Bureau of. Legal Provisions Governing the Practice of Medicine in the Various States. Rep. 1902, 1 : xcvii.

DENTAL

Fillebrown, Thomas. Shall Dentistry be Taught as a Medicine? Harv. Grad. Mag. 4 : 214–220. New York (State) University — College Department Dentistry. In its Professional Education, Ser. 1900, v. 9. — *Parsons*, J. R. Dentistry. In Butler's Education in the United States, 1900, 2 : 62–69.

PHARMACEUTICAL

New York (State) University — College Department Pharmacy. In its Professional Education in the United States, Ser. 1900, v. 10. — *Parsons*, J. R. Pharmacy. In Butler's Education in the United States, 1900, 2 : 70–78. — United States Education, Bureau of. Pharmacy in the United States. Rep. 1894–1895, 2 : 1239–1241.

TRAINING OF NURSES

McMurdy, Robert. An Interesting Experiment. Outl. 69 : 662. (Training School for Colored Nurses in Chicago). — North, Franklin H. A New Profession for Women. Cent. 3 : 38–47. (Bellevue Training School for Nurses, New York). — *Nutting*, Adelaide. The Working Hours of Pupil Nurses. Char. Rev. 5 : 239–246.

CHAPTER XVII

TECHNICAL AND AGRICULTURAL EDUCATION

TECHNICAL SCHOOLS

WITHIN our country, schools of applied science, whether the application be to industry and the mechanic arts or to agriculture, are, with but one or two exceptions, the growth of the last half of the nineteenth century. The first half of the century had seen the accumulation of a considerable mass of scientific fact. Great progress has been made in physics, especially in electricity and chemistry; what had been at first but a chaotic mass of unrelated facts was fast becoming a science that was not without its effect upon the industry of the time. But the discoveries along these lines were being made in the laboratories of the classical colleges, for those were the only institutions in any way equipped for scientific work, and in a classic atmosphere. Yet such institutions had never as yet contributed in any important way to the progress of industrial development, and were not considered capable, it must be acknowledged, by the industrial world, of doing so. Theirs was supposed to be a different field. Occasional attempts had, however, been made at a few of the older institutions to apply their scientific instruction to practical needs. As early as 1792 Samuel L. Mitchell was appointed in Columbia College with the title of Professor of Natural History, Chemistry, and Agriculture, though what instruction he offered in the last subject is uncertain. Much of the work which Silliman did at Yale was of the greatest value in pointing out the relation between the facts of chemistry and the affairs of everyday life, and we must consider him one of the pioneers in the field of applied science. Except, however, for the United States Military Academy at West Point, New York, which is in a sense a technical school of high rank, no special school for the study of applied science was established until 1824. This was the Rensselaer Polytechnic Institute at Troy, New York. Many years elapsed before its example was followed. The professions of engineering and architecture developed slowly; and not until they were considered as more than trades to be learned, was there any demand for technical education. This point reached, the growth of technical education was rapid, and to-day we have 147 higher institutions offering courses in the various fields of engineering and architecture, or agriculture, or both.

Ren. Pol. Inst.
p. 345.

Although each of these institutions differs from all the others in some particulars, they fall into four distinct classes, so far as organization is concerned.

    a. Technical schools upon private foundations (7).
    b. Technical schools supported in part or wholly by national or state appropriations (36).
    c. Technical schools or departments connected with colleges and universities (102).
    d. The national military and naval academies (2).

The following table shows, for the various geographical divisions of the country, the year of establishment of classes *a* and *b*, and so many of class *c* as are receiving national support from the legislative acts of 1862 and 1890 (28). It was not possible in all cases to determine the date upon which technical work was begun in the established colleges.

YEAR	N. ATLANTIC	S. ATLANTIC	S. CENTRAL	N. CENTRAL	WESTERN	TOTAL
1890–1902	3	5	2	2	6	18
1881–1889	1	3	3	3	2	12
1871–1879	2	2	6	4	2	16
1861–1869	8	3	3	7	1	22
1851–1859	1	—	—	1	—	2
1841–1849	—	—	—	—	—	—
1831–1839	—	—	—	—	—	—
1821–1829	1	—	—	—	—	1
Total	16	13	14	17	11	71

It must be borne in mind that this table covers only about one-half of the higher academic institutions, offering technical courses, though, with the exception of perhaps a dozen, such as Harvard, Yale, Columbia, Chicago, Leland Stanford, all the important ones are included. Although agricultural education has run parallel in many respects to that in science, applied to manufacture and arts, I shall treat the two separately.

a. Technical Schools upon Private Foundations

As has been indicated, this was the first class to enter the field. Rensselaer Polytechnic Institute at Troy, New York, the oldest technical institution, opened its doors in 1825. It was founded by Stephen Van Rensselaer, a descendant of the original "patroon" who had gained possession of a considerable portion of eastern New York early in the seventeenth century. He was a Harvard graduate, and was the first to propose a canal from the Hudson River to Lake Erie, and as a commissioner of the state, made the first survey in 1811. The founder states his purpose for the school in a letter dated November 5, 1824: —

"I have founded a school at the north end of Troy," he says, "for the purpose of instructing persons who may choose to apply themselves in the application of science to the common purposes of life. My principle object is to qualify teachers for instructing sons and daughters of farmers and mechanics, by lectures or otherwise, on the application of experimental chemistry, philosophy [physics], and natural history to agriculture, domestic economy, the arts, and manufactures."

He further says : —

"These are not to be taught by seeing experiments and hearing lectures according to the usual methods. But they are to lecture and experiment by turns, under the immediate direction of the professor, or competent assistant. Thus, by a term of labor, like an apprentice to a trade, they are to become operative chemists."

Sherwood, p. 484.

It is plain that Van Rensselaer did not have in mind the preparation of a professional class in the establishment of the school. The first senior professor was Amos Eaton, who had a great influence in the early popularization of scientific studies in the North. Upon his death, in 1842, the course of study was reorganized and strengthened, and the school became more distinctly one of civil engineering. At present the degree of civil engineer (C.E.) is offered in that course, and that of bachelor of science (B.S.) in general science. The entrance requirements are not so high as in some other schools of technology.

The next separate school of technology was established in 1868, in Worcester, Massachusetts, as the Worcester Polytechnic Institute, through the generosity of John Boynton of Templeton, Massachusetts.

During the more than forty years which had elapsed since the founding of the school at Troy, great strides had been taken in technical education. The Morrill bill had been passed, and nearly twenty states had availed themselves of its privileges. The Massachusetts Institute of Technology was well started (discussed under class *b*), and engineering as a profession had become an accomplished fact.

P. 350.

A distinctive characteristic of the Worcester school is the large use made of workshops and laboratories. In the former, the students construct and place upon the market machines of considerable elaborateness, many of which were invented by themselves or their instructors. In this way the final test of proficiency in manual work is reached through commercial competition. Although the course for mechanical engineers is perhaps the strongest in the institute, four others are offered, each of four years: civil engineering, electrical engineering, sanitary engineering, and general science. The state of Massachusetts maintains forty scholarships at the school, while there are about thirty more to which only residents of Worcester County are eligible.

The third school of class *a* to be established is the Stevens Institute of Technology, at Hoboken, New Jersey, which was opened in 1871. Professor Henry Morton was brought from the University of Pennsylvania as its first president; and in connection with R. H. Thurston, later of Cornell, as Professor of Mechanical Engineering, and others of prominence upon the faculty, soon built up a very strong school. Stevens offers but one course, that for mechanical engineers; but in connection with it are introduced many elaborate tests, especially with locomotives and steam-engines which are not possible in institutions where the equipment is divided among several departments.

The Case School of Applied Science in Cleveland, Ohio, was established in 1881. Leonard Case was its founder, and directed that in the school should be taught "by competent professors, and teachers, mathematics, physics, engineering — mechanical and civil — chemistry, economic geology, mining, metallurgy, natural history, drawing, and modern languages, and such other kindred branches of learning as the trustees of said institution may deem desirable." Eight courses are maintained: civil, mechanical, electrical, and mining engineering, physics, chemistry, architecture, and general science, each leading to the B.S. degree at the end of four years with the M.S. conferred for one year more of work. The school has about $2,000,000 in productive funds and $350,000 in buildings and grounds.

Two years after the establishment of the Case School (1883), the Rose Polytechnic Institute was opened at Terre Haute, Indiana, through the generosity of Chauncey Rose. Dr. Charles O. Thompson, who had been instrumental in building up the polytechnic institute at Worcester, Massachusetts, was its first president; and, although he died shortly after accepting the position, he nevertheless had had time to establish the school upon similar lines. Four courses of study are offered: mechanical and electrical engineering, civil engineering and architecture, and in chemistry, each of four years, granting the B.S. degree. The M.S. is conferred two years after graduation, if one of them has been spent in practice and the other in graduate study.

The next technical school to be established upon private foundation, the Armour Institute of Technology, is also in the West, at Chicago. It was founded by Philip D. Armour, in 1893, his gifts to the institute exceeding $2,500,000. It offers a full four-year course in technical instruction.

The latest entry into the lists of private technical schools is the Clarkson School of Technology at Potsdam, New York, established in 1896.

b. Technical Schools supported in part or wholly by National or State Appropriations

There are thirty-six such schools in the country, by far the greater number of which owe their origin to the Morrill Act of 1862. When this is the case, scientific agriculture and military instruction are required by law to have place in the curriculum.

When the various states received their portions of land-grant scrip, each with more or less haste disposed of a considerable proportion, and proceeded to establish courses of instruction as the money realized, permitted. Some whose quotas were too small to finance a separate institution, turned the funds over to some already established college or university which should comply with the provisions of the law. In this way Rhode Island gave hers to Brown; Connecticut to Yale; New Hampshire to Dartmouth, and New Jersey to Rutgers.

Many states which had received a larger share, but still not enough to carry out the act in all its particulars, founded purely agricultural colleges, as instanced by Michigan and Iowa. Others divided the funds between two separate institutions: one for the agricultural branches, favorably located in a farming community, and another for the courses in the mechanic arts. Massachusetts, with its national grant divided between its Institute of Technology and the Agricultural College at Amherst, is an example of such division of interests.

Still another class of states, each with a large share of the scrip, determined to carry out the provisions of the act in the broadest and fullest possible way by applying it all to a single institution which, although the mechanic arts branches should receive full attention, should be a university in the broadest sense. To this class belong New York and Illinois. These various methods of utilizing the national grant for technical purposes have, on the whole, worked well. Only in a few cases has the fund been mismanaged, and the many-sided institutions which have resulted present all phases of usefulness. Of the separate institutions for scientific study of any sort — and these are the only ones we are considering in this class — ten are designated as colleges of agriculture, pure and simple, and thirteen by some title indicating some combination of agriculture with the other applied sciences, for instance, the Rhode Island College of Agriculture and Mechanic Arts, Mississippi Agricultural and Mechanical College, and the Washington Agricultural College and School of Science. All are, however, primarily agricultural in their interests, and will be considered under agricultural colleges. Of the remainder, three, the Alabama Polytechnic Institute, the Massachusetts Institute of Technology, and Purdue University, the State School of Technology for Indiana, are primarily schools of technology, though in some instances offering agricultural instruction. Four are designated as schools of mines, as the Colorado, New Mexico, and South Dakota State Schools of Mines, and the Michigan College of Mines.

The two remaining schools, although offering technological courses, put the stress upon military training, at least in their titles, as the South Carolina Military Academy and the Virginia Military Institute. Not all of these institutions receive support from the land-grant, but all are state institutions.

Of those designated as schools of technology, the Massachusetts Institute is the oldest, and has exerted by far the most important influence upon the development of scientific education. In fact, there is probably no other institution of any of the classes considered, which has surpassed it in this respect. Although a beneficiary of the Morrill Act, it was incorporated in 1861, before the passage of the act, yet instruction was not actually begun until after the Civil War, in 1865. The institute owes its origin to William B. Rogers, who became its first president, and directed its interests, with the exception of an interval from 1870 to 1878, until 1881, when ill health forced him to retire from the work, and General Francis A. Walker, one of the foremost educators of our times, accepted the responsibility. The institute offers thirteen distinct courses, each of four years : civil, mechanical, electrical, mining, chemical, and sanitary engineering, architecture, chemistry, biology, physics, geology, naval architecture, and general studies. Since the latter includes most of the academic branches usually taught in a college or university, it is possible to pursue a broader course at the Massachusetts Institute than at any of the other separate technical schools. It is by far the largest of its class in point of student body. It receives but one-third of the state apportionment of the land-grant fund, the rest of its income being from tuition and private bequest.

The school of next importance in the strictly technical schools of this class is Purdue University at Lafayette, Indiana. It is in reality the technological department of the State University, though not in the same city with the academic departments. It was established in 1874. Five special courses are offered: mechanical and electrical engineering, agriculture, general science, and pharmacy. Except for the latter, each is of four years, and leads to the B.S. degree.

The four institutions whose names imply a special application of science to the needs of the mining engineer are all situated in states of great mineral resources, where the interests of the miner are paramount, and where ample facilities for studying mining operations are at hand. Of them, the Colorado institution is the oldest, having been founded in 1873; Michigan coming next in 1885; North Dakota following in 1886; and New Mexico in 1893. Although the principal stress is placed upon the courses of the mining engineer, other courses are in every case offered, and work of the highest order is being done. The students accompany their instructors to mining centres, and in some instances spend considerable periods of time in service within the mines themselves. This class of schools is proving of the greatest value in furnishing intelligent directors for the development of our mineral resources.

c. Technological Schools connected with Colleges and Universities

Within this class of schools, which is at once the largest as well as the most diversified of any so far as courses are concerned, come some of the oldest as well as the best technical institutions in our country. In breadth of offering they vary from the small college, which has combined with its academic work a single technical course of a professional character, to institutions like Columbia University, with eleven distinct courses, Cornell with ten, and the University of Illinois with seven. Only twenty-eight of the whole hundred or more receive support from the land-grant; a small proportion of the remainder are state institutions, but the great majority are upon a private foundation.

Yale Col. p. 244.   Of them all, the Sheffield Scientific School at Yale, although opened in the same year (1847) as the scientific school at Harvard, may perhaps with justice be considered the oldest, since it was but a continuation of the important scientific work of Silliman and his colleagues which had been carried on for a quarter of a century earlier. The school is what its name implies — a scientific school rather than a school of technology pure and simple, the stress being rather placed upon science than upon its application. The courses include civil, mechanical, and electrical engineering, chemistry, agriculture, natural history, mineralogy, biology, mining, and metallurgy. The undergraduate course is of but three years, though the entrance requirements are so much higher than most of the separate schools of technology as to make graduates practically equivalent. The faculty of the school is distinct from that of the university, though some of the instructors are connected with both.

Harvard Col. p. 232.   The Lawrence Scientific School at Harvard was also established in 1847. For many years it was maintained practically as a separate institution, but had gradually become more closely united with the university, until now it is an integral part of it. It has no separate faculty, and its degrees are conferred by the university. The school offers eleven distinct courses: civil, mechanical, electrical, and mining engineering, architecture, geology, chemistry, biology, science for teachers, anatomy, and physiology. Its entrance requirements are high; practically the same as those for the academic departments of the university. With the advantages which come from the unsurpassed library, museum, and laboratory facilities at Harvard, Lawrence is enabled to offer advantages to the student in the less purely applied lines of scientific study which are impossible to the smaller institution.

Four years after the establishment of scientific departments at Harvard and Yale (1851), the Chandler School of Science was founded at Dartmouth College, through a bequest by Abiel Chandler, to set up "a permanent school of instruction in the college in practical and useful arts of life." Its course is broadly scientific rather than technical. The Thayer School of Civil Engineering, also at Dartmouth, is a graduate department, established through a gift by General Sylvanus Thayer in 1867. Owing to the requirements for entrance, the number of students is small, but the work is of a very high character. The only degree given is that of civil engineer. Dartmouth Col. p. 268.

Other scientific departments of the same general class as the Sheffield and the Lawrence schools, in that they are connected with colleges and universities upon private foundations, are the John C. Green School of Science at Princeton University, founded in 1873 — besides general science courses, it graduates students in civil and mechanical engineering — the Towne Scientific School of the University of Pennsylvania, founded in 1874, which offers five separate engineering courses Princeton Col. p. 245 *et seq.* Univ. of Pa. p. 250 *et seq.*

in addition to those in general science, and special scientific or technological schools at Union College, Washington University (St. Louis, Missouri), Tulane University, Brown University, Leland Stanford University, Johns Hopkins University, the Polytechnic Institute of Brooklyn, University of Cincinnati, Lehigh University, Vanderbilt University, and the University of Virginia.

The most elaborately organized scientific department at any of the private universities is that under the faculties of pure and applied science at Columbia University, offering, all together, ten separate professional courses, besides a large number of less direct vocational application. The School of Mines was opened as early as 1864, and has stood practically at the head of such institutions ever since. Other schools of architecture, engineering, and of chemistry are maintained. Nearly fifteen hundred students have graduated from these various schools.

Of the state universities, nearly all of which are beneficiaries of the Morrill Act of 1862, thirty maintain technical courses. Of them, one course each is offered by the universities of Montana and North Carolina; two by those of Alabama, Arizona, Georgia, Iowa (has a state college of agriculture and mechanic arts in addition, at which four courses are offered), North Dakota, South Dakota, Texas, Utah, and Wyoming; three each at the universities of Arkansas, Colorado, Idaho, Louisiana, Maine, Mississippi, Nebraska, Tennessee, and West Virginia; four at the University of Wisconsin; five each at Kansas, Ohio, Oregon, and Washington state universities; six at California and Minnesota; seven at the University of Illinois; and eight at that of Missouri. In their equipment for technological work, the variation among the institutions is even greater than in the number of courses, though generally speaking it is better than among the colleges upon private foundation.

Of them all, Michigan was the first to offer technological courses, which were begun in 1853, though included within the offerings of the college of literature, science, and arts, until 1895, when an engineering college was established. All courses lead to the B.S. degree. The universities of Illinois and Minnesota established technical courses at the start (1868), and the University of Wisconsin in 1870. These three institutions are, perhaps, the leaders among the state universities in matters of technical instruction. Each has a magnificent equipment, large numbers of students, and maintains courses of the highest character. It is probably safe to say that the general average of technical work done in the state universities as a class is higher than that in the colleges upon a private foundation, though marked exceptions to this occur.

d. The National Military and Naval Academies

The United States Military Academy at West Point was established in 1802, though as early as 1783, at the close of the Revolution, the question of founding such an institution was considered. Although its aim is the production of the efficient military officer, it is realized only through four years of vigorous training, both physical and mental, and its courses include much that is found in our best technical schools, of which it might with justice be considered the oldest. In fact, until the establishment of the Rensselaer Institute, it was the only institution in the country offering engineering courses. Its courses were at first not of a high order of excellence, but during the superintendency of General Sylvanus Thayer, who was appointed in 1817, they were fully reorganized and placed upon the footing of the best military colleges in Europe. This high standard it has since maintained. It has graduated in all 4806 students, who have immediately, upon leaving the school, received appointments as second lieutenants in the regular army.

Unlike the other schools of our country, except the Naval Academy at Annapolis, admission to West Point is only by the Secretary of War, through the nomination of a senator or representative in Congress, or by the President. In the case of congressional appointments there may or may not be a competitive examination for the position. Each congressional district, territory, and the District of Columbia is entitled to have one student at the academy, as well as is each senator, while the President of the United States appoints forty, usually the sons of army officers who have no fixed residence.

Both physical and mental examinations must be passed by the appointee; and these are so rigid as not infrequently to debar a candidate from admission, even though the formality of the appointment has been made. An allowance of $609.50 per year is made each student, which is sufficient, with economy, to defray all expenses. During the summer the cadets live in camp, but one leave of absence being allowed for the four years.

First year: mathematics, modern languages, history, geography, and ethics, drill regulations of artillery and cavalry, use of the sword.

Second year: mathematics, modern languages, drawing, drill regulations of artillery, infantry, and cavalry.

Third year: natural and experimental philosophy, chemistry, mineralogy and geology, drawing, drill regulations and practical military engineering.

Fourth year: civil and military engineering and science of war, modern languages, law, history, geography, and ethics, practical military engineering, drill regulations and ordinance and gunnery.

Students who are deficient in their studies are peremptorily discharged, and the discipline, on the whole, is even more rigid than in the regular army.

The United States Naval Academy at Annapolis, Maryland, was established in 1845. During the Civil War it was removed to Newport, Rhode Island; but was returned to its old location in 1865. Appointments to it are made upon practically the same basis as to West Point, except that there are but ten presidential appointees. The allowance is $500 annually for each student. The course of instruction is for six years, the last two of which must be spent at sea.

For the first four years it is as follows : —

First year : mechanical drawing, algebra, geometry and descriptive geometry, English and French, or Spanish.

Second year : a continuation of these subjects, with the addition of trigonometry, conic sections, differential calculus, astronomy, elementary physics and chemistry.

Third year : seamanship, astronomy, elements of mechanism, mechanical processes, marine engines, metal mechanics, mechanical drawing, physics, including electricity and magnetism, chemistry, and international and military law.

Fourth year : seamanship and naval tactics, navigation and surveying, instructions for infantry and artillery, gunnery, drill, ordinance, experimental engineering, including boilers, naval designing, and construction, and special instruction in physiology and hygiene. The summers are spent by the cadets in cruises upon the practice ship.

In 1897 a graduate course in naval architecture was established. A full reconstruction of the buildings at Annapolis is now going on. When completed, the academy will be one of the finest naval training schools in the world.

The Course of Study

With very few exceptions, the course of study at the technological schools is four years, and has been since their

Rep. Com. Ed.
1901, 2 : 1813.

establishment.   In other respects there is the greatest
diversity.   In the separate schools, whether private or
public, the curriculum is largely restricted to the pure and
applied sciences, together with English and modern languages.   In the Massachusetts Institute of Technology,
however, one finds nearly all the subjects of the college
curriculum, though this is an exception.   In the schools
of mines, metallurgical studies receive much attention,
though in other respects the work does not vary materially from other technical schools.   In the departments
of science and engineering in colleges and universities
the possibilities for the student to broaden his course
are almost unlimited, so far as offerings go, and in those
institutions where the technical course permits of election
— though this unfortunately is not the case in many of
the schools whose courses are primarily for engineers—
many of the more broadly academic subjects are taken.
This is especially true in the so-called schools of science
connected with the large Eastern colleges, which are less
purely professional than the departments of engineering
of the great state universities.   In the matter of shop
work, in courses especially for mechanical engineers,
there is much variation.   In a majority of the schools it
is placed in a very subordinate position in the curriculum, in some even hardly figuring at all; while in schools

P. 346.

of the Worcester type, manual construction work occupies as much as one-fourth of the student's time.

The prime centres of activity in all the schools with
anything like an adequate equipment are the laboratories.   These include those of chemistry and physics,
which in associated departments are used in common
with the academic students, and the drawing and draught-
ing rooms.   Besides these are an increasing number of
special laboratories for the application of pure science to
the needs of the professional practitioner.   These laboratories and their equipment are very expensive, but are
the characteristic features of the technical school, and

are the bases of its particular usefulness. The entrance requirements, especially in the separate technological institutions, do not presuppose so many years of preparation as those of the higher academic institutions. The classical languages are not included, and only in a comparatively few schools, modern languages; yet in mathematics the requirements are rigid. In the scientific and technical departments of the academic institutions, the prerequisites are usually approximate to, and in some universities identical with, the other departments, making them, generally speaking, a little higher than those of the separate schools.

In 1902, sixteen separate professional courses, not counting agriculture and closely allied subjects, were being offered in the technical schools of all classes. The following table shows the number of institutions offering each one of these courses : —

Architecture	19
Civil engineering	95
Chemical engineering	21
Electrical engineering	79
Irrigation engineering	2
Mechanical engineering	85
Metallurgical engineering	7
Mining engineering	36
Marine engineering	4
Sanitary engineering	11
Naval architecture	6
Textile engineering	4
Railway engineering	5

The number of these courses offered by each one of the institutions is as follows : —

Offering one course	31
Offering two courses	20
Offering three courses	30
Offering four courses	18
Offering five courses	11

Offering six courses	.	.	.	.	7
Offering seven courses	.	.	.	.	1
Offering eight courses	.	.	.	.	3
Offering ten courses	.	.	.	.	1

In many cases, agriculture, forestry, domestic science, or horticulture are offered, but these courses are not included in the list.

AGRICULTURAL EDUCATION

Although agricultural interests have always been paramount in the United States, more than two centuries of colonial and national life had passed before there were any serious attempts made to establish institutions for scientific agricultural instruction. When land could be had for the asking, and there was no necessity for making it produce more than a small percentage of its possible crop, there was no need for scientific method in its cultivation. Mere scratching of the surface and a dropping in of seed brought reasonable results, and when a piece of land was worked out, more was to be had.

Some inducements to care in farming were held out through the prizes offered at fairs, and even before the commencement of the nineteenth century, societies for the promotion of agriculture were formed in some of the Eastern states (New York, 1791; Connecticut, 1792), which, with their descendants, the granges, and other associations of rural agriculturalists, have undoubtedly had a very important influence upon agricultural progress, though only in a remote way contributing to agricultural instruction. Allusion has already been

P. 343.

made to the attempt at Columbia at about this time to establish courses in agriculture; but they came to naught, and so far as we know were not again attempted anywhere for nearly half a century. It was at a university, however, that the second attempt was made: this time at Yale, in connection with the Sheffield school, one of the first instructors (1847) having the title of Professor of Agricultural Chemistry, Vegetable and Animal Physiology. But previous to this time the national government had interested itself to the extent of carrying on a free distribution of seeds (Department of Agriculture not established until 1872), and in many states the farmers were urging the establishment of schools for agricultural instruction. In 1838 in New York State a petition was presented to the legislature, containing six thousand signatures, urging the establishment of such a school, and stating that "there is no school, no seminary, no department of any school in which the science of agriculture is taught." A number of small private schools seem to have resulted from this public expression of need, but certainly none by state enactment for many years. In fact, the first school of such a character did not come in the East after all; but it remained for the West, where action has usually followed more closely upon conviction in matters educational, to establish the first agricultural college. This was the Michigan State Agricultural College, opened at Lansing, Michigan, in 1857. It was given a site embracing 676 acres of heavily timbered land, and buildings to the cost of $100,000 were immediately erected. In 1862 the college was made the recipient of the state's allotment of land-grant scrip, and has ever since been one of the strongest agricultural colleges of the country.

Maryland was the next state to found such a college, which was opened in 1859, near the city of Washington.

Public agitation for such an institution was seriously begun in Massachusetts in 1849, though a charter was not granted until 1856, and actual instruction not begun until 1869. The College of Agriculture is situated at Amherst, though it is not in any way connected with Amherst College; it receives but two-thirds of the land-grant income of the state. Pennsylvania followed with an agricultural college in 1859. These four prac-

Dabney, p. 606.

Bost. Inst. Tech. p. 350.

tically complete the list up to 1862, the year of the Morrill Act.

Pp. 282, 348.

With the passage of the Morrill Act, an immediate impetus was given to agricultural education, since the act specifically required that institutions founded under it should teach such branches of learning as are related to agriculture and the mechanic arts. The twenty-six colleges so established and bearing the title "Agricultural," either alone or in connection with some other designating term, are distributed as follows, with the year of establishment of each: —

Virginia (Hampton)	1862
Kansas (Manhattan)	1863
Kentucky (Lexington)	1866
New Hampshire (Durham)	1867
Iowa (Ames)	1868
Oregon (Corvallis)	1870
Mississippi (Westside)	1871
Georgia (Athens)	1872
Virginia (Blacksburg)	1872
Texas (College Station)	1876
Colorado (Fort Collins)	1879
Mississippi (Agricultural College)	1880
Connecticut (Storrs)	1881
Florida (Lake City)	1884
South Dakota (Brookings)	1884
North Carolina (W. Raleigh)	1889
Rhode Island (Kingston)	1890
Utah (Logan)	1890
North Dakota (Agricultural College)	1891
Oklahoma (Stillwater)	1891
South Carolina (Clemson)	1893
New Mexico (Merella Park)	1891
Washington (Pullman)	1892
North Carolina (Greenboro)	1894 (colored)
Oklahoma (Sangston)	1897 (colored)
South Carolina (Orangeburg)	1896 (colored)

In addition to the strictly agricultural courses that are offered in all these colleges, one or more of the engineering courses, discussed in the first part of the chapter, are usually maintained. In addition to these, domestic science is taught in fourteen, forestry in one (Michigan), and horticulture in four. These courses cover in a general way the strictly agricultural offerings; yet many of the institutions are broadly industrial, and include within their curricula a great variety of work. Especially is this true in the South. For example: the Alabama Agricultural and Mechanical College (colored), besides the usual agricultural courses and a normal course of four years, announces the following industrial courses: carpentry, iron-working, shoemaking, sewing, and printing, each of three years; nurse training, cooking, and laundering, of two years each; broom making, chair-bottoming, millinery, and shorthand, each one year. The school is not, however, a fair type of the American agricultural college.

In the following fifteen states and territories, the agricultural college is a part of the State University: Arizona, Arkansas, California, Idaho, Illinois, Louisiana, Maine, Minnesota, Missouri, Nebraska, Nevada, Ohio, Tennessee, Wisconsin, and Wyoming. Except in method of organization, these departments do not vary materially from the separate agricultural colleges.

In ten colleges and universities, established upon a private foundation, agricultural courses are offered: four of these, Delaware College, Cornell University, Chapter XV. Rutgers College, and the University of Vermont, receive support from the land-grant. The other six, Berea and Knoxville colleges, Harvard, Yale, and Howard universities, and the University of Virginia, are the only institutions in which strictly voluntary or non-state supported courses in agriculture are maintained in the country. Of these ten institutions, Cornell makes the most extensive offerings in agriculture, and is in some ways the leader in scientific agricultural instruction in the country. At Harvard the agricultural department Harvard Col. is known as the Bussey Institution, and is situated at P. 233.

Yale Col. p. 244. Jamaica Plain, a suburb of Boston. At Yale, the agricultural courses are given in the Sheffield Scientific School. At both Harvard and Yale much is made of the courses in forestry. In the other private institutions of the list varying amounts of agricultural work are offered, though, except in those receiving incomes from the land-grant, it is usually small.

Entrance to Agricultural Colleges

In the various states these vary materially. The feeling is somewhat general that if the agricultural college is to be of most benefit to the rural communities, the preparation of rural communities must be accepted; that is, the same as that required for admission to a first-class high school. This is true very generally in the South and some parts of the West. When more is demanded by the separate agricultural colleges, a preparatory department is frequently maintained. For admission to the departments of agriculture connected with the colleges and universities more is usually required, in some cases equaling that demanded for admission to the other departments. This is true at Cornell and the University of Illinois. When, however, one is not a matriculant for a degree, this requirement is not usually made. At a recent meeting of representatives of the various agricultural colleges of the country, the question of admission was fully discussed, and the following list of subjects made out " as a standard series of entrance requirements to be adopted as soon as possible ": —

Physical geography; United States history; arithmetic, including the metric system; algebra to quadratics; English grammar and composition, together with the English requirements of the New England association; Rep. Com. Ed.
1896–1897, I : 429. plane geometry, one foreign language; one of the natural sciences, and ancient, general, or English history.

Course of Study

In most institutions, the full agricultural course is four years in length, and is usually quite fully prescribed. This course leads to the B.S. degree in science or the degree B.Ag. There are, however, quite generally maintained what are known as short courses, not leading to a degree. In many cases these are general courses of two years, or (rarely) one year, for students who can devote only a limited amount of time to study, but who wish a general survey of the field and to get in touch with scientific method.

Again, still shorter courses are offered in many institutions, permitting the student to devote all his time, or a considerable portion of it, to a single subject. Such courses are usually offered in the winter time, when work upon the farm is not pressing; and they are open to all mature applicants, irrespective of academic qualification. Thus at Cornell are offered twelve weeks' courses in agriculture and in dairying, and of a single term in forestry; and at the Michigan Agricultural College, a twelve weeks' course in chemistry, six weeks' courses in beet sugar production, dairy husbandry, creamery management, and live stock husbandry, and a four weeks' course in cheese-making.

In the full four years' course there is the greatest variation in the different institutions. In part this diversity is brought about by conditions peculiar to the state. In the arid regions of our country, irrigation-engineering takes a prominent place, and in most states the peculiarities of the soil and the character of the staple crop are made the bases of specializations : in the corn belt, giving rise to special courses in corn culture; in the beet sugar regions, to the beet; and in fruit and grain states, to those products. That there might be less variation in the fundamental branches which should form a basis for such variations, the association of agricultural colleges has framed the following outline of studies, the relative prominence to be given each of which is given in hours : —

	Hours
Algebra	75
Geometry	40
Trigonometry	40
Physics (classroom)	75
Physics (laboratory)	75
Chemistry (classroom)	75
Chemistry (laboratory)	75
English	200
Modern language	340
Psychology	60
Ethics or logic	40
Political economy	60
General history	80
Constitutional law	50
	1285

The total number of hours included in a four years' course, allowing 15 hours per week for 36 weeks, would be 2160, with ten hours' laboratory or practicums added, 3600.

The committee suggests 1740 hours additional to those given in the list in applied science, as follows : —

Agriculture	480
Horticulture and forestry	180
Veterinary science	180
Agricultural chemistry	180
Botany	180
Zoölogy, including entomology . . .	120
Physiology	180
Geology	120
Meteorology	60
Drawing	60

It is safe to say that but few agricultural colleges are as yet following this programme fully, though many of those connected with large academic institutions find it possible, and are approximating it.

Experiment Stations

A most important feature of the modern college of agriculture is the experiment station. Involving, as it does, the experimental farm as well as many special laboratories, it is an essential part of the equipment, but is proving of perhaps greater general value as a place for the scientific investigation of agricultural problems. The general farmer, who must make his land pay, does not go far from the beaten path of agricultural procedure. In the experiment station, a single crop, upon a limited area, may be sacrificed, if thereby something of value may be learned; and vast contributions are coming from these stations annually, which are doing much to put agriculture on a sound, scientific foundation.

The first serious attempts at investigation in connection with an agricultural school were made at the Bussey Institution (Harvard), in 1871, and published in the following year. In 1873 Professor W. O. Atwater, at Wesleyan University (Connecticut), established an experiment station which has ever since been one of the most productive centres of investigation. North Carolina followed in 1877; New York (Cornell), in 1879; New Jersey, in 1880; and Tennessee, in 1882. Up to 1887, when the so-called Hatch Act was passed by Congress, appropriating $15,000 annually to each state for purposes of agricultural investigation, seventeen such stations had been established. Now, each state and territory has one. Several hundred reports come annually from these stations embodying the results of special researches, most of them in such form as to be easily made use of by the farmers. The importance of these scientific contributions to the material prosperity of our nation can hardly be overestimated.

Elementary Agriculture

The introduction of agricultural instruction in the public schools has presented another problem to the educator. The widespread interest in this subject may be judged from the large number of recent texts on elementary agriculture, special leaflets and bulletins from the experiment stations, together with discussions and outlines of the work in school journals, farmers' institutes, and teachers' associations. In a number of states teachers are required to pass an examination in elementary agriculture; in some the law requires them to teach it. To meet this new condition, certain of the state normal schools, as those of Missouri, have introduced courses in practical and theoretical agriculture, and the subject is taking a prominent place in teachers' institutes. Minnesota and Nebraska have each established an agricultural high school. Alabama has an agricultural school of secondary grade in each of its nine congressional districts. Each of these schools has a farm connected with it. Wisconsin has established a system of county schools of agriculture and domestic science, and also offers some work along the same line in the county training school. In some of the states, as in Illinois, agriculture has been included in the state course of study, private schools have included it in their curricula, and the extension work of the agricultural colleges is reaching every part of the state.

All these agencies for the preparation of teachers for elementary agricultural instruction are producing valuable results. While some states are discussing the problem of ways and means for its introduction into the rural schools, others are boldly making the experiment with great success. It is now being given in all the schools of North Carolina. Georgia, Alabama, and Louisiana, too, have taken steps in the same direction ; and we may safely predict that in the near future scientific agricultural instruction of an elementary character will find a place in the better class of rural schools throughout the entire country.

REFERENCES

TECHNICAL EDUCATION

Allensworth, Capt. A. Military Education in the United States. N. E. A. 1891 : 221–234. — Barnard, Charles. New Roads to a Trade. Cent. 1 : 285–288. — Bond, A. Curtis. Technical Education. Pop. Sci. Mo. 23 : 475. — *Burstall*, F. W. American Higher Technical Education. Nature, 61 : 299–301. — Cogswell, Edward. Technical Education. N. A. Rev. 146 : 223. — *Davidson*, T. Technical Education. Forum, 6 : 382. — Deyo, M. Tendency of Technological Instruction. Ed. 8 : 252. — Drown, T. M. Technical Training. J. Frankl. Inst. 116 : 329–354. Electrical Education. Engin. Mag. 23 : 771–772. *Entrance Requirements for Engineering Colleges.* Rep. Com. Ed. 1896–1897, 1 : 891. — *Holden*, E. S. The United States Military Academy at West Point. Rep. Com. Ed. 1891–1892, 2 : 767–774. — *Richetts*, P. C. Rensselaer Polytechnic Institute. Rep. Com. Ed. 1891–1892, 2 : 757–766. — *Riedler*, A. American Technological Schools. Rep. Com. Ed. 1892–1893, 1 : 657–686. — Rigg, J. H. Technical Instruction in America. Contemp. 46 : 208–223. — *Rogers*, H. J. Education and Commercial Development. Ed. Rev. 23 : 486–502. — Scudder, H. E. Education by Hand. Harper, 58 : 406–418. — Sooysmith, Charles. American and German Polytechnic Instruction. Nation, 39 : 479–480. Technical Education. Science, 8 : 381–382. — *Thurston*, R. H. Evolution of Technical Education. J. Frankl. Inst. 149 : 112–122. Professional and Academic Schools. Ed. Rev. 17 : 19. Technical Schools : their Purpose and Accomplishments. Sch. Rev. 1 : 523. — *Tyler*, H. W. Technical Education in the United States. Forum, 12 :.18. United States Military Academy. Rep. Com. Ed. 1901, 2 : 2421. — *Walker*, Francis A. The Place of Schools of Technology in American Education. Ed. Rev. 2 : 209. The Relation of Professional and Technical Schools to General Education. Ed. Rev. 8 : 417. — White, H. Technical Education. Nation, 45 : 129–130. — *Woodward*, C. M. Change of Front in Education. Science, N. S., 14 : 474–482.

AGRICULTURAL EDUCATION

Bailey, L. H. Farmer's Reading Courses. United States Agriculture Department Farmer's Bulletin, No. 109. The Revolution in Farming. World's Work, 2 : 945–948. — Bogen, B. D. Courses of Study in Agriculture. Ed. 22 : 89. Briarcliff School of Farming. Pub. Opin. 8 : 727. — Butterfield, K. L. An Untilled Field in American Agricultural Education. Pop. Sci. Mo. 63 : 257–261. — Craig, John. Teaching Farmers at Home. Cur. Lit. 31 : 27. Farm Institutes. Ind. 53 : 284–285. Farmer's Reading Courses. Chaut. 30 : 470–471. — Dabney, C. W. Agriculture. In Butler's Education in United States. — Fawcett, Waldon. Women Students of Agriculture. Pub. Opin. 30 : 812–813. Graduate School of Agriculture. Pop. Sci. Mo. 61 : 475–477. — *Halstead*, Murat. The Story of the Farmer's College. Cos. 22 : 280–288. — Harris, Sallie Vawter. The Hart Farm School. Pub. Opin. 27 : 652–653. — Kiehle, D. L. The Plan and Function of the Agricultural College. N. E. A. 1890 : 213. A Minnesota Plan. Outl. 65 : 656. Nature Study for Farmers. Pop. Sci. Mo. 53 : 139. — *Stewart*, J. A. Science and Agricultural Experiment. Sci. Am. Sup. 51 : 21295–21296. To Teach Farming. Outl. 66 : 234–235. — *True*, A. C. Education and Research in Agriculture in the United States. United States Agricultural Year-book, 1894, pp. 81–116. University Extension in Agriculture. Forum, 28 : 701–707. — *United States Education*, Bureau of. Methods of Instruction in Agriculture, Rep. 1897–1898, 2 : 1575–1622. Curriculum of the Land-grant Colleges. Rep. 1896–1897, 1 : 427–456. — Women at a College of Agriculture. Pub. Opin. 25 : 662.

CHAPTER XVIII

THE PREPARATION OF TEACHERS

THE machinery of our educational system did not provide for the special preparation of the teacher until well into the nineteenth century. Teachers there had of course been since the beginning of schools; persons of considerable dignity, too, in the New England towns, ranking next to the minister in social importance, and sharing with him certain of the ministerial functions. In the earlier colonial days grammar-school teachers **P. 80.** were almost universally college men, but beyond a knowledge of the academic subjects they were to teach, with no special pedagogical preparation whatever. In the colonies other than those of New England, schools were less frequent, and, generally speaking, the teachers less fully educated. The wealthy planters in some instances brought educated men from England to act as tutors in their own families; and not infrequently these eventually established neighborhood schools. Among the re- **Pp. 58, 65.** demptioners of early days was occasionally a man of learning who was pressed into the service of the schools, and so the very few schools which had been established in the seventeenth century were fairly well provided for. During the next century the colleges, though few, were sending out graduates in increasing numbers, nearly all of whom were either ministers or teachers, or both, for it was very common to combine the two callings. In those days, too, as with us now, many men who looked forward to the professions of law or medicine, spent a few years after graduation from college as teachers. John Adams, William Ellery Channing, and, somewhat later, William H. Seward, Daniel Webster, and Salmon P. Chase were among those who passed an apprenticeship in the schoolroom, and we may well imagine with what excellent success. Besides these two classes of teachers—college graduates who made teaching a lifework, and those who taught but temporarily — was another important class, made up of undergraduate students in the colleges, who spent the long winter vacations in the schoolroom. Until comparatively recently many of the Eastern colleges so divided the year as to make this possible, throwing into the school market their entire student body for as much as three of the colder months. This proved a benefit to the schools, many of those in the smaller districts being thus able to secure bright, energetic young men who proved the greatest inspiration to the pupils. It is a matter of doubt even, if the same schools have ever had as good teachers as a class since, even with our modern facilities for the preparation of the teacher. With the growth of the private academy came another source of supply for the teaching force, not so good as the colleges, yet supplementing them in a way, and in the few instances of coeducational academies, for the first time making women available as teachers. But until about the beginning of the third decade of the nineteenth century, there had been only occasional expressions of opinion that any other than a purely academic training was needed by the teacher, and up to that time absolutely no facilities had been provided for any other training anywhere in the country. As

Gordy, p. 9.

early as 1789 an article ascribed to Elisha Ticknor had appeared in the Massachusetts magazine, in which it was urged that a grammar school be established in each county "to fit young gentlemen for college and school keeping." It was advocated that a board of supervisors be appointed which "should annually examine young gentlemen designed for school masters, in reading, writing, arithmetic, and English grammar, and if they are found qualified for the office of school keeping, and able to teach these branches with ease and propriety, to recommend them for the purpose." Wise as such a proposition was, public sentiment was not ready for it. Not only were no immediate results produced, so far as a school for teachers is concerned, but even the plan seems not to have been mentioned again for nearly thirty years. This was at a Yale commencement, when Denison Olmstead, afterward Professor of Natural Philosophy in that institution, discussed somewhat fully the plan for an "academy for schoolmasters" in his oration. Two or three other papers upon the same general subject appeared within the next few years, but no actual attempt was made to found such a school until 1823, and then it was a private institution established by Samuel R. Hall at the little village of Concord, Vermont. Hall was a preacher, sent to the place by the Missionary Society of Vermont, but on his refusing longer to stay, unless allowed to try the experiment of a teachers' school, he was given permission. Soon his modest enterprise was attracting more than local attention. He maintained a practice school for his teacher pupils, and in many ways anticipated the methods of the normal schools of to-day. After some years' experience in the work, Mr. Hall published a book entitled *Lectures on School Keeping*, which met with an immediate success; at least two states (New York and Kentucky) purchasing a copy for each teacher in the state. Mr. Hall continued to maintain a school for teachers until 1840, though in 1830 he removed it to Andover, and in 1837, to Plymouth.

The move for the professional training of teachers was now under way, public sentiment in favor of such training had become aroused, and even during the earlier years of Hall's venture in Vermont, in at least two other states agitation was spirited in the direction of some adequate provision for it. The moves were,

Gordy, p. 10.

however, in two different directions; in Massachusetts, toward the establishment of special institutions for the training of teachers; and in New York, toward the modification of the courses of study in the existing academies in such a way as to make them especially meet the needs of the teacher. Both these moves originated at about the same time, though with the priority of a year or two in Massachusetts. In that state James G. Carter may with justice be called the father of the movement. In 1820 he published in pamphlet form an essay treating, among other educational matters, an "institution for the training of teachers." One year later he put his plan into practice at Lancaster, Massachusetts. The town did not appreciate his efforts, and the institution was short-lived. Not so Mr. Carter's interest, however; and, upon being elected in 1835 to the state legislature, he immediately began a campaign for a similar institution to be supported by the public.

P. 98.

In 1837 he drew the bill providing for a state board of education, and without doubt his speeches, more than anything else, brought about the Normal School Act in 1838. Another man whose influence was great in the move for normal schools in Massachusetts was Mr. Charles Brooks. Impressed with the perfection of the Prussian school system in which they were prominent, entirely upon his own initiative, he called a meeting of all interested in school reform in Plymouth, Massachusetts, in 1835, and so impressed his hearers with the importance of normal schools in the country, that considerable money was then and there subscribed for the purpose. During the next two years Mr. Brooks lectured in nearly all the New England states, as well as in some others, "riding in his chaise over two thousand miles" in his missionary tour, his subject being ever the same: that of the normal school and its needs. It is

Horace Mann, ch. vi.

not strange, then, that when Horace Mann began his active campaign for the establishment of such schools, he found the public, at least, not unfamiliar with the idea.

The move for normal schools had not yet been made in any state outside of New England, but New York was solving the problem of teachers' training through its academies. In 1827 the legislature of that state passed an act, which, among other things, was " to promote the education of teachers "; but since it was not specified how this should be done, the law was productive of no results.

One year later the report of the regents contained this statement : —

" The academies have become, in the opinion of the regents, what it has always been desirable that they should be, fit seminaries for imparting instruction in the highest branches of English education, and especially for qualifying teachers of the common schools."

It would be difficult to say in what particulars they were especially fit at that time for the fulfilment of the latter function ; but the expression of confidence on the part of the regents seemed to have the proper effect, for in 1831 the Canandaigua and St. Lawrence academies report "principles of teaching" as among the subjects offered ; the next year two other academies were maintaining similar courses, and in 1834 the fifth was added to the list.

In 1832 the board of regents fully discussed the plan of training teachers in connection with the academies, expressing their reasons for believing it to be a better method than through the establishment of normal schools. Special appropriations of school funds were made annually until 1844, for the support of these teachers' courses, and up to that time nearly four thousand students were graduated from them. But upon the motion of State Superintendent Young in that year they were discontinued, as not fulfilling the expectations of their promoters, and the bill establishing the State Normal College at Albany passed. So closed in New

Regents' report for 1832, or Gordy, p. 27, *et seq.*

York the experiment of using the academies as training schools for teachers.

In Massachusetts, the first public normal schools in the country had been opened in 1839: one in Lexington for women and the other in Barre for both sexes. At the opening of each, Governor Edward Everett delivered a masterly oration, in which he outlined fully the course of study which was to be offered. The schools had been made possible largely through the generosity of Edmund Dwight, who gave $10,000 upon the agreement that the legislature should appropriate an equal amount. The school at Lexington was opened first upon July 3, 1839, with three students; that at Barre following upon September 5 of the same year.[1] Of the school at Lexington, Rev. Cyrus Pierce was chosen principal; and to his tact and untiring devotion is due, in large part, not only the success of this school, but that of the whole normal school movement, which depended so largely upon it.

The minimum course of study was fixed at one year, though two might be devoted to it. The subjects of the first curriculum were as follows: —

(1) Orthography, reading, grammar, composition and rhetoric; (2) writing and drawing; (3) arithmetic (mental and written), algebra, geometry, bookkeeping, navigation, and surveying; (4) geography with chronology, statistics and general history; (5) physiology; (6) mental philosophy; (7) music; (8) constitution and history of Massachusetts and the United States; (9) mental philosophy and astronomy; (10) natural history; (11) the principles of piety and morality; (12) the science and art of teaching with reference to all these subjects.

Students who spent but a year at the school made a selection of studies from those offered, determined by the character of the school they intended to teach. A model school was established at the start, and has been

Barnard, 13 : 758.

Pierce.

---

[1] For full account of the early conditions of these schools, see Gordy, Ch. III.

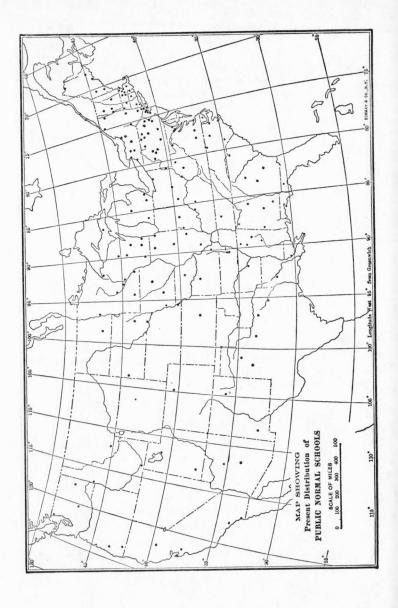

MAP SHOWING
Present Distribution of
PUBLIC NORMAL SCHOOLS

SCALE OF MILES
0   100   200   300   400   500

an important feature of the schools, which have taken that at Lexington as a pattern. The location of the first two Massachusetts normal schools did not prove adapted to the best results, and in 1844 that at Lexington was removed to West Newton, and later to Framingham, and the Barre school, to Westfield. In 1840 a third school had been established at Bridgewater. The beneficial effects of the schools upon the teaching force of the state were soon apparent, and other states were not slow to follow the example set in Massachusetts, until to-day every state save Delaware is supporting one or more state normal schools; although in some instances they are maintained as departments of the state universities. In all there are 535 institutions (other than high schools) offering courses especially for teachers, with 114,353 students enrolled in such courses. These institutions are of five classes:—

   a. State normal schools.
   b. Private normal schools.
   c. City training schools.
   d. Pedagogical departments in colleges and universities.
   e. Teachers' colleges.

a. STATE NORMAL SCHOOLS

The distribution by states, of schools of this class (also public normal schools upon other foundations), together with the year of establishment of each, is given in the following table:—

Alabama	4	1873, 1875, 1883 (2).
Arizona	2	1889, 1899.
Arkansas	1	1877.
California	4	1862, 1882, 1897, 1899.
Colorado	1	1899.
Connecticut	4	1849, 1889, 1893, 1903.
District of Columbia	2	1873, 1877.

Florida	3	1887 (2), 1901.
Georgia	1	1895
Idaho	2	1893 (2).
Illinois	5	1857, 1869, 1895 (2), 1899.
Indiana	1	1865.
Iowa	4	1876.
Kansas	1	1863 (auxiliaries, 1902–1903).
Kentucky	3	1880, 1886.
Louisiana	2	1877, 1885.
Maine	3	1864, 1867, 1879.
Maryland	1	1866.
Massachusetts	10	1839 (2), 1840, 1854, 1873, 1874, 1895, 1897 (3).
Michigan	4	1849, 1895 (2), 1903.
Minnesota	5	1860, 1868, 1869, 1889, 1902.
Mississippi	1	1871.
Missouri	3	1871 (2), 1873.
Montana	1	1897.
Nebraska	2	1867, 1903.
New Hampshire	1	1871.
New Jersey	1	1855.
New Mexico	2	1891, 1898.
New York	12	1844, 1865, 1867, 1868, 1869 (2), 1871 (2), 1886, 1889, 1890.
North Carolina	6	1877, 1881 (2), 1884, 1891.
North Dakota	2	
Oklahoma	3	1891, 1897, 1903.
Oregon	3	1882, 1896, 1898.
Pennsylvania	12	1859, 1861, 1862, 1866, 1869, 1871, 1873, 1874, 1875, 1877, 1887, 1889.
Rhode Island	1	1854.
South Carolina	1	1886.
South Dakota	1	1883.
Tennessee	1	1875.
Texas	5	1879, 1901, 1903.
Utah	2	1869, 1897.
Vermont	3	1866, 1867, 1868.
Virginia	1	1884.
Washington	3	1890 (2), 1898.
West Virginia	4	1867, 1868, 1873 (2).
Wisconsin	7	1859, 1866, 1868, 1871, 1875, 1885, 1896.

As may be seen by the table, the first state to follow Massachusetts in the establishment of a normal school was New York, the first having been founded in Albany in 1844. This has now developed into an institution to which the title "college" is applicable, and will be mentioned under that head. Connecticut followed in 1849, Michigan in 1850, Rhode Island in 1852, but the school was discontinued after a few years; Massachusetts again in 1854 with a school at Salem; New Jersey in 1855, Illinois in 1857, Pennsylvania and Minnesota in 1859, with a much larger number during the next decade and each succeeding one. Not until the close of the war, however, was one established in the South, though since that time they have been quite fully introduced.

In 1875 there were 70 state normal schools in operation with 17,698 students, the states of Delaware, Georgia, Kentucky, Louisiana, North Carolina, Ohio, Oregon, and Utah, of those then in the Union, being without such a school. In 1880 the number was 84, with 15,289 students; in 1885, 103, with 21,070 students. At present there are 143 state normal schools; but for late years no statistics covering enrolment are available which differentiate the state schools from others supported by public taxation, *i.e.* class, c.

Admission to State Normal Schools

With one or two exceptions, all are open to both sexes, and women students largely predominate. Tuition is free to students of the state. The academic qualifications for entrance vary materially in the different states, though a great majority of the schools accept students with a common school preparation; that is, the equivalent of eight years' schooling. In some states, notably Massachusetts, a four years' high school course or its equivalent is demanded for admission. According to the recommendations of the National Educational Association committee on normal schools, the minimum requirement for entrance to the state schools in general, should include a reasonable proficiency in the following subjects: arithmetic, English, grammar, geography, United States history, physiology and hygiene, drawing, civil government, music, grammar school algebra, nature study, reading, penmanship, spelling, and English. In states where the rural schools predominate, these requirements are not usually maintained. When high schools are easily accessible to most of the pupils in the state, they are, in many cases, exceeded. Frequently the model or practice school is made the fitting school for the normal.

N. E. A. Normal School report, p. 11.

The Course of Study

The greater number of the state normal schools offer a four years' course of study intended for students who come with the minimum of preparation. Besides this, or in combination with it, is in many instances a two years' course for high school graduates, and not infrequently a course of a single year, almost entirely professional in its character, for college graduates. In the relative amounts of academic and professional instruction, the schools differ greatly. In some, and this is particularly true of the Pennsylvania schools, the academic largely predominates; so much so as to make them differ but slightly from the old New York academies in the times when teachers' courses were maintained.

Appendix E.
In many of the others professional courses are much more prominent, though in all a considerable amount of academic work is found to be a necessity.

The National Educational Association committee on normal schools recommends the following as a four years' course: arithmetic, elementary algebra, plane geometry, English grammar, English, elements of rhetoric, zoology, botany, physiography, physics, chemistry, nature study, penmanship, drawing, manual training (either domestic science or sloyd, or both), reading, music, fine arts, sociology, history, civics, economics, folklore, general physical education, gymnastics, games, school sanitation, psychology, pedagogy, observation, and teaching in the training school. Each of the last four subjects are to be taken for an entire year, giving them a time value of at least one-fourth of the entire course. It is doubtful if any school follows this programme in detail, though some few approximate it. Frequently, the course of study is determined by characteristics peculiar to the state; either the conditions of the local schools or the requirements for certification to teach. For instance, in the New England states, purely professional courses predominate, since the high schools easily furnish all that is required along academic lines. In the Southern states, where the negro population must be considered, and where also secondary education is deficient, industrial and academic courses abound. In the Pennsylvania schools this is also true, and each of the thirteen schools maintains a preparatory department. In the Mississippi Valley and the Western states, fewer normal schools are maintained than in the East, and, as a consequence, some have large numbers of students in attendance; that of Kansas having nearly fifteen hundred, and the Iowa school at Cedar Rapids, considerably more. Academic subjects are taught, but only as made necessary by the requirements of the professional courses. Regarding the course of study in the state normal schools, the N. E. A. committee says: —

N. E. A. Normal School Rep. p. 29.

" All these observations lead to the conclusion that there has been constant progress in the three-quarters of a century the state normal schools have existed. That progress has been both experimental and evolutionary. The changes that have come to the possibilities and needs have always found the normal school ready to adapt itself to the new conditions. The normal school has been so near the public thought all this time that it is more nearly to-day an actual exponent of public sentiment than any other public institution of equivalent magnitude. It is specially sensitive to public demand, and sincerely endeavors to do for the people what is assumed to be essential to prepare teachers for the public schools. This accounts for much of the variation that is known to exist at present, and it is evident that, with a better knowledge of what has been accomplished in the different states in the preparation of teachers, and what ideals prevail in producing the different characteristics of strength and successful results now known to be attained, there will be found more satisfactory and uniform results, more sympathetic relation among the workers in this great field of labor, and a loftier conception of what the American teacher must become to fill the place of destiny conferred by democracy and Christianity."

Observation and Practice Schools

The practice school is the characteristic feature of our state normal schools, and that which distinguishes them from the purely academic institutions. They are in some instances maintained in connection with private normal schools ; and, in fact, with each of the four other classes of professional schools for teachers, but not as a rule. With the state normal schools, however, the plan was adopted at Lexington with the first school, and has since become almost universal. In the practice school, the prospective teachers constituting the student body of the normal school are given opportunity, not only to observe the work of expert teachers, but also themselves to teach, under the scrutiny of those same experts who serve as critics. The development of the practice school has closely paralleled that of the normal, though the administrative relations between the two differ in different institutions. In fact, four distinct plans are in vogue in the normal schools throughout the country for securing practice facilities for their students. The most common of these (and it is the one made use of by considerably more than one-half of the schools), is to maintain a complete practice department, comprising all the grades, and in many instances, a kindergarten, within the buildings of the normal school, and entirely under the control of the normal school authorities. Usually a small tuition is charged for attendance at the practice schools, and the fact that they can survive in competition with the free public schools is a tribute to the excellence of the instruction offered within them.

The second plan is that of utilizing the school system of the city or town in which the normal school is situated for purposes of observation and practice. In about one-sixth of the state normals the plan is in vogue, all being situated in comparatively small towns and cities. The financial relations are adjusted in various ways; sometimes the normal school furnishes the teachers, while the town bears the other expenses of maintaining the school. Again, in some instances, the normal contributes only a part of the teachers' expenses; while a third plan is for the town to pay to the normal school an annual sum, equal to the ordinary amount expended for school purposes.

A third method of maintaining a practice school is but a modified form of the plan just mentioned. Under it, certain schools of the town are set apart for the uses of the normal schools, the relations between those schools and the normal being the same as those between it and all the schools in the other plan. This plan is made use of in about one-tenth of the state normal schools. With the rest of the normal schools a city ward-school is conducted in the normal building, practically full privileges being given in the way of practice and observation.

The amount of practice teaching done by the normal students before graduation is usually not far from two hundred hours; that is, one hour per day for one school year. This is usually divided among several grades; or, in the case of teachers who are preparing to be specialists, among some few subjects. The teaching is usually in the presence of the critic teacher, whose duty it is to note any glaring defects and discuss them with the student teachers at some subsequent meeting.

b. PRIVATE NORMAL SCHOOLS

Despite the rapid growth of state normal schools and other public means for the training of teachers, they have not met the demands of our public school system, and large numbers of private normal schools have sprung up in all parts of the country. In 1875 there were 56 such schools, with 9328 students. Ten years later the number was 132, with 23,005 students, and, is in 1902, 118, with 23,573 students. They are most abundant in the Middle West, nearly one-half of the whole number, with about two-thirds of the student enrolment, being in the North Central states. These schools vary so greatly in all particulars as to make an exact characterization of them, impossible. In the earlier days, before the general establishment of state normal schools, some of them, particularly in the South, did pioneer work of the greatest value, and some few are undoubtedly of high character to-day; but too large a number are but short cuts to the teaching profession. Usually no prerequisites to admission are made, other than sufficient maturity; the courses are undefined and short, and the accomplishments are superficial. Not infrequently such schools are but subordinate departments of commercial schools. From the standpoint of the teaching profession, their only excuse as a class, for being, is that the facilities for the training of teachers are as yet inadequate, and that even the training that the poorest of them give, is better than none. The schools are now decreasing in number, and the student body is no larger than it was twenty years ago.

c. CITY TRAINING SCHOOLS

Most of the larger cities, and not a few of the smaller ones, are in part providing their own schools with trained teachers through normal or training schools of their own maintenance. In 1880 there were 21 such schools, with 2941 students; in 1885 the number was 25, with 4549 students; in 1902 special teachers' courses were maintained in no less than 44 cities and towns in the United States, either as a part of the high school curriculum, or in especially organized training schools. More than 10,000 pupils are taking these courses, and nearly 9000 more are doing similar work in connection with the private secondary schools. The simplest form of city training school consists of little more than a fifth year of high school work, made up mostly of pedagogical courses, together with observation and practice-teaching in the grades. Although usually not in any sense the equivalent of the normal school course, it is nevertheless an efficient means of furnishing the grades with teachers. In the city training schools lately established in New York City, two years instead of one are devoted to the course.

The Girls' Normal School of Philadelphia seems to have been the earliest of this class, having been organized by Joseph Lancaster in the earlier years of the last century. The Boston Normal School was founded in 1852, and has ever since been one of the best. The Normal College of the City of New York combines academic instruction with its professional courses in such a way as to provide the girls instruction of practically the same character as that offered the boys in the College of the City of New York. It grants the bachelor's degree in arts as well as in pedagogy, and even the advanced degrees. A high school education, or its equivalent, is demanded for entrance. The latter is true also for the Chicago Normal School, which won renown under the direction of Colonel Francis Parker, who was a long time its president.

d. PEDAGOGICAL DEPARTMENTS IN COLLEGES AND UNIVERSITIES

The institutions for the training of teachers already discussed are primarily for providing the elementary and rural schools with a properly prepared teaching force. It is true that many of their graduates find their way into the secondary schools, and do efficient service there, but academically, the normal and city training schools are little more than of secondary grade themselves, and are not intended to develop the extended scholarship that is a desideratum for the best high school work. This fact being recognized, the higher academic institutions are attempting quite generally to solve the problem of the preparation of the secondary school teacher through the establishment of pedagogical departments, or by offering courses especially adapted to the professional needs of the teacher. This move is practically one of the last thirty years, not more than three or four attempts having been made longer ago than that. The first seems to have been in the University of the City of New York (now New York University) in 1832–1833, when for about a year pedagogical courses were offered. Brown University next tried the experiment in 1850, continuing such courses for five years, after which they were discontinued. In 1873 Iowa University established teachers' courses which were open to seniors; and in 1878 opened its College of Normal Instruction, primarily for graduates, and offered courses in the history of education, national systems of education, practical educational topics, school economy, and the principles of education. The whole was under the direction of Dr. N. S. Fellows, and led to the degree of Bachelor of Pedagogics. In 1879 the University of Michigan founded a chair of science and art of teaching, which has, since its inception, been occupied by but two men — Professors W. H. Payne and B. A. Hinsdale.

P. 274.
Kinneman,
p. 336.

P. 263.

From that time there was a rapid increase in the number of higher institutions offering pedagogical instruction. In 1884 there were six, the universities of Iowa, Michigan, Missouri, Nebraska, Wisconsin, and Johns Hopkins. In 1893 the number was 83; in 1894, 174; in 1897, 220; in 1899, 244; and in 1902, 247. The pedagogical courses offered in these institutions vary so greatly, both in number and character, as to make any general statement of them impossible. In some, but a single course is maintained; and this is usually offered by an instructor connected with the philosophical or other department. In others, several instructors give their whole time to the work, a sufficient number of courses being offered in the department to make it possible for the student to devote the last two years of his course largely to professional work, or even to take an advanced degree in it. The courses most frequently offered may be summarized under four general heads: (*a*) philosophical, (*b*) historical, (*c*) courses in organization and administration, and (*d*) courses in special methods; under the first, as variously stated, come courses in the philosophy of education; principles of education; general pedagogy; educational theory; educational aims; educational foundations; and educational æsthetics: the second comprises, besides the general history of education, the history of education in special countries, as Grecian, Roman, German, and English; the development of the American school system; the comparative study of national school systems; and the study of educational classics. The courses in organization and administration usually have special reference to secondary school work, though sometimes they are of broader application. Under "methods," a vast number of special courses are offered, though generally with direct secondary school applications. Every important subject of the high school curriculum is, in some institutions, made the subject of study, the courses not infrequently being offered by instructors connected

Rep. Com. Ed. 1883–1884, p. cxiii.

with the various academic departments of the college. Besides these courses most frequently offered, others in school hygiene, educational psychology, and child study are sometimes given by the pedagogical departments, though more often by those of psychology.

On the whole, the pedagogical departments in the higher institutions are doing most valuable work in the preparation of teachers for the secondary schools. They are not as yet so well organized as they should be, and furnish very little adequate facility for observation or practice work on the part of the students. In some few institutions, as at Harvard and Brown, arrangements are made with public school systems in the vicinity, that the students may have practical experience in school work, but such instances are altogether too few. In this respect, the normal schools, through their practice schools, are far in advance of the universities.

e. TEACHERS' COLLEGES

Within this class there are as yet but few institutions, though the tendency seems to be for the pedagogical departments of the colleges and universities to develop into such; and we may expect many more within the next decade. It is, moreover, difficult to say just what constitutes a teachers' college. Many of the normal schools are officially known as universities, as the two older schools in Illinois, and a still larger number, as colleges, but these titles have only a historical significance. Among the whole number of institutions for the professional training of teachers there are, however, a half-dozen or so varying greatly among themselves, but still in every case doing work of a manifestly higher grade than the normal schools as a class, and having a sufficiently distinct organization to warrant treating them in a separate class from the normal schools, or the university departments of pedagogy. One of these

institutions is an advanced normal school, — the New P. 375.
York State Normal College at Albany, — while the
others are connected with universities. These are
the Teachers College, connected with Columbia; and
the schools of pedagogy, and of education, connected,
respectively, with New York University and the University
of Chicago. Clark University may, perhaps, be
mentioned as a sixth, though it has no specially organized
pedagogical department. It offers, however,
every facility at its command for the study of advanced
educational problems, and many valuable contributions
come from it.

The New York State Normal College, for nearly a
half-century of its existence as an institution, varied but
little from the ordinary type of normal school. But in
1891 its courses were reorganized and the school put
upon a wholly professional basis, no academic subjects
being taught except as features of courses in special
methods of teaching. A high school diploma, or its
equivalent, is required for admission. The college offers
a so-called English course, a classical course, and a kindergarten
course, each of two years, and a special course
for school superintendents and college graduates, of one
year. The degree of Bachelor of Pedagogy is granted.

The Teachers College at Columbia is the most elaborately Columbia,
equipped and fully organized professional school P. 259.
for teachers in the country. It was founded as a separate
institution in 1888, but has by gradual stages
been absorbed by Columbia, until now it ranks with the
schools of law, medicine, and applied science, as one of
the professional departments of the university. The
college has magnificent buildings adjoining the Columbia
campus, maintains the Horace Mann School with all
grades, from kindergarten to high school, as an observation
school, besides the Speyer School, an admirably
equipped elementary school for purposes of practice.
The college offers a four years' course, the last two

being largely professional, at the end of which a bachelor's diploma is awarded. The course is divided into special groups of subjects, so arranged as to prepare the student to be a specialist, either in (*a*) the elementary schools, (*b*) the kindergarten, (*c*) any one or more of the usual academic subjects in the secondary school curriculum, (*d*) domestic science, (*e*) domestic art, (*f*) fine art, (*g*) manual training, (*h*) music, (*i*) physical education. The master's and doctor's diploma, also, are granted for graduate work. Furthermore, the relationships are such that work in the college is accepted for any of the degrees granted by Columbia University, making it possible for a student to take his advanced university degree at the same time as his diploma in the college. Probably no training school for teachers in the world has a finer equipment than the Teachers College, or is doing work of a higher grade. Its teaching force numbers about seventy, many of whom are also members of the Columbia faculty.

N. Y. Univ.
p. 274.
The School of Pedagogy of New York University was established as one of the graduate schools of the university in 1890. Its aim, as stated in its announcement, is "to furnish thorough and complete professional training for teachers. For this purpose it brings together all that bears on pedagogy from the history of education, from analytical, experimental, and physiological psychology, from the science of medicine, from ethics, from philosophy, from æsthetics, from sociology, from the principles and art of teaching, and from a comparative study of the national systems of education. It unifies this knowledge into a body of pedagogical doctrine, and points out its application to the practical work of the educator." It offers courses leading both to the master's and doctor's degrees in pedagogy, as well as certain other courses intended to qualify students for the more advanced work. Extension lectures are also offered. The rooms occupied by the school are in

the heart of New York City, facing Washington Square, and are easily accessible to thousands of teachers, who are more and more fully availing themselves of its advantages.

The School of Education of the University of Chicago is the latest to enter the ranks of teachers' colleges. It was established in 1901 by the union of the Chicago Institute, founded by Mrs. Emmons McCormick Blaine, with the university. In its organization it comprises the College of Education with a faculty of twenty-seven, and the University High School and elementary school. Courses are offered (*a*) in arts and technology, (*b*) in special work for kindergartens, elementary school teachers, critic teachers, and departmental supervisors in elementary schools, and (*c*) in special work for secondary school teachers. The degrees of A.B., S.B., Ph.B., and Ed.B. (Bachelor of Education) are given. The school has magnificent quarters in a new building adjoining the university campus, containing full equipment for every branch of its work, including the observation schools.

Univ. of Chi. p. 278.

TEACHERS' CONTINUATION COURSES

Although the institutions for the preparation of the teachers of various classes enumerated have large numbers of students enrolled, and are annually sending quite an army of trained instructors into the schoolroom, it is nevertheless true that the great majority of American teachers enter it entirely lacking in any special pedagogical preparation. That this must be true is shown by the fact that in 1871 our entire teaching force numbered upward of 180,000, while there was an enrolment of but 10,922 in the training schools. In 1880 the numbers were 282,644 and 43,077; in 1890, 363,935 and 64,440; while in 1902 the numbers were 439,596 and 94,157 — the latter figures including those in the pedagogical courses in colleges and universities. It is plain, then, that since the demand for teachers so far outruns the output of the training schools, that some methods must be made use of to supply, at least in part, the lack of preparation before entering the schoolroom, through professional study after the work of teaching has been taken up ; and also to furnish an inspiration to some form of continuation study on the part of those who have had a professional preparation.

Such work is being carried on by at least three agencies.

　a. Teachers' institutes.

　b. Teachers' meetings, under the direction of principal or superintendent.

　c. Reading circles.

a. Teachers' Institutes

Appendix I. These are essentially brief, normal sessions, held at different times of the year, usually under the direction of the county superintendent of schools, or of some other school official. They had their origin when the normal schools were in their infancy, and when the proportion of trained teachers was vastly smaller even than to-day. They have been in the past a source of great good, and, when properly conducted, have not by any means outlived their usefulness. The first teachers' institute of which we have any record was held in Hartford, Connecticut, in October, 1839, under the direction of Henry Barnard, then secretary of the state board of education. Twenty-six young men were in attendance, and the session lasted for six weeks. No others were held within the state for several years. New York State held its first institute in 1840. This was really the first meeting of teachers under that name, since the term "institute" was not used in connection with the Hartford gathering. Both Massachusetts and Rhode Island took up the work in 1845; New Hampshire and Vermont in 1846, and Maine a year later.

The following table shows the years, so far as I have been able to determine them, of the beginnings of institute work in the various states.

ORIGIN OF TEACHERS' INSTITUTES

Connecticut	1839	Wisconsin	1848
New York	1840	Illinois	1854
Massachusetts	1845	Pennsylvania	1854
Ohio	1845	Iowa	1858
Rhode Island	1845	Minnesota	1860
Indiana	1846	Kansas	1863
Michigan	1846	Nebraska	1869
New Hampshire	1846	North Carolina	1872
Vermont	1846	Colorado	1885
Maine	1847	Florida	1886

The earliest institutions have left few definite records of themselves. Attendance was, however, voluntary; and since no public provision had been made for their support, the necessary expenses were met by the teachers themselves. The work was almost entirely academic in its character, a condition necessitated by the scarcity of schools above the common grade, and the consequent ignorance of the teachers, as a class, of anything above the common branches. The importance of such voluntary teachers' meetings was early recognized by the states. Massachusetts appropriated money for their support as early as 1846, New York, in 1847, and soon every state in which they were conducted, was contributing to their support. Throughout the South the Peabody fund was in many instances made available.

The work was undoubtedly disconnected and fragmentary, as indeed was all the school work of the time, and is too fully the case with much institute work today; yet it was extremely profitable for the teachers, not only from the standpoint of academic instruction, but from that of inspiration. The sessions were not generally so long as was that of Barnard's first institute, yet somewhat longer than is the average to-day. As time went on, and the academic preparation of the teachers improved, institutes of the better class have taken on more of a professional aspect. It became evident to the leaders, that one week, or even two or three, devoted to the study of a school subject, amounted to but little; while in that time a vast amount of inspiration could be gained, together with not a little insight into the problems of school organization and administration and the other more particularly pedagogical subjects; and except in instances where a short-sighted county superintendent makes the institute a cramming institution pure and simple, for his teachers' examination, that class of subjects is now made prominent, and educators of the highest class are often heard upon the institute platform. In Massachusetts the agents of the state board of education devote a considerable part of their time to institute work, and in New York State a special institute faculty is maintained. In most of the other states, members of the state normal school faculties address the institutes; in some, this being a part of their regular duties.

The subjects included in the institute programmes cover a wide range, no less than 72 titles being given to the offerings in the institutes of Massachusetts alone for the year 1886–1887. In the printed announcement of 17 county institutes (all that issued such announcements) in Illinois for the summer of 1902, 26 subjects are mentioned, as follows: history, music, and primary work in 12; arithmetic and reading in 11; geography, grammar, and pedagogy or psychology in 9; English literature, psychology, and school management in 6; drawing in 4; nature study and science in 3; botany, civics, language, physics, school decoration, and zoölogy in 2; while agriculture, biology, bookkeeping, library work, and spelling each appeared once. Of those same institutes, four had 6 instructors; two had 5; four had 4; and three each 3 and 2. Eight out of the 17 had one or more lectures by persons outside the regular corps of institute instructors.

Particulars regarding the present organization and support of teachers' institutes are given in Appendix I, which is compiled from the recent school laws of the various states, together with statements made by the state superintendents of public instruction.

b. TEACHERS' MEETINGS

The national and state teachers' associations are touched upon in Chapter XXVIII and need not be mentioned here, unless it be to say that American teachers flock together as do those of no other country in the world. Especially is this true in the West and Middle West, and it augurs well for the earnestness and professional spirit of the profession. Within the single state of Illinois, more than seven thousand were in attendance at the state teachers' association and four separate meetings of divisional associations for the year 1902–1903. But aside from these great meetings of teachers, ever since the office of city superintendent of schools was established, there have been held, in connection with nearly every particular school system, meetings of the corps of teachers under the direction of the superintendent for purposes of study and discussion. In many instances, the superintendent has practically made his teaching force in this way, and often made it well, for such meetings, when frequently held, constitute what is essentially a teachers' training school. The exact character of the meetings depends entirely upon the interest and efficiency of that supervising officer. In some instances they are mere unprofitable discussions of the clerical details of administration; in others, some special book of pedagogical import is read and critically discussed; in others, the superintendent lectures; and in still others, specialists from outside the local circle occupy the time. In correspondence with 36 superintendents in cities of small and medium size throughout the Middle West, it was found that all hold teachers' meetings of some sort at regular intervals: in 3 instances, weekly; in 7, bi-weekly; in 22, monthly; in 3, bi-monthly; and in 1, quarterly. Nine superintendents state that special meetings for the grade teachers are also held, either under their own direction or that of the principals of the ward schools. Eleven state that they (the superintendents) usually occupy the time either in lecture or reading; 2, that occasional lectures are given by educational experts; and 1, that such is regularly the custom. Twenty-eight say that the meeting is of such a character that the teachers are expected to participate in discussions of a pedagogical nature, in a few instances regular assignments having been previously made. In but one instance is attendance at the meetings tacitly compulsory on the part of the teachers, though it is probably virtually so in many more.

Undoubtedly many sins have been committed under the sanction of the teachers' meeting, but we cannot doubt that it is, when properly conducted, an efficient means of pedagogical instruction.

c. TEACHERS' READING CIRCLES

These are believed to have had their origin in an idea presented in a paper read before the Ohio State Teachers' Association, in 1882. The plan, which closely resembled some features of the Chautauqua scheme, met with immediate acceptance on the part of the Ohio teachers, and a circle was organized the following year, which in a short time comprised a membership of two thousand teachers.

It was under the auspices of the State Teachers' Association, with the direct management in the hands of a special committee. The Ohio circle was followed in its plan by the teachers in other states, until now similar organizations exist in many of the Western states. Hinsdale (I), p. 389.

Usually the state board of directors selects the books to be read, prepares questions for suitable examinations, and issues certificates to those who pass the examinations.

The local circles are conducted by the superintendents of schools or some teacher selected because of special fitness for the work. Not infrequently, too, educational journals add efficiency to the work, by publishing articles having an especial bearing upon the books studied. It is probable that at least fifty thousand teachers throughout the Middle West are doing the prescribed work in reading circles, with most valuable results.

The Certification of Teachers

From the early times, wherever any formal recognition of the schools was taken or support given to them by the civil authorities, it has been the custom to require some sort of a certificate of proficiency of the teacher. Even in the Dutch schools of New Amsterdam this was done, and the difficulties which Van Corler experienced in securing a license to teach were truly pathetic. The exact character of the requirements imposed have, however, varied very greatly, both as to quality and quantity. In some instances they have been purely religious, orthodoxy in some special form of religion being the prerequisite : in others nationality was the determining factor, and in others — and fortunately for the schools it was the larger number — academic proficiency was the desideratum. Appendix H. P. 15. P. 76.

In Massachusetts, the school ordinance of 1647 decreed that the schoolmaster must be of "discreet conversation, well versed in tongues." The provisions of this act applied also to New Hampshire, at that time united with Massachusetts. It was enacted in 1701 that every grammar school master must be approved by the minister of the town and also by the ministers of the two adjacent towns. The ministers were, however, not permitted to hold the position themselves. By the law of 1712 the schoolmaster was required to secure the approbation of the selectmen of the town. A later law (1789) requires that masters of schools must be graduates of a college or university, though a certificate of proficiency from some learned minister might be taken in lieu of this.

Pp. 81, 137, 149.

In Connecticut it was decreed in 1714 that "the selectmen in every town should examine the teachers as to their qualifications."

A similar law was in force at this time in New Jersey. To just what hardships the early aspirants for teachers' honors were subjected by those early officials, many of whom we have every reason to believe could themselves neither read nor write, cannot now be said. No doubt an uncertainty on this point, on the part of the aspirants themselves, tended to lessen the number of unqualified teachers; but beyond this we doubt the efficiency of the test. When during the last century state systems of schools were established in every instance, the door to the schoolroom was guarded by some form of teachers' examination.

In many states three classes of teachers' certificates are now issued based upon general legislation.

1st. County certificates, usually good but for one or two years, elementary in their character, and intended for teachers in the rural schools.

2d. State certificates good for a definite period — frequently five years — and of a much more advanced character than the county certificates.

3d. State life certificates, given only after a some-what rigid examination in all the common school branches, together with some subjects of a higher grade. In all three examinations some knowledge of educational theory and practice is demanded. There is no exact uniformity among the different states either in the character of the examination or in the method of its administration. Besides these state and county tests of efficiency, most large cities and towns demand special examinations of applicants for positions within their schools, but such have only a local bearing.

In many states, though not by any means all, a normal school diploma, or a certificate from a college or university is accepted in place of the general teachers' examinations.

Certain particulars regarding the present methods of certification of teachers throughout the country are given in Appendix H.

REFERENCES

Barnes, Earl. Teachers' Classes. N. E. A. 1895 : 173. — Barnett, P. A. Making of the Teacher. In Common Sense in Education and Teaching, pp. 289–310. — *Blodgett*, J. H. Teachers' Examination and Certificates in the Various States. Rep. Com. Ed. 1897–1898, 2 : 1659. — Boone, R. G. Preparation of Teachers. In Education in the United States, pp. 117–157. — *Burk*, Frederick. Normal Schools and the Training of Teachers. At. Month. 81 : 769. — *Butler*, N. M. Training of Teachers. Cent. 16 : 915. A College for Teachers. Dial, 25 : 249–251. — *Cook*, John W. Professional Training of Teachers in Normal Schools. N. E. A. 1894 : 86. — Gordy, J. P. Rise and Growth of the Normal School Idea in the United States. Circ. Inf. No. 8, 1891. — *Hall*, G. Stanley. American Universities and the Training of Teachers. Forum, 17 : 148. The Training of Teachers. Forum, 10 : 11. — Hanus, Paul H. Preparation of the High School Teacher of Mathematics. In Educational Aims and Values, pp. 141–163. — Hervey, W. L. New York College for Training of Teachers. R. of R.'s. 5 : 424–428. — Hinsdale, B. A. (I). Training of Teachers. In Butler's Education in the United States, 1 : 361–407. The Teacher's Academical and Professional Preparation. N. E. A. 1891 : 713. The Certification of College and University Graduates as Teachers in the Public Schools. Sch. Rev. 7 : 331. — *Hollis*, A. P. The Present Status of Teaching in State Normal Schools. Ped. Sem. 8 : 495. — Hughes, Mrs. E. P. The Professional Training of Teachers for the Secondary Schools. N. E. A. 1893 : 217. —*Jacobs*, W. B. The Training of Teachers for Secondary Schools. Ed. Rev. 11 : 245. —*Jones*, L. H. Teachers' Reading Circles. N. E. A. 1895 : 179. — **Kinneman**, A. J. Pedagogy in our Colleges and Universities. Ped. Sem. 9 : 366. — *Maxwell*, W. H. Teachers' Salaries. Ed. Rev. 2 : 73. —*Newell*, M. A. Contributions to the History of Normal Schools in the United States. Rep. Com. Ed. 1898–1899, 2 : 2263.— Nightingale, A. F. Preparation of Teachers for Secondary Schools. Sch. Rev. 4 : 129. — Olin, Arvin S. Teachers' Institutes. N. E. A. 1895 : 165. — Olmstead, Denison (biog.). Am. Jour. Ed. 5 : 367. — *O'Shea*, M. V. The Professional Training of Teachers. Pop. Sci. Mo. 45 : 796. — *Parker*, Francis W. The Training of Teachers. N. E. A. 1895 : 969. Training of Teachers. Science, 9 : 564–567. — *Payne*, W. H. The Training of the Teacher. Ed. Rev. 16 : 469. — Pierce, Cyrus (biog.). Am. Jour. Ed. 4 : 275. — *Rice*, J. M. Talent *vs.* Training, in Teaching. Forum, 34 : 588–607. — *Russell*, J. E. The Training of Teachers for Secondary Schools. N. E. A. 1899 : 285 ; 1901 : 636. — Sabin, Henry. What Present Means are Available for the Preparation of Teachers? N. E. A. 1891 : 505. — *Schaeffer*, N. C. One-sided Training of Teachers. Forum, 32 : 456–459. — *Shepherd*, H. E. Examining and Certificating of Teachers. Ed. 1 : 237. — *Smith*, W. Tolman. Teachers' Salaries and Pensions, Ed. Rev. 2 : 335. — Tappan, E. T. The Examination of Teachers. N. E. A. 1883 : 3. Teachers' Pensions and Annuities. Rep. Com. Ed. 1899–1900, 2 : 2569. — United States Education, Bureau of. Teachers' Institutes. Circ. Inf. No. 2, 1885, p. 206. Training of Teachers. Reports, 1880 : lxxxvii–c ; 1881 : cxxviii–cxxxiii ; 1882 : xcvi–cii ; 1883 : cix–cxvii ; 1884 : cxxxvii–cxliii ; 1886 : 396–452 ; 1887 : 379–458 ; 1889 : 1015–1020 ; 1893 : 469–487 ; 1894 : 650–663 ; 1896 : 865–870. — Welldon, J. E. C. Teacher's Training of Himself. Contemp. 63 : 369–386.

CHAPTER XIX

ART AND MANUAL EDUCATION

a. ART EDUCATION

ALTHOUGH since the time of Benjamin Franklin there have been earnest advocates of drawing and various forms of manual training as school subjects, such can hardly be said to have received a respectable hearing on the part of the people until so late as 1870. It is true that previous to that time there had been established in various cities of the country, drawing and art schools of a more or less nondescript character, and that there were in operation a few creditable institutions ; but the mass of the people had not yet been touched, and there was probably some justification in the European characterization of us, as an inartistic people. In fact, previous to 1870 there were but ten institutions in the country giving instruction in any department of the fine arts, of sufficient promise to be considered by the commissioner of education in his later reports. Of these, the three oldest were in Philadelphia, that in connection with the Philadelphia Academy of Fine Arts having given free instruction in drawing and modelling in clay since 1806. The second to open its doors was the Franklin P. 559. Institute of Philadelphia, which offered courses in mechanical, architectural, and topographical drawing in semi-weekly classes for a small fee. It began the work in 1824. The third was a school entirely for women, opened by the Philadelphia School of Design in 1847, and giving free instruction in drawing and painting, as well as modelling in clay. The next to open was the night school

401

of the Maryland Institute, giving training in elementary and mechanical drawing to members of the institute only. The day school was not opened until 1860. In 1852 the Cooper Union in New York City opened its women's courses, and in 1857 its free school of art. This institution has been doing a work in popular education in New York City, hardly equalled by any other of its character in the country, if indeed in the world. It was founded by Peter Cooper, a wealthy merchant of the city. The character of the man may be gathered from the following extract from his address delivered at the dedication of the building which he had given : —

"Believing that instruction in the science and philosophy of a true republican government, formed, as it should be, of the people and for the people, in all its operations, is suited to the common wants of our nature, and absolutely necessary to preserve and secure the rights and liberties of all; that such a government rightly understood and wisely administered, will most effectually stimulate industry and afford the best means possible to improve and elevate our race, by giving security and value to all forms of human labor; that it is on the right understanding and application of this science based as it is on the golden rule; that eternal principle of truth and justice that unites the individual, the community, the state and the nation in one common purpose and interest binding all to do unto others as they would that others should do unto them: thus deeply impressed with the great importance of instruction in this branch of science, I have provided that it shall be continually taught, as of preëminent importance to all the great interests of mankind."

His school has been one of the most enduring monuments ever erected by man.

According to its by-laws, the work of the union is as follows : —

"The trustees shall establish and maintain a school for the instruction of respectable females in the arts of designs and such other branches of knowledge as in their judgment will tend to the elevation and employment of female labor . . . 'a free reading room in the large hall of the third story for the use of the working classes of both sexes and their families' . . . free courses of instruction at night in the elementary principles of science and their application to the practical business of life . . . shall always include chemistry, physics, mechanics, and mechanical drawing . . . an annual course of lectures upon the principles of government and political economy . . . as soon as the income of the corporation will warrant, establish, and maintain a thorough polytechnic school."

All this has been, and is being done. In the free night school of art courses are offered in free hand, perspective, industrial, architectural, and mechanical drawing, drawing from the form, and from the cast, and modelling in clay.

Other institutions for instruction in the fine arts were established in the United States as follows, up to the year 1870 : —

    1856. School of Design of the Ohio Mechanics Institute, Cincinnati.
    1861. The Free School of Design of the Brooklyn Art Association.
    1865. Pittsburg School of Design for Women.
    1869. School of Design of the University of Cincinnati.

What makes the year 1870 memorable in the art annals of our country is the introduction of drawing into the public schools of Boston. Attempts had been made previous to this time to have the subject taught in the schools in other cities ; but they had come to naught, or for various reasons been productive of few results. In Baltimore, as far back as 1849, drawing was given a place in the school programme, but was continued only for a brief period. Cleveland, too, tried the experiment in the same year, but little resulted from it. Boston was, however, fortunate in securing no less an artist and organizer than Walter Smith as "art director" for its schools, and since in the same year (1870), by state law, drawing was made a required study in all towns in the state having five thousand and more inhabitants, the subject came immediately into prominence. The State

Normal Art School was established at Boston in 1873 as a source of supply for adequately prepared teachers. The Centennial Exhibition of 1876 was made the occasion of an elaborate exhibit of what had been accomplished, and since the people were ready for it, an immediate wave of art enthusiasm spread over the country which since that time has steadily gained in volume, until now no public school system is without its art instruction, nor without a competent specialist as director, unless prevented by financial reasons.

In the public high schools of the fifty largest cities of the country, where this consideration would have little force, no less than 53,234 pupils out of a total of 109,-029 are taking courses in drawing, a larger number than for any other subject, save Latin, algebra, rhetoric, and English literature. Statistics are not at hand for the high schools in the smaller cities nor for the elementary school systems, but certainly for the latter they would far exceed these figures.

Meanwhile special institutions for art instruction have gone on multiplying in the same proportion. Several of these are in connection with our great museums of fine arts, as the Boston Art Museum, and the Corcoran Art Gallery in Washington, while others are maintained as departments in colleges and universities. Of the 422 such institutions in 1901, 47 were offering courses in fine arts (this and many of the following facts are taken from Frederick), the enrolment in the subjects being a little over 5000 out of a total student body of 47,000. Yale was the first to establish fine arts instruction, and has been a leader in the movement, standing in a class by itself to-day in the success with which it deals with the problems of the artist as well as with those of the general student body. It is one of two of the larger universities, the other being Leland Stanford, which gives a degree for work in the department.

Bibliography.

Yale Col. p. 245.

Fine arts instruction has been a matter of gradual

introduction during the last two decades, usually without any special change in university organization, except in the establishment of the new department. It is often impossible to say just when it did find place in the curricula of particular institutions. As it is at present taught, however, the character of the courses present four somewhat distinct types. First, we find that of lectures merely, upon the history of fine arts and æsthetics, with little or no technical instruction. Such is the nature of the work at Bryn Mawr, Princeton, Chicago, and the state universities of Maine, Missouri, and Wisconsin. The course at Brown, which is typical of the class, is as follows: (1) ancient art, chiefly Greek; (2) Roman and mediæval, including Byzantine; (3) renaissance, chiefly Italian; (4) art of seventeenth and eighteenth centuries; (5) nineteenth century art; (6) theory and criticism. A second class, including Wellesley, Harvard, and the state universities of Michigan and Indiana, while putting much stress upon the lecture side of instruction, provide studio courses for those who desire them. Of the work at Harvard, Professor Frederick says:—

"Of all our universities and colleges, Harvard comes the nearest to what may be called fine art instruction, of any American university. Having no technical nor professional aim in view, the study is really cultural: and is made so by a unison of theory and practice."

The following are Harvard's courses: (1) principles of delineation, color, and (2) principles of design in architecture, sculpture, and painting, (3) history of Greek art, (4) the fine arts of the Middle Ages and the renaissance; also an advanced course in classical archæology. This is made possible by the collection of the Fogg Art Museum and the Boston Museum of Fine Arts. It may be said here that it is as impossible to teach fine arts without examples as to conduct a school of agriculture upon a desert island. Many institutions, although putting some stress upon art for art's sake, nevertheless offer art courses largely because of the bearing they have upon architectural and other forms of professional instruction. Among such should be classed Columbia, Cornell, Johns Hopkins, Leland Stanford, Pennsylvania, the United States Military Academy, and the University of Illinois, as well as the various schools of technology. Many of these institutions have admirably equipped art departments, and are doing work of the highest character.

b. Musical Education

From the earliest days of the district school, music, or what passed for it, has had a place in the curriculum. Not that technical instruction was given, for the itinerant singing master with his evening singing school looked after that, but " examination day " came with regularity, and songs for the occasion had to be prepared. These were practised industriously and sung with vigor.

Not until about the middle of the nineteenth century did the real pedagogical value of music begin to be recognized, and the schools set to work to introduce it from that point of view. As kindergartens were introduced, they did much to popularize the subject, and now it is practically universal, taken alike by the musical and unmusical. In 1885, when a special study of the teaching of music in the public schools was made by the bureau of education, the following were found to be the conditions : —

Circ. of Inf. 1 : 1886.

Pupils in schools in which music is not taught	128,738
Pupils in schools in which music is taught by the regular teaching force . . .	251,769
Pupils in schools in which music is taught by special teachers only	21,032
Pupils in schools in which music is taught by special teachers and regular teachers .	795,314

As will be seen by the figures, at that time only about one-eighth of the pupils were without instruction in music; and to-day the proportion is much less. Besides the public school facilities for musical instruction, private teachers are abundant in every locality, and each considerable town has one or more conservatories where extended instruction is offered. Many of the colleges and universities, too, maintain musical departments; in some instances seminaries for women having so emphasized them as to have become little other than conservatories of music. Singing societies and choral unions must not be disregarded as important factors in municipal education, and too much cannot be said in praise of such men as Henry L. Higginson, whose generosity has made possible for these many years the Boston Symphony Orchestra. In the matter of artists' concerts, we are now but little behind the European nations, and in the musical productions made possible at the Metropolitan Opera House in New York, far in the lead.

c. MANUAL EDUCATION

Those forms of education which are primarily intended to produce in the pupil a dexterity of movement, rather than intellectual development of an academic or professional nature, have arisen as a result of two distinctly different demands on the part of the people. The first is largely an economic one, and calls for skilled labor. The result has been the various trade schools. The second has come from the educational leaders, and has called for the various forms of manual instruction, not so much because of their vocational, as their educational value; and has resulted in the introduction of departments of manual instruction of a general nature, in our public schools and other educational institutions. It is true that neither one of these classes of schools disregards the primary aim of the other, for the educational value of trades instruction in the purely industrial schools is fully recognized, as is the vocational nature of much of the manual work in the other class of schools; yet that their aims are distinct cannot be denied, nor should it be.   Schools of the industrial type have been touched upon in the chapter on technical education. Those of manual instruction for educational ends are a later development, and have their *raison d'être* in the changing social conditions.   When the population was largely rural, and the boys and girls were factors in the household economy, helping with the "chores" and the housework, besides doing the many little mechanical jobs which arise about the house, the proper motor control of the various parts of the body was acquired without the necessity of help on the part of the machinery of the schools.   But with the increase of urban population, and the more intricate organization of the affairs of the household, the boys and girls were deprived of this home education in manual and domestic service to the undoubted detriment, not only of the active side of their education, but of the purely intellectual as well, for one cannot suffer without injury to the other.   These facts being recognized, the leaders in educational thought cast about for some remedy, and in the early '70's, soon after the first enthusiasm was manifested in the question of drawing in the public schools, and perhaps somewhat dependent upon it, manual instruction for other than purely vocational purposes had its origin.   Such work seems to have been first offered at the Illinois Industrial University, now the University of Illinois, in 1871, under the direction of N. C. Ricker, now dean of the College of Engineering.   In that year both wood and iron shops were in operation.   During the next year (1872) similar shops were established by C. M. Woodward, a leader in manual instruction ever since, at the Washington University in St. Louis.   Even previous to this time, the merits of the so-called "Russian" method of tool work, formulated by Della Vos in St. Petersburg, had been discussed on this side of the water, yet had not been actually introduced. But in 1873 Professor Ricker, during a visit to Europe, made a careful study of its methods and results, modified it to meet the wants of his department, and put it into practice in 1875. Specimens of work done under his direction were exhibited at the Centennial Exhibition in 1876. At the same exhibition an elaborate display of models illustrating the method was made by the Russian school, and we may perhaps date the real beginning of educational manual training from that year. Schoolmen from all parts of the country went home from the exhibition enthusiastic over the possibility of manual instruction; and, so far as possible, took steps to introduce it into their schools. The move, so far as the public schools are concerned, has taken on two forms: (1) that of the introduction of manual branches into the regular curricula of the schools, and (2) that of the establishment of separate manual training high schools. Where the latter is done, the simpler manual branches are taught in the grades in connection with the regular work.

Manual Training in the Grades

So rapid was the introduction of this feature of educational work into the public schools, that in 1889 some form of it was in operation in 28 cities and towns in the country, in 9 of which it was offered in all the grades. In the others it was about evenly distributed over the primary and intermediate classes; and was usually given three times a week for an interval of one hour, though many variations from this plan were shown. Besides the subject of drawing, which was very frequently included with the manual work, all gave some form of wood work, 21, sewing; 11, cooking; 9, modelling in clay; 6, paper folding; 5, printing; and 4, work in iron. In 1901 similar courses were being given in 232 cities of over 8000 inhabitants, and in a large number of smaller towns. The tendency seems to be to put the courses in the later rather than the earlier grades, where they are given at all, about six times as many schools having them in the 5th, 6th, 7th, and 8th, as in the first four grades. Cooking has also been more generally introduced.

Manual Training Schools

Beginning with the St. Louis Manual Training School, which opened in 1880, the number of special schools of this character has rapidly increased, being 18 in 1889, and 153 in 1901, though the last figure includes a considerable number of trades schools, among them, 35 for Indians. Of the 100 or so in which the vocational element is made subservient to the more broadly educational, 25 are elementary in their character; 24 cover both the elementary and secondary fields of instruction; 48 are purely secondary; 4 combine work of a secondary grade with the higher; 4 do work of a collegiate grade only, while 2 cover all grades of work from the lowest elementary, through the college. Of those giving instruction of a secondary grade only, nearly all are public manual training high schools supported in every way, as are any other parts of the public school system. The move for the establishment of such schools was not under way until well into the '80's, but in 1884 Chicago and Baltimore established them, and New York City made provision for manual instruction in its city college. The next year (1885) the Central Manual Training High School was opened in Philadelphia, and early in 1886 the Cleveland School. Omaha, New Orleans, Cincinnati, Denver, New Haven, Louisville, Brooklyn, Kansas City, and Boston soon followed with similar schools, the latter naming its school the Mechanics Arts High School. These schools are all of one general type, though each retains an individuality of its own. The entrance requirements are usually the same as for the English and classical high schools, in the same cities, the courses of the same length, and the requirements for graduation equivalent. Modern lan- Appendix E. guages are taught, though not the ancient; English is not neglected, while mathematics is emphasized. The physical and chemical sciences receive much attention, and the laboratory facilities for teaching them are generally better than in the academic high schools. Besides the departments for wood and iron working, which are primarily, though not exclusively, for the boys, those of the domestic arts and sciences, including sewing, dressmaking, millinery, cooking, and even household sanitation and æsthetics are maintained in the coeducational schools. In the manual training high schools and manual training departments of the other high schools in the fifty largest cities of the country are enrolled 10,146 students, which is about one-tenth of the total number in those schools. Of these 2687 are girls.

The private secondary schools of manual training do not differ materially from the public, except that in many instances their offerings are more extensive, combining the manual instruction with a greater amount of art work and even courses for library and business training.

The few schools which combine the secondary grade of instruction with the higher are all private institutions. Among them are the Lewis Institute, Chicago, the Bradley Polytechnic Institute, Peoria, Illinois (1896), the Lowell Textile School of Lowell, Massachusetts, Drexel Institute of Philadelphia (1891); schools of the highest order of excellence.

Of the two institutions of a collegiate grade, one is a state institution — the State Manual Training School of North Dakota at Ellendale; the other, the Pennsylvania Museum School of Industrial Arts. Although the former is essentially an institution for instruction in the manual arts, the latter offers them only as a department in connection with commercial and other branches. Besides these two special institutions of collegiate rank, manual training is taught in all the land-grant colleges and in many of the other institutions which were discussed in Chapter XVII. Courses in domestic science, though formerly not included in their curricula, are being rapidly introduced, and are now given in the following: the state universities of Minnesota, Nebraska, Ohio, Illinois, Missouri, and Nevada; the agricultural colleges of Alabama (colored), Colorado, Connecticut, Florida, Iowa, Kansas, Michigan, Montana, North Carolina (colored), North Dakota, Oregon, South Dakota, and Utah; the Branch Normal of Arkansas, Hampton Institute, and the West Virginia Colored Institute. These institutions, together with Pratt Institute, the Teachers College (Columbia), the manual training schools, wholly or partially of a collegiate grade, and a few normal schools, form the source of supply for teachers of this branch.

REFERENCES

ART

Art Decorations in School Rooms. Rep. Com. Ed. 1894–1895, 1 : 793–804; 1895–1896, 1 : 1363–1412. — *Clarke*, I. E. Art and Industrial Education. In Butler's Education in United States, pp. 705–767. — *Carter*, C. M. The Extension of Art Education. N. E. A. 1895 : 810–814. — Dewey, John. The Æsthetic Element in Education. N. E. A. 1897 : 329. — **Frederick,** Frank Forrest. The Study of Fine Arts in American Colleges and Universities. N. E. A. 1901 : 695. — Goodyear, W. A. Some Principles of Decorative Art. Rep. Com. Ed. 1895–1898, 2 : 1326–1329. — *Hoppin*, James M. Art in Popular Education. Forum, 7 : 331–338. — *MacAlister*, James. Art Education in the Public Schools. Rep. Com. Ed. 1894–1895. 1 : 793–803. — *Maxwell*, W. H. Art Teaching in Schools. N. E. A. 1897 : 266–274. Study of Art and Literature in Schools. Rep. Com. Ed. 1898–1899, 1 : 687–706. — *Thompson*, L. S. Evolution of Systems of Drawing in the United States. N. E. A. 1889 : 641–646. — United States Education, Bureau of. Art Education. In various reports.

MUSIC

Bull, W. S. An Ignis Fatuus in School Music. Music, 22 : 246–250. — *Crane*, J. E. Some Salient Points in Public School Music. Music, 14 : 220. — Fairbanks, H. W. Music Credits in High Schools. Music, 2 : 298–303. — *Lagerquist*, Charles. Music in the Country Schools. Music, 14 : 328–332. — Mathews, J. L. Music for Grade and Rural Teachers. Music, 12 : 254–257. — Mathews, W. S. B. A Few Thoughts on School Music. Music, 20 : 351–352. — Regal, M. L. How One City trains Music Lovers. Music, 17 : 138–149. — *Rice*, C. I. School Music in the Primary Grades. Music, 19 : 11–119. — Smith, C. B. Education of the Supervisor. Music, 21 : 252–256. — United States Education, Bureau of. Music in Schools. In various reports. Music in the Public Schools. Circ. Inf. 1 : 1888.

MANUAL TRAINING

Carter, C. M. Industrial Idea in Education. Cent. 14 : 679–684. Cities in which Manual Training is given. Rep. Com. Ed. 1901, 2 : 2233. — *Charles*, I. E. Art and Industrial Education. In Butler's Education in United States, pp. 705–767. — Goodnough, W. S. Æsthetic Element in Manual Training. Rep. Com. Ed. 1895–1896, 2 : 1323–1325. — *Hartman*, W. N. Manual Training in the Elementary School. N. E. A. 1890 : 842. — *Ham*, C. H. Manual Training. Harper, 72 : 404–412. — Leipziger, H. M. The Progress of Manual Training. N. E. A. 1894 : 877. — *Leland*, C. G. Industrial Art in Education. Critic, 9 : 85–86. Handwork in Public Schools. Cent. 2 : 890–896. — *Magnus*, Philip. Manual Training in School Education. Contemp. 50 : 696–706. — *Richards*, C. R. Limitations to Artistic Manual Training. Rep. Com. Ed. 1895–1896, 2 : 1325. — Stebbins, H. W. Industrial Education as a Social Force. Ed. 23 : 462–467. — *Thorpe*, F. N. Manual Training as a Factor in Modern Education. Cent. 16 : 920–927. — *Typical Institutions Offering Manual or Industrial Training.* Rep. Com. Ed. 1895–1896, 2 : 1001–1152. — United States Education, Bureau of. Various annual reports. Industrial Education in South Carolina. Circ. Inf. No. 5, 1888–1889, 86 p. — Winston, G. I. Industrial Education and the New South. Rep. Com. Ed. 1900–1901, 1 : 509–513. — *Woodward*, C. M. Manual Training. Rep. Com. Ed. 1893–1894, 1 : 877–950. The Rise and Progress of Manual Training. Rep. Com. Ed. 1893–1894, 1 : 877. Manual Training Schools. Cassier, 5 : 478–480.

DOMESTIC SCIENCE

Lake Placid Conference on Home Economics. Ed. Rev. 24: 426–427. — Home Economics, 1900 (New York State University. Home Education Department, Syllabus, No. 82). — Watson, Mrs. K. H. Outline of Study to use in Women's Clubs prepared for the National Household Economic Association (see Campbell, Helen. Household Economics. Ed. 2, N.Y., 1898, pp. 257–259). — Winnington, Laura. Kitchen Garden. Outlook, 68:52.

CHAPTER XX

COMMERCIAL EDUCATION

INSTITUTIONS offering courses of training for business are of four classes.

a. Commercial and business schools.

b. Public high schools.

c. Endowed secondary schools, usually more or less industrial and technical in their nature.

d. Colleges and universities.

a. COMMERCIAL AND BUSINESS SCHOOLS

This class of schools, supporting themselves entirely from fees and conducted purely as business ventures, were first in the field, having had their origin soon after the middle of the nineteenth century. In their inception they were very simple institutions, having in many instances but one teacher, and as equipment, nothing more than a single room, usually in some business block, and a few tables and chairs. The course was short, of a few months at most, and consisted of penmanship, business arithmetic, and bookkeeping.

There can be no doubt, however, that such institutions met a business need; for they multiplied very rapidly, took on more complete forms of organization, and in some instances developed into schools of considerable size, or into systems of affiliated schools situated in different cities, but under the same general management. The Packard schools and the Bryant and Stratton schools are evidences of this tendency to form "chains," no less than fifty having been at one time under the latter name.

In 1870 the number of private commercial schools in the country was 26, with 5824 pupils. In 1875 the numbers were 131, and 26,109, respectively. In 1880, 162, and 27,146; in 1890, 263, and 78,982; while in 1901, there were 407 such schools with a total enrolment of 110,031 students, and a teaching force of 2434. The greatest variation is found among these institutions. Several have but 1 instructor, a considerable number but 2, while 26 have between 10 and 19; 6 between 20 and 29; and 1 upwards of 30; the remainder having between 3 and 9 upon the teaching force. As prerequisites to admission, the common branches only are demanded. All except a very few schools maintain a general commercial course; and all save 75, courses in stenography. In addition, a general course in the English branches is offered in about one-half the schools, while telegraphy is taught in about one-fourth. But 36 of the schools offer courses of twelve months or over (one 36 and another 30), the average length being six months. A great majority hold sessions in the evening as well as in the daytime. Many are elaborately equipped with all the business offices for the transaction of commercial business—including bank, clearing house, etc. — and the students carry on business transactions through the mail with those in other affiliated schools. Although it cannot be denied that the schools of this class have done valuable work, they can hardly be classed as educational institutions in the broadest sense, since their primary aim is to turn out pupils who are proficient in some particular system of bookkeeping or of stenography, rather than to develop intellectual power. What they pretend to do, however, they in many instances do well, and even an apprentice system pure and simple has some place in our economic development.

b. COMMERCIAL EDUCATION IN PUBLIC HIGH SCHOOLS

Courses for business gained their admission to the American high school through the introduction, in some instances two or three decades ago, of courses in bookkeeping, typewriting, and sometimes stenography, offered as electives. In many schools this represents precisely the status of business studies to-day. There is, however, a widespread move in the direction of better organization of the work and the arrangement of definite curricula covering three or four years, which shall bring about as full an intellectual development as do any of the secondary school courses; though utilizing as the basis of such a development the purely and allied commercial branches. Whether this is entirely possible remains to be seen; but many cities are struggling with the problem, and in so many different ways that if the problem is capable of a solution, it will be discovered in some one of them. Although it is too early in the move to predict results, it seems probable that the best plan for commercial education in the high school is through the establishment of entirely separate schools for the purpose — the plan which has proved so successful in the case of manual training. Washington, District of Columbia, and New York City are as yet the only ones to do so (Washington since 1890, New York since 1900); but Chicago has the matter under consideration, and will undoubtedly soon take definite action. In Boston a two years' commercial course is given in connection with some of the regular high schools. In Pittsburg, the course is of but one year. In Omaha, the course is spread over four years, no one of which is intensively commercial in its character, and a similar course is pursued in the Central High School of Philadelphia. James, pp. 676–677.

A study of the curricula of public high schools in various parts of the country, for the years of 1890 and 1900, throws an interesting light upon the changes in commercial branches during the ten years' period. Fifty schools were selected for the study, from the larger and medium-sized cities, and every part of the country was represented. The facts were taken from the printed courses of study and are expressed in the following table: —

UNITED STATES	BOOK-KEEPING		BUS. PRAC.		CIV. GOV.		COM. LAW		COM. ARITH.		COM. GEOG.		STENOG-RAPHY	
	1890	1900	1890	1900	1890	1900	1890	1900	1890	1900	1890	1900	1890	1900
No. of schools studied, 1890, 46; 1900, 56														
Per cent offering study . .	64	74	9	23	59	52	13	25	26	72	4	28		22
Per cent offering one-half year	33	36	—	6	54	46	11	17	7	44	4	7	—	—
Per cent offering one year .	24	19	7	8	5	6	2	8	19	28	—	21	—	6
Per cent offering two years .	9	19	2	10	—	—	—	—	—	—	—	—	—	16
Per cent offering study first year	26	35	4	8	15	16	—	2	7	26	4	18	—	—
Per cent offering study second year	28	39	7	12	24	17	9	13	17	30	—	6	—	—
Per cent offering study third year	13	19	—	12	7	8	2	6	2	16	—	4	—	—
Per cent offering study fourth year	8	4	—	2	13	11	2	4	—	—	—	—	—	—
Per cent offering a full course, 1890, 8; 1900, 23														
Per cent offering no studies, 1890, 24; 1900, 19														

As may be seen, the full commercial course is given in about three times as many of these schools in 1900 as was the case in 1890. The specific subjects which have been especially emphasized are stenography, commercial geography, commercial law, and business practice.

The commercial courses in the high schools differ from those in the private commercial schools in being less technical, and in the introduction of these subjects, and in some instances the ethics of business, which tend to give a broad foundation for the mastery of the fundamentals of commercial relations.

The number of students pursuing commercial branches in our public high schools for as many years as figures are given for by the commissioner of education is as follows: 1893–1894, 15,220; 1894–1895, 25,539; 1895–1896, 30,330; 1896–1897, 33,075; 1897–1898, 31,633; 1898–1899, 38,134; 1899–1900, 68,890; 1900–1901, 84,412.

c. COMMERCIAL EDUCATION IN PRIVATE ENDOWED INSTITUTIONS OF SECONDARY GRADE

There are many institutions of this class, and among them a few which must be recognized as leaders among secondary schools in commercial education, such as the Pratt Institute in Brooklyn, and the Drexel Institute of Philadelphia. The latter has an especially elaborate organization and extended course. Rep. Com. Ed. 1901, 1 : 1167.

In all, 867 private academies offer commercial courses, with a total enrolment of 15,649 pupils. The courses do not vary materially in most instances from those in the public high schools.

Many of the normal schools, too, both public and private (seventy-five in all), make provision for commercial students.

d. COMMERCIAL EDUCATION IN COLLEGES AND UNIVERSITIES

The most recent move in commercial education, and the most hopeful one, since it aims to produce leaders rather than mere journeymen, is that which is just now taking place in our higher academic institutions. Our commercial and economic development is in the direction of great business enterprises, the success or failure of which depend upon the good judgment and farsightedness of their leaders, not in their expertness as bookkeepers. In recognition of this, our colleges and universities have set themselves to the task of graduating men of power, the basis of whose education is commercial, rather than classical or technically scientific. The move started but little more than a decade ago, and gained hardly any momentum until within the last five years. Previous to that time commercial branches had been taught in the colleges, but the treatment was academic rather than professional, and amounted to little.

Univ. of Pa.
p. 250 *et seq.* The University of Pennsylvania was the first higher institution to arrange definite courses of study for students anticipating business careers. This was made possible through a gift of $100,000 made by Mr. Joseph Wharton, which was devoted to the establishment of a school of finance and economy in the university, bearing the name of the founder. Besides certain mathematical, historical, and linguistic studies, the course in the Wharton school includes, in the freshman year, physical and economic geography, practical economic problems, economic literature, and legislative and executive documents. In the sophomore year the professional studies are business law, money, and banking, business practice, theory and geography of commerce, American and European constitutional law, political economy, and legislative organization and procedure. The juniors study comparative politics, modern legislative problems, business practice and banking, economic history, sociology with field work, English constitutional history, logic, and ethics; while the last year of the course comprises the history of law and legal concepts, local and municipal institutions, political economy, statistics, public finance, transportation, and advanced sociology.

No other great institution followed the example set by Pennsylvania until 1898, when two, both in the West, established colleges of commerce. These were the universities of California and of Chicago. In each the course is four years. In the former the studies are divided into ten groups, viz.: philosophical, legal, political, historical, economic, linguistic, geographical, mathematical, and technological, covering (*a*) the materials of commerce and (*b*) transportation.

At Chicago the prescribed studies for the first two years comprise economics and social history, commercial geography, civil government, history, modern languages, English, and science. In the last two: principles of political economy, elements of jurisprudence, constitutional law of the United States, Europe in the nineteenth century, recent American history, and psychology. The remainder of the course, amounting to somewhat more than one-fourth, is selected from fifty-six special offerings which are open for election.

Univ. of Chicago, p. 278.

In 1900 the Amos Tuck School of Administration and Finance was opened at Dartmouth College. The course of study extends through two years, and is intended to be graduate work, though it may be taken in part by seniors in the college. The subjects covered are modern languages, advanced history, advanced economics, law and diplomacy, sociology and statistics, administration, accounting and auditing, business organization and procedure, commerce, transportation, money and banking, public finance, corporation and financial insurance, and a thesis to be presented by each student.

Dartmouth Col. p. 265 *et seq.*

At the University of Illinois, what is practically a school of commerce was organized in 1902, offering courses for business under the following general heads: (*a*) general courses in business training, (*b*) courses in banking, (*c*) courses in transportation, (*d*) courses for journalism, (*e*) courses in insurance. In connection with these general courses, there are in economics, commerce, and industry, thirty-five special offerings: in government, one; in history, six; in law, six; in insurance, one; in materials of commerce, five; in mechanical technology, six; besides mathematical, philosophical, and linguistic subjects.

These outlines will serve to show the kind of commercial work that is at present being done in those colleges and universities in which it has been most fully organized. Several others are, however, offering courses of much the same character; in all (1901), a dozen or more in addition to those mentioned. Among them are the state universities of Michigan, Wisconsin, Louisiana (Tulane), Vermont, West Virginia, Nevada, and Wyoming.

It is too early to say just what particular direction the development of these schools may take, but there can be no doubt of their general efficiency, nor that they are bound to play an important part in our business and economic development as a nation.

As yet they have not turned themselves prominently in the direction of preparation for journalism, but the recent gift of Mr. Joseph Pulitzer of New York to Columbia University for the foundation of a school of journalistic training, cannot fail to turn public attention in that direction, and we may expect important developments within the next few years.

Columbia
p. 259.

REFERENCES

Ashley, W. J. Universities and Commercial Education. N. A. Rev. 176 : 31–38. — *Business Education.* N. Y. Univ. Regents Bull. Oct. 1898, pp. 366–417. Business Education in the United States. Ed. 23 : 116–117. — *Business Training for College Men.* World's Work, 5 : 2922. — *Eliot*, Charles W. Commercial Education. Rep. Com. Ed. 1898–1899, 1 : 677–681. On Higher Commercial Education. Ann. Am. Acad. 14 : 396–397. — *Ellis*, C. B. Commercial Education in Secondary Schools. Ed. 22 : 631–637. Purpose of a Good Business Department in a Public High School. Sch. Rev. 11 : 123–137. — Haskins, C. W. Business Education. Harp. W., 46 : 1688, 1705, 1719. — Herrick, Cheesman A. Higher Commercial Education. Ann. Am. Acad. 21 : 511–513. — *Irish*, C. W. Place of Commercial Studies in the High School. Sch. Rev. 10 : 550–557. — James, Edmund J. Commercial Education. In Butler's Education in the United States, 1900, v. 2. Plea for the Establishment of Commercial High Schools, 1893. — Jones, E. D. Preparing College Students for Business. World's Work, 6 : 3686. — National Educational Association. Report of Committee on Courses of Study for Business Colleges. Rep. Com. Ed. 1898-1899, 2 : 2163-2174. — Organ, T. A. Systematic Commercial Education. Rep. Com. Ed. 1897-1898, 1 : 334-338. — Robinson, E. L. Commercial Work in the School. Ed. 23 : 410-418. — *Thwing*, Charles F. Some Truths about Colleges of Commerce. Ind. 52 : 14. — United States Education, Bureau of. *Commercial and Business Colleges.* See various reports. — Waldo, Frank. The New Movement in Commercial Education. Cent. 66 : 798-799. — Whitfield, E. E. Commercial Education in Theory and Practice, 1901.

CHAPTER XXI

THE·EDUCATION OF WOMEN

WE have little evidence that our forefathers of early colonial days felt the importance of educating their daughters. Doubtless in the home, many of them became familiar with at least the first two of the "three R's," and occasionally a girl in some of the larger settlements seems to have prevailed upon some fortunate brother, of grammar school privileges, to share with her his knowledge of the third, but such cases were extremely rare.

The Dame schools were, however, open to her from the first, and although their special function seems to have been to provide the boys, destined for grammar school honors, with the rudiments of English which were a prerequisite, girls attended in considerable numbers. The Dame schools were at first private elementary schools; taught by women usually in some room in their own homes.

Crabbe has described the school as follows: —

> "When a deaf poor patient widow sits
> And awes some twenty infants as she knits —
> Infants of humble, busy wives who pay
> Some trifling price for freedom through the day,
> At this good matron's hut the children meet
> Who thus becomes the mother of the street:
> Her room is small, they cannot widely stray
> Her threshold high, they cannot run away:
> With bands of yarn she keeps offenders in,
> And to her gown the sturdiest can pin."

The school was of the most elementary as well as the most primitive character, though it was the only source of book-learning for the girls, as well as for most of the boys, during at least a century of our colonial history. There were no desks, maps, blackboards, nor any other equipment for schoolkeeping, save a teacher,—who in many cases knew little beyond the letters she was teaching,—and perhaps a single copy of the *horn book*. The Dame school was at first a private venture; but as time went on, and it proved its usefulness as an institution, it was not uncommonly supported, at least, in part, by the town. As an instance of this, we find record of action taken at Springfield, Massachusetts, in 1682:—

"The select men agreed with Goodwife Mirick to encourage her in the good work of training up of children, and teaching children to read, and that she should have three pence a week for every child that she takes to perform this good work for." Swett, p. 21.

In Woburn, Massachusetts, in 1869: "Paid for boarding school dame, at three shillings per week," and considerably later in Winchendon, Massachusetts, "Paid for a horse to carry the school dame up and bring her down again." So it was that the Dame school became in a sense a part of the public school system of the early New England colonies, though it was never held as an institution of much consequence or dignity. In it the boys got what little learning was required for entrance to the grammar schools, and the girls, all that it was thought they needed.

As time went on, and grammar schools were estab- P. 25 *et seq.* lished in greater numbers, we find occasional, but only occasional, instances in which girls were in any way admitted to their privileges, until nearly the beginning of the nineteenth century. Superintendent Small studied Small. the records of nearly two hundred towns in New England, and found, for the first century of colonial history, less than a dozen instances. Deerfield, Massachusetts, voted in 1698 that "all families having children, either male or female between the ages of six and ten years shall pay by the poll" for their schooling. There are references to similar action in the towns of Northampton and Hatfield in 1680; in Meriden, Connecticut, in 1678; in Rehoboth, Massachusetts, in 1699; and in Deerfield one year earlier. Such instances were, however, extremely rare, and the sentiment of the times regarding the admission of girls to boys' grammar schools seems to be expressed in the ruling for the Hopkins School in New Haven made in 1684. It reads: —

Am. Jour. Ed.
28 : 303.

". . . and all girls be excluded as improper and inconsistent with such a grammar school as ye law injoines and as is the Designe of this settlement."

Yet when the first school was set up in Dorchester, Massachusetts, the question was raised as to whether the "maydes shall be taught with the boys or not," though not settled in the affirmative for nearly a century and a half.

And so matters stood, with the Dame schools supreme in matters of female education, until well toward the time of the Revolution. Then concessions were made, though somewhat slowly, by the boys' schools, through admitting girls at odd times. Medford votes in 1766 that "the committee have power to agree with the school master to instruct girls two hours in a day after the boys are dismissed." The master was paid a salary for six months, "part of which time he schooled the girls as well as the boys." Gloucester with true feeling, passes this resolution in 1790: —

Small, p. 534.

"And also that the master be directed to begin his school from the first day of April to the last day of September at eight o'clock in the morning and close at six o'clock in the afternoon, or any eight hours in the twenty-four as shall be thought the most convenient, and that two hours, or a proportionable part of that time be devoted to the instruction of females — as they are a tender and interesting branch of the community, but have been much neglected in the public schools of this town."

In Norwich, Connecticut, the morning hours "from 5 to 7 A. M." were given to the girls. Nathan Hale, while schoolmaster in New London in 1774, writes in a letter:—

"I have kept during the summer, a morning school between the hours of 5 and 7, of about twenty young ladies: for which I have received twenty shillings a scholar by the quarter."

Toward the end of the eighteenth century many other New England towns made similar provisions for the instruction of girls; but that the two sexes were rarely together in the same school is to be inferred by a memorandum made by Benjamin Mudge. He says:—

"In all my school days which ended in 1801 I never saw but three females in public schools in my life and they were only in the afternoon to learn to write."

Dorchester had, however, in 1784, inserted the wedge which eventually, though only after many years, opened the door of the public school to girls. In that year the town voted "that such girls as can read the psalter be allowed to attend the grammar school from the first day of June to the first day of October." Previous to this time they had been admitted only to the general annual catechising.

In Portsmouth, New Hampshire, one David McClure was employed by the selectmen in 1773 to take care of a girls' school, and makes this interesting note in his diary:—

Am. Jour. Ed.
28 : 148.

"Opened school, consisting the first day of about 30 Misses. Afterward they increased to 70 and 80; so that I was obliged to divide the day between them and one half came in the forenoon and the other in the afternoon. They were from 7 to 20 years of age. . . . I attended to them in reading, writing, arithmetic and geography principally. This is, I believe, the only female school (supported by the town) in New England, and is a wise and useful institution."

In 1789, Boston established the first of the so-called "Double-headed" schools, in which girls were given the same privileges as the boys, though the two sexes were taught separately. They were reading and writing schools, with the programmes so arranged that one half-day was given up to each subject; the girls taking one, the boys the other. These were the common girls' schools in the city until about the time of the girls' grammar school in 1826.

The eagerness with which the girls availed themselves of any educational privilege accorded them was not overlooked by private teachers. Toward the latter part of the eighteenth century, several private schools for girls were opened. In New Haven, two Yale students, during the time that college work was suspended in 1779–1780, taught each a class of young women for a brief period. Jedidiah Morse had a similar school there in 1783. Two years later Timothy Dwight, afterward president of Yale, opened an academy, to which both sexes were admitted, at Greenfield Hill. At Medford, Massachusetts, an institution for girls, dignified with the title of "Academy," was opened in 1789, and is said to have been the first of its kind in New England. The famous New England academies were by this time being established and, although the greater number of them were for boys only, Leicester Academy (1784) and Westford Academy were coeducational from the start. Bradford Academy, also founded in the Merrimac Valley in 1803, originally admitted both sexes; but the girls gradually displaced the boys, and for many years now it has been one of the best-known schools for girls in the East. In its early days the course of study consisted of Morse's *Geography*, Murray's *Grammar*, Pope's *Essay on Man*, Blair's *Rhetoric*, composition, embroidery on satin, and the study of the Bible. In 1818, the Rev. Joseph Emerson, believing that girls should be better educated, opened his academy at Byfield, Massachusetts, and offered girls an opportunity to study philosophy and other branches, which before this had been open only to boys.

Academies, ch. vi.

In 1821, Emma Willard established her female seminary at Troy, New York, and in 1837 it was chartered. It made no pretensions to collegiate rank. In 1822, Catherine Beecher founded a girls' school at Hartford, Connecticut. One year later the Adams' Academy was established at Derry, New Hampshire, as the first in New England, incorporated expressly for the education of girls. Mrs. Willard and Miss Mary Lyon were both teachers there, the latter becoming subsequently the distinguished founder of Mt. Holyoke Seminary at South Hadley. Abbot Academy, at Andover, Massachusetts, was established in 1829.

In other parts of the country we find even less willingness on the part of schools to admit girls to their privileges, than was the case in New England. In the South, the wealthier classes provided tutors for the boys, and the girls seem in some cases to have shared the educational privileges with their brothers, with sometimes a visit to Europe to ensure the proper social polish. The home was, however, generally thought to be school enough for them, and the housewifely duties, a sufficiently extended curriculum; so it is not strange that we find that for a considerable part of the eighteenth century not more than one-fourth of the women who had occasion to sign legal documents could do so, except through the device of making their "mark."

A few academies for girls had, however, sprung up. The Moravians, in connection with their religious establishment at Nazareth, Pennsylvania, had maintained a school for girls since before 1750, and such was the reputation of the school that students were sent to it from all the colonies.

In Philadelphia an academy for girls was started by Dr. Rush, and in the same city, the Penn Charter School had admitted both sexes. In Lexington, Kentucky, a girls' school was opened very early, and in various other parts of the country sporadic attempts were made to establish similar institutions, most of which were but ephemeral. Some few, however, continued to the present. In 1875, there were 311 separate schools for girls of a secondary grade, but the number is somewhat less to-day, owing to the fact that a considerable proportion of them were public high schools which have been merged with those for boys, and also to the fact that competition with the public schools has caused others to close their doors. There are, however, many admirable schools for girls scattered throughout the country, not a few of which are convent schools belonging to the Roman Catholics.

Coeducation in the Common Schools

The custom of teaching the sexes together in the public schools of our country arose through convenience and for reasons of economy, rather than because of any feeling on the part of those in charge, that it was the best plan. In its later development it has been supported by pedagogic principle, but in the beginning that was lacking. Provision for the education of boys antedated by nearly two centuries of our history that for girls. When need for the latter arose, the plan of admitting them to the boys' school was, in many places, the only practicable one; and was followed, since the expense of separate establishments was out of the question. Where economic conditions allowed, separate schools were maintained, as in Boston and the older coast cities, and in some instances remain till to-day. When this was done, the girls were the sufferers, so far as the character of the work was concerned, for it was not of so high a standard in the girls' schools as in the boys'. This is amply shown by the girls' high schools of Boston, which, up to 1878, did not provide sufficiently advanced courses to prepare its students for entrance to college, although the boys' schools had done so for more than twenty-five years. In Baltimore, too, in 1900, the two girls' high schools did not complete the ordinary college entrance work, though the boys' schools had been sending their students to Johns Hopkins for years. Meanwhile the coeducational high schools in the smaller cities and towns of the country had been for a generation offering the girls the same advantages as the boys.

But the coeducational experiment, undertaken in the older schools in the East through stress of circumstances, was made the working plan throughout the West as settlements were made, through preference. It was fully in accord with the democratic ideas on educational matters, and has been followed out in nearly all the towns there from the beginning. The South has been somewhat more conservative, and has only gradually adopted the system of coeducation; but it is practically in full possession of the field there to-day. The move there has been made, as indeed it has in the East, somewhat largely through the device of dividing a school building into the so-called "boy side" and "girl side"; that is, by making essentially two separate buildings out of one by means of a division wall. The next step, when it was found that there were no dangerous results from teaching boys and girls within the same structure, was to demolish the wall, and teach both sexes in the same rooms. In some few schools the wall still stands.

The development of coeducation in the common schools, to its present extent, has been a very gradual one, and one not easy to trace in its details. It began in the first decades of the nineteenth century, and is still going on. Within the last decade it has made progress in eight different states; the only reason that the number is not larger is that it was already complete in so many.

In 1902 the status of coeducation in the public primary and secondary schools throughout the country was as follows: —

Adapted from a table based upon 628 cities given in Com. Ed. 1901. 2 : 1220.

The following states teach the two sexes together in all schools reported : Colorado, Connecticut, Delaware, Florida, Illinois, Indiana, Iowa, Kansas, Louisiana, Maine, Michigan, Minnesota, Missouri, Montana, Nebraska, Nevada, New Hampshire, North Dakota, Ohio, Oklahoma, Oregon, Rhode Island, South Dakota, Tennessee, Utah, Washington, West Virginia, Wisconsin, and Wyoming. Of the twelve states not included in this list, — Alabama : in Montgomery the sexes are taught separately in the high schools. California has two grammar schools and one high school, exclusively for girls, all in San Francisco. Georgia : in Atlanta separate high schools are maintained. Kentucky : in Covington the eighth grade pupils and a part of the seventh grade are separately taught. In Louisville there are separate high schools for boys and girls, and in some of the grades the sexes are separate. Maryland has a number of towns in which the sexes are separated in high school work. Massachusetts : in Boston there are three high schools for boys, two for girls, and seven which are coeducational; also twelve grammar schools each for boys and girls, and thirty-four for both sexes together. The lower schools are all coeducational. In Salem there is one grammar school and one primary school for each sex. In the high school both sexes recite together, but study in separate rooms. In Newburyport "during the past ten years many of our schools have been changed from separate schools to those for both sexes." Mississippi : the schools in two cities have the sexes separate. New Jersey : three towns have separate schools in part. New York : in New York City several of the high schools admit but a single sex, and in the grades instruction is frequently in separate classes, though usually within the same building. In two other towns in the state the same custom prevails. North Carolina : in Raleigh there is no high school. The pupils in the fourth, fifth, sixth, and seventh grades are in separate schools, though, upon request of parents, girls may be sent to the boys' schools. Boys, however, are not admitted to girls' schools. Pennsylvania: In Philadelphia separate schools are maintained for boys and girls. In six or seven other towns in the state a partial separation of the sexes is maintained. Texas and Virginia each has one town in which the sexes are separated in high school work. The statistics furnished by the commissioner of education show that as a result of the century of progress toward full educational privileges for women the move is thorough and complete. No class of schools is closed to them, and, so far as the number of individual institutions is concerned, considerably more exclude men than women. In the public elementary schools, in 1892, 55.9 per cent of the enrolment was of girls: in 1898 it was 56.5. From these figures we cannot doubt that the girls are making the most of their opportunities.

Higher Education of Women

When it had been proved beyond a doubt by the academies and seminaries for women which sprang up during the earlier decades of the nineteenth century, that sex differences were not of so much importance in education as had been supposed, it was not a long step to the establishment of institutions of a still higher grade for women. Some of the academies added a year or more to their course of study, and took on the more pretentious name of college or seminary; while at the same time, new institutions made their appearance in considerable numbers. The colleges for men, too, since the public secondary schools demonstrated the entire feasibility of coeducation, opened their doors to women, and we have to-day, as the result of all the moves in the direction of the higher education of women, three classes of institutions admitting them.

a. Colleges for women upon distinct and separate foundations.

b. Women's colleges affiliated with universities for men.

c. Coeducational institutions in which both sexes have equal privileges.

a. COLLEGES FOR WOMEN UPON DISTINCT AND SEPARATE FOUNDATIONS

Of these three classes, the first was the earliest in the field, the third but a little later, while the second is the product of the last few years of the nineteenth century. In point of numbers, the coeducational institutions far exceed the separate colleges, while as yet there are but few of the affiliated colleges for women. The following table shows the decades of organization, as well as the geographical distribution, of classes *a* and *b* taken together : —

COLLEGES FOR WOMEN

Years	N. Atlantic	S. Atlantic	S. Central	N. Central	Western	Total
1890–1901	—	8	8	1	—	17
1880–1889	2	3	6	1	—	12
1870–1879	4	11	6	—	1	21
1860–1869	5	3	7	2	—	17
1850–1859	5	10	22	2	—	39
1840–1849	—	7	5	2	—	15
1830–1839	2	2	3	—	—	7
Total	18	44	57	8	1	128

As will be seen from the table, the decade from 1830 to 1839 saw the beginning of higher education for women in our country. Of the twenty-two institutions taking their origin before 1850, but two were in the North

Atlantic states, and but two — Mt. Holyoke College at South Hadley, Massachusetts, and Rockford College, Rockford, Illinois — have arisen to any prominence or are to-day doing work of the standard done in the colleges for men. Of these, Rockford College is the oldest, having been opened as a seminary in 1849 and chartered as a college in 1892. Its student body is not large.

Mt. Holyoke owes its origin to Mary Lyon, a former student at Byfield, and a woman of exceptional ability. Impressed with the importance of the higher education of women, she gave her whole life to the cause — many years to the creation of a public sentiment in favor of her project, and the remainder to the duties of president of the institution which she founded. Mt. Holyoke was opened as a seminary in 1837, was chartered as a seminary and a college in 1888, and in 1893 took on a full college organization, doing work of the highest class. It has a splendid equipment and a large faculty. It varies from the other women's colleges of high grade in that the students are required to assist materially with the simpler domestic duties connected with the dormitory life. Lyon.

Just previous to the establishment of the school at South Hadley, several institutions for women, of somewhat more than secondary grade, had been established in the South. Among these, the Wesleyan Female College at Macon, Georgia, was authorized to grant degrees. In all, before 1850, Georgia had four so-called women's colleges, Alabama, Missouri, North Carolina, and Tennessee, each two, while one each had been founded in Maine, Massachusetts, Ohio, Illinois, South Carolina, and Texas. The preponderance of such institutions throughout the South is noticeable in this list, and is even more prominent for the next decade. Out of thirty-nine women's colleges founded between 1850 and 1859, thirty-two were in that region. But in other parts of the country, coeducation was by this time well under way,

and schools for both sexes were making less necessary
the establishment of special schools for girls. Of the
women's colleges founded in the decade of the '50's,
but one has arisen to full college rank, so far as scholarship goes, though all are locally influential and doing
valuable work. This is Elmira College, at Elmira, New
York, established in 1855. It has been claimed that at
the time of its organization it was the only real college
for women in the country, those which preceded it not
having as yet reached a grade of scholarship which
would warrant the use of the term. The courses at Elmira have, from the first, been nearly the equivalent of
those in most of the colleges for men. As outlined at
its opening, the course for the freshman year included
Cicero's *Orations*, Greek grammar, university algebra,
descriptive astronomy, critical reading of the English
poets, ecclesiastical history, botany, physical geography,
and the philosophy of history, with the courses for the
others based upon this as a beginning. In the decade
from 1860 to 1869 came the Civil War, and with it a
crushing blow to education, especially in the South.
Although less than one-half as many colleges for women
date their origin to this period as to the one just preceding, at least two of the number, Vassar College, at Pough-
keepsie, and Wells College, at Aurora, both in New York,
have arisen to first rank.

The former was founded in 1865 through the generosity of Matthew Vassar (*q.v.*). For the first two years
the 352 students which were enrolled were unclassified,
but at the end of that time a complete reorganization had
been effected and a full course of study arranged.
The prerequisites for admission to the freshman class at
Vassar, as announced in the first catalogue (1867–1868),
compare favorably with those of men's colleges of the
time, and have been considerably stiffened since: in
Latin, they included four books of Cæsar, four orations
of Cicero, and six books of Virgil; Robinson's *University*

Vassar.

Sherwood, p. 451.

Algebra to equations of the second degree; rhetoric, and outlines of general history. In addition to these subjects, which were required of all, entrance to the classical course presupposed a knowledge of Greek grammar and syntax, together with three books of Xenophon's *Anabasis;* for the modern language course, French was accepted in place of Greek.

At its opening the college had two buildings, the main hall and the observatory, the latter made famous by its director Maria Mitchell.

Vassar has had but three presidents in its history, and these have all been men, although its faculty is made up of both sexes, women preponderating. In value of buildings and grounds Vassar stands first, and in number of students second among the higher women's colleges of our country; and in the importance of its influence upon the general trend of higher education for the past forty years, certainly is unsurpassed by any.

Of Vassar, President Thomas of Bryn Mawr says : — Thomas, p. 336, footnote.

"To any one familiar with the circumstances, it does not admit of discussion that in Vassar we have the legitimate parent of all future colleges for women which were to be founded in such rapid succession in the next period. It is true that in 1855, the Presbyterian synod opened Elmira College in Elmira, N.Y., but it had practically no endowment and scarcely any college students. Even before 1855, two famous female seminaries were founded and did much to create a standard for the education of girls. In 1821 Mrs. Emma Willard (*q.v.*) opened at Troy a female seminary, still existing as the Emma Willard school. In 1837 Mary Lyon opened in the beautiful valley of the Connecticut, Mt. Holyoke Seminary where girls were educated so cheaply that it was almost a free school. This institution has had great influence in the higher education of women : it became in 1893 Mt. Holyoke College. These seminaries have often been claimed as the first women's colleges, but their curriculum of study proves conclusively that they had no thought whatever of giving women a collegiate education, whereas, the deliberations of the board of trustees whom Mr. Vassar associated with himself show clearly that it was expressly realized that here for the first time was being erected a woman's college as distinct from the seminary or academy."

Wells College, also founded in the same decade as Vassar, and in the same state, opened its doors in 1868 as Wells Seminary. Two years later it was chartered as a college, and has since that time been doing work of a high grade. For many years the number of students was limited to seventy-five; but of late that number has been considerably exceeded, though it has never been large. Its presidents have all been men, though women have been in a majority on the faculty.

Among the 21 women's colleges founded in the decade of 1870 to 1879 we have 3 which have arisen to the highest collegiate rank. Mills College, in California, and Smith and Wellesley colleges, both in Massachusetts. The first of these was opened as a seminary in 1871, and chartered as the only woman's college in the states west of the Rocky Mountains. Although it maintains a large preparatory department, less than 50 college students are in registration; full evidence that in the Western part of the country coeducational institutions are looked upon as meeting the demands of higher education. The faculty at Mills College includes both sexes.

Both Smith and Wellesley colleges opened their doors in 1875. They are within a little more than 100 miles of one another; yet each has risen to the very highest rank among colleges for women. The two combined had, in 1902, considerably more than one-third of the students registered in the collegiate departments of the 13 institutions ranked by the United States Commissioner of Education as first class. Henry F. Durant founded Wellesley (at Wellesley, Massachusetts) as "a college for the glory of God, by the education and culture of women." For the first five years a preparatory department was maintained; but since 1880 only collegiate courses have been offered. The college has a beautiful campus of more than 400 acres, including a lake for boating, and every facility is provided for outdoor games and recreations. Its main building is a large and imposing structure, containing, besides lecture rooms, living accommodations for 250 students. Besides this are a chapel, an observatory, a chemical laboratory, an art building, a music building, and 10 residence halls. The presidents have all been women. Smith College, at Northampton, Massachusetts, was founded by a woman, Sophia Smith, to provide "means and facilities for education equal to those which are afforded in our colleges for young men." It has had but one president, and that a man. Its campus is not large (40 acres), but well supplied with buildings, including 2 lecture halls, a gymnasium, a general science building, a chemical laboratory, an observatory, a conservatory, a music building, and 13 residence halls, with accommodations for 500 students.

Although the decade from 1880 to 1889 saw the establishment of twelve higher institutions for women in our country, but two of these — Bryn Mawr College, and the Woman's College of Baltimore — are placed in the first class by the Commissioner of Education. The former of these is situated at Bryn Mawr, in Pennsylvania, a few miles from Philadelphia, and opened its doors to students in 1885. It was founded by Joseph W. Taylor, with the expressed purpose of providing "an institution of learning for the advanced education of women, which should afford them all the advantages of a college education which are so fully offered to young men." This, Bryn Mawr has done to an extent perhaps unequalled by the other women's colleges. Its productive funds are larger than those of any of the others, and its equipment, especially along scientific lines, is unexcelled. Although its undergraduate courses are of a high order, its graduate work is particularly well organized, and a larger number of students are pursuing advanced work there than in all the other separate colleges for women, of first rank, taken together. Bryn Mawr has had but two presidents, the first a man, while the present incumbent of the office is a woman. No preparatory department has ever been maintained. The Woman's College of Baltimore, founded in 1888, is a Methodist institution, in its early years maintaining a large preparatory department which in 1891 became the Girls' Latin School of Baltimore. Since that time only work of a collegiate grade has been carried on in the college. The institution has had but two presidents, both of whom have been men.

The last decade of the nineteenth century saw the establishment of seventeen separate women's colleges, only one of which, the Randolf-Macon Woman's College at Lynchburg, Virginia, opened in 1893, has attained highest rank. It is a denominational institution, supported by the Methodists.

b. Women's Colleges affiliated with Universities for Men

The great strides in the direction of the higher education of women made during the last half-century, could not be ignored by the older colleges for men. Throughout the West they have accommodated themselves to the movement by opening their doors fully to both sexes, and becoming generally coeducational. This plan is not without its followers in the East and South, yet there, conservatism in matters of educational organization is strong, and in several of the older universities a compromise has been reached by the establishment of colleges for women under the same board of control as those for the men, and usually with the same faculties, but in which the women are separately instructed. There is considerable diversity in the detail of organization and affiliation among such colleges, yet each is an integral part of the organization with which it is affiliated. Five such women's departments are in operation : three in the Eastern states, and one each in the North Central and South Central divisions.

The H. Sophie Newcomb Memorial College for Women, affiliated with Tulane University, New Orleans, Louisiana, was the first of the kind to be established, and was opened in 1886. Although the South had been active in the foundation of separate seminaries, as has already been shown, no one of them had attained high rank, and with the sentiment not strong for coeducation, the plan of an affiliated college was tried as the most favorable means of providing full collegiate instruction for women. The buildings used by the college are in another part of the city from those of Tulane University. The same trustees officiate for both institutions, though the productive funds are in part, separate. The president and faculty are also distinct. The graduate department of the university has been open to the students of the college without restriction since 1890. *[margin: Tulane Univ. p. 275.]*

The College for Women at Western Reserve University, Cleveland, Ohio, was established in 1888. From 1872 up to that date women had been enrolled as students in the university, though without formal authorization; but in that year, through action of Adelbert College, the undergraduate department, they were excluded. The university, however, immediately made provision for them through the establishment of the woman's college. The latter has separate buildings, though in immediate proximity to the university campus, and a separate faculty. The university graduate department is fully open to the women of the college. and the degrees are conferred by the university. Certain of the laboratories of the men's college are open to the undergraduates of the woman's college. *[margin: West. Res. Univ. p. 274.]*

Barnard College, the woman's college of Columbia University, was founded in 1889, and is in reality an independent corporation, so far as maintenance is concerned, though academically under the control of Co- *[margin: Columbia Col. p. 253 et seq.]*

lumbia University. Since 1900 it has borne the same relation to it as an undergraduate college for women, as does Columbia College, the undergraduate college for men. The requirements for admission and standard of scholarship are the same for both.

The greater part of the undergraduate instruction is carried on in the Barnard College buildings, though some of the senior courses are taken in Columbia in the same classes with the men. After 1904 the latter practice will be discontinued, except for courses in the teachers' college. All degrees are conferred by the university. Since the graduate school of the university is open to women, Barnard offers no graduate courses.

Brown Univ.
p. 259 *et seq.* At Woman's College, Brown University, Providence, Rhode Island, instruction was informally begun in 1892, and fully organized as a college, under the direction of the university trustees in 1897. An advisory council for women was established to aid the president of the university and dean of the college in matters of administration. The entrance requirements and courses are the same for the women in the college as for the men students, and the same degrees are conferred by the university. Undergraduate instruction is given the two sexes in separate classes, though in the graduate course both are together. The faculty of the woman's college is made up entirely of members of the university faculty. The college occupies a separate building — Pembroke Hall — several blocks from the Brown campus.

Harvard Col.
p. 225 *et seq.* Radcliffe College, the affiliated woman's college of Harvard University, was started as a separate woman's college in 1879 by the Society for Collegiate Instruction, though not chartered with power to confer degrees until 1894. It may, perhaps, with justice, however, be considered the first of the affiliated colleges for women, since it was brought into existence by the efforts of a number of members of the Harvard faculty. For many years, though known as the "Harvard Annex," it had no official connection with the university. Its board of trustees and financial management are separate from those of Harvard, though its faculty is entirely composed of Harvard instructors. The college confers its own undergraduate degrees and offers graduate courses leading to the A.M.; but since Harvard does not confer degrees upon women, no Ph.D. degrees are open to Radcliffe students. Since 1893 Harvard has admitted women to its graduate courses, so such students may pursue advanced work without any hope of academic recognition. The Radcliffe buildings are not upon the Harvard campus, though at no great distance from it.

Besides these five officially affiliated colleges for women, at least two other colleges and universities are attempting to solve the problem of woman's education by other methods than those of full coeducational privileges. In both the change has been from coeducation to the present plan. The first of these, Colby College, at Waterville, Maine, in 1890, instituted the plan of teaching the women in separate classes from the men, and of debarring them from certain student honors. The complete separation which was at first planned did not prove practicable; and from the beginning of the sophomore year the two sexes are together in all elective work. From 1871 till 1890 Colby had been fully coeducational. The other attempt to modify the plan of coeducation was instituted at the University of Chicago in 1902. This institution had admitted both sexes on a coeducational basis since its foundation, but the plan, not proving satisfactory to all, so-called " segregation " of the sexes was instituted. Under it the two sexes are taught separately, though by the same instructors, for the first two years of the course. Separate buildings are provided for the men and women of the " junior college," each with its quadrangle; and, academically, the two sexes are not brought into contact with one another in that college. Much objection has been raised to the

Colby Col. p. 273.

Univ. of Chicago, p. 278.

plan by devotees of coeducation, but it cannot be denied that it has some good features.

During the half-century and more since separate colleges for women were first established in this country, the rapid increase in the number of students enrolled, has amply proved that the nation was ready for them. Although not equalling in number the women enrolled in coeducational institutions, they form, nevertheless, quite an army of educated womanhood.

The reports of the United States Commissioner of Education gives us the following figures for the women's colleges since 1875. The statistics for students do not include the preparatory departments, which in many instances were very large.

WOMEN STUDENTS IN NON–COEDUCATIONAL COLLEGES

Year	Institutions	Undergrad.	Graduate	Faculty
1902	131	16,544	326	2463
1901	132	15,977	304	2397
1895	163	14,049	301	2445
1890	179	11,811	181	2299
1885	227	12,333	208	2554
1880	227	11,422	204	2106
1875	222	9,572	—	2187

As is shown by the table, the number of institutions classified by the commissioner as of collegiate rank, has decreased more than one-third in the twenty-five years, while the student body has increased about the same amount in the same time. The decrease in schools is due to two causes: first, that the method of classification has altered within the period covered, and a considerable number which were at its beginning placed with the colleges are now included with the secondary schools; and second, many which were really little more than secondary schools have been forced, through competition with the public high school, to close their doors. The table is on the whole extremely encouraging, for the number of schools is not as important a matter as is the quality. One-third of the entire number of students within the 132 schools are registered in the dozen or more of undoubted college rank, while twenty-four years ago scarcely one-twentieth were in such institutions.

A noticeable fact in the development of the separate colleges for women is the tendency to make the courses within them as nearly as possible like those of the colleges for men. In their inception they had certain characteristics which distinctly characterized them as women's colleges; music and art were prominent in their curricula, and there were evident attempts to modify the intellectual training then in operation in the colleges for men. Such attempts have gradually been given up in the best women's colleges — whether wisely or not, I should not wish to say. Another gradual movement has been the elimination of the preparatory departments, and the cutting down of the number of special students, which formed a large part of the early enrolment. In 1870, 19.6 per cent of the students at Vassar were enrolled as specials, to 3.9 per cent in 1898. Smith and Bryn Mawr do not admit them at all.

Thomas, p. 341.

c. WOMEN IN COEDUCATIONAL INSTITUTIONS

Coeducation in higher institutions of learning is a Western product, and although it crossed the Alleghanies and is the practice in many institutions in the East, it is in the West that it is practically in full possession of the field. Oberlin Collegiate Institute — since 1850, Oberlin College at Oberlin, Ohio — opened its doors in 1833 to men and women alike, and must be given credit for being the first fully coeducational institution of college grade in the world. Twenty years elapsed before

P. 101.

another followed its example, and this time it was within the same state; Antioch College, under the presidency of no less renowned an educator than Horace Mann, who had waged such a battle for the public schools in Massachusetts. The influence of such a man gave the movement for coeducation a great impetus, and many other colleges and universities soon followed the example. The state universities which were being founded throughout the West were the leaders, and almost without exception those established since 1862, when the Morrill Bill was enacted, have admitted both sexes on equal terms. Even before that time, in 1856, the State University of Iowa had done so. The following table gives the dates of foundation of each of the state universities, as well as the year they became coeducational: —

State Univ.
p. 284.

University of Alabama,	Opened 1831,	Coeducational 1893.
University of Arkansas,	Opened 1872.	
University of California,	Opened 1870,	Coeducational from beginning.
University of Colorado,	Opened 1877,	Coeducational from beginning.
University of Florida,	Opened 1903,	Coeducational.
University of Idaho,	Opened 1872,	Coeducational from beginning.
University of Illinois,	Opened 1868,	Coeducational 1870.
University of Indiana,	Opened 1820,	Coeducational 1868.
University of Iowa,	Opened 1856,	Coeducational from beginning.
University of Kansas,	Opened 1866,	Coeducational from beginning.
University of Kentucky,		Coeducational 1889.
University of Maine,	Opened 1868,	Coeducational 1872.
University of Michigan,	Opened 1837,	Coeducational 1870.
University of Minnesota,	Opened 1868,	Coeducational from beginning.
University of Mississippi,	Opened 1848,	Coeducational 1882.
University of Missouri,	Opened 1870,	Coeducational from beginning.
University of Montana,	Opened 1895,	Coeducational from beginning.

University of Nebraska,	Opened 1871,	Coeducational from beginning.
University of Nevada,	Opened 1886,	Coeducational from beginning.
University of North Carolina,	Opened 1795,	Coeducational 1896.
University of North Dakota,	Opened 1884,	Coeducational 1884.
University of Ohio,	Opened 1873,	Coeducational from beginning.
University of Oregon,	Opened 1876 (?),	Coeducational from beginning.
University of South Carolina,	Opened 1805,	Coeducational 1894.
University of South Dakota,	Opened 1884,	Coeducational from beginning.
University of Tennessee,	Opened 1794.	
University of Texas,	Opened 1883,	Coeducational from beginning.
University of Utah.		
University of Washington,	Opened 1862,	Coeducational from beginning.
University of West Virginia,	Opened 1868,	Coeducational 1897.
University of Wisconsin,	Opened 1850,	Gave some instruction to women 1860. Coeducational 1874.
University of Wyoming,	Opened 1887,	Coeducational from beginning.
University of Arizona,	Opened 1891,	Coeducational from beginning.
University of New Mexico,	Opened 1892,	Coeducational from beginning.
University of Oklahoma,	Opened 1892,	Coeducational from beginning.

The state universities of Virginia, Georgia, and Louisiana are still closed to women. The influence of the state universities in the West and South was so great, that as other colleges were established throughout the region upon private foundation, they were in nearly every instance coeducational; so that to-day the college for men alone is the exception.

In the East, Cornell was the pioneer coeducational institution, and although its influence upon the others has been great, Eastern conservatism has stood in the way of a large following there. The following table shows, for the geographical divisions made use of by the commissioner of education, the number of higher institutions, other than those for women, which are for men alone and are coeducational: —

| N. Atlantic | | S. Atlantic | | S. Central | | N. Central | | Western | | Total | |
Men	Coed.	Men	Coed.	Men	Coed.	Men	Coed.	Men	Coed.	Men	Coed.
50	37	34	36	21	61	34	157	7	33	146	324

As is shown by the table, 146 of the entire 470 colleges admit men only, or 31 per cent. If we deduct the 64 Roman Catholic institutions included, all of which are for men only, we find that of the other — and they are those generally patronized by the Protestants who form the bulk of our population — but 20 per cent are non-coeducational.

In the proportion of coeducational institutions there has been a marked change, as might be expected, the percentage in 1870 being 30.7 of the whole number. In 1880 it was 51.3; in 1890, 65.5 and in 1902, 72 per cent; in each case with the Roman Catholic colleges included.

Although the increase in the proportion of coeducational institutions has been very rapid, a little more than doubling in the thirty years, that in the number of women students in attendance has been much more so, as is shown by the following table: —

WOMEN STUDENTS IN COEDUCATIONAL COLLEGES

| Year | Students | | Year | Students | |
	Under-grad.	Graduate		Under-grad.	Graduate
1901–1902 . .	21,151	2065	1884–1885 . .	3107	——
1900–1901 . .	19,959	1602	1879–1880 . .	2750	——
1894–1895 . .	13,222	718	1874–1875 . .	3044	——
1889–1890 . .	7,847	228	1869–1870 . .	——	——

Here we have shown a growth of from 3044 to 21,151 in undergraduate women enrolled in the coeducational colleges in twenty-five years — an increase of considerable more than six times.

By reference to the table showing the entire enrolment of these institutions — both male and female — it may be seen that this increase is twice as great for the women students as for those of both sexes, the latter having increased only about three times (1875, 26,352; 1901, 81,084). Another comparison is also of interest — that between the increase of women students in the coeducational institutions and women students in separate colleges. The former, as has been stated, has increased more than six times, while the latter has grown Table, p. 444. only from 9572 to 16,554, or less than doubled in the twenty-five years.

This fact would seem to be an expression of a preference on the part of women for the coeducational plan of instruction; though not necessarily so, since by far the greater proportion of coeducational institutions, notably the state universities, have no charge for tuition. The showing may be one of economic necessity rather than of personal preference.

Although the plan of coeducation in colleges and universities has, in most instances, fulfilled the highest expectation of its promoters, it cannot be denied that there is a feeling of uncertainty in some quarters as to its ultimate results. Although little dissatisfaction has been Univ. of Chicago, p. 443 expressed by the students of either sex, the governing bodies of some institutions seem fearful as to its possible outcome. Colby Col. p. 443. The intellectual equality of woman is not questioned; but the disproportionate increase in the number of women students points to a time when the student body may be over feminized. Already, in a number of colleges, women outnumber the men, and in at least two (Northwestern University, which has limited the number of women students to the capacity of its dormitories, and Leland Stanford, which has arbitrarily limited them to five hundred) steps have been taken to prevent any disproportion of women students. Theoretically, the same instruction for both sexes is right, only if the aim of education is identical for the two, *i.e.* if they are to be competitors in the same kinds of work. Otherwise, some form of specialization is demanded. In the larger coeducational institutions, where a wide choice of electives is offered, this specialization is, in effect, being brought about through selection of courses, some of which are largely taken by women, while others are the choice of the men. This is as it should be, and can be depended upon in the end to solve the question of what instruction is best adapted to women more wisely than could any prescribed courses theoretically formulated in special institutions for the single sex.

Graduate Instruction for Women

P. 443.

In all the fully coeducational institutions, and in the affiliated colleges, with the exception of that at Harvard, all the privileges of graduate instruction are as fully open to women as to men. Moreover, of the great universities for men which do not admit women to their undergraduate courses, but two (Princeton and Johns Hopkins) still have their graduate schools closed to them. In addition, they have access, of course, to what graduate instruction is offered in the special colleges for women; so, as far as the number of institutions goes, they are considerably better off than their brothers. That they are availing themselves of their opportunities in rapidly increasing numbers is shown by the tables upon pages 444 and 448.

The figures upon the former table should probably carry but little weight, showing, as they do, considerable numbers of graduate students in 1880 and 1885, since to-day even, very few of the separate colleges for women are in a position to offer work of a strictly university grade, and none other should be classed as graduate — and it is doubtful if any were, two decades ago. The figures upon page 448, however, are interesting. A comparison of them with those upon page 296, which give the total graduate enrolment in coeducational colleges and those for men, shows that in 1890 women made up about one-eighth of the total number; in 1895, about one-sixth; and in 1901, roughly, one-fourth. Approximately, one-tenth of the Doctorates of Philosophy, conferred by our higher institutions within the last four years, have been upon women.

Thomas, p. 350.

Regarding graduate scholarships and fellowships for women, Miss Thomas says : —

" In 1899 there were open to women 319 scholarships varying in value from $100 to $400 (50 of them exclusively for women); 81 resident fellowships of the value of $400 or over (18 of these exclusively for women); 24 foreign fellowships of the value of $500 and upwards (12 of these exclusively for women)."

The Professional Education of Women

With the battle for the higher education of women, won in the academic institutions, the professional schools have very generally welcomed them, and to-day nearly all are coeducational. In medicine there was a strong prejudice against such action to be overcome, and four or five women's medical schools were organized, which contain about one-third of the women medical students in the country. Other than these, there exist no professional schools for women only.

The following table shows the enrolment of women in the professional schools of the country as far back as records are available : —

WOMEN IN PROFESSIONAL SCHOOLS

YEAR	THE-OLOGY	MEDICINE	LAW	DENTIS-TRY	PHAR-MACY	NURSES
1902	108	1177	165	162	218	
1901	181	1219	170	106	206	10,202
1900	181	1456	151	160	196	9,969
1898–1899	—	—	—	—	—	8,004
1897–1898	193	1397	147	162	174	8,004
1896–1897	—	1583	131	150	131	6,705
1895–1896	—	1471	77	143	140	4,661
1894–1895	—	1399	64	53	83	3,607
1893–1894	—	1411	52	88	88	2,485
1892–1893	—	1275	—	—	—	2,214
1889–1890	—	884	—	53	60	1,449

Previous to 1890 very few women were pursuing professional courses. Except in the training schools for nurses, the numerical increase in enrolment has not been very great; not so great, in fact, as to lead us to believe that woman is to be, at least in the near future, an important factor in the learned professions. In medicine there were 400 more women students enrolled in 1897 than five years later; in law there has been an increase of but 34 students in the last five years; in dentistry, no change; and in pharmacy, an increase of 75. In fact, in the four professions of medicine, law, dentistry, and pharmacy, there has been an actual decrease of 274 in enrolment since 1897. Meanwhile, women enrolled in academic institutions have increased 5892 in number. We can hardly interpret these facts in any other light than that the learned professions offer but few attractions to women.

The following table summarizes the statistics of the education of women in all classes of institutions in our country for the years 1891–1892 and 1901–1902: —

	1891–1892		1901–1902	
	Students	Per Cent	Students	Per Cent
Secondary schools:				
Public	126,379	59.7	323,697	59.
Private	48,406	47.9	53,154	51.7
Colleges and seminaries for women	24,611	100	25,289	100
Normal schools	22,480	76.7	37,194	75.3
Universities and colleges for men and both sexes:				
Preparatory	12,572	29.6	14,508	23.8
Undergraduate	10,021	19.1	21,051	25.3
Graduate	369	12.7	1,610	26.3
Professional	530	2.8	1,450	3.

REFERENCES

EDUCATION OF WOMEN

Angell, J. R. Reaction from Coeducation. Pop. Sci. Mo. 62 : 5–26. — Barnett, P. A. Girl's Schools. In Common Sense in Education and Teaching, 1901, pp. 125–130. — *Bibliography of Coeducation*. Rep. Com. Ed. 1901, 2 : 1310. — Boone, R. G. Higher Education of Women. Education in the United States, pp. 362–382. — **Earle**, Alice Morse. A Boston School Girl in 1771. At. Mo. 72 : 218. — Freeman, M. L. Vassar College. Ed. 8 : 73. — *Jordan*, D. S. Higher Education of Women. Pop. Sci. Mo. 62 : 97–107. — Lyon, Mary (biog.). Am. Jour. Ed. 10 : 647. — Nutting, Mary O. Historical Sketch of Mt. Holyoke Seminary. Springfield, 1878. — *Palmer*, Alice F. A Review of the Higher Education of Women. Forum, 12 : 28. Reminiscences of Female Education. Am. Jour. Ed. 16 : 137. — **Small**, H. W. Girls in Colonial Schools. Ed. 22 : 552. — Smith, Charles Foster. The Higher Education of Women in the South. Ed. Rev. 8 : 287. — *Stephens*, Kate. Advanced Education for Women. Forum, 7 : 41. — *Taylor*, J. M. Education of Women. World's Work, 6 : 3751–3753. — **Thomas**, M. Carey. Education of Women. In Butler's Education in the United States, 1900, 1 : 319–358. — *Thwing*, C. F. College Education of Young Women. Pub. Opin. 16 : 9. University Degrees for Women. Fortn. 63 : 895–903. — Vassar, Matthew (biog.). Am. Jour. Ed. 11 : 53. — Willard, Mary (biog.). Am. Jour. Ed. 6 : 125. — Woodward, Mary V. Women's Education in the South. Ed. Rev. 7 : 466.

CHAPTER XXII

EDUCATION OF THE NEGRO AND OF THE INDIAN

a. NEGRO EDUCATION

THE history of negro education in the United States goes back no farther than the Civil War. Previous to that time in the South the teaching of the blacks, whether they be slaves or free, was forbidden by law, and in some states made an offence for which the pupil might be fined and whipped, at the discretion of the court, and the teacher be fined or imprisoned. In the North no such penalty was imposed, but since no special schools were provided for the blacks, and public sentiment opposed their admission to other schools, they were practically without educational advantages. It is true that both in the South and North negroes occasionally were taught the rudiments of learning in the so-called "clandestine schools"; still such instances were rare, and cannot be said to qualify the general statement that in *ante bellum* days, the negroes were uneducated. When, however, they were given full rights as citizens, the problem of their education was immediately taken up, and is being solved as rapidly as social and economic conditions, together with the capability of the colored race, will allow. The first move of any magnitude was made through the Freedman's Bureau, established by act of Congress in 1865. General O. O. Howard was the first commissioner of the bureau, and under his direction a work of immense magnitude began. At the end of five years, when the bureau was discontinued, the report showed that 4239 schools for colored pupils had been established through-

Miller, p. 743.

out the South, under the direction of 9307 teachers, and
having an enrolment of 247,333 pupils. The move had
cost $6,513,955. The schools were largely elementary,
for the work had to be begun from the bottom; but as
pupils were ready for them, those of higher grade were
established, and in 1879, 61 intermediate or grammar
schools for blacks were in operation, and no less than
74 high and normal schools, the latter with an enrolment of 8174 students. The freedmen themselves contributed about one-fifth of the expense of these higher
schools. The remainder of the funds came from the Federal government or from private bequests in the North.
Among the latter, and they have been many, that of
George Peabody, known as the Peabody Fund, has been
productive of the most good. It consisted of $2,000,000,
one-half given in 1867 and the remainder in 1869, which
was placed in the hands of trustees with the instruction
that "the income thereof shall be applied in your discretion for the promotion and encouragement of intellectual,
moral or industrial education of the young of the more
destitute portions of the southern and southwestern
states of our Union; my purpose being that the benefits
intended shall be distributed among the entire population without other distinction than that of their needs
and the opportunities of usefulness to them." The fund
has always been well invested, and under the trusteeship
of leading educators of our country. Up to the present
time it has made available for use, nearly $3,000,000,
which, with the exception of a comparatively small
amount devoted to the maintenance of higher institutions of learning in various states, has been turned
over to the most needy public schools throughout
the entire South. Besides the Peabody Fund are two
others, both due to the generosity of Northern citizens:
the Slater Fund of $1,000,000, given by Mr. John
Fox Slater in 1882, administered through a board of
trustees, as is the Peabody Fund, and devoted largely to

the promotion of industrial education; and the "Daniel Hand Educational Fund for Colored People" of $1,000,-894.25, given by Mr. Daniel Hand of Guilford, Connecticut, in 1888. The American Missionary Association is made the custodian of the latter fund, which is devoted to purposes of general education throughout the South. Aided by these great benefactions and a multitude of smaller ones, the South is doing its best to solve the problem of the education of its nearly 3,000,000 colored children of school age, and at the same time to provide higher institutions of learning for those who wish to carry their studies farther.

It is doing so almost entirely through separate schools, for whites and blacks. So far as elementary education is concerned, in no one of the Southern states are mixed schools generally maintained, though in most of the Northern states colored pupils are admitted to all the public schools. Although this duplication of schools for the two races involves extra expense, it is the avowed policy of the South, and one which the white citizens generously support by an extra heavy taxation; for in no one of the sixteen former slave states is the cost of negro schools met by the taxation of the freedmen, themselves.

Miller, p. 749.

In those states the cost of such schools, with the per capita expense of educating the negro children, is shown by the following table for certain years: —

Year	Expense for Colored Schools	Colored Pupils	Cost Per Pupil
1900–1901	6,000,000	2,734,223	$2.19
1897–1898	6,451,935	2,844,570	2.87
1894–1895	5,011,362	2,761,205	1.81
1890–1891	5,444,625	2,551,511	2.13
1886–1887	4,420,323	2,382,570	1.86
1882–1883	3,632,533	2,221,930	1.63
1878–1879	2,050,590	2,042,150	1.00
1874–1875	1,723,954	1,794,870	.96
1870–1871	780,306	1,578,170	.49

In all, it is estimated that the South has expended about $121,000,000 upon the education of the negro since the war; a sum sufficiently large to prove conclusively that the problem of negro education is not being neglected there, and also to make the contributions from the North seem not at all excessive.

Although by far the greater amount of the sum has been spent upon the common schools, since the population of the South is so largely rural, yet in the cities, colored high schools are maintained in large numbers. In 1880 there were 36 such schools, with 5237 pupils; in 1890 the number was 53, with 11,480 pupils; while in 1901 there were 100, with 12,202 pupils enrolled. The courses of study in these schools compare favorably with those in the schools for the white pupils in the same cities. The teachers are mostly colored, though reasonably well prepared, through the normal schools which exist in considerable numbers throughout the South.

Normal Schools

Although the negro has demonstrated over and over again his capability for advanced academic education, it was early seen that the great hope lay along the lines of industrial and vocational training, and as a result, industrial schools, or normal schools offering, besides the courses intended for teachers, many of an industrial character, were early established. In 1877 there were 27 such institutions, with an enrolment of 3785; in 1880 the numbers were 44 and 7408; in 1899, 41 and 7642, and in the year 1901 there were 793 students in the graduating classes of such schools. Among schools of this class, the Hampton Normal and Industrial Institute at Hampton, Virginia, is perhaps the best known.

Of its enrolment, about one-eighth are Indians. It was chartered in 1870, in 1872 was given one-third of Virginia's share of the Morrill grant, and has since been supported largely by public bequest, receiving considerable financial aid from the American Missionary Association and Peabody Fund. Besides the normal courses, it offers others in carpentry, harness-making, shoe-making, house-painting, printing, tailoring, plumbing, and the trades of the blacksmith, the tinsmith, the wheelright, and the machinist.

A descendant of the Hampton Institute is that at Tuskegee, Alabama, which has been made famous by its president, Booker T. Washington, who has perhaps done more for negro education than has any other man of his race. It was opened in 1881 with 1 teacher and 30 students; it has now a faculty of 44 (all colored) and an enrolment of more than 1200 students. Besides academic instruction, courses are given in twenty-six different industries. Its large number of buildings were nearly all erected by the students themselves. On the whole, the Tuskegee institute probably represents the highest type of efficiency in schools for the colored race.

Higher Institutions

The colored race is not wanting in colleges and universities. With a few exceptions they are all denominational in their support, and in many instances have large numbers of students doing secondary and even primary work; yet in an important manner they are holding out to the colored youth the possibility of higher academic education. The leading institutions of the class, together with the dates of establishment, are as follows: —

Lincoln University, Lincoln University, Pa.	1864
Wilberforce University, Wilberforce, Ohio	1868
Howard University, Washington, D.C.	1868
Berea College, Berea, Ky.	1869
Leland University, New Orleans, La.	1870
Benedict College, Columbia, S.C.	1870
Fish University, Nashville, Tenn.	1871
Atlanta University, Atlanta, Ga.	1872

Biddle University, Charlotte, N.C.	1872
Southland College, Southland, Ark.	1872
Roger Williams University, Nashville, Tenn.	1873
New Orleans University, New Orleans, La.	1874
Shaw University, Raleigh, N.C.	1874
Rust University, Holly Springs, Miss.	1874
Straight University, New Orleans, La.	1874
Branch College, Pine Bluff, Ark.	1878
Claflin University, Orangeburg, S.C.	1778
Knoxville College, Knoxville, Tenn.	1879
Clark University, South Atlanta, Ga.	1879
Wiley University, Marshall, Tex.	1880
Paine University, Augusta, Ga.	1882
Allen University, Columbia, S.C.	1883
Talledaga College, Talledaga, Ala.	1885
Virginia Collegiate Institute, Petersburg, Va.	1885
Paul Quin College, Waco, Tex.	1885
Lincoln Institute, Jefferson City, Mo.	1890
Morris Brown College, Atlanta, Ga.	1890
Atlanta Baptist College, Atlanta, Ga.	1893
Georgia Industrial College, College, Ga.	1894
Delaware State College, Dover, Del.	1894
Philander Smith College, Little Rock, Ark.	1894

In these institutions and others of the class there were, in 1902, 1600 students pursuing classical courses, 842 scientific courses, 9972 English courses, and 402 courses for business. ^{Miller, pp. 834-835.}

In the matter of entrance requirements and courses of study these institutions vary greatly, a few being on a par with the better colleges for white students in the North; while in a great majority they are decidedly lower, some of them being little more than of secondary grade. That the occasional negro at least is capable of doing academic work equal to that of the best white students is shown by the stand they have taken in the Northern universities. These are open to them almost without exception, and colored students have been graduated with honors from Harvard, Yale, Cornell, Columbia, Pennsylvania, and nearly all the other institutions of rank in the North and East, in some instances having been elected to Phi Beta Kappa.

Rep. Com. Ed. 1901, I: 839; 1902, I: 191-229.

Phi Beta Kappa, p. 237.

Professional Education

In those professions which require a definite certification as a prerequisite to practice (medicine and law) the number of negroes is comparatively small. Nor can it be said that the colored man is taking the place in those professions that he might be expected to take.

The reasons for this are, however, largely social. The white population does not care to employ him, and this is largely true of persons of his own race, the feeling seemingly being prevalent that white service is more efficient. The professional training of the colored physicians and lawyers has been largely in the regular schools which are open to both races; though a few professional schools, for colored students only, are maintained. A considerable number of the colleges support theological departments, providing the colored people with educated ministers, while the normal schools are responsible for the large numbers in the teaching profession.

The Education of Negro Women

Practically all the educational advantages are open equally to negroes of both sexes. This is fully true for the elementary, secondary, and normal schools, while but two of the higher institutions are closed to women. In the public elementary schools the girls slightly outnumber the boys. In the secondary schools, including the normals, this is also true, though not in purely academic subjects. The normal courses, and those in sewing, laundering, and general housekeeping, are the ones most fully patronized by them. In the higher academic institutions the women are not found in large numbers, but 170 having been graduated from those wholly for colored students up to 1898. The proportion is, however, rapidly increasing. Up to the same year 82 colored women had graduated from women's colleges and coeducational institutions in the North, 55 from Oberlin, with Vassar, Wellesley, Mt. Holyoke, Cornell, and Michigan, represented among 16 other institutions. Miller, p. 826.

b. INDIAN EDUCATION

Although many crimes may be charged up against the white settler in America on the score of his treatment of the Indian, that of a neglect of his intellectual and spiritual welfare, at least in the earlier colonial days, is not one of them. The very first school planned in the colonies — the projected Henrico School of 1618, which came to naught through the Indian himself — was for "the training up of the children of those infidels, P. 2. in true religion, moral virtue and civility, and for other godliness"; and the stories of the hardship of Marquette and his companions, of John Eliot, the Indian apostle, of Sergeant and of Wheelock are sufficient proof of the sincerity of the early attempts in that direction. P. 265. In fact the history of colonial times is full of evidences that our forefathers felt a deep interest in the spiritual, if not in the intellectual, welfare of the aborigines; and showed that interest in the establishment of missionary schools, as well as through making special provision for the admission of Indian children to many of the regularly established public schools. It was not, however, until nearly forty years after the establishment of our independence as a republic that the national conscience was touched in the matter; or that any general provision was made for the education of our Indian wards through the establishment of schools. This was, perhaps, stimulated by the religious revival which swept over the country in the first quarter of the nineteenth century, inspiring the various denominational societies with a new interest in missionary work, and eventually moving Congress itself to act. This was in 1819, and the first appropriation was $10,000, which was repeated the next year, and has been considerably increased each succeeding year. In 1823 the government contributed $12,000 out of $80,000 expended in the maintenance of 21 schools, religious denominations and private individuals making up the remainder. In 1825 the number had increased to 38, to which the government gave $25,000. By 1848 there were in operation 16 industrial schools and 87 of an elementary nature, all under denominational influence, but supported in part by governmental appropriation. This method of national participation in Indian education was practically the only one in vogue until 1873, there being, up to that time, with the exception of a few unimportant day schools, none whatever under direct government control.

From that time it has been the policy to control more and more fully the schools receiving any part of the government appropriation, until now, save for a few missionary schools, the entire machinery for the education of the Indians belongs to the national government. The move has been an expensive one. Whereas, in 1880 the appropriation for the purpose was but $75,000, in 1885 it was $992,800; in 1890, $1,364,568; in 1895, $2,060,695; in 1899, $2,638,390; and in 1903, $2,837,786.

These immense sums are expended in support of schools of the following classes : —

  a. Non-reservation boarding schools.
  b. Reservation boarding schools.
  c. Day schools.
  d. Contract schools.
  e.[1] Mission schools (privately supported).

a. Non-reservation Boarding Schools

These are the most advanced of the Indian schools, as well as the most cosmopolitan, since pupils from

[1] Since 1901 no government appropriations have been made to mission schools.

many tribes are brought together in a single school, often to the obliteration of long-standing hereditary prejudices. They are usually, too, situated near towns and cities of considerable size, thus bringing the pupils in contact with white civilization in a way that none of the strictly reservation schools can do. Each school of the class has a full instructional and dormitory equipment, providing a home for the Indian youth for the considerable number of years of his attendance. Usually, he has been through some of the reservation schools before entering this, and, since the more elementary branches do not need to be taken, the time can be devoted to such subjects as arithmetic, geometry, geography, history, and civil government. Many of these schools are so fully equipped for training pupils in domestic science and the trades as to be essentially industrial schools.

Among the best known of this class of schools are those at Carlisle, Pennsylvania; Chilocco, Oklahoma; Genoa, Nebraska; Albuquerque, New Mexico; Lawrence, Kansas (the Haskell Institute); Grand Junction, Colorado; Sante Fé, New Mexico; Phœnix, Arizona; and Fort Shaw, Montana. All of these schools are largely industrial in their nature, though three of them, the Carlisle, the Lawrence, and the Sante Fé schools, have normal departments. Each has its dormitories and other buildings, besides ample facilities for agricultural work, which forms a large part of the course.

In all, the government now maintains twenty-five non-reservation boarding schools, the particulars for each of which are shown in the following table : —

U. S. Rep. on Indian affairs, 1902.

LOCATION, CAPACITY, ATTENDANCE, ETC., OF NON-RESERVA-
TION INDIAN SCHOOLS DURING FISCAL YEAR ENDING
JUNE 30, 1902

LOCATION OF SCHOOLS	DATE OF OPENING	NUMBER OF EMPLOYEES [a]	CAPACITY	ENROLMENT	AVERAGE ATTENDANCE
Carlisle, Pa	Nov. 1, 1879	90	[b] 950	1086	1023
Chemawa, Ore. (Salem)	Feb. 25. 1880	50	550	660	556
Chilocco, Okla	Jan. 15, 1884	49	400	509	429
Genoa, Neb.	Feb. 20, 1884	28	325	355	307
Albuquerque, N.M.	Aug. —, 1884	34	300	368	331
Lawrence, Kan. (Haskell Institute)	Sept. 1, 1884	61	700	871	690
Grand Junction, Col.	—— —, 1886	20	175	176	160
Santa Fé, N.M.	Oct. —, 1890	29	300	379	349
Fort Mojave, Ari.	Dec. —, 1890	21	170	173	168
Carson, Nev.	Dec. —, 1890	23	200	271	232
Pierre, S. Dak.	Feb. —, 1891	16	150	175	152
Phœnix, Ari.	Sept. —, 1891	57	700	763	655
Fort Lewis, Col.	Mar. —, 1892	37	300	341	266
Fort Shaw, Mont.	Dec. 27, 1892	34	300	340	310
Perris, Cal.	Jan. 9, 1893	19	150	265	226
Flandreau, S. Dak. (Riggs Institute)	Mar. 7, 1893	34	350	460	352
Pipestone, Minn.	Feb. —, 1893	14	150	136	120
Mount Pleasant, Mich.	Jan. 3, 1893	23	300	321	243
Tomah, Wis.	Jan. 19, 1893	21	225	257	204
Wittenberg, Wis.[c]	Aug. 24, 1895	11	100	120	106
Greenville, Cal.[c]	Sept. 25, 1895	8	90	76	63
Morris, Minn.[c]	Apr. 3, 1897	16	160	181	151
Chamberlain, S. Dak.	Mar. —, 1898	13	100	114	105
Fort Bidwell, Cal.	Apr. 4, 1898	8	100	56	45
Rapid City, S. Dak.	Sept. 1, 1898	12	100	115	111
Total		728	7345	8568	7354

[a] Excluding those receiving less than $100 per annum.
[b] 1,500, with outing pupils.
[c] Previously a contract school.

b. RESERVATION BOARDING SCHOOLS

This type of Indian school is much more numerous
than the preceding, nearly every reservation having two
or three, with an average capacity of about 125 pupils.
Of the 90 now in operation, 5 were established in the

decade between 1860 and 1869; 25 between 1870 and 1879; 21 between 1880 and 1889; 26 between 1890 and 1899; and 11 since 1900. Each school is in charge of a superintendent and corps of instructors, as well as the necessary domestic servants. The cook, seamstress, and laundress instruct the girl pupils in their respective lines of work, while a head farmer, a tailor, a shoemaker, a carpenter, and a blacksmith, at least in the larger schools, perform a similar service for the boys.

In 1894 kindergartens were made so successful a feature of the work that now more than one-half the schools have installed them. The aim of the schools, so far as instruction is concerned, is to give the pupils the ability to read simple English, to perform the simple mathematical computations, and to acquire a rudimentary knowledge of geography, history, the laws of hygiene, and habits of bodily as well as domestic cleanliness. The school is a home for the pupil during his most impressionable years, and it is more in this capacity than as a means of merely academic instruction that it is accomplishing its best results. The total enrolment in reservation boarding schools was, in 1902, 11,506.

c. THE DAY SCHOOL

These schools do not differ materially from the ungraded country schools in white communities. Each is in charge of a single teacher— usually a man — with some provision made for a housekeeper. They are located in Indian villages or camps, but not on reservations.

Both a morning and afternoon session of the school is held, and in the poorer communities a simple noonday lunch is served the pupils by the housekeeper, at government expense. The housekeeper is also expected to teach the girls the simpler household duties, as well as to visit the homes of the parents and endeavor in every way to influence them in the direction of better living.

At present (1903) 134 day schools are maintained, having an enrolment of 3223 pupils.

d. Contract Schools

The plan of placing Indian children in the public schools of the villages near where they live has not proven very successful, though theoretically the very best method for their civilization. In a few instances it is, however, done; at present 110 pupils are in sixteen different public day schools throughout the country, the government paying their tuition. It also pays for 120 Indian students in the Hampton Institute.

P. 457.

e. Mission Schools

The preceding classes of schools are the only ones through which the government attempts to educate its Indian wards. The missionary work of the various Christian denominations for the adult Indians is, however, supplemented by schools for the children, conducted under their auspices. A majority of them are reservation boarding schools, in which religious training is combined with that of a secular nature. The total number of such schools is 49 (2 of which are day schools). Of them, 33 (including the day schools) are supported by the Roman Catholics, 4 by the Presbyterians, 5 by the Episcopalians, 3 by the Congregationalists, and 1 each by the Reformed Presbyterian and Methodist denominations, and by the Society for the Propagation of the Gospel. The enrolment in all these schools is 3853 (1902). The schools do not differ materially from the reservation boarding schools under government support, except for the religious character of the work.

The schools of the so-called "five civilized nations" of Indian Territory are not included within the foregoing discussion, since these, by special treaties, are practically under local control.

In the Cherokee nation the schools are under the immediate supervision of its own board of education, acting in conjunction with the United States supervisor of schools for the nation. Within the nation are 140 day schools, 1 colored high school, an orphans' academy, and academies for males and females. The enrolment in these schools is 5383.

Within the other nations, except the Seminole which has sole control, the administration does not differ materially from the Cherokee; a general classification of the schools, together with the enrolment, is given in the following table: —

SCHOOLS IN THE "FIVE NATIONS"

	DAY SCHOOLS	OTHER SCHOOLS	ENROLMENT
Cherokee	140	4	5383
Creek	52	10	2754
Choctaw	190	7	4788
Chickasaw	16	4	939
Seminole	No statistics	No statistics	No statistics

NEGRO EDUCATION

Andrews, C. G. Education of the Colored Race. Ed. 6 : 221. — *Atkins*, S. G. History and Status of Education among the Colored People. Circ. Inf. No. 3, 1888, 158–163. — Blair, Henry W. The Negro Problem. Ind. 54 : 442–444. — Bradford, Amory H. Among Colored Educational Institutions. Outl. 56 : 454–457. — Curry, J. L. M. (1) Difficulties, Complications, Limitations, connected with the Education of the Negro. (2) Education of the Negroes since 1860. Rep. Com. Ed. 1894–1895, 2 : 1366–1384. — *Du Bois*, W. E. B. A Negro Schoolmaster in the New South. At. Mo. 83 : 99–104. On the Training of Black Men. At. Mo. 90 : 289–297. The Education of the Negro. Pub. Opin. 22 : 150 151. — Fussel, H. B. Hampton Normal and Agricultural Institute. Rep. Com. Ed. 1901, 2 : 2463. The Training of Negro Teachers. N. E. A. 1900 : 482. —

Future of the Colored Race. Rep. Com. Ed. 1898–1899, 1 : 1227–1248. — The Hampton Conference. Outl. 67 : 752–753. — *Harris,* W. T. Education of the Negro. At. Mo. 69 : 721. — *Keating,* J. M. Twenty Years of Negro Education. Pop. Sci. Mo. 28 : 24. — Kirke, Edmund. How shall the Negro be Educated ? N. A. Rev. 143 : 421. — *Merriwether,* Colyer. Education of the Negro. Circ. Inf. No. 4, 1888 : 122–126. — **Miller,** Kelley. The Education of the Negro. Rep. Com. Ed. 1901, 1 : 731–859. The Function of the Negro College. Dial, 32 : 267–270. — *Poe,* Clarence. Should Southern Whites aid Negro Schools ? (A Southerner's view.) Outl. 71 : 1010–1013. — Salisbury, Albert. Some Conclusions concerning the Education of the American Negro. Andover Review, 6 : 256–264. — *Scarborough,* W. S. Booker T. Washington and His Work. Ed. 20 : 270. The Negro and the Higher Education. Forum, 33 : 349. — Stetson, George R. The New Basis of National Education. Andover Review, 14 : 254–260. — Thrasher, M. B. Tuskegee : Its Story and Its Work, with an Introduction by B. T. Washington. Boston, 1901. Tuskegee Institute and Its President. Pop. Sci. Mo. 55 : 592–610. — United States Bureau of Education. Bibliography. Education of the Colored Race. Rep. 1893–1894, 1 : 1038–1061. See also Education of the Colored Race in other Reports. — Villard, Oswald Garrison. An Alabama Negro School. R. of R.'s, 26 : 711–714. — *Washington,* B. T. Education will solve the Race Problem. N. A. Rev. 170 : 220. Education of the Negro. In Butler's Education in the United States, 2 : 895–936. The Future of the American Negro. Boston, 1900. Light in the South. Ind. 51 : 175–176. Why push Industrial Education in the South ? Pub. Opin. 20 : 750–751. — Willis, Rev. S. T. Education of the Colored Race. Outl. 56 : 262–263.

INDIAN EDUCATION

Armstrong, S. C. Education of the Indian. N. E. A. 1884 : 177. — Barrows, William. The Education of the Indians. Andover Review, 16 : 479–491. — *Blackmar,* F. W. Haskell Institute as Illustrating Indian Progress. R. of R.'s, 5 : 557–561. — Carlisle Indian School. Rep. Com. Ed. 1892–1893, pp. 1090–1095. — Creelman, G. C. Indian Industrial Education. Outl. 67 : 234–236. — *Eastman,* Elain G. A New Method of Indian Education. Outl. 64 : 222–224. — Education of the Indians. Rep. Com. Ed. 1885–1886, pp. 657–660. — *Finley,* Blanche. Kindergarten Work among the Indians. N. E. A. 1900 : 705. — Garland, Hamlin. The Red Man's Present Needs. N. A. Rev. 174 : 476–488. — *Hailmann,* William N. Education of the Indians. In Butler's Education in the United States, 1900, 2 : 937–972. — *James,* James Alton. Early Provisions for Indian Education. Johns Hopkins Univ. Studies, 12 : 509–517. — Ludlow, Helen W. Indian Education at Hampton and Carlyle. Harper's Mag. 62 : 659–675. — *Montezuma*, Dr. Carlos. The Indian Problem from an Indian's Standpoint. Rep. Com. Ed. 1896–1897. — *Morgan*, T. G. The Education of the American Indian. Ed. 10 : 246. — Murphy, M. The Day School, the Gradual Uplifter of the Tribe. N. E. A. 1901 : 913. — *Rogers*, F. K. The Teaching of Trades to the Indian. N. E. A. 1900 : 698. — *Sheldon*, H. D. The Evolution of the Indian School System. Ed. 16 : 7. — *Spencer*, Frank Clarence. Education of the Pueblo Child ; a study of arrested development. New York, 1899. — *Thwing*, Charles F. The Education of the Indian. Ed. 3 : 385. — Bureau of Education. Indian Education and Civilization. (Special Report, 1888, by Alice C. Fletcher.) United States Interior, Department of. Office of Indian Affairs. See various reports.

CHAPTER XXIII

THE EDUCATION OF DEFECTIVES

No system of public education is complete which fails to make provision for those children whom nature has but imperfectly equipped, as to special sense organs or brain, for fitting into the complicated social mechanism of modern life. The common school can adapt itself to a considerable variation in these respects among its pupils, and is called upon to do so; but beyond certain limits of organic deficiency they cannot accept pupils without positive detriment to the schools; nor would the admission of such pupils be of much benefit to themselves. Yet there are three distinct classes of defectives, tolerated throughout all the preceding centuries of the world's history as mere clogs to the wheels of progress, which the more scientific and more humanitarian spirit of to-day is trying, and with success, not only to make self-supporting, but even to contribute in no small degree to the world's advancement. These are the deaf, the blind, and the feeble-minded, as well as persons embodying any unfortunate combinations of these three defects.

a. THE DEAF

The first school for the deaf in this country, indeed the first school for any of the three classes of defectives, was opened at Hartford, Connecticut, in 1817, with seven pupils. Through the influence of a physician in that city whose daughter was deaf, interest had been aroused in such a school, some two years previously; and

Thomas Hopkins Gallaudet (*q.v.*), a Yale theological Gallaudet
graduate, sent to study the methods for teaching the
deaf as practised in Europe. After fruitless efforts to
gain admission to the schools of Great Britain, which
were private and conducted for gain, as private monopo-
lies, he visited the schools of Paris; and, besides making
a study of them, induced Laureat Clerk, a deaf mute
himself, though accomplished and an instructor in the
Paris school, to return with him and undertake the work
of establishing a similar school in America. These two
are the parents of the education of the deaf in our
country. Upon their return to this country, they travelled extensively, lecturing upon and demonstrating the
possibility of such education through the living example
of Clerk himself, and aroused a general interest throughout all the Eastern states. As a result, one year later
(1818), New York followed the example set at Hartford, employing a teacher from that school. In 1819
Philadelphia saw the establishment of a similar school.
In the same year Massachusetts, through state appropriation, sent 20 pupils to the Hartford school, and in
1825 New Hampshire and Vermont adopted the same
policy, which was soon followed by other states. The
first of such schools west of the Alleghanies was
founded in Kentucky in 1822; and thereafter their establishment was comparatively rapid: Ohio following in
1827, Virginia and Illinois in 1839, Indiana in 1844,
Tennessee and Georgia in 1846, North Carolina in 1847,
and South Carolina in 1849; making in all 13 institutions
previous to 1850. In 1874 the number was 41, in 1890
it was 48, and in 1901 the total number of schools of all
classes was 118, 57 of which are state institutions.
The total number of pupils in all these schools is
11,343.

The state institutions are in every case boarding
schools, to which pupils are admitted upon the recommendation of the principal or some other authorized

person ; and upon the completion of the regular course, the students are graduated as are those from any other school. Industrial courses are prominent in the curriculum, 333 of a total of 1035 teachers being occupied with trades courses. Kindergartens are maintained in connection with 30 of the institutions, and are found to be very effective.

P. 166.

Of the total number of 118 schools for the deaf, 46 are public day schools, maintained for the most part exactly as are the common schools of learning, except that special teachers are employed, and special methods, of course, followed. This is a comparatively recent move, but it is proving eminently successful in reaching large numbers of children who would, otherwise, be entirely without instruction. Thirty-five cities and towns throughout the country now support such schools, Chicago taking the lead with twelve. As a state, Wisconsin has surpassed any other in providing instruction for its deaf mutes in this way, furnishing a special teacher at state expense wherever a little circle of such children can be gathered near their homes. In this way, fifteen towns in the state are provided with special schools. Of the whole number of day schools for the deaf, but one, the Horace Mann School of Boston, is east of Ohio.

Besides these two classes of schools, the state and the public day school, there are several private institutions where admission is only by tuition, and where excellent work is being done ; and the Gallaudet College of Washington, D.C., which stands in a class by itself. This was established in 1857 as the Columbia Institution, in 1864 was given the name, National Deaf Mute College, and later, the one it now bears. Besides a department resembling very much the State Institutions for the Deaf, it has one for advanced work, in which degrees are given. It is the principal source of supply for teachers.

Methods of Instruction

Owing to the inability of Gallaudet to gain admission to the English and Scotch schools in 1817, the purely P. 471. manual method of the French was introduced in America and remained supreme for forty years. In it, all communication is through the sign language, no attempts at oral articulation being introduced. But in 1843 Horace Mann and Dr. Howe of the Perkins Institute for the Blind at Boston, while in Europe, investigated the merits of the oral method which had been introduced there, and being favorably impressed with it, Mann urged its general introduction in his next annual report. This was the beginning of a controversy which is not yet settled, and which has divided the ranks of teachers of the deaf into two opposing schools. By the oral method, articulate speech is taught, even to those who have been totally deaf since birth. The advantages of this method seemingly more than overbalance its disadvantages, which latter rest principally upon the greater age which pupils must have reached before instruction is possible, and it is gradually gaining ground. At present, it is in practice in nearly all the public and private day schools in the country ; and in the state institutions 3748 pupils are being taught by that system alone, 4292 by a combination of it with the manual, while 2979 are studying the manual system alone.

b. The Blind

Owing, perhaps, to the fact that the sightless do not seem to be so fully cut off from the world as do the deaf, public sympathy was not aroused in the United States to the point of establishing an institution for their instruction for nearly fifteen years after the opening of the American School for the Deaf at Hartford. In 1829 the New England Asylum for the Blind was incor-

Howe.

porated in Boston, but it was three years before Dr. Samuel G. Howe (*q.v.*), who was selected to be its head, could make the necessary investigation abroad and open the school. When this was done, in 1832, an institution in New York City had already been opened, antedating that in Boston by a few months. The next year (1833) a similar school was opened at Philadelphia. These three pioneer institutions were all private corporations, and remain so to this day. Pupils from these schools, and especially the Perkins school (Boston), were exhibited in various parts of the country until public interest was fully aroused and the states began to take action through the establishment of schools of their own. Ohio was the first to do so, in 1837; Virginia followed in 1839; Kentucky, in 1842; Tennessee, in 1846; Indiana, in 1847; Illinois, in 1849; and Wisconsin, in 1850.

Allen, p. 793.

By 1860, 10 more had followed. In 1874 the total number of institutions was 29; in 1890, was 33; and in 1901, was 39, with a total of 4199 pupils. All these schools belong to one class — the boarding school — and all are maintained in part or wholly by public taxes. In them all, manual and industrial courses have a prominent place, not only because of the importance of teaching the pupil a trade which might provide support after graduation, but because it is by doing and constructing that the blind especially learn best. Sloyd has been found to be well adapted to their needs. A great many trades have at one time or another found place in the curricula of the schools; but only a few, and those the simple ones, such as chair caning, hammock making, broom making, carpet weaving, and a few others have proved wholly suitable.

Music has a place in every school, not only because it opens up a wide vocational field to the blind, but because of the delightful diversion it provides. Many of the blind are unusually gifted and are graduated as organists, teachers of music, and piano tuners. Only those pupils who show aptitude are allowed to specialize in music, and not even those, at the expense of the academic subjects.

The kindergarten is an almost universal part of the school for the blind, and no other educational method has been found so effective as the Froebelian. The games and occupations seem to meet exactly the needs of coördination between the senses still active, and the little pupils seem to miss but little that the perfect child gains.

In the matter of literature for the blind, three distinct systems of raised printing are in vogue. The oldest is the system of embossed letters, differing but little from the lower case letter of an ordinary printed page, invented by Dr. Howe. It has the advantage of being easily read by the seeing eye without special training, but requires an extremely delicate sense of touch to decipher with the finger tips. So much so that Superintendent Wait of the New York Institution has said that "only 34 per cent of them [the blind] will ever be able to read it with pleasure or profit." The next system to be introduced, the New York Point, was invented by Mr. Wait, and consists of an arbitrary arrangement of embossed dots, easily readable through the sense of touch, though requiring special training to be read by the eye. The latest is a combination of this system with the French Braille system, and is known as the American Braille. The two last-mentioned systems are those principally in use to-day. Typewriters have been invented for writing in them, and also a modified typewriter for printing upon brass plates, from which any number of copies can be struck off. Printing houses have been established, one subsidized by Congress, for the printing of books for the blind; and in all, there are more than one hundred thousand volumes in the libraries of the schools for the blind.

c. THE DEAF-BLIND

It is in the instances of the few unfortunates lacking both the senses of hearing and of sight, that the really wonderful possibilities in the education of defectives has shown itself most forcibly. Laura Bridgeman, who spent more than fifty years of her life at the Perkins Institute, is the historic case, though her accomplishments are made to pale before those of Helen Keller, the Southern girl, who is successfully completing her course at Radcliffe College. But instances of this sort are not frequent enough to warrant their consideration in a volume of this character, and I must refer any particularly interested to the bibliography at the end of the chapter.

d. THE FEEBLE-MINDED

It was not until 1846 that any movement in the direction of providing schools for the mentally deficient, or idiots, as they were then universally called, was made in this country, and the interest began almost simultaneously in Massachusetts and New York. The former state, however, seemed most ready to act, and in 1848 an experimental school was opened in Boston under the direction of Dr. Howe of the Perkins Institute. In the same year a private school of the same general character was founded at Barre, Massachusetts. New York followed in 1851 with a state institution situated at Syracuse; Pennsylvania, in 1853, at Media; Ohio, in 1857, at Columbus; Kentucky, in 1860, at Frankfort; and Illinois, in 1865, at Jacksonville.

The growth of these schools has never been rapid. In 1890 there were 17 public and 10 private schools in the country, while in 1901 the numbers were 20 and 12 respectively, with a total of 11,149 pupils in the former and 468 in the latter. There is no regular course in these institutions from which the pupils graduate at a specified time; in fact, the most that can be hoped for in the education of many of the pupils is to teach them so much as to make it possible for them to lead a happy life within the institution; in others a certain degree of usefulness may be developed, while with the milder cases some considerable academic education is possible. The kindergarten is an important factor, and many pupils never get beyond it. Entertainments are frequent, and highly enjoyed. The brighter pupils learn to read and write and to use some few of the arithmetical processes, but seldom to reason in the abstract. The girls — and all the pupils are boys and girls, no matter what the age — are taught to do the cooking, sewing, and washing for the school, while the boys work upon the farm, make the shoes, and even in one institution (Indiana) the bricks of which the buildings are constructed. In this way, the institutions are at least in part, self-supporting, and their further development is by far the most economical way for the support of this class of unfortunates, which has always been so largely a dead weight upon the community.

REFERENCES

Allen, E. E. Education of Defectives. In Butler's Education in the United States, 1900, 2 : 771–819. — Barr, M. W. The Training of Mentally Deficient Children. Pop. Sci. Mo. 53 : 531. — Bell, A. G. Education of the Deaf. N. E. A. 1897 : 96. — *Blind, Institutions for, in the United States.* Am. Jour. Ed. 1 : 370, 1 : 447, 11 : 390. — Boone, R. G. Education of Unfortunates. In Education in the United States, pp. 243–250. — Booth, F. W. Statistics of Speech-teaching in Schools for the Deaf in the United States. N. E. A. 1900 : 668. — *Brandt*, T. B. The State in its Relation to the Defective Child. N. E. A. 1901 : 876. — *Brocket*, L. P. Blind, Institutions for the. Am. Jour. Ed. 4 : 127. — Crouter, A. L. E. and Gallaudet, E. M. Higher Education of Deaf and Dumb. Science, 19 : 199–200, 231–233. — Crouter, A. L. E. Instruction of Deaf. Science, 17 : 141–144. — Deaf Mutes, Education of, in the United States (statistics for 1850). Am. Jour. Ed. 1 : 420, 444. — Gallaudet, T. H. (biog.). Am. Jour. Ed. 1 : 433. — *Gallaudet,*

E. M. Instruction of Deaf Mutes. Ed. 1:279. The Deaf and their Possibilities. N. E. A. 1898:207.—*Greely*, A. W. Higher Education of Deaf in America. R. of R.'s, 6:57–62. — **Howe**, S. G. (biog.). Am. Jour. Ed. 11:389.—*Johnson*, A. Education and Care of Feeble-minded. Am. Jour. Sociol. 4:463–473. — Johnston, E. R. On the Training of the Feeble-minded. N. E. A. 1900: 677.—Jones, M. C. Education of Blind. Scrib. Mag. 12:373–387.—*Macey*, J. A. Teaching of the Deaf. World's Work, 6: 3840–3842. Manual Training for Defective Classes. Rep. Com. Ed. 1895–1896:1095–1097.—Morton, A. Instruction of Deaf Mutes. Ed. 18:417.—*Peet*, W. B. Education of Deaf and Dumb. Scrib. Mag. 12:463–474. — Ritter, J. D. How the Blind are Taught. Chaut. 15:65–73.—United States Education, Bureau of. Defective Classes. Various Reports. — Wright, J. D. Speech and Speech Reading for the Deaf. Cent. 31:331–343.

PART THREE

EDUCATIONAL EXTENSION

THE history of education in a country like ours would
not be complete without a consideration of certain institutions entirely outside the organized machinery of the
chools, which contribute largely to the general culture
and extended scholarship of great masses of the people.
Schools are primarily for the youth. Of necessity, the
greater number in attendance upon them must depend
upon others for their support; cannot themselves be
producers; are members of the leisure class, so far as
contribution to the world's economic progress goes.
Since, however, no social mechanism can support profitably too large a leisure class, nor a leisure class for too
long, the time comes when the youth must enter the
ranks of producers, leaving the school days behind.
The exact stage at which this change must take place is
determined by the general economic conditions of the
country.

In 1800 the daily per capita production of wealth
for the United States was about ten cents. In 1850 it
had arisen to thirty cents, in 1880 to forty-four cents, in
1890 to fifty-two cents, and is to-day (1903) upward of
sixty cents.

Harris, N. E. A.
1901, p. 180.

This increased productiveness has been at the bottom
of the rapid increase in secondary and higher education;
since, with the greater earning capacity of the head of
the family, the youth — especially the boys — could be
longer spared to avail themselves of advantages which
the schools offer.

Yet these facts make possible the postponement for a

few years only of the cessation of active school work. Eventually it must come, and thereafter education be an avocation, rather than a vocation; a by-product rather than the principal aim of life.   Yet the maximum of usefulness on the part of the individual demands that educative processes be continued, and it is a recognition of this fact that has given rise to those institutions which make such continuation possible.

These may be divided into two general classes: —

1st. Those that may be made use of entirely within the home.

    a. *Libraries.*
    b. *Newspapers and periodicals.*

2d. Those which take one outside the home, yet which do not seriously interfere with business occupations.

    a. *Summer schools and assemblies.*
    b. *Evening and correspondence schools.*
    c. *Learned societies.*
    d. *Lecture courses and lyceums.*

CHAPTER XXIV

LIBRARIES

PUBLIC libraries, in the sense of collections of books purchased and maintained by public taxation for the free use of the people, are a development of the last half of the nineteenth century. As far back as 1803, the town of Salisbury, Connecticut, received by bequest the private library of Caleb Bingham, and made some additions to it by town grant, but the collection of books is no longer in existence, and can hardly be said to have figured at all prominently in the general library movement. The town of Peterborough, New Hampshire, lays claim, and perhaps with some justice, to having been the birth- _{Fletcher, p. 102.} place of the public library. In 1833 that town voted to use a certain sum of money received from the state as the proceeds of a general taxation of banks, for the purchase of books for a town library to be free to the people of the town. Since this was sixteen years before a law was passed in any state providing for a library tax, it is probable that it was not only the first publicly supported library in the country, but also in the world. This does not mean, however, that there were not at this time many collections of books under corporate ownership, and even accessible, with some restrictions, to the public at large. The colleges and universities had from the _{Colleges and Universities, Chapter XV.} first established libraries for the use of their students and faculties, though these have figured but slightly as forces contributing to the general development of the public library of to-day. Although the library of Harvard College, founded in 1638, was without doubt the first in our land to be used by any constituency larger than a single family, it is to the learned society and the private corporation that we must look for the direct antecedent of libraries for the people; and our study takes us back to Benjamin Franklin — the originator of so many useful

P. 550.

institutions — and the American Philosophical Society in Philadelphia. The story of the foundation of this so-

Franklin, VI, p. 220.

ciety, the oldest of its kind in the country, and its library, are delightfully told by Franklin in his autobiography. The first books purchased were received from London in 1732, and were kept in the rooms of Robert Grace, one of Franklin's friends, and an associate in the establishment of the library. An attendant was on duty for one hour on Wednesdays, and two hours on Saturdays, and was allowed, as the record shows, to permit "any civil gentleman to peruse the books of the library, in the library room, but not to lend or suffer to be taken out of the library, by any person who is not a subscribing member, any of the said books, Mr. James Logan only

Adams, p. 5.

excepted."

Here we have the first evidence of a willingness on the part of library authorities to allow any kind of public participation in their privileges. It is doubtful if they were much bothered by a reading public, for both inclination and ability to read were lacking on the part of the great mass of the community, but the spirit, nevertheless, meant much. Here and there a library followed their plan, for the eighteenth century saw as many as a dozen collections of books under society ownership in various parts of the country.

Notable among them, both for its generosity and the cumbrousness of its statement, was the Redwood Library of Newport, Rhode Island, founded in 1747. Its charter states it to be "a library whereunto the curious and impatient enquirer after resolution of doubts, and the bewildered ignorant, might freely repair for discovery and

Fletcher, p. 12.

demonstration to the one and true knowledge and satisfaction to the other; nay, to inform the mind in both, in order to reform the practice."

It is interesting to note the humanitarian and public-spirited views of these promoters of subscription libraries of the eighteenth century. They seem, however, for the most part, in spite of their literary benevolence, to have been possessed of the belief that books were things to be hoarded rather than to be used; and moreover that the people as a class had little use for such things, or such things for the people. In the latter particular they were probably not far from correct. The ability to read books must precede their usefulness, and in addition, economic conditions must be such as to provide leisure for their perusal. Seemingly these two conditions were slow in being attained, for it was more than a century after the American Philosophical and the Redwood Libraries had opened their doors that the public library movement was really under way. Libraries had sprung up, meanwhile, in most of the large cities of the country, and in many of the smaller towns, but they failed to touch the people. They were supported and patronized by what might be called a literary aristocracy, and the masses felt that they had no share in them. It was no doubt, in part, due to the prevalence of the lyceum in the fourth and fifth decades of the nineteenth century, bringing the masses, as it did, into new fields of thought; and, in part, to the increased leisure resultant upon a less rigorous struggle for existence, that organized attempts were made about the middle of the century to provide more general library facilities through state action.

Adams, pp. 2–37.

The American Lyceum, p. 569.

School District Libraries

This move took form in the establishment of district school libraries, New York State taking the lead in 1835, and being followed by twenty-one other states. The plan does not seem to have been successful. The unit of administration was too small, and, except as it paved the way for other methods through familiarizing the peo-

Rep. Com. Ed. 1895–1896, 6 : 254.

ple with the idea of free books for everybody to read, the district library hardly fulfilled the great expectations of its promoters. This being the case, the ardent believers in the efficiency of books as instruments of education (and there were many such, even at this time), began to cast about for some more satisfactory plan. It took the form of a law enabling *towns* to establish and maintain libraries by public taxation. This proved to be the right thing at the right time.

TOWN LIBRARIES

To New Hampshire, the state in which public funds had first been devoted to library purposes sixteen years earlier, falls the honor of the first enactment of such a law in 1849, though that state perhaps got the idea from a bill passed by the Massachusetts legislature one year previous, granting similar privileges to the city of Boston. The New Hampshire law of 1849 was very simple in form, and its main features remain unchanged. Under its authority any town may raise and appropriate money for establishing and maintaining a library without limitation as to amount, the money to be raised by ordinary taxation.

Idem, pp. 523–597.

Fundamentally the library laws of all the other states do not differ from the New Hampshire law of 1849, though in some, notably New York, other concessions to library interests have been made, and the wonderful developments at the end of the nineteenth century, which have given rise to its characterization as the Age of Libraries, are directly attributable to them.

The following states have passed permissive library laws: —

New Hampshire	1849	Ohio	1867
Massachusetts	1851	Colorado	1872
Maine	1854	Illinois	1872
Vermont	1865	Wisconsin	1872

New York	1872	Wyoming		1886
Indiana	1873	North Dakota		1887
Iowa	1873	South Dakota		1887
Texas	1874	Pennsylvania		1887
Connecticut	1875	Washington		1890
Rhode Island	1875	Mississippi		1892
Michigan	1876	Utah		1896
Nebraska	1877	North Carolina		1897
California	1879	Tennessee		1897
Minnesota	1879	Maryland		1898
New Jersey	1879	Georgia		1898
Montana	1883	Delaware		1899
New Mexico	1884	Arizona		1899
Missouri	1885	Oklahoma		1899
Kansas	1886			

In addition to this legislation of a purely permissive nature, many states, mostly in the East, have passed laws, tending directly to encourage the growth of public libraries through special grants of money and in other ways.

In this move Massachusetts led, by the appointment in 1890 of a special commission of five persons to look after library interests and foster their growth throughout the state. In the first report made by this commission special attention was called to those towns which had no public libraries. The effect of this undesirable prominence was such that during the year 1891 thirty-six towns established them, and at the end of ten years only four or five towns and less than one-half of one per cent of the population were without their influence.

New Hampshire followed a year later with similar legislation, and again in 1893 took the lead in library legislation by enacting the law that "each town *shall* assess annually a sum to be computed at the rate of thirty dollars for every dollar of the state tax apportioned to each town . . . to be appropriated to the sole purpose of establishing and maintaining a free public library within said town." It also provided that in case this sum be less than $100, the state should make it up to that amount. The influence of this legislation was what might be expected, and other states were not slow to fall in line, some twenty having in the next ten years appointed library commissions and made specific moves toward library encouragement.

The effect of all this has been, not only to multiply libraries, but to increase in many ways their efficiency. The best thought has been bestowed upon the problem; and, whereas even a generation ago the public library had a comparatively small constituency, it is now a force directly felt by the vast majority of people in nearly every community. This has been brought about largely through changes or innovations, the most important of which has been the making of books more accessible to the people.

Fletcher, p. 27.

LIBRARY EXTENSION

In Bulletin No. 40 of the Home Education Department of the University of New York, Melvil Dewey, its director, says : —

"The original library was a storehouse in which books could be preserved, and passed on to posterity. To get and to keep were the chief functions, while to use was subordinate. Only a favored few had access to the books. Then a broadening process began. Those who could pay a certain fee might use the library. Then came the broad thought of making it free to all, but only for use in the building, as the present museum is used. The old librarian would have been as much shocked at the suggestion of taking a book from the building, as would the modern curator of a museum if an interested child should ask to carry home the bird of paradise. Then came the lending to the favored few, then to all who could pay the fee, and finally the great thought of lending free to all. But this was by no means the end realized that if they were to do the best work they must have this aggressive spirit, and adopt the aggressive methods of those who make other enterprises most successful. Then came the branch in the larger cities in order to reduce the difficulties of inaccessibility, and get within a reasonable distance of each home a collection of books and an inviting reading room. The more widely scattered delivery stations followed, so that the workman could readily return his book in the morning and get a new one on the way back without going much out of his usual course. Then books were sent out for a trifling fee to those who could not conveniently come after them. . . . Yet all this did not meet the demand, and we realized that the new conditions brought about by cheap and quick transportation demanded new methods in solving our problem of 'the best reading for the largest number at the least cost.' "

This result was the travelling library.

Open Shelves

The first move in the direction of accessibility was the open shelf. The old adage, " If you don't see what you want, ask for it," will not work with the mass of modern public library users, for a great majority do not know well enough what they want to ask for it. It worked well enough when the patrons were few and trained, but not to-day. The shopkeeper has solved the problem through the show window, so arranged as to create a desire, even if it did not previously exist. The modern, up-to-date librarian has done the same by throwing open his book stacks, at least a part of them, to the public. It is of course necessary to preserve the most valuable works and the rare editions from excessive handling, but this in no way interferes with the plan which has become quite general, and is undoubtedly an important factor in increasing the clientage of the modern public library.

There are still some large libraries which are more conservative than others, as, for instance, those of Boston, Chicago, and St. Louis; but in Cleveland, Buffalo, Philadelphia, Milwaukee, Denver, Kansas City (Missouri), Toledo, and Springfield (Massachusetts), and many other cities, the plan has been so successful as to make it a safe one to follow. Cleveland was the first city (1886) to make use of it, and now 100,000 of its 150,000 volumes are freely accessible to the public. The Philadelphia public library is the largest with the open-shelf system, having nearly all of its 234,000 volumes freely accessible. Of the plan Mr. Thompson, its librarian, says : —

"I have no hesitation whatever in saying that there is no limit whatever to the number of books to be placed on the open shelves. If open shelves had been risky, then there is no doubt that the danger would have been felt in a city the size of Philadelphia. In small cities and towns the readers are known to the attendants ; in cities like Chicago, New York, and Philadelphia, of course the larger number are unknown. The loss from theft has in our case proved insignificant. The number of books lost in one year does not amount in volume to the salary of one employee. The safeguard of closed shelves would require the services of several attendants, and the difference between closed and open shelves, so far as the service to the public is concerned, does not admit of discussion. Persons using libraries by means of the catalog or cards only, cannot gain one-third of the benefit that is procurable by a person who has free access to the books themselves."

Similar reports come from other librarians who are in a position to observe the benefits of the open shelf. At the Wardner's Library in Springfield, Massachusetts, not a single book was lost from 25,000 to which the public had free access, in the course of a whole year.

LIBRARY SUB-STATIONS

The next move in library extension, after that of getting the people to the books, as exemplified by the open-shelf plan, was that of getting the books to the people. It soon became evident that in spite of the tremendous increase in the number of libraries, they were still too far from the mass of the people to be of the greatest use. The remedy was the institution of branch libraries and charging stations, so located with reference to the principal residence centres and factories in the larger cities, as to make it possible for any one to get and return books without going much out of his way. The plan has wrought havoc with many of the pet ideas of the old-school librarians, but it is in the line of greater efficiency, and is being developed in nearly every large city; and in some rural communities, as rapidly as funds will permit. The general idea has already taken form in the following ways:—

a. Branch libraries containing permanent collections of books and performing all the functions of a small, independent library.

b. Delivery stations where books may be ordered from the main library, and through which they may be returned, but where no permanent collection is kept.

c. Deposit stations, to which small collections of books are sent from the main library to be freely circulated, and then returned as a whole for a new collection.

These offshoots of the public library are as logical a growth in the larger centres of populations as are the ward school buildings. There is no more reason why all the books should be housed in a central library building than that all the children should go to some one common schoolhouse. In fact, the reasons are equally good why neither should be the case.

a. Branch Libraries

Of the three forms of library extension mentioned above, that of the branch library is undoubtedly the most efficient, as it carries with it the services of a trained librarian. Since the function of the library is to interest the reader, as well as to provide books, this is a matter of no small consequence. From the standpoint of this influence, the branch has an advantage over the main library, since its clientage is small, and the librarian can better know the interests of each individual, and cater to them. The readers, too, have a feeling of ownership in a small library, simply equipped, which they never feel in going into a magnificent building. The rapidity with which branch libraries have been established in the larger cities renders it impossible to make any statement of their number which would be valid for more than a few months. In 1902 Boston had 10; New York City, 13; Philadelphia, 8; Buffalo, 2; Chicago, 6; Pittsburg, 6; and Brooklyn, 18, as yet without a central library. New York and Washington, with their magnificent Carnegie gifts, will soon take a lead in the matter of branch libraries which will place them far in advance of any other city.

It is an interesting indication of the incompleteness with which the central library had covered its field, to note that with the establishment of branches, a new impetus was given the circulation of the main library. In the case of Boston, during the two years following the establishment of the first branch, the circulation in the main library had increased 90,880 volumes, as compared with an increase of 35,236 for the two years next preceding. The report of the Cleveland library also states that one-half its circulation is through branches, without lessening the use of the main library.

b. Delivery Stations

The type of delivery station almost universal, is that located in a grocery, dry-goods, or drug store, or any place of business which can be secured for the purpose. The proprietor of the store forwards to the main library orders for the books, with the reader's card, and delivers the books to him when they arrive. His responsibility is slight, and he has nothing to do with the charging of books. As a compensation, he receives a small stated sum from the library fund, or in some cities a certain amount for each book handled.

In spite of the fact that the plan of delivery stations is being constantly extended, their desirability is sometimes questioned.

The president of the New York Mercantile Library says : —

"We believe the system of home delivery to be far preferable and more advantageous in every way for our members than the plan of delivery stations."

The authorities of the Cleveland Public Library also say : —

"The system seems indispensable, but continues to be the most expensive and least satisfactory work that we do."

This is because the work is all done at arm's length. The borrowers have no opportunity of seeing the books, which they are obliged to select from the catalogue, and the assistants at the library have no opportunity to see the borrowers, whose wants they try to fill.

In spite, however, of these difficulties, present library administration seems to demand them. Chicago has nearly 70, St. Louis, 48, Buffalo, 8, Cincinnati, 33, and Cleveland, 4 delivery stations.

c. Deposit Stations

In the deposit station many of the disadvantages of the mere delivery station are wanting. It has all the merits of a small branch library, except that of a trained librarian. Books may be handled and taken out; and, with some care on the part of the library authorities in the selection of books, a better class may be put in circulation than by the other plan.

The more common places for such stations are fire-engine houses, police stations, factories, street railway barns, social settlements, homes, public schools, and public parks. In each case a collection of books varying in number from a dozen to several hundred is sent in a suitable case and left until it has fulfilled its purpose, when it is exchanged for another. In the engine houses they have worked particularly well. The men have, under ordinary circumstances, plenty of leisure and make the fullest use of the books which they would probably not take the trouble to go to the library to secure. Buffalo has 84 such stations, Boston, 41, Cleveland, 26, and New York City, nearly 100. Neither police stations, railway trains, nor factories seem to have been as fully used for deposits of books as have engine houses, but the move in the direction of their fuller utilization is under way in many of the large cities. In the plan of home deposits, the Carnegie Library of Pittsburg seems to have taken the lead. In 1901 there were reported twenty-six such deposits with a membership of 401. In locating these centres for library extension, the school-teacher has been of much help. Most of the deposits are scattered through the city in districts not reached by the central library nor by any of its branches.

School Deposits

If we may judge by their prevalence, by far the most efficient deposit of books is that in the public school. We can, in fact, hardly estimate the educational importance of this plan of library extension. The reading habit, if formed at all, will, in nine cases out of ten, be formed during childhood. It cannot, however, be acquired without books, and will not, in most cases, if the child must go to the books. The books, then, of the right sort must go to the child, and since libraries are among the last things to which the ordinary school board will devote funds, the public libraries are supplying the lack, and doing so most generously. They are following one of two plans: either that of making deposits of books in each separate room, under the direction of its teacher; or of furnishing some general library room, either within each building or in the public library, to be used by all the pupils. The former plan has been in

vogue in Detroit for about fifteen years, and at
present 80 boxes, containing in all about 10,000 volumes, are circulating in all grades above the fourth.
Buffalo has 457 such classroom libraries, with 20,346
volumes, which in the year 1900 were charged 194,045
times for withdrawal. Mr. Crunden of the St. Louis
public library, while employing the general plan of
sending to the schools selections of books, has supplemented it by depositing enough copies of certain ones
to supply each pupil in the room. Of this plan he
says : —

"It is better to send thirty copies of the same book than thirty
different books for two reasons : first, because it enables the teacher
to have class exercises ; second, because the interest of each pupil is
greatly intensified when all his classmates are reading the same
book. It gives them all a common subject of conversation and edi-
fying topics to supplant the vulgarities of boys and the vanities of
girls. And this is one of the incidental benefits of literature in a
school, which is of no small importance."

These sets of thirty are sent to the schools on request
of the principal for a period of two weeks, with the privilege of renewal. Three hundred sets are in circulation. Crunden[1], p. 109.
The second plan mentioned for school deposits has
been very fully worked out by the Brookline, Massachusetts, public library. In its report for 1900 we find : —

"The most important development of the Brookline public library
has been an extension of its work done with the public schools. The
chief characteristics of the work have been : 1st, Visiting the schools
by an assistant to train the minds of the pupils and teachers. 2d, Issuing to teachers, beside the seven books allowed for their personal
use, twenty or more books each, drawn either from the special collection in the school reference room which contains many duplicates
or from the general library, to be used by the pupils in school or
home, in connection with their lessons or simply for recreative reading. 3d, The special assistant has charge of the school reference
room during the afternoon, and assists pupils who resort there for
the purpose of looking up topics of study or for collateral reading.
4th, Systematic instruction in the use of the library is given by the
assistant in charge of the pupils of the eighth and ninth grades of

the grammar schools and the first year of the high school, who are brought there in classes, accompanied by their teachers. The lowest grade is taught about the makeup of a book, the title page, copyright, table of contents, index, and how to use them; also the chief facts about the binding and the use of the commoner reference books. The next grade takes up the more advanced reference books and learns the use of the card catalogue; while the high school students are doing some simple bibliographical work."

From the standpoint of the educator this would seem to be the most helpful correlation possible between the library and the school. As valuable as the schoolroom deposits are proving, there is the danger that the pupil will associate them wholly with the school, and through their exclusive use, fail to come in contact with the general library. In that case, the reading habit, even though acquired, might be lost with the school days. The schoolroom deposit might make the pupil a stranger to the public library and never give him a "smell of the leather," which meant so much to Lowell and others who have so loved the crowded alcove.

The latest move of the deposit stations has been to the public park and recreation grounds. The plan has not yet been developed to its full possibility in any city, though beginnings have been made in several. The first attempt seems to have been made in Tompkins Park, Brooklyn, in the summer of 1899, at which time a collection of one thousand books for children was installed in the pavilion. It is too soon to say what the scheme may lead to. But it would seem as if this might be one of the most useful forms of library extension.

TRAVELLING LIBRARIES

Although our country cannot claim to be the birthplace of the travelling library, it is with us that the plan is being developed to its fullest usefulness. The scheme of sending boxes of books from place to place in order to reach those who would otherwise be without reading matter, is not one of recent date. As long ago as 1825, one Samuel Brown of the East Lothian region of Scotland instigated a move which placed in circulation no less than nineteen so-called " itinerant libraries," each containing fifty volumes and making a circuit of fifteen stations, each with its own librarian. On this side of the water, the manager of the American Lyceum first P. 569. made use of the plan in 1831, and since that time certain railroad corporations, as well as the Seaman's Friend Society, have employed it. In each case, however, the books were only for the favored few : either those who had become regular subscribers through the payment of a fee, or the beneficiaries of the company or association owning the libraries. It was in New York State that the scheme was first applied to the free public library, and it is within that state that it has seen its. fullest development. The rules adopted under the legislature of 1892 provide that a collection of one hundred books may be lent from the state library for six months to any public library of the state ; or where no library exists, anywhere upon the petition of twenty-five resident taxpayers, provided some person owning real estate will hold himself responsible for the books. A fee of $5 is demanded to cover the cost of transportation and incidental expenses. A later rule is made to cover a selection of twenty-five books, the fee being $3.

The first library went out in February, 1893. The plan met with a success unhoped for even by its ardent advocates, and was 'rapidly extended, 35,624 volumes having been sent out from the state library at Albany during the university year 1899–1900. Besides, public libraries, and groups of twenty-five tax-payers, school extension centres, summer schools, study clubs, and private guarantors participated in the plan. Moreover, books, pictures, lantern slides, and lanterns for projection purposes were similarly loaned. By these means the library at Albany is making itself felt throughout its constituency as is no other state library in the country. Following its leadership, several other state libraries, not a few city libraries, and several clubs and associations of a private character maintain travelling libraries. In 1901, some one or more of these agencies were maintaining travelling libraries in the states of Maine, Vermont, Massachusetts, Rhode Island, Connecticut, Pennsylvania, New Jersey, Delaware, Maryland, Virginia, North Carolina, Georgia, Alabama, Louisiana, Texas, Tennessee, Kentucky, Ohio, Indiana, Illinois, Michigan, Wisconsin, Minnesota, Iowa, Missouri, Kansas, Nebraska, North Dakota, Montana, Colorado, Oregon, Idaho, and Washington.

An interesting elaboration of the scheme has been worked out by the New York state library in the form of a book wagon. A large covered wagon is used, holding a number of separate libraries with different selections of books, and a definite route is covered at stated intervals. A trained librarian is in charge. The supposition is that he, through conversation with the people in his route, will discover their special interests and be of service in the selection of books which shall meet the wants of each.

With this, plans for making the library accessible to the people seem to have reached the maximum of development — a development remarkable indeed when we consider that from the stage of no libraries to this of the itinerant "missionary of the book" only the brief space of fifty years has elapsed. It is true that but a few counties in a single state have as yet heard the clank of his wagon wheels; but, with a people as ready as ours to see the good and to appropriate it, we need hardly expect another fifty years to have elapsed before the book wagon will be as familiar a sight, even in the remotest regions, as is Uncle Sam's rural delivery cart.

CHILDREN'S ROOMS

A recent library move of much importance educationally is the establishment of children's rooms. Most libraries have had an age limit to the borrowers of books. As a result, children could enjoy their advantages only through the courtesy of an adult; and, even then, without that feeling of equal participation which is such an important factor. The public library of Brookline, Massachusetts, deserves the credit, in 1890, for being the first to open a special room for the little folks. From this modest beginning — for it was only an unused basement room which was devoted to the purpose — has sprung one of the most promising forms of library extension, in some libraries even rivalling the department for adults in its prominence. With the initial step taken at Brookline, other cities were not slow in following the example. Minneapolis, in 1893, opened a similar room, though much more invitingly arranged; and in 1894 the public libraries of Denver, Colorado, and Cambridge, Massachusetts, made similar provisions for the wants of the child. Since that time the development has been too rapid to follow.

The children's room, as ordinarily maintained, performs a twofold function; that of reading room, and of circulating department. though the latter is not always a feature. From three hundred volumes to ten times as many, carefully selected for the children's wants, are upon the shelves — which are in every case open to the children — in the various children's rooms of different libraries, and one or more special librarians are in most cases in constant attendance. Suitable magazines are taken and are on file; and in every possible way the rooms are made as attractive as possible for the little folks. Tables, chairs, reading desks, and shelves are of sizes best adapted to their needs: the pictures upon the walls and other decorations of the rooms are of such a character as to meet their appreciation.

The whole move is in too early an infancy properly to estimate, but if we may be allowed to predict, it must take rank in the very forefront of important steps in library extension.

Private Bequests to Libraries

The American people has of late years shown its appreciation of the public library movement, not only by its willingness to devote public funds to its furtherance, but also by generous private bequests. Hundreds of cities and towns throughout the country owe their library buildings either wholly or in part to the latter. The magnitude of recent gifts for library purposes is shown by the following table.

Gifts to libraries in the United States during the last eleven years : —

1892	$ 4,092,000
1893	6,330,700
1894	3,012,000
1895	532,433
1896	1,452,000
1897	1,218,000
1898	1,166,500
1899	5,012,400
1900	2,961,000
1901	15,388,752
1902	4,970,800
Total	$46,136,585

Although this unprecedented munificence comprises gifts from hundreds of persons, those of Mr. Andrew Carnegie so far surpass those of any other person — in fact, those of all other persons put together — as to make him a veritable colossus among library benefactors.

Previous to the year 1899, he had given $5,811,000 to the cause. In 1899 his gifts amounted to the sum of

$3,503,500; in 1900, to $640,000; in 1901, to $12,888,-
500; in 1902, to $2,598,500; and in 1903 to $5,633,500,
making a grand total of $31,075,000. His first benefactions were to the city of Pittsburg, Pennsylvania, and towns in its immediate vicinity; but later they have been extended, until no part of the country is without his influence. His custom is to erect the library building in whatever town or city he deems worthy, after investigation, stipulating only that a suitable site be provided, and that adequate funds be raised by taxation for its maintenance. In this way more than three hundred libraries have been endowed by him. Some communities have refused this aid, asserting that its tendency was to pauperize, rather than to stimulate a healthy library interest. Such refusals have, however, been few. Generally the wisdom of the gifts has been recognized, and we cannot doubt that by them interest in libraries has been tremendously stimulated.

A library movement which has established its commercial success, as well as its educational value, was started in Philadelphia, in March, 1900, under the title, The Booklover's Library. Its founder was Mr. Seymour Eaton, and he has ever since been the prime mover in the undertaking. It is conducted as a private club, to which membership is by election. It now has centres in nearly every city of any size in the country. At each of the principal centres is a library, from which books are sent, by special carriers, to all the members residing within the city or its suburbs, and to those at a distance by express. This feature of home delivery has given to the Booklover's Library an almost phenomenal growth, as, according to its latest reports, it is sending out to its patrons more than ten million volumes a year. Membership in the library is of several classes, with a sliding scale according to the number of books which one may receive at a time. Special attention is taken to keep the volumes fresh and clean. To this end, each is enclosed in a neat pasteboard case. Branches of the library are to be found on many railroad trains and steamboat lines, and prove of great convenience to the travelling public, since a volume drawn from one branch may be returned at any other, and another drawn in its place.

In connection with the Booklover's Library is the Tabard Inn Library, having many more centres for exchange, but lacking the home delivery feature. Membership in the latter is less expensive than in the former. We cannot doubt that both these libraries, though primarily commercial in their inception, are important factors in general library extension. They are perhaps the strongest evidences we have that books must be both attractive and easily accessible to be widely circulated.

Conclusion

The following summary of important events in library development and extension, modified from that given in Dr. H. B. Adams's Monograph on *Public Libraries and Popular Education* may serve as an aid to the memory.

Adams, pp. 138–140.

1. Parish libraries instituted in North Carolina, 1705.

2. The Philadelphia Library Company, founded 1732.

3. Library of the American Philosophical Society, Philadelphia, 1743.

4. The first medical library, Pennsylvania Hospital, Philadelphia, 1763.

5. The first foreign nationality to establish a library, the German Society of Philadelphia, 1764.

6. Library of the American Academy of Arts and Sciences, Boston, 1780.

7. The first theological library at St. Mary's Theological Seminary of St. Sulpice, Baltimore, Maryland, 1791.

8. The first state historical library, Boston, 1791.

9. The first formal state library, New Jersey. 1796.

10. The Congressional Library, founded, Washington, 1800.

11. The first law library, Bar Association of Philadelphia, 1802.

12. The young men's mercantile libraries founded, Boston and New York City, 1820.

13. The first free public library, Petersborough, New Hampshire, 1833.

14. The first law establishing school district libraries, New York State, 1835.

15. First city ordinance authorizing a tax for public library, Boston, 1848.

16. First state law authorizing a tax for public libraries, New Hampshire, 1849.

17. First state library commission appointed, Massachusetts, 1890.

18. First state law authorizing travelling libraries, New York, 1892.

19. First state law *requiring* taxation for public libraries, New Hampshire, 1893.

REFERENCES

Adams, Herbert B. Public Libraries and Popular Education. Bull. No. 31. Home Education Department, University of the State of New York, 1900 (full bibliography). — American Library Association Handbook. January, 1899. — Boston, Public Library. Rep. of the Fine Arts Dep. on Art Exhibitions, 1899, 60–64. — Bostwick, Arthur E. Branch Libraries. L. J. 23 : 14–18. — Brett, William Howard and others. Discussion of Open Shelves in the Light of Actual Experience. L. J. 24 : C 136–142. — *Canfield*, J. H. Public Libraries and the Public Schools. N. E. A. 1901 : 836. — Carpenter, Edmund J. The Story of the Boston Public Library. N. E. Mag. 18 : 737–756. — **Crunden**, F. M. The School and the Library. N. E. A. 1901 : 108. Travelling Libraries. St. Louis Lib. Mag. 5 : 90–96. — *Dana*, John Cotton. Library Primer. — *Cutter*, C. A. The Development of Public Libraries. Rep. Com. Ed. 1899–1900, 2 : 1352. — *Dewey*, Melvil. The Place of the Library in Education. N. E. A. 1901 : 858. The Extension of the University of the State of New York. N. Y. Regents' Report, 1890, 103 : 73–115. — **Edwards**, Edward. Free Town Libraries in America. 1869. — **Fletcher**, William Isaac. Public Libraries in America. — *Flint*, Weston. Statistics of Public Libraries in the United States and Canada. Rep. Com. Ed. 1893. — Foote, Elizabeth L. The Children's Home Library Movement. Outl. 57 : 172–173. — **Franklin**, Benjamin. Autobiography. — Gilbert, Charles B. The Public Library and the Public School. N. E. A. 1903 : 948. — *Haines*, Helen E. The Rapid Growth of Public Libraries. World's Work, 5 : 3086–3090. — *Harrison*, Joseph Le Roy. The Public Library Movement in the United States. New Eng. Mag. 16 : 709–722. — *Hutchins*, F. A. The Present Condition of School Libraries in Rural Schools and Villages of less than 2500. N. E. A. 1899 : 501. — Larned, J. N.

The Mission and the Missionaries of the Book. New York State University. Convocation, 1896. — Libraries as Related to the Educational Work of the State of New York. University Convocation, 1888. — Miller, Joseph Dana. Libraries and Librarians. Bookman, 6 : 407–415. — Meader, C. L. The Most Essential Books for a High School Library. Sch. Rev. 4 : 149. — Methods of Children's Library Work. L. J. 22 : C 28–31. — *McMurray*, Charles A. The Relation of the School to Libraries. N. E. A. 1899 : 472. — New York State University. Various Bulletins of the Public Library, and Home Education Departments. — *Poole*, William Frederick. The Public Library of Our Time. L. J. 12 : 311–320. — *Presnell*, H. Library Legislation in the United States. Rep. Com. Ed. 1895–1896, I : 523. — Public Libraries and Popular Education. New York State University. Bulletin 31 : 1900. — *Putnam*, Herbert. The Great Libraries of the United States. Forum, 19 : 484–494. — Reading Rooms for Children. Public Libraries, 2 : 125–131. — Rhees, William Jones. Manual of Public Libraries, Institutions, and Societies in the United States and British Provinces of North America. — *Scudder*, Horace. School Libraries. At. Month. 72 : 678. — *Smith*, Allen. History of Petersborough, New Hampshire. — Thompson, John. Travelling Libraries. L. J. 21 : C 29–31. — *Tyler*, Moses Coit. The Historic Evolution of the Free Public Library in America, and its True Function in the Community. L. J. 9 : 40–47. — Education, United States Bureau of. Public Libraries in the United States, Their History, Condition, and Management. Washington, 1876. Statistics of Libraries and Librarians in the United States. 1897. Relations of Public Libraries to Public Schools. Rep. 1899–1900, I : 663. The Public School and the Public Library. Rep. 1897–1898, I : 673–692. Report of Committee of the National Educational Association on the Relation of Public Libraries to Public Schools. Rep. 1899–1900, I : 663–719. See Libraries in various reports. — *Zueblin*, Charles. Public Libraries. See his American Municipal Progress. 1902, pp. 173–205.

CHAPTER XXV

NEWSPAPERS AND PERIODICALS

a. NEWSPAPERS

POWERFUL as is the library as a factor in educational extension, we must in all probability give first place to the public press. It would be hard to determine in any definite and precise way, the magnitude of its influence, but it is safe to say that in shaping public opinion, if not in furnishing the food for intellectual progress, it had more to do than has any other influence. Dr. W. T. Harris, in an address before the Congregational Club, in Washington, has said : —

"Far surpassing our libraries in educative influences are our own daily newspapers and magazines. Our people are far more freely supplied with newspapers than are the people of any other nation. We are governed by public opinion, as ascertained and expressed in the newspapers to such an extent that our civilization is justly to be called a newspaper civilization."

Like all our great social and institutional growths, the newspaper has its beginnings far back in colonial days. Not so far as the public school, yet antedating the public library. In respect to age, indeed, our own public press is not so very far behind that of Europe. Depending, as it does, upon the printing press, it was impossible before the time of that invention, and even then was forced to wait until an appetite for news had been created. So it was probably not until 1622 that the first regularly printed sheet appeared in England, and eighty years later (1702) that a daily paper was started.

Rep. Com. Ed.
1871, p. 553.

In the colonies, the first newspaper issued was in 1690, at Boston. Its publication was, however, declared contrary to law by the colonial legislature, since it was charged with containing "reflections of a very high nature," and a second issue was never made. So far as is known, but one copy is in existence, and that is in the state paper office in London. It is a small sheet of four quarto pages, one of them blank.

The next essay into the newspaper field was more successful. On the 24th of April, 1704, appeared in the same city, *The Boston News Letter*, edited by the postmaster, John Campbell; and since its sole predecessor did not live to draw its second breath, this may well be considered the parent of the American public press. It was a half sheet, twelve inches by eight. It continued to be issued weekly until 1776. Until 1719 the *News Letter* had the entire field in the colonies, but in that year two other papers made their appearance, *The Boston Gazette* and *The American Weekly Mercury*, of Philadelphia, the former being printed, though not controlled, by James Franklin, elder brother of Benjamin. It was continued for many years, finally falling a victim to the Stamp Act. In 1721, James Franklin severed his connection with the *Gazette* and established *The New England Courant*, the third paper in Boston, and it was in connection with this sheet that his brother Benjamin got his first taste of letters. Of his connec-

Palfrey, p. 283.

tion with it J. G. Palfrey says: —

"But the master spirit of the *Courant's* better days was Franklin's brother Benjamin, then a boy apprenticed in the office. The paper provoked the severe displeasure of the clergy and the government, which the latter did not fail to manifest in process of legislature and judicial action. All this might have continued, with good management and a portion of the favor, to brave or evade and thrive upon, but Franklin was indiscreet enough to quarrel with his brother, and with his elopement to Philadelphia the glory departed from the *Courant*, and its weak life soon expired."

In addition to the papers already mentioned, there were established in Boston, previous to 1750, three others: *The Weekly Rehearsal*, *The Weekly Post Boy* (1734), and *The Independent Advertiser* (1748). In the other colonies there had been meanwhile enough others started to bring the number up to that of the original states — thirteen — though their distribution was not by any means of the same breadth. Philadelphia had, besides *The Weekly Mercury*, *The Pennsylvania Gazette*, purchased by Benjamin Franklin, in 1729, a year after its establishment, and published by him for thirty years. In Newport, Rhode Island, was *The Rhode Island Gazette*, started in 1732; Annapolis had *The Maryland Gazette* (1728); and Charleston, South Carolina, *The South Carolina Gazette* (1731). These, and two or three others of an ephemeral type, constituted the entire news circulation of the colonies at the middle of the eighteenth century; and no one of these was a daily. Such a thing, in fact, was hardly dreamed of, and did not make its appearance until 1784, in Philadelphia, with the issuing of *The Pennsylvania Packet*, subsequently called *The Daily Advertiser*, and printed under that name until 1837.

It would be out of place to discuss here in detail the development of the newspaper press later than 1750. From that time on its growth was much more rapid, as is shown by the accompanying table: —

TABLE SHOWING GROWTH OF NEWSPAPERS AND
PERIODICALS IN THE UNITED STATES

State	1750	1775	1810	1828	1871	1903
Maine	—	—	—	29	66	164
Massachusetts . .	6	7	32	78	280	565
New Hampshire . .	—	1	12	17	56	90
Vermont	—	—	14	21	44	74
Rhode Island . . .	1	2	7	14	26	56
Connecticut . . .	—	4	11	33	87	164
New York	1	4	66	161	894	1953
New Jersey . . .	—	—	8	22	138	376
Pennsylvania . . .	2	9	71	185	584	1381
Delaware	—	—	2	4	18	38
Maryland	1	2	21	37	96	198
District of Columbia .	—	—	6	9	25	72
Virginia	1	2	23	34	116	226
North Carolina . .	—	2	10	20	65	246
South Carolina . .	1	3	10	16	59	138
Georgia	—	1	13	18	123	344
Florida	—	—	1	2	25	145
Alabama	—	—	—	10	78	233
Mississippi	—	—	4	6	93	224
Louisiana	—	—	10	9	90	188
Tennessee	—	—	6	8	104	269
Kentucky	—	—	17	23	105	310
Ohio	—	—	14	66	411	1173
Indiana	—	—	—	17	264	832
Michigan	—	—	—	2	139	792
Illinois	—	—	—	4	499	1688
Missouri	—	—	—	5	289	984
Arkansas	—	—	—	1	51	256
Kansas	—	—	—	—	112	693
Nebraska	—	—	—	—	46	604
California	—	—	—	—	187	684
Nevada	—	—	—	—	15	30
Oregon	—	—	—	—	32	200
Minnesota	—	—	—	—	104	705
West Virginia . . .	—	—	—	—	58	203
Wisconsin	—	—	—	—	201	677
Texas	—	—	—	—	123	770
Territories	—	—	—	—	73	319
Colorado	—	—	—	—	—	347
Idaho	—	—	—	—	—	85
Montana	—	—	—	—	—	91
North Dakota . . .	—	—	—	—	—	177
South Dakota . . .	—	—	—	—	—	273
Utah	—	—	—	—	—	77
Wyoming	—	—	—	—	—	38
Total	13	37	358	851	5983	20,483

Neither in 1750 nor 1775 was there a single daily paper published in the colonies. In 1820 there were 27 dailies and an annual issue of 22,321,000 copies. In 1828 the latter had increased to 68,117,796; and in 1871 to 1,499,922,219.

The earlier papers were ordinarily printed on a half sheet, folded either once or twice, though with no great uniformity in this respect. Occasionally, when there was a press of news, the modern supplement was anticipated by the use of an entire sheet. Although advertisements were inserted, they were not frequent. One appeared in the first issue of the *News Letter* and two in the second. This paper contained from time to time some interesting intimations that the editor of that day had troubles not unlike those of his modern prototype. In one of the issues of the year 1709 we find the following editorial dun : —

" All persons in town or country are hereby desired now to pay or send it in with their resolution that they would have it continued and proceeded on the fifth year, life permitted,"

and later, the outline of an artful advertising scheme which would put to shame even the most up-to-date business manager of a modern sheet. It should be remembered that the editor was also postmaster. He says : —

" If he does not print a sheet every other week this winter time, he plans to make it up in the spring when ships do arrive from Great Britain. And for the advantage of the postoffice, an entire sheet of paper, one half with the news and the other half, good writing paper to write on, may also be had there for every one that pleases to have it every Monday."

b. MAGAZINES

For many years these old papers of the earlier eighteenth century served the double purpose of news carrier, and the more dignified medium for discussion of the graver, philosophical, religious, and political questions. In the course of time, however, a differentiation took place. Some of those already established took on more nearly the character, though not the form, of the modern magazine, and became less ephemeral in their nature. As early, too, as 1743, there appeared quite a pretentious publication of more than fifty octavo pages, under the title of *The American Magazine and Historical Chronicle* which was issued monthly at Boston for more than three years. In 1758, in the same city, was born *The New England Magazine of Knowledge and Pleasure*, sixty pages 12mo, which in spite of its poetical advertisement, or perhaps, because of it, failed to survive its fourth monthly number.[1]

During the twenty-five years preceding 1775 no less than six similar essays into the magazine field, mostly at Philadelphia, proved abortive; but in that year, *The Pennsylvania Magazine*, edited by Robert Aiken, got a foothold, largely through the contributions of Thomas Paine. If we may believe the editor, the problems of the sanctum were hardly less complicated in those days than they are at present. He explains that on one occasion, being ready to issue, and out of copy, he induced Paine to accompany him home.

Palfrey, p. 202.

" I seated him at the table," he says, " with the necessary apparatus which always included a glass and a decanter of brandy. The first glass put him in a train of thinking; I feared the second glass would disqualify him or render him untractable; but it only illuminated his intellectual system; and when he had swallowed the third glass he wrote with great rapidity, intelligence, and precision; and his ideas appeared to flow faster than he could commit them to paper. What he penned from the inspiration of brandy, was perfectly fit for the press without any correction or alteration."

But even this method seems not to have given his magazine sufficient strength to weather the storms of

[1] " With something suited to each different ged,
To humor him and her, and me and you."

the Revolutionary period, and it went under, together with every one of its contemporaries on this side of the water.

The nineteenth century opened more auspiciously. Within its first decade began the growth of periodical literature, which has meant much to us as a people. The first, and perhaps the only one of that decade to have any considerable influence upon the literary tastes of the country, was *The Portfolio*, published by Dennie, in Philadelphia, from 1801 till 1825. In 1815 we have the birth of *The North American Review*, the first of all our list which is anything more than a myth to the present generation. For many years it was published in Boston as a quarterly, but later it was moved to New York City and has, since 1819, appeared as a monthly. It has had in its editorial chair in succession Tudor (its founder), Channing, Dana, Everett, Sparks, H. H. Everett, Palfrey, Bowen, Peabody, Lowell, Norton, Henry Adams, A. T. Rice. With such leaders of thought at its head, it is not strange that it ranks as probably first among American periodicals in its influence upon American thought.

A close second to *The North American Review*, if indeed we should give it second place, is *The Atlantic Monthly*, founded in Boston in 1857, and ever since published there. First edited by James Russell Lowell, and followed by James T. Fields, William D. Howells, Thomas Bailey Aldrich, and having as regular contributors such men as Longfellow, Holmes, Emerson, Whittier, Trowbridge, and nearly every other man of prominence in American letters, it met with immediate recognition, and has maintained its high standard to the present time.

During the first half of the century many other magazines of more or less temporary renown had made their appearance. Notable among these was *The Casket*, published in Philadelphia from 1821 to 1839, and continued as *Graham's Magazine* till 1850; *The Gentle-man's Magazine*, also from Philadelphia, 1837–1840; *The Dial*, the organ of the transcendentalists in Boston from 1821 to 1844; and *The Knickerbocker Magazine* in New York, established in 1832. *Harper's Magazine*, established in New York in 1850, was the first periodical in America to make illustrated articles a regular feature. It has had much to do with the tremendous advance of the last half-century in the methods of book and magazine illustration. Beginning at a time when the uncouth wood-cut was the only picture made use of, its files furnish a most complete record of every step, to a stage of perfection which, by common consent, makes our American magazines the best illustrated in the world. Aside from its pictures, *Harper's Magazine* is in the front rank of the more popular literary periodicals.

In 1871 *Scribner's Magazine* appeared as a competitor to *Harper's* along the same lines. On the death of its first editor, J. G. Holland, in 1881, its name was changed to the *Century*, which we know to-day as one of our leading magazines.

Within the last quarter-century so many magazines of merit have been established as to make impossible any discussion of them within the limits set for this work. In 1903 there were in all 15,129 weekly publications; 281 semi-monthly; 2824 monthly; and 163 quarterly, issued in the United States.

Scientific Magazines

Appendix L.   Specialization was for many years a slow movement in the case of American periodicals, and it was not until 1818 that we had a scientific journal. In that year *The American Journal of Science* was first issued at New Haven, Connecticut, under the editorship of the elder Silliman. For fifty years it practically had the field to itself, and served for the publication of the scientific productions of the country. In 1867 the *American Naturalist* made its appearance; and five years later, *Appleton's Popular Science Monthly* (now the *Popular Science Monthly*). In 1883 *Science* was established, a weekly publication of greatest value in the field of general science.

A. A. A. S. p. 554.

The Scientific American, also weekly, first published in 1846, should not be omitted from any list of general scientific journals of wide influence. Although it publishes few, if any, lengthy scientific papers, it has probably done more for the lay reader than has any one of the others mentioned, unless it be the *Popular Science Monthly.*

An important move by our public press, hardly noticeable more than a decade ago, is that of publishing regular courses of study, and special articles with a direct educational purpose. This represents a stage in journalism at which an important educational factor becomes conscious that it is such, and plans, in a definite manner, to increase its influence. It makes education one of its aims, rather than a mere by-product, as it had formerly been.

Although the more pretentious magazines are participating in the move, it seems to be the daily and weekly newspapers that are making the most of it. Of the latter, a great majority of the better class discuss regularly the Sunday school lessons, and not a few have special departments devoted to literature, art, music, and science.

The most elaborate attempt which has yet been made to give a direct educational value to the daily paper is through " The Home Study Circle " established in 1897, by Dr. Seymour Eaton of the Drexel Institute. Under its direction, two or three columns of some of the principal daily papers of Chicago, Cleveland, Cincinnati, Buffalo, Pittsburg, Louisville, Memphis, Minneapolis, St. Louis, Denver, Los Angeles, besides many smaller cities, are, or have been, devoted to regular courses of study prepared by some of the leading thinkers of the country. Nearly one hundred separate courses have been offered under the direction of the Circle, and it has been conservatively estimated that more than one hundred thousand people follow the work, either closely or incidentally.

Rep. Com. Ed.
1899-1900.

The form and style of presentation have been direct and simple, making it possible for any person of average intelligence to follow it. Although such work cannot be considered as in any way an equivalent of proper study done under the immediate personal influence of a competent instructor, it is, nevertheless, not to be ignored in any catalogue of our educational forces.

REFERENCES

American Newspaper Press. Critic, 21 : 98–100. American Periodicals. Dial, 13 : 203-204. — *Bellew*, F. H. J. Old Time Magazines. Cosmopolitan, 12 : 343. — Deland, Margaret. A Menace to Literature. N. A. Rev. 158 : 157. — Dutton, F. S. Educational Resources of the Community. Ed. Rev. 21 : 17–25. — *Eaton*, C. H. Decade of Magazine Literature. Forum, 26 : 211–216. *Education by Newspapers.* R. of R.'s, 26 : 233. Education through the Press and Public Organizations. Ed. 23 : 270-276. Growth of Magazine Literature. Harper, 70 : 165-168. *Half Forgotten Magazines.* Chaut. 33 : 28-33. Influences of Colleges and Newspapers. Dial, 31 : 501-502. List of American Magazines published in the Eighteenth Century. L. J. 14 : 373-376. *Newspaper Press, History of.* Eclec. Rev. 91 : 720. — *Palfrey*, J. G. Periodical Literature of the United States. N. A. Rev. Oct., 1834, 39 : 277-301. — Porter, Noah, in Books and Reading (chapter on newspaper and periodicals), 341-359. — *Powell*, E. P. Home Education. Ed. 14 : 10-15. Use of Periodicals. L. J. 20 : C 12-16.

CHAPTER XXVI

THE summer schools of our country are a growth of the present generation, and are the natural and logical result of conditions which have only come with the later years of our history. The most fundamental of these is the long summer vacation, for summer instruction is essentially vacational — and the summer vacation enjoyed to-day by so many is not a very ancient institution: next important as a factor which has given rise to the summer school is the increasing desire on the part of the people to utilize to the best advantage the leisure time, which changing social conditions have left at their disposal; and a third which has undoubtedly been an influencing factor in summer instruction at the colleges and universities, is the desire to have the great educational plants used all the year round, and not a part of the year only. Such being the conditions, and the feelings of the people, the educational machinery was certain to adapt itself to them, and the present heterogeneous mass of institutions for summer instruction was the result, as indigenous to the soil as is our indian corn, and nearly as prolific. The varying needs of many classes of people have given rise to institutions of many types. Dr. Stephen B. Weeks classifies them as follows: —

Rep. Com. Ed. 1894–1895, pp. 1483–1503.

(1) Schools that teach only a single branch of knowledge; as ancient and modern languages, religion, philosophy, library economy, natural sciences, etc.

(2) Schools of the arts; as drawing, industrial art, manual training, music, oratory, etc.

(3) Professional, normal, or schools of methods, where the training of teachers is the main idea — summer schools of pedagogy.

(4) General; where all or nearly all the subjects of the school curriculum are treated, and where the idea of study is combined with that of rest and recreation.

(5) Summer sessions at colleges and universities.

Again from the standpoint of control and maintenance they may be divided into several classes: —

(1) Private, including all schools maintained wholly by fees or tuitions paid by the students; or by endowment made especially for carrying on summer work. This class includes by far the greater number of summer schools, varying from the modest coaching establishment, to Chautauqua and the great national summer schools.

(2) College or university, which are usually general in their character.

(3) State, which are generally devoted to the training of teachers, and include the so-called teachers' institutes of all kinds.

In the matter of fees, they range all the way from those asking a sufficient sum to place the institution upon a paying financial basis, to the state schools, which are usually free, or practically so.

The variation in length of session is as great as that of fee, in some cases being but a week or even less, while in others covering the whole three summer months.

These various institutions have before them the task of providing instruction: —

(1) For those persons who are desirous of adding to their intellectual attainments, but are otherwise unable to obtain professional assistance in their studies. The instruction, when it has this end, is generally popular in its character, and limited to those subjects in which

instruction of a fairly satisfactory character can be obtained without the necessity of a prolonged and continuous effort; and in which the advantages of summer study can be supplemented by reading pursued during the rest of the year. Schools especially intended for this class of students usually restrict their courses to such subjects as literature, history, physical training, elocution, etc. In these schools, too, the element of recreation is an important one. The various Chautauqua assemblies and popular schools at summer resorts belong to this class.

(2) For undergraduate college students and others seriously working for an academic degree. Many such students are thus enabled to save time in gaining academic distinction, and others to gain such distinction which would otherwise be impossible. The schools of this class are usually directly associated with some degree-conferring institution.

(3) For students pursuing some definite branch of instruction, but unable because of local peculiarities or geographical difficulties to carry on the work desired. The seaside and lakeside laboratories, as well as schools for geological study and surveying, located especially for those ends, belong to this class.

(4) For teachers, who wish to place themselves in line for promotion by devoting their time to general pedagogical study or to academic subjects closely associated. In this class of schools the element of inspiration is an important one. In them teachers of all classes, from the college to the kindergarten, meet and profitably exchange experiences, doing much to help each other out of the ruts into which the teacher is prone to fall. The Martha's Vineyard Summer Institute is a type of this class of school, at which 80 per cent or more, of all in attendance, are teachers.

In treating in detail some of the more important summer schools of the past and present, I shall roughly follow the first classification given above.

1. Schools at which but a Single Branch is Taught

a. Biological Sciences

This class of schools, though not so numerous to-day as some of the others, was the first to enter the field. The principal *raison d'être*, especially of those of science, has been some particularly favorable geographical location. As may be seen from the table on page 538, in the rapid increase in the number of institutions for summer work from 1890 to 1896 and the subsequent decline in numbers, schools of this class have much more than maintained their proportion of the whole, being 13 per cent in 1893, and 21 per cent in 1900.

Such schools originated as circles for investigation, with instruction only an incident to the other more important feature. As early as 1869 a group of professors and advanced students, mostly from the scientific schools of Harvard, made a trip to Colorado for the purpose of investigation; and during the next four years groups of students under Professor Marsh and other Yale instructors made similar excursions, carrying on scientific investigations of much value and collecting material which is deposited in the Museum of Natural History at New Haven. It was also the custom at about this time for Professor Orton, of Vassar College, to spend a part of each summer with a number of his students in different places of geographical interest; but these instances of educational instruction, though of much real value, can hardly be dignified with the title of Summer Schools.

It remained for Louis Agassiz, the great teacher and naturalist of Harvard University to take the next step, — in collaboration with his colleague Dr. N. S. Shaler, — by the establishment of the Anderson School, on Penikese Island. We can hardly overestimate the influence of this school, short-lived though it was, upon the development of scientific thought in our country; and since it was the first American summer school, it is deserving of more than passing mention.

It was first opened in the summer of 1873, with forty-three students in attendance.

For years Agassiz had been convinced that if any real advance was to be made in the biological sciences, it must be through the study of the lower forms of marine life, and that to study them successfully one must do more than make an occasional collecting excursion to the seaside. He believed that nothing less than a seaside laboratory, where the investigator might spend at least the summer months in residence, would answer the purpose, and he set about to secure such a laboratory. His first thought was that the island of Nantucket would be the most suitable place for such an enterprise, and even at the time of issuing his first printed announcement, expected to hold the session there. The Massachusetts legislature, however, after urgent appeal, devoted the little island of Penikese—one of the westernmost of the Elizabeth islands, south of Buzzards Bay and about halfway from Woods Holl, Massachusetts, and Newport, Rhode Island—to the purpose.

Through the generosity of Mr. John Anderson of New York City, Agassiz was able to erect a large, though cheaply built structure, for laboratory and dormitory purposes, and the dream of his later years was fulfilled. The prospectus of the first session contains the names of many men since famous as biologists, and shows the character of the work attempted. But for one summer, and one summer only, was the great naturalist the visible inspiration of the laboratory at Penikese. Before the next he had died, and although the laboratory was kept open under the direction of his son, Alexander Agassiz, the genial, moving spirit was gone, and at the end of that season the whole project was abandoned.

Of the man himself, but a word is necessary: As a

Rep. Com. Ed. 1891-1892, p. 899.

Richard Bliss,
Pop. Sci. Mo.
4 : 618.

naturalist, Professor Agassiz was untiring in his devotion to his favorite pursuits. He worked early and late, often denying himself the most necessary rest and recreation, and his remarkably strong constitution sustained him under a strain that would have quickly proved fatal to a man of less vigor. His mind was preëminently great. Gifted with a wonderfully retentive memory, he combined with it a power of generalization and quick perception that places him next to Cuvier, whose disciple he was, and whom he seemed to imitate. In his methods of investigation he was thoroughly honest, and though many might differ from him in his conclusions, none could deny the absolute integrity of his convictions. In his intercourse with his fellow-men he was extremely affable and genial, and especially so to the young. With inexperience he was most patient and painstaking, never wearying in his efforts to aid.

Tolerant of ignorance when associated with modesty, he had little patience with arrogance and ignorance combined. His students will all bear witness to the unvarying cheerfulness and ready sympathy in him they had learned to look up to as their master.

Of his last summer at the Penikese *The Nation* said, editorially : —

Nation, 4 : 175.

" Professor Agassiz himself worked as he always does, hard and almost uninterruptedly : in fact too hard for his health. He was almost constantly in the laboratory encouraging and aiding alike the students and the other teachers, or spending hours in elucidating points in the structure of animals which he had studied all his life : and he lectured nearly every day, at times even twice a day, for he attended every lecture given by others, and at its close, or even in its course, would rise to add a word of confirmation or doubt and, as upon several occasions, would continue for half an hour upon matter suggested by the lecture. In fact nothing could be more genial than the intercourse between the respected chief and all connected with the school. From what has been said it will be seen that the enumeration of Agassiz's subjects would not be easy. A series of admirable lectures upon glaciers, embodying much that has never been published, and a course upon radiates, and a third upon the egg, formed nuclei, around which were grouped discourses upon general topics and special questions such as were never before brought within the same time. And when it is to be remembered that the school opened July 8 and the last student departed August 28, and that during these seven weeks, Professor Agassiz was absent less than one week, it will be evident that when he asked coöperation of others he did not mean to rest content with directing their labors : but it is to be hoped that another year he may be willing to give himself more of the rest he so sadly needs." (Written three months before Agassiz's death.)

Although the laboratory itself at Penikese was but short-lived, the spirit which actuated it still survives in a considerable line of descendants. Of these, the one most closely related is, perhaps, Professor Alexander Agassiz's laboratory established in Newport, Rhode Island, in 1877. Although elaborately appointed for work in biological investigation, it is private, and since but very few students are admitted, and those only under special terms, it can hardly be legitimately classed among the summer schools of the country. In 1879 a summer school of biology was established at Salem by the Peabody Academy of Science, but after holding five sessions, was discontinued. Another early revival of the Penikese idea was the Chesapeake Zoological Laboratory of the Johns Hopkins University. This has been essentially migratory in its nature, the first two sessions (1878–1879) being held at Fort Wood, an artificial island of some six acres in extent, situated in Chesapeake Bay, near Hampton Roads ; the next five or six, for the most part at Beaufort, North Carolina ; and then, after a few years' discontinuance for want of financial support, was reorganized in 1891. Since its beginning this school has been under the direction of Dr. W. K. Brooks of Johns Hopkins, and its contributions to science contain many of the strongest papers ever prepared by American investigators.

It was not until 1881 that facilities were offered to others than trained investigators or advanced students at any of the summer laboratories. During that summer and a few succeeding ones, a laboratory was conducted at Annisquam, Massachusetts, at which elementary work was offered. It was supported in part by the Boston Society of Natural History, and in part by the Women's Educational Association of the same city. These societies, after having conducted the Annisquam Laboratory successfully for six years, felt that they were warranted in calling upon the patrons of science for financial aid in support of larger things, and in 1888, through a combination of interests, The Marine Biological Laboratory was established at Woods Holl, Massachusetts, and the work at Annisquam discontinued. Since that time the laboratory at Woods Holl has been the leading summer biological workshop of the country. The buildings are large, commodious, and adequately equipped, while a steam launch and rowboats are kept constantly in service for collecting purposes. Private rooms in the laboratory building, furnished with aquaria and other apparatus, are provided for investigators of repute free of charge. Both advanced and elementary instruction are provided in general laboratories, and students may spend nearly the entire three summer months at the laboratory upon special arrangement, though the instruction is for but six weeks. General evening lectures are of frequent occurrence, and on the whole, the laboratory has done invaluable service to the cause of biological instruction and investigation in our country.

During the last decade and a little more, many admirable summer schools of science, similar to those which we have discussed, have sprung up wherever conditions seemed to be especially favorable for scientific investigation. Of these, the Brooklyn Institute Biological Laboratory, founded at Cold Spring Harbor in 1890, is among the best. From the beginning, instruction has been given in elementary zoology and botany, comparative embryology and bacteriology, although the laboratory by no means neglects the side of original investigation. At South Harpswell, Maine, and in the Blue Hills of Milton, Massachusetts, modest centres for biological study have been started. In Rhode Island a summer school for nature study has been maintained since 1899 at Kingston. In the Middle West, the University of Illinois conducted a freshwater laboratory at its biological station on the Illinois River for two or three seasons, and the University of Indiana has maintained a similar laboratory at Winona Lake, Indiana, since 1890. Still farther west, the State University of Montana established a biological station at Big Forks in 1899, and on the Pacific coast, the Hopkins Seaside Laboratory has been open for students since 1892.

b. Philosophy

Another early summer school of the class giving instruction in a single subject, of much importance in its day because of the eminent men associated with it was the Concord Summer School of Philosophy, established in 1879 at Concord, Massachusetts, under the direction of Mr. Bronson Alcott. There were associated with him in the work Mr. S. H. Emery, B. F. Sanborn, Dr. W. T. Harris, Dr. B. F. Jones, Ralph Waldo Emerson, Thomas Wentworth Higginson, Benjamin Pierce, Thomas Davidson, Noah Porter, Mrs. Julia Ward Howe, and a whole galaxy of other notables. Ten sessions were held, the work being discontinued upon the death of Mr. Alcott; but during its life the school stood for the highest type of extra-university instruction.

The following paragraph shows the importance of the task to which the school devoted itself.

" Exactly what we are about, what is the value of our civilization, and toward what ideals we are working, are things not so clear as they might be, and there is great need of keener analysis and more careful thinkers to prevent our drifting blindly — to prevent, that is, not by obstructive conservatism, but by progressive comprehension. To educate for this purpose, then, is another object of the school. In order to know what to teach and what to receive we must seek through philosophy the one central principle on which the world — the universe — rests. Then we have to trace this back again from that, through all its manifestations in religion, governments, literature, art, science, and manners. This is manifestly a large job, and the Concord School does not expect to carry it out so that it will never have to be done again, but rather to set people in the right path, so that they can keep on doing it forever. At a time when Germany is overpowered by the influence of Mill, Spencer, and Darwin, and the genius of materialism is getting so strong a hold everywhere, it is interesting to find that the Concord School reasserts with breadth and penetration the supremacy of the mind. . . . But it must not be supposed that the school is hostile to science; on the contrary, it approves and heartily sympathizes with it in its great work, which, properly regarded, it considers tributary to the highest ends of existence."

Harper's Weekly, Aug. 19, 1881.

After the closing of the Concord Summer School, Mr. Thomas Davidson, the well-known philosopher and educational interpreter, took up the idea, and for some years conducted a similar school at Farmington, Connecticut. Later he removed it to the little village of Glenmore, in the heart of the Adirondacks. The scope was finally somewhat broadened, and covered the whole field of the culture sciences. The aim was stated as both scientific and practical.

" The former it seeks to reach by means of lectures on the theory and history of the culture science, and by classes, conversations, and carefully directed private study. The latter it endeavors to reach by encouraging its members to conduct their lives in accordance with the highest ascertained ethical laws, to strive after 'plain living and high thinking, to discipline themselves in simplicity, kindliness, thoughtfulness, helpfulness, regularity, and promptness.'"

For the single session of 1892 there were, among other lecturers at this school, Hon. W. T. Harris, Thomas Davidson, Professor Josiah Royce, John Dewey, and J. Clarke Murray. The school is not now in existence.

The School of Applied Ethics at Plymouth, Massachusetts, started in 1892, was similar in character to the last two mentioned. Professor Felix Adler of New York City was its organizer and first director. The main purpose of the school was the promotion of historical and scientific study in those branches of knowledge which relate to human conduct. During the three sessions of the school — for that of 1895 was its last — there were present as lecturers among others the now presidents Wilson of Princeton, Wheeler of California, Andrews of Nebraska, and Wright of Clark College; Albert Shaw of the *Review of Reviews*, Professors Giddings, Burgess, Smith, and Jackson of Columbia, Jencks of Cornell, and Taussig of Harvard.

The school was a success to the end, and at the close of its last session it was fully expected to resume the work the next season; but circumstances arose which made that seem unwise.

Of a nature somewhat similar to these schools of philosophy was the Monsalvat School of Comparative Religion, established at Eliot, Maine, in the summer of 1896, at which the history of religious beliefs, both Oriental and Occidental, was made a special object of study. The school was discontinued in 1901.

Important among the summer gatherings of religious students is the Northfield Summer Conference for college students, first called together in 1886 by Dr. Moody, the evangelist, at his home at Mt. Vernon, Massachusetts. On that occasion more than 250 students, representing 225 different institutions, met to spend a part of their vacation in the study of the Bible and of practical methods in Christian work. The place has become memorable as the birthplace of the student volunteer movement for foreign missions. Much of the time of those in attendance at the conference is spent in athletic pursuits, although regular courses of lectures are given, as well as special addresses upon many phases of religious work. The work at Northfield proved of so much value that similar summer institutes have been started in other parts of the country; that at Lake Geneva in 1888 and another at Knoxville, Tennessee, in 1892. Through platform addresses, Bible-class sessions, conferences for the consideration of special topics, and informal discussions, the following ends are sought: " Promotion of more thorough Bible study, both on the part of the individual student and in class work; development of a more effective form of organized Christian work in colleges and universities; training of picked men who shall be qualified to be leaders in such organizations." In connection with the Lake Geneva Conference is held the Y. M. C. A. Secretarial Institute and Training School.

c. Languages

The Sauveur Summer College of Languages was the first of its kind to be established in this country, and is, according to its founder, "the parent and prototype of all the schools of the same order that have since been established." The first session was held at Plymouth, New Hampshire, in 1876; those from 1877 to 1883 at Amherst, Massachusetts, where it has held sessions, with the exception of one or two summers, ever since. It is the aim of the school to supply the wants of the following classes : —

First: American teachers of foreign languages who wish to gain hints and suggestions on the best methods of teaching those languages.

Second: Professional and business men and women who would like to devote a brief vacation to the study of the humanities.

Third: Students who desire to begin the study of a language, or to make up deficiencies, or to gain a greater familiarity with languages.

Although the work of the school is primarily linguistic, other branches are offered. In 1895 the school was joined with the Amherst College Summer School. For four years, beginning with 1887, there was a so-called Berlitz Summer School of Languages held at Asbury Park, New Jersey, with a faculty of a dozen or more. Beyond these there have been no attempts, more than local in their character, to maintain summer schools devoted exclusively to the languages.

d. Library Science

Although special summer instruction in library science has been offered in the Amherst College Summer School by the librarian, Mr. W. I. Fletcher, continuously since 1891, and at the summer session of the State University of Wisconsin since 1895, it was not until 1896 that a summer school was established devoted entirely to the needs of the library. This was at Albany, New York, in connection with the New York State Library. Melvil Dewey is its director. The session is six weeks in length, and the subjects offered include cataloguing and the classification of books, practical work in the reference and loan departments, bookbinding and library economy.

Summer courses in library science were offered in the Ohio State University in 1898; at Chautauqua Lake and in the University of Iowa since 1901; and by the Indiana Public Library commission at Indianapolis beginning with 1902.

2. Schools of the Arts

Such subjects as art, music, oratory, and the various æsthetic handicrafts were found to adapt themselves readily to the conditions of summer work, and schools of this class were early in the field, though never in large numbers. Among the first was the Lexington (Massachusetts) Normal Music School. This school, established in 1883, soon had a national reputation.

The School of Expression, founded at Martha's Vineyard three years later, and with subsequent sessions in Boston, Saratoga Springs, Lancaster (Massachusetts), and Newport (Rhode Island), was also very successful with its work. Vocal training, phonology and articulation, vocal expression, physical training, pantomimic expression, extemporaneous speaking, public reading, methods of training the voice, vocal expression, the history of pedagogy in its relation to expression, as well as the study of various English classics, formed the basis of its courses.

The Boston School of Oratory, for special instruction in the synthetic philosophy of expression held a summer session in 1890.

The Monroe College of Oratory, also of Boston, which held a summer session in 1887, was later merged with the Martha's Vineyard Summer Institute, and bears the name of the Emerson School of Oratory. In 1900 there were nine summer schools coming under this class.

3. SCHOOLS OF PEDAGOGICAL METHODS

Since school-teachers, as a rule, are more certain of a long summer vacation than are any other classes of intellectual workers, the summer schools early found them their most numerous and enthusiastic patrons. Questions having to do with the theory and practice of teaching are of such a character, too, as to admit of profitable discussion under summer school conditions, and a very large and increasing proportion of our public school teachers are spending at least an occasional summer in study.

The proportion of summer institutions which are especially catering to their needs is very rapidly increasing. The table given later in this chapter shows that in 1893 but six per cent of the centres for summer study laid the principal stress upon pedagogical courses, while in 1900 the percentage was nineteen, with a steady and gradual increase from one to the other. These figures do not include county and other institutes for teachers, required by the laws of the various states.

Among the summer schools catering principally to the needs of the teachers, the Martha's Vineyard Summer Institute ranks among the first, not only in point of time, but in the importance of its work. It must be placed second only to the great assemblies at Chautauqua in the breadth of its influence and in the number of students who have been in attendance. The school was started in the summer of 1878, and has continued its work uninterruptedly ever since.

The originator of the enterprise was Colonel Homer B. Sprague, at that time master of the Girl's High School in Boston. In 1882 he was succeeded by Dr. W. J. Rolfe, the Shakespearian editor, and later by Dr. W. D. Morey.

More than fifty courses of instruction have been offered during a single season. These may be roughly divided into (1) methods for elementary studies, (2) methods for secondary studies, (3) academic branches. Among the latter are the natural sciences, modern and ancient languages, mathematics, English literature, history and civil government, vocal and instrumental music, drawing, painting, and sloyd. The school has several substantial buildings of its own, is incorporated under the laws of Massachusetts, and is, on the whole, one of the most substantial institutions for summer work in the country outside of the larger universities. During its history, nearly every educator of note in the country has appeared upon its platform, and the inspiration to the teachers in general from such a contact is incalculable.

In the summer of 1885 there was founded at Saratoga, New York, the National Summer School of Methods. Since the school at Martha's Vineyard did not restrict its offerings solely to the needs of the teachers, this was the first distinct and special summer school of methods in the country, and grew out of the belief that many teachers, anxious to learn better methods, could improve their work by observing the work of others of long experience, and by studying the art of teaching under practical educators of national reputation.

The faculty was made up of educational experts from all parts of the country. After three seasons, this school united with the one at Round Lake, and sessions were held at both places. In 1890 the two schools combined with a summer school for teachers at Glens Falls, where sessions were continued until 1897.

Another similar institution for teachers of more than local influence was the Virginia Summer School of Methods, at Bedford, Virginia. The first of its seven or eight sessions was in 1888. The school was strictly pedagogic in its character, and the needs and capacities of all grades of teachers were considered.

In addition to these more pretentious schools for pedagogical instruction, less important ones have sprung up in large numbers in every part of the country, many of them leading a precarious existence for a season or two, only to go under, or, as in some instances, to coalesce with some other institution. The state has, however, in many cases, recognizing the earnest desire on the part of the teaching force for good instruction during the summer months, more than made up for the depletion in the ranks of private schools of pedagogy by establishing summer sessions at the state normal schools, and also by improving the character of the work done at the county institutes for teachers.

Of these two methods of state instruction during the

summer months, the former would undoubtedly be the more efficient, if generally carried out. At present, scarcely more than a dozen public normal schools have a summer session, but as is the case with the state universities, the feeling is growing that the valuable equipment should not lie idle for a third of the year, and without doubt the number doing so will rapidly decrease.

Where summer work is carried on, it does not vary materially from that of the regular school year.

The first teachers' institute — so called — was held by J. S. Denman, superintendent of schools for Tompkins County, New York, in 1843, lasting two weeks. During the activity of Horace Mann in Massachusetts they flourished, and his writings upon the subject are among his most interesting contributions to educational literature.

N. Y. School
Report, 1843.
p. 613.

Teachers' Inst.
p. 392.
Appendix I.

4. SUMMER SCHOOLS HAVING A GENERAL COURSE

This class of schools has been from the beginning by far the most numerous. The table on page 538 shows that in 1893 76 per cent of all the schools tabulated were within it. Although their proportion is decreasing, in 1900 more than one-half of the whole number in the field gave courses of a general nature. In the table already alluded to, this class of schools has been subdivided into three groups: First, Private and proprietary schools other than the Chautauqua; second, Chautauqua; third, General summer sessions at colleges and universities.

The relative distribution of these three groups within the class has changed materially within the last four years, the tendency being away from the usually poorly organized and equipped *omnibus* summer assemblies, and in the direction of the summer facilities offered by the colleges and universities. In 1893, 39 per cent of the summer schools were in general of the former type, while but 10 per cent were in the field seven years later. Meanwhile, at the beginning of the same period, the colleges furnished but 8 per cent of the summer institutions for study, ending it with 24 per cent in 1900. This readjustment means much. Not necessarily that the former type did not occupy a field of usefulness, for no one can question that they did, but that they have, as a class, served as appetizers to large numbers of persons who could not satisfy their intellectual hunger upon the viands provided, and have moved on to better furnished tables. They have, in fact, created a demand which will in the end be supplied almost entirely through the summer sessions of old, established institutions. The summer school has found itself and has come down to business. There are, however, among the survivors of this class of summer schools, some relatively ancient and certainly honorable institutions, while equally as worthy have fallen by the wayside. Among the survivors of prominence to-day is the Catholic Summer School of America. This school owes its origin to a demand on the part of Catholics for an institution similar to Chautauqua, where busy men and women might find opportunity for needed improvement either by summer assemblies or courses of winter reading. The first session was held at New London, Connecticut, in 1892. In 1893 the organization was incorporated under the laws of New York, and what has to-day the aspect of a permanent and valuable centre of summer work established at Plattsburg, New York, on the shores of Lake Champlain. The school enjoys all the privileges granted to any institution by the University of the State of New York, and is a part of its extension department.

Besides the general literary courses, series of lectures are offered each year by men prominent in the Catholic church, upon religious topics. Meetings of the various societies of the church are also held during the session of the school. It is intended that the institution shall become the quasi parent of a great series of Catholic summer schools throughout the English-speaking world. To meet the demand for such institutions, Catholics of the West have established the Columbian Catholic Summer School at Madison, Wisconsin; and another similar institution, meeting in the winter, holds its sessions at New Orleans, Louisiana.

At Colorado Springs, Colorado, in 1892, a very promising institution of the general type was started under the title of the Colorado Summer School of Science, Philosophy, and Languages. Situated as it was at the foot of Pike's Peak, with every facility for associated outing, it attracted large numbers of people during the five or six years of its existence. It had as instructors and lecturers, Presidents Woodrow Wilson, E. B. Andrews, W. De Witt Hyde, William L. Slocum, and J. H. Baker. Professors William James, R. T. Ely, C. E. Bessey, E. W. Bemis, W. B. Rolfe, Katharine Lee Bates, Katharine Coman, W. D. Todd, and many others.

Chautauqua

The most elaborate organization offering summer work in this country, if not the most comprehensive educational organism in the world, is that comprehended under the Chautauqua movement. A variety of methods for the popularization of education are embraced by it. The almost marvellous growth of the movement within a few years offers a striking example of what the economists characterize as an "effective demand" for higher education. One writer has said : —

" The ramifications of Chautauqua would stagger belief did we not know steam and electricity have developed the world into the round table of these latter days, and with their weaver's shuttle laced together the thoughts of men. Chautauqua is a marvellous illustration of the fact that often great social and economic forces flow with The New Eng. Mag. 8 : 94.

a tidal sweep over communities only half conscious of them. Its one hundred thousand registered students, half of whom are between the ages of thirty and forty years, and its practically endless courses, make the home college the realization of a World University, the summer assembly being its visible centre. About one in every thousand of the people of the United States owns the shibboleth Chautauqua, while more than one in every hundred visits its yearly gatherings. It exists in every state and territory of the Union."

Historically speaking, the whole movement is the outgrowth of a religious camp-meeting which resolved itself into a Sunday School Assembly in the summer of 1874, at Chautauqua Lake, New York.

The regular summer meetings have been held there during the months of July and August every year since. The Chautauqua Literary and Scientific Circle (C. L. S. C.) was organized in 1878, the summer college in 1879, and the correspondence college in 1885. The whole movement looks toward general culture, not special training. The following tabular statement of the Chautauqua system explains its many ramifications.

Home reading and study

1 *The Chautauqua literary and scientific circle.* A four years' course of general reading. [Certificate granted. Does not count for degree.]

2 *Specialized courses* for continued reading and study. [Certificate does not count for degree.]
- History.
- Literature.
- Science.
- Art.
- Pedagogy. Teachers' reading union.

3 *School of theology.* Correspondence instruction. [Degree B.D.] Rigid examinations personally supervised. No honorary degrees.]
- Hebrew and Old Testament.
- Greek and New Testament.
- Biblical and doctrinal theology.
- Ecclesiastical history.
- Homiletics and pastoral theology.
- Christian science, life and literature.

4 *College of liberal arts.* Correspondence instruction in preparatory and college studies. [Degrees of B.A., etc.]
- Latin, Greek, French, German, English, mathematics, psychology, political economy, history, physical science, geology, and biology.

Sixteen courses and rigid personally supervised examinations are required to secure the degrees B.A., B.S., etc.

Correspondence and residence combined complete a system of academic study looking toward the degrees of B.A. and B.S.

Summer study and rational recreation at Chautauqua

1 *College of liberal arts.* [No degrees except through correspondence department.] Personal instruction by well-known men in all departments mentioned under (4) above.

2 *School of methods in teaching.*
- Psychology.
- Pedagogic principles.
- Applications and methods.

3 *Schools of sacred literature.* Study of the Bible as a great classic and inspired book.

4 *Classes in* Art, music, physical culture, elocution, kindergarten, etc.

5 *Lecture courses* on the university extension model. Progressive courses by one lecturer. No extra fee is charged. The attendance is large.

6 *Public lectures and addresses* by men and women prominent in various departments of life.

7 *Recreative and æsthetic elements,* concerts, dramatic recitals, stereopticon entertainments, etc.

At the more recent summer meetings the courses —
and there are scores if not hundreds of them — are
given under the following divisions : —

1. School of English Language and Literature.
2. School of Modern Languages.
3. School of Classical Languages.
4. School of Mathematics and Science.
5. School of Psychology and Pedagogy.
6. School of Religious Pedagogy.
7. School of Music.
8. School of Fine Arts.
9. School of Expression.
10. School of Physical Education.
11. School of Domestic Science.
12. School of Practical Arts.

In each department the strongest men and women
from every part of this country and abroad are secured,
and nearly every one of eminence has been heard from
the Chautauqua platform.   For years President William
Harper of the University of Chicago was at the head
of the whole movement, and later Bishop John H. Vincent has been the chancellor.   Chautauqua degrees
are given, and diplomas are granted those who have
pursued certain courses of study for a series of years.
The coördinating instrument of the organization is *The
Chautauquan*, a monthly magazine of much merit, which
contains, in part, the required reading for those regularly registered and following the prescribed courses.
An important feature of the Chautauqua movement is
the system of branch assemblies which are held all over
the country, and which follow as closely as may be the
plan of the central meeting at Chautauqua Lake.   In
1900 there were sixty-six such assemblies, nearly every
state in the Union being represented in the list.

Prominent among them is the Jewish Chautauqua at
Atlantic City, New Jersey.   In it the study of Jewish lit-

erature and history is made a prominent feature, though the regular Chautauqua courses are offered.

Summer Work at Colleges and Universities

The rapid growth in numbers of the institutions, as well as students in attendance, would lead us to believe that here lies the hope of the future in the matter of summer instruction. It had its initiative at Harvard, if we may consider the earlier scientific attempts already mentioned in the chapter as coming within the meaning of the term "Summer School," in 1868. Agassiz and his Penikese experiment, which was really under Harvard control, led to the establishment of scientific courses at Cambridge. Amherst was the next to take up summer work, through the Sauveur School of Languages in 1876. A summer library school only, is now maintained. In 1877 the University of Virginia established summer work in chemistry, and in 1895, in physical training. Nearly ten years elapsed after the first Virginia experiment with summer work, before it found a place in other higher institutions of learning; and then it was the Ohio Wesleyan University at Delaware, Ohio, that took it up. After this date (1886) its growth was comparatively rapid in the colleges and universities, as shown by the following table, which gives years of beginning in most of the institutions in which it is conducted.

Harvard	1868	Ohio University	1892
Amherst	1876	University of Nebraska	1893
University of Virginia	1876	University of North Carolina	1894
Ohio Wesleyan	1886	University of Michigan	1894
University of Wisconsin	1887	University of Missouri	1895
University of Indiana	1890	University of Wooster	1895
Drake University	1890	University of Illinois	1896
University of Chicago	1891	University of California	1899
University of Minnesota	1891	Columbia University	1900
Clark University	1892	University of Cincinnati	1900

This list is not complete, owing to the inability to determine in some cases the year of establishment of summer work. It is, however, approximately correct, other colleges and universities now offering summer courses having begun them since 1900.

In the universities of Chicago and West Virginia, the work of the year is practically continuous, being divided into four terms or "quarters," one of which is in the summer. In all the others a comparatively short summer session is conducted, of from three to nine weeks, bearing no very intimate relation to the work of the remainder of the year. Usually not all departments offer instruction, the selection being determined by local conditions, though pedagogical courses are frequently included. A tuition fee is charged even in the state universities, where instruction is free for the remainder of the year.

Although the summer teaching force is largely made up of instructors from the regular faculty, and the student body to a considerable extent from the undergraduates, the custom is in vogue of popularizing the summer work by means of general lectures, either singly or in courses, thus giving, even to the summer sessions of our colleges and universities, some points of resemblance to schools of the Chautauqua type. Chicago and California have found this plan especially useful in building up an attendance, and it seems fully to meet the needs even of the most studious class of patrons.

In the various bulletins of the Home Educational Department of the University of the State of New York are to be found the most complete statistics bearing upon summer schools, and from them we are able not only to determine at least approximately the number and character for any year of a considerable period of time, but also to note the trend.

Blanks were sent out each year from 1893 to 1900 by the summer school division, and the returns which would indicate roughly the number of schools being maintained were as follows : —

Year,	1893	1894	1895	1896	1897	1898	1899	1900
Schools,	105	180	159	251	181	106	118	105

A mere glance at these figures shows that there has been of recent years a rapid falling off in the number of institutions offering summer work. The climax came in 1896. Dr. Dewey, in discussing these facts says : —

" More careful study shows that the apparent diminution is what we ought to expect and hope for, as the institution takes its place as a permanent factor in our educational system. By checking ●ff the 251 schools in the report for 1896 with the 105 for 1900, it will be seen that the disappearance from the list are largely those of camp-meetings and temporary experiments, made sometimes by well-meaning enthusiasts, sometimes more from commercial motives. Some of these did more harm than good, and their disappearance is itself a gain. Others served a temporary purpose in arousing public interest to a point where the strong endowed institutions were willing to take up the work. They were a *culture*, as the bacteriologists would say, for a new idea, performing the same functions as the briars, poplars, and pinchberries do in the forest after a fire, making it possible for the valuable maple, birch, and beech to get a sound foothold in the soil." Bul. 39, Home Ed. Dept. Univ. of N. Y. p. 402.

In order to determine more specifically just what type of summer school has been worsted in the struggle for permanency and recognition, I went through all the figures in the various reports, and find the percentages of institutions of each of the general classes which have formed the basis of the discussion of this chapter, so far as any characterization is given, to be as follows for each of the years covered by the data : —

	Single Academic Subjects	Religion	Art, Oratory, Music, etc.	Pedago-gical	General		
					Occasional	Chautauqua	College
1893	8	5	4	6	39	29	8
1894	10	11	5	6	32	28	9
1895	11	9	6	6	24	30	13
1896	10	7	6	15	18	24	20
1897	8	8	9	11	16	28	22
1898	12	8	8	17	13	17	23
1899	12	9	10	12	12	19	24
1900	12	8	9	19	10	17	24

This table has been referred to at various points in the chapter and need not be discussed here further than to say that it emphatically supports the above quotation.

In 1893, 68 per cent of the summer schools were of the general or Chautauqua type, while in 1900 but 27 per cent so characterized themselves. Meanwhile summer work offered at the colleges and universities had come up from 8 per cent of the whole number to 24 per cent. The exact number of colleges reporting in the latter year was 26, in 14 of which the summer session is made one of the regular terms of the college year. In 12 it is connected with the institution, but its work forms no part of the regular course.

In 1900, 17 summer schools gave certificates of attendance or statement of work done; 37 gave certificate of proficiency or credit in the institution connected; 10 gave diplomas; 9 issue no certificate or diploma.

Financial support is wholly or in part from the following sources: fees 55, state 20, endowment 3.

Many have no special admission requirements; several say "ability to do the work." In a few cases, the applicants must be teachers. In most of the higher institutions where the session is one of the regular terms, other than matriculated university students are admitted to the work, though only the latter receive credit.

The following table gives the general distribution of summer schools in 1900, together with decades of organization:—

Location	1868–1880	1881–1885	1886–1890	1890–1896	1896–1900	No. of Schools
Northwestern states .	6	2	7	17	10	42
Southern states . . .	1	1	2	5	—	9
North Central states .	4	4	9	16	6	39
Western states . . .	1	—	2	5	2	10
Pacific states . . .	1	—	—	3	2	6
Total	13	7	20	46	20	106

Of those of the Northeastern states, New York leads with 18, followed by Massachusetts with 15. In the Southern states, Virginia had 4 and North Carolina 3. Of the North Central states, Illinois had 12, Ohio, 8, Michigan, 7, and Wisconsin, 6; in the West, Colorado claims 4, and on the Pacific coast 5 of the 6 were in California.

Regarding the trend of summer work in this country, it seems safe to predict that the present tendency away from the disorganized, superficial, camp-meeting type, in the direction of the adequately equipped and maintained institutions where intensive work of dignity and value can be carried on, will continue; and that with some, as is the case now in a few universities, the summer students will more than outrank in numbers those of the rest of the year. Such institutions must, however, be favorably located, as far as climate and other surroundings are concerned, for the element of recreation cannot be neglected.

It is also probably true that the Chautauqua and its type of assemblies will continue to flourish; but except for the mother institution at Chautauqua Lake, and a very few of the other better maintained assemblies, the summer work will soon cease to figure educationally, unless we use that word in its broadest possible meaning.

REFERENCES

Adams, Herbert B. Chautauqua; a Social and Educational Study. Rep. Com. Ed. 1894–1895, 1 : 977–1065. Catholic Summer School of America; ditto, 1065–1077. Summer Schools and University Extension. In Butler's Education in the United States, 1900, 2 : 834–843 (bibliography, pp. 859–860). *Conventions and Summer Gatherings.* American Summer Schools. R. of R.'s, 1892–1903, 5 : 421–422 ; 7 : 539–542 ; 9 : 539–543 ; 11 : 530–534 ; 13 : 553–555 ; 15 : 554–555 ; 17 : 541,668 ; 19 : 583–585 ; 21 : 557–561 ; 23 : 588 ; 25 : 582–585 ; 27 : 590–592 (title not always the same). Democracy of Summer Schools. Ind. 54 : 1911–1913. Friends' Summer School of Religious History. Outl. 65 : 611. Harvard Summer School of Theology. Outl. 68 : 10. — King, Gray R. The Summer School of the South. Outl. 72 : 233–234. — *Lawton*, W. C. Extension and Intension. Dial, 20 : 228–229. New York (State) University. Annual Report of Regents, No. 115, Summer Schools in Index. Home Education. Bulletins of Summer Schools, 1894–1900, Nos. 8, 9, 13, 19, 25, 30, 36, and recent numbers. — *Mullaney*, John F. Summer Schools and their Relation to Higher Education. New York (State) University. Annual Report of Regents, 1893, 107 : 484–490. — *Raymond*, J. H. Continuous University Sessions. N. E. A. 1899 : 819. Select Types of Summer Schools. Rep. Com. Ed. 1899–1900, 1 : 320–324. Some Notes on the Summer Schools. Critic, 11 : 173. Summer Scholarships for Teachers. Nation, ·63 : 384–385. The Summer School. Dial, 18 : 313–315. Summer School in Philanthropic Work. Ann. Am. Acad. 12 : 319–323 ; 20 : 463–465. Summer School of the Illinois Botanical Station. Science, N. S., 7 : 768–769. Summer Schools, 17 : 168. Lit. W. Summer Schools. Music, 18 : 389–390 ; 20 : 273–274. Summer Schools. Rep. Com. Ed. 1890–1891, 1 : 850–852. Summer Schools of Methods. Music, 12 : 621–622. University Summer Term. Ind. 52 : 1879–1880. — **Weeks**, Stephen B. Check List of American Summer Schools. Rep. Com. Ed. 1894–1895, 2 : 1483–1503 (with bibliography). — *Willoughby*, W. W. History of Summer Schools in the United States. Rep. Com. Ed. 1891–1892, 2 : 893–959. — Zueblin, Charles. World's First Sociological Laboratory. Am. J. Sociol. 4 : 577–582.

CHAPTER XXVII

EVENING AND CORRESPONDENCE SCHOOLS

a. EVENING SCHOOLS

IT is impossible to say when evening schools had their origin in America. In a contract made with the schoolmaster of Flatbush, New York, in 1682, the "evening school" is mentioned; but it is probable that Appendix A. allusion is made to the afternoon session of the school, which began at 1 P.M. It is certain, however, that in 1773 evening schools were conducted as private ventures in Salem, Massachusetts, especially for instruction in the mariner's art, although some poor boys were taught to "cypher and to write." It would be strange, too, if similar schools had not existed in other places as modifications of the tutorial plan of instruction which was common; but if so, we have no record of them.

The beginning of the public evening school movement of the present day, which has spread to every part of the country and is represented by nearly one thousand separate schools and more than two hundred thousand pupils, was at Louisville, Kentucky. What seems to have been the first evening school in the country in any way connected with public education, or having any bearing upon its subsequent development, was opened there upon the first Monday in November, 1834, in the basement of one of the city school buildings, and continued in session for four months. It had two teachers, both connected with the day schools, and twenty-two boys as pupils. The school was continued for another year under practically the same conditions, the enrolment being twenty-four boys, most of whom were apprentices in the shops of the city. From that year (1836) until after the Civil War, evening schools were only occasionally opened in Louisville, and then, if the meagreness of attendance is any measure, without much success. Since 1882 there has been no discontinuance of the work.

The next evening school to be established in the country seems to have been a benevolent enterprise, though the only information I can gain regarding it is from Martin's *Evolution of the Massachusetts Schools*, page 218, in which is the statement: —

"In connection with the philanthropic work of the Warren St. Chapel in Boston seems to have been the first evening school in this country, with two pupils."

In 1848, the city of Worcester, Massachusetts, established free evening schools, which have been continued ever since, marking what may be considered the beginning of their successful operation in the country. The example there set was followed but slowly by other cities, for in 1868 the following statement was made by Henry Barnard: —

Barnard, Am. Jour. 19: 439.

"Evening or night schools in elementary branches for pupils over fifteen years of age and in several cities, under special conditions to be determined by the school board, for pupils under fifteen, are provided as a part of the system of public instruction in Chicago, Brooklyn, New York, Lowell, Newark, New Orleans, Providence, Salem, San Francisco, and St. Louis.

As has been shown, Worcester had them previous to this time; and, since they were established in Scranton, Pennsylvania, in 1866, and in Philadelphia and Cambridge, Massachusetts, in 1868, it is evident that Dr. Barnard's statement does not cover all instances. We may therefore presume that the work had been begun in other cities.

The instruction was generally of an elementary character, though the evening high school of New

York, established previous to 1867, was an exception. In this school, grammar, reading, declamation, penmanship, arithmetic, bookkeeping, algebra, geometry, trigonometry, natural philosophy, chemistry, astronomy, history, and political science were taught.

In 1877, eight evening schools were in operation in Baltimore, though they were not continued throughout the winter. In the same year, those in Albany were reported to "have proved almost an entire failure." In Boston, one evening high school was in operation with 1100 pupils, and 16 elementary schools, besides 6 of drawing. New York City was maintaining 222 evening classes with 19,802 pupils enrolled. Since of those who entered, 1111 could not read, and 1374 could not write, the elementary character of the work is evident. In Cincinnati there was one evening high school and 15 elementary schools, with 60 teachers, while Chicago had one high school and 7 elementary schools. The course in the former, in addition to the common branches, included mechanical drawing, bookkeeping, and stenography. St. Louis had in the same year 34 evening schools, and San Francisco, 13.

In 1881 evening schools were in operation in 32 cities, those in Boston having reached an enrolment of about 2500 pupils. The curriculum had broadened, drawing was made much of, and several courses in stenography introduced. In 1890, 808 separate evening schools were in operation in 165 cities and towns, the enrolment being 150,770.

Of these schools Philadelphia had 54; New York (and Brooklyn), 43; Chicago, 38; Cleveland, 38; Scranton, 32; Pittsburg, 24; Boston, 22; and Lawrence, Massachusetts, 20.

For later years it is impossible to tell how many public evening schools are in operation, except in cities of 8000 inhabitants and over. In such, the number was 921 in 1901, with a total of 5115 teachers and 203,000 pupils,

121,886 of whom were males. The North Atlantic states are those in which the evening school movement has gained most headway, seven-ninths of the schools being in that region, and more than four-fifths of the pupils. In the South it is hardly yet under way, there being but 45 schools in all that region; and even in the North Central states, which lead in most classes of school statistics, there are less than 20,000 pupils in the evening schools.

In most of the public evening schools the session is from seven till nine, for a period varying from twelve to twenty-four weeks, usually beginning early in October. In those of an elementary grade, instruction is given in all the common school branches from the A B C's, up. In those cities where there is a rapidly increasing foreign population they are largely patronized by recent immigrants, and the average age of the pupils far exceeds that for any grade of the day schools.

Besides these publicly supported evening schools which form a part of the city school systems, there are in many cities evening schools upon private foundations, and those maintained by religious and philanthropic associations as well as schools of a professional and technical character.

P. 401.

To the former class belongs that of the Cooper Union in New York City, opened in 1859, which has been of inestimable value to thousands of students since. To the second class belongs the system of evening classes maintained in almost every great city of the country, by the Young Men's Christian Association. To the last class belong evening schools of drawing and the fine arts as conducted by art leagues and museums of fine arts all over the country, as well as evening colleges of law, medicine, and pharmacy. As early as 1848 the

P. 400.

Maryland Institute of Art and Design opened its evening classes. And its example has been followed by others.

Along professional lines, twenty-seven schools of law now offer evening courses, while there are nine evening schools of pharmacy, six of medicine, and four of dentistry. Altogether, there are probably three hundred thousand pupils in evening schools of all kinds throughout the country; not a large number when compared with those in the day schools, still an army of earnest workers not to be neglected in any review of educational forces.

b. CORRESPONDENCE SCHOOLS

Instruction through correspondence upon anything like a general plan had its origin in the Chautauqua movement. In the autumn of 1879, at the close of the session of the school of languages, a number of the students, wishing to continue their work through the winter months, prevailed upon their instructor to outline a course of study and direct them through the mails. For want of thorough organization, the plan did not prove a success, largely, no doubt, owing to the fact that no financial contract was involved, the students undervaluing the importance of the direction which they were getting for nothing, and the instructors not feeling called upon to devote much time to gratuitous instruction. Two years later the plan was again taken up, this time upon the basis of a stipulated fee of $3 for each course taken. A director of correspondence work was appointed who should have direct supervision over it, seeing that some regularity of direction and reply was maintained; but this time, too, the plan failed, probably because the fees paid were too small to be an incentive to pupil or teacher.

But the next year the defect was remedied; the fee raised to $10 for each course, and the custom adopted of sending out assignments of work at regular intervals, rather than waiting for a request for such, as had pre-

viously been the case. This plan proved successful.
The interest of the students was maintained, and in 1883
correspondence work was made the basis of instruction
in the Chautauqua University, organized in 1883 and
continued under that name until 1885, when the scope
was broadened and the title changed to the College of

P. 531.

Liberal Arts. Elaborate arrangements were made for
the conduct of its work, and upon its faculty were en-

Rep. Com. Ed.
1902, 1 : 1076.

rolled some of the most eminent educators of the country.   The fees in the college were $5 for matriculation
and $10 for each course. This sum was not sufficient
to defray the expenses connected with the work. Nevertheless, it was continued with success for fifteen years,
until 1900, when in a readjustment of the Chautauqua
affairs, all correspondence work was dropped, thus ending the first successful attempt of the kind made in the
country.

Correspondence work, as it is now carried on, is offered by two distinctly different classes of institutions.
First, colleges and universities which maintain it as a
subordinate department of their regular instructional
work; and second, correspondence schools pure and
simple, which offer no courses for students in residence.

Neither of these two classes is large; but the first is
especially limited in numbers, largely, no doubt, owing
to the lack of time to be devoted to the work on the part
of their instructional force. It is true that in all institutions where students are registered *in absentia*, instruction of a character analogous to that in the
correspondence school is given; but this is usually of
an extremely indefinite nature and can hardly be considered under the head of correspondence courses.
Some few have, however, in the past made, or are at
present making, definite announcement of such work
with the intent of attracting students to it. The state
universities of Wisconsin and West Virginia, Taylor
University at Upland, Indiana, and the Rhode Island

Agriculture College are among those which have tried the experiment and given it up. In but one of the great higher institutions of learning (the University of Chicago) are correspondence courses now emphasized. Impressed with the possibilities of the work during his connection with Chautauqua, President Harper early introduced it at Chicago and has given it complete organization. Twenty-five separate courses were offered in 1902 under the direction of 103 instructors. Among the subjects offered are philosophy, education, history and the political sciences, modern and ancient languages, mathematics, the biological sciences, and theology. The total number of students enrolled for the various years was as follows: 1892–1893, 93; 1893–1894, 209; 1894–1895, 31; 1895–1896, 481; 1896–1897, 641; 1897–1898, 881; 1898–1899, 1015; 1899–1900, 1158; 1900–1901, 1311; 1901–1902, 1485.

The Armour Institute, also in Chicago, is making an important feature of correspondence courses.

In addition to these two Western institutions at least three others in various parts of the country mention correspondence courses in their catalogues. One of these, the Pennsylvania State College, confines its offerings, thirty in all, to agriculture and domestic science. Printed lesson sheets are used, and sent without tuition charge to all enrolled, each sheet being accompanied by questions which must be answered before another will be sent. College certificates in the following general subjects are granted upon the completion of a definitely prescribed amount of work: general agriculture (nine courses), animal industry (seven courses), horticulture (four courses), dairying (six courses), and domestic science subjects (four courses).

In 1897 Baylor University at Waco, Texas, first announced correspondence courses. Two plans are followed: that of direction of the work by means of printed outlines as at Pennsylvania State College; and, second, that of informal direction from time to time as occasion demands. Fees of from $10 to $12 are charged for courses, according to their character.

The New England states seem to be represented in this class of correspondence work solely by the state normal school at Willimantic, Connecticut. Students doing the work are enrolled as non-resident; and any completing the course in a given subject are exempted from the examination in it for the state teachers' certificate. American history, botany, civil government, drawing, English, general history, geography, literature, mathematical geography, mineralogy, penmanship, and physics are the offerings. Sheets containing assignments of work are sent to the student, who does the required reading, and remails the completed lesson. This, accepted, is replaced by another. No course may be extended beyond a year.

The second class of correspondence schools mentioned, that which conducts no residence work, is considerably larger than the first, although just how large, it is impossible to say, since many of them are extremely simple and informal in their character and not included in any list of educational institutions. In some instances they are nothing more than non-resident tutoring establishments of uncertain value and unfixed location, conducted by a single individual. No school within the class is maintained by the public, or even endowed, so far as I can discover, each being conducted as a business enterprise, as are the private commercial schools. On the other hand, there is at least one school within the class having an instructional force of nearly four hundred, and an enrolment of more than three hundred and fifty thousand students within the first ten years of its existence. The real educational value of the work done by such schools has been a matter of debate among students of education. No one could be so impressed with its merits as to consider it the equivalent of study done in residence at the better colleges and special schools; yet we must, it seems to me, recognize them as important factors in educational extension. Probably five hundred thousand persons, the greater number of whom are young men, have made use of the opportunities which they offer within the last ten years, very few of whom would have done any systematic study except for them. Such facts are not to be disregarded in their educational bearing, and although there have been many "get-wise-quick" schemes as well as "get-rich-quick" schemes exploited under the guise of correspondence schools, when all is said, we cannot deny that as a class they have been productive of much good.

There were in 1900, twenty-five separate correspondence schools in operation in the United States. Of these, six were in New York State, seven in the other Eastern states, two in the Southern, and ten in those of the Middle West. In three the courses were largely theological in their nature, in three primarily dealing with the fine arts, in four literary and linguistic, in three legal, in two engineering, while in the others a variety of subjects was given.

Bulletin 276, Univ. of the State of New York.

REFERENCES

Boone, R. G. Evening Schools. In Education in the United States, pp. 269–272. — *Emerson*, R. Development of Evening Schools. Jour. of Ed. 48 : 235. Evening Schools. Bliss Encyclopedia of Social Reform, p. 566. Evening Schools. Circ. Inf. 1885 : 32–40. Evening Schools in the United States. Am. Jour. Ed. 19 : 439. — Fuchs, Otto. Evening Industrial Training Schools. N. E. A. 1885 : 307–310. — *Marble*, A. P. Evening Schools. N. E. A. 1887 : 186. — *Correspondence Schools*. Rep. Com. Ed. 1902, 1 : 1069. United States Education, Bureau of, Evening Schools, in various annual reports.

CHAPTER XXVIII

LEARNED SOCIETIES AND ASSOCIATIONS

In 1743 Benjamin Franklin brought together a little circle of friends at an alehouse in Philadelphia and informally organized a society called *The Junto*, for the discussion of philosophic and scientific questions. In his autobiography he says: —

Franklin, Vol. I, p. 81

"The rules that I drew up required that every member should in turn produce one or more queries on any point of morals, politics, or natural philosophy, to be discussed by the company, and once in three months produce and read an essay of his own writing on any subject he pleased. Our debates were to be under the direction of a president, and to be conducted in the sincere spirit of truth, without fondness for disputes, or desire of victory."

There were but six original members of The Junto, and its meetings were finally discontinued, without any of its proceedings having been published. The interest which had been aroused by it was, however, directly responsible for the establishment, some years later, of *The American Philosophical Society held at Philadelphia for Promoting Useful Knowledge*, incorporated in 1780, which claims as the year of its birth that of the original Junto, 1743. Franklin was the first secretary, and afterward president up to the time of his death. This society, which is still in existence, may justly lay claim to being parent of the very numerous progeny of more than five hundred societies and associations of men and women, who meet at stated intervals for the discussion of problems in every field of human knowledge. Since many of their discussions are printed and accessible to the general reader, our learned societies and associa-

Libraries, p. 482.

tions are proving a veritable clearing-house of scientific thought, the value of which can hardly be overestimated.

The evolution of these societies shows the same tendencies toward specialization that are noticeable in educational organizations. In The Junto, papers might be read upon any subject of the author's choice. Even before the close of the eighteenth century, the few similar circles which had been organized turned their faces, either in the direction of general scientific problems, or of historical discussion. With the growth of special professional classes having restricted interests, this differentiation went on, until now no line of thought is without its learned societies.

All these, with very few exceptions, are voluntary in their nature, having arisen through the natural desire of persons whose interests are similar, to congregate. They have, with one exception, no connection with any branch of the national or state government.

This exception is the *National Academy of Sciences*, which was established by act of Congress in 1863. It is, in a sense, the scientific advisory board of the national government, being required to investigate and report upon scientific questions as requested by Congress. In scientific circles it occupies in this country about the same position as does the Academy of Sciences in France, and the Royal Society in England, election to it being considered the highest honor attainable along scientific lines. Originally the membership was limited to fifty ; but in 1870 the limit was removed, and of late years four new members have been elected annually, giving a total number of nearly one hundred, selected from all branches of science.

The headquarters of the Academy are in Washington, where a stated meeting is held annually. Although the government has but seldom made use of the Academy for scientific purposes, it has served as a valuable stimulus to scientific research throughout the country.

For purposes of study, the other learned societies and associations may be classified roughly under the following heads : —

a. General scientific societies.

b. Historical societies, and those of allied interests.

c. Societies of natural history and the biological sciences.

d. Associations for the study of special subjects.

e. Professional associations.

f. Teachers' associations.

The following table shows the number of existing societies and associations under these various heads, together with the decade of organization of each. It is not complete for the last decade : —

	a	b	c	d	e	f	Total
1890–1900	8	22	6	5	4	12	57
1880–1889	18	43	19	21	20	9	130
1870–1879	15	28	13	7	13	4	83
1860–1869	7	18	6	4	4	9	48
1850–1859	5	18	4	—	4	3	34
1840–1849	2	8	1	1	6	3	21
1830–1839	1	7	2	2	—	—	12
1820–1829	3	6	1	—	5	—	15
1810–1819	1	1	1	—	1	—	4
1800	—	1	—	—	1	—	2
Before 1800	3	1	—	—	—	—	4
Total	63	153	53	40	58	50	410

a. GENERAL SCIENTIFIC SOCIETIES

Of this class the oldest representative, except the American Philosophical Society already mentioned, is the *American Academy of Arts and Sciences* of Boston, Massachusetts, founded in 1780, largely through the influence of John Adams, and having among its charter members, John Hancock, Robert Treat Paine, and Joseph Willard. The stated object was "to promote and encourage the knowledge of antiquities in America, and of the natural history of the country, and to determine the uses to which the various natural productions of the country may be applied; to promote and encourage medical discoveries, mathematical disquisitions, philosophical inquiries and experiments, astronomical, meteorological, and geographical observations, and improvements in agriculture, arts, manufacture, and commerce, and, in fine, to cultivate every art and science which may tend to advance the interest, honor, dignity, and happiness of a free, independent, and virtuous people." The academy has published many volumes of proceedings, and has a large library.

The *Connecticut Academy of Arts and Sciences*, organized in 1799, was the next to follow. Timothy Dwight was its first president, with Noah Webster as secretary, and many notables of New Haven — among them, Governor Trumbull — as original members. This society has been maintained largely through the activity of members of the Yale faculty.

In 1817 the *New York Academy of Sciences* was established. It was the first of a considerable number of societies in various cities to adopt the name "Academy of Science." Four meetings are now held each month, from which have come voluminous reports.

In Brooklyn a similar society was established in 1823, known as the *Brooklyn Academy of Arts and Sciences*, and has been ever since very active in all lines of scientific work. No less than twenty-five sections, each representing a particular field of thought, have been organized, each with special officers and programmes. The *Albany Institute* (1824) was next to be founded, with the *Maryland Academy of Sciences* following in 1826, and the *Delaware County Institute of Science* (Media, Pennsylvania), in 1833.

The year 1848 saw the beginning of the *Essex Institute* at Salem, Massachusetts, and the *American Association for the Advancement of Science*, the latter of which is probably the largest and most influential of the general science associations of our country. Its objects are

"By periodical and migratory meetings, to promote intercourse between those who are cultivating science in different parts of our country; to give a stronger and more general impulse and more systematic direction to scientific research, and to procure for the labors of scientific men increased facilities and wider influence."

All these aims have been reached to an unusual extent. Annual meetings have been held in various parts of the country, until 1900, in the summer time; since then, during the Christmas holidays. At these meetings several hundred members are usually in attendance, and a large number of papers are read before the several sections. The association has numbered among its presidents many of the leading scientists of the country. The monthly magazine *Science* is the organ of the association, and is received by all its members.

Am. Lyceum, p. 569.

Within the class of general scientific societies are more than sixty representatives, nearly every state having one or more. Many of these are the direct result of the American Lyceum movement, being organized as continuations of local lyceums, and at about the time the latter were declining in influence. This accounts for the unusual number founded in the later decades of the nineteenth century, as shown by the table.

b. Historical Societies, and those of Allied Interests

Associations of a purely historical nature were early in the field, the *Massachusetts Historical Association* having been founded in Boston in 1791. Its object was the study of the history of New England. Most other societies of this class interest themselves in the consideration of historical matters connected with some particular region. In 1804 the *New York Historical Society* was founded. In 1822 both Rhode Island and Maine founded similar associations, New Hampshire in 1823, and Connecticut in 1825. Nine other states have followed their examples. In a few, among them Wisconsin and Nebraska, the societies have official connection with the state government.

In all, there are now upward of fifty separate historical associations. Besides the state and city societies (more than fifty of the latter), a considerable number have to do with particular nationalities, as the *Holland Society of New York* (1885), and *American Jewish Historical Society* (1902). Another class is denominational in its characteristics, as the *American Congregational Society* (Boston, 1853); and a much larger class is primarily memorial in its nature, though historical in a very valuable sense, since particular epochs in our national history are made the objects of study. The *Pilgrim Society* (Plymouth, 1820) and the *Society of Colonial Wars*, with branches in several states, illustrate this class, of which there are more than twenty members.

The one national historical society, *The American Historical Association*, dates only from 1884. It is truly national in its character, since, pursuant to the act of Congress which established it, reports must be made annually to the government, through the Smithsonian Institution, concerning the condition of historical study in America. The society must also stand in readiness to make special investigations of any historical subject at the request of Congress. The headquarters of the society are in Washington. The character of the men composing its membership may be gathered from a mention of the names of its first board of officers. They were, president, Andrew D. White; vice-presidents, Justin Winsor and Charles Kendall Adams; secretary, Herbert B. Adams.

Among the societies closely allied to the historical, the *American Antiquarian Society*, national in its interests, though with its collections and library in Worcester, Massachusetts, is the oldest, having been founded in 1812. It has published extensively over the signatures of many of the leaders in historical thought, who are among its members.

In geography and geology the *American Geographical Society of New York*, founded in 1852, is the oldest of six similar societies, two of which are in Washington, two in San Francisco, and one in Rochester, New York.

Ethnology is represented by the *American Ethnological Society*, organized in New York City in 1842; folklore, by the *American Folklore Society* (Cambridge, Massachusetts, 1888); archæology, by the *Archæological Institute of America* (New York, 1879). There are also a number of numismatic and philatelic societies in various parts of the country.

c. SOCIETIES OF NATURAL HISTORY AND THE BIOLOGICAL SCIENCES

This class numbers upwards of fifty societies, distributed through every portion of our country. Many of them are general in their character, — the descendant of the American Lyceum, — while others confine their attention to narrow fields of study.

Of them all, the *Academy of Natural Sciences* of Philadelphia (1812) is the oldest, with the *Providence* (Rhode Island) *Franklin Society* (1821), the *Boston Society of Natural History* (1830), the *Lyceum of Natural History* of Williams College (1835), the *Portland* (Maine) *Society for Natural History* (1843), and the *Worcester* (Massachusetts) *Natural History Society* (1852), following in that order, all established for the general study of natural history.

Quite generally, in connection with these societies,

museums were established, that of the Boston society having grown to large proportions. Membership did not presuppose any extended scientific knowledge; but simply an interest in the subjects to be considered. In connection with them, many of our leading scientists of to-day got their initial training.

The oldest of the special associations having to do with biological branches is the *American Entomological Society* (1859), a national society which publishes some four hundred pages of proceedings annually. The *American Ornithologist's Union* (1843) and the *American Microscopical Society* (1878) are also national societies of this class. The former publishes *The Auk.* The *American Society of Naturalists* (1883) is another important biological association which holds annual meetings, usually in connection with the *American Association for the Advancement of Science.*

d. ASSOCIATIONS FOR THE STUDY OF SPECIAL SUBJECTS

Under this class I have placed mathematical, chemical, psychological, philosophical, economic, and linguistic societies.

Of the first, the *American Mathematical Society* (New York, 1888), with its Western branch, is the only important representative.

In chemistry the *American Chemical Society* (Brooklyn, New York, 1874), with its several branches, is the most important.

The *American Psychological Association* (New York, 1892), and the *American Philosophical Association*, each with Western branches, occupy their respective fields.

In economics and allied branches the *American Statistical Society* is the oldest, having been established in Boston, in 1839, "to collect, pursue, and diffuse statistical information in the different departments of human knowledge." It is national in its scope. The two societies within this field which are the most active along lines of social science are the *American Economic Association* (Ithaca, New York, 1865) and the *American Academy of Political and Social Science of Philadelphia* (1889). Each has published extensively, though the latter, through its *Annals*, a quarterly magazine, is one of the most prolific of all our learned societies.

In the field of literature the *American Oriental Society* (New Haven, Connecticut, 1842) is the oldest, confining its attention to Asiatic and African languages and literature.

The *American Philological Association*, founded in 1869, comes next, with the *Modern Language Association of America* following in 1883.

These comprise the more influential literary societies of more than local importance, though in all there are upwards of twenty-five. Of these, about one-third confine their studies to Shakespeare, and nearly as many to Browning.

e. PROFESSIONAL ASSOCIATIONS

In the field of medicine the *American Medical Association* is the leading representative (1847), and has proved an immense stimulus to medical research. It has a very large membership, including many of the leading physicians of the country. Annual meetings are held at different places, the full proceedings of which are published. A weekly journal, also, is issued by the association.

The *American Dental Association* (1859) holds a similar position in that branch of surgery. Of both these classes of associations there are many state and city representatives.

In legal matters the *American Bar Association* (1878) is the leading society, with many others of a similar character, but of local influence, in the field.

The profession of engineering in its various branches is represented by many strong and influential societies. The oldest of these is the *Franklin Institute* of the state P. 401. of Pennsylvania, founded in 1824, for "the promotion of the mechanics arts." During its entire history, it has issued a monthly report, the files of which contain many of the most important contributions to engineering literature.

The *Maryland Institute for the Promotion of the Mechanics Arts* (1826) was the next society of this class to be established. Its particular interests are in the direction of manufactures and the useful arts.

The first evidence of differentiation into the special fields of engineering is shown by the organization of the *Boston Society of Civil Engineers* (1848), followed by a National Society in 1852. The *American Institute of Mining Engineers* was organized in 1871, of *Mechanical Engineers* in 1881, and of *Electrical Engineers* in 1884, though local societies in each of these branches had preceded them. They are all important societies, and publish voluminous reports.

In the field of art the *Pennsylvania Academy of the Fine Arts* was established in 1804, and the *National Academy of Design* in 1820. Each has exerted an important influence.

The *Architectural League* of New York (1888) and the *National Sculpture Society* (New York, 1893), are young but flourishing societies.

f. TEACHERS' ASSOCIATIONS

With the exception of certain of the historical and of the national history societies, associations of the classes so far discussed are for the most part patronized by the leaders of thought, the scholars within the various specialties. Although the latter are perhaps usually the leaders in the teachers' associations, the bulk of the membership (and the membership is vast) is composed of the rank and file of the teaching profession. It is, in fact, to such that the greatest good from such associations comes ; not so much through instruction and information along the lines of advanced educational method, as through inspiration from the contact of minds interested in similar pursuits, even though those minds be but little better trained than their own. So, it has come about that American teachers flock to society and association meetings of all sorts, beyond all precedent in any other country, or in any other profession. A great proportion of our four hundred thousand and more teachers belong to one or more associations, the meetings of which they attend religiously.

When teachers in this country began to meet more or less informally for mutual improvement, can hardly be determined with exactness ; but it was undoubtedly long before any formal organization of sufficient dignity had been perfected to leave record of itself. So far as is known, the *Middlesex County Association for the improvement of the common schools*, organized at Middletown, Connecticut, is the oldest. The *American Institute of Instruction* was organized in 1830, and has had a long life of greatest usefulness. The oldest state organization is the *New York State Teachers' Association*, founded in 1845, with the avowed purpose of promoting "the interests of public education and the elevation of the profession of teaching." Other states, especially in the West, were not slow to follow the example set by New York. Illinois and Iowa both organized state associations in 1854, Virginia in 1861, Kentucky in 1865, Georgia in 1867 ; and to-day nearly every state in the Union has one or more such societies. All are conducted along practically the same lines ; at least one annual meeting is held, this usually coming at the Christmas holidays ; the programme is divided into several sectional meetings with one or two sessions only, reserved for the general association meetings. Not infrequently, the greater part of three days is devoted to the meeting.

The great national society of teachers, the *National Educational Association*, was organized under its present name in 1870; and since it is the largest, as well as perhaps the most influential organization of the kind in the world, it merits more than passing mention.

The first call for a national meeting was sent out in 1857, over the signatures of the presidents of a number of the state teachers' associations, the American Association for the Advancement of Education, and other influential societies of teachers. This call invited "all practical teachers in the North, South, East, and West, who are willing to unite in a general effort to promote the general welfare of our country by concentrating the wisdom and power of numerous minds, and by distributing among all the accumulated experiences of all, who are ready to devote their energies, and their means to advance the dignity, respectability, and usefulness of their calling, and who believe that the time has come when the teachers of the nation should gather into one educational brotherhood." Copies were sent to the officers and workers in the teachers' associations of the whole country, asking for their coöperation. Only ten presidents responded. In compliance with the call a number of teachers assembled in Philadelphia, on August 26, 1857, and the *National Teachers' Association* was organized.

The constitution provided for the government of the association by a board of directors elected at the annual meeting. This board was to consist of a large number of councillors, one from each state, district, or territory, together with the president, secretary, treasurer, and twelve vice-presidents. It also became the practice, even from this early meeting, to appoint a large nominating committee, consisting of one member from each state represented in the convention.

The directory of the newly formed association voted to meet at Cincinnati in August, 1858. Of the thirty-eight signers of the constitution at the time of its adoption, only five were present at the first annual meeting.

At the Cleveland meeting in 1870, the name was changed from the National Teachers' Association to the National Educational Association. The constitution was also amended at this meeting so as to admit the coöperation of two other educational associations, the *National Superintendents' Organization*, and the *American Normal Association*. According to the terms of this amendment, other departments could be organized, and the Department of Higher Instruction, and the Department of Primary or Elementary Instruction were organized immediately. These departments elected their own officers, and provided their own programmes for the annual meeting. Up to this time all the educational topics had been discussed before the whole association. Since then, each department holds its own meeting and discusses such topics as relate to its work. There are now, in all, eighteen different departments : Superintendence, Normal Schools, Elementary Education, Higher Education, Manual Training, Art Education, Kindergarten Education, Music Education, Secondary Education, Business Education, Child Study, Physical Education, Natural Science Instruction, School Administration, Library Department, Education of Deaf, Blind, and Feeble-minded, Indian Education, and National Council of Education.

The membership of the association is made up of annual members, who pay $2 a year; of life members, who pay $20; of life directors, who pay $100; and of perpetual directorships, which are usually secured by boards of education or associations through the payment of $100. There are three classes of annual members, active, associate, and corresponding. Teachers, and all who are actively associated with the management of educational institutions, including libraries and periodicals, may become active members upon application indorsed by two active members, the payment of an enrolment fee of $2, and the annual dues for the current year. All others who pay an annual membership fee of $2 may become associate members. Eminent educators not residing in America may be elected by the directory to be corresponding members. The number of corresponding members cannot exceed fifty, according to the constitution, but the limit has never been reached. All life members and life directors are denominated active members, and enjoy all the powers and privileges of such members, without the payment of annual dues. The annual membership of the association is changeable, because of the migratory character of the meetings.

A new movement was inaugurated in the association at the Saratoga meeting in 1892, by the appointment of the special Committee of Ten to investigate and report on the course of study for secondary schools. The committee, after a preliminary discussion, organized conferences, each consisting of ten members, on the following subjects: Latin; Greek; English; other modern languages; mathematics; physics, astronomy, and chemistry; natural history (biology, including zoology, botany, and physiology); history, civil government, and political economy; geography (physical geography, geology, and meteorology). The result was a report of nearly 250 printed pages which has become an educational classic, and is one of the most valuable contributions ever made to the literature of education.

In 1893 the Committee of Fifteen, on elementary education, was appointed. The members of the committee were divided into three sub-committees — on the training of teachers; on the correlation of studies in elementary education; and on the organization of city school systems. The report was presented to the Department of Superintendence in 1895, and has proved of hardly less value than its predecessor.

In 1895 the Committee of Twelve on Rural Schools was appointed by the council. Their report was made to the council in 1897, and published in the volume of proceedings of the Milwaukee meeting. The Committee of Twelve was divided into four sub-committees, and assigned the following topics for investigation and report : School Maintenance; Supervision; Supply of Teachers ; Instruction and Discipline. The reports of these sub-committees were adopted by the whole committee at Chicago in 1896, and were published, together with an appendix containing reports from various persons connected with rural schools, in 1897.

The Committee on College Entrance Requirements was appointed in 1895 ; that on Normal Schools in 1895 ; and that on the Relations of Public Libraries to Public Schools in 1898. These three committees reported at the Los Angeles meeting in 1899, and the reports are all included in the Los Angeles volume.

The annual volume of proceedings embodies the results of the work of the association from year to year, and is therefore its most important contribution. It has been the aim of the successive publication committees to confine it to a single volume of one thousand pages.

The association is now in a most prosperous condition. More than thirty-two thousand members of all classes were in attendance at the Boston meeting in 1903. A permanent salaried secretary is maintained, who devotes his whole time to its interests, and the association stands without a rival in influence and usefulness.

The only other society of teachers in any way approaching the National Educational Association in breadth of influence is the *Southern Educational Association*, organized in 1890. Although comparatively small, it is a power for much good throughout the South.

In special departments of education a number of flourishing associations exist. Prominent among them is the *Western Drawing Teachers' Association* (1893), and the *American Manual Training Association* (1896).

The common interests of the college and secondary schools are subserved in various parts of the country by the *New England Association of Colleges and Preparatory Schools* (1885), the *Association of Colleges and Preparatory Schools of the Middle States and Maryland*, and the *Association of Colleges and Preparatory Schools of the Middle West*.

About 1892 the *National Herbart Society* was organized, with a limited membership, mostly composed of devotees to the Herbartian doctrines, which were at that time especially prominent in educational thought. The society held two meetings annually for some years, the proceedings of which were published in the form of year-books. Some very valuable papers appeared in this form. In 1901 the society was discontinued, but its membership was absorbed by the *National Society for the Scientific Study of Education*, organized in that year. This society practically continues the general plan of its predecessor, though with its field of discussion somewhat broadened. Papers for discussions at its meetings are prepared in advance, and distributed to the members. Its meetings are held in connection with those of the National Educational Association and of the Department of Superintendence of that association, which comes annually in February. This society is, perhaps, the most exclusively scientific of our educational associations.

Admission to the Learned Societies

This varies greatly with the different societies. At one extreme stands the National Academy of Sciences, election to which is purely honorary, and reserved for the few of unusual achievement. As might be supposed, application for membership to the Academy would be a grave breach of decorum. It, however, stands practically alone in this respect, application to most of the others being in order; though eligibility usually presupposes some particular interest in the subject covered by the society. In some instances, too, special accomplishment or position is a prerequisite. Only in certain of the patriotic societies, such as the Sons of the American Revolution, is ancestry the determining factor. Applications for membership must usually be made in writing, with the indorsement of one or more active members. The annual dues vary from a small sum — $1 or even less — to many times that amount, though for most of the purely literary and scientific associations the dues do not exceed $5 annually, though where extended publications are furnished the members, they are sometimes more than this amount.

The Value of Learned Societies

The greatest value of such associations comes, perhaps, through the printed proceedings of the meetings, and through the occasional or irregular publications of other material. This is truly enormous, amounting annually to something like fifty thousand printed pages. No specialist in any literary or scientific subject can keep abreast of the times without access to this material, and no library of any pretension can be without it.

Of little less importance is the stimulus which comes from the meetings themselves. It is the unusual man or woman who can keep up a full head of intellectual steam for any length of time upon the fuel of the study alone. The mutual inspiration which comes from these gatherings is often little short of revivalistic in its influence. Though the actual instruction which comes from the meetings themselves is probably exceeded by that from the printed proceedings, such is certainly not true of the inspiration, and this latter is not to be neglected. On the whole, it is probably true that no professional man can make the most of himself without the information or inspiration which comes from direct association with his fellow-specialists; and the learned societies have done much to furnish opportunities for this association.

Study Clubs

Of quite a different character from the learned societies, yet not to be neglected as factors in education, are the local associations of persons — largely of women — for the pursuance of certain lines of general or special study. Women's clubs, and societies of every kind, except those purely social in their nature, come under this head. Hardly a city or town of any size in our land is without one or more such clubs, and in spite of the fact that they have been subjected to much ridicule, their educational value is not slight. In New York State they have been organized under the Home Education Department of the University of the State of New York, which furnishes books for study, travelling libraries, mounted pictures, and, in some instances, lanterns and lantern slides. In 1900 there were 391 such study circles in the state, with a membership of many thousands; and averaging somewhat more than twenty meetings each during the year.

REFERENCES

Bourland, Mrs. Clara P. Women's Clubs and their Relation to the Public Library Movement. Public Lib. 2 : 316–319. — Cattell, J. McK. Scientific Societies and Associations. In Butler's Education in the United States, 2 : 867–891. — *Channing*, Walter. Beginnings of an Educational Society. Ed. Rev. 14 : 354–359. — *Croly*, Mrs. Jane (Cunningham). The History of the Women's Club Movement in America, 1898. — *Harris*, W. T. The National Educational Association: Its Organization and Functions. N. E. A. 1891 : 443–451. — *Henrotin*, Ellen M. Coöperation of Women's Clubs in the Public Schools. N. E. A. 1897 : 73. — *Maxwell*, W. H. Report of the Committee of Ten. N. E. A. 1894 : 232–237. — Michigan State Library Study Clubs (Library Bulletin, No. 1 L (course of study of 113 clubs). — *N. E. A. Report on Public Libraries.* Rep. Com. Ed. 1899–1900, 1 : 663–719. — New York (State) University Study Club Division. Extension Bulletin, 1895. — *Pickard*, J. L. Report of the Committee of Fifteen. Ed. 15 : 603 (full report in Rep. Com. Ed. 1893–1894, 1 : 469–556). — Pierce, J. M. American Psychological Association. Ed. 17 : 346–350. — *Snyder*, Z. X. Report of the Committee on Normal Schools. N. E. A. 1899 : 837–903. — **Weeks**, S. B. A Preliminary List of American Learned and Educational Societies. Rep. Com. Ed. 1893–1894, 2 : 1493–1661. — Welch, Margaret Hamilton. Club Women and Club Work. Harper's Bazaar, 1897 : 30, to date. — *White*, E. E. History of the Department of Superintendence of the National Educational Association. N. E. A. 1901 : 233–236.

CHAPTER XXIX

LYCEUMS, POPULAR LECTURES, AND MUSEUMS

THE *American Lyceum* was a popular institution of immense educational influence, which flourished during the second and third quarter of the nineteenth century. It originated in a local society of thirty or forty farmers and mechanics, which met for study and mutual improvement in the town of Milbury, Massachusetts, about 1826. Their example was contagious, and within the next few years a dozen or more of the surrounding towns had formed similar circles, subsequently uniting to form the Worcester County Lyceum.

The system spread rapidly throughout New England, then into New York; and by 1831, the date of the first national convention of lyceum workers, it had established itself in the South, and as far west as Jacksonville, Illinois, then practically the Western limit of civilization. In fact, so rapid had been the growth of the lyceum movement, that in 1831, according to the minutes of the convention, there were " not less than eight or ten hundred town lyceums, fifty or sixty county societies, and several state lyceums." Such a rapid development seems almost incredible.

According to the general constitution, the American Lyceum was "to favor the advancement of education, especially in the common schools, and the general diffusion of knowledge."

The organization was well worked out at the national conventions, which were held for many years, and consisted of: 1st, town, district, or village lyceums; 2d, county lyceums; 3d, state lyceums; and 4th, the national lyceum.   Each had its proper officers, and representation in the higher organization.

At various times, the national lyceum approved the following measures : —

1. Formation of a central cabinet or museum of natural history, by means of local contributions.
2. A system of exchanges for local museums.
3. Promotion of coöperation between schools.
4. Introduction of apparatus for illustrating lectures.
5. Addition of vocal music to the school curriculum.
6. Study of American history and constitutional law.
7. Study of natural history.
8. Town maps and local museums.
9. Preservation of materials for local history.
10. Uniform plan for keeping meteorological data.
11. Beautifying the village scenery.
12. Text-books for schools and tracts for the people.
13. Travelling libraries.

A mere glance at this list is enough to show that we have in this movement the forerunner and parent of many of our most valuable institutions to-day.   The United States Weather Bureau, library extension, the museum of natural history, the scientific laboratory, free text-books, the village improvement society, all are there foreshadowed ; and there can be little doubt that the National Educational Association, and the American Association for the Advancement of Science were both more or less directly the outgrowth of the lyceum movement.

Rep. Com. Ed.
1899–1900, I :
186–187.
I cannot do better in attempting to describe the American lyceum than to quote Herbert B. Adams.

"The constitutional objects of the town lyceums were mutual improvement and the general diffusion of knowledge.   The means for effecting these objects were meetings for reading, conversation, discussions, dissertations illustrating the sciences, or other exercises which should be thought expedient; a cabinet consisting of books; apparatus for illustrating the sciences; plants, minerals, and other natural or artificial productions. Annual membership was rated at $2; life membership at $20. Persons under eighteen years of age could enjoy for $1 per annum all the privileges of the society, except voting.

"*Lyceum Proceedings.* — These varied somewhat in different localities, but it was a very general custom to have weekly meetings, with alternate lectures and debates. Popular science was a favorite subject of public instruction, and no lyceum was properly equipped unless it possessed a so-called 'philosophical apparatus' for experiments in physics or natural philosophy. The favorite subjects of public discussion were practical and economic; for example, the utility of railroads, which came into vogue at the very time that lyceums and education were rising in popular favor.

"Lectures and discussions were often extempore, but sometimes elaborated by local appointees and read from manuscript, with copious citations from good authorities. Home talent and self-help were the life principles of a village or town lyceum. A community which could not produce its own lecturers and debaters could not support a good lyceum. It was a training school for adults, and many Americans received from it a decisive impulse toward public life. It fostered in no small degree that gift for public speaking for which Americans have long been famous.

"*Junior Members.* — It is becoming necessary in country towns for the first class, or the oldest pupils in each of their schools, to become members of lyceums, not merely to witness the illustrations or other exercises performed by adults, but to take part in them, to which they have found themselves equal, greatly to the satisfaction and sometimes to the astonishment of their parents and other friends.

"*Influence of the Community.* — The village or town lyceum was a helpful and uplifting power for various classes in local society. 'Teachers are accommodated with the room, apparatus, specimens, books, etc., of lyceums for their mutual improvement in relation to their schools. Farmers and mechanics also have their special lyceums under the patronage of a general society. In the summer season ladies' lyceums are conducted, one afternoon in a week, under the same arrangement.' Here are clearly foreshadowed the teachers' associations, farmers' institutes, and women's clubs of more recent times."

Such was the American Lyceum in its palmy days. As time went on, the element of entertainment, which had always been present to a legitimate extent in the form of occasional lectures by men of renown from outside the local circle, began to grow at the expense of mutual participation, and we have the last important stage, that of the popular lecture course. Valuable as this has been and is, it cannot compare in educational importance with that which preceded it.

During the stirring years from 1860 to 1865, but little time was given to individual or community improvement, and the lyceum went down with most other forms of educational extension. When resuscitated, it was in a quite different form. Nearly every village in the North had considerable numbers of returned soldiers, in a way unfitted for immediate participation in community affairs, but in whom the excitement of war had developed tremendous appetites for entertainment. That want, the lyceum soon began to supply through the medium of popular lectures. Each lyceum was now eager to secure the best speakers from away, as it had formerly been to develop them from within. America had such to give, and the names of Everett, Emerson, Phillips, Curtis, Garrison, Sumner, Lowell, Hale, Taylor, Douglas, Gough, and Greeley were frequently seen upon the lyceum bills. Some of these speakers, in fact, devoted their entire time to the work. It is said that John B. Gough alone spoke no less than ninety six hundred times to audiences numbering in the aggregate nine million. Women, too, proved themselves to be popular with lyceum audiences. Julia Ward Howe, Susan B. Anthony, Elizabeth Cady Stanton, Anna Dickinson, and Mary A. Livermore, besides many others of lesser note, were always in demand.

But the lyceum had not only by this time lost nearly every vestige of its former self, but in most places, even its name. It is true that the agency which provided speakers of almost any description and cost, was known as a lyceum bureau, but it bore no relation to the American Lyceum. The lectures were usually given in the various cities under the title of "Star Courses." Early in the '70's music began to figure prominently in them, with the famous Ole Bull as the first, and perhaps greatest success. Camilla Urso, another violin virtuoso, was popular, as were Clara Louise Kellogg, Emma Thursby, and Anna Louise Cary as vocalists.

Since that time, both the lecture and the concert, as well as the author's reading, have been popular, and practically all the larger towns and cities support courses which usually contain them all.

What bids fair to rival the old American lyceum at its best in matters of instruction, though not in the important element of mutual participation, is the present popular lecture movement being conducted by the boards of education in some of our larger cities.

In this, New York City has taken the lead, and a description of what is being done there will show the maximum of accomplishment in this line.

The move originated in 1888 by an act of the New York legislature empowering the city of New York to expend public moneys to provide for lectures for the working men and women of the city. The board of education immediately appropriated $15,000 for the purpose, and from June 1 to April 1, 1889, 186 lectures were given in six different schoolhouses situated in the more densely populated portions of the city. The total attendance at these lectures was 22,149. So successful was the work considered, that more elaborate arrangements were made for the next winter, when 329 lectures were delivered, though with a total attendance but slightly larger than for the previous season.

The next year the work was placed under the direction of Dr. Henry M. Leipziger, who has since had it in charge, and to whom much of its extraordinary success is due.

He immediately took steps for giving the lectures a

wider advertisement; secured a large corps of specialists to lecture upon popular subjects; engaged suitable halls when the school buildings did not contain adequate rooms; provided lanterns and slides for projection, and in every way made the offerings attractive to the class of people for whom they were intended. The effect of all this was remarkable.

The total number of lectures given each season since 1890, together with the total number of persons in attendance, is as follows: —

Years	Lectures	Attendance	Years	Lectures	Attendance
1890–1891	185	78,295	1896–1897	1065	026,927
1891–1892	287	122,243	1897–1898	1595	509,571
1892–1893	310	130,830	1898–1899	1923	519,411
1893–1894	383	170,368	1899–1900	1871	538,084
1894–1895	502	224,123	1900–1901	1963	553,558
1895–1896	1040	392,733	1901–1902	2243	585,908
			1902–1903	2536	620,524

These figures are for the Borough of Manhattan alone. Beginning with 1901–1902, lectures have been delivered in three other boroughs of greater New York — Brooklyn, Queens, and Richmond. These gave an additional attendance of 342,342 for the first season, and 583,602 for the second.

These figures are stupendous, giving us a total attendance of nearly 7,000,000 for the fifteen years the lectures have been given.

During the winter of 1902–1903 lecture centres were maintained at fifty-five different points throughout the city, thirty-two of which were school buildings. Among the others were the Cooper Union, Columbus Hall, American Museum of Natural History, Young Men's Hebrew Association, Harlem Young

Men's Christian Association Hall, and the Hall of the Board of Education. Of the entire number of lectures for the season, 2911 were illustrated by means of the lantern, 267 by experiments, while 1043 were not illustrated in any way. The general subjects covered by the lectures were: physiology and hygiene, including first aid to the injured, natural science, electricity, physics, chemistry, astronomy, sociology and kindred subjects, education, literature, history, biography, descriptive geography and travel, commercial geography, music, and art. Twelve lectures were given in Italian, eleven in Yiddish, and five in French. Of the free lecture course Dr. Leipziger has said:—

"The free lecture system is a veritable godsend to a great city like ours. In sections where the poor dwell, what glad hours these lecture hours are. . . . What a delight to see a hall in the Bowery crowded with men, following, after a hard day's work, a course in electricity! What a pleasure to see in these halls, man and wife, brother and sister, meeting at the temple of learning, and having a wider horizon given, not only to the present, but the coming generation. . . . It is the hope of all interested in this movement that it shall extend to all portions of our city, making the lecture centre a force that shall develop in the greater New York, loftier civic pride and nobler individual ideals."

In this matter of public lectures, supported by the city, New York has been practically alone.

Many of the larger cities, and a few of the smaller ones, have provided occasional lectures, but nothing that in any way approximates the movement in New York City. The question of fuller utilization of the school buildings for general educational purposes is, however, being agitated in many places, and we may soon expect to see material results.

In the city of Boston, public evening lectures maintained by the board of education have been given occasionally for many years, but under no systematic plan until the season of 1901–1902, when forty special lectures were given in the evening schools. The speakers were all members of the teaching force of the city; and, except upon a few occasions, only the pupils of the evening schools were admitted. During the next winter (1902–1903), the plan was entirely changed, and the lectures were thrown open to the public. Fifty-six were given with almost phenomenal success, no less than 40,000 persons being in attendance, or an average of 715 at each lecture. The subjects were all of a literary character, or of travel, the scientific lines, along which New York City had been so successful, not having been followed. Much more elaborate preparations are being made for the future conduct of the work, and we cannot doubt that in Boston it will prove of the same great value as in the city of its origin.

In Chicago, the University of Chicago has coöperated with the board of education, and has given many public lectures, usually in courses, in the different school buildings of the city.

The board of education of Albany, New York, has, since 1894, maintained series of illustrated lectures, primarily for the pupils in the schools, but which are occasionally given in the evening to general audiences. In Syracuse, New York, two or three such lectures are provided for the public annually. In the winter of 1902–1903, the city of Milwaukee offered the first course of public lectures under the auspices of the school board, and the plan is to be continued. Denver, Colorado, offered such courses during the winters of 1897, 1898, 1899, but not since.

Another great source of popular education through the public lecture plan is the University Extension movement. In the University of the State of New York, where it was begun in 1891, it is made to include much more than this (extension lectures, libraries, study clubs, and summer schools); but in higher institutions of an instructional nature, it is mainly through courses of lectures given at various so-called extension centres, by members of the regular faculty. Many colleges and universities have undertaken the work, with varying degrees of success.

At the University of Chicago nearly 150 members of the instructional force are connected with the extension division, and " centres " have been established throughout the Middle West.

The lectures are arranged in courses of six or twelve, travelling libraries, and other illustrative materials are provided, and under some conditions university credit is given for attendance upon the work.

In many of our larger cities the museums have made important contributions to public education through popular lectures, as well as in other ways. The centre of museum interest in the country is perhaps the Smithsonian Institution of Washington. This was established through the bequest of about $500,000 made by Joseph Smithson, an Englishman, in 1829, but not available until 1838. As stated by the founder, the object of the institution was "to increase the diffusion of knowledge," and most nobly is it serving its purpose. This is done largely through its publications, numbering nearly three hundred volumes of most valuable scientific material, though the popular lecture feature is not neglected. Its large museum, housed in a peculiarly picturesque building near the Capitol, and always open to the public, is now supported by the government. It has been of greatest service to the meteorological, the geological, and the coast and geodetic bureaus, while that of ethnology is under the administration of the institution. The United States National Museum, with its collections in a building adjoining that of the Smithsonian Institution, supplements the latter, through its immense mass of anthropological, geological, and biological material, relics of prehistoric man, aboriginal modes of living, the occupations, arts, and industries of native and foreign races are exhibited in most instructive ways. Duplicate collections are frequently lent or given to local museums in various places, thus making the museum an educational influence throughout the entire land. For the support of the museum, the government annually appropriates somewhat more than $200,000.

The great scientific museum of New York City is the American Museum of Natural History, with an enormous collection, unparalleled in its arrangement; and with $75,000 each year to be devoted to the enlargement of its collections, it is doing work second in importance only to that of the Smithsonian Institution.

At this museum much is made of educational extension. On Tuesday and Saturday evenings throughout the fall and winter, the museum, in coöperation with the Department of Education of the city, offers, free to the public, a course of lectures on travel, geography, and natural science. Through Professor A. S. Bickmore (and under a grant from the state) it gives to the public school-teachers, on Saturday mornings during the winter, a series of lectures on geographical topics, illustrated by means of lantern slides. These lectures are repeated on legal holidays for the benefit of the general public. In coöperation with various scientific societies of the city, — the Audubon and Linnæan societies, New York Academy of Sciences, etc., — the museum provides lectures on scientific subjects to which the public is always welcome. In order to bring about a more intimate relation between the museum and the school-teachers, the museum has prepared sets of birds, insects, and various invertebrates, which are loaned to the schools for periods of three weeks or more, to assist in the nature study work. Teachers and their classes are admitted to the museum at all times, and specimens are removed from the cases to classrooms in the building for special study. In addition to the lectures above mentioned, the museum periodically coöperates with Columbia University in providing lectures upon various scientific subjects, and has also very recently made an arrangement whereby public school-teachers may come to the museum and find a very large series of lantern slides which they are at liberty to use in the assembly rooms, for lectures given by them to their students. The museum is also doing an important work for the teachers of the state in distributing, through the Department of Public Instruction, various sets of lantern slides with accompanying lecture notes.

The Field Columbian Museum of Chicago, established through the gifts of Marshall Field and other citizens of the city, was opened in 1894, in one of the buildings erected for the Columbian Exposition. Its growth has been rapid, and its collections are fast nearing the scope of the two museums already mentioned. About twenty popular lectures upon scientific subjects are given each year.

Aside from these three, the only other museums of the country are maintained by scientific societies, educational institutions, and by the various states. In most instances the latter are unimportant. Of the societies and associations, the Boston Society of Natural History, the Academy of Natural Sciences of Philadelphia, and the San Francisco Academy of Sciences have large and valuable collections. At Harvard are the Agassiz Museum of Comparative Zoology, and the Peabody Museum of Archæology and Ethnology, unsurpassed by those of any educational institution; and at Yale, the Peabody Museum, containing one of the most important paleontological collections in the world. Many other colleges and universities have collections of considerable merit, and in some instances unsurpassed, in the value of material illustrative of local conditions. With our immense unstudied fields, we have every opportunity for scientific exploration and research, and museums in every quarter are being rapidly enriched. With the present tendency to utilize to its fullest extent every possible educational agency, we may well expect that their importance to the people will be rapidly increased.

REFERENCES

Blackmar, Frank W. Educational Work in the National Museum. Circ. Inf. 1890, 71–72. Importance of Museums in Education. Circ. Inf. 1890, 65–66. Public Lectures at Smithsonian Institution. Circ. Inf. 1890, 74. — *Farrington*, O. C. The Museum as an Educational Institution. Ed. 17 : 481. — Field Columbian Museum Work of the Year. Pop. Sci. Mo. 63 : 89–91. — *Flower*, W. H. Suggestions for the Formation and Arrangement of a Museum of Natural History in Connection with a Public School. Nature, 41 : 177–178. — *Goode*, G. Brown. Museums of the Future. 1891, 427–445 (Reprinted from Report of the National Museum). — *Greenwood*, T. Place of Museums in Education. Science, 22 : 246–248. — Iles, George. How a Great Free Lecture System Works. World's Work, 5 : 3327–3334. — *Leipziger*, H. M. Free Lectures. Critic, 28 : 329–330. Lecture System in New York City. Munic. Aff. 3 : 462–472. — McCormick, S. D. Lecture System in New York City. Outl. 64 : 121–124. — *Mayer*, A. G. Educational Efficiency of Our Museums. N. A. Rev. 177 : 564–569. — Meldola, R. Museums. Nature, 58 : 217–219. — *Pond*, J. B. Great Authors and the Lyceum. Cosmopol. 21 : 247–256. The Lyceum. Cosmopol. 20 : 595–602. — Smith, A. Tolman. The National Museum at Washington. Ed. 9 : 277. — *Starr*, Frederick. The Museum in Educational Work. Ed. Rev. 3 : 254. United States Education, Commissioner of, Lectures, Lyceums, and Museums Reports, 1890–1891 : 843–848 ; 1891–1892 : 752, 1206 ; 1894–1895 : 1567 ; 1045–1046. — *Wallace*, A. R. American Museums. Fortn. 48 : 347–359, 665–675. — Willis, S. T. Free Lecture System. Cosmopol. 25 : 661–669. — *Winchell*, N. H. Museums and Their Purposes. Science, 18 : 43–46.

APPENDIX A

" SCHOOL SERVICE. — I. The school shall begin at eight o'clock,
and go out at eleven; and in the afternoon shall begin at one
o'clock and end at four. The bell shall be rung when the school
commences.

" 2. When the school begins, one of the children shall read the
morning prayer, as it stands in the catechism, and close with the
prayer before dinner; in the afternoon it shall begin with the prayer
after dinner; and end with the evening prayer. The evening school
shall begin with the Lord's prayer, and close by singing a psalm.

" 3. He shall instruct the children on every Wednesday and
Saturday in the common prayers, and the questions and answers
in the catechism, to enable them to repeat them better on Sunday
before the afternoon service, or on Monday, when they shall be
catechised before the congregation. Upon all occasions, the schoolmaster shall be present, and shall require the children to be friendly
in their appearance, and encourage them to answer freely and
distinctly.

" 4. He shall be required to keep his school nine months in succession, from September to June, in each year, in case it should be
concluded upon to retain his services for a year or more, or without
limitation; and he shall be required to be regulated by these articles,
and to perform the same duties which his predecessor, Jan Thibaud,
above named, was required to perform. In every particular therefore,
he shall be required to keep school according to this seven months
agreement, and shall always be present himself.

" CHURCH SERVICE. — I. He shall keep the church clean, and
ring the bell three times before the people assemble to attend the
preaching and catechism. Also before the sermon is commenced,
he shall read a chapter out of the Holy Scriptures, and that between

581

the second and third ringing of the bell. After the third ringing he shall read the ten commandments, and the twelve articles of our faith, and then take the lead in singing. In the afternoon after the third ringing of the bell, he shall read -a short chapter, or one of the Psalms of David, as the congregation are assembling, and before divine service commences, shall introduce it, by the singing of a Psalm or Hymn.

" 2. When the minister shall preach at Brooklin or New Utrecht, he shall be required to read twice before the congregation, from the book commonly used for that purpose. In the afternoon he shall also read a sermon or the explanation of the catechism, according to the usage and practice approved by the minister. The children as usual, shall recite their questions and answers out of the catechism, on Sunday, and he shall instruct them therein. He, as chorister, shall not be required to perform these duties, whenever divine service shall be performed in Flatlands, as it would be unsuitable, and prevent many from attending there.

" 3. For the administration of Holy Baptism, he shall provide a basin with water, for which he shall be entitled to receive from the parents, or witnesses, twelve styvers.[1] He shall at the expense of the church, provide bread and wine, for the celebration of the Holy Supper. He shall be in duty bound promptly to furnish the minister with the name of the child to be baptized, and with the names of the parents or witnesses. And he shall also serve as messenger for the consistory.

" 4. He shall give the funeral invitations, dig the grave ; and toll the bell, for which service he shall receive for a person of fifteen years and upwards, twelve guilders, and for one under that age, eight guilders. If he should be required to give invitations beyond the limits of the town, he shall be entitled to three additional guilders, for the invitation of every other town, and if he should be required to cross the river, and go to New York, he shall receive four guilders.

" School Money. — He shall receive from those who attend the day school, for a speller or reader, three guilders a quarter, and for a writer, four guilders. From those who attend evening school, for a speller or reader, four guilders, and for a writer, six guilders shall be given.

" Salary. — In addition to the above, his salary shall consist of four hundred guilders, in grain, valued in Seewant, to be delivered at Brooklyn Ferry, and for his services from October to May, as above stated, a sum of two hundred and thirty-four guilders, in the same kind, with the dwelling house, barn, pasture lot and meadows, to the school appertaining. The same to take effect from the first day of October, Instant.

[1] A styver is equal to about two cents.

" Done and agreed upon in Consistory, under the inspection of the Honorable Constable and Overseers, the 8th of October, 1682.

Constable and Overseers	*The Consistory*
CORNELIUS BARRIAN.	CASPARUS VAN ZUREN, Minister.
RYNIER ÆRTSEN.	ADRIÆN REYERSE.
JAN REMSEN.	CORNELIUS BARENT VANDWICK.

" I agree to the above articles, and promise to perform them according to the best of my ability.

" JOHANNES VAN ECKKELEN."

APPENDIX B

IMPORTANT COLONIAL SCHOOL ORDINANCES

MASSACHUSETTS SCHOOL ORDINANCE OF 1642

" This court, taking into consideration the great neglect of many parents and masters in training up their children in learning and labor, and other employments which may be profitable to the commonwealth, do hereupon order and decree that in every town the chosen men appointed for managing the prudential affairs of the same shall henceforth stand charged with the care of the redress of this evil, so as they shall be sufficiently punished by fines for the neglect thereof upon presentment of the grand jury, or any other information or complaint in any court within this jurisdiction ; and for this end they, or the greater number of them, shall have the power to take account from time to time of all parents and masters, and of their children, concerning their calling and employment of their children, especially of their ability to read and understand the principles of religion and the capital laws of this country, and to impose fines upon such as shall refuse to render such accounts to them when they shall be required ; and they shall have power, with consent of any court or the magistrate, to put forth apprentices the children of such as they shall [find] not to be able and fit to employ and bring them up. They shall take . . . employing them . . . up, nor shall take course to dispose of . . . themselves ; and they are to take care of such as are set to keep cattle be set to some other employment withal, as spinning upon the rock, knitting, weaving tape, &c., and that boys and girls be not suffered to converse together, so as may occasion any wanton, dishonest, or immodest behaviour. And for their better performance of this trust committed to them, they may divide the town amongst them, appointing to every of the said townsmen a certain number of families to have special oversight of. They are also to provide that a sufficient quantity of materials, as hemp, flax, etc., may be raised in their several townes, and tools and implements provided for working out the same ; and for their assistance in this so needful and beneficial employment, if they meet with any difficulty or opposition which they cannot well master by their own power, they may have recourse to some of the magistrates, who shall take such course for their help and encouragement as the occasion shall require according to justice; and the said townsmen, at the next court in those limits, after the end of their year, shall give a brief account in writing of their proceedings herein, provided that they have been so required by some court or magistrate a month at least before, and this order to continue for two years, and till the court shall take further order."

MASSACHUSETTS SCHOOL ORDINANCE OF 1647

" It being one of the chief projects of that old deluder Satan to keep men from the knowledge of the Scriptures, as in former times by keeping them in an unknown tongue, so in these latter times by persuading from the use of tongues, that so at least the true sense and meaning of the original might be clouded by false gloss is of saint-seeming deceivers, that learning may not be buried in the grave of our fathers in the church and commonwealth, the Lord assisting our endeavors:

" *It is therefore ordered,* That every township in this jurisdiction, after the Lord hath increased them to the number of fifty householders, shall then forthwith appoint one within their town to teach all such children as shall resort to him to write and read, whose wages shall be paid either by the parents or masters of such children, or by the inhabitants in general, by way of supply, as the major part of those that order the prudentials of the town shall appoint: *Provided,* Those that send their children be not oppressed by paying much more than they can have them taught for in other towns; and

" *It is further ordered,* That where any town shall increase to the number of one hundred families or householders, they shall set up a grammar school, the master thereof being able to instruct youth, so far as they may be fitted, for the university: *Provided,* That if any town neglect the performance hereof above one year, that every such town shall pay five pounds to the next school until they shall perform this order."

A DECLARATION CONCERNING THE ADVANCEMENT OF LEARNING IN NEW ENGLAND BY THE GENERAL COURT OF MASSACHUSETTS, 1652

" If it should be granted that learning, namely, skill in the tongues and liberal arts, is not absolutely necessary for the being of a Commonwealth and churches, yet we conceive that, in the judgment of the godly wise, it is beyond all question not only laudable, but necessary for the well-being of the same; and although New England (blessed be God) is completely furnished (for this present age) with men in place, and upon occasion of death or otherwise, to make supply of magistrates, associates in courts, physicians, and officers in the Commonwealth, and of teaching elders in the churches, yet for the better discharge of our trust for the next generation, and so to posterity, seeing the first founders do wear away apace, and that it grows more and more difficult to fill places of most eminence as they are empty or wanting; and this court, finding by manifest experience that though the number of scholars at our college doth increase, yet as soon as they grow up ready for public use they leave the country, and seek for and accept of employment elsewhere, so that if timely provision be not made it will tend much to the disparagement, if not to the ruin, of this Commonwealth: It is therefore ordered and hereby enacted by this court, that a voluntary collection be commended to the inhabitants of this jurisdiction for the raising of such a sum as may be employed for the maintenance of the president, certain fellows, and poor scholars in Harvard College, and for that purpose do further order, that every town of this jurisdiction do choose one meet person to take the voluntary subscriptions of such as shall underwrite any sum or sums of money for that purpose, and to make return thereof to the next court; and forasmuch as all the colonies are concerned therein; this court doth order the secretary to signify to the governor of the several colonies our endeavors herein, and to commend the same unto them for their help and furtherance in so good a work."

Amendment to the Law of 1647, passed in 1671

"Whereas the law requires every town, consisting of one hundred families or upward, to set up a grammar school, and appoint a master thereof, able to instruct youth so as to fit them for the college, and upon neglect thereof the said town is to pay five pounds per annum to the next Latin school until they shall perform that order, the court, upon weighty reasons, judge meet to declare and order, that every town of one hundred families and upwards that shall neglect or omit to keep a grammar school, as is provided in that law, such town shall pay ten pounds per annum unto the next town school that is set according to that law.

"Whereas in the law, title Townships, the several towns and selectmen of the said towns have power to impose penalties as the law directs; and whereas many constables question whether it be their duty to serve warrants from the selectmen for persons to appear before them and to levy fines for the removal of such doubts, and, as an addition to the said law, this court doeth order and require that all constables respectively shall serve all warrants from the selectmen, and levy all such fines as shall be imposed by the said towns or selectmen."

AMENDMENT PASSED 1683

" That every town consisting of more than five hundred families or householders shall set up and maintain two grammar schools and two writing schools, the masters whereof shall be fit and able to instruct youth as said law directs.

" And whereas the said law makes the penalty for such towns as provide not schools as the law directs to pay to the next school ten pounds : This court hereby enacts that the penalty shall be twenty pounds when there are two hundred families or householders."

PLYMOUTH COLONY ENACTMENT OF 1677

" 1677. fforasmuch as the Maintainance of good litterature doth much tend to the advancement of the weale and flourishing estate of societies and Republiques.

" This Court doth therfore order ; That in whatsoeuer Townshipp in this Gourment consisting of fifty familier or vpwards ; any meet man shalbe obtained to teach a Gramer scoole such townshipp shall allow att least twelue pounds in currant marchantable pay to be raised by rat on all the Inhabitants of such Towne and those that haue the more emediate benifitt therof by theire childrens going to scoole with what others may voulentarily giue to promote soe good a work and generall good, shall make vp the resedue Nessesarie to maintaine the same and that the proffitts ariseing of the Cape ffishing ; heertofore ordered to maintaine a Gramer scoole in this Collonie, be distributed to such Townes as haue such Gramer scholes for the maintainance therof ; not exceeding fiue pounds p annum to any such Towne vnlesse the Court Treasurer or other appointed to manage that affaire see good cause to adde thervnto to any respectiue Towne not exceeding fiue pounds more p annum ; and further this Court orders that euery such Towne as consists of seauenty families or vpwards and hath not a Gramer scoole therin shall allow and pay vnto the next Towne which hath such Gramer scoole kept vp amongst them, the sume of fiue pounds p annum in currant Marchantable pay, to be leuied on the Inhabitants of such defectiue Townes by rate and gathered and deliuered by the Constables of such Townes as by warrant from any Majestrate of this Jurisdiction shalbe required."

CONNECTICUT LAWS OF 1650

Children

" Forasmuch as the good Education of Children is of singular behoofe and benefitt to any Commonwealth ; and whereas many

parents and masters are too indulgent and negligent of theire duty
in that kind ; —

" *It is therefore ordered by this Courte and Authority thereof,* that
the Select men of euery Towne in the several precincts and quarters
where they dwell, shall have a vigilant eye over their brethren and
neighbors, to see, first, that none of them shall suffer so much bar-
barism in any of their families, as not to endeavor to teach by themselves or others, their children and apprentices so much learning as
may enable them perfectly to read the English tongue, and knowledge
of the capital laws, upon penalty of twenty shillings for each neglect
therein ; also, that all masters of families, do, once a week, at least
catechise their children and servants, in the grounds and principles
of religion ; and if any be unable to do so much, that then, at the
least, they procure such children or apprentices to learn some short
orthodox catechism, without book, that they may be able to answer to
the questions that shall be propounded to them out of such catechisms
by their parents or masters, or any selectmen, when they shall call
them to a trial of what they have learned in this kind ; and further,
that all parents and masters do breed and bring up their children
and apprentices in some honest lawful [calling,] labor, or employment, either in husbandry or some other trade profitable for themselves
and the commonwealth, if they will not nor can not train them up in
learning, to fit them for higher employments, and if any of the selectmen, after admonition by them given to such masters of families,
shall find them still negligent of their duty, in the particulars afore-
mentioned, whereby children and servants become rude, stubborn
and unruly, the said selectmen, with the help of two magistrates, shall
take such children or apprentices from them, and place them with
some masters for years, boys until they come to twenty-one, and
girls to eighteen years of age complete, which will more strictly look
unto and force them to submit unto government, according to the
rules of this order, if by fair means and former instructions they will
not be drawn unto it."

Schools

" It being one chief project of that old deluder, Satan, to keep men
from the knowledge of the Scriptures, as in former times, keeping
them in an unknown tongue, so in these latter times, by persuading
them from the use of tongues, so that at least, the true sense and
meaning of the original might be clouded with false glosses of saint
seeming deceivers ; and that learning may not be buried in the grave
of our forefathers, in church and commonwealth, the Lord assisting
our endeavors :

" *It is therefore ordered by this court and authority thereof,* That
every township within this jurisdiction, after the Lord hath increased

them to the number of fifty householders, shall then forthwith appoint one within their town to teach all such, children, as shall resort to him, to write and read, whose wages shall be paid, either by the parents or masters of such children, or by the inhabitants in general, by way of supply, as the major part of those who order the prudentials of the town, shall appoint ; provided, that those who send their children be not oppressed by paying more than they can have them taught for in other towns.

"*And it is further ordered*, That where any town shall increase to the number of one hundred families, or householders, they shall set up a grammar school, the masters thereof being able to instruct youths, so far as they may be fitted, for the university, and if any town neglect the performance hereof above one year, then every such town shall pay five pounds per annum, to the next such school, till they shall perform this order.

"*And it is ordered*, That two men shall be appointed in every town within this jurisdiction, who shall demand what every family will give, and the same to be gathered and brought into some room, in March ; and this to continue yearly, as it shall be considered by the commissioners."

APPENDIX C

THE FIRST RULES FOR THE GOVERNMENT OF THE
STUDENTS OF HARVARD UNIVERSITY, PRINTED IN
1642.

(From New England First Fruits. Mass. Hist. Col. I, pp. 242–246)

" Rules and Precepts that are observed in the Colledge.

" 1. When any Schollar is able to understand Tully, or such like classicall Latine author extempore, and make and speake true Latine in verse and prose, *suo ut aiunt Marte:* and decline perfectly the paradigms of nounes and verbes in the Greek tongue : let him then, and not before, be capable of admission into the Colledge.

" 2. Let every student be plainly instructed and earnestly pressed to consider well the main end of his life and studies is, to know God and Jesus Christ, which is eternall life, John XVII, 3, and therefore to lay Christ in the bottome, as the only foundation of all sound knowledge and learning. And seeing the Lord only givest wisdom, let everyone seriously set himselfe by prayer in secret to seek it of him. Prov. II, 3.

" 3. Every one shall so exercise himselfe in reading the Scriptures twice a day, that he shall be ready to give such an account of his proficiency therein, both in theoreticall observations of the language, and logick, and in practicall and spiritual truths, as his Tutor shall require according to his ability : *seeing the entrance of the word giveth light, it giveth understanding to the simple.* Psalm CXIX, 130.

" 4. That they eschewing all profanation of Gods name, attributes, word, ordinances and times of worship, doe studie with good conscience carefully to retain God and the love of his truth in their mindes, else let them know that (nothwithstanding their learning) God may give them up to strong delusions and in the end, to a reprobate minde. 2 Thes. II, 11, 12. Rom. I, 28.

" 5. That they studiously redeeme the time : observe the generall hours appointed for all students and the special houres of their *classis :* And then diligently attend the lectures without any disturbance by word or gesture. And if in anything they doubt, they shall enquire as of their fellowes so, (in case of non-satisfaction) modestly of their Tutors. •

"6. None shall, under any pretense whatsoever frequent the company and society of such men as lead an unfit and dissolute life.

"Nor shall any without his Tutor's leave, or (in his absence) the call of parents or guardians go abroad to other townes.

"7. Every schollar shall be present in his Tutor's chamber at the 7th hour in the morning, immediately after the bell at his opening the Scripture and prayer, so also at the 5th hour at night, and then give account of his own private reading, as aforesaid, in particular the third, and constantly attend lectures in the hall at the hours appointed. But if any (without necessary impediment) shall absent himself from prayer or lectures, he shall be lyable to admonition if he offend above once a week.

"8. If any schollar shall be found to transgresse any of the laws of God or the schoole, after twice admonition, he shall be lyable, if not *adultus* to correction, if *adultus*, his name shall be given up to the Overseer of the College, that he may be admonished at the public monethly act.

"The times and order of the studies, unless experience shall show cause to alter.

"The second and third day of the week, read lectures as followeth.

"To the first yeare at 8th of the clock in the Morning Logick, the first three quarters, Physicks the last quarter.

"To the second yeare, at 9th houre, Ethicks and Politicks at convenient distances of time.

"To the third year, at the 10th, Arithmetick and Geometry the three first quarters, Astronomy the last.

" *Afternoone*

"The first yeare disputes at the second hour.

"The 2d yeare at the 3d houre.

"The 3d yeare, at the 4th everyone in his art.

"The 4th day reads Greeke.

"To the first yeare, Etymologie and Syntax at the eighth hour.

"To the 2d at the 9th houre, Prosodia and Dialects.

" *Afternoone*

"The first yeare, at 2nd houre, practice the precepts of Grammar, in such authors as have a variety of words.

"The 2nd yeare perfect their theory before noon and exercise Style, Composition, Imitation epitome both in prose and verse, afternoon.

" The fifth day read Hebrew and Easterne Tongues.

" Grammar to the first yeare, houre the 8th.

" To the 2d Chaldee at the 9th houre.

" To the 3d Syriach at the 10th houre.

" *Afternoone*

" The first yeare practice in the Bible the 2nd houre.

" The 2nd in Ezra and Daniel at the 3rd houre.

" The 3d at the 4th houre in Trostin's New Testament.

" The 6th day reads Rhetorick to all at the 8th houre.

" Declamations at the 9th.   So ordered that any schollar may declame once a month.

" The rest of the day *vacat Rhetoricis studiis*.

" The 7th day reads Divinity Catechetical at the 8th houre, common places at the 9th houre.

" *Afternoone*

" The first houre reade History in the winter.

" The nature of plants in the summer.

" The summe of every lecture shall be examined before the new lecture is read.

" Every schollar, that on proof is found able to read the originale of the Old and New Testaments into the Latin tongue and to resolve them logically: withall being of Godly life and conversation: and at any publick act hath the approbation of the Overseers and Master of the Colledge, is fit to be dignified with the first degree.

" Every schollar that giveth up in meeting a System of Synopsis, or summe of Logick, naturall and morall Philosophy, Arithmatick, Geometry and Astronomy: And is ready to defend his Theses or positions, Withall skilled in the originalls as above said: And of godly life and conversation: And so approved by the Overseers and Master of the Colledge, at any publicque Act, is fit to be dignified with his 2nd degree.

" The manner of the late Commencement expressed in a letter sent over from the Governor, and divers of the ministers their own words these.

" The students of the first classis that have beene these four yeares trained up in University training (for the ripening in the knowledge of toungues, and arts) and are approved for their manners, as they have kept their publick Acts in former years, ourselves being present at them: so have they lately kept two solemn Acts for their Commencement when the governor, Magistrates and the Ministers from all parts, with all sorts of schollars, and others in great numbers were present and did hear their exercise: which were Latin and Greek orations and Declamations and Hebrew Analysis, Grammaticall, Logicall, and Rhetoricall of the Psalms: And their answers and disputations in Logicall, Ethicall, Physicall, and Metaphysicall questions: and so were found worthy of the first degree (commonly called Batchelors) *Pio more Academiarum in Anglia* : Being first presented by the President to the Magistrates and Ministers and by him. upon their approbation, solemnly admitted unto the same degree, and a booke of artes delivered unto each of their hands, and power given them to read lectures in the Hall upon any of the arts, when they shall be thereunto called, and a liberty of studying in the library.

"Boston New England, Sept the 26th 1642."

[This is an account of the first commencement at Harvard.]

APPENDIX D

"ORDERS OF YE COMMITTEE OF TRUSTEES FOR THE GRAMMAR SCHOOLE AT NEW HAVEN TO BE OBSERVED AND ATTENDED IN YE SAID SCHOOLE, MADE, AGREED· UPON AND PUBLISHED IN YE SD SCHOOLE IN YE YEARE 1684."

(Am. Jour. Ed. 4 : 710)

"1. The Erection of ye sd Schoole being principally for ye Institucion of hopeful youth in ye Latin tongue, and other learned Languages soe far as to prepare such youths for ye Colledge and publique service of ye Country in Church, & Commonwealth. The Chiefe work of ye Schoole-Mr. is to Instruct all such youth as are or may be by theire parents or Friends sent, or Committed unto him to yt end wth all diligence faithfulness and Constancy out of any of ye townes of this County of New haven upon his sallary accompt only, otherwise Gratis. And if any Boyes are sent to ye Mr of ye said Schoole from any other part of ye Colony, or Country, Each such boy or youth to pay ten shillings to ye Mastr at or upon his entrance into ye said Schoole.

"2. That noe Boyes be admitted into ye sd Schoole for ye learning of English Books, but such as have been before taught to spell ye letters well & begin to Read, thereby to perfect theire right Spelling, & Reading, or to learne to write, & Cypher for numeracion, & addicion, & noe further, & yt all others either too young & not instructed in letters & spelling, & all Girles be excluded as Improper & inconsistent wth such a Grammar Schoole as ye law injoines, as is ye Designe of this Settlemt, And yt noe Boyes be admitted from other townes for ye learning of English, without liberty & specially licence from ye Comitte.

"3. That the Master & Schollars duly attend the Schoole Houres viz. from 6 in ye morning to 11 o Clock in ye forenoone, And from 1 a Clock in the afternone to 5 a Clock in the afternoone in Summer & 4 in Winter.

"4. That the Mr shall make a list or Catalogue of his Schollars names And appoint a Monitor in his turne fore one week or longer tyme as the Mr shall see Cause, who shall every morning & noone et at least once a day at ye set tyme Call over ye names of ye Schollars and Note down the Late Commers, or Absent, And in fit season Call such to an accompt That the faulty, & truants may be Corrected or reproved, as their fault shall desearve.

"5. That the Schollars being called together the Mr shall every morning begin his work with a short Prayer for a blessing on his Laboures & theire Learning.

"6. That the prayer being ended the Master shall Assigne to every of his Schollars theire places of Sitting according to theire degrees of learning. And that (having theire Parts, or Lessons appointed them) they keep theire Seates, & stir not out of Doors, with [out] Leave of the Master, and not above two at one tyme, & soe successively: unless in Cases of necessity.

"7. That ye Schollars behave themselves at all tymes, especially in Schoole tyme with due Reverence to theire Master, & with Sobriety & quietnes among themselves, without fighting, Quarrelling or calling one anothr or any others, bad names, or useing bad words in Cursing, taking the name of God in vaine, or other prophane, obscene, or Corrupt speeches which if any doe, That ye Mr Forthwith give them due Correcion. And if any prove incorrigible in such bad manners & wicked Corrupting language & speeches, notwithstanding formr warnings, admonishions & Correcion that such be expelled ye Schoole as pernicious & dangerous examples to ye Rest.

"8. That if any of ye Schoole Boyes be observed to play, sleep, or behave themselves rudely, or irreverently, or be any way disorderly at meeting on ye Saboath Daye or any other tyme of ye Publiqe worships of God That upon informacion or Complaint thereof to ye due Conviccion of the offender or offenders, The Master shall give them due Correccions to ye degree of ye Offence. And yt all Correccions be wth Moderacion.

"9. That noe Lattine Boyes be allowed upon any pretence (sickness, and disability excepted) to withdraw, or absent themselvs from the Schoole, without liberty graunted by the Master, and yt noe such liberty be granted but upon ticket from ye Parents or frends, & on grounds sufficient as in Cases extraordinary or absolute necessity.

"10. That all the Lattin Schollars, & all other of ye Boyes of Competent age and Capacity give the Mr an accompt of one passage or sentence at least of ye sermons the foregoing Saboth on ye 2d day morning. And that from 1 to 3 in ye afternoone of every last day of yeweek be Improved by ye Mr in Catechizing of his Schollars yt are Capeable."

APPENDIX E

REPRESENTATIVE COURSES OF STUDY FOR EDUCATIONAL INSTITUTIONS OF VARIOUS CLASSES

WORCESTER ACADEMY, WORCESTER, MASS.

NOTE. — Exercises that require no preparation outside the classroom are designated by the numbers in the right-hand column.

CLASSICAL

First year: PERIODS

English	5
Latin	5
History (Greece)	3
Mathematics (Algebra, to Quadratics) . . .	5
Manual Training	3

18 | 3

Second year:

English	3
Greek	5
Latin	5
History (Rome)	2
Mathematics (Algebra and Plane Geometry) . .	5

20

Third year:

English	3
Greek	5
Latin	5
French or German	4
History (Review)	2
Mathematics (Review)	2

21

NOTE. — At the end of the third year regular students are expected to pass college preliminary examinations in (1) Elementary Greek, (2) Elementary Latin, (3) Elementary French, (4) Classical History, (5) Mathematics (Algebra and Plane Geometry).

Fourth year:

	PERIODS
English .	
Greek .	3
Latin .	5
French or German .	5
French ⎫	
German ⎬ for beginners .	3 | 1
Mathematics (Solid Geometry)	2
Science (Physics) .	3 | 2
	21 | 3

NOTE. — A student who enters the fourth year without having had a modern language may take French or German ; he cannot, however, be a candidate for a diploma.

LATIN-SCIENTIFIC

In general this programme is developed from the classical by the substitution of scientific studies for Greek, thus :

(First year the same as in the classical programme)

Second year:

Physiography in place of Greek.

Third year:

Physics in place of Greek.

Fourth year:

Chemistry or Advanced Physics in place of Greek; Trigonometry and Advanced Algebra in place of Physics.

SCIENTIFIC

First year:

	PERIODS
English .	4
French .	4
Mathematics (Algebra, to Quadratics)	5
Science (Zoology, Physiology, Botany)	5 | 2
Manual Training .	3
	18 | 5

Second year:

English .	
French .	3
History (Ancient and Mediæval)	3
Mathematics (Algebra and Plane Geometry)	3
Science (Physiography) .	5
Science (Mechanical Drawing)	3 | 2
Manual Training .	2 | 2
	2
	19 | 6

Third year: PERIODS

    English   3

    French . . . .

    French } for beginners . . . . . . } 4

    German }

    History (Modern European and English) . . . 4

    Mathematics (Review) 3

    Science (Physics) . . . . . . 4 | 2
                                        18 | 2

NOTE. — At the end of the third year regular students are expected to pass college preliminary examinations in (1) Elementary French, (2) in case they have passed this. Advanced French, (3) Mathematics (Algebra and Plane Geometry), (4) Laboratory Physics.

Fourth year:

    English . , ... 3

    French or German . . . . . .

    French } for beginners . . . . . } 3 | 1

    German }

    History (United States, with Civil Government) . 3

    Mathematics (Advanced) 5

    Science (Advanced Physics), or Science (Chemistry) 5 | 5
                                        19 | 6

NOTE. — A student who enters the fourth year without having had a modern language may take French or German · he cannot, however, be a candidate for a diploma.

THE CLEVELAND HIGH SCHOOL, CLEVELAND, OHIO

FIRST YEAR

NOTE. — In elective subjects, classes will not generally be formed with fewer than fifteen pupils.

COMMERCIAL COURSE	SCIENTIFIC COURSE	CLASSICAL COURSE
Bookkeeping, Business Forms, and Commercial Correspondence . . 5	Natural History or Manual Training 5	Latin 4
English Composition, Reading, Literature . . . 4	English Composition, Reading, and Literature . 4	English Composition, Reading, and Literature . 4
Algebra 5	Algebra 5	Algebra 5
Natural History or Manual Training 5	Latin, or German, or American History . . . 4	German 4, or Natural History . 5

SECOND YEAR

COMMERCIAL COURSE	SCIENTIFIC COURSE	CLASSICAL COURSE
Bookkeeping, Arithmetic, and Commercial Law . . 5	Physical Geography or Manual Training . . . 5	Latin 5
English Composition, Reading, and Literature . 4	English Composition, Reading, and Literature . 4	Greek or German 5
Geometry . . . 5	Geometry . . . 5	Geometry . . . 5
English History or Manual Training 5	Latin, or German, or English History 5	English 4

NOTE. — Oratory is required one hour of each week in the third and fourth years. Music, one hour each week, and Drawing, two hours, are elective, except for students who expect to attend the normal school.

THIRD YEAR

COMMERCIAL COURSE	SCIENTIFIC COURSE	CLASSICAL COURSE
Bookkeeping, Business Practice, and Commercial Geography . . . 4	Physics 5	Latin 5
English Literature or German . . 5	Latin, German, or English Literature 5	Greek or German . 5
Physics 5	History 4	History 4, or Physics 5
Stenography and Typewriting or Manual Training 5	College English or Mathematics . 3	College English . 3

FOURTH YEAR

COMMERCIAL COURSE	SCIENTIFIC COURSE	CLASSICAL COURSE
Office Practice, Banking and Higher Accounting 4	Chemistry or Physiology and Botany 4	Latin 4
Economics and Civics 4	Economics and Civics . . . 4	Greek or German . 4
Stenography and Typewriting, with Commercial Correspondence . . 5	History or Advanced Mathematics . . . 4	French or Physics 5
Spanish 5, or German or American Literature . . . 4	French 5, or Latin, German, or American Literature 4	History or Mathematics . . . 4
	English 2	English 2

COURSES		FIRST YEAR		SECOND YEAR		THIRD YEAR		FOURTH YEAR	
		First Term	Second Term	First Term	Second Term	First Term	Second Term	First Term	Second Term
ENGLISH AND COMPOSITION	I	Lessons in English and Composition	Lessons in English and Composition	American Classics and Essays	American Classics and Essays	Rhetoric, American Literature and Essays	Rhetoric, American Literature and Essays	English Literature, Note Book and Essays	English Literature, Note Book and Essays
SCIENCE	II	Physiography	Physiography			Physics	Physics	Chemistry	Chemistry
	III	Zoology	Zoology	Botany	Botany	Physiology	Meteorology	Mineralogy or Psychology	Geology
	IV							Steam	Electricity
MATHEMATICS	V	Constructional Geometry	Algebra and Plane Geometry	Algebra and Plane Geometry	Algebra and Plane Geometry	Algebra and Solid Geometry	Algebra and Plane Trigonometry	Descriptive Geometry	Surveying
DRAWING	VI	Free Hand	Mechanical	Illustrative	Mechanical	Perspective	Mechanical	Elective	Elective
	VII	Free Hand	Cast	Natural Forms	Conventionalizing	Applied Design	Historic Ornament	Elective	Elective
MANUAL TRAINING	VIII	Joinery	Joinery	Turning	Moulding and Pattern Making	Forging	Forging	Machine Shop Practice	Machine Shop Practice
	IX	Sewing	Sewing	Dressmaking	Domestic Economy	Millinery	Domestic Economy	Cooking	Household Economy
HISTORY AND ECONOMICS	X	Ancient	Mediæval	Modern	English	American	American	Civil Government	Political Economy
LANGUAGE	XI	German	German	German	German	German	German	German	German
	XII	French	French	French	French	French	French	French	French
	XIII	Latin	Latin	Latin	Latin	Latin	Latin	Latin	Latin
BUSINESS	XIV	Arithmetic Bookkeeping	Business Forms Bookkeeping	Business Forms Bookkeeping	Typewriting Business Law	Stenography	Stenography	Stenography	
MUSIC	XV	Voice Culture	Voice Culture	Singing	Singing	Singing	Singing	Chorus Singing	Chorus Singing
ELOCUTION	XVI	Voice Culture	Extemporaneous Speaking	Reading	Speaking				
PHYSICAL TRAINING	XVII	Class Drills Gymnastics and Games	Class Drills Gymnastics and Games	Class Drills Gymnastics and Games	Class Drills Gymnastics and Games	Fencing Gymnastics and Games	Fencing Gymnastics and Games		

By a course of study is meant a line of work in any single department, logically arranged. Several are taken at the same time. Forty terms ("points") are required for graduation. Of these eight are required in English, six in Mathematics, six in Science, eight in Manual Training, and four in Drawing. Pupils may not graduate with fewer than twenty-four academic points, exclusive of Manual Training, Drawing, Physical Culture, Typewriting, and Singing.

CALIFORNIA STATE NORMAL SCHOOL, LOS ANGELES, CALIFORNIA

PRELIMINARY

First Year

First Term

Grammar, Classic Myths, Composition	4*
Ancient and Mediæval History	4
Physics	5
Algebra	4
Reading	3
Music	2
Physical Training	3
	Total, 25 units.

Second Term

Composition, Wood-work, and Literature	4
Geography	4
Botany	5
Algebra	4
Drawing	2
Manual Training	2
Music	1
Spelling	1†
Physical Training	3
	Total, 26 units.

Second Year

First Term

American Literature, Poetics	4
English History	4
Physiology	5
Geometry	5
Drawing	2
Manual Training	2
Physical Training	3
	Total, 25 units.

* The numbers indicate the recitations or exercises per week for the full term.

† Spelling may be passed by examination unless written work shows deficiency.

Second Term

English Literature, Shakespeare	5
United States History and Government	5
Chemistry or Physics	5
Geometry	4
Drawing	2
Manual Training	1
Music	1
Physical Training	2

Total, 25 units.

PROFESSIONAL

(Admission based on University Entrance Requirements.)

COURSE I

This course of study leads to a diploma on which a teacher's elementary certificate will be granted by county boards.

FIRST YEAR

First Term

Composition	3
Biology	5
History	4
Reading and Spelling *	5
Drawing and Manual Training	4
Music	2
Physical Training	3

Total, 26 units.

Second Term

Psychology	6
Literature	3
Geography	4
Arithmetic	5
Drawing and Manual Training	4
Music	2
Physical Training	2

Total, 26 units.

* Spelling may be passed by examination unless written work shows deficiency.

SECOND YEAR

First Term

Teaching in Training School	5
Child Study and Pedagogy	5
Grammar	3
Nature Study	3
Drawing	2
Domestic Science	3
Music	2
Physical Training	2

Total, 25 units.

Second Term

Teaching in Training School	10
School Law and School Economy	2
History of Education	3
Special Method in Common School Subjects in connection with discussion of the work in Training School	10

Total, 25 units.

COURSE II

(Kindergarten)

In addition to the requirements for admission to Professional Course (I), applicants will be required to pass an examination in music: —

(*a*) Instrumental: ability to read simple airs with reasonable facility, in good time, and with fair touch.

(*b*) Vocal: ability to sing simple songs with accuracy and expression.

FIRST YEAR

First Term

Composition	3
Biology	5
Reading	4
Drawing	3
Music	2
Kindergarten Theory	5
Observation in Kindergarten	3

Total, 25 units.

Second Term

Psychology	6
Literature	3
Nature Study	3
Drawing	3
Music	2
Kindergarten Theory	5
Observation in Kindergarten	3

Total, 25 units.

SECOND YEAR

First Term

Child Study and Pedagogy	5
Music	1
Kindergarten Theory	4
Teaching in Kindergarten	15

Total, 25 units.

Second Term

History of Education	3
Music	1
Kindergarten Theory	6
Kindergarten Teaching	15

Total, 25 units.

PRINCETON THEOLOGICAL SEMINARY, PRINCETON, N.J.

FIRST YEAR

Old Testament Literature: General Introduction, Special Introduction to the Pentateuch, Hebrew, Sacred Geography and Antiquities, Old Testament History. New Testament Literature: General Introduction, Special Introduction to the Gospels, Exegesis of selected Epistles of Paul. Didactic Theology: Prolegomena and Theology proper. Relations of Philosophy and Science to the Christian Religion: Theism, Theological Encyclopedia, General Introduction to Apologetics. Homiletics. Elocution.

SECOND YEAR

Old Testament: Unity of the Book of Genesis, Special Introduction to the Historical and Poetical Books, Exegesis, Biblical Theology. New Testament: Life of Christ and Exegesis of the Gospels. Didactic Theology: Anthropology and Soteriology (Christology).

Relations of Philosophy and Science to the Christian Religion: Evidences of Christianity. Church History: Ancient and Mediæval. Government and Discipline of the Church. Homiletics: Criticisms of Sermons. Elocution. Missions.

THIRD YEAR

Old Testament: Special Introduction to the Prophets, Exegesis. New Testament: Acts of the Apostles, Special Introduction to the Epistles, Biblical Theology. Didactic Theology: Soteriology (Pneumatology) and Eschatology. Church History: Mediæval and Modern. Relations of Philosophy and Science to the Christian Religion: Christian Ethics and Christian Sociology. Church Government and Discipline; Pastoral Care; Ordinances of Worship; Homiletical Criticism and Analysis of Texts. Elocution. Missions.

The regular course is completed in three years; students may, however, remain a fourth, taking a minimum of twelve hours per week from what are known as extra curriculum courses.

HARVARD LAW SCHOOL, CAMBRIDGE, MASS.

FIRST YEAR

Contracts: Three hours a week. Criminal Law and Procedure: Two hours a week. Property: Two hours a week. Torts: Two hours a week. Civil Procedure at Common Law: One hour a week.

SECOND YEAR

Agency: Two hours a week. Bills of Exchange and Promissory Notes: Two hours a week. Evidence: Two hours a week. Jurisdiction and Procedure in Equity: Two hours a week. Property: Two hours a week. Sales of Personal Property: Two hours a week. Trusts: Two hours a week. Admiralty: Two hours a week during the first half-year. Bankruptcy: Two hours a week during the second half-year. Carriers: Two hours a week during the first half-year. Damages: One hour a week. Law of Persons: One hour a week. Quasi-contracts: Two hours a week during the second half-year.

THIRD YEAR

Conflict of Laws: Two hours a week. Constitutional Law: Two hours a week. Corporations: Two hours a week. Insurance —

Marine, Fire, and Life: One hour a week. International Law as administered by the Courts: Two hours a week. Partnership: Two hours a week. Property: Two hours a week. Roman Law — selected topics: Two hours a week. Suretyship and Mortgage: Two hours a week. Jurisdiction and Procedure in Equity; Two hours a week in the first half-year. Comparative Jurisprudence: One hour a week.

Extra Courses

A number of extra courses are offered, which do not count toward a degree.

Every candidate for a degree is required to take all the subjects of the first year, and ten hours a week in each of the last two years.

COLLEGE OF PHYSICIANS AND SURGEONS, COLUMBIA UNIVERSITY, NEW YORK CITY

First Year

1. Physics: Lectures, combined with demonstrations, *3; laboratory work (3-hour exercise), 1, first half-year. 2. General Chemistry: Lectures, 2, throughout the year; Conferences and laboratory work, 2, for the first half-year. 3. Anatomy: Demonstrations to sections, 5; laboratory work in dissection. 4. Normal Histology: Laboratory work (2-hour exercises), 5. 5. Physiology: Lectures, combined with demonstrations, 3; laboratory work, in sections, 3; demonstrations and recitations, in sections, 1, all in the second half-year.

Second Year

1. Anatomy, finished: Lectures, combined with demonstrations, 3; demonstrations to sections, 4; laboratory work with dissection. 2. Physiology, finished: Lectures, combined with demonstrations, 3; laboratory work, in sections, 3; demonstrations and recitations, in sections, 1, all in the first half-year. 3. Physiological Chemistry: Lectures, with occasional demonstrations, 1; conferences, combined with recitations, 1; laboratory work, with demonstrations (2-hour exercises), 3, all for one half-year. 4. Pathological Anatomy, begun; the technique of autopsies: Attendance at autopsies, with practical instruction, 2, for eight weeks. 5. Bacteriology and Hygiene: Laboratory work (2-hour exercises), 3, for one-fourth the year. 6. Materia Medica and Therapeutics, begun: Recitations, 2.

* Numbers are for exercises per week for the year, except when otherwise indicated.

7. Obstetrics, begun: Recitations to sections, 1. 8. Medicine, begun: Recitations to sections, 1. 9. Surgery, begun: Recitations to sections, 2, last half-year. 10. Minor Surgery: Practical clinical instruction to sections at the Vanderbilt Clinic and Out-patient Department of the Roosevelt Hospital, 12 exercises. 11. Physical Diagnosis: Practical clinical instruction to sections, 12 exercises.

THIRD YEAR

1. Materia Medica and Therapeutics: Lectures and clinics, 3, the first half-year. 2. General Pathology and Pathological Histology: Laboratory work (2-hour exercises), 4, for one-half the year. 3. Pathological Anatomy, finished: Demonstrations to sections, 1. 4. Clinical Pathology: Laboratory work (2-hour exercises), 3, for eight weeks. 5. The Practice of Medicine: Lectures, 1; recitations, 2; clinical lectures at the Vanderbilt Clinic, 2; clinical lectures or instruction in the wards at the Roosevelt Hospital, 1, — at the New York Hospital, 1; physical diagnosis, 24 lessons. 6. Diseases of the Mind and Nervous System, begun: Lectures, 1, first half-year. 7. The Principles and Practice of Surgery: Lectures, 2; recitations, 3, for one-half the year; surgical demonstrations, at the Presbyterian Hospital, 1; clinical lectures, at the Vanderbilt Clinic, 2; clinical lectures and the witnessing of operations at the Roosevelt and Presbyterian hospitals, 2, — at the New York Hospital, 1; minor surgery, practical clinical instruction at the Vanderbilt and Outpatient Department of Roosevelt Hospital, 24 exercises; optional — clinical lectures and the witnessing of operations additional to the above at the following hospitals: The New York, Presbyterian, St. Luke's, and the General Memorial Hospital. 8. Obstetrics, continued: Lectures, 3 (2 didactic and 1 clinical), first half-year. 9. Gynecology, begun: Recitations, combined with demonstrations, to sections, 1, first half-year; lectures, 3 (2 didactic and 1 clinical), second half-year. 10. Genito-Urinary Diseases: Clinical lectures at the Vanderbilt Clinic, 1, last half-year; clinical lectures and the witnessing of genito-urinary operations at Bellevue Hospital, 1; practical clinical instruction to sections, 10 exercises. 11. Diseases of the Eye: Clinical lectures at the Vanderbilt Clinic, 1, last half-year; practical instruction, 10 exercises. 12. Diseases of the Ear: Practical clinical instruction, from 6 to 8 exercises; four didactic lectures on general aural pathology and therapeutics. 13. Diseases of Children: Lectures, 1, last half-year; practical clinical introduction to sections, 10 lessons.

FOURTH YEAR

1. Materia Medica and Therapeutics: Clinical Lectures, 1, first half-year. 2. The Practice of Medicine, finished: Lectures, 1;

Bedside Instruction to sections in the wards of the Roosevelt or Presbyterian Hospital (2-hour exercises) 3, for four weeks; Clinical Lectures at the Vanderbilt Clinic, 2; Clinical Lectures or Instruction in the wards of the Roosevelt, Bellevue, or Presbyterian Hospital (2-hour exercises) 3, for eight weeks. Practical Instruction to sections in infectious diseases in the wards of the Willard Parker and Riverside Hospitals. Optional — Clinical Instruction in Bellevue and Presbyterian Hospitals, 2. 3. The Diseases of the Mind and Nervous System, finished: Lectures, 1, first half-year; Clinical Lectures at the Vanderbilt Clinic, 1; Practical Clinical Instruction, 10 exercises. 4. The Principles and Practice of Surgery, finished: Clinical Lectures at the Vanderbilt Clinic, 2. Required — (1) Clinical Lectures and the witnessing of operations by sections at the Roosevelt Hospital, 2, or at the New York Hospital, 1; (2) Practical Clinical Instruction in the wards at Roosevelt and Presbyterian Hospitals for 2 hours 3 days a week for eight weeks; at Bellevue Hospital for 2 hours 3 days a week for four weeks; (3) Operative Surgery on the Cadaver, 12 lessons. Optional — Clinical Lectures and the witnessing of operations at the New York Hospital, additional to the above, and at the Presbyterian, Bellevue, St. Luke's, St. Mary's, and General Memorial hospitals. 5. Obstetrics, finished: Two weeks' residence at the Sloane Maternity Hospital and attendance upon confinements, each student delivering personally at least one case; Practical Clinical Instruction to sections, at the Sloane Maternity Hospital, daily for one week for each student. 6. Gynecology, finished: Minor Operations and Demonstrations to small sections, at the Roosevelt Hospital, 3, for two weeks; Practical Clinical Instruction to sections, at the Vanderbilt Clinic, 3, for four weeks; Operative Clinics at the Roosevelt Hospital, 1. 7. Diseases of the Nose and Throat: Lectures at the Vanderbilt Clinic, 1. November to April; Practical Clinical Instruction, 10 lessons. 8. Diseases of Children, finished: Lectures, 1, second half-year; Clinical Lectures at the Vanderbilt Clinic, 1; Bedside Instruction to sections at the New York Foundling or Babies' Hospital, 2; Bedside Instruction to sections in the Roosevelt Hospital, 2; Clinical Instruction in the wards of St. Mary's Free Hospital for Children, 1, for eight weeks. 9. Diseases of the Skin: Clinical Lectures at the Vanderbilt Clinic, 1, first half-year; Practical Clinical Instruction, 10 lessons. 10. Orthopedic Surgery: Clinical Lectures at the Vanderbilt Clinic, 1; Practical Clinical Instruction, 10 exercises. Optional — Clinical Lectures and the witnessing of orthopedic operations at the Hospital for Ruptured and Crippled, Tuesdays, at 8.30 A.M.

APPENDIX F

A TABULATION OF FACTS RELATING TO SCHOOL ORGANIZATION AND ADMINISTRATION IN THE VARIOUS STATES AND TERRITORIES

(Prepared by E. C. Converse, Educational Seminar, University of Illinois)

State	Unit	Number of Officers	Term Years	Employ Teachers	Levy Taxes	How Chosen	By Whom	Qualifications	Special Power
Alabama	Town	3	2	Yes	No	Appointed	County Supt.	Freeholders Householders	
Arizona	District	3	3	Yes	Yes	Elected	People	Tax-payer Resident	
Arkansas	District Cities	3 6, or 2 per ward	3 3	Yes Yes	No No	Elected	People		Employ city supt. Exam. teachers
California	District Cities	3 Special	3	Yes Yes	No	Elected	People		Exam. teachers
Colorado	District — 1st class 2d class 3d class	5 3 3	5 3 3	Yes Yes Yes	Yes No No	Elected	People		
Connecticut	District Cities	3 6, 9 or 12	3 3	Yes Yes	Yes Yes	Elected	People	Resident	Exam. teachers
Delaware	District Independent District	3 6	3 6	Yes Yes	Yes Yes	Elected	People	Voters	
Florida	County Divided into Districts	3 3	2 2	Yes	Yes	Elected	People		
Georgia	County	5	4	Yes	No	Appointed	Grand jury	Freeholders	Exam. teachers

State	District type	No.	No.			Selection	By whom	Voters	Duties
Idaho	District / Independent District	3 / 6	3 / 6	Yes / Yes	Yes / Yes	Elected	People	Voters	Exam. teachers
Illinois	District / Cities — / a. 1000+ / b. 100,000+	3 / 6+3 per 10,000 / 21	3	Yes / Yes	Yes / Yes	Elected / Appointed	People / Mayor	Voters / Resident / Read and write	
Indiana	District	1	1	No	No	Elected	People		Employ supt.
Iowa	Township / Independent district	1 per sub-district / 3–5–7	3 / 3	Yes / Yes	No / No	Elected	People		
Kansas	District / Cities — / 1st class / 2d class	3 / 3 per ward / 2 per ward	3 / 3 / 2	Yes / Yes / Yes	Yes	Elected	People		
Kentucky	District / Cities — / 1st and 2d class / 3d and 4th class	3 / 2 per ward	3 / 2 / 4	Yes / Yes / Yes	Yes / Yes	Elected	People	21 years old / Voter / Read and write	Cities, 2d, 3d, and 4th classes, choose city supt.
Louisiana	Parish / New Orleans	5+ / 20	4 / 4	Yes / Yes	No / No	Appointed / Appointed	State board / Governor	Moral citizens	Employ supt. / Employ city supt.
Maine	Town	3	3	Yes	Yes	Elected	People		
Maryland	District	3	1	Yes	No	Appointed	County bd.		
Massachusetts	Town	3 or multiple	3	Yes	Yes	Elected	People		Exam. teachers / Employ supt.
Michigan	District / Town / Graded school district	3 / 4 / 5	3 / 2 / 3	Yes / Yes / Yes	Yes / Yes / Yes	Elected	People	Voters	

State	Unit	Number of Officers	Term Years	Employ Teachers	Levy Taxes	How Chosen	By Whom	Qualifications	Special Powers
Minnesota	District	3	3	Yes	Yes	Elected	People		Employ supt.
	Township	5	3	Yes	Yes				
	Independent district	6	3	Yes	Yes				
	Cities	2 per ward	3	Yes	Yes				
Mississippi	District	3	3	Yes	No	Elected	People	Read and write. Be persons of good character	
	Independent district	5	5	Yes	No				
Missouri	District	3	3	Yes	No	Elected	People	Citizens Taxpayers Voters	
	Cities	6	3	Yes	No				
Montana	District —								
	1st class	7	2	Yes	Yes	Elected	People	Voters	
	2d class	5	2	Yes	Yes				
	3d class	3	2	Yes	Yes				
Nebraska	District	3	3	Yes	Yes	Elected	People	Voters	
	Cities (small)	5	3	Yes	Yes				
	Cities more than 40,000	15	3	Yes	Yes				
Nevada	District	3	2 & 4	Yes	No	Elected	People		
	1500 + voters	5	2 & 4	Yes	No				
New Hampshire	Town	7+	3	Yes	No	Elected	People	Voters	Employ supt.
New Jersey	Township	3–9	3	Yes	No	Elected	People	Voters Taxpayers Read and write	Employ city supt.
	Towns	3–9	3	Yes	No				
	Cities	9	3	Yes	No				
New Mexico	District	3	3	Yes	Yes	Elected	People	Voter Taxpayer	Employ city supt.
	Cities	3, or 2 per ward	3	Yes	Yes				

								Voter Read and write Resident	
New York	District Free union district	3 3–9	3 3	Yes Yes	Yes Yes	Elected	People		
North Carolina	District	3	2	Yes	No	Appointed	Town Trustees		
North Dakota	District or Township Cities	3 5, or 1 per ward	3 3	Yes Yes	Yes Yes	Elected	People		Employ city supt.
Ohio	Special district Township 1st class cities 2d class cities	3–6 Varies Special 3–6	3 3 Special 3	Yes Yes Yes Yes	Recom- mend	Elected	People	Voters	Employ city supt.
Oklahoma	District Cities	3 1 per ward	3 3	Yes Yes	Yes Yes	Elected	People		Employ city supt.
Oregon	District Cities	3 5	3 5	Yes Yes	Yes Yes	Elected	People	Voters	Exam. teachers
Pennsylvania	District (township, borough, city, or district)	6	3	Yes	Yes	Elected	People		Elect county supt.
Rhode Island	Town	5–8	1	Yes	Yes	Elected	People	Voters	
South Dakota	District Cities	3 2 per ward + 1	3 3	Yes Yes	Yes Yes	Elected	People		
South Carolina	County Divided into Districts Cities	3 3 Special	2 2 Special	No Yes	Yes No	Appointed Appointed	State board County bd.		

APPENDIX F — *Continued*

State	Unit	Number of Officers	Term Years	Employ Teachers	Levy Taxes	How Chosen	By Whom	Qualifications	Special Powers
Tennessee	District	3	3	Yes	No	Elected	People	Resident	
	Cities	6	3	Yes	No	Elected	People	Read and write	
Texas	District	3	2	Yes	No	Elected	People	Voters	
	Independent district	6	4	Yes	No	Elected	People	Read and write	
Utah	District	3	3	Yes	Yes	Elected	People		
	Cities —								
	1st class	2 per ward	4	Yes	Yes	Elected	People		Employ city supt.
	2d class	1 per ward	4	Yes	Yes	Elected	People		
Vermont	Town	3	3	Yes	Yes	Elected	People	Citizen	
	Villages	5–7	2	Yes	Yes	Elected	People		Employ town supt.
	Incorporated districts	Special							
Virginia	District	3	3	Yes	No	Appointed	Electoral bd.	Resident	
	Towns	3	3	Yes	No		Council		
	Cities	3 per ward	3	Yes	No		Council		
Washington	District	3	3	Yes	Yes	Elected	People	Read and write	
	Cities	5	3	Yes	Yes	Elected	People		Employ city supt.
West Virginia	Magisterial districts Divided into	3	4	No	Yes	Elected	People		
	Districts	3	3	Yes	No	Appointed	County		
	Independent district	3	4	Yes	Yes	Elected	People		
Wisconsin	Town	Varies Clerk of sub-district	3			Elected	People		
	District	3	3	Yes	Yes	Elected	People		
Wyoming	District	3	3	Yes	No	Elected	People		
	Districts with 10,000+ inhabitants	6	3	Yes	No	Elected	People		

APPENDIX G

A TABULATION OF FACTS RELATIVE TO THE OFFICE OF
STATE SUPERINTENDENT OF PUBLIC INSTRUCTION IN
THE STATES AND TERRITORIES [1]

(Prepared by C. C. Burford, Educational Seminar, University of Illinois)

	Year Office Established	SELECTION		Term of Office	Member of State Board of Education	REPORTS		Oath or Bond
		Popular Election	Appointment			Annual	Biennial	
Alabama . . .	1854	×		2 yrs.			×	$15,000
Arkansas . . .	1874	×		2 yrs.	Secretary	×		×
Arizona . . .	1870		Governor	2 yrs.	Secretary	×		2,000
California . .	1851	×		4 yrs.	Secretary		×	×
Colorado . . .	1861	×		2 yrs.	President		×	5,000
Connecticut . .	1839		Board of Education	1 yr.	Secretary	×		
Delaware. . .								
Florida . . .	1868	×		4 yrs.	Secretary		×	
Georgia . . .	1868	×		2 yrs.	Chairman	×		×
Idaho	1864	×		2 yrs.	President		×	2,000
Illinois . . .	1854	×		4 yrs.	Secretary		×	25,000
Indiana . . .	1852	×		2 yrs.	×		×	
Iowa	*1841	×		2 yrs.	President		×	2,000
Kansas . . .	1859	×		2 yrs.	×		×	10,000
Kentucky . .	1837	×		4 yrs.	Chairman		×	2,500
Louisiana . .	*1847	×		2 yrs.	Secretary		×	×
Maine . . .	1846		Governor	3 yrs.		×		×
Maryland . .	*1825							
Massachusetts .	1837		Board of Education	1 yr.	Secretary	×		
Michigan . .	1836	×		2 yrs.	Secretary		×	
Minnesota . .	1858		Governor	2 yrs.	Secretary		×	×
Mississippi . .	1868	×		4 yrs.	President		×	5,000

[1] Office not always under that title.

615

FACTS RELATIVE TO THE OFFICE OF STATE SUPERINTENDENT OF PUBLIC INSTRUCTION — *Continued*

	Year Office Established	Selection		Term of Office	Member of State Board of Education	Reports		Oath or Bond
		Popular Election	Appointment			Annual	Biennial	
Missouri . . .	1839	×		4 yrs.	President	×		10,000
Montana . . .	1866	×		4 yrs.	Secretary		×	10,000
Nebraska . .	1869	×		2 yrs.	×	×		50,000
Nevada . . .	1866	×		4 yrs.	Secretary		×	
New Hampshire	1846		Governor	2 yrs.			×	
New Jersey . .	1845		Governor	5 yrs.	Secretary	×		
New Mexico .	*1890		Governor	2 yrs.	×	×		2,000
New York . .	*1813		General Assembly	3 yrs.	Regent	×		×
North Carolina .	1852	×		4 yrs.	Secretary		×	
North Dakota .	1867	×		2 yrs.			×	
Ohio	1837	×		3 yrs.	×	×		5,000
Oklahoma . .	1891		Governor	2 yrs.	President	×		5,000
Oregon . . .	1872	×		2 yrs.	Secretary		×	
Pennsylvania .	1833		Governor	4 yrs.		×		
Rhode Island .	1843		General Assembly	1 yr.	Secretary	×		
South Carolina .	1868	×		2 yrs.	Secretary	×		5,000
South Dakota .	1867	×		2 yrs.			×	2,000
Texas	1871	×		2 yrs.	Secretary		×	×
Tennessee . .	1867		Governor	2 yrs.	Secretary	×		10,000
Utah	1852	×		4 yrs.	×	×		
Vermont . . .	*1827		General Assembly	2 yrs.			×	×
Virginia . . .	1870		General Assembly	4 yrs.	President	×		
Washington . .	1872	×		4 yrs.	President	×		
West Virginia .	1869	×		4 yrs.	×	×		2,500
Wisconsin . .	1849	×		4 yrs.			×	×
Wyoming . .	1869	×		4 yrs.			×	

* Not continuous since establishment.

APPENDIX H

TABULATION OF FACTS RELATIVE TO THE CERTIFICATION OF TEACHERS IN THE DIFFERENT STATES AND TERRITORIES

(Prepared by J. R. Benson, Educational Seminar, University of Illinois)

| | STATE CERTIFICATES | | | | | | | | | | | COUNTY CERTIFICATES | | | | | | | | Given without examination |
| | Life | | | | | Limited Term | | | | | | | First Grade | | | | Second Grade | | | |
	States granting	No. of subjects required	Given to graduates of state institutions without examination	Given on papers from other states	Years of experience required	States granting	No. of subjects required	No. of years good	Given to graduates of state institutions without examination	Given on papers from other states	Years of experience required	No. of grades issued	Years in force	Required average	Years of experience required	Additional subjects	Years in force	Required average	Additional subjects	
Alabama	X	3	X		10	X	5	6		X	5	2	4	80		2	2	70	1	X
Arizona	X	12		X	2	X	5	6			2	3	2			2	1		1	X
Arkansas	X			X	5							4	6				6		8	
California	X		X		2	X		1				3	3			2	2		2	
Colorado [a]	X		X									3	3							X
Connecticut [a]			X			X		5	X											X
Delaware	X				3	X	10	5	X		3	3	10	90		4	5	90		
Florida	X					X		5			3	3	4	80		3	3	75	3	
Georgia	X					X	12	5			5	3	3	90		1	2	80		
Idaho	X	10			5	X		8 or 6				2	3				2			
Illinois	X	16				X	6	5			5	4	2			3	1		3	
Indiana	X	13				X	7	5				2	4		1	4	3		4	
Iowa	X	17			5	X											1			

[a] Colorado; Connecticut

TABULATION OF FACTS RELATIVE TO THE CERTIFICATION OF TEACHERS — *Continued*

| | COUNTY CERTIFICATES | | | | | | | | | STATE CERTIFICATES | | | | | | | | | | |
| | SECOND GRADE | | | | FIRST GRADE | | | | | LIMITED TERM | | | | | | LIFE | | | | |
State	Given without examination	Additional subjects	Required average	Years in force	Additional subjects	Years of experience required	Required average	Years in force	No. of grades issued	Years of experience required	Given on papers from other states	Given to graduates of state institutions without examination	No. of years good	No. of subjects required	States granting	Years of experience required	Given on papers from other states	Given to graduates of state institutions without examination	No. of subjects required	States granting
Kansas		2	90	3	5	4	90	1	3	2	X	X	5 or 3		X	2		X	7	X
Kentucky		2	75	2	4		85	4	3			X	8		X	6				X
Louisiana		3		3	6			5	3				4		X	7				
Maine[a]		2		1	4	1			2				5	5	X	2	X	X		X
Maryland								5	2							1	X	X		X
Massachusetts[a]		2	75	3	3	1	75				X	X	5		X	6				
Michigan	X	4	85		4	1	90	4	3	1		X	5 or 2		X	10		X		X
Minnesota		8		1	6	3		2	2		X		3		X	3	X	X	21	X
Mississippi				2	5	1		2	3		X	X		3		10	X	X	8	X
Missouri	X	3	70	3	15			3	3	5		X	6	2	X			X		
Montana		3	75	1		1		4	4	1		X	3		X			X	7	X
Nebraska			80	3	6			2	3						X			X	9	X
Nevada								4	3				6 or 5	2	X	5				X
New Hampshire[a]				3	7	2				2		X	1	6	X			X	8	X
New Jersey	X			2		4	90	5	3				10 or 7		X				8	X
New Mexico				3			75	3	3				3		X					
New York				1		2	90	10	3								X			X
North Carolina				2				1	2										6	X
North Dakota					5	2		3	4	2	X	X	5			2		X		X

State																				
Ohio	×	11	×		6							5	8		3	4	5			
Oklahoma				×		×		5	×			3	3	90	2	1	2	80	1	
Oregon	×	10	×	×	6	×	6	5	×			4	3	90	1		2	80		
Pennsylvania [a]	×			×	3	×		2	×			2	1		1	1	1			
Rhode Island [a]		16			15	×	14	3 or 2	×	×								70		
South Carolina			×	×		×			×	×	3	2	2	80			2			
South Dakota					10	×	12	5	×			3	3				2			
Tennessee	×	8				×		4 or 2	×									75	3	
Texas	×	13	×		5	×	2	5	×	×		3	life	85	1	8	2			
Utah	×				2	×		10 or 5	×			2	1		1	1	1			
Vermont					3	×	11	7	×	×		3	5		1	3	2		1	
Virginia	×					×		5	×		3	3	3				2	75		
Washington					1	×		12 or 6	×			4	5	85			2			
West Virginia	×		×	×		×	4	5	×	×		3	5		1		3	80		
Wisconsin		9				×	9	5	×	×		4	5	90		9	3			×
Wyoming	×		×	×		×						3	2			8	1	85	5	

[a] Issuing town certificates.

APPENDIX I

A TABULATION OF FACTS RELATING TO TEACHERS' INSTITUTES

(Prepared by C. G. Wilson, Educational Seminar, University of Illinois)

State	Organization	Minimum Length	Time of Year	Attendance	Payment	Director
Alabama	District	1 week	Summer	Not stated	State	State Supt.
Arkansas	County	Not stated	September	Compulsory	State	County Supt.
	District					State Supt.
California	County	20 days	To be arranged	Compulsory	Not stated	County Supt.
	County	3 days	Not stated	Compulsory	County	County Supt.
					Certificate fee	
Colorado	13 districts	2 weeks	Summer	Optional	Institute fee	County Supt.
Connecticut . . .	Various	Not stated	Not stated	Not stated	State	State Board of Education
Delaware	County	3 days	Not stated	Compulsory	State	County Supt.
Florida	County	Not stated	Not stated	Not stated	Certificate fee	State Supt.
Georgia	County	1 week	Generally Summer	Compulsory	Certificate fee	State School Committee
Idaho	County	5 days	Optional	Compulsory	County Certificate fee	County Supt.
Illinois	County	1 week	Generally Summer	Optional	County	County Supt.
Indiana	County	5 days	Not stated	Not stated	County	County Supt.
Iowa	County	1 week	Summer	Optional	Certificate fee	County Supt.
Kansas	County	4 weeks	Summer	Optional	Fee County State	County Supt.
Kentucky	County	5 days	Summer	Compulsory	$1 to $2 fee	County Supt.

State		Length	Time	Attendance	Support	Held / certified by
Louisiana	Normal	Not stated	Summer	Compulsory	State	State Supt.
Maine	Parish	Not stated	Not stated	Not stated	State	State Supt.
Maryland	County	5 days	Optional	Not stated	Not stated	County Examiner, State, Normal
Massachusetts	Not stated	Not stated	Optional	Optional	State	State Board
Michigan	County, District	3 days	Summer	Optional	Certificate fee, County	State Supt. or assistant
Minnesota	County	1 week	Not stated	Compulsory	State	State Supt.
Mississippi	County	5 days	Not stated	Not stated	State Fee	County Supt.
Missouri	County	3 days	Sept, Oct, Nov, or Dec.	Compulsory	County, 30% of certificate fees	State Board of Education
Montana	County	3 days	Summer	Compulsory	Certificate fees	State Supt.
Nebraska	Normal	Optional	Optional	Compulsory	Appropriation	County Supt.
Nevada	County	Not stated	Not stated	Compulsory	Certificate fee	State Supt.
New Hampshire	State	3 days	Optional	Not stated	County	County Supt.
New Jersey	County	Not stated	Not stated	Optional	Not stated	State Supt.
New York	County	Not stated	Not stated	Compulsory	County	County Supt.
North Carolina	District	Optional	Optional	Compulsory	State	Commissioner
North Dakota	County	Not stated	Not stated	Compulsory	Appropriation, County	County Supt.
Ohio	County	4 days	Not stated	Optional	State $50, Bequests	State Supt., County Supt.
Oregon	Judicial	Not stated	Not stated	Not stated	Not stated	Teacher or County Supt.
Pennsylvania	County	3 days, 5 days	Not stated	Optional	County, $1 for each 3 days attendance	State Supt., County Supt., County Supt.

A TABULATION OF FACTS RELATING TO TEACHERS' INSTITUTES—*Continued*

STATE	ORGANIZATION	MINIMUM LENGTH	TIME OF YEAR	ATTENDANCE	PAYMENT	DIRECTOR
Rhode Island	Not stated	Not stated	Not stated	Not stated	State	Commissioner
South Carolina	County	Not stated	Not stated	Not stated	State	County Supt.
South Dakota	County	5 days	April 1 to Sept. 15	Compulsory	County	County Supt.
Tennessee	County	3 days	Generally Summer	Optional	State institute fund	County Supt.
Texas	County	3 sessions of 2 days each	Not stated	Not stated	Not stated	County Supt.
Utah	County	2 days	Summer	Compulsory	County $100	County Supt.
Virginia	County	Not stated	Not stated	Not stated	Not stated	County Supt. City Supt.
Vermont	County	4 days	Not stated	Not stated	State	State Supt. or County Supt.
Washington	County { singly or jointly	1 week	Not stated	Compulsory	County	County Supt.
West Virginia	County	1 week	Optional	Compulsory	State	State Supt.
Wisconsin	County	Optional	Optional	Optional	Normal and General State fund	County Supt.
Wyoming	County	4 days	Optional	Compulsory	County	County Supt.
Arizona	County { singly or jointly	Not stated	Not stated	Not stated	Not stated	County Supt.
New Mexico	County	2 weeks	Not stated	Compulsory	Fee	County Supt. Territorial Supt.
Oklahoma	Territorial	Not stated	Not stated	Not stated	Territorial	Territorial Board
	County	2 weeks	Not stated	Not stated	Fee and Appropriation	County Supt.

APPENDIX J

LAWS RELATING TO COMPULSORY SCHOOL ATTENDANCE AND CHILD
LABOR, IN THE SEVERAL STATES AND TERRITORIES

(Adapted from Rep. Com. Ed. 1901, 2 : 2410 *et. seq.*, corrected for 1902)

| State | COMPULSORY EDUCATION | | | CHILD LABOR |
	Age	Annual Period	Penalty on Parents for Neglect	Age under which Specified Employments are Forbidden
Alabama	—	—	—	10 years, in mines.
Alaska	—	—	—	21 years, in bar-rooms.
Arkansas	—	—	—	14 years, in mines.
California	8–14	Two-thirds full term; 12 consecutive weeks.	First, not exceeding $20; subsequent, $20 to $50, with costs.	10 years. Certificate of age required under 16.
Colorado	8–14	12 weeks; 8 consecutive. Full term not less than 20 weeks in districts of first and second class.	$5 to $25.	14 years, in any underground works; 12 years in coal mines. No girls employed in coal mines.
Connecticut	8–16[a]	Full term.	Not exceeding $5.	14 years.
District of Columbia	8–14	12 weeks; 6 consecutive.	Not exceeding $20.	
Idaho	8–14	12 weeks; 8 consecutive.	First, not less than $5; subsequent, $10 to $50, with costs.	14 years, in mines (state constitution).
Illinois	7–14	16 weeks; 6 consecutive. Time to commence with beginning of first term of school year for pupils under 10 years of age, and not later than December 1 of said year for pupils over 10.	$1 to $5 and costs; stand committed till paid. Penalty for false statements as to age or attendance, $3 to $20.	14 years, in any mercantile institution, etc. Girls may not work in mines at any age. Certificate of age required under 16.[b]
Indiana	7–14	Full term.	$5 to $25, and, in discretion of court, imprisonment 2 to 90 days.	14 years, in any manufacturing or mercantile establishment, etc. Certificate of age required under 16.

623

COMPULSORY SCHOOL ATTENDANCE AND CHILD LABOR — *Continued*

| State | COMPULSORY EDUCATION | | | CHILD LABOR |
	Age	Annual Period	Penalty on Parents for Neglect	Age under which Specif Employments are Forbid
Iowa	—	————	————	12 years, in mines (bo
Kansas	8–12	12 weeks; 6 consecutive.	First, $5 to $10; subsequent, $10 to $20.	12 years, in coal mines
Kentucky	7–14	8 consecutive weeks.	First, $5 to $20; subsequent, $10 to $50.	14 years, in any worksh factory, or mine, with written consent of ent or county judge
Louisiana	—	————	————	12 years (boys), 14 ye (girls), in any fact warehouse, or w shop.
Maine	7–14	Full term.	Not exceeding $25, or imprisonment not exceeding 30 days.	12 years, in any ma facturing or mercan establishment. Cer cate of age requi under 16.
Maryland *c*	8–12 *d*	Full term.	Not exceeding $5.	14 years, in mills and tories (except cann establishments), un self, widowed mot or invalid father, so dependent upon s employment. Ninet counties exempt fr law.
Massachusetts . . .	7–14 *e*	Full term.	Not exceeding $20.	14 years, in factories, wc shops, or mercantile lishments, and in other employment wages, during sch hours; 18 years, h dling intoxicating uors (except in d stores). Certificate age required under
Michigan	8–15 *f*	4 months; full term in cities having a duly constituted police force.	Fine of $5 to $50, or imprisonment 2 to 90 days, or both.	14 years, in manufactur establishments, hot or stores. Certific of age required un 16. (Law does not ply to canning or ev orating works.)
Minnesota	8–16	12 weeks; 6 consecutive.	First, $25; subsequent, $25 to $50.	14 years, in factories, wo shops, or mines; years, in mercantile tablishments, telegra telephone, or pub messenger compan' 16 years, in any occu tion dangerous to l limb, health, or mora

COMPULSORY SCHOOL ATTENDANCE AND CHILD LABOR — *Continued*

	COMPULSORY EDUCATION			CHILD LABOR
State	Age	Annual Period	Penalty on Parents for Neglect	Age under which Specified Employments are Forbidden
Mississippi	—	——	——	Children under 21 (boys), under 18 (girls), may not be employed away from home without consent of legal guardian.
Missouri	—	——	——	14 years, in manufacturing or mechanical establishments, or where work would be dangerous to health of child.
Montana	8–14	12 weeks; 6 consecutive.	$5 to $25.	14 years, in mines.
Nebraska	7–14	Two-thirds school term.	$5 to $25.	10 years, in manufacturing, mechanical, industrial, or mercantile establishments; under 12 years, not more than four months in the year in railway shops, factories, shops, or mines. Certificate of age under 16 years.
Nevada	8–14	16 weeks; 8 consecutive.	First, $50 to $100; subsequent, $100 to $200, with costs.	
New Hampshire . . .	8–14	Full term.	First, $10; subsequent, $20 or imprisonment 5 to 90 days.	12 years, in any manufacturing establishment.
New Jersey	7–12	Full term.	$1 to $25, or imprisonment 5 to 90 days.	14 years (girls), 12 years (boys), in factories, workshops, mines, or manufacturing establishments.
New Mexico	8–16	12 weeks.	$1 to $25, or imprisonment not exceeding 10 days.	
New York	8–16	Full term (Oct. 1 to June 1) between ages of 8 and 12; 80 days ages between 12 and 14; when unemployed, 14 and 16.	First, not exceeding $5; subsequent, not exceeding $50, or imprisonment not exceeding 30 days, or both fine and imprisonment.	14 years, in factories and in mercantile establishments in villages and cities over 3000 inhabitants. Certificate of age, school attendance, etc., required under 16.
North Carolina . . .	—			Under 21 may not be employed out of state without consent of legal guardian.

COMPULSORY SCHOOL ATTENDANCE AND CHILD LABOR — *Continued*

	COMPULSORY EDUCATION			CHILD LABOR
State	Age	Annual Period	Penalty on Parents for Neglect	Age under which Specified Employments are Forbidden
North Dakota . . .	8–14	12 weeks; 6 consecutive.	First, $5 to $20; subsequent, $50, with costs.	12 years, in mines, factories, and workshops (constitution of state).
Ohio	8–14 [g]	Full term, 24 weeks.	In no case less than $5 to $20; on default, imprisonment from 10 to 30 days.	14 years, in factories, shops, mercantile or other establishments; 15 years, in mines.
Oregon	8–14	12 weeks; 8 consecutive.		
Pennsylvania	8–16 [h]	Full term; but school board of each district has power to reduce this to not less than 70 per cent of term.	First, not exceeding $2; subsequent, not exceeding $5; on default, imprisonment; first, not over 2 days; subsequent not over 5.	13 years, in factories, manufacturing or mercantile establishments; 14 years, in mines (boys). Girls may not work in mines. Certificate of age required under 15.
Rhode Island	7–15 [i]	Full term.	Not exceeding $20.	12 years, in factories, manufactures, or mercantile establishments. Certificate of age required under 15.
South Dakota . . .	8–14	12 weeks; 8 consecutive.	$10 to $20, and costs; stand committed till paid.	14 years, in mines.
Tennessee	—	—	—	14 years, in workshops, mills, factories, or mines.
Utah	8–14	20 weeks; 10 consecutive.	First, not exceeding $10; subsequent, not exceeding $30, with costs.	14 years, in mines (constitution of state). Girls may not work in mines.
Vermont	8–14	20 weeks.	$5 to $25.	10 years, in manufacturing or mechanical institutions.
Washington	8–15 [j]	12 weeks.	$10 to $25; defective children, $50 to $200.	14 years, in mines (boys). Girls may not work in mines.
West Virginia . . .	8–14	16 weeks.	First, $2; subsequent, $5.	12 years, in mines, factories, workshops, manufactories, or establishments where goods or wares are manufactured.

COMPULSORY SCHOOL ATTENDANCE AND CHILD LABOR — *Continued*

| State | COMPULSORY EDUCATION | | | CHILD LABOR |
	Age	Annual Period	Penalty on Parents for Neglect	Age under which Specified Employments are Forbidden
Wisconsin	7–14	12 weeks.	$5 to $20.	14 years, in mines, factories, or workshops, and in mercantile establishments, except in vacation of public schools. Certificate of age required under 16.
Wyoming	6–21 *k*	12 weeks.	Not exceeding $25.	14 years, in mines (constitution of state). Girls may not work in mines.
United States Laws for Territories	—	——	——	12 years in the underground workings of any mine.

a Not applicable to children over 14 lawfully employed and not enrolled at school.

b This certificate must contain: Name, place, and date of birth of child; in New York and Massachusetts and some other states, a statement of school attendance, personal description of child, and other data.

c Provisions tabulated for Maryland are those of the compulsory attendance of 1902, whose operation is limited to Baltimore City and Alleghany County.

d To 16, unless regularly employed to labor at home or elsewhere.

e To 16 if wandering about public places without lawful occupation.

f In cities 7 to 15, and to 16 if wandering about public places without lawful occupation.

g To 16 if unemployed.

h Not applicable to children over 13 who can read and write and are regularly employed in useful service.

i Not applicable to children over 13 who are lawfully employed.

j 6 to 21 in case of defective children.

k Penalty only for child 7 to 16, or one living idly and loitering about public places.

APPENDIX K

EDUCATIONAL STATISTICS FOR 1902 BY DIVISIONS, STATES, AND TERRITORIES

(Compiled from various tables in Rep. Com. Ed., 1902)

	U. S. Totals	N. Atlantic States	S. Atlantic States	S. Central States	N. Central States	Western States	Alabama
COMMON SCHOOLS (Public)							
1. Whole numbers of pupils enrolled	15,925,887	3,733,683	2,279,290	3,156,590	5,866,396	889,928	365,171
2. Percentage of total population enrolled	20.28	17.12	21.31	21.45	21.80	19.93	19.03
3. Percentage of school population (5–18 years) enrolled	71.54	70.05	67.02	65.37	77.25	80.28	57.01
4. Length of school year, in days	145.1	177.3	115.8	100.6	156.5	143.9	102.5
5. Average number of days attended by each pupil	100.1	130.2	73.4	66.9	109.4	99.2	67.4
6. Number of teachers	439,596	108,070	51,385	65,500	187,843	26,796	6,303
7. Percentage of male teachers	27.8	16.7	38.1	46.8	25.6	22.2	49.2
8. Average monthly salary of male teachers	$49.45	$59.01	$30.50	$44.28	$50.85	$65.90	$31.00
9. Average monthly salary of female teachers	$39.77	$40.17	$28.60	$36.88	$39.60	$33.73	$27.00
10. Total number of school buildings	254,076	43,467	37,672	51,715	107,265	13,957	7,058
11. Total value of all public school property	$601,571,307	$243,150,933	$25,109,903	$29,875,383	$250,393,396	$53,132,592	$2,200,000
12. Total amount expended for schools in the year	$235,208,465	$91,242,162	$14,159,390	$16,780,141	$93,654,876	$19,371,896	$1,057,906
13. Expenditure per capita of population	$2.99	$4.18	$1.32	$1.14	$3.48	$4.39	$.55
14. Expenditure per capita of school attendance	$21.38	$31.28	$9.79	$8.00	$22.84	$31.59	$4.41
15. Permanent common school funds	$164,955,190	$22,482,565	$4,190,777	$40,077,525	$87,937,288	$10,267,035	$2,564,462
(Private)							
16. Total number of pupils enrolled	1,218,600	429,300	126,200	179,800	430,100	53,200	26,722
17. Percentage of pupils in private schools	7.11	10.31	5.25	5.39	6.83	5.64	7.87
HIGHER AND PROFESSIONAL SCHOOLS							
18. Number of colleges for men and both sexes	464	85	73	77	190	39	6
19. Number of colleges for women	131	19	45	46	19	2	7
20. Students in colleges for men	24,560	15,482	3,474	1,885	3,046	673	320
21. Students in colleges for both sexes	59,021	10,050	4,236	7,054	31,090	6,591	371
22. Students in colleges for women	24,963	7,024	6,881	7,161	3,020	278	831
23. Value of buildings and grounds of class 18	$154,529,288	$64,519,288	$16,352,083	$12,205,092	$50,795,024	$10,747,769	$988,000
24. Value of buildings and grounds of class 19	$16,990,359	$7,855,692	$4,402,950	$2,139,000	$2,059,737	$538,000	$431,000
25. Number of schools of theology	148	52	19	14	58	5	3
26. Number of students in schools of theology	7,343	2,915	903	534	2,910	81	47
27. Number of schools of medicine	154	26	23	26	67	12	2
28. Number of students in schools of medicine	26,821	6,514	3,609	4,995	10,693	1,100	240
29. Number of schools of law	102	18	21	17	39	7	1
30. Number of students in schools of law	13,912	4,598	2,138	796	5,851	529	67
31. Public normal schools, number	173	62	4, 25		40	2?	6
32. Number of students in public, normal schools	49,403	17,24?	4,083	5,261	18,6?7	3,910	1,386

EDUCATIONAL STATISTICS FOR 1902 BY DIVISIONS, STATES, AND TERRITORIES — *Continued*

	Arkansas	Arizona	California	Colorado	Connecticut	Delaware	District of Columbia
COMMON SCHOOLS (*Public*)							
1. Whole number of pupils enrolled	340,695	19,203	278,330	130,369	161,545	36,895	48,432
2. Percentage of total population enrolled	25.18	13.77	18.07	21.34	16.91	19.98	16.73
3. Percentage of school population (5–18 years) enrolled	74.56	53.24	79.16	86.38	73.74	75.32	76.98
4. Length of school year, in days	91.5	125.	167.4	135.	188.89	170.1	176.
5. Average number of days attended by each pupil	57.7	74.9	125.9	85.6	138.	116.6	138.1
6. Number of teachers	7,723		8,072	3,947	4,318		1,323
7. Percentage of male teachers	56.8	25.8	15.8	19.3	13.8	25.3	12.9
8. Average monthly salary of male teachers	$36.17	$85.51	$87.01	$66.97	$99.29	$30.60	$94.98
9. Average monthly salary of female teachers	$32.75	$71.75	$67.19	$53.05	$44.51	$34.08	$64.31
10. Total number of school buildings	5,063	275	3,697	1,331	1,586	550	141
11. Total value of all public school property	$2,901,212	$654,942	$21,105,141	$6,950,808	$11,741,073	$1,043,997	$4,600,810
12. Total amount expended for schools in the year	$1,592,110	$376,685	$613,708	$3,100,855	$3,556,442	$453,670	$1,094,255
13. Expenditure per capita of population	$1.18	$2.70	$4.94	$5.08	$3.72	$2.46	$5.85
14. Expenditure per capita of school attendance	$7.41	$32.72	$36.37	$37.50	$30.13	$17.93	$44.59
15. Permanent common school funds	$1,143,000		$3,641,200	$1,251,901	$3,054,541	$350,000	
(*Private*)							
16. Total number of pupils enrolled	9,680	1,531	24,350	2,515	35,063		5,000
17. Percentage of pupils in private schools	2.76	7.38	8.04	1.89	17.83		10.53
HIGHER AND PROFESSIONAL SCHOOLS							
18. Number of colleges for men and both sexes	7	1	12	4	3	2	7
19. Number of colleges for women	1		2				1
20. Students in colleges for men			424	30			174
21. Students in colleges for both sexes	890	69	3,705	893	2,038	110	566
22. Students in colleges for women	121		278		309	28	45
23. Value of buildings and grounds of class 18	$576,000	$123,434	$5,899,597	$1,402,300	$7,231,700	$140,000	$4,807,607
24. Value of buildings and grounds of class 19	$45,000		$538,000				?
25. Number of schools of theology			4		3		3
26. Number of students in schools of theology			49		191		110
27. Number of schools of medicine	1			3	1		5
28. Number of students in schools of medicine	220		635	196	147		610
29. Number of schools of law	1		2	2			6
30. Number of students in schools of law	35		301	123	249		1,138
31. Public normal schools, number		2	5	1			2
32. Number of students in public normal schools	65	63	1,758	289	634		178

EDUCATIONAL STATISTICS FOR 1902 BY DIVISIONS, STATES, AND TERRITORIES — Continued

	FLORIDA	GEORGIA	IDAHO	ILLINOIS	INDIANA	INDIAN TERRITORY	IOWA
COMMON SCHOOLS (Public)							
1. Whole number pupils enrolled	112,384	502,887	46,117	971,841	560,224	22,121	560,173
2. Percentage of total population enrolled	20.02	22.29	25.54	19.67	22.16	4.83	25.09
3. Percentage of school population (5–18 years) enrolled	64.71	66.83	89.20	71.88	80.08	14.16	88.07
4. Length of school year, in days	94.	113.	124.2	167.	146.	159.	160.
5. Average number of days attended by each pupil	70.9	70.9	80.9	131.5	110.3	97.2	106.90
6. Number of teachers	2,799	10,519	1,238	27,186	16,039	618	29,073
7. Percentage of male teachers	32.1	38.3	29.	25.	43.7	39.	14.30
8. Average monthly salary of male teachers	$39.68	—	$56.11	$64.55	$66.80	—	$43.66
9. Average monthly salary of female teachers	$33.67	—	$44.83	$54.18	$48.	—	$30.17
10. Total number of school buildings	2,336	6,536	836	12,865	9,987	450	13,931
11. Total value of all public school property	$1,066,904	$2,995,809	$1,459,092	$52,764,922	$24,182,052	$67,150	$18,989,923
12. Total amount expended for schools in the year	$792,919	$2,184,670	$689,636	$19,025,258	$9,216,082	$425,026	$9,213,707
13. Expenditure per capita of population	$1.41	$.97	$3.82	$3.85	$3.65	$.93	$4.13
14. Expenditure per capita of school attendance	$10.41	$6.73	$22.97	$24.87	$21.78	$31.42	$24.63
15. Permanent common school funds	$794,678	—	$441,780	$7,031,544	$10,874,326	—	$4,724,804
(Private)							
16. Total number of pupils enrolled	2,000	27,285	—	144,471	4,560	1,698	43,715 [a]
17. Percentage of pupils in private schools	1.75	6.16	—	12.94	.80	7.13	7.21 [a]
HIGHER AND PROFESSIONAL SCHOOLS (1901)							
18. Number of colleges for men and both sexes	5	11	1	31	13	2	25
19. Number of colleges for women		10		3			
20. Students in colleges for men	32	733		835	674	—	254
21. Students in colleges for both sexes	196	557	146	5,585	2,237	23	2,946
22. Students in colleges for women		1,971		501			
23. Value of buildings and grounds of class 18	$576,000	$1,553,000	$200,000	$11,777,926	$4,140,970	$85,000	$3,118,498
24. Value of buildings and grounds of class 19		$940,250		$385,000			
25. Number of schools of theology		2		15	3		4
26. Number of students in schools of theology		86		1,111	153		120
27. Number of schools of medicine		2		7	3		4
28. Number of students in schools of medicine		380		2,694	428		656
29. Number of schools of law	1	3		8	6		3
30. Number of students in schools of law	15	89		1,047	634		383
31. Public normal schools, number	2	4	2	5	2		3
32. Number of students in public normal schools,	192	853	255	2,700	2,259		2,232

EDUCATIONAL STATISTICS FOR 1902 BY DIVISIONS, STATES, AND TERRITORIES— *Continued*

	KANSAS	KENTUCKY	LOUISIANA	MAINE	MARYLAND	MASSACHU-SETTS	MICHIGAN
COMMON SCHOOLS (*Public*)							
1. Whole number of pupils enrolled	389,272	498,989	198,896	133,537	224,004	468,188	510,031
2. Percentage of total population enrolled	26.18	22.58	13.80	19.06	18.60	16.39	20.86
3. Percentage of school population (5–18 years) enrolled	88.17	72.94	42.40	82.27	66.62	73.79	77.11
4. Length of school year, in days	125.7	104.3	120.	147.	190.	185.	164.2
5. Average number of days attended by each pupil	88.3	66.	84.6	108.9	114.9	146.6	106.7
6. Number of teachers	11,709	9,501	4,271	6,634	5,036	13,622	16,054
7. Percentage of male teachers	28.9	48.8	31.5	14.2	21.3	8.9	18.9
8. Average monthly salary of male teachers	$44.24	$50.90	$36.09	$36.05		$140.94	$48.68
9. Average monthly salary of female teachers	$36.55	$39.18	$31.14	$27.24		$52.75	$36.68
10. Total number of school buildings	9,106	8,328	3,267	3,964	2,535	4,421	8,066
11. Total value of all public school property	$11,660,470	$5,818,545	$2,450,000	$4,728,743	$4,790,000	$48,979,719	$20,404,388
12. Total amount expended for schools in the year	$4,804,563	$2,851,651	$1,236,648	$1,794,505	$2,549,497	$14,179,947	$7,965,700
13. Expenditure per capita of population	$3.23	$1.29	$.86	$2.56	$2.12	$2.12	$3.26
14. Expenditure per capita of school attendance	$17.59	$9.04	$8.82	$18.14	$18.81	$38.21	$22.21
15. Permanent common school funds	$7,531,732	$2,315,027		$442,758		$4,470,548	$6,533,112
(*Private*)							
16. Total number of pupils enrolled		19,274	12,905			82,325	53,046
17. Percentage of pupils in private schools		3.72	6.09			14.95	9.42
HIGHER AND PROFESSIONAL SCHOOLS							
18. Number of colleges for men and both sexes	20	11	8	4	11	9	9
19. Number of colleges for women	1	10	3	2	1	5	
20. Students in colleges for men	147	289	568	254	646	3,720	
21. Students in colleges for both sexes	1,969	1,007	579	831	249	768	78
22. Students in colleges for women	112	1,712	292	267	343	3,108	2,609
23. Value of buildings and grounds of class 18	$3,370,000	$1,562,615	$2,453,000	$1,587,819	$234,127	$9,973,271	$2,740,657
24. Value of buildings and grounds of class 19	$200,000	$449,000	$105,000	$268,000	$697,000	$3,559,000	
25. Number of schools of theology	2	2	1	1	6	8	4
26. Number of students in schools of theology	32	294	4	41	461	494	103
27. Number of schools of medicine	3	6	2	2	7	3	5
28. Number of students in schools of medicine	210	1,360	445	101	1,650	876	959
29. Number of schools of law	1	2	1	1	3	2	3
30. Number of students in schools of law	173	77	78	46	329	1,161	1,069
31. Public normal schools, number	1	1	5	5	1	1	4
32. Number of students in public normal schools	1,833	154	566	641	385	1,800	2,165

631

EDUCATIONAL STATISTICS FOR 1902 BY DIVISIONS, STATES, AND TERRITORIES — *Continued*

	Minnesota	Mississippi	Missouri	Montana	Nebraska	Nevada	New Hampshire
COMMON SCHOOLS (*Public*)							
1. Whole number of pupils enrolled	414,671	387,488	703,057	42,400	289,468	6,952	67,250
2. Percentage of total population enrolled	22.32	24.51	21.97	16.21	26.80	16.17	16.05
3. Percentage of school population (5-18 years) enrolled	75.95	72.12	74.57	72.80	88.77	75.95	74.39
4. Length of school year, in days	153.9	97.6	143.00	107.	138.	155.6	140.05
5. Average number of days attended by each pupil	98.1	57.4	96.50	74.3	105.50	112.2	102.6
6. Number of teachers	12,605	8,515	16,347	1,221	9,629	319	2,376
7. Percentage of male teachers	15.7	40.4	34.	15.6	19.30	11.9	8.7
8. Average monthly salary of male teachers	$53.56	$32.18	$42.67	$73.86	$49.15	$100.84	$43.58
9. Average monthly salary of female teachers	$37.21	$26.69	$42.89	$50.11	$38.51	$61.58	$29.11
10. Total number of school buildings	8,598	6,790	10,320	712	6,813	273	1,847
11. Total value of all public school property	$19,433,862	$1,840,000	$21,210,897	$7,400,250	$10,281,548	$304,090	$4,155,616
12. Total amount expended for schools in the year	$6,697,589	$1,472,433	$8,169,288	$879,882	$4,286,528	$209,484	$1,107,464
13. Expenditure per capita of population	$3.60	$0.93	$2.55	$3.36	$3.97	$4.87	$2.79
14. Expenditure per capita of school attendance	$25.34	$6.48	$17.28	$33.97	$23.08	$41.78	$23.69
15. Permanent common school funds	$15,050,425	$1,052,004	$12,795,517	$571,881	$7,706,593	$1,809,256	
(*Private*)							
16. Total number of pupils enrolled	20,073 [a]	14,021	17,671	1,816		343	11,543
17. Percentage of pupils in private schools	5.39 [a]	3.67	2.45	4.11		4.7	14.65
HIGHER AND PROFESSIONAL SCHOOLS							
18. Number of colleges for men and both sexes	9	4	22	1	10	1	2
19. Number of colleges for women	1	11					
20. Students in colleges for men	155	175	402		71		
21. Students in colleges for both sexes	2,394	347	2,356	60	1,850	203	690
22. Students in colleges for women	28	2,187					
23. Value of buildings and grounds of class 18	$2,777,215	$515,000	$4,827,000	$125,000	$1,917,100	$197,961	$1,150,000
24. Value of buildings and grounds of class 19	$40,000	$471,000					
25. Number of schools of theology	7		5		1		1
26. Number of students in schools of theology	336		413		17		72
27. Number of schools of medicine	2		11		2		
28. Number of students in schools of medicine	500		2,249		300		
29. Number of schools of law	3	2	5		2		
30. Number of students in schools of law	599	71	633		178		
31. Public normal schools, number	5	5	3	1	1		1
32. Number of students in public normal schools	1,120	367	2,045	124	630		140

a 1894-1895.

632

EDUCATIONAL STATISTICS FOR 1902 BY DIVISIONS, STATES, AND TERRITORIES — *Continued*

	NEW JERSEY	NEW MEXICO	NEW YORK	NORTH CAROLINA	NORTH DAKOTA	OHIO	OKLAHOMA
COMMON SCHOOLS (Public)							
1. Whole number of pupils enrolled	336,664	40,184	1,268,625	464,669	83,677	832,044	131,591
2. Percentage of total population enrolled	16.95	18.30	16.80	23.76	22.51	19.63	25.32
3. Percentage of school population (5–18 years) enrolled	67.82	59.76	70.21	71.41	75.13	74.24	80.83
4. Length of school year, in days	186.	85.	177.	86.9	147.	165.	95.
5. Average number of days attended by each pupil	125.2	57.8	133.2	50.3	86.10	121.1	59.9
6. Number of teachers	7,938	710	30,636	8,731	4,586	26,410	2,915
7. Percentage of male teachers	13.1	54.2	13.1	45.5.	26.10	37.5	41.6
8. Average monthly salary of male teachers	$87.15	$64.77		$26.77	$42.70	$42.20	$31.93
9. Average monthly salary of female teachers	$52.06	$64.77	$64.77	$23.80	$37.14	$37.00	$26.20
10. Total number of school buildings	1,932	710	11,889	7,293	2,885	13,125	2,192
11. Total value of all public school property	$18,065,764	$1,125,598	$92,207,473	$1,469,440	$2,899,184	$48,257,961	$1,618,850
12. Total amount expended for schools in the year	$6,976,118	$241,227	$37,737,654	$1,287,276	$1,677,874	$14,868,999	$1,116,231
13. Expenditure per capita of population	$3.51	$1.09	$5.00	$.66	$4.51	$3.51	$2.15
14. Expenditure per capita of school attendance	$31.15	$8.83	$41.54	$4.79	$34.25	$24.35	$13.44
15. Permanent common school funds	$5,461,789		$8,587,661	$194,159	$1,418,629	$4,003,677	
(Private)							
16. Total number of pupils enrolled	47,453	4,553	168,057	26,198		27,133	
17. Percentage of pupils in private schools	12.82	10.18	11.70	7.25		3.16	
HIGHER AND PROFESSIONAL SCHOOLS							
18. Number of colleges for men and both sexes	5	1	23	14	3	34	1
19. Number of colleges for women			5	9		3	
20. Students in colleges for men	1,582		3,676	643		265	
21. Students in colleges for both sexes		10	3,608	981	158	545	
22. Students in colleges for women			2,212	1,524		450	76
23. Value of buildings and grounds of class 18	$4,046,500	$75,000	$23,326,637	$2,100,000	$2,582,000	$11,356,266	$150,000
24. Value of buildings and grounds of class 19			$2,566,862	$783,000		$571,737	
25. Number of schools of theology	5		16	2		13	
26. Number of students in schools of theology	407		958	24		421	
27. Number of schools of medicine			7	3		8	
28. Number of students in schools of medicine			2,227	223		957	
29. Number of schools of law			8	3	1	6	
30. Number of students in schools of law			2,434	131	20	805	
31. Public normal schools, number	4	2	17	5	2	3	3
32. Number of students in public normal schools	907	229	6,119	752	376	468	933

EDUCATIONAL STATISTICS FOR 1902 BY DIVISIONS, STATES, AND TERRITORIES — *Continued*

	Oregon	Pennsylvania	Rhode Island	South Carolina	South Dakota	Tennessee	Texas
COMMON SCHOOLS (Public)							
1. Whole number of pupils enrolled	100,659	1,163,599	69,357	272,443	105,591	499,591	712,629
2. Percentage of total population enrolled	23.65	17.80	15.38	19.71	24.69	24.41	22.33
3. Percentage of school population (5–18 years) enrolled	86.83	67.12	65.46	56.94	79.76	76.32	66.74
4. Length of school year, in days	158.	166.40	192.	87.3	129.	93.	101.91
5. Average number of days attended by each pupil enrolled	104.8	124.7	141.6	66.8	91.20	63.	74.9
6. Number of teachers	4,510	30,640	2,002	5,832	5,052	9,484	16,170
7. Percentage of male teachers	25.3	28.	8.6	43.5	19.90	51.6	43.6
8. Average monthly salary of male teachers	$47.58	$44.92	$116.1	$25.96	$40.03		$61.00
9. Average monthly salary of female teachers	$37.61	$33.78	$51.99	$23.20	$33.52		$49.55
10. Total number of school buildings	2,125	15,016	540	4,843	4,380	7,241	11,326
11. Total value of all public school property	$3,561,737	$55,994,604	$5,476,951	$978,000	$3,643,384	$3,591,069	$9,288,557
12. Total amount expended for schools in the year	$1,802,227	$23,027,678	$1,708,412	$985,394	$1,847,783	$1,811,454	$5,216,672
13. Expenditure per capita of population	$4.23	$3.52	$3.79	$.71	$4.31	$.89	$1.63
14. Expenditure per capita of school attendance	$26.99	$26.41	$33.82	$4.73	$25.37	$5.17	$9.95
15. Permanent common school funds	$769,299		$254,137		$4,084,507	$2,512,500	$30,489,932
(Private)							
16. Total number of pupils enrolled	7,416	42,990	18,480	—	1,888[a]	45,428	—
17. Percentage of pupils in private schools	6.86	3.56	21.04	—	2.10[a]	8.52	—
HIGHER AND PROFESSIONAL SCHOOLS							
18. Number of colleges for men and both sexes	8	35	1	9	5	24	14
19. Number of colleges for women	—	7	—	9	—	10	4
20. Students in colleges for men	—	3,452	—	212	—	320	213
21. Students in colleges for both sexes	556	3,306	826	723	242	2,189	1,572
22. Students in colleges for women	—	1,436	—	1,461	—	1,710	774
23. Value of buildings and grounds of class 18	$569,000	$15,168,393	$1,200,000	$1,034,500	$426,650	$3,745,477	$2,130,000
24. Value of buildings and grounds of class 19	—	$1,496,810	—	$599,500	—	$425,000	$240,000
25. Number of schools of theology	1	18	—	3	—	7	1
26. Number of students in schools of theology	32	824	—	48	—	179	10
27. Number of schools of medicine	2	6	—	2	—	10	4
28. Number of students in schools of medicine	107	2,245	—	89	—	2,116	497
29. Number of schools of law	2	4	1	1	—	8	2
30. Number of students in schools of law	37	677	31	32	—	293	174
31. Public normal schools, number	4	15	1	1	3	1	4
32. Number of students in public normal schools	286	6,487	209	306	539	575	1,215

a 1892–1893.

EDUCATIONAL STATISTICS FOR 1902 BY DIVISIONS, STATES, AND TERRITORIES — *Continued*

	UTAH	VERMONT	VIRGINIA	WASHINGTON	WEST VIRGINIA	WISCONSIN	WYOMING
COMMON SCHOOLS (*Public*)							
1. Whole number of pupils enrolled	74,578	35,008	381,561	136,624	236,015	446,247	14,512
2. Percentage of total population enrolled	26.07	18.79	20.26	22.11	24.09	21.22	15.68
3. Percentage of school population (5–18 years) enrolled	80.02	80.43	64.08	87.43	78.11	77.11	65.67
4. Length of school year, in days	147.	154.	122.7	126.3	118.	169,	110.
5. Average number of days attended by each pupil	112.1	116.6	72.2	77.7	76.1	105.6	73.3
6. Number of teachers	1,593	3,906	9,008	4,159	7,306	13,356	570
7. Percentage of male teachers	34.9	11.7	30.	35.	544	17.	15.6
8. Average monthly salary of male teachers	$66.81	$40.54	$32.66	$54.79	$45.85	$53.33	$73.68
9. Average monthly salary of female teachers	$48.12	$29.13	$26.46	$45.85	$26.46	$39.52	$43.36
10. Total number of school buildings	712	2,272	7,417	2,262	6,021	7,179	524
11. Total value of all public school property	$3,220,160	$1,800,000	$3,663,634	$6,896,497	$4,561,390	$16,574,795	$453,607
12. Total amount expended for schools in the year	$1,399,186	$1,093,942	$2,012,359	$2,805,455	$2,199,350	$5,881,473	$253,551
13. Expenditure per capita of population	$4.89	$3.16	$3.07	$4.54	$2.24	$2.80	$2.74
14. Expenditure per capita of school attendance	$26.06	$22.23	$8.91	$30.72	$14.45	$21.10	$24.95
15. Permanent common school funds	$291,205	$211,131	$1,747,527	$1,442,513	$1,104,413	$5,582,452	$48,000
(*Private*)							
16. Total number of pupils enrolled	2,814	6,401	2,100	4,892	1,894	55,789	175
17. Percentage of pupils in private schools	3.55	8.96	5.22	3.46	.86	11.11	1.53
HIGHER AND PROFESSIONAL SCHOOLS							
18. Number of colleges for men and both sexes	2	3	11	7	3	9	1
19. Number of colleges for women			1			1	
20. Students in colleges for men	267	70	924	219		265	
21. Students in colleges for both sexes		402	501	545	435	2,899	77
22. Students in colleges for women			260			225	
23. Value of buildings and grounds of class 18	$420,477	$835,000	$2,950,000	$1,485,000	$240,000	$2,674,842	$250,000
24. Value of buildings and grounds of class 19			$127,000			$158,000	
25. Number of schools of theology			3			4	
26. Number of students in schools of theology			174			204	
27. Number of schools of medicine		1	3			2	
28. Number of students in schools of medicine		210	562			290	
29. Number of schools of law			3	1	1	2	
30. Number of students in schools of law			287	68	117	310	
31. Public normal schools, number	1	3	3	3	7	8	1
32. Number of students in public normal schools	200	305	519	658	898	2,540	45

APPENDIX L

SCIENTIFIC

Anthropology

The Anthropologist (1888), New York, quarterly journal of the
American Folklore Society (1888), Boston, quarterly.

Astronomy

Astronomical Journal (1849), Cambridge.
Astrophysical Journal (1895), Chicago, monthly.
Popular Astronomy (1893), Northfield, Minn., monthly.

Botany

Bulletin of the Torrey Botanical Club (1870), New York, monthly.
Botanical Gazette (1876), Chicago, monthly.

Chemistry

American Chemical Journal (1879), Baltimore, monthly.
Journal of the American Chemical Society (1887), Easton, Penn.,
monthly.
Journal of Physical Chemistry (1896), Utica, N.Y., nine numbers.

Education

American School Board Journal (1902, Vol. 22), New York, monthly.
Child Garden (Kindergarten, 1902, Vol. 10), Chicago, monthly.
Education (1902, Vol. 23), Boston, monthly.
Educational Review (1902, Vol. 22), New York, monthly.
Intelligence (1902, Vol. 22), Oak Park, Ill., semi-monthly.
Journal of Education (1902, Vol. 54), Boston, weekly.
Journal of Pedagogy (1902, Vol. 18), Lansing, Mich., quarterly.
Kindergarten Magazine (1902, Vol. 15), Chicago, monthly.
School and Home Education (1902, Vol. 21), Bloomington, Ill.,
monthly.
School Review (1902, Vol. 10), Chicago, monthly.

Geology and Geography

American Geologist (1888), Minneapolis, monthly.
Journal of Geology (1893), Chicago, semi-quarterly.
National Geographic Magazine (1888), Washington, monthly.
Bulletin of the American Geographical Society (1892), New York, five numbers.

History

The American Journal of Archæology (1885), New York, bi-monthly.
The American Historical Review, New York.

Mathematics

American Journal of Mathematics (1878), Baltimore, quarterly.
Annals of Mathematics (1884), Cambridge.
Bulletin of the American Mathematical Society (1893), New York, monthly.

Philology

American Journal of Philology (1879), Baltimore, quarterly.
Modern Language Notes (1886), Baltimore, eight numbers.

Philosophy

The Monist (1890), Chicago, quarterly.
The International Journal of Ethics (1890), Philadelphia, quarterly.
The Philosophical Review (1891), New York, bi-monthly.

Physics

Physical Review (1893), New York, monthly.
Terrestrial Magnetism and Atmospheric Electricity (1895), Baltimore, quarterly.

Physiology and Pathology

American Journal of Insanity (1843), Baltimore, quarterly.
Journal of Comparative Neurology (1890), Granville, Ohio, quarterly.
Journal of Experimental Medicine (1895), New York, bi-monthly.
American Journal of Physiology (1898), Boston, monthly.

Psychology

American Journal of Psychology (1887), Worcester, Mass., quarterly.
Psychological Review (1890), New York, bi-monthly.

Zoology

The Auk (1876), New York, quarterly.
Journal of Morphology (1887), Boston, irregular.

INDEX

(For all private or endowed institutions of learning, see under class to which particular institution belongs: as Harvard under COLLEGES; Tuck School of Finance under COMMERCIAL EDUCATION, etc. For all publicly supported institutions as State Universities, Normal Schools, etc., see under the several states.)

Academia Virginiensis et Oxoniensis, 5.

ACADEMIES, courses of study, 93, 596; early conditions, 90; land grants, 92; statistics, 430; teachers' courses, 375; in the various states, 94-96; Arkansas, 130; Florida, 139; Georgia, 72; Kentucky, 126; Louisiana, 132; Mississippi, 136; Ohio, 104; South Carolina, 70; Tennessee, 128; Academy, Abbot, 429; Adams', 429; Batesville, 130; Bradford, 428; Davidson, 128; Dummer, 91; Germantown, 61; Lebanon, 84; Leicester, 92, 428; Madison, 109; Nazareth, 429; Newark, 58; at Philadelphia, 90; Phillips, at Andover, 91, 92, 94, 95; at Exeter, 91; Talcon, 128; Washington (Miss.), 135; Washington (Ill.), 109; Westford, 428; Wilmington, 68; Worcester (Mass.), course of study, 596.

Adams, H. B. (quoted), 2, 570.

Agassiz, Louis, 163, 516.

AGRICULTURAL EDUCATION, 360 et seq.; bibliography, 369-370; courses of study, 365 et seq.; elementary, 163, 368; entrance requirements, 364; experiment stations, 367; short courses, 365; Colleges in various states, 362-363; Bussey Institution, 233, 363; Cornell, 363.

"Akron Law," 106.

Alabama, academies, 96; coeducation, 432; compulsory education laws, 623; first schools, 136; newspapers, 506; normal schools, 377; organization, school, 610; state university, 284, 354, 456; statistics, educational, 628; superintendent of public instruction, 615; teachers, certification, 617; teachers' institutes, 620; women's colleges, 435.

Albany (N.Y.), superintendent established, 193.

Andover (Mass.), Phillips Academy at, 91.

Andrew, Samuel, 239.

Arizona, agricultural college, 363; first schools, 148; legislation, school, acts of 1864, 1868, 148; library legislation, 485; normal schools, 377; organization, school, 610; teachers, certification, 617; teachers' institutes, 620; territorial university, 285, 354, 363, 447; statistics, educational, 629; superintendent of public instruction, 615.

Arkansas, academies, 96, 130; agricultural college, 363; compulsory education laws, 623; first schools, 130; legislation, school, acts of 1829, 1843, 1867, 130; newspapers, 506; normal schools, 377; organization, school, 610; state university, 284, 354, 363, 446; statistics, educational, 629; superintendent of public instruction, 615; teachers, certification, 617; teachers' institutes, 620; text-book legislation, 219.

ART EDUCATION, 401 et seq.; bibliography, 412; in high schools, 404; in various colleges, 406; Brown, 405; Cincinnati School of Design, 403; Cooper Institute, 402; Franklin Institute (Philadelphia), 401; Harvard, 405; Ohio Mechanics Institute (Cincinnati), 403; Philadelphia

Library
Sampson Technical Institute